STUDIES IN EVANGELICAL HISTORY AND THOUGHT

Conscience and Compromise

Forgotten Evangelicals of Nineteenth-century Scotland

STUDIES IN EVANGELICAL HISTORY AND THOUGHT

A full listing of all titles in this series appears at the close of this book.

STUDIES IN EVANGELICAL HISTORY AND THOUGHT

Conscience and Compromise

Forgotten Evangelicals of Nineteenth-century Scotland

Patricia Meldrum

Foreword by David Bebbington

Eugene, Oregon

Wipf and Stock Publishers
199 W 8th Ave, Suite 3
Eugene, OR 97401

Conscience and Compromise
Forgotten Evangelicals of Nineteenth-century Scotland
By Meldrum, Patricia
Copyright©2006 Paternoster
ISBN 13: 978-1-55635-248-5
ISBN 10: 1-55635-248-4
Publication date 2/2/2007
Previously published by Paternoster, 2006

Paternoster
9 Holdom Avenue
Bletchley
Milton Keyes, MK1 1QR
Great Britain

STUDIES IN EVANGELICAL HISTORY AND THOUGHT

Series Preface

The Evangelical movement has been marked by its union of four emphases: on the Bible, on the cross of Christ, on conversion as the entry to the Christian life and on the responsibility of the believer to be active. The present series is designed to publish scholarly studies of any aspect of this movement in Britain or overseas. Its volumes include social analysis as well as exploration of Evangelical ideas. The books in the series consider aspects of the movement shaped by the Evangelical Revival of the eighteenth century, when the impetus to mission began to turn the popular Protestantism of the British Isles and North America into a global phenomenon. The series aims to reap some of the rich harvest of academic research about those who, over the centuries, have believed that they had a gospel to tell to the nations.

Series Editors

David Bebbington, Professor of History, University of Stirling, Stirling, Scotland, UK

John H.Y. Briggs, Senior Research Fellow in Ecclesiastical History and Director of the Centre for Baptist History and Heritage, Regent's Park College, Oxford, UK

Timothy Larsen, Professor of Theology, Wheaton College, Illinois, USA

Mark A. Noll, McManis Professor of Christian Thought, Wheaton College, Wheaton, Illinois, USA

Ian M. Randall, Deputy Principal and Lecturer in Church History and Spirituality, Spurgeon's College, London, UK, and a Senior Research Fellow, International Baptist Theological Seminary, Prague, Czech Republic

For my husband, John

Contents

List of Graphs	xii
List of Maps	xiii
List of Tables	xiv
Foreword	xvii
Preface	xix
Abbreviations	xxiii

Chapter 1 Introduction — 1
The Rise of Evangelicalism in Nineteenth-Century Scottish Episcopalianism — 6
Scottish Episcopal Evangelicals — 15
English Episcopal Evangelicals — 22
Early Lay Scottish Evangelical Episcopalianism — 22
Strength of Evangelical Episcopalianism in Scotland — 23
History of the Scottish Episcopal Church — 29

Chapter 2 Geographical Distribution — 37
Church Missionary Society Visits — 45
Conclusion — 56

Chapter 3 Social Class — 67
Choosing the Records — 70
Classification Scheme — 73
    St Paul's, Aberdeen — 78
    St Peter's, Montrose — 79
    St James's, Edinburgh — 79
    St Thomas's, Edinburgh — 80
    St James's, Aberdeen — 81
    St Vincent's, Edinburgh — 81
    St Silas's, Glasgow — 82
    St Jude's, Glasgow — 82
    St Silas's Partick Mission, Govan, Glasgow — 83
    St Paul's, Carrubber's Close, Edinburgh — 83
Analysis — 83
Skilled Working Class in Evangelical Episcopal Churches — 84
Unskilled Working Class in Evangelical Episcopal Churches — 87
Upper Middle Class in Evangelical Episcopal Churches — 91
Lower Middle Class in Evangelical Episcopal Churches — 93
Conclusion — 93

Chapter 4 Theology — 117
Core Theology — 117
  Conversionism — 117
  Activism — 122
  Crucicentrism — 129
  Biblicism — 131
Wider Evangelical Theology — 133
  Incarnation Theology — 133
  Sanctification — 136
  Election — 139
  Millenarianism — 143
  Inspiration of Scripture — 147
Conclusion — 151

Chapter 5 Lifestyle — 153
Femininity and Masculinity — 154
Children — 159
Philanthropy — 164
Sabbatarianism — 170
Temperance — 174
Recreation — 177
Conclusion — 182

Chapter 6 Doctrinal and Practical Issues — 183
Anti-Catholicism — 183
Baptism — 193
Architecture — 205
Ritualism — 210
Conclusion — 212

Chapter 7 The Doctrine of the Scottish Communion Office — 215
The History of the Scottish Communion Office — 220
Disputes Over The Scottish Communion Office of 1764 — 224
  The Prayer of Oblation — 226
  The Prayer of Invocation — 228
  Minor Points of Difference — 232
  Bagot's Analysis — 232
  High Church Response to Craig, Drummond and Bagot — 235
  Scottish Evangelical Episcopal Response — 237
Conclusion — 244

Contents xi

Chapter 8 Secession **247**
Introduction 247
The First Disruptions 258
  Arradoul 258
  Edinburgh 259
    Events 259
    Factors Surrounding the Conflict 265
Conclusion 278

Chapter 9 Continuing Disruption **281**
St Paul's, Aberdeen 284
St Jude's, Glasgow 289
Other English Episcopal Chapels, 1845-1855 293
Internal Disruptions, 1854-1865 302
Later Disruptions, 1861-1887 308
Consolidating Factors, 1845-1887 310
Evangelicalism and English Episcopalianism 314
Conclusion 316

Chapter 10 From Secession to Partial Union, 1846-1900 **319**
Concessions from the Church of England, 1845-1863 320
The Duke of Buccleuch's Bill, 1864 331
Aftermath, 1864-1869 332
Attempt at Reconciliation, 1870-1872 336
Divisions within English Episcopalianism 343
An English Episcopal Bishop 352
Moves to Unite, 1882 354
Revision of Liturgy and Canons, 1890 357
After 1890 360
Conclusion 363

Chapter 11 Conclusion **365**

Bibliography **385**

Index **407**

List of Graphs

Graph 3.1	Members, St Paul's, Aberdeen	105
Graph 3.2	Baptismal Presenters, St Paul's, Aberdeen	105
Graph 3.3	Heads of Families with Voting Rights, St Peter's, Montrose	106
Graph 3.4	Baptismal Presenters, St James's, Edinburgh	106
Graph 3.5	Baptismal Presenters, St Thomas's, Edinburgh	107
Graph 3.6	Baptismal Presenters, St James's, Aberdeen	107
Graph 3.7	Baptismal Presenters, St Vincent's, Edinburgh	108
Graph 3.8	Baptismal Presenters, St Silas's, Glasgow	108
Graph 3.9	Baptismal Presenters, St Jude's, Glasgow	109
Graph 3.10	Baptismal Presenters, Partick Mission, Govan, Glasgow	109
Graph 3.11	Baptisms, St Paul's, Carrubber's Close, Edinburgh	110
Graph 9.1	English Episcopal Chapels	282

List of Maps

Map 2.1	Evangelical Episcopal Congregations and Laypeople, 1800-1818	58
Map 2.2	Evangelical Scottish Episcopal Congregations, 1821-1830	59
Map 2.3	Evangelical Scottish Episcopal Congregations, 1831-1842	60
Map 2.4	Evangelical Episcopal Congregations, 1842-1898	61
Map 2.5	Scottish Episcopal Churches subscribing to CMS, 1816-1835	62
Map 2.6	Scottish Episcopal Churches subscribing to CMS, 1841	63
Map 2.7	Episcopal Churches subscribing to CMS, 1847	64
Map 2.8	Episcopal Churches subscribing to CMS, 1859	65
Map 2.9	Episcopal Churches subscribing to CMS, 1896	66
Map 3.1	Skilled and Unskilled Working Class, St Thomas's and St Vincent's, Edinburgh, 1869-1900	111
Map 3.2	Skilled Working Class, St James's and St Paul's, Aberdeen, 1854-1879	112
Map 3.3	Unskilled Working Class and Single Mothers, St James's, Aberdeen, 1854-1871	113
Map 3.4	Upper and Lower Middle Class, St Thomas's and St Vincent's, Edinburgh, 1869-1900	114
Map 3.5	Upper and Lower Middle Class, St James's and St Paul's, Aberdeen, 1854-1879	115
Map 3.6	Class Distribution, St Silas's, Glasgow, 1864-1900	116

List of Tables

Table 1.1	Evangelical Scottish Episcopal Clergy, 1800-1900	9
Table 1.2	English Episcopal Evangelicals, 1842-1900	11
Table 1.3	Evangelical Laypeople, 1808-1819	25
Table 1.4	Strength of Evangelical Episcopalianism, 1800-1890	26
Table 2.1	Population (in thousands) of the Largest Cities in Nineteenth-Century Scotland and their Order after London	38
Table 2.2	Subscriptions from Scottish Episcopal Congregations to Church Missionary Society, 1816	46
Table 2.3	Subscriptions from Scottish Episcopal Congregations to Church Missionary Society, 1821-1828	47
Table 2.4	Visits by Church Missionary Society to Scottish Episcopal Congregations, 1834-1835	48
Table 2.5a	Planned Visits to Scottish Episcopal Congregations by Church Missionary Society, 1841	49
Table 2.5b	Accomplished Visits to Scottish Episcopal Congregations by Church Missionary Society, 1841	50
Table 2.5c	Subscriptions from Scottish Episcopal Congregations to Church Missionary Society, 1841	51
Table 2.6	Subscriptions from English and Scottish Episcopalians to Church Missionary Society, 1847	52
Table 2.7	Subscriptions from English and Scottish Episcopalians to Church Missionary Society, 1859	52
Table 2.8	Subscriptions from English and Scottish Episcopalians to Church Missionary Society, 1896	53
Table 3.1	Division of Scottish Labour, 1867	67
Table 3.2	Individuals with Middle-class Occupations in Scotland as a Percentage of the Occupied Population	68
Table 3.3	Baptisms at St Paul's, Aberdeen, 1870-1880, 1889	72
Table 3.4	Members, St Paul's, Aberdeen	95
Table 3.5	Baptismal Presenters, St Paul's, Aberdeen	96
Table 3.6	Heads of Families with Voting Rights, St Peter's, Montrose	97
Table 3.7	Baptismal Presenters, St James's, Edinburgh	98
Table 3.8	Baptismal Presenters, St Thomas's, Edinburgh	99

List of Tables

Table 3.9	Baptismal Presenters, St James's, Aberdeen	100
Table 3.10	Baptismal Presenters, St Vincent's, Edinburgh	101
Table 3.11	Baptismal Presenters, St Silas's, Glasgow	102
Table 3.12	Baptismal Presenters, St Jude's, Glasgow	103
Table 3.13	Baptismal Presenters, Partick Mission, Govan, Glasgow	104
Table 3.14	Baptismal Presenters, St Paul's, Carrubber's Close, Edinburgh	104
Table 3.15	Class Distribution in the Presbyterian Churches of Glasgow, 1845-1865	83
Table 3.16	Baptismal Record of St Andrew's, Back of Castle, Edinburgh, 1857-1862	91
Table 6.1	Episcopal Committee Members of the Scottish Reformation Society, 1851-1880	190
Table 6.2	Residents living 1/2 Mile from St Thomas's Canongate Mission, Edinburgh, 1841-1851	192
Table 7.1	Types of Invocation	222
Table 7.2	Collation of Communion Offices	378
Table 9.1	English Episcopal Chapels, 1842-1988	283
Table 10.1	Ritualism in Scotland, 1860-1880	335
Table 10.2	Ritualism in Scotland, 1900	345

Foreword

The provinces of the Anglican communion have traditionally possessed a distinctive flavour. Thus the Church of the Province of Southern Africa has been predominantly High Church while the Church of the Province of Uganda has been overwhelmingly Evangelical. Within the British Isles, whereas the English provinces of Canterbury and York have been notably mixed in churchmanship, Wales, erected into a separate province in 1920, has been principally High Church. So has Scotland, where Episcopalianism has maintained its particular usages down the generations. In the nineteenth century the Scottish Episcopal Church contained contrasting parties, but the chief contestants for its soul were all High Churchmen – whether they were defenders of the traditional liturgy, accommodators with the Church of England or innovators moulded by Tractarianism. Scotland seemed to be a High Church bastion.

That reality has obscured the part played in Scottish Episcopal life by the Evangelical party. From the early years of the century there was a rising tide of Evangelicalism within the Scottish Episcopal Church. Much later than in the Church of England, but roughly in parallel with similar developments in Ireland, the clergy who proclaimed a gospel of conversion gradually gathered sympathetic congregations. It was part of the process of cultural convergence that marked the United Kingdom during the century. The clergy, who were often Englishmen themselves, naturally looked to the Church of England, and especially to its strong Evangelical party, for their inspiration. With their uncompromising rejection of certain High Church beliefs such as baptismal regeneration, they created tensions within the church. They never managed to achieve the degree of success of their Irish contemporaries. Yet, as this book reveals, the Evangelicals within the Scottish Episcopal Church did establish a significant number of congregations in Scotland, some of them large and influential.

A proportion of Evangelical Episcopalians, however, left the church to form their own separate denomination. The chief leader of a secession, David Drummond, was forced out reluctantly in 1842 because he held weeknight meetings without the liturgy. His Edinburgh church, St Thomas's, became the flagship of a new English Episcopal body which abandoned distasteful High Church practices, endorsed revivals and even secured the services of a retired colonial bishop. Although most of its chapels falteringly returned to the Scottish Episcopal Church before the century was over, this denomination was represented by strong congregations in the cities of Scotland and a sprinkling of lesser groups elsewhere. This volume, which carefully analyses the phenomenon, shows that as many as two dozen congregations belonged to English Episcopalianism.

Pat Meldrum here explores the role of Evangelicals both inside and outside the Scottish Episcopal Church in nineteenth-century Scotland. With exemplary thoroughness, she identifies each known congregation, putting the reasons for its existence into context. She examines the theological and liturgical issues that separated Evangelicals from other Scottish Episcopalians, showing that some of the apparently minor technicalities were rooted in major disagreements. And she investigates the social composition of the Evangelical congregations, asking who their members were and how they lived. This is a book about people as well as ideas. Pat Meldrum has written a comprehensive study of the Evangelical movement in nineteenth-century Scottish Episcopalianism.

David Bebbington,
University of Stirling
March 2006

PREFACE

The topic for the thesis, which forms this book, came to mind after completion of an undergraduate degree with the Open University. I had especially enjoyed a course entitled Religion in Victorian Britain, and therefore the subject of nineteenth-century Scottish Episcopalianism was immediately appealing. But, in particular, it was the Evangelical aspect that caught my attention. At the age of seventeen I came to know Christ as my Saviour and friend through the witness and teaching of Evangelical Anglicanism and, since moving to Edinburgh, had been a member of St Thomas's church, the focus of Scottish Evangelical Episcopalianism in the nineteenth century. In some ways such personal connections made the task, which required a dispassionate approach, more difficult. Nevertheless, the journey on which I embarked proved to be unusually rewarding and the process of becoming acquainted with Churchmen and women of various shades of belief, living and labouring in Scotland so many years ago, has been enriching beyond all expectation.

I have been extremely fortunate in having Professor D. W. Bebbington of the Department of History, University of Stirling, as my supervisor. His expertise, enthusiasm and untiring efforts to improve my performance have been an inspiration. Without his help I would probably have relinquished all hopes of completing the thesis long ago. Together with his professional skills I would like to pay tribute to Professor Bebbington's unfailing personal kindness, his encouragement in times of difficulty, and his insistence on achieving the best possible results, while never disparaging my tentative or erroneous ideas. He has animated every supervision and I can never express adequately the debt I owe to him. It is thus important to emphasise that any errors in the text of this book are entirely my own.

I would also like to thank others in the History Department at Stirling: Professor G. C. Peden for his oversight of my period of study and Dr I. G. C. Hutchison for some helpful suggestions early in my research. Appreciation is also due to Linda Bradley, departmental secretary, and Annabelle Hopkins, departmental assistant, for the careful attention to the myriad of official regulations surrounding postgraduate degrees and for their patient understanding of my mishaps in this field.

There are many others to whom I am indebted. Unfortunately I am sure to miss out some, and for this I apologise. Among historians I particularly thank Dr D. M. Bertie who generously gave me a list of English Episcopalians he had compiled during the course of his own research and in advance of the publication of his book, *Scottish Episcopal Clergy, 1689-2000*. He thus gave me an invaluable head start in my own investigations. Dr Rowan Strong helpfully pointed me towards various archive deposits and provided me with some photocopies. The late Rev Canon David McCubbin explained aspects of Scottish Episcopalianism with which I was unfamiliar. Dr Gavin White sent me a chapter, dealing with English Episcopalianism, from his book *The Scottish Episcopal Church: A New History*, and shared his knowledge with me. Professor John Wolffe pointed me to the deposit at the Scottish Reformation Society. Sara Stevenson provided me with photocopies of archive and other material from the Scottish National Portrait Gallery. Rev Dr Eric Culbertson allowed me extended loan of his thesis 'Evangelical Theology, 1857 to 1900'. Rev Dr K. S. Jeffrey informed me of archives concerning English Episcopalianism in Aberdeen. Rev Dr Alan Munden gave useful preliminary suggestions for pursuit. From Edinburgh University, others have been particularly helpful. My husband, Dr J. D. P. Meldrum, Reader in Pure Mathematics, gave me advice on mathematical sampling and tutored me in all aspects of computing. Dr Chris Merchant, lecturer in the Department of Geo Sciences, provided me with outline maps of Scotland. I thank all these people for their time and expertise.

The staff at the National Library of Scotland and New College Library, Edinburgh, have been noteworthy for their advice, for the efficient supply of my orders for material and for the welcome smile day-by-day. They will remain long in my memory for all that is best in dealing with customers in a pleasant and knowledgeable manner. It was a pleasure, also, to use the facilities of the British Library, in particular the newspaper department at Colindale where the staff, again, were exceptionally helpful. Similar thanks are due to Lambeth Palace Library, Aberdeen University Library and the Central Library, Dundee, who provided assistance, often over the telephone, and photocopied archive material for me. Again special appreciation goes to Edinburgh City Library, the Mitchell Library, Glasgow, and the Public Libraries at Huntly, Montrose, Nairn and Perth.

Curators of archives are likewise remembered gratefully. Among them Dr Tristram Clark and his colleagues at the National Archives of Scotland, together with the staff of Aberdeen City Archives, the Derbyshire Record Office, the Diocesan Synod, Edinburgh, and Edinburgh City Archives are thanked. Again, Rev A. Sinclair Horne of the Scottish Reformation Society gave much helpful advice. It is appropriate to highlight the search made by John Howard, archivist at St Mary's Cathedral, Edinburgh, who eventually, after a year, located the Dawson Collection in a tower underneath a pile of correspondence concerning drains and plumbing. Perusal of the thesis will reveal the importance of this archive.

I would also like to thank the Royal Historical Society for a generous grant. It enabled the photocopying of much of the newly available Drummond archive at the Derbyshire Record Office which allowed many special additions to be made to the thesis.

I am indebted to various clergy for allowing me to consult archives held in their churches. Rev Canon Mike Parker very kindly permitted me to store the material from St Thomas's, Edinburgh, in my home. His generosity saved me much time. Thanks are also recorded to Rev H. G. C. Lee, Crieff; Rev Canon R. A. Grant, St Vincent's, Edinburgh; Rev K. F. Scott and Joanna McLennan, St James's, Edinburgh; Rev D. W. McCarthy, St Silas's, Glasgow; Rev S. A. Fellows and members of the congregation, Huntly; Rev and Mrs J. L. Evans, Fochabers; Rev and Mrs A. A. Sinclair, St John's, Inverness; Rev B. A. Hutton and Judy Page, Holy Trinity, Paisley; Rev R. C. Fyffe and members of the congregation, St John's, Perth.

While I am conscious of the many shortcomings in the finished work, I thank God for spiritual aid in its completion and for providing family and friends who have helped me along the way. I gratefully acknowledge the constant encouragement of my late parents, Kathleen and Jack Sealey, and of my children Elizabeth and David together with their spouses Marius and Beverley. My fellow research student, Alison Kennedy, has been a special joy, always ready in an instant to give advice, enthuse, sympathise and minister to me as a constant and cheerful friend. Again, Julia Park will never realise how much her lively interest has meant, and how valuable her help was in typing up some of the Dawson Collection. Special thanks are again expressed to Rev Canon Mike Parker for his zeal for the project. Likewise, Isabel Murphy and Margaret Leask from the Open University, Chris and Jim Smith, Mary Graham, Susan Southam, Elizabeth Lawson, Jean Todd and many others from St Thomas's, Edinburgh, have supported me. I owe a great debt to my husband, John, for his prayers, patience and help, even in times of his own heavy workload and illness. His encouragement has been a golden thread through the years. I dedicate this book to him.

Abbreviations

CMS	Church Missionary Society
DC	Dawson Collection
DRO	Derbyshire Record Office
ENCS	Denotes duplication with Rowan Strong, *Episcopalianism in Nineteenth-Century Scotland* (Oxford, 2002). See Chapter 1, p. 33 of this book for further explanation.
LPL	Lambeth Palace Library
Memoir	D. T. K. Drummond, *The Last Scenes in the Life of our Lord and Saviour* with *A Sketch of his Life and Labours, by Professor Balfour* (London, 1878).
NAS	National Archives of Scotland
NLS	National Library of Scotland

Chapter 1

Introduction

The history and development of the Evangelical movement in nineteenth-century Scottish Episcopalianism has received little attention from historians. Whereas the background of the Scottish Episcopal Church in general is well documented,[1] the contribution of Evangelicals to Episcopalianism in Scotland has not been researched fully. Since the period was one of intense activity among Evangelicals in Britain, leading to a notable influence on society in the communication of religious faith, accepted moral values and philanthropy,[2] there is ample justification for exploring the part played by those Evangelical Episcopalians living in the northern part of Britain.

An Evangelical Churchman is one who adheres to the characteristic theology of Evangelicalism. In this book the term 'Evangelical' will be used to describe anyone, regardless of denomination, who held or holds these particular beliefs. As D. W. Bebbington explains, Evangelicalism, which emerged as a distinct Protestant movement in the eighteenth century, put a particular emphasis on the need for religious conversion leading to a personal relationship with God. This was understood to be a transforming experience because those who passed through it claimed to have come to know God in a totally new way. Starting from the point that human beings are naturally sinful, Evangelicals preached that lives could be changed when people acknowledged their sin and accepted, by faith, the atoning death of Christ on the cross. Whether this was a gradual or sudden event, individuals were aware of a difference in their lives. Evangelicals believed that this process of conversion was taught in the Bible. As such, it was part of their biblicism – the belief that scripture, supremely, rather than Church fathers, popes or priests, taught the substance of the Christian faith. The centre of their theology was the cross, for it was there that Christ was believed to have gained salvation for all those who came penitently to him. As a result, Evangelicals were typically activist and missionary-minded in

---

[1] George Grubb, *An Ecclesiastical History of Scotland* (Edinburgh, 1861). Frederick Goldie, *A Short History of the Episcopal Church in Scotland* (Edinburgh, 1976). Marion Lochhead, *Episcopal Scotland in the Nineteenth Century* (London, 1996). Gavin White, *The Scottish Episcopal Church: A New History* (Edinburgh, 1998). Rowan Strong, *Episcopalianism in Nineteenth-Century Scotland* (Oxford, 2002).

[2] D. W. Bebbington, *Evangelicalism in Modern Britain* (London, 1993).

their efforts to pass on their faith because they believed it to have life-changing properties.³ J. C. Ryle, Bishop of Liverpool from 1880 to 1900, described these tenets as the 'principal things in Christianity', emphasising that it was not that other Churchmen failed to preach them but, rather, that they did not give them the same prominence as Evangelicals did.⁴ Although the order of priority of the categories tended to change depending on the religious climate of the age,⁵ Evangelicalism has thus displayed a distinct theology.

Historians sometimes use the term 'evangelical' to apply to any Protestant Churchmen in the sixteenth and seventeenth centuries. But Evangelicalism as a movement, rather than as a term describing certain Reformation beliefs, began only at a later date in America, Wales, England and Scotland in originally unrelated events. In 1727 Jonathan Edwards, a Congregational minister in Northampton, Massachusetts, experienced what he described as a new awareness of God. Under his preaching many in his congregation came to similar faith themselves, and a series of such conversions in other New England churches from 1740 until 1743 escalated into The Great Awakening. Quite independently, in 1735, Howell Harris, a schoolmaster at Talgarth in Wales, was deeply affected when reading books published by the Society for Promoting Christian Knowledge. At a communion service on Whit Sunday he, too, professed a new relationship with God. He gathered a following which was to develop into the Calvinistic Methodist society in Wales, the term Methodist referring to the system whereby its followers met regularly for Bible study and prayer. Although never ordained, Harris inspired events throughout South Wales in a movement which became known as the Welsh Revival. In the spring of 1745 George Whitefield, while a student at Oxford, underwent a similar experience to those of Edwards and Harris. He was subsequently ordained into the Church of England and, in 1741, embarked on a round of preaching which took him to Scotland. Notably, the Cambuslang Revival there in 1742 saw many professing refreshed belief. In 1743 Whitefield founded the English Calvinistic Methodist Connexion, uniting those who had been influenced by his preaching. John and Charles Wesley had been affected likewise in 1738. Their combined ministry, with John as an itinerant preacher and Charles as composer of hymns, marked the onset of the

---

³ Bebbington, *Evangelicalism*, pp. 2-17. Chapter 4 of this thesis elaborates on some of the characteristics of Evangelical faith among nineteenth-century Episcopalians in Scotland.

⁴ J. C. Ryle, *Knots Untied* (London, 1959), p. 13.

⁵ In the eighteenth century the stress was on conversion and the doctrine of the cross. J. C. Ryle at the end of the nineteenth century laid more emphasis on the supremacy of the Bible, in reaction to assaults on biblical inspiration from the 1860s onwards. See Bebbington, *Evangelicalism*, p. 3.

Introduction 3

eighteenth-century Revival in England and the development of the Arminian Methodist society from 1743. Evangelicalism, introduced into Britain by the ministry of Harris, was perpetuated by the Wesleys and Whitefield.[6]

By 1795 the Wesleyan Methodists separated from the Church of England, and the Calvinistic Methodists had largely disappeared after Whitefield's death in 1770, apart from an enduring presence in Wales. In the Church of England itself neither kind of Methodism, despite Anglican roots, affected many clergy or their associates. However, some were touched by the new religious climate as a result of private reading and prayer. These individuals generally emerged as moderate Calvinists, Samuel Walker, incumbent of Truro from 1746 to 1761, William Grimshaw of Haworth from 1742 to 1763, and William Romaine, Rector of St Anne's, Blackfriars, London, from 1766 to 1795, being typical of those who heralded the advent of Anglican Evangelicalism. Numbers grew steadily, bound together by personal correspondence and regular meetings and, by 1769, John Wesley reported between fifty and sixty such Anglican clergy. Thus the Evangelical movement in the Church of England did not derive directly from Methodism, but was held by its supporters to be a distinct response to the spiritual mood of the age.[7]

In Scotland, Methodism was never well established although the Wesleyans had sixteen preachers ministering to over one thousand members by 1790.[8] But Evangelical emphases were readily grafted on to the Calvinisitic theology of the Presbyterians. In the Church of Scotland John Maclaurin, of Ramshorn, Glasgow, from 1723 to 1754, corresponded with Jonathan Edwards and learnt early of the American revival. He influenced others of whom Thomas Gillespie of Dunfermline and Thomas Boston of Jedburgh left the Church in 1761 over the issue of patronage and the right of a congregation to choose its own minister. The resulting Relief

---

[6] Chapter 4, pp. 139-143 discusses the differences between Calvinism and Arminianism. See Bebbington, *Evangelicalism*, pp. 27-34 for the history of Methodism.

[7] Bebbington, *Evangelicalism*, pp 20-31. Nigel M. de S. Cameron, *Dictionary of Scottish Church History and Theology* (Edinburgh, 1993) p. 306. Kenneth Hylson-Smith, *Evangelicals in the Church of England, 1734-1984* (Edinburgh, 1988), pp. 10-21.

[8] Anglican Evangelicals who had a strong sense of Church order, for example Charles Simeon of Holy Trinity, Cambridge, were wary of Methodism. See Chapter 8, p. 248. However, it is possible that some Methodist preachers were instrumental in the conversion of Scottish Episcopalians. Duncan Wright ministered in Aberdeen, Perth and Greenock and Robert Dall was active in Peterhead, Fraserburgh, Forres, Elgin, Cromarty and Dingwall. Nigel M. de S. Cameron, *Dictionary of Scottish Church History and Theology* (Edinburgh, 1993), p. 560. See Chapter 1, p. 23 which lists Anne Robertson of Dingwall as an early nineteenth-century Scottish Episcopal Evangelical, Chapter 1, p. 17 for the movement at Greenock, and Chapter 8, pp. 258-259 for Evangelicalism at Arradoul, near Elgin.

Church, which was notable for its Evangelical beliefs, existed alongside the Secession Church, formed in 1733 for similar reasons. The latter, which was also home to a number of Evangelicals, was responsible for inviting Whitefield to Scotland in 1741.[9]

The Scottish Episcopal Church, by contrast, appears to have been relatively unaffected by the Evangelical Revival of the eighteenth century. While it is likely that some individual laypeople came to the new brand of faith,[10] possibly through contact with Whitefield, or as a result of the itinerant ministries of evangelists such as the Anglican, Rowland Hill of Surrey Chapel, Blackfriars, in 1799 and 1800,[11] or through Methodist preachers, other churches, or when visiting England, there are no accounts of a similar movement among the clergy. The southern clergy, who were mainly English, Irish or Anglicized Scots, were generally analogous to High Churchmen in the Church of England. They typically stressed the pre- and post-Reformation Catholic beliefs of baptismal regeneration, sacramental grace in the eucharist, and the apostolic succession of the ordained priesthood with its authority to preach and administer the sacraments. They were faithful to the Book of Common Prayer and, additionally, were strong upholders of Church authority and discipline. Although believing in the supremacy of scripture, they looked also to the teaching of the early fathers of the church rather than relying on individual interpretation of biblical doctrine.[12] While loyal to the Thirty-Nine Articles, some like George Gleig, the future Bishop of Brechin and Primus in 1816 to 1837, were so anti-Calvinist as to espouse semi-Pelagianism.[13] The clergy of northern Scotland, however, were mostly Scottish. While also adhering to High Church doctrine, they were typically Virtualist theologians, holding to the theology of the eighteenth-century English Nonjurors[14]. Their communion service, composed in 1764, differed

---

[9] Bebbington, *Evangelicalism*, pp. 33-34. Cameron, *Dictionary*, pp. 560-561, 702-703.

[10] See Chapter 1, pp. 22-23.

[11] Rowland Hill, *Journal Through the North of England and Parts of Scotland with Remarks on the Present State of the Established Church* (London, 1799). On p. 104 Hill alludes to a single visit to an Episcopal church in Scotland by Charles Simeon of Cambridge. Rowland Hill, *Extracts of a Journal of a Second Tour from England through the Highlands of Scotland and the North Western Parts of England* (London, 1800).

[12] Chapter 4, p. 119 and Chapter 6, pp. 193-205 discuss baptismal regeneration. *Cf.* White, *Scottish Episcopal Church*, p. 12. P. B. Nockles, *The Oxford Movement in Context* (Cambridge, 1994), pp. 25-26.

[13] Chapter 4, p. 118, discusses Gleig's theology.

[14] The term 'Virtualist' in this thesis is written with an upper case following C. W. Dugmore, *Eucharistic Doctrine in England from Hooker to Waterland* (London, 1942);

considerably from the Book of Common Prayer. While eschewing transubstantiation, it stressed a sacrificial aspect and placed an emphasis on the eucharistic elements becoming the body and blood of Christ in virtue, power and effect, capable of conveying grace.[15] The Scottish Episcopal Church, dominated by these two groups of High Churchmen, was thus markedly unreceptive to Evangelical belief at the time of the eighteenth-century Revival.

In the early nineteenth century some High Churchmen began to show a lack of fervour and vigour in their preaching and beliefs and, as a result, were known as the 'High and Dry' party.[16] Such parched ground was evident in Scotland. Although possibly partisan in his comments, Rowland Hill remarked after his Scottish tour of 1799 that the prerequisite for an Episcopal clergyman there was that he 'should be a good reader...should not squall...and should produce nothing from the pulpit but what is made easy to the practice of the present age'.[17] While acknowledging that there was one incumbent in 'the north of Scotland...who gives most flattering promises that he will become a burning and shining light', he dismissed the rest as preaching 'undecided doctrines'.[18] Similarly, in 1844 the Evangelical newspaper, the *Record*, accused the majority of Scottish Episcopal clergy of 'lulling their congregations asleep among the dissipation and worldliness of fashionable life'.[19] In the same year the *Christian Remembrancer*, the periodical of the High Church Tractarian party whose adherents from 1833 sought to breathe new life into the Church by stressing a Catholic interpretation of the Book of Common Prayer and the Thirty-Nine Articles, was likewise critical. While approving the over-riding doctrinal stance of the Nonjuring Scottish Communion Office, it condemned the Scottish Episcopal Church as being 'without the energy which gives life and reality to the beautiful theory which she

---

A. J. MacDonald, *The Evangelical Doctrine of Holy Communion* (London, 1936); Peter Toon, *Evangelilcal Theology 1833-1856: A Response to Tractarianism* (London, 1977).

[15] Strong, *Episcopalianism*, pp. 17-19. White, *Scottish Episcopal Church*, pp. 3-5. Chapter 7 discusses the issue of the communion service. White suggests that many Scottish Virtualists were followers of the Yorkshireman, John Hutchinson (1674-1737). Hutchinsonianism, which spoke against the appeal to reason and natural religion, emphasised instead that truth was to be found only by direct revelation from the Bible or even from classical literature. Its view of the miraculous aspect of God's intercourse with mankind had similarities to Evangelicalism, but led to a heightened sacramentalism while Evangelicalism stressed the life-changing doctrine of conversion. Cameron, *Dictionary*, p. 419.

[16] Nockles, *Oxford Movement*, p. 193.

[17] Hill, *Remarks on Present State*, pp. 103-104.

[18] *Ibid.*, pp. 103-105. The exception was probably William Ward of Old Deer (1798-1800). See Chapter 1, p. 15.

[19] *Record*, 17 November 1842.

teaches'.[20] Certainly there were exceptions to the general rule. The Evangelical clergyman D. T. K. Drummond of Edinburgh reminisced in 1873 that the ministry of the High Churchman, E. B. Ramsay at St George's Chapel, Edinburgh, from 1824 to 1826, had exhibited 'faithful preaching and stirring appeals...attractiveness of style and manner'.[21] But, overall, by the nineteenth century it appears that the Scottish Episcopal Church was noted for its rather staid and formalised stance. Such ground provided an environment in which more vibrant expressions of Christianity could take root. Thus Evangelicalism and Tractarianism both attracted adherents in nineteenth-century Scotland, each offering new, although opposing, versions of faith. The tension between such Protestant and Catholic doctrinal emphases was to play a major part in the developing face of Scottish Evangelical Episcopalianism at that time.

The Rise of Evangelicalism in Nineteenth-Century Scottish Episcopalianism

In order to trace the development of Evangelicalism in Scottish Episcopalianism it is first necessary to construct a method which enables accurate identification of Evangelicals. Various criteria can be applied when ascertaining churchmanship. Noting what contemporaries thought of a person is useful; if he or she were generally labelled as an Evangelical it would seem safe to assume likewise. This is particularly appropriate when considering clergy since the public nature of their views exposed them to classification by their contemporaries. But there are dangers in this method. For instance some might have declared themselves as Evangelicals in an effort to extract support for a cause. Conversely, in the fervour of theological polemic, one party might have disowned another unjustly. Personal assessments are not totally reliable.

An added verification can be made by checking if the individual is entered in *The Blackwell Dictionary of Evangelical Biography* which records some of the best-known Evangelicals, clerical and lay. But since it sometimes has to rely on the opinion of contemporaries, it is not always reliable and is of little use for lesser-known people. An alternative method is to study the writings of a person. If these clearly display the doctrines of Evangelicalism as discussed above[22] – the belief that spiritual conversion rather than baptism signifies the beginning of Christian life, the centrality of the cross in preaching, devotion to the Bible, and a burning desire to spread the gospel to others – it is reasonable to suppose that the person was

---

[20] *Christian Remembrancer*, Volume vii, January 1844, p. 80.

[21] Charles Rogers, *Memorial and Recollections of the Rev. Edward Bannerman Ramsay* (London, 1873), pp. 58-59.

[22] See Chapter 1, p. 1.

Introduction 7

an Evangelical. But expression of only one or two of these categories is not enough to classify a person as a clear Evangelical. An individual might have preached the doctrine of conversion, for instance, but was not necessarily labelled as an Evangelical by fellow Churchmen, whereas others who preached similarly were. This was particularly true by the later decades of the nineteenth century when some Anglo-Catholic teaching bore a marked similarity to Evangelicalism in calling for conversion beyond baptism.[23] Likewise, many High Churchmen were assiduous workers in spreading the gospel, and looked to the Bible for their model of faith.[24] Another difficulty is scarcity of writings and, since Evangelicals did not necessarily preach their characteristic beliefs in every sermon, it can be difficult to ascertain churchmanship from available texts. Sometimes Evangelicals changed their views over time. For example some, like J. H. Newman, either became Tractarians or veered towards the movement in the 1830s and 1840s. It is not inevitably the case that an Evangelical in the 1820s, say, remained one later on. Evidence of Evangelical beliefs expressed in written texts, therefore, has to be treated cautiously and examined over a span of years. It is not always a precise pointer to churchmanship.

Allegiance to the Church Missionary Society (CMS), an Evangelical Anglican organisation founded in April 1799, can sometimes determine churchmanship. But, again, this is not foolproof. Evidence for multi-party involvement with CMS will be given later,[25] but at present it is sufficient to note that the society had a policy of visiting any church willing to issue it with an invitation, and so it collected money from Anglican churches of various types – inclusion of a church on the CMS list of subscriptions does not mean that its incumbent was definitely an Evangelical. Similarly, publications by the society give the names of private subscribers, both clerical and lay. While it seems reasonable to assume that such people were Evangelicals, this was not always the case because, again, some non-Evangelicals probably gave to the society. CMS data is not a foolproof guide when identifying Evangelicals.[26]

Therefore it is obvious that there are difficulties in classifying accurately all those who were Evangelicals in the nineteenth century. However, with

---

[23] *Cf.* Dieter Voll, *Catholic Evangelicalism* (London, 1963), pp. 50-84. For an example of Evangelical High Churchmanship in Scotland, see Bishop J. R. A. Chinnery-Haldane's sermon, 'Conversion of the Heart', *Scottish Guardian*, September 25 1885. Haldane was Bishop of Argyll and the Isles, 1883-1906. He was the son of Alexander Haldane, editor of the *Record*. See D. M. Bertie, *Scottish Episcopal Clergy 1689-2000* (Edinburgh, 2000), p. 208.

[24] Chapter 4, pp. 119, 122, 132 and Chapter 3, p. 90 give examples of such clergy.

[25] Chapter 2, pp. 46-56.

[26] *Cf.* Strong, *Episcopalianism*, p. 219.

the onset of various theological disputes in the 1820s, but mainly in the 1830s as Tractarianism emerged, beliefs were sharpened and people tended to ally themselves more distinctly with parties. Thus by 1840 it is much easier to isolate Evangelicals. In Scotland the added dimension of several secessions from the Scottish Episcopal Church from the 1840s onwards, analysed in Chapters 8 and 9, facilitates the task. These problems began in 1842 when D. T. K. Drummond of Holy Trinity, Edinburgh, left the Scottish Episcopal Church with a substantial number of his congregation after C. H. Terrot, Bishop of Edinburgh, challenged him over the use of non-liturgical evangelistic meetings. As a result, Drummond founded St Thomas's which opened in Edinburgh in 1843. It was completely separate from the Scottish Episcopal Church, designating itself as loyal to the Church of England and taking on the title of English Episcopal in order to make its allegiance clear. While some Evangelicals remained within the Scottish Episcopal Church, the majority joined this 'English Episcopal' movement after it became apparent that there were doctrinal difficulties with the Scottish Communion Office of 1764, the official liturgy of the Church. In the process these Churchmen enunciated their beliefs clearly, and they emerged as a distinct group of Evangelicals who, while Episcopalian, relinquished all links with the Scottish Episcopal Church. Using all these tools – reputation, writings, allegiance to CMS, and involvement with the English Episcopal movement – it is possible to construct a list of people who can be classified as Evangelical Episcopalians in nineteenth-century Scotland. The results are recorded in Table 1.1, which shows Evangelical clergy in the Scottish Episcopal Church in the nineteenth century, and in Table 1.2, which lists the Evangelical English Episcopalians from 1842 to 1900.

Introduction

Table 1.1 Evangelical Scottish Episcopal Clergy, 1800-1900

DATE	CHURCH	INCUMBENT
c. 1800	Old Deer qualified chapel, Aberdeenshire	William Ward [E]
1817-45	Holy Trinity, Paisley	W. M. Wade [?]
1818-21	St Paul's, Carrubber's Close, Edinburgh	Edward Craig [E]
1821-35	St James's, Edinburgh	Edward Craig
1828-39	St Mark's, Portobello, Edinburgh	G. M. Drummond [S]
1829-31	St John's, Greenock	T. H. Wilkinson [E]
1832-37	St Paul's, Carrubber's Close, Edinburgh	D. T. K. Drummond [S]
1834-36	Fochabers	W. P. McFarquhar [I]
1835-43	St James's, Edinburgh	Daniel Bagot [I]
1837-43	St Jude's, Glasgow	Robert Montgomery [E]
1838-42	Holy Trinity, Edinburgh	D. T. K. Drummond
1840-45	St John's, Dumfries	W. P. McFarquhar
1842-43	St Paul's, Aberdeen	Sir William Dunbar [S]
1842-45	Huntly	J. D. Hull [I]
1843-1844	St Jude's, Glasgow	C. P. Miles [E]
1843-45	Aberdour	John Hitchcock [E]
1845-46	St James's, Edinburgh	J. H. Crowder [E]
1845-1900	Fasque	Possibly variable Churchmanship
1848	Crieff and Muthill	J. H. P. A. M. Maynard [E]
1848-53	Holy Trinity, Edinburgh	Robert Payne Smith [E]
1851-85	Holy Trinity, Edinburgh	V. G. Faithfull [E]
1857-1905	St Andrew's, Edinburgh	C. R. Teape [I]
1839-42 (Overseas)	CMS Bombay, India	J. S. S. Robertson [S]
1843-44	Dunblane	
1844-48	Aberdour	
1847-48	Lecturer in Hebrew and Oriental Languages, Trinity College, Glenalmond	
1848-57 (Overseas)	CMS Nazikh and Bombay, India	
1858-78	CMS Secretary	
1862-64	Pitlochry	

1864-65	St Peter's, Edinburgh	
1865-83	Chaplain to Lord Rollo, Duncrub	
1877-78	Dunning Mission	
1879-81	St Andrew's, Edinburgh	
1866-71	St Columba's, Crieff	E. F. D. Hutton [E/S]
1871-78	St Paul's, Glasgow	James McCann [E]
1872-86	Bishop of Edinburgh	Henry Cotterill, [E] uncertain Churchmanship
1873-1875	Diocesan Chaplain, Edinburgh	Thomas Worthington [E]
1882-88	St Vincent's, Edinburgh	T. K. Talon [I]
1890-1921	St Peter's, Edinburgh	E. C. Dawson [E]
1885-1920	Christ Church, Morningside, Edinburgh	C. M. Black [I]
1897-99	St James's, Aberdeen	A. M. MacKay [E/S]
1899-1907	Holy Trinity, Edinburgh	A. M. MacKay
1898-1908	St Paul's, Aberdeen	E. E. Marshall [E]

Total Number of Evangelical Scottish Episcopal Clergy: 28
Nationality: [E] 15 English, [I] 6 Irish, [S] 4 Scottish, [E/S] 2 Anglo-Scottish
Source: D. M. Bertie, *Scottish Episcopal Clergy, 1689-2000* (Edinburgh, 2000).

Introduction

Table 1.2 English Episcopal Evangelicals, 1842-1900

CHURCH	INCUMBENT	CURATE/ASSISTANT
Arradoul (independent church, intermittently)	Visiting clergy and lay people, 1831-54	
St Thomas's, Edinburgh and Canongate Mission	D. T. K. Drummond, 1842-75 [S]	S. C. Baker, 1844-45 [E] W. Wade, 1846-53 [?] Richard Hibbs, 1852-54 [E] Francis Richardson, 1854-58 [S] George Hamilton, 1858-64 [I] A. H. R. Hebden, 1864-65 [E] George Forrester, 1867-68 [E] W. C. Hughes, 1868-70 [?] W. S. Moncrieff, 1870-75 [S]
	G. W. Butler, 1876-78 [E] E. C. Dawson, 1878-90 [E] W. L. Holland, 1891-95 [E] H. J. Colclough, 1895-1919 [I]	Henry Armstrong, 1897-99 [E] D. C. O'Connor, 1898-1901 [I]
St Paul's, Aberdeen	Sir William Dunbar, 1843-55 [S] Joshua Kirkman, 1855-58 [E] F. W. B. Bouverie, 1858-69 [F] Samuel Clark, 1870-75; 1878-1886 [I] T. W. Bray, 1875-78 [E] G. W. Rowntree, 1886-1894 [E] William Fairclough. 1894-1898 [E] E. E. Marshall, 1898 [E]	J. D. Miller, 1845-48 [?] S. A. Walker, 1848-53 [I] S. R. Carter, 1854-55 [E]

St Jude's, Glasgow	C. P. Miles, 1844-58 [E]	C. B. Gribble, 1845-47 [E] W. Marrable, 1847-48 [E] George Stanham, 1854-58 [E]
	G. K. Flindt, 1858-68 [E]	W. Marshall, 1858-59 [?] T. Birch, 1861-63 [?]
	James McCann, 1869-70 [E] John Bennett, 1876-78 [E] Frederick Courtenay, 1870-76 [E/S] William Williams, 1879-84 [E] William Robinson, 1885-88 [E] P. E. Phelps, 1888-90 [E] W. E. Hodgkinson, 1890-91 [E]	
Dunoon	Visiting clergy, 1845-1900	
Huntly	J. D. Hull, 1845-54 [I]	
Nairn	John Hitchcock, 1845-48 [E] J. Roberts, 1854-60 [?] E. C. Wrenford, 1866-79 [E]	
Gask	Private chapel, 1845-55	
Fochabers	G. F. Williamson, 1847-49 [I]	
Galloway House	John Nunn, 1848-? [E] *	
Crieff	A. C. Rainey, 1849-54 [?]	
Corrimony	Private chapel, 1850-54	
Old Deer	Visiting clergy and lay people, 1853-58	

Introduction 13

St James's, Aberdeen	Abel Woodroofe, 1854 [I] Richard Jones, 1854-58 [E/A] John Goodwin, 1858-62 [E] T. B. Wrenford, 1862-67 [E] William Acraman, 1868-71 [E] Thomas Worthington, 1871-73 [E] F. R. Stratton, 1873-74 [E] John Lockwood, 1874-76 [E] Robert Allen, 1877-80 [I] C. M. Black, 1880-85 [I] A. M. MacKay, 1886-97 [E]	
Selkirk	J. Harris, 1854-56 [?] George Robinson, 1856-58 [?]	
St Vincent's, Edinburgh	Richard Hibbs, 1857-60 [E] Matthew Churton, 1860-67 [E] T. K. Talon, 1867-82 [I]	
Wemyss Bay	Visiting clergy, 1861-1932 **	
St Silas's, Glasgow and Partick Mission	W. T. Turpin, 1863-65 [?] J. M. Maynard, 1865-71 [E] E. F. D. Hutton, 1871-80 [E/S] Frederic Peake, 1880-86 [I] Sholto Douglas-Campbell Douglas (Lord Blythswood), 1886-99 [S]	Horatio Moule, 1873-75 [E] J. T. Loftus, 1875-77 [?] L. J. Fish, 1893-94 [E] G. A. Stephenson, 1893-94 [I] A. G. Townshend, 1895-99 [E] H. Johnson 1898-99, (Partick Mission) [?]
St John's, Dundee	Various clergy, 1868-69 Ambrose Lawson, 1869 [I] D. J. Mulkerns, 1869-78 [I] – Lane, 1878 [?]	
Hunter's Quay	Visiting clergy, 1870-1905	

Cally	C. T. Moor, 1872-77 [E]	
	O. F. Walton, 1877-83 [E]	
	H. E. Eardley, 1884-85 [E]	
Johnstone	A. E. Daniel, 1874-77 [E]	
Balmacara	Visiting clergy, 1887-1916	
St Peter's, Montrose (Qualified 1712-1920)	J. Wade, 1845-50 [?]	
	R. Wade, 1850-51 [?]	
	W. P. Macdermott, 1851-58 [I]	
	H. J. Marshall, 1859-60 [E]	
	W. J. Pollock, 1860-62 [I]	
	R. J. Iagoe, 1864-67 [E]	
	H. E. Preston, 1868-72 [E]	
	H. J. Knapp, 1874-76 [E]	
	A. E. Daniel, 1877-79 [E]	
	T. S. Connolly, 1881-1913 [I]	

Total Number of English Episcopal Clergy: 91
Nationality: [E] 50 English, [I] 18 Irish, [S] 5 Scottish, [F] 1 French, [E/S] 2 Anglo Scottish, [E/A] 1 Anglo Australian, [?]14 Unknown
Bishops Officiating in Scotland for English Episcopalians
    1856 Samuel Gobat (Bishop of Jerusalem, 1846-79)
    1877-1887 E. H. Beckles (Bishop of Sierra Leone, 1860-69)
Bishops Officiating in England for English Episcopalians
    1856-60 H. M. Villiers (Bishop of Carlisle, 1856-60)
    1860-69 Samuel Waldegrave (Bishop of Carlisle, 1860-69)
    1869-75 Charles Baring (Bishop of Durham, 1861-79)
    1885-1900 J. C. Ryle (Bishop of Liverpool, 1880-1900)
*The Earl of Galloway, c. 1848, joined the English Episcopal movement with John Nunn as his chaplain at Galloway House, Wigtonshire. Further information has not been found.
**1860-90: Visiting Clergy at Wemyss Bay, apart from English Episcopalians: 102
Sources: *Edinburgh Almanack* (Edinburgh, 1843-1900). D. M. Bertie, *Scottish Episcopal Clergy 1689-2000* (Edinburgh, 2000), pp. 655-658. Edwin Hodder, *Sir George Burns Bart.* (London, 1892), pp. 371-372. *Revised Report of the Debate in the House of Lords* (London, 1849), p. 232.

Scottish Episcopal Evangelicals

Table 1.1 shows that at least twenty-eight Evangelical clergy served in the Scottish Episcopal Church during the nineteenth century. Of those with identifiable national origins, fifteen were English, six Irish, four Scottish and two Anglo-Scottish. Scottish Episcopal Evangelicalism was thus very much an English implant. The first reference to a clergyman clearly recognised by his contemporaries as an Evangelical occurs in 1798 at the qualified[27] church at Old Deer, Aberdeenshire, when William Ward from Norfolk became its incumbent. Possibly, Ward was the clergyman identified as an Evangelical by Hill in 1799.[28] Whatever the case, William Walker, of neighbouring Monymusk, described him in 1883 as 'a narrow minded and intolerant Calvinist [who] preached a doctrine of conversion'.[29] Walker noted that the High Churchman, John Skinner, a contemporary of Ward's at nearby Longside, 'ridiculed' this teaching on conversion, countering Ward's estimation of himself and others who did not adhere to it as 'without the pale of the Gospel – heathen men, in short'.[30] Thus Old Deer, under Ward until 1800, was probably the first Episcopal Evangelical congregation in nineteenth-century Scotland, but it is impossible to judge whether later incumbents were also Evangelicals because they have left no available writings.[31]

By 1818 Scottish writers were beginning to note a definite Evangelical movement in Edinburgh. G. T. Noel, vicar of Rainham, Kent, and a well-known Evangelical who had been educated in Edinburgh,[32] officiated in St Paul's, Carrubber's Close, Edinburgh, during a vacancy there in 1818. In the same year he introduced the congregation to a newly ordained English Evangelical clergyman, Edward Craig, who was thereupon appointed to the incumbency. In 1861 the Scottish Episcopal historian George Grubb recorded Noel and Craig as misleading 'many ill-informed persons...by the new doctrines'.[33] J. M. Neale, the nineteenth-century Anglo-Catholic clergyman, also pinpointed them as the first to introduce Evangelicalism

---

[27] See Chapter 1, pp. 30-31 for definition of qualified chapels.

[28] See Chapter 1, p. 5.

[29] William Walker, *The Life and Times of the Rev John Skinner at Linshart, Longside* (London, 1883), pp. 140-141.

[30] *Ibid.*

[31] These incumbents were: Alexander Allardice (1800-1816), W. Lawson (1816-1827), H. S. Beresford (1827-1829), Thomas Addison (1829), T. J. Green (1829-1831). D. M. Bertie, *Scottish Episcopal Clergy 1689-2000* (Edinburgh, 2000), p. 652.

[32] Donald M. Lewis (ed.), *The Blackwell Dictionary of Evangelical Biography*, Volume II (Oxford, 1995), p. 831.

[33] George Grubb, *An Ecclesiastical History of Scotland* Vol IV (Edinburgh, 1861), p. 174.

into Scotland,[34] and Walker of Monymusk, in 1878, noted them as 'eloquent and earnest men' preachers of 'new views...[who] did not fail to create a sensation and secure a following'.[35] Thus Noel and Craig appear to have launched an Evangelical movement in the Scottish Episcopal Church in 1818.

The congregation at St Paul's grew under Craig's ministry. By the spring of 1820, after an acrimonious debate with George Gleig, Bishop of Brechin, over Craig's alleged Calvinist views,[36] Craig and some supporters decided to form a distinctly Evangelical Scottish Episcopal congregation in Edinburgh. The chapel, St James's, was opened on 15 May 1821 at Broughton Place, occupying the first floor of a tenement building, after a sum of more than £4000 had been raised.[37] Its churchmanship was firmly secured with the inclusion of not only Noel and Craig as trustees but also of the prominent Evangelical Charles Simeon, Fellow of King's College, and vicar of Holy Trinity, Cambridge. The trustees were enabled to maintain the Evangelical status of St James's because they had voting rights on the affairs of the chapel and on the appointment of new clergy.[38] Although coming after Ward's ministry at Old Deer, the foundation of St James's, Edinburgh, in 1821 seems to have marked the institutional planting of Evangelicalism in the Scottish Episcopal Church in the nineteenth century.

Craig remained at St James's until 1835, when he returned to England to take up a post at Burton Latimer, Kettering, Northamptonshire. By then St James's was a vibrant centre of Evangelicalism with a congregation of eight hundred which was able to support the incumbent with an annual salary of £400.[39] An advertisement in the *Record* in 1835 asked for a man 'of sound Evangelical views' to replace Craig.[40] Accordingly Daniel Bagot, from the diocese of Dromore, Ulster, was appointed.[41]

Other Evangelicals moved into the Scottish Episcopal Church in the late 1820s and 1830s. G. M. Drummond took the incumbency of St Mark's, Portobello, Edinburgh, from 1828 to 1839. His early subscriptions of £1.0.0 to CMS in 1825 to 1826 while a student at Oxford, and the support of St Mark's for the society during his time there suggest his allegiance to the

---

[34] J. M. Neale, *The Life and Times of Patrick Torry* (London, 1856), p. 141.
[35] William Walker, *Memoirs of Bishops Jolly and Gleig* (Edinburgh, 1878), p. 106.
[36] See Chapter 8, p. 248.
[37] The money was donated by Evangelicals of various denominations in Scotland and by friends of Craig in England. Craig made up the deficit with a loan at 4%. For the history of St James's see St James's Minute Book, October 1835, St James's Church, Edinburgh, Archives.
[38] *Ibid.*, 10 January 1836.
[39] *Ibid.*, 11 September 1835-1 October 1835, *passim*.
[40] *Ibid.*, 1 October 1835.
[41] *Ibid.*, 12 October 1835.

Introduction

party.[42] His brother, D. T. K. Drummond, from the diocese of Bristol, became incumbent at St Paul's, Carrubber's Close, Edinburgh, in 1832. By 1835, at the age of thirty, he was recognised as a leading Evangelical, being considered as a replacement for Craig.[43] Sir William Dunbar, incumbent at Stoke on Trent, and of a similar age to Drummond, was also recommended for the post.[44] Drummond became assistant minister at Trinity Chapel, Dean Bridge, Edinburgh, in 1838, and Dunbar was appointed to St Paul's, Aberdeen, in 1842. Robert Montgomery, an Evangelical clergyman from Shropshire, joined the newly built St Jude's, Glasgow, in 1837.[45]

A further centre of Evangelicalism revolved around the Duchess of Gordon who had been converted in the 1820s.[46] She and her husband built the Gordon chapel at Fochabers, which was left under the control of the Duchess since the Duke attended the Church of Scotland.[47] She appointed clergy to Fochabers, of whom W. P. McFarquhar (1834-1836) preached Evangelical doctrines.[48] Her chaplain J. D. Hull, also an Evangelical, became the incumbent of nearby Huntly in 1842.[49] Craig, Bagot, the Drummonds, Montgomery and the history surrounding Fochabers represent a core of Evangelicalism within Episcopal Scotland by the 1830s and early 1840s.

But Evangelicalism was never a monochrome movement. Earlier, in 1831, the minute book of St John's, Greenock, near Glasgow, revealed that its incumbent, T. H. Wilkinson, was a follower of Edward Irving, minister of the Church of Scotland congregation at Hatton Row, London.[50] His particular brand of Evangelicalism, which included speaking in tongues and dramatic healings, does not appear to have been followed by other Evangelical Scottish Episcopal clergy, and he emerges as a clear, although extreme, member of the party. Again, at Arradoul, in the diocese of Aberdeen, others were concerned about the doctrine of the Scottish Communion Office and formed a breakaway independent church in

---

[42] *Proceedings of the Church Missionary Society for Africa and the East* (London, 1825, 1826), AN XIX.

[43] St James's Minute Book, September 1835, St James's Church, Edinburgh, Archives.

[44] *Ibid.*

[45] See Chapter 9, pp. 289, 293.

[46] A. Moody Stuart, *Life and Letters of Elisabeth, Last Duchess of Gordon* (London, 1865), pp. 67-78.

[47] See Chapter 9, p. 298.

[48] See Chapter 4, p. 122, n. 27 for W. P. McFarquhar. No writings have been found for other incumbents at Fochabers: Charles Bigsby, 1836-1840, Johnathan Douphrate, 1840-1847.

[49] See Chapter 4, p. 120 for Hull's Evangelicalism.

[50] St John's Minute Book, February-April 1831, St John's Church, Greenock, Archives.

protest.⁵¹ At the opposite end of the scale there was the less robust Evangelicalism of W. M. Wade at Holy Trinity, Paisley, who became Dean of Glasgow and Galloway in 1843. Although Noel and Craig were regarded as the innovators of Evangelicalism in the Scottish Episcopal Church, Wade's sermons of 1822 display clear teaching on conversion as 'renouncing your own righteousness...falling in humble, sorrowing penitence at the foot of the cross'. But at the same time he deviated somewhat from the crucicentric emphasis of Evangelicals, preaching that the term 'altar' may be 'properly applied' since 'ever anew and anew...the clergyman emblematically offers up in the elements the like sacrifice [of Christ]'.⁵² Together with the inclusion of Holy Trinity in deputation visits for CMS in 1824 and 1841,⁵³ Wade's teaching probably marks him out as an Evangelical, although of a less firm theological complexion than Noel and Craig.

From the 1840s more Evangelicals entered the Scottish Episcopal Church. The duration among the stricter representatives of the party tended to be short. McFarquhar left Fochabers in 1836 without trace, but was appointed to St John's, Dumfries from 1840 to 1845.⁵⁴ J. H. Crowder, in 1845 to 1846, seems to have been the last Evangelical to serve at St James's, Edinburgh. Its previous incumbent, Bagot, declined to take the church into the English Episcopal movement, and Crowder found it increasingly uncomfortable to exercise his ministry in the Scottish Episcopal Church.⁵⁵ C. P. Miles served at St Jude's, Glasgow, for a few months from 1843 to 1844 before joining the English Episcopalians. In 1843 John Hitchcock defected to the English Episcopal church at Nairn in 1845,⁵⁶ having served at Aberdour, the private chapel of George Philip Stuart, the fourteenth Earl of Moray, for two years.⁵⁷ J. H. P. A. M. Maynard lasted less than a year at Crieff and Muthill in 1848, becoming the incumbent at St Silas's English Episcopal Church, Glasgow, from 1865 to 1871. Likewise, E. F. D. Hutton,⁵⁸ a nephew of the Drummond brothers, was the incumbent at the newly erected St Columba's, Crieff, from 1866 to 1871. He left over a dispute concerning his right to overrule in the

---

⁵¹ See Chapter 8, p. 258-259.

⁵² W. M. Wade, *Ten Sermons Preached in Trinity Episcopal Chapel, Paisley*, (Paisley, 1839), pp. 102, 145.

⁵³ See Chapter 2, pp. 47, 49.

⁵⁴ D. M. Bertie, *Scottish Episcopal Clergy 1689-2000* (Edinburgh, 2000), p. 346.

⁵⁵ See Chapter 9, p. 295.

⁵⁶ *Ibid.*, p. 297.

⁵⁷ Bertie, *Scottish Episcopal Clergy*, p. 419. H. A. Doubleday (ed.), *The Complete Peerage* Vol. IX (London, 1936), p. 192.

⁵⁸ See Chapter 3, pp. 122-123 for examples of his theology.

Introduction 19

appointment of vestrymen and took up the incumbency of St Silas's.[59] Only J. S. S. Robertson, Hitchcock's successor at Aberdour in 1845, stayed for any time. His involvement with CMS from 1839 to 1878, as depicted in Table 1.1, together with his writings, reveals that he was a strong Evangelical.[60] Nevertheless, he turned out to be a roving figure holding only short incumbencies at Dunblane from 1843 to 1844, at Aberdour in 1844 to 1848, at Pitlochry from 1862 to 1864, at St Peter's, Edinburgh, from 1864 to 1865 and at St Andrew's, Edinburgh, from 1879 to 1881, the last two appointments coinciding with his chaplaincy to Lord Rollo at Duncrub from 1865 to 1883.

However, strict Evangelicals were more permanent in the Scottish Episcopal Church after 1870. The demotion of the Scottish Communion Office to a secondary position in 1863 encouraged some defections from the English Episcopal movement. Thomas Worthington, after a stormy disagreement with the managers of St James's, Aberdeen, concerning congregational matters,[61] was appointed as Diocesan Chaplain to Edinburgh from 1873 to 1875. Similarly, James McCann left St Jude's, Glasgow, to set up St Paul's as part of the Scottish Episcopal Church in the city from 1871 to 1878. After a declaration by the Scottish bishops in 1882, legalised in 1890, allowing more freedom in evangelism and confirming that subscription to the canon law did not thereby indicate endorsement of all the doctrines held by the Church,[62] other English Episcopalians absconded. T. K. Talon served at St Vincent's, Edinburgh, within the Scottish Episcopal Church from 1882 to 1888; C. M. Black resigned from St James's English Episcopal Church, Aberdeen, in 1885 to become the incumbent of Christ Church, Morningside, Edinburgh, until 1920.[63] E. C. Dawson left St Thomas's, Edinburgh, to take up a position at St Peter's, Edinburgh, from 1890 to 1921.[64] A. M. MacKay united St James's, Aberdeen, with the Scottish Episcopal Church in 1899,[65] whereupon he left and was appointed to Holy Trinity, Edinburgh, until 1907. E. E. Marshall became the incumbent at the reunited St Paul's, Aberdeen, from 1898 to 1908.[66] All these clergy contributed to an Evangelical presence in the Church in the latter part of the century, but whether Talon's successors at St Vincent's were strong Evangelicals is not clear.

---

[59] *Strathearn Herald*, 23 September, 7 October, 14 October 1871. *Scottish Guardian*, 1 November, 1 December 1871.
[60] See Chapter 4, pp. 119, 122, 128.
[61] See Chapter 10, pp. 338-340, 343.
[62] *Ibid.*, pp. 355-357, 359.
[63] St James's Minute Book, 1885 *passim*, St James's Church, Aberdeen, Archives.
[64] See Chapter 10, p. 361.
[65] St James's Minute Book, 1896 *passim*, St James's Church, Aberdeen, Archives.
[66] Bertie, *Episcopal Clergy 1689-2000*, p. 656. Chapter 10, p. 355.

Unlike strict Evangelicals, milder representatives tended to stay longer in the Scottish Episcopal Church before 1870. The chapel at Fasque, the family home of the Gladstones, in the diocese of Brechin, was built in 1845 for private use by John Gladstone, the father of W. E. Gladstone – who himself contributed £1,000 to the project.[67] Although John was a mild Evangelical, the churchmanship of William was in evidence when the chapel was dedicated by the High Churchman, Samuel Wilberforce, Bishop of Oxford, in 1847.[68] It was served by a succession of clergy who left no writings or other documents to enable identification of their beliefs. Robert Payne Smith, the Syriac scholar, was the incumbent of Holy Trinity, Edinburgh, from 1848 to 1853. His writings of the 1860s identify his Evangelicalism, but the only surviving sermon from his days at Holy Trinity does not clearly place his views.[69] It is possible that his career in Edinburgh led him into Evangelicalism, but there is no proof of this assumption. Other clergy at Holy Trinity are likewise difficult to classify. Certainly, in 1882 the High Churchman, D. F. Sandford of St John's, Edinburgh, described V. G. Faithfull, serving there from 1851 to 1885, as an Evangelical. But W. F. Skene, the Historiographer Royal for Scotland, who was an Evangelical himself and the benefactor of St Vincent's English Episcopal Church, did not agree – although failing to give his reasons.[70] Thus the clergy at Holy Trinity can be categorised only as sympathetic to the movement, or possibly as very mild Evangelicals. Similar doubt is cast on C. R. Teape of St Andrew's, Edinburgh. From 1880 to 1885 he was a member of the Evangelical Alliance, founded in 1846 in an attempt to unite Evangelicals of different denominations. His late and transitory involvement, although evidence for adherence to Evangelicalism, possibly places him as a tardy and speculative convert to the movement, compared to D. T. K. Drummond who joined the newly formed Edinburgh branch in 1850, remaining a member until his death in 1877.[71] Again, Sandford

---

[67] S. G. Checkland, *The Gladstone: A Family Biography* (Cambridge, 1971), p. 342.

[68] *Ibid.*, p. 360. Thomas Gladstone, eldest son of the family, inherited Fasque when his father died in 1851. He retained Evangelical beliefs and it is likely that Charles Aitken (1852-1858), G. F. H. Foxton (1858-1871) and A. H. Belcher (1872-1909), incumbents of Fasque, were Evangelicals. *Ibid.*, pp. 377-380. Bertie, *Episcopal Clergy*, pp, 157, 174, 262. For Sir John Gladstone see Lewis, *Dictionary*, Vol. I, pp. 446-447.

[69] See R. Payne Smith, 'The Powers and Duties of the Priesthood', in G. H. Sumner (ed.), *Principles at Stake* (London, 1868). R. Payne Smith, *Sermon Preached at Trinity Episcopal Chapel, Edinburgh, 27th June* (Edinburgh, 1852). Sidney Lee, 'Robert Payne Smith', *Dictionary of National Biography*, Vol. XV (London, 1909), pp. 570-572.

[70] Daniel Sandford to W. F. Skene, 10 April 1882, DC. See Chapter 9, pp. 303-305 for history of St Vincent's.

[71] *Edinburgh Almanack* (Edinburgh, 1850, 1880, 1884, 1885), pp. 509, 915, 980, 962.

Introduction

referred to Teape as an Evangelical,[72] but Skene, as before, objected to the designation. Teape, like Faithfull, thus remains obscure. Overall, then, it appears that before 1870 Evangelicals who remained in the Scottish Episcopal Church tended to be of mild views.

The problems of identifying Evangelicals are clearly shown in the case of Henry Cotterill, Bishop of Edinburgh from 1872 to 1886. The *Blackwell Dictionary of Evangelical Biography* refers to him as an Evangelical.[73] Again, J. G. Cazenove, in a memoir, revealed that his mother had been a friend of the Evangelical author Hannah More, and had assisted her in writing descriptions of scenery in her book *Coelebs in Search of a Wife*, published in 1800. Cazenove's admiration for Cotterill's acceptance of a chaplaincy in Madras with the East India Company in 1836, when a glittering double first at Cambridge might have conceivably provided more lucrative employment, gives credence to the idea that Cotterill was perhaps an Evangelical with a strong sense of mission.[74] Although the *Record*, the organ of outspoken Anglican Evangelicalism from the 1830s, omitted to reveal his churchmanship when he became Bishop of Grahamstown, South Africa, in 1856, the High Church *Guardian* remarked on his death in 1886 that the appointment had been made in the 'Evangelical interest', to act as a counterbalance to the Tractarianism of Robert Gray, Bishop of Cape Town.[75] However, it seems likely that Cotterill's combined efforts with Gray in creating the autonomous Church of the Province of South Africa in 1870, and their joint condemnation in the 1860s of the liberal views of J. W. Colenso, Bishop of Natal, drew Cotterill towards High Churchmanship. Gray himself bore witness to this in 1871 when he mourned the 'loss of the strong sense of ripened views of a faithful colleague' on Cotterill's call to Edinburgh.[76] Cotterill's theological writings certainly indicate a possible drift of position. On the topic of baptism, in 1872, he appeared to follow High Church doctrine declaring, 'those who believe must be baptised in order to be members of the kingdom of heaven...by which initiatory ordinance they are brought into a state of salvation'.[77] In 1863 he regarded disputes concerning the theology of the service of Holy Communion, such as those in which the English Episcopalians were involved, as 'never a profitable subject', acknowledging in 1871 that the biblical text 'produces very different effects on different minds' and that all ideas are 'mutually illustrative and confirm each other, and are necessary to the completeness

---

[72] Daniel Sandford to W. F. Skene, 10 April 1882, DC.

[73] Lewis, *Blackwell*, Volume I, pp. 255-256.

[74] J. G. Cazenove, *Bishop Cotterill. Reprinted from the Proceedings of the Royal Society of Edinburgh* (Edinburgh, 1888), pp. 151-155.

[75] *Record*, 22 April 1886.

[76] *Ibid.*

[77] Henry Cotterill, *The Genesis of the Church* (Edinburgh, 1872), pp. 151, 237.

of true spiritual knowledge'.[78] Yet just before he died in 1886, Cotterill seems to have been harking back to Evangelicalism, mourning 'the great danger of the present day [as] lukewarmness – there is so little Evangelical fervour, so little single-hearted devotion to Christ'.[79] Cotterill is thus difficult to place. He was possibly an Evangelical who drifted into some expressions of High Churchmanship while always having an affinity with Evangelicals. He is included in Table 1.1 on this basis.[80]

English Episcopal Evangelicals

The strictest of the Evangelical Episcopalians left the Scottish Episcopal Church from 1842 onwards to become English Episcopalians, as listed in Table 1.2. Evidence of their churchmanship will be given in the forthcoming chapters. The strength of the movement is apparent in that it involved over ninety-one clergy, compared to only twenty-eight in the Scottish Episcopal Church. Again, clergy from south of the Border dominated the movement. Of those whose background is identifiable, fifty were English, eighteen Irish, five Scottish, two Anglo-Scottish, one French, and one Anglo-Australian. Bishops H. M. Villiers (Carlisle, 1856), Samuel Waldegrave (Carlisle, 1860), Charles Baring (Durham, 1861) and J. C. Ryle (Liverpool, 1880), agreed to confirm English Episcopal candidates, and E. H. Beckles, the retired Bishop of Sierra Leone, ignored censure by the Convocations of York and Canterbury in April 1877, and regularly visited the English Episcopal congregations up to 1885.[81] The movement thus represents the main thrust of Evangelical Episcopalianism in Scotland in the nineteenth century, and its history will form the core of this book.

Early Lay Scottish Evangelical Episcopalianism

Although the dawn of Scottish Evangelical Episcopalianism has been shown to have occurred around 1818 with the arrival of Noel and Craig, they came to a country where there were already some isolated Evangelical laypersons. Perusal of the *Proceedings of the Church Missionary Society for Africa and the East* from 1800 to 1820 indicates the presence of a

---

[78] Henry Cotterill, *Charge of the Lord Bishop of Grahamstown at his Third Visitation* (Grahamstown, 1863), p. 16. Henry Cotterill, *A Charge Delivered in the Cathedral Church, Grahamstown, June 29, 1871* (Grahamstown, 1871), p. 10.

[79] *Scottish Guardian*, 28 May 1886. Report of a sermon by T. I. Ball, incumbent of St Michael's, Edinburgh.

[80] Similar arguments may surround Cotterill's stepbrother, J. M. Cotterill, incumbent of St Mark's, Portobello, Edinburgh, 1873-1902, but no evidence has been found to substantiate this supposition.

[81] See Chapter 10, p. 352.

Introduction

scattering of such people, as shown in Table 1.3.[82] It can be assumed that Robert Wardlaw (1816) and Mr and Mrs James Johnstone (1816 and 1817), with their later connection to St James's, Edinburgh, were Episcopal Evangelicals. While Robert Morris (1811), the owner of the mansion and estate at Craig, Ayrshire,[83] and R. Plenderleath cannot be identified as Episcopalians, and Morris's membership of CMS indicates only a possible Evangelicalism, Plenderleath's Evangelicalism is substantiated. In 1831 he was involved with Edward Craig and Thomas Chalmers, of the Church of Scotland, in the Evangelical Edinburgh Association in Aid of the United Brethren's Moravian Mission.[84] The other inclusions are more speculative. For instance, Mrs Drummond of Strageath and Edinburgh (1819) is recorded in the list because she was the mother of G. M. and D. T. K. Drummond. When resident at her home of Aberuchill Castle, near Crieff, she would have been a neighbour of Lady Campbell, and it is thus possible to suppose that both might have been Episcopal Evangelicals. Again, Elizabeth Kirkhill of Aberdeen and Lady Murray of Edinburgh cannot be positively identified as Evangelicals.

Apart from these supporters of CMS, Anne Robertson of Dingwall, the wife of John Gladstone and mother of W. E. Gladstone, was a notable Evangelical from before her marriage in 1800.[85] It is not clear how she became an Evangelical since none of the Scottish Episcopal clergy in Dingwall was known to be of that persuasion, but, whatever the case, her Evangelicalism is well documented. Thus there was a scattered base of Evangelical laypeople in the Scottish Episcopal Church early in the nineteenth century, before Noel and Craig laid the firm foundation.

Strength of Evangelical Episcopalianism in Scotland

Table 1.4[86] shows the strength of Evangelicalism within Episcopal Scotland in the nineteenth century. It can be seen that, from 1838 to 1842, Scottish Episcopal Evangelicals were becoming a significant force. By this time their numbers had risen since 1800 by a factor of 9, albeit from a small base, compared to only 1.2 for Scottish Episcopalians generally. The trend continued from 1842 to 1854 when there were twenty times as many Evangelical congregations in Scotland as there had been at the beginning of the century, whereas the total of Scottish Episcopal congregations had only slightly more than doubled. Of these, the percentage of English

---

[82] See Chapter 1, p. 25.

[83] F. H. Groome, *Ordnance Gazetteer of Scotland*, Vol. II (London, n.d.), p. 292.

[84] *Ninth Report of the Edinburgh Association in Aid of the United Brethren's Mission for the Year 1831* (Edinburgh, 1832), p. 1.

[85] Checkland, *The Gladstones*, pp. 38-39.

[86] See Chapter 1, pp. 26-28.

Episcopalians outstripped that of Evangelical Scottish Episcopalians by 6.7%. This peak of Evangelical representation in Episcopal Scotland corresponded with the zenith of Evangelical strength in the Church of England by mid-century.[87] Although by 1885 to 1890 the Scottish Episcopal Church had grown markedly to around three hundred and ten establishments, this still represented only a four and a half-fold increase since 1800. At the corresponding time Evangelical congregations numbered sixteen, of which English and Scottish Episcopalians numbered eight churches each. This was representative of a slight drop in their growth and, by 1899, there was a sustained decline when Evangelical congregations numbered only twelve.

However, the actual number of Evangelical Episcopalians, both of the English and Scottish variety, in Scotland was never great. Overall, Scottish Episcopalians constituted only a small national presence. In 1851 they amounted to approximately 44,000 adherents compared to 566,000 in the Church of Scotland, the corresponding figures in 1900 being 116,000 and 662,000 respectively.[88] While in 1842 to 1854 Evangelicals were a significant force, they nonetheless accounted for only 13.3% of all Episcopalians in Scotland, falling to a mere 3.7% by 1899. But although Evangelical Episcopalians in Scotland were a minority group in the nineteenth century, it will be shown in the following chapters that they wielded considerable influence and commanded noteworthy support both north and south of the Border.

---

[87] B. E. Hardman, 'The Evangelical Party in the Church of England, 1855-1865', (Cambridge University Ph. D. thesis, 1964), Chapter 2. G. R. Balleine, *A History of the Evangelical Party in the Church of England* (London, 1951), pp. 210-211.

[88] Strong, *Episcopalianism*, p. 29.

Table 1.3 Evangelical Laypeople, 1808-1819

Date	Name	Abode	Amount given to CMS
1806	Mrs Stewart	Edinburgh	£2.2.0
1808-11	R. Plenderleath	Edinburgh	£6.0.0
1811	Robert Morris	Craig, Ayrshire	Life Member £10.0.0
1816	Robert Wardlaw	Tillicoultry House, Stirling Vice President Edinburgh CMS 1818 Trustee St James's, Edinburgh, 1821	£21.0.0 Life Member £10.0.0
	Mrs Johnstone	Alva, Alloa, Stirling	£1.1.0
1817	Lady Campbell	Aberuchill, Perthshire, and Broughton Street, Edinburgh	£1.1.0
	James Johnstone	Alva, Alloa, Stirling Vice President Edinburgh CMS 1818 Trustee St James's, Edinburgh, 1821	
1818	Mrs Elizabeth Kirkhill	Aberdeen	£1.1.0
	Rt Hon. Lady Murray	Edinburgh	£1.1.0
1819	Mrs Drummond	Strageath, Perthshire, and Edinburgh. Mother of G. M. and D. T. K. Drummond	£1.1.0

Source: *Proceedings of the C. M. S. for Africa and the East*, (London, 1807-1818), pp. 107, 387, 146, 262, 286, 11, 326, 710, AN XVII, AN XVIII, ANXIX. St James's, Edinburgh, Minute Book, *passim*, St James's Church, Edinburgh, Archives.

Table 1.4 Strength of Evangelical Episcopalianism, 1800-1890

Date	Scottish Episcopal Churches	Episcopal Churches served by Evangelicals	% served by Evangelicals
1800	c. 71	Old Deer	1.4
1821	c. 75	St James's, Edinburgh	1.3
1830-38	c. 84	St James's, Edinburgh Holy Trinity, Paisley Greenock Arradoul St Paul's, Carrubber's Close, Edinburgh St Mark's, Portobello Fochabers	By 1838: 9.5
1838-42	c. 85	St James's, Edinburgh Holy Trinity, Paisley St Jude's, Glasgow Holy Trinity, Edinburgh St John's, Dumfries Aberdour St Paul's, Aberdeen Fochabers Huntly	By 1842: 10.6
1842-54	c. 150	St James's, Edinburgh Holy Trinity, Edinburgh Fasque Dunblane Aberdour St Thomas's, Edinburgh [EE] St Paul's, Aberdeen [EE] St Jude's, Glasgow [EE] Dunoon[EE] Nairn[EE] Gask[EE] Huntly [EE] Fochabers [EE] Galloway House[EE] Crieff[EE] Corrimony[EE Arradoul [EE] Old Deer[EE] St James's, Aberdeen[EE] Selkirk[EE]	By 1854: 13.3 [3.3% Scottish Episcopal 10% English Episcopal]

Introduction

1860-75	c. 201	St Andrew's, Edinburgh St Columba's, Crieff Holy Trinity, Edinburgh Fasque Pitlochry St Peter's, Edinburgh St Paul's, Glasgow Diocesan Chaplain, Edinburgh St Thomas's, Edinburgh[**EE**] St Paul's, Aberdeen[**EE**] St Jude's, Glasgow[**EE**] Dunoon[**EE**] Nairn[**EE**] St James's, Aberdeen[**EE**] St Vincent's, Edinburgh[**EE**] Wemyss Bay[**EE**] St Silas's, Glasgow[**EE**] St John's, Dundee[**EE**] Hunter's Quay[**EE**] Cally[**EE**] Johnstone[**EE**]	By 1875: 10.4 [4.0% Scottish Episcopal 6.5% English Episcopal]
1885-90	c. 310	Duncrub St Vincent's, Edinburgh St Andrew's, Edinburgh Holy Trinity, Edinburgh Fasque St Peter's, Edinburgh Cally Christ Church, Morningside, Edinburgh St Thomas's, Edinburgh[**EE**] St Paul's, Aberdeen[**EE**] St Jude's, Glasgow[**EE**] Dunoon[**EE**] St James's, Aberdeen[**EE**] Wemyss Bay[**EE**] St Silas's, Glasgow[**EE**] Balmacara[**EE**] [St John's, Dundee joined Church of Scotland 1885]	By 1890: 5.2 [2.6% Scottish Episcopal 2.6% English Episcopal]

1897-1899	c. 316	St Vincent's, Edinburgh St Andrew's, Edinburgh Christ Church, Morningside, Edinburgh Holy Trinity, Edinburgh St Peter's, Edinburgh St Paul's, Aberdeen St James's, Aberdeen St Thomas's, Edinburgh [EE] Dunoon [EE] Wemyss Bay [EE] St Silas's, Glasgow [EE] Balmacara [EE]	By 1899: 3.7 [2.2% Scottish Episcopal 1.6% English Episcopal]

[EE] English Episcopal Source: D. M. Bertie, *Scottish Episcopal Clergy 1689-2000* (Edinburgh, 2000).

History of the Scottish Episcopal Church

Before an analysis of Scottish Evangelical Episcopalians can be undertaken it is necessary to consider the background of the Scottish Episcopal Church. Much of this history was to have an important bearing on events in the nineteenth century. After the Reformation parliaments of 1560 and 1567, the next hundred years saw the state religion of Scotland alternating between Episcopalianism and Presbyterianism. Under James VI of Scotland, Episcopacy gained the upper hand and by 1637, in the reign of Charles I, Archbishop Laud of Canterbury, much influenced by James Wedderburn, Bishop of Dunblane, produced a prayer book for Scotland. It was strongly resisted by Presbyterians because of its lack of warrant by the Scottish parliament and its leaning towards the Catholic theology of Edward VI's first liturgy of 1549.[89] Presbyterian distaste for it led to riots in Scotland but, in the nineteenth century, Laud's prayer book was to play an important role when Scottish Evangelical Episcopalians and High Churchmen tried to reach a compromise over the existing authorised liturgy of the Scottish Communion Office which had been produced in 1764.

In 1688 the Roman Catholic, James II of England, and VII of Scotland, fled to France. When William and Mary of Orange came to the throne in 1689, the Scottish bishops still supported James as their rightful king. In 1690 William enacted an exclusively Presbyterian system for Scotland, loyal to himself. Some Episcopalians also agreed to the terms of the 1690 settlement and prayed for William and Mary, but a Nonjuring faction remained particularly strong in the Aberdeen area. In effect the Nonjurors were illegal, but the other clergy, who used the Book of Common Prayer and prayed for William and Mary, and later for Queen Anne on her accession in 1702, were allowed to proceed unhindered.

In 1707 the Treaty of Union placed Scottish affairs under the control of Parliament in London which, in 1712, passed the Toleration Act ensuring that those Episcopal clergy who had been ordained by a Protestant bishop, used the Book of Common Prayer and prayed for the British royal family, should have freedom of worship.[90] Many Episcopal clergy, who were thereafter described as 'qualified' for ministry, accepted the conditions of the act. But most of the Nonjurors refused to comply and continued to pray for the exiled Scottish monarch James Edward Stuart, VIII of Scotland and

---

[89] See Chapter 7 for an analysis of Laud's service.

[90] The direct cause of the Toleration Act arose from problems encountered by a Scottish Episcopalian clergyman, James Greenshields, in carrying on his ministry in Edinburgh. The Presbyterian Church had objected to his presence and ordered his imprisonment on the grounds that he had no authority to minister and had introduced innovations in public worship. See Goldie, *Short History*, pp. 40-41.

son of James II. The act was to be an important tool for Evangelical English Episcopalians in 1842 when they sought to prove their legality as congregations separated from the Scottish Episcopal Church.

When George I became king in 1714, many of the Jacobite Nonjurors rose in rebellion against him in favour of James Edward Stuart. After the rebellion had been quelled, disciplinary measures were taken. Twenty-one Edinburgh clergy were fined and thirty-six Episcopal clergy were deprived of their pulpits in the Aberdeen diocese. By 1719 a Penal Act was drawn up which forbade Nonjuring clergy to officiate in the presence of more than nine people beyond their own household. If they refused to pray for the monarch, they were to be imprisoned for six months. All the bishops and some of the clergy declined the terms of the act while others who agreed to it were, again, officially recognised as qualified.[91]

At the beginning of the eighteenth century some of the disqualified Nonjuring Scottish Episcopalians, such as James Gadderar, Bishop of Aberdeen from 1725 to 1733, and John Falconar, College Bishop[92] from 1709 to 1723, forged links with the 'usager' party of the English Nonjurors. By 1764 the descendants of these Virtualist theologians, who were doctrinally more Catholic than orthodox High Churchmen, had produced a communion service for Scotland, similar to Laud's service of 1637, but differing markedly from that of the Anglican Book of Common Prayer.[93] But, because only the northern clergy used the service, its contents were not widely known and most people assumed that Laud's liturgy was the operative one, a situation which continued even in 1811 when the 1764 office was adopted as the official liturgy of the Scottish Episcopal Church.[94]

In 1745 Charles Edward Stuart, the grandson of James II, landed in Scotland in a bid to claim his ancestral throne. After his defeat at Culloden in the spring of the following year, the resulting penal laws against Nonjurors in 1746 and 1748 were even stricter than those of 1719. All orders granted by Scottish bishops were annulled and ordinations by bishops of only the English or Irish Church were regarded as valid. The oath of allegiance was made obligatory and the Scottish Episcopal laity was

---

[91] *Ibid.*, pp. 44-45.

[92] During the 1720s and 1730s the Scottish Episcopal bishops formed two parties. The older, or 'college' party, sought to perpetuate the system developed since 1689 and to govern the church by the bishops acting collectively as a college, with the bishops elected solely by royal nomination. The diocesan party wanted re-establishment of a diocesan structure with the bishops elected by diocesan clergy. See Strong, *Episcopalianism*, p. 14.

[93] See Chapter 7, pp. 228-234.

[94] Chapter 7 examines this point in detail. Dowden, *Scottish Communion Office*, pp. 64-65. D. T. K. Drummond, *Historical Sketch of Episcopacy from 1688 to the Present Time* (Edinburgh, 1845), pp. 62-64.

Introduction

barred from voting, from taking seats in Parliament, and from universities. In response, Episcopal congregations became scattered and many of the laity began to attend the Church of Scotland. Sir Walter Scott's words, transmitted through his character Peter Pleydell in *Guy Mannering*, 'I am a member of the suffering and Episcopal Church of Scotland – the shadow of a shade now', aptly sum up the circumstances in Scotland by 1750.[95]

When Charles Edward Stuart died in 1788 leaving no lawful issue, the *raison d'être* of the Jacobites disintegrated.[96] Many prayed without scruple for the king, George III, who, for his part, showed no leaning towards repression of Scottish Episcopalianism. Congregations again began to build chapels, and Juring and Nonjuring clergy alike went openly about their business. In 1792 the Penal Acts were repealed but a clause remained whereby Scottish priests not ordained by English or Irish bishops were debarred from officiating in England. All Scottish Episcopal clergy had to swear allegiance to the British throne and assent to the Thirty-Nine Articles of the Church of England.

After 1792 the Nonjuring clergy with their more Catholic theology were still very reluctant to subscribe to the Thirty-Nine Articles. They regarded Article XVII on predestination and Article XXV on the sacraments as too Calvinistic. At the convocation of Laurencekirk in 1804 the Primus, Alexander Jolly, Bishop of Moray, persuaded the Nonjurors, who accounted for around sixty congregations, to subscribe to the Thirty-Nine Articles, albeit with some reservations. Additionally, thirteen out of the twenty-four qualified clergy agreed to recognise the authority of their local bishop in return for the use of the Book of Common Prayer and joined the Scottish Episcopal Church. By 1818 only seven qualified congregations remained, falling to two – Perth and Montrose – by 1843.[97]

At the General Synod of 1811 a distinctly High Church personality was stamped on the Scottish Episcopal Church after pressure from clergy in the Aberdeen diocese in particular. The surplice rather than the black gown was recommended as the proper sacerdotal vestment; the Scottish Communion Office of 1764 was elevated to primacy and was to be used in consecrations of bishops, although the English service was permissible in those congregations, mainly in southern Scotland, which were accustomed to it. In 1840 an act was passed forging closer links between the Scottish Episcopal Church and the Church of England whereby Scottish-ordained clergy were permitted to officiate in England for a maximum of two days.[98] Evangelical Episcopalianism, introduced by Noel and Craig in 1821, and

---

[95] Sir Walter Scott, *Guy Mannering or the Astrologer*, Vol. II, with introductory essay and notes by Andrew Lang (London, 1892), p. 88.

[96] Charles Edward Stuart's brother, a cardinal, survived.

[97] Bertie, *Scottish Episcopal Clergy*, p. 649.

[98] Drummond, *Sketch of Episcopacy*, p. 129.

perpetuated thereafter by a succession of clergy, was born into and grew within this milieu.

The existing secondary literature concerning the nineteenth-century Evangelical movement in the Scottish Episcopal Church is sparse. In particular, no extensive analysis has been made of Evangelical objections to the Scottish Communion Office. P. B. Nockles in 'Scottish Episcopal Church and the Oxford Movement', *Journal of Ecclesiastical History*, 47 (1996), provides a valuable insight into the eventual opposition of the Scottish Nonjurors to the Tractarian movement, highlighting the differences between their Virtualist theology and the more advanced Anglo-Catholic teaching of the latter by the 1850s. But there is no dissection of the views of Evangelicals to explain their reasons for regarding the 1764 office as 'popish' compared to that of the Book of Common Prayer. Instead, Nockles focuses particularly on Drummond stating, without extended analysis, that his objections were primarily 'a useful theological cloak for his secession, and provided a stick with which he could beat his theological opponents'.[99] Similarly, Rowan Strong in *Episcopalianism in Nineteenth-Century Scotland* (Oxford, 2002), highlights that Evangelicals opposed the office because of the 'supposed transubstantiation' of the prayer of invocation,[100] but, like Nockles, he makes no examination of what Evangelicals were, in reality, arguing concerning Virtualist theology and the way in which they understood it could be adapted to more advanced doctrine. Reginald Foskett takes a similar line in 'The Drummond Controversy 1842', *Records of the Scottish Church History Society*, 16 (1967). Evangelical theology, compared to that of the Scottish Virtualists, has not been fully analysed.

Some writers have highlighted other aspects of the English Episcopal movement, but again with little acknowledgement of the rationale of Evangelical belief. Gavin White, in *The Scottish Episcopal Church: A New History* (Edinburgh, 1998), while granting that the Scottish invocation did raise 'all sorts of new problems'[101] considers the English Episcopal movement to have concentrated on the state connection with the Church of England to the detriment of Christ's headship over the Church.[102] He elaborates this point in 'The Nine Lives of the Episcopal Cat: changing self-images of the Scottish Episcopal Church', *Records of the Scottish Church History Society*, 28, (1998), positing that the English Episcopal movement was 'more establishment than anything else', and tending to

---

[99] P. B. Nockles, 'Scottish Episcopal Church and the Oxford Movement', *Journal of Ecclesiastical History*, 47 (1996), pp. 676-677.

[100] Strong, *Episcopalianism*, p. 221.

[101] White, *Scottish Episcopal Church*, p. 27.

[102] *Ibid.*, p. 78.

Introduction

denigrate its Evangelicalism.[103] Foskett highlights the illegality of Drummond's evangelistic meetings, comparing him to John Wesley who took 'the whole world for his parish'.[104] But he does not analyse the difficulties for Evangelicals in pursuing their theology within the Scottish Episcopal Church after the ruling of the 1838 synod which led to this position, and thus the resulting picture is distorted.

Strong gives a synopsis of some of the events surrounding the development of English Episcopalianism, extending previous works considerably. But it is by no means complete and contains some inaccuracies. A small part of the information presented in the thesis which preceded this book was completed without consultation with Strong and before his *Episcopalianism in Nineteenth-Century Scotland* was published. Where duplication occurs it is noted by *ENCS* in the footnotes. An extension of Strong's work is thus offered together with answers to two serious allegations he makes concerning Drummond: it is said that he was 'opinionated' and that he 'rather gloried' in his separation from the Scottish Church. Since Strong does not offer a sustained analysis of Drummond's arguments or of the level of support he had in Britain, it may be that this particular emphasis needs to be reconsidered in the light of new evidence.[105]

Apart from these publications dealing directly with Scottish Evangelical Episcopalianism, some secondary literature elucidates further areas of interest. D. W. Bebbington's *Evangelicalism in Modern Britain* (London, 1993) and W. J. C. Ervine's 'Doctrine and Diplomacy: Life and Thought of Anglican Evangelical Clergy in the Church of England 1797 to 1837' (Cambridge University Ph.D. thesis, 1979) show the differences between strict and mild nineteenth-century Evangelicals over issues such as the inspiration of scripture, millenarianism, the incarnation, baptism and anti-Catholicism.[106] Eric Culbertson's 'Evangelical Theology 1857-1900' (London Ph.D. thesis, 1991) provides analysis of later Evangelical doctrine. He shows how there was some movement of thought concerning the mode of Christ's presence in the communion service. Comparison can be made with Evangelical Episcopalians in Scotland to ascertain if they had a similar range of thought by the end of the nineteenth century. Again, Anne

---

[103] Gavin White, 'The Nine Lives of the Episcopal Cat: Changing Self-images of the Scottish Episcopal Church', *Records of the Scottish Church History Society*, 28 (1998), p. 88.

[104] Reginald Foskett, 'The Drummond Controversy 1842', *Records of the Scottish Church History Society*, 16, (1967), p. 99.

[105] Strong, *Episcopalianism*, pp. 220, 230.

[106] Bebbington, *Evangelicalism*, pp. 75-97. W. J. C. Ervine, 'Doctrine and Diplomacy: Some Aspects of the Life and Thought of Anglican Evangelical Clergy 1797-1837' (Cambridge University Ph. D. thesis, 1979), pp. 64-86, 107-144, 295-296.

Bentley's 'Transformation of the Evangelical Party in the Later Nineteenth Century', (Durham University Ph.D. thesis, 1971) has an important section on the involvement of Evangelicals in church missions alongside High Churchmen[107] which can be used to ascertain if there was similar accommodation of belief and practice among Scottish Evangelical Episcopalians. Affinities between Scottish Evangelical Episcopalians and Scottish Presbyterian beliefs can be gathered from A. C. Cheyne's *The Transforming of the Kirk* (Edinburgh, 1983). This body of secondary works enables the construction of a doctrinal profile of Scottish Evangelical Episcopalians throughout the nineteenth century to be made, which in turn informs the reasons for their disputes with the Scottish Episcopal Church.

Various works explain the nature of Tractarianism. Peter Toon's *Evangelical Theology, 1833-1856* (London, 1977) discusses the Evangelical response to the movement concerning the doctrines of baptism, Holy Communion and innovations in worship, showing how many became more extreme in their views. It thus provides a study of the religious climate of the time and indicates the sorts of areas of concern with which Scottish Evangelical Episcopalians were likely to have been involved. Alf Härdelin's *The Tractarian Understanding of the Eucharist* (Uppsala,1965) explains the evolving theology of the Oxford Movement and helps to elucidate the doctrinal differences between it and Evangelical theology on the communion service. C. W. Dugmore in *Eucharistic Doctrine in England from Hooker to Waterland* (London, 1942) is helpful in explaining the Virtualist eucharistic understanding, as is W. Jardine Grisebrooke in *Anglican Liturgies of the Seventeenth and Eighteenth Centuries* (London, 1958). These works all shed light on the reasons behind the disputes between Evangelicals and High Churchmen in Scotland.

Ian Bradley's *Call to Seriousness* (London, 1976), Ford K. Brown's *Fathers of the Victorians* (Cambridge, 1961), and D. M. Rosman's *Evangelicals and Culture* (London, 1984) give gauges against which to examine the way in which Evangelical Episcopalians in Scotland conducted their family lives, missionary work and philanthropy, showing how their theology was worked out in day-to-day affairs. Peter Hillis in 'Presbyterianism and Social Class in Mid-Nineteenth Century Glasgow', *Journal of Ecclesiastical History*, Vol. 32, (1981), and C. G. Brown's *Religion and Society in Scotland since 1707* (Edinburgh, 1997) found that skilled working-class people were represented in the congregations they investigated. Their methods open up the way for a similar study of the congregations examined in this book. Finally, similarities between the breakaway English Episcopal Evangelicals and other Evangelical protesters

---

[107] Anne Bentley, 'The Transformation of the Evangelical Party in the Church of England in the Later Nineteenth Century (Durham University Ph. D. thesis, 1971), pp. 301-311.

in the nineteenth century can be made by reference to a variety of texts.[108] Clashes over issues such as baptism and Tractarianism can be further elucidated in the light of these analyses.

The following chapters are constructed to examine various aspects of Scottish Evangelical Episcopalianism in the nineteenth century and to answer questions raised in previous works. *Chapter 2* will establish the geographical distribution of Evangelicalism in the Scottish Episcopal Church during the nineteenth century, showing the locations in which it flourished and the reasons for its success in these places. *Chapter 3* is a survey of the social composition of Scottish Evangelical Episcopalian congregations in order to ascertain whether they made a substantial impact among the working-class population, or whether they were the province of the middle classes. Comparisons will be made with the social structure of some Presbyterian churches. *Chapter 4* will explore the beliefs of the group as revealed in their written works, marking out those who held to a distinct Evangelical theology. Affinities with High Churchmanship and Presbyterianism will also be examined. *Chapter 5* will discuss the outworking of Evangelical theology in the lifestyle of some of the Scottish Evangelicals in order to show whether their private personas matched their public pronouncements, and to reveal some of the philanthropic enterprises with which they were involved.

Chapter 6 provides an insight into various issues facing Scottish Evangelical Episcopalians. The analysis will concentrate firstly on the consolidation of Roman Catholicism during the century and the way in which it enhanced the Protestantism of the group. The doctrine of baptism will be explored, highlighting the conflict between Evangelical and High Church understandings in Scotland. The expression of Evangelical belief in church architecture and the conduct of services will be shown to have been a factor in giving the group a distinct personality within the Scottish church scene. *Chapter 7* will continue the study of issues with an exploration of the theology of the Scottish and Anglican Communion Offices, and the reasons why the former was not acceptable to some Scottish Episcopal Evangelicals in a time of advancing Tractarian beliefs. An analysis of Nonjuring doctrine will help to display the doctrinal problems facing Evangelicals in the Scottish Episcopal Church. *Chapter 6* and *Chapter 7* thus form the basis for

---

[108] Grayson Carter, *Anglican Evangelicals: Protestant Secessions from the Via Media c. 1800-1850* (Oxford, 2001). R. D. Fenwick, 'The Free Church of England, otherwise called the Reformed Episcopal Church circa 1845 to 1927' (Lampeter Ph. D. thesis, 1995). Peter Hinchliff, *Anglican Church in South Africa: An Account of the History and Development of the Church of the Province of South Africa* (London, 1963). Anthony Ive, *A Candle Burns in Africa: The Story of the Church of England in South Africa* (Natal, 1992). *A History of the Free Church of England Otherwise Called the Reformed Episcopal Church* (no author, Free Church of England Publications Committee, 1960).

Chapter 8, which explains the first disruption in 1842 of Evangelicals from the Scottish Episcopal Church and the foundation of St Thomas's, Edinburgh, under the incumbency of D. T. K. Drummond. Subsequent disruptions will be discussed in *Chapter 9*. The background against which the continuing controversy between Evangelicals, High Churchmen and others in the Scottish Episcopal Church evolved will be discussed in *Chapter 10*. It will explain the sustained influence of Tractarianism on events in the 1860s and the later impact of Ritualism. The struggle for recognition from the Church of England by the Scottish Episcopal Church and the independent, breakaway Evangelical chapels will be analysed. The later demise of the English Episcopal chapels at a time of increasing accommodation of belief and practice within British Evangelicalism will be discussed. Finally, the problems which faced the Scottish Episcopal Church in providing a liturgy acceptable to both its own High Churchmen and Evangelicals in the English Episcopal movement will be investigated. *Chapter 11* will provide a summary of the arguments of the preceding chapters. Thus a detailed analysis of Evangelical Episcopalianism in Scotland, covering doctrine, social issues, image and its contribution to Scottish religious life will emerge.

Chapter 2

Geographical Distribution

In Chapter 1 it was shown that the Evangelical Episcopal presence in Scotland evolved from small beginnings, starting in 1800 with the chapel at Old Deer, Aberdeenshire. Additionally, there were a few lay people connected with Evangelicalism resident in the country up to about 1818 as shown in Table 1.3.[1] The locations of these early Evangelicals are shown on Map 2.1[2] where it is evident that, until 1818, the movement was a scattered one, although there was a developing nucleus around Edinburgh.

However, when the Evangelical, Edward Craig, was appointed to St Paul's, Carrubber's Close, Edinburgh, in 1818 he was not breaking into the heartland of Scottish episcopacy which was located in the northeast of the country. Incumbencies were sometimes multiple, but in that year the Diocese of Aberdeen numbered twenty-one served churches; Moray, Ross and Caithness, further to the north, had twelve; nearby Brechin contained nine; and central Scotland, represented by St Andrews, Dunkeld and Dunblane, numbered fifteen. In the south the Edinburgh diocese was composed of nine congregations, while Glasgow had only three and Galloway just one. Thus Craig and his mentor Gerard Noel, who had been active at St Paul's before him, both heralded as introducing Evangelicalism into Episcopal Scotland, entered by way of Edinburgh, an area not abounding in Scottish Episcopal churches.

Although Craig's position in Edinburgh was a direct consequence of his friendship with Noel, Edinburgh was, in reality, a far more suitable choice than northeastern Scotland for the positioning of an Evangelical congregation. Certainly there were pockets of Evangelical activity at Old Deer, Aberdeenshire, and Dingwall, Ross and Cromarty, but High Churchmen who were loyal to Nonjuring theology and the Scottish Communion Office of 1764 dominated the area, and it was thus not fertile ground for Evangelicalism. Additionally, most of the churches in the northeast were situated in small villages. Although the Episcopal church in Peterhead, Aberdeenshire, in 1843, could claim seven hundred and sixty-three sittings, most of the others in the Aberdeen diocese were below the

---

[1] See Chapter 1, p. 25.
[2] See Chapter 2, p. 58.

three hundred level.[3] In comparison St Paul's, Carrubber's Close, despite being one of the smallest Edinburgh churches, with only three hundred and sixty seats,[4] had all the advantages that a distinguished university city, cultural and theological centre could offer. In 1818, with the nucleus of nearby Evangelical laypeople shown on Map 2.1, and Noel's previous visits to St Paul's which had prepared the way for the acceptance of Evangelical preaching there, Edinburgh was thus a natural choice in which to establish an Evangelical congregation.

The Scottish cities were growing in size during the nineteenth century, and were certainly able to provide sufficient numbers to form viable congregations. While Evangelical churches might spring up in other places such as those endowed by individual moneyed patrons or groups of exceptionally rich members, or appear purely fortuitously, densely populated areas were likely to have provided fertile ground in which churches could take root. Table 2.1 records the population growth in Glasgow, Edinburgh, Aberdeen and Dundee during the nineteenth century. It shows that Glasgow, Scotland's largest city throughout the nineteenth century, came second only to London in terms of population in 1871. Edinburgh followed closely at the beginning of the century, although its growth rate fell off compared to Glasgow by 1851. Numbers rose sharply in Dundee by 1851, when it overtook Aberdeen as Scotland's third largest city. The four major Scottish cities were thus vibrant centres of population in the nineteenth century, and likely places in which Evangelicals would be found.

Table 2.1 Population (in thousands) of the Largest Cities in Nineteenth-Century Scotland and their Order after London

	1801	1821	1851	1861	1871	1881
	000s	000s	000s and [Order after London]	000s and [Order after London]	000s and [Order after London]	000s and [Order after London]
Glasgow	84	147	375 [3]	443 [2]	568 [1]	673 [1]
Edinburgh	82	138	202 [6]	203 [7]	244 [7]	295 [7]
Aberdeen	27	44.6	72 [16=]	74 [21=]	88 [23]	106 [24]
Dundee	27	30.5	79 [15]	91 [17]	119 [16]	140 [10]

Sources: T. C. Smout, *A History of the Scottish People 1560-1830* (London, 1969), p 243. Geoffrey Best, *Mid-Victorian Britain 1851-75* (London, 1971), p. 29.

---

[3] J. P. Lawson, *History of the Scottish Episcopal Church from the Revolution to the Present Time* (Edinburgh, 1843), pp. 485-574.

[4] *Ibid.*, p. 509.

Geographical Distribution 39

Maps 2.2-4, derived from Tables 1.1 and 1.2[5] show the locations of Evangelical Episcopal churches from 1821 to 1898. They demonstrate that Edinburgh, Glasgow, Aberdeen and Dundee were, indeed, all home to such congregations. Cities were important locations for Evangelical Episcopalians.

Part of the reason for the success of city churches was that they were centres for the wealthy classes. St Jude's, Glasgow, for instance, although set up partly in the hope of attracting the poor, drew mainly on the upper social groups.[6] But the diverse nationalities represented in the Scottish cities also contributed to the viability of Evangelical congregations. The nineteenth century saw increasing numbers of Irish and English immigrants in Scotland. The Irish were the more numerous. Starting in the 1820s, with the problems of over-population in Ireland and the incentive of cheap fares to the mainland, and exacerbated by the potato famine of 1845 to 1847, numbers of Irish people arrived in Britain, many of whom were poor. In 1841 they accounted for 5% of the total Scottish population, rising to 10% by 1851. At the latter date, 19% of the total population of Dundee was Irish, and in Glasgow the figure was 18.2%. English immigrants were far fewer. In 1841 they made up only 1.5% of the total population of Scotland, reaching 3.5% by 1911,[7] but were particularly noticeable in Edinburgh by 1835.[8] Aberdeen, by contrast, had less Irish and English immigrants. Out of the population of 72,000 in 1851, only 1,270 were Irish, together with a similar number of English.[9] But, overall, the nineteenth century saw a marked growth of Irish and English people taking up residence in Scotland.

Some of the Irish, often coming to take up jobs in the textile industries, were Orangemen from Ulster. Their Low Church background was conducive to Evangelicalism and at St John's, Dundee, founded in 1868, the congregation was mainly made up of such Irish workers.[10] The English

---

[5] See Chapter 2, pp. 59-61. See also Chapter 1, pp. 9-14.

[6] Lawson, *Scottish Episcopal Church*, p. 503. Michael Russell, *An Affectionate Address to the Managers and Congregation of St Jude's* (Glasgow, 1844), pp. 4-5.

[7] W. Hamish Fraser and R. J. Morris (ed.), *People and Society in Scotland, 2. 1830-1914* (Edinburgh, 1987), pp. 17-18.

[8] *Stephen's Episcopal Magazine*, January-December 1835, Vol. III, p. 32. In 1845 out of a total of 138,194 people resisdent in Edinburgh, 9,012 (6.5%) were English and 7,100 (5.1%) were Irish. See J. Gordon (ed.), *The New Statistical Account of Scotland* (Edinburgh, 1845), p. 650.

[9] A. A. MacLaren, *Religion and Social Class. The Disruption Years in Aberdeen* (London, 1974), p. 6.

[10] Although Evangelicals by the mid-nineteenth century were often called Low Churchmen, the terms Low Church and Evangelical are not necessarily synonymous. Low Churchmen in the Church of England give a 'low' place to the claims of the episcopate, priesthood, sacraments and ceremony in worship but do not always preach the doctrine of conversion with the same emphasis and fervency as Evangelicals. Thus

newcomers to Edinburgh in 1835 were, unlike the Irish, predominantly professional people, army personnel, businessmen, and families seeking education for their children in Scotland together with their governesses and servants. They were reported as swelling the Scottish Episcopal congregations in the city,[11] and the Evangelical churches were likely to have been among those attracting a number of English people used to the Anglican prayer book. By contrast, the qualified congregation of St Paul's, Aberdeen, in 1840, was attended mainly by native Scots who, nevertheless, provided Sir William Dunbar, appointed in 1843, with a well-established base supportive of Low Anglicanism and receptive to Evangelicalism.[12] Cities which were home to the wealthy middle classes, Irish and English immigrants of mixed social status, or, occasionally, to qualified congregations, were productive areas of Evangelical growth.

Map 2.4 shows the success of Evangelical Episcopalianism in the Scottish cities from 1842 to 1898. Edinburgh had nine such congregations, Glasgow, four, Aberdeen, two, and Dundee, one. Of these the English Episcopal churches, which represented the most distinct form of Evangelicalism in the period after 1842, were the most enduring. Table 1.2 shows that St Thomas's, Edinburgh, existed for one hundred and forty-five years in a state of separation from the Scottish Episcopal Church, followed by St Silas's, Glasgow (one hundred and twenty-three years), St Paul's, Aberdeen (fifty-five years), St Jude's, Glasgow (fifty years), and St James's, Aberdeen (forty-three years). Whereas the congregation at St John's, Dundee, was mainly Irish working-class and survived only eighteen years, the other congregations were placed in locations which would have supplied influential, moneyed and well-educated members conversant with theological debate, and who would have provided the impetus for continued separation. While cities were generally viable places for Evangelicalism to take root, English Episcopal congregations in particular survived best in sophisticated environments.

Flourishing towns such as Paisley, Greenock, and Johnstone, all situated near Glasgow, together with Dumfries in southwestern Scotland, and Montrose, in Forfar, recorded in Tables 1.1, and 1.2, provided, like cities, fertile ground for Evangelical congregations. They are shown on Maps 2.1 -

---

the difference between the groups is often subtle, but an Evangelical, while holding much in common with a Low Churchman, would not always regard him as a true counterpart. This probably explains why C. R. Teape of St Andrew's, Back of Castle, Edinburgh, was not acknowledged as an Evangelical. See Chapter 1, pp. 20-21. See also F. L. Cross, *The Oxford Dictionary of the Christian Church* (London, 1958), p. 824.

[11] *Stephen's Episcopal Magazine*, January-December 1835, Vol. III, p. 32.

[12] See Chapter 9, pp. 284-289.

Geographical Distribution 41

2.4.[13] Paisley was the sixth most populous town in Scotland by the end of the nineteenth century. It was a centre for the textile industry, attracting many Irish workers.[14] Greenock was home for a variety of immigrants. Irish textile workers, hatters from Lancaster, earthenware manufacturers from the English potteries, glass blowers from Newcastle, chain cable makers from Liverpool, and sugar boilers from Germany all flocked in during the 1830s and 1840s.[15] Likewise, Johnstone was a centre for the textile industry, providing jobs for Irish immigrants.[16] While it is not certain that the Evangelical Episcopal churches there attracted these working-class people, many of the wealthy factory owners probably attended and were likely to have influenced their employees.[17] Dumfries, popularly named Queen of the South, was the metropolis for its area. Early in the century it was reported to be populated by an unusually large proportion of educated and wealthy inhabitants, and its association with the poet, Robert Burns, drew large numbers of visitors each year.[18] Montrose, home to a qualified congregation, was noted for flax spinning, and the weaving of sheets and canvas. It was an important port and customhouse in the 1860s and 1870s. In 1868 there were one hundred and twelve ships, mostly belonging to Montrose, passing through it and trading with the Baltic, Norway and Australia. Imports were of timber, coal, flax, hemp and wheat, the trade in wood being second only to that on the Clyde. With fishing providing another important industry,[19] Montrose, too, could support an Episcopal congregation with Evangelical leadership in 1845. But Evangelical chapels in smaller towns tended to run into difficulties. For instance Huntly, Aberdeenshire, was a relatively isolated market town, unlikely to attract holidaymakers or immigrants.[20] The foundation of the Evangelical English

---

[13] See Chapter 2, pp. 58-61. Regional names follow the pattern given in *Map of August 1 1879, Published under the Committeee of General Literature and Education Appointed by the Society for Promoting Christian Knowledge and of the National Society* (London, 1879). Map L.16.14, National Library of Scotland.

[14] F. H. Groome, *Ordnance Gazetteer of Scotland. A Survey of Scottish Topography, Statistical, Biographical and Historical*, Vol. V (London, 1894), pp. 145-155. Gordon, *Statistical Account*, Volume 11, p. 281.

[15] Lawson, *Scottish Episcopal Church*, pp. 431-432.

[16] Groome, *Gazetteer*, Volume IV, pp. 334-335.

[17] Lawson, *Scottish Episcopal Church*, p. 432.

[18] Groome, *Gazetteer*, Volume II, pp. 390-397. Gordon, *Statistcal Account*, Volume 4, p. 15 notes a mainly agricultural population at Dumfries with a small amount of manufacturing of hats and stockings.

[19] Groome, *Gazeteer*, Volume V, pp. 51-58. Gordon, *Statistical Account*, Volume 11, p. 281.

[20] Groome, *Gazeteer*, Volume III, pp. 278-279. Gordon, *Statistical Account*, Volume 12, p. 1041 notes of manufactures at Huntly, 'there are none in this parish worth naming'.

Episcopal church there owed its existence to the influence of the Duchess of Gordon and her protégé, J. D. Hull. It was very much a local phenomenon, not likely to be fuelled by a regular influx of new people and, when Hull left, a replacement incumbent was not forthcoming. Similarly Selkirk, a Border market town, owed the existence of its English Episcopal chapel to the Murray family at nearby Philiphaugh,[21] and was short-lived. However, towns with a vibrant economy were generally attractive and viable places for Evangelical Episcopal congregations.

Watering places and centres for holidaymakers were similarly notable for Evangelical activity. The English Episcopal churches at Dunoon, Hunter's Quay, Wemyss Bay, Nairn, Crieff and Balmacara, together with the Scottish Episcopal churches at Portobello, Pitlochry and Dunblane illustrate this. Dunoon and Hunter's Quay, in Argyllshire, had steamboat piers and were situated close to the Royal Clyde Yacht Club. They were notable resorts patronised by invalids and, in 1869, the West of Scotland Convalescent Home opened in Dunoon with two hundred beds.[22] Wemyss Bay on the Clyde, in Renfrewshire, was another yachting centre and beauty spot.[23] Nairn, in northeastern Scotland, was recommended by London physicians as suitable for invalids requiring a dry, bracing, yet moderate climate. It became known as 'the Brighton of the North' and was the haunt of Londoners and the southern English who supplied half the total of annual visitors.[24] Crieff, Perthshire, was a summer resort for tourists and sportsmen, popular because of its pure, dry climate and exquisite surroundings.[25] Balmacara, Ross and Cromarty, overlooked the Highland Loch Alsh and had a hotel for summer yachtsmen and other holiday makers.[26] Visitors to such places were likely to have been numerous enough to help supply viable congregations to which local residents would also have been attracted, and where the Evangelical message was communicated – at Balmacara the concern was: 'that those who come only thinking of nature, may be led to Nature's God'.[27] But these churches had a problem if many of their people were present for only part of the year. This, together with the likelihood that fashions could change with respect to holiday resorts, meant such chapels would be subject to decay, especially

---

[21] See Chapter 9, p. 300.

[22] Groome, *Gazetteer*, Volume II, pp. 306-308, 443-445. Gordon, *Statistical Account*, Volume 7, p. 613 notes that the population of Dunoon doubled during the summer and autumn because of the influx of visitors.

[23] Edwin Hodder, *Sir George Burns Bart. His Times, His Friends* (London, 1892), pp. 226-227.

[24] Groome, *Gazetteer*, Volume V, pp. 91-93.

[25] *Ibid.*, Volume II, pp. 306-308. Crieff became known as the Montpelier of Scotland because of its mild climate. See Gordon, *Statistical Account*, Volume 10, p. 498.

[26] *St Silas's Magazine* August 1889, St Silas's Church, Glasgow, Archives.

[27] *Ibid.*

Geographical Distribution

by the latter part of the century when new resorts were opening up. The closure of the English Episcopal chapels at Nairn (1879), Dunoon (1900), Hunter's Quay (1905), Balmacara (1916) and Wemyss Bay (1932) was probably partly due to this trend.

For the Scottish Episcopalian Evangelicals, Portobello, with its fine beach and proximity to Edinburgh, was also attractive as a fashionable watering place.[28] Pitlochry, Perthshire, gained fame when Queen Victoria visited Blair Castle in 1845, and as a result the Royal Physician, Sir James Clarke, was struck by Pitlochry's healthy climate and advised invalids to visit the town.[29] Neighbouring Dunblane was probably a source of interest for its Scottish Episcopalian incumbent, J. S. S. Robertson, because it was home to Archbishop Leighton's library with 1,400 volumes available for consultation.[30] But unlike the Clyde resorts, which depended mainly on the yachting fraternity, Pitlochry's royal connection and Portobello's proximity to Edinburgh provided a more sustained prosperity which enabled the congregations to survive. Towns with specific attractions were home to Evangelical Episcopal congregations.

Again, it should be noted that Scottish cities and towns were host to a variety of congregations outside the mainstream of the Established Church. At Edinburgh, in 1845, besides twenty-nine parish churches there were twenty-three Free Churches, together with nine Secession, eight Episcopal, six Baptist, five Relief, three Independent, two Associate Synod, two Roman Catholic congregations and one each of Methodist, Quaker and Unitarian gatherings. Huntly, likewise, apart from a Church of Scotland congregation, also numbered an Episcopal, Seceeder, Independent and Roman Catholic church. English Episcopal churches, in such a religious climate, were very likely to thrive.[31]

---

[28] Groome, *Gazetter*, Volume V, pp. 216-217. Local people of Portobello were involved mainly with agriculture. Gordon, *Statistical Account*, Volume 1 p. 392.

[29] Groome, *Gazetter*, pp. 205-206. Trading of various types was also important at Pitlochry by 1845 due to good connections by road north and south. Gordon, *Statistcal account*, Volume 10, p. 660.

[30] Groome, *Gazetter*, Volume II, pp. 409-410.

[31] I thank Dr Helen Dingwall of Stirling University for directing me to this consideration. For Edinburgh, see *Statistical Account*, Volume 1, pp. 650, 666-668. For Huntly, see *Statistical Account*, Volume 12, pp. 1042-1043. Similar information can be obtained for further centres of English Episcopal activity in 1845. Glasgow, sittings at churches: 30,928 Church of Scotland: 42,497 Seceders, Dissenters, Episcopalians, Roman Catholics. *Ibid.*, Volume 6, p. 188. Aberdeen churches: 12 Church of Scotland in 6 parishes; 3 Congregationalist: 3 United Associate Synod; 2 Baptist; 1 Relief; 1 Weslyan Methodist; 1 English Episcopal; 1 Scottish Episcopal; 1 Roman Catholic; 1 United Christian Church. *Ibid.*, Volume 12, pp. 33-35. Dundee churches: 8 Church of Scotland; 2 United Secession; 2 Episcopal; 1 Associate Synod of Original Burghers; 1 Associate Synod of Original Seceders; 1 Congregational Union; 1 Scotch Independent;

Some English Episcopal churches owed their existence to wealthy patrons. W. F. Burnley, a member of St Jude's and subsequently of St Silas's, Glasgow, owned Dunoon. Wemyss Bay was the property of George Burns, founder of the Cunard shipping line and a member of St Jude's, Glasgow, and eventually of St Silas's.[32] Hunter's Quay was the project of C. J. Anderson, possibly another member of St Silas's. Local wealthy landowners provided funds for Nairn and Crieff, and the businessman C. H. Bousefield founded the church at Johnstone.[33] Balmacara, although partially funded by St Silas's, was dependent on its wealthy owner who had gifted it for summer use.[34] A more random distribution of Evangelical congregations occurred when aristocratic and wealthy lay Evangelicals set up churches at their homes, and the location of these was purely a factor of where the benefactors lived. The church at Fasque, Brechin, built in 1845

---

1 Relief; 1 Methodist; 3 Baptist; 1 Glassite; 1 Roman Catholic. *Ibid.*, volume 11, pp. 42-43. Old Deer could number 714 families belonging to the Church of Scotland; 83 Episcopalian; 157 Original or United Secession; 30 Dissenting, chiefly Congregationalists. *Ibid.*, Volume 12, p. 151. Families at Nairn: 730 of Established Church; 100 Dissenting and Seceding; 1 Episcopalian; 1 Roman Catholic. *Ibid.*, Volume 13, p. 5. Dunoon churches: 2 Church of Scotland; 1 Associate Synod. *Ibid.*, Volume 7, p. 567. Montrose churches: 1 Church of Scotland; 2 Episcopalian (including the English Episcopal church); 2 United Associate Synod; 1 Methodist; 1 Baptist; 1 Glassite; 1 Independent. *Ibid.*, Volume 11, p. 285. Crieff churches: 1 Church of Scotland; 1 United Secession; 1 Original Seceders; 1 Roman Catholic. Selkirk churches: 1 Church of Scotland; 1 Associate Synod. *Ibid.*, Volume 3, p. 7. Fochabers churches: 1 Church of Scotland; 1 Episcopal; 1 Roman Catholic 4 miles away. *Ibid.*, Volume 6, p. 122. Cally families: 373 Church of Scotland; 23 Roman Catholic; 12 Independents; 7 Associate Synod; 3 Reformed Presbyterian; 1 Episcopalian. *Ibid.*, Volume 4, p. 307. Parish of Sorbie, Galloway House: 1 Church of Scotland; 1 Independent. *Ibid.*, Volume 4, p. 33. By contrast, Johnstone recorded only 1 Church of Scotland, built in 1823. *Ibid.*, Volume 7, p. 203.

Concerning locations of Evangelical Scottish Episcopal Churches in 1845: Portobello churches: 1 Church of Scotland; 1 United Associate; 1 Relief; 1 Episcopalian; 1 Independent; 1 Roman Catholic. *Ibid.*, Volume 1, p. 395. Aberdour families: 357 Church of Scotland; 70 Dissenting or Seceding; 1 Episcopalian; 1 Roman Catholic. *Ibid.*, Volume 9, p. 719. Dumfries churches: 2 Church of Scotland; 2 United Secession; 1 Cameronian; 1 Relief; 1 Independent; 1 Methodist; 1 Episcopalian. *Ibid.*, Volume 4, pp 14-15. Pitlochry: 1 Church of Scotland; 3 Episcopalian families; 3 Baptist families; 1 Independent family. *Ibid.*, Volume 10, pp. 659-660. Fasque: 1 Church of Scotland. Additionally, 14 people belonged to the Independent Church, 13 to Episcopal Church, 14 to Berean Church, 6 to United Associate Synod, 2 to Annabaptist, 2 to Relief Synod, 1 to Roman Catholic Church. *Ibid.*, Volume 11, p. 125.

[32] Edwin Hodder, *Sir George Burns Bart, His Times and Friends* (London, 1892), pp. 136-146, 161-174, 260-279.

[33] See Chapter 9, p. 310.

[34] *Ibid.*

Geographical Distribution 45

by John Gladstone, was part of his estate.[35] The Earl of Moray and Lord Rollo were the owners of the chapels at their Fifeshire estates at Aberdour and Duncrub respectively.[36] English Episcopal churches were built by the Duke and Duchess of Gordon at Fochabers, near Elgin, at Gask, Perthshire, by the Oliphant family, and at Galloway House by the Earl of Galloway. Similarly, Cally, in Kirkcudbrightshire, Selkirk, Old Deer, Corrimony, in Ross and Cromarty, and Arradoul, near Elgin, also depended on landed gentry as patrons.[37] Like watering places, however, such locations were subject to decay. If the patron changed allegiance, as was the case with the Duchess of Gordon at Fochabers and Henrietta Oliphant at Gask, both of whom joined the Free Church, the chapel was likely to close. The death of a patron would also cause trouble for such chapels if the heir did not continue to support them. This was possibly the case at Old Deer and Arradoul. Wealthy patrons provided Evangelical churches but these were not necessarily long-lasting.

It can be seen from Maps 2.1-4 that there was no penetration of Episcopal Evangelicalism into northwestern Scotland apart from the patron-endowed Balmacara and Corrimony. The Free Church was the mainstay of Evangelicalism here, owing much of its success to its comparatively large numbers compared to the Episcopal Evangelicals. The large body of the Free Church enabled it to set up its Sustentation Fund which could support minor congregations, especially those in the Highland region. The small group of Episcopal Evangelicals was unable to do likewise, in particular after its large defection into the English Episcopal movement, which was unable to apply to funds such as the Scottish Episcopal Church Society and Equal Dividend Scheme which distributed money to poorer congregations,[38] helping in the maintenance of around eighteen churches in the northwestern Highlands after 1860.[39] Evangelical Episcopalianism generally took root in places of denser population.

Church Missionary Society Visits

Apart from these centres of activity, there were some scattered Scottish Episcopal churches which, while not overtly Evangelical, nonetheless

---

[35] S. G. Checkland, *The Gladstones. A Family Biography 1764-1851* (Cambridge, 1971), pp. 342-343.

[36] See Chapter 1, p. 18.

[37] See Chapter 8, pp. 258-259. Chapter 9, pp. 298-301, 310.

[38] Frederick Goldie, *A Short History of the Episcopal Church in Scotland* (Edinburgh 1976), pp. 87-91. Scottish Episcopal Church Society was set up in 1838. It had only limited powers and was replaced by the Equal Dividend Scheme in 1871.

[39] D. M. Bertie, *Scottish Episcopal Clergy, 1689-2000,* (Edinburgh, 2000), pp. 537-548.

appear to have been touched by the movement. This is evident from the data surrounding deputations from the Church Missionary Society (CMS). Tables 2.2 - 8 and Maps 2.5 - 9 display some of the Scottish churches, both Evangelical and non-Evangelical, which subscribed to the society, or were visited by it, from 1816 to 1896.[40]

Table 2.2 Subscriptions from Scottish Episcopal Congregations to Church Missionary Society, 1816

DATE	CHURCH	INCUMBENT	AMOUNT	AMOUNT as %
1816	Cowgate, Edinburgh	Archibald Alison	£30.9.2 1/2	13.0
	Blackfriars Wynd, Edinburgh	Robert Adam	£26.13.4 1/2	11.4
	St George's, Edinburgh	R. Q. Shannon	£20.3.7 1/2	8.6
	Carrubber's Close, Edinburgh	William Elstob	£9.10.0	4.1
	Haddington	C. H. Terrot	£7.5.3	3.1
	Musselburgh	William Smith	£9.17.10	4.2
	Leith	Michael Russell	£10.4.0	4.4
	Glasgow	William Routledge	£64.14.0	27.7
	"	"	£22.9.4	9.6
	Old Deer	Alexander Allardice	£11.4.2	4.8
	Tillicoultry		£21.0.0	9.0

Source: *Proceedings of the Church Missionary Society for Africa and the East* (London, 1816), p. 326, AN XVI.

---

[40] See Chapter 2, pp. 46-53, 62-66.

Table 2.3 Subscriptions from Scottish Episcopal Congregations to Church Missionary Society, 1821-1828

DATE	CHURCH	INCUMBENT	AMOUNT	% not given – entries appear unreliable
1821	St James's, Edinburgh	Edward Craig	£92.16.10	
1822	"	"	£72.16.0	
	"	"	£103.14.2 Annual Sermon	
1823			£87.11.8 Annual Sermon	
	"	"	£15.9.1	
	"		£23.17.6	
	"		£33.16.6 Annual Meeting	
	Perth	H. A. Skete	£7.3.0	
1824	St James's, Edinburgh	Edward Craig	£49.9.10	
1825	Haddington	C. H. Terrot	£17.16.0	
	Holy Trinity, Paisley	W. M. Wade	£13.11.0 (collected by Edward Craig)	
	Greenock	W. D. Carter	£16.19.0. £13 11.0 (collected by Edward Craig)	
	Dingwall	Duncan MacKenzie	£15. 5. 0	
	East Lothian	-	£15.13.0	
	Glasgow	-	£10.19.6	
1826	East Lothian	-	£20.16.0	
	Glasgow	-	£15.13.4	
1827	Berwicksire	-	£10.0.0	
	East Lothian	-	£20.16.0	
	Dingwall	Duncan MacKenzie	£20 5.0	
	Glasgow St Andrew's St Mary's	William Routledge H. J. Urquhart George Almond	£36.13.4	

Source: *Proceedings of the Church Missionary Society for Africa and the East* (London, 1821-1828), AN XXII, XXIII, XXIV, XXV, XXVI, XXVII, XXVIII.

Table 2.4 Visits by Church Missionary Society to Scottish Episcopal Congregations, 1834-1835

DATE	CHURCH	INCUMBENT	AMOUNT	AMOUNT as %
August 1834	St James's, Edinburgh	Edward Craig	£29.14.7, £11.3.2	9.9 3.7
	Musselburgh	Thomas Langhorne	£6.8.6	2.1
	Portobello, St Mark's	G. M. Drummond	£9.6.0	3.1
	Portobello, St John's	John Housby	£6.12.4	2.2
	Greenock	Richard Martin	£8.10.0	2.8
10 August	Glasgow St Andrew's St Mary's	William Routledge George Almond	£42.0.11	13.9
18 August	Dundee St Paul's St John's	Heneage Horsley, John Hetherton Samuel Hood	£9.0.0	3.0
19 August	St Paul's, Carrubber's Close, Edinburgh	D. T. K. Drummond	£68.7.0	22.7
29 March 1835	Edinburgh St James's, St Paul's, Carrubber's Close	Edward Craig D. T. K. Drummond	£32.2.9 £16.0.0	10.7 5.3
	Portobello	G. M. Drummond	£6.11.0	2.2
30 March 1835	Musselburgh	Thomas Langhorne	£7.1.0	2.3
	Haddington	James Trail	£9.10.6	3.2
31 March	Edinburgh	Various	£24.2.8	8.0
	St John's, Edinburgh	E. B. Ramsay J. H. Hughes	£12.10.0	4.1
	Dundee	Heneage Horsley, John Hetherton, Samuel Hood	£2.11.6	0.9

Source: *Church Missionary Society Record*, (London, 1835), pp. 19, 87.

Table 2.5a Planned Visits to Scottish Episcopal Congregations by Church Missionary Society, 1841

DATE	CHURCH	INCUMBENT
18-20 April 1841	Various, Edinburgh	-
21 April 1841	Ayr	W. S. Wilson
22 April 1841	Paisley	W. M. Wade
"	Montrose St Peter's, Qualified chapel Scottish Episcopal Congregation	John Dodgson Patrick Cushnie
23 April 1841	Glasgow St Mary's St Jude's	 George Almond, A. L. Courtenay Robert Montgomery
25-26 April 1841	Greenock	G. T. Mostyn
27 April 1841	Dumfries	W. P. McFarquhar
8-26 August 1841 Sunday	Kirkcaldy	Norman Johnston
"	Haddington	James Trail
"	St Mark's, Portobello	H. S. Beresford
Monday	St James's, Edinburgh	Daniel Bagot
Tuesday	St Mark's, Portobello	H. S. Beresford
Wednesday	St Paul's, Dundee	Heneage Horsley
Thursday	Montrose St Peter's, Qualified chapel Scottish Episcopal congregation	John Dodgson Peter Cushnie
Friday	Peterhead	Charles Cole
Sunday	Inverness	Charles Fyvie
	Elgin	W. C. A. Maclaurin
Monday	Elgin	W. C. A. Maclaurin
	Dingwall	Duncan MacKenzie
Tuesday	Inverness	Charles Fyvie
Wednesday	Blair Atholl	Thomas Walker
Thursday	Perth	H. A. Skete
Sunday	Stirling	Robert Henderson
	Alloa	John Hunter
Monday	Alloa	John Hunter

Sources: Proceedings of the Church Missionary Society for Africa and the East (London, 1841), pp. 52-53. *Church Missionary Society Record*, (London, 1841), p. 175.

Table 2.5b Accomplished Visits to Scottish Episcopal Congregations by Church Missionary Society, 1841

DATE	CHURCH	INCUMBENT	MISSIONER AND AMOUNT	AMOUNT as %
22 April 1841	Montrose St Peter's Scottish Episcopal	John Dodgson Peter Cushnie	£7.2.0	4.1
25 April 1841	Glasgow St Mary's	George Almond, A. L. Courteney	Francis Close £39.12.0	22.9
	St Jude's	Robert Montgomery	£38.6.6	22.2
"	Greenock	G. T. Mostyn	£7.1.9	4.1
26 April 1841	Glasgow, St Mary's St Jude's	George Almond Robert Montgomery	£11.12.0 £6.2.11	6.7 3.6
15 August 1841	Dingwall	Duncan MacKenzie	D. T. K. Drummond £10.0.0	5.8
24 August 1841	Inverness	Charles Fyvie	£14.0.0	8.1
25 August 1841	Elgin	W. C. A. McLaurin	C. Bridges £7.0.0	4.0
"	Huntly	James Walker, J. D. Hull	C. Bridges £10.0.0	5.8
29 August	Holy Trinity, Edinburgh	George Coventry, D. T. K. Drummond	C. Bridges £22.0.0	12.7

Source: Church Missionary Society Record, (London, 1841), pp. 129, 222.

Table 2.5c Subscriptions from Scottish Episcopal Congregations to Church Missionary Society, 1841

DATE	CHURCH	INCUMBENT	AMOUNT	AMOUNT as %
1841	Glasgow St Mary's St Jude's	George Almond Robert Montgomery	£189.4.8	42.4
	Edinburgh Holy Trinity	George Coventry, D. T. K. Drummond	£56.16.0	12.7
	St James's	Daniel Bagot	£6.15.6, £43.8.9 (Juvenile Association)	11.2
	St Mark's, Portobello	H. S. Beresford	£46.8.9	10.4
	Greenock	G. T. Mostyn	£26.7.6	5.9
	Montrose St Peter's Qualified Chapel Scottish Episcopal	John Dodgson Patrick Cushnie	£25.16.0	5.8
	Haddington	James Trail	£19.4.1	4.3
	Dumfries	W. P. McFarquhar	£8.17.8	2.0
	St Paul's, Aberdeen	Sir William Dunbar	£8.15.5	2.0
	Perth Qualified Chapel	H. A. Skete	£6.13.2	1.5
	Huntly	James Walker, J. D. Hull	£5.0.0	1.1
	Dunfermline	E. B. Field	£2.0.0	0.4
	Forres	Alexander Ewing	£2.0.0	0.4
	East Lothian	-	£1.0.0	0.2

Source: Proceedings of the Church Missionary Society for Africa and the East (London, 1841), AN XLIII.

Table 2.6 Subscriptions from English and Scottish Episcopalians to Church Missionary Society, 1847

DATE	CHURCH	INCUMBENT	AMOUNT	AMOUNT as %
1847				
English Episcopal	St Thomas's, Edinburgh	D. T. K. Drummond	£301.3.8	49.9
	St Jude's, Glasgow	C. P. Miles	£132.5.2	21.9
	St Paul's, Aberdeen	Sir William Dunbar	£59.2.7	9.8
	St Peter's, Montrose	John Wade	£30.1.1	5.0
	Huntly	J. D. Hull	£3.10.0	0.6
Scottish Episcopal	St Mark's, Portobello	John Boyle	£37.13.8	6.2
	Glasgow	-	£33.11.8	5.6
	Inverness	Charles Fyvie	£4.16.6	0.8
	Banff	Alexander Bruce	£1.10.9	0.3

Source: *Proceedings of the Church Missionary Society for Africa and the East* (London, 1848), AN L, pp 163-164.

Table 2.7 Subscriptions from English and Scottish Episcopalians to Church Missionary Society, 1859

DATE	CHURCH	INCUMBENT	AMOUNT	AMOUNT as %
1859				
English Episcopal	St Thomas's, Edinburgh	D. T. K. Drummond	£271.5.1	42.0
	St Jude's, Glasgow	G. K. Flindt	£132.10.0	20.5
	St Paul's, Aberdeen	F. W. B. Bouverie	£54.7.1	8.4
	St James's, Aberdeen	John Goodwin	£45.4.8	7.0
	Montrose	H. J. Marshall	£18.1.4	2.8
Scottish Episcopal	St Mark's, Portobello	C. S. Absolom	£21.10.0	3.3
	Private Subscriptions		£102.14.7	15.9

Source: *Proceedings of the Church Missionary Society for Africa and the East* (London, 1860), pp. 214-215.

Table 2.8 Subscriptions from English and Scottish Episcopalians to Church Missionary Society, 1896

DATE	CHURCH	INCUMBENT	AMOUNT	AMOUNT as %
1896				
English Episcopalians	St Silas's, Glasgow	Sholto Douglas-Campbell Douglas	£189.13.3	29.3
	St Thomas's, Edinburgh	H. J. Colclough	£180.4.6	27.9
	Hunter's Quay	-	£74.11.0	11.5
	St Paul's, Aberdeen	William Fairclough	£3.16.1	0.6
	St James's, Aberdeen	A. M. Mackay	£1.7.3	0.2
Scottish Episcopalians	Cally	Walter Plant	£43.0.0	6.6
	St Peter's, Edinburgh	E. C. Dawson	£41.8.11	6.4
	Holy Trinity, Edinburgh	Rayner Winterbotham	£32.8.5	5.0
	Annan	Frank Coleby	£30.5.6	4.7
	Kirkcaldy		£10.0.0	1.5
	St Vincent's, Edinburgh	P. W. Hulbert	£9.17.9	1.5
	Broughty Ferry	George Mackness	£8.7.6	1.3
	St Cuthbert's, Colinton	X. P. Massy	£7.3.8	1.1
	Duncrub	John Stevenson	£5.5.0	0.8
	Crieff	W. R. Cosens	£3.0.0	0.5
	St Andrew's, Edinburgh	C. R. Teape	£2.14.10	0.4
	Culross	William Bruce	£2.2.0	0.3
	Cathedral, Edinburgh	J. F. Montgomery	£1.11.0	0.2

Source: Proceedings of the Church Missionary Society for Africa and the East (London, 1897), AN XCVIII, p. 272.

In 1816 Table 2.2 shows that Old Deer qualified chapel was the only overtly Evangelical Episcopal church to be supportive of CMS, contributing 4.8% of the giving. But additional random support came from various non-Evangelical congregations in Edinburgh together with nearby Haddington, Musselburgh, Leith, and, notably, Glasgow which provided 27.7% of the total collection. The pattern continued in 1823 to 1827 as shown in Table 2.3, although there appear to be discrepancies since St James's, Edinburgh, and Holy Trinity, Paisley, are not noted after 1824 and 1825 respectively. For this reason the percentage giving has not been calculated. While the Evangelical Episcopal churches of St James's, Edinburgh, and Holy Trinity, Paisley, supported the society, other Scottish Episcopal churches, not under Evangelical incumbencies, at Perth, Haddington, Greenock, Dingwall, East Lothian, Glasgow and Berwickshire were also involved in the work.

Likewise, in 1834 to 1835, Table 2.4 records that St Paul's, Carrubber's Close, Edinburgh, St James's, Edinburgh, and St Mark's Portobello, under the Evangelical incumbencies of D. T. K. Drummond, Edward Craig and G. M. Drummond respectively, gave amounts accounting for 22.7%, 13.6% and 3.1% of the total. But the contribution (13.9%) from the non-Evangelical Glasgow churches of St Andrew's and St Mary's in 1834 also suggest substantial allegiance to the society, while the small collections at St John's, Portobello (2.2%), St Paul's and St John's, Dundee (3.0% and 0.9%), Haddington (3.2%) and St John's, Edinburgh (4.1%), indicate some support.

Map 2.6 illustrates that CMS had an enlarged sphere of influence in 1841. As Table 2.5a shows the society, in that year, planned widespread visits to Ayr, Greenock, Kirkcaldy (Fife), Haddington, St Paul's, Dundee, Peterhead (Aberdeenshire), Inverness, Elgin, Blair Atholl (Perthshire), Perth, Stirling and Alloa (Clackmananshire), none of which can be identified as being under Evangelical leadership. Although it seems that the society could not supply the necessary staff to man all the deputations, Table 2.5b indicates that, in April to August 1841, the non-Evangelical incumbencies of Montrose (4.1%), St Mary's, Glasgow (22.9% and 6.7%), Greenock (4.1%), Dingwall (5.8%), Inverness (8.1%) and Elgin (4.0%), were visited and contributed money, along with the Evangelical St Jude's, Glasgow (22.2% and 3.6%) and Holy Trinity, Edinburgh (12.7%).[41] Table 2.5c shows all the Scottish churches paying annual subscriptions to the society in 1841. While the Glasgow and Edinburgh churches, which included Evangelical congregations, were the largest contributors at 42.2% and 23.9% respectively, it is apparent for instance that Haddington, under

---

[41] Francis Close, the well-known Evangelical incumbent of Holy Trinity, Cheltenham, was a gifted evangelist who would have contributed to the input of Evangelicalism in the Glasgow churches in April 1841. See Kenneth Hylson-Smith, *Evangelicals in the Church of England 1734-1984* (Edinburgh, 1988), pp. 145-147.

Geographical Distribution 55

James Trail and contributing 4.3%, continued to offer some support to CMS. But the Elginshire church at Forres (0.4%), provided little.

Table 2.6 shows that support for the society from Scottish Episcopal churches tailed off by 1847 when, although sizeable sums from St Mark's, Portobello (6.2%) and the Glasgow congregations (5.6%) were given, the English Episcopalians at St Thomas's, Edinburgh, St Jude's, Glasgow, and St Paul's, Aberdeen, outstripped them with 49.9%, 21.9% and 9.8% of the giving respectively. However, as Map 2.7 indicates, the society travelled the long distance to Inverness and Banff despite the apparent low level of support from the Scottish Episcopalians there. By 1859, Table 2.7 indicates that allegiance in the Scottish Episcopal churches, apart from St Mark's, Portobello, which accounted for 3.3% of the collections, had diminished even further, with only £102.14.7, less than the amount collected in 1834 to 1835, being contributed by private individuals throughout Scotland. By contrast, St Thomas's, Edinburgh, alone gave 42% of the total.

In 1896 the donations recorded in Table 2.8 show that St Silas's, Glasgow, and St Thomas's, Edinburgh, constituted the centres of support with collections of 29.3% and 27.9% of the total respectively. There was a reasonable contribution at the previously English Episcopal church at Cally where 6.6% of the total was donated, and at St Peter's, Edinburgh, with 6.4%, but the former was probably due to the continued support of its patron, Horatio Murray Stewart, and the latter to the defection to St Peter's of some members of St Thomas's along with their incumbent E. C. Dawson.[42] The congregation of Holy Trinity, Edinburgh, contributing 5.0% to the society, also appears to have increased its interest, as did Annan, near Dumfries, in the diocese of Glasgow and Galloway, with 4.7%. Thus, at the end of the century, although there was a continuing strand of support for CMS from churches not known for Evangelicalism, most loyalty was to be found from the Evangelical English Episcopal movement, which contributed 69.5 % of the giving.

Various inferences can be drawn from this information. Firstly, CMS data is only a rough measure of Evangelical allegiance. Non-Evangelicals were involved with, and donated to, the society. In 1820, George Gleig, Bishop of Brechin, pointedly described C. H. Terrot, the incumbent of Haddington, as 'not of [the Evangelical] party' although he was secretary of the Edinburgh branch of CMS from 1818 to 1831.[43] While CMS

---

[42] See Chapter 10, pp. 356, 361.
[43] *Correspondence between the Rt. Rev. Bishop Gleig and Rev. Edward Craig Respecting an Accusation Lately Published in a Charge Delivered to the Clergy of the Episcopal Communion of Brechin* (Edinburgh, 1820), p. 25. *Proceedings of the Church Missionary Society for Africa and the East* (London, 1818), AN XVIII. *Edinburgh Almanack* (Edinburgh, 1831), p. 379.

contributed to an Evangelical presence in Scotland, it is impossible to conclude that all connected with the society were Evangelicals.

Secondly, despite this, giving to CMS from non-Evangelical congregations probably often came about through the efforts of local Evangelicals. In 1816 it is feasible to conclude that Robert Wardlaw and James Johnstone[44] wielded influence in the Edinburgh area. Again, at Greenock, there seems to have been Evangelical influence in 1825, before T. H. Wilkinson's ministry from 1829 to 1831. The movement surrounding Anne Robertson's family in Dingwall, Ross and Cromarty, in the early decades of the century,[45] possibly generated the considerable effort required for deputations in 1825 and 1827 to travel the long distance to the northern towns as indicated in Map 2.5. The small contributions collected at Montrose and Elgin in 1841 again suggest local Evangelical influence. Similar inferences may be drawn from the data for Inverness and Banff in 1847, St Mark's, Portobello, in 1859 and Annan and Crieff in 1896. It is also noteworthy that, despite better roads and railways by the end of the century, the society did not visit further north than Aberdeen (Map 2.9) possibly because Evangelical influence in the region had waned. Thus it is reasonable to conclude that a few scattered Evangelicals attended their local Scottish Episcopal churches, stimulating interest in CMS in the nineteenth century.

Thirdly, referring to Maps 2.5 – 2.9, important cities such as Glasgow, Edinburgh and Dundee, together with prosperous towns such as Montrose, Elgin and Perth, home to a qualified congregation since 1730 and an important shipbuilding and garrison centre,[46] and holiday centres like Blair Atholl and Crieff were noteworthy places of possible Evangelical influence within non-party congregations. But overall it appears that there was only a scattered, small representation of Evangelicalism within non-Evangelical Scottish Episcopal churches in the nineteenth century.

Conclusion

Evangelical Episcopalian congregations were evident throughout Scotland in the nineteenth century, although they made little progress in the northwest. CMS records indicate that some isolated Evangelicals possibly attended local Episcopal churches in a variety of locations, where they probably fostered Evangelicalism. However, although CMS certainly preached the Evangelical message at these places, possibly gaining converts, it is impossible to gauge the level of genuine party commitment as

---

[44] See Chapter 1, p. 25.
[45] See Chapter 1, p. 23.
[46] Bertie, *Scottish Episcopal Clergy*, pp. 652-653. Groome, *Gazetteer*, Volume V, pp. 177-188.

Geographical Distribution

illustrated by the involvement of the non-Evangelical, C. H. Terrot, at Haddington. The main thrust of Evangelical Episcopalianism in Scotland, both before and after the advent of English Episcopalianism, has been shown to have occurred in cities, towns, and holiday centres where the population was large enough to support a congregation financially and where the inhabitants were accustomed to a variety of religious denominations. Places where wealthy patrons could supply a viable economic base for a relatively small group were also home to such churches. But Evangelical Episcopalianism in Scotland, being a minority section of the religious community, was unable to sustain a substantial widespread geographical distribution.

58   *Conscience and Compromise*

Map 2.1
Evangelical Episcopal Congregations and Laypeople, 1800-1818

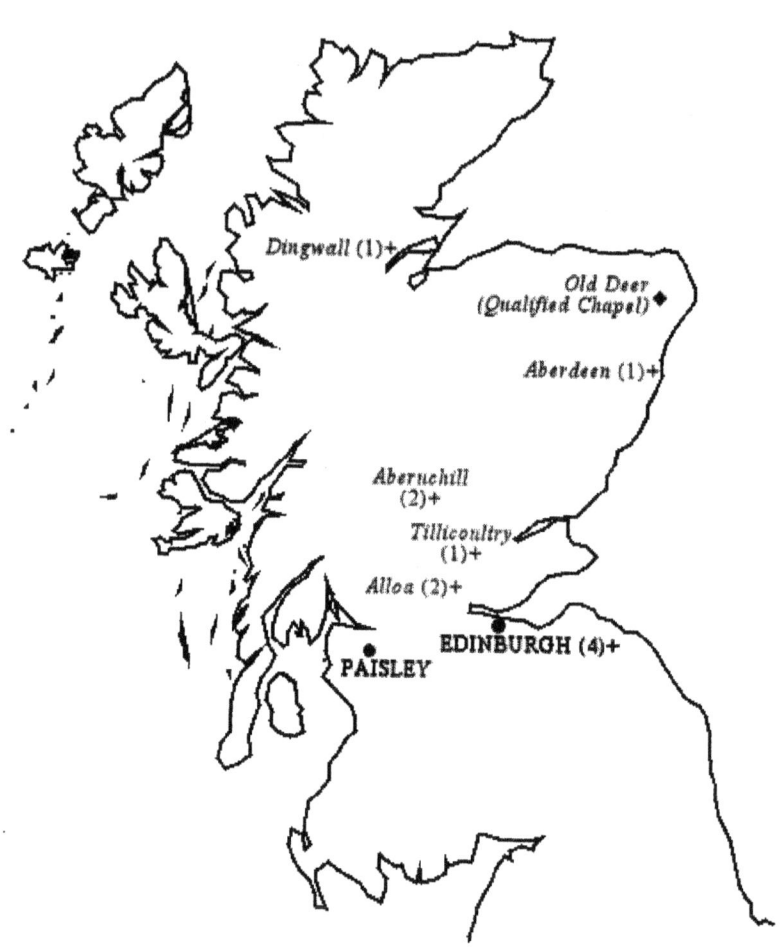

Scottish Episcopal Congregation IN CAPITALS
+ *Lay people supportive of CMS. Numbers in (brackets)*
♦ Qualified Chapel

Geographical Distribution

**Map 2.2
Evangelical Scottish Episcopal Congregations, 1821-1830**

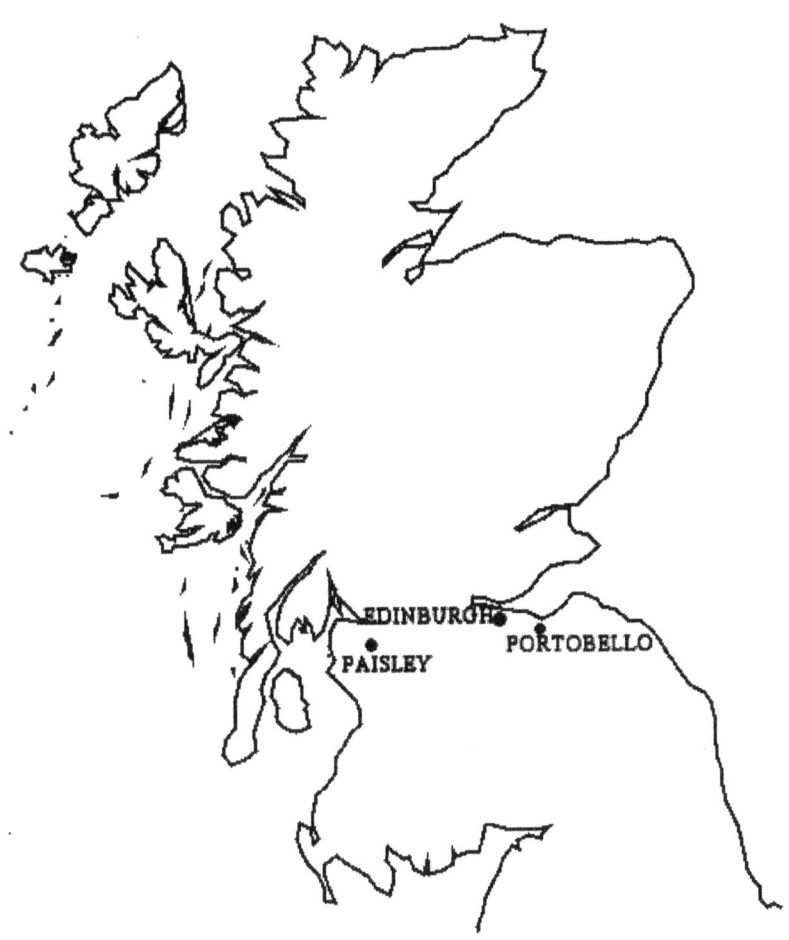

Scottish Episcopal Congregation IN CAPITALS

Map 2.3
Evangelical Scottish Episcopal Congregations, 1831-1842

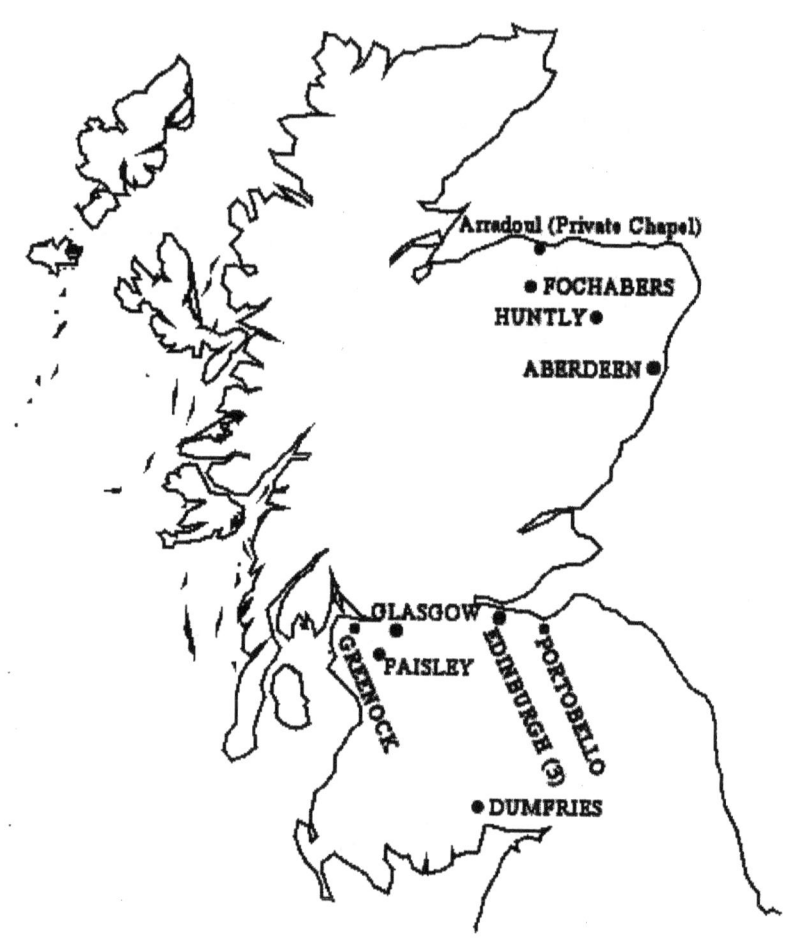

Scottish Episcopal Congregation IN CAPITALS

Geographical Distribution

Map 2.4
Evangelical Episcopal Congregations, 1842-1898

English Episcopal Congregation, 1842-1898　　▲ Watering Places
SCOTTISH EPISCOPAL CONGREGATION, 1840-1898　▼ Church with a Patron

N. B. The total of 6 Evangelical Scottish Episcopal Churches in Edinburgh should not be taken to represent a significant movement in that Church. Of the Edinburgh Churches St James's lost its Evangelical status after 1846 (Ch. 9, p. 305), Holy Trinity, Edinburgh, was only mildly Evangelical (Ch.1, p. 20), J. S. S. Robertson was at St Peter's for only one year and at St Andrew's for 2 years, in the capacity of an assistant (Ch.1, p. 9), St Vincent's and St Peter's (1880-1890) were direct descendants of the English Episcopal movement (Ch. 10, pp. 366-367, 371).

Map 2.5
Scottish Episcopal Churches subscribing to CMS, 1816-1835

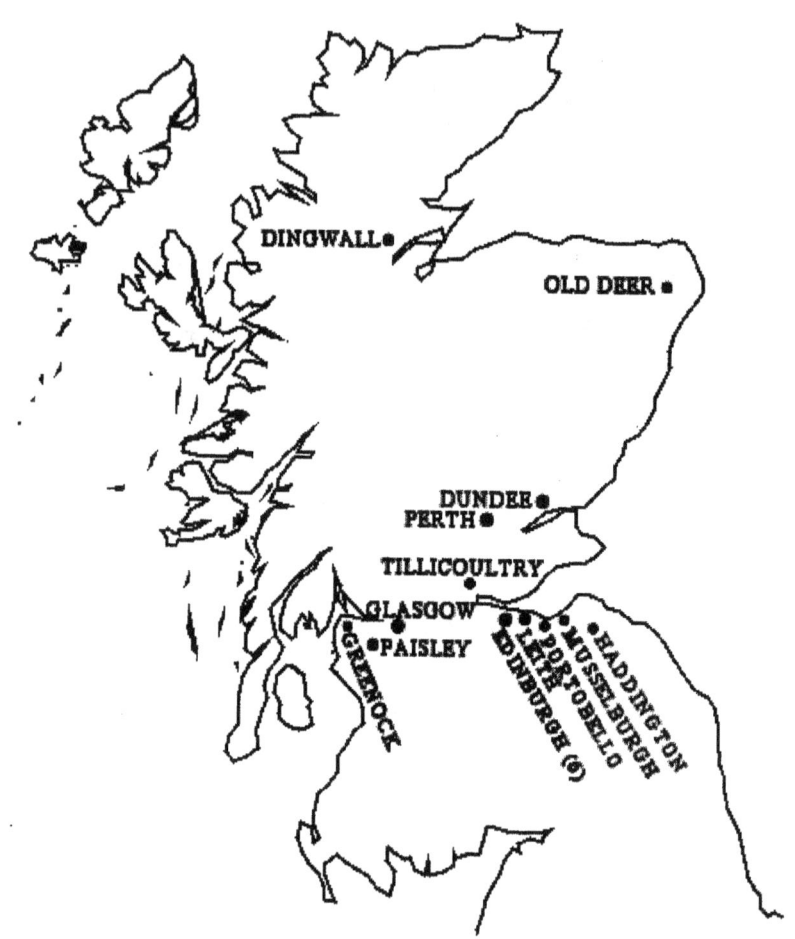

Map 2.6
Scottish Episcopal Churches subscribing to CMS, 1841

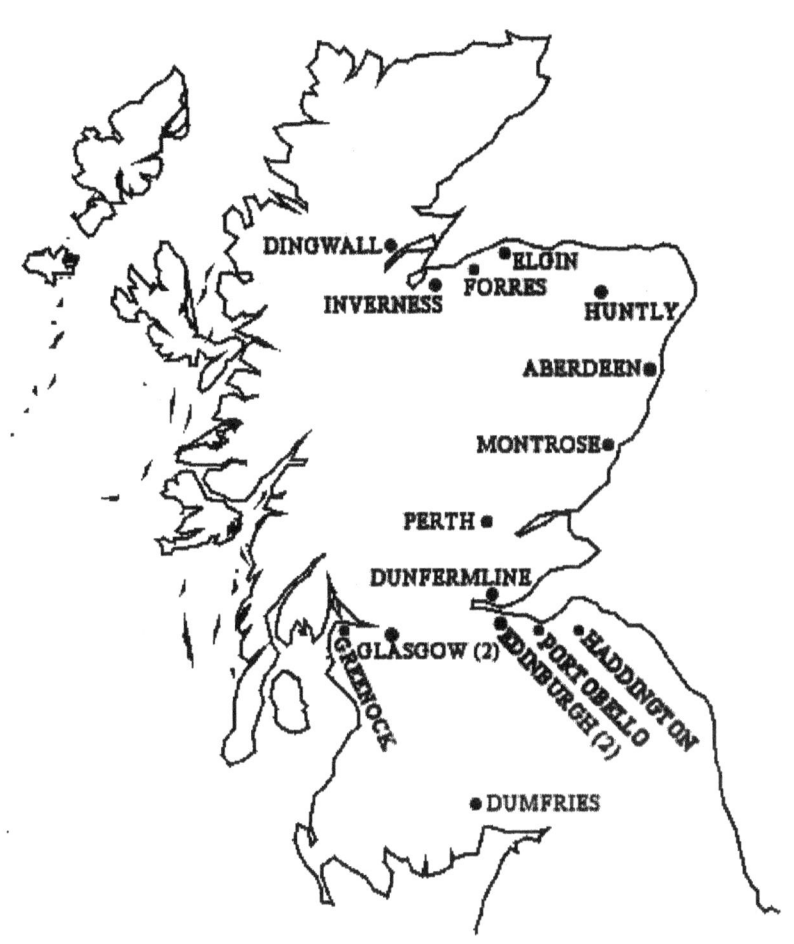

Map 2.7
Episcopal Churches subscribing to CMS, 1847

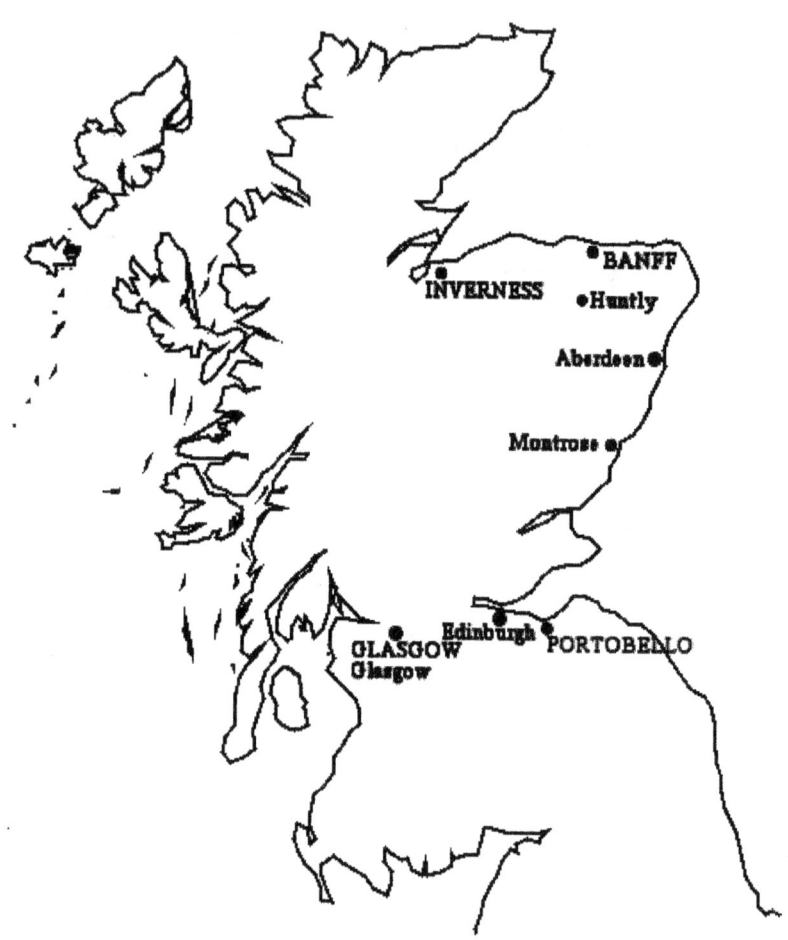

English Episcopal Congregation
SCOTTISH EPISCOPAL CONGREGATION

Geographical Distribution

**Map 2.8
Episcopal Churches subscribing to CMS, 1859**

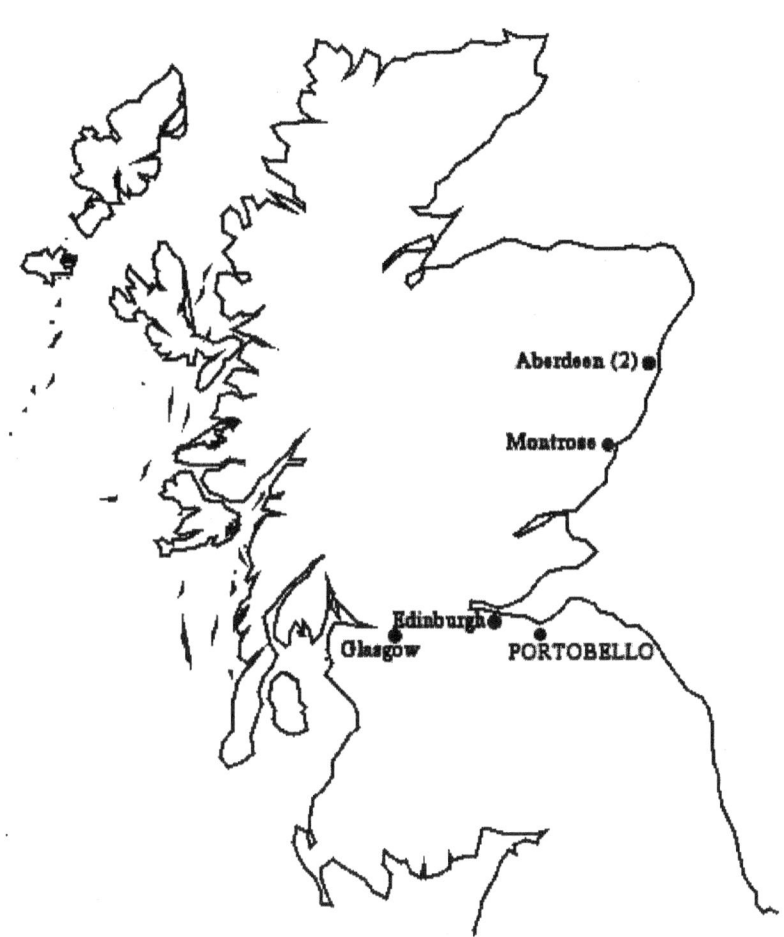

English Episcopal Congregation
SCOTTISH EPISCOPAL CONGREGATION

Map 2.9
Episcopal Churches subscribing to CMS, 1896

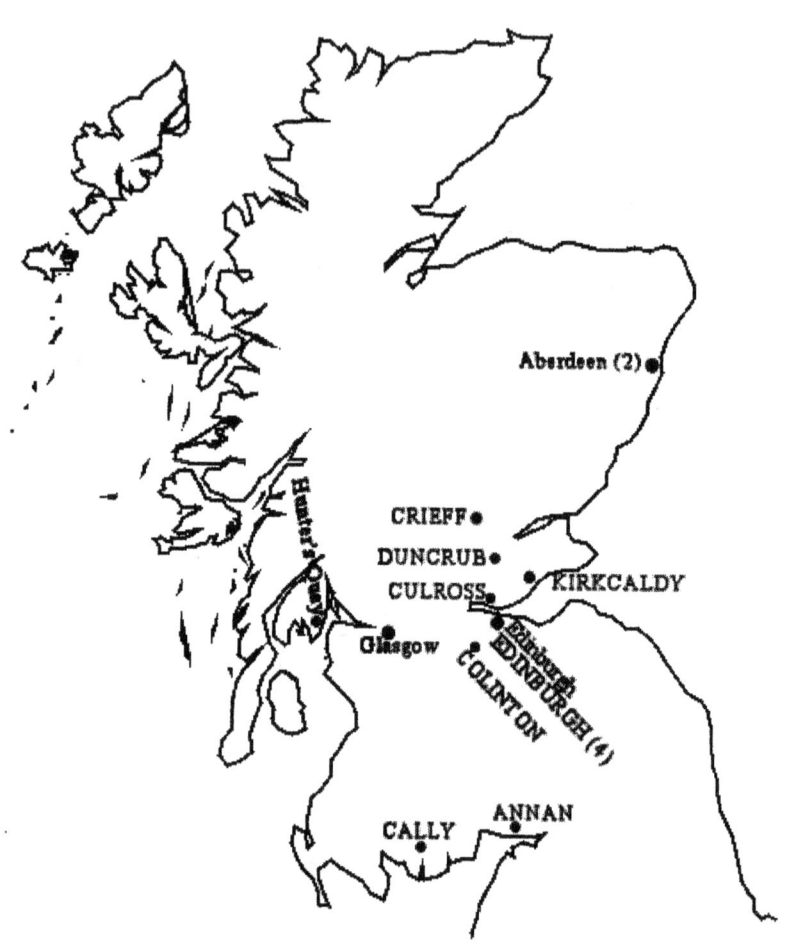

English Episcopal Congregation
SCOTTISH EPISCOPAL CONGREGATION

Chapter 3

Social Class

Scottish class distribution in the nineteenth century followed the national pattern of a society with a large base of lower-skilled and unskilled workers and an apex of a small number of upper-class individuals. Although the proportion of working-class people dropped as the century progressed, when some acquired the expertise to enable them to rise to middle-class status, they remained the numerically dominant group. This is clearly illustrated in Table 3.1, which shows the results derived from R. D. Baxter's summary of the division of Scottish labour in 1867, and in Table 3.2, which plots middle-class presence in Scotland from 1861 to 1911.[1]

Table 3.1 Division of Scottish Labour, 1867

Classification	Yearly Income	Number of Productive Persons	% of Working Population
Upper Middle Class	£1000+	4,700	0.33
Middle Middle Class	£100-£1000	111,300	7.95
Lower Middle Class	Up to £100	156,000	11.19
Higher Skilled Working Class	£50+	137,000	9.82
Lower Skilled Working Class	£40-£50	558,000	40.02
Unskilled Working Class	Under £40	427,000	30.63

Adapted from T. C. Smout, *A Century of the Scottish People 1830-1950* (London, 1987), p. 111.

---

[1] The percentage of middle-class people in Scotland given in Table 3.1 for 1867 is larger than that suggested by Geoffrey Best of between 10.3% and 11.4%. However, the overall point is that the proportion of middle-class people was rising during the nineteenth century. Geoffrey Best, *Mid-Victorian Britain 1851-1875* (London, 1987), p. 106.

Table 3.2 Individuals with Middle-class Occupations in Scotland as a Percentage of the Occupied Population

	1861	1881	1911
Aberdeen	22.5	27.2	30.4
Dundee	11.6	17.1	17.8
Edinburgh	29.3	36.0	37.0
Glasgow	17.6	16.4	27.6
All Scottish Towns	16.6	23.5	Not Available
Scotland	21.6	23.2	25.1

Source: Nicholas Morgan and Richard Trainor, 'The Dominant Classes', in W. Hamish Fraser and R. J. Morris, *People and Society in Scotland, Volume II, 1830-1914* (Edinburgh, 1990), p. 106.

It can be seen from Table 3.1 that, in 1867, the combined working classes made up roughly 80% of Scottish society while the middle classes accounted for only 20%. Similar figures are shown in Table 3.2 to have held for the remainder of the century with only a slight rise in the middle-class level to about 23% in 1881 and 25% in 1911. The social structure of Scotland was heavily based on the working classes in the nineteenth century

Additionally, it can be seen from Table 3.2 that Edinburgh and Aberdeen, throughout the period 1861 to 1911, had a higher proportion of middle-class people than the national average, while Glasgow and Dundee fell below this figure. Another factor, not apparent in the tables, is that the composition of the working-class groups was fluid during the century. Although the proportion of people in these categories dropped slightly when some rose to middle-class status, as indicated in Table 3.2, the skilled working-class group increased as the unskilled learnt the talents required by new industries.[2] Class distribution varied with location and time.

One challenge for the churches in the nineteenth century was to reach the large group of working-class people. The Royal Commission on Religious Instruction in Scotland for 1836 to 1839 published statistical details concerning the state of Scottish churches. The data for Episcopalianism showed a divide between many rural and urban congregations. In the former category it was reported that a high number of poor and working-class people often attended church. For instance, at Cuminestone, Aberdeenshire, five-sixths of the attenders were of the labouring class. At Huntly, in the diocese of Moray, Ross and Argyll, the incumbent, James Walker, claimed that 'the greater part of the congregation are of the working classes'. Similar sentiments were forthcoming from the diocese of

---

[2] Best, *Mid-Victorian Britain*, pp. 117-118.

Brechin, where the church at Muchalls reported the congregation, with few exceptions, to be 'all poor people...fishermen and their families'.[3] Episcopal allegiance in the rural northwestern Highlands was, however, low. Shortage of Gaelic-speaking clergy was a problem, although a congregation met regularly at Ballachulish, Appin.[4] In cities and towns there was more variation. While at St John's, Edinburgh, the poor and working class accounted for one fifth of the congregation, neighbouring St Peter's included very few. Likewise, in Glasgow, while the Evangelical, Robert Montgomery, of St Jude's, ministered to a church 'chiefly composed of the upper classes', his fellow Evangelical W. M. Wade, at Paisley, noted that his people were mainly poor and working-class 'with the exception of from fifteen to twenty families'.[5] Such variation between rural and urban churches is not surprising. Labourers in farming and fishing communities would have made up the bulk of the population, with only a few local proprietors contributing to the upper classes. Poor people in such locations would not have felt the same social uneasiness about attending church as their counterparts in urban areas where the upper and middle classes were likely to have been present in far greater numbers. Again, it could not be expected that a church situated in a fashionable urban area would attract many poor people. But while churches probably tended to serve the locations in which they were set, the case of St John's, Edinburgh, situated at the wealthy West End of Edinburgh, suggests non-uniformity. Its mixed congregation indicates that some poorer people were not always reluctant to attend well-to-do places, presumably because the ministry offered appealed to them. Generally, then, it seems that the Scottish Episcopal Church attracted a number of poor people in rural areas in the 1830s, but in cities the situation was patchy.

By mid-century working-class church attendance in rural Scotland appears to have been largely maintained, although revivalist activity after 1859 tended to scatter Scottish Episcopal fisherfolk in Aberdeenshire to the Brethren and Baptist churches.[6] In towns, however, some feared that the situation was worsening. Horace Mann's analysis of the statistics of church

---

[3] Reports of the Commissioners of Religious Instruction, Scotland, *PP* (1836-1839) quoted in J. P. Lawson, *History of the Scottish Episcopal Church from the Revolution to the Present Time* (Edinburgh, 1843), pp. 488, 495, 496. *Cf. ENCS*, pp. 47-48.

[4] Rowan Strong, *Episcopalianism in Nineteenth-Century Scotland* (Oxford, 2002), pp. 86-88. Itinerant Evangelists and Evangelicals from the Church of Scotland had built up congregations in the area in the late eighteenth and early nineteenth centuries, which in turn led to a deficit of Gaelic Episcopal clergy. *Ibid.*, p. 84.

[5] Lawson, *Scottish Episcopal Church*, pp. 503-504, 508-509.

[6] Strong, *Episcopalianism*, pp. 62-63. Efforts in the 1830s by Church of Scotland Evangelical clergy such as James Brewster at Ferryden, Aberdeenshire, in conjunction with the evangelistic activities of D. T. K. Drummond at nearby Usan, also contributed to Scottish Episcopal erosion in these areas. See Chapter 8, p. 251.

attendance in Britain, based on the Religious Census of 30 March 1851, led him to warn that while 'labouring myriads of our country have been multiplying with our multiplied material prosperity, it cannot...be stated that a corresponding increase has occurred in the attendance of this class in our religious edifices'.[7] Certain modern historical research of urban congregations supports Mann's view. A. A. MacLaren argued that, in mid-century Aberdeen, while the working classes continued to hold an allegiance to the Presbyterian churches, they were not regular attenders and were certainly not evident on the membership lists.[8] By contrast, the more recent research of P. L. M. Hillis and C. G. Brown, consisting of a detailed numerical analysis, suggests that the skilled working class was attracted in fairly large numbers to the Presbyterian churches in Glasgow at this time.[9] Conversely, Rowan Strong suggests that the middle classes often dominated urban Episcopal churches and that the working class, whom he identfies as mainly Irish and English, exercised absenteeism if it felt marginalized by superior social groupings.[10]

Records of rural Evangelical Episcopal churches have not survived in sufficient detail to enable a study of their class distribution to be made. However, the archive material of some strongly Evangelical Episcopal urban churches in nineteenth-century Scotland is available, of which an analysis will be made in this chapter in order to compare the attendance of working-class people with other social groups. The examination will range over the years before 1842, when the churches were part of the Scottish Episcopal Church, and after that date when many had left to form independent English Episcopal congregations.

Choosing the Records

Three obvious sources reveal the social make-up of a congregation. Baptismal lists, as used by Hillis and Brown, membership lists and congregational data all provide information of varying types. Membership of a church entitled people to vote on congregational issues, while baptismal involvement alone did not.[11] In some of the independent

---

[7] *B. P. P. 1851 Census Great Britain, Population* Volume II (London, 1853), p. 93.

[8] A. A. MacLaren, *Religion and Social Class: the Disruption Years in Aberdeen* (London, 1974), pp. 126-127, 137-138, 162.

[9] P. L. M. Hillis, 'Presbyterianism and Social Class in Mid-Nineteenth Century Glasgow: a Study of Nine Churches', *Journal of Ecclesiastical History*, 32, (1981), p. 54. C. G. Brown, *Religion and Society in Scotland since 1707* (Edinburgh, 1997), pp. 95-122.

[10] Strong, *Episcopalianism*, p. 297.

[11] Perusal of the minute books of the Evangelical Episcopal chapels makes it clear that only members had voting rights.

Social Class

Evangelical English Episcopal chapels, such as St James's, Aberdeen, membership was not granted until a person had been an attender for over a year.[12] It might thus be expected that membership lists would furnish a picture of the committed section of a congregation. But they are not entirely without drawbacks. For instance Hillis points out that, in many non-established Presbyterian churches, membership involved an additional donation of money above that collected from pew rents in order to keep the church viable and to enable the undertaking of various projects. This was very likely to have also been the case in the English Episcopal chapels which were independent of the Scottish Episcopal Church after 1842 and had no access to money apart from that provided by their congregations. Such a system was obviously unfavourable to the less well off.[13] Hence, while working-class people might have attended these churches, and even bought seats, they would not necessarily have been members because of monetary constraints. Membership lists, which are therefore likely to be skewed towards the wealthier middle classes, will omit certain people.

This assertion is indicated by the minute book of St Paul's, Aberdeen, which reveals that, in 1870, there were seven hundred and twenty-six sittings at the church, and one hundred and eleven members.[14] The number of individuals making up families of members is unknown, but, assuming an estimate of four people per family to allow for those with no, or few, children, a total of four hundred and forty-four seats occupied by members and their families in 1870 might have been a likely figure. This would have left a further two hundred and eighty-two seats available for non-members. Membership lists are by no means totally reliable guides to congregational composition.

Baptismal registers are useful in ascertaining church attendance. It seems very fair to assume that, given the strict ideas of Evangelicals regarding the relevance of infant baptism for only believing families,[15] the rite was not administered indiscriminately and that many families appearing in the baptismal lists were also regular attenders at church.[16] Reference to the

---

[12] St James's, Aberdeen, Minute Book, 1870, *passim*, St James's Church, Aberdeen, Archives.

[13] Hillis, 'Social Class', p. 57.

[14] St Paul's Minute Book, 24 January 1870, 28 March 1870, St Paul's Church, Aberdeen, Archives.

[15] See Chapter 6, pp. 193-205.

[16] Credence for this assumption is substantiated by Hillis, 'Presbyterianism and Social Class', pp. 49-50 which argues that this was the case for Presbyterians. Again, Strong, *Episcopalianism*, pp. 196, 199, 209, shows that many Scottish Episcopal clergy, notably David Aitchison at Christ Church, Calton, Glasgow, (1835-1840), enforced this requirement, leading to a loss of working-class people from the congregations. There seems to be no reason to assume that Evangelical Episcopal clergy behaved differently, in particular those of the English Episcopal movement who were strongly Evangelical.

records of St Paul's, Aberdeen, indicates that this group of people was not negligible. Table 3.3 shows the number of infant baptisms at St Paul's in the years 1870 to 1880 and in 1889, and the membership status of the fathers of the children. While members' children accounted for around only one third of the total baptisms – although there were exceptions: 50% in 1875 and 12% in 1880 – the majority of baptisms in these years were performed for non-members. Baptismal rolls thus provide the names and occupations of a sizeable group of people many of whom were likely to have been regular churchgoers but who do not appear on membership lists. However, despite the assumptions registered here it is necessary to allow for the possibility that some on the baptismal registers had only casual church links, and so an analysis using them probably indicates congregational trends rather than precise figures.

Table 3.3 Baptisms at St Paul's, Aberdeen, 1870-1880, 1889

Year	Baptisms	Members' Children Baptised	% Members' Children Baptised
1870	32	11	34
1871	34	14	41
1872	29	11	38
1873	29	4	14
1874	32	13	41
1875	18	9	50
1876	27	11	41
1877	27	6	22
1878	22	8	36
1879	17	4	24
1880	26	3	12
1889	14	6	43

Source: St Paul's, Aberdeen, Baptismal Roll and Minute Books, 1870-1880, 1889. Aberdeen University Library MS 3320/8.

There are other drawbacks with baptismal rolls. Firstly, they provide the names and occupations of only fathers or single mothers – most unmarried people do not appear in them. Additionally, the lists are concentrated on the younger church attenders since, although there would have been some fathers who were older, in the main it can be expected that they would have been younger men. Again, some upper-class members might well have had

---

(See, Chapters 3, 8, 9). However, it may be the case, for example, that the large number of working class baptisms at St Paul's, Aberdeen, recorded in Table 3.5 indicates some indiscriminate baptisms, and thus working-class church attendance might be lower than the discussion here suggests.

baptisms performed in their own homes or private chapels, rather than in church, and so would not necessarily appear in the baptismal records. In some of the English Episcopal churches, such as St Thomas's, Edinburgh, there is also the consideration that many seat holders belonged to the Free Church,[17] where they would almost certainly have had their children baptised, and thus be absent from the baptismal lists of the chapels under consideration. Sometimes baptisms were not entered in the register when they clearly should have been. This is evident, for instance, in the many gaps left in the St Thomas's records of the 1850s, and such occurrences make baptismal records rather unreliable. Added to all these difficulties is the fact that, as J. A. Banks has shown, the lower social classes tended to have more children than the upper classes in the later nineteenth century.[18] Although all social groups were having fewer children by the end of the century, the baptismal figures will generally be higher for the lower classes than for the middle classes, giving the impression that they were the largest group in the congregation. Care has to be taken not to assume this. However, given the lower birth rate for the upper classes it is likely that, if their baptismal figures are the highest in a sample, then they probably constituted the largest group in the congregation under consideration. Overall then baptismal rolls, like membership lists, provide only a partial picture of the social make-up of a church. They illustrate patterns rather than absolute numbers in the various congregational social groups. Ideally it would seem that records listing all the people in church Sunday-by-Sunday, would give the most accurate assessment. But these do not exist for the Evangelical Episcopal chapels under consideration. Apart from St Paul's, Aberdeen, and St Peter's, Montrose, membership data is not available either. For this study it is therefore necessary to rely mainly on baptismal rolls along the lines of Hillis and Brown.

Classification Scheme

The method of classification adopted by MacLaren, Hillis and Brown was used in this investigation.[19] This will enable comparisons to be made with the Presbyterian churches. Additionally, Rowan Strong's suggestion that middle-class dominance of the leadership roles in urban Episcopal

---

[17] See Chapters 8 and 9, *passim*.

[18] Banks estimates that the average number of children for upper-class people in 1871-1881 was 4.79, falling to 3.46 in 1881-1891. For skilled working-class families the figures were generally over 6.0 and 3.5 respectively. For unskilled workers the figures were over 6.6 and 5.3 respectively. J. A. Banks, *Victorian Values. Secularism and the Size of Families* (Aldershot, 1994), pp. 98-107.

[19] Hillis, 'Social Class', pp. 48-49. MacLaren, *Social Class*, pp. 218-219. Brown, *Religion and Society*, p. 108.

congregations led to working-class absenteeism will be clarified.[20] At the same time a partial survey of the nationality of working-class attenders will be given, and compared with Strong's assertion that they were mainly Irish and English.

However, it was decided to give the categories the names upper middle class, lower middle class, skilled working class, unskilled working class, and others – which are not the terms used by Hillis and MacLaren. Their names of high and low status to describe the middle classes were considered to be less clear, while Brown's lack of a name for the upper middle class, and a split of the skilled working class into two groups, did not give an instantly accessible categorisation. The simplified terms used in this study are considered to be generally more useful, but their relation to Hillis's classification [A] to [I] is shown below. The categories clergy, gentlemen and landed gentry, not included by Hillis, often appeared in the baptismal records of the Evangelical Episcopal churches, and were put into the upper middle-class groups [A] and [D].

UPPER MIDDLE CLASS AND ABOVE

[A] *Professional Group* (generally university graduates.)
1. Advocates, partners in legal firms.
2. Professors, lecturers, physicians and surgeons.
3. Principals, rectors, headmasters of important educational establishments.
4. Clergymen.

[B] *Commercial Group.*
1. Bankers, bank managers and agents.
2. Cashiers, principal clerks, accountants, insurance company managers, brokers and agents, company treasurers.

[C] *Large Merchant-Manufacturing Group.*
1. Suppliers of capital goods, timber, etc., construction companies, iron founders, textile manufacturers, wholesalers and importers, distillers, company managers.
2. Suppliers of consumer goods and services catering for the middle class, silversmiths, silk mercers.
3. Suppliers of food and wines, grocers, vintners, etc.
4. Commission merchants, ship agents.

---

[20] Strong, *Episcopalianism*, p. 297.

Social Class

[D] *Retired-Rentier Group.*
1. Shipowners.
2. Landlords, those retired and living on income from rented property, shares or capital.
3. Farmers.
4. Gentlemen and landed gentry.

LOWER MIDDLE CLASS

[E] *Public Servants.* (I)
1. Druggists.
2. Local government officials, building inspectors, architects, surveyors, house factors.
3. Shipmasters, marine and civil engineers.

[F] *Public Servants.* (II).
1. Teachers, divinity students who were also often city missionaries.
2. Clerks, writers.

[G] *Small Merchant-Tradesmen Group.*
1. Shopkeepers.
2. Self-employed tradesmen, agents living in premises, commercial travellers.
3. Foremen, overseers.
4. Retired tradesmen and shopkeepers.

SKILLED WORKING CLASS

[H] *Artisans.*
1. Engineers, boiler-makers, joiners, smiths, etc.

UNSKILLED WORKING CLASS

[I] *Unskilled Workers.*
1. Labourers, carters, porters, chimney sweeps, etc.

It was necessary to make some additions to the list. Preliminary designations were made following the scheme of W. A. Armstrong.[21] The list below shows these occupations.

UPPER MIDDLE CLASS

Owners/directors of ship building firms.

LOWER MIDDLE CLASS

Hotelkeepers, photographers.

SKILLED WORKING CLASS

Van drivers, policemen, chamberlains, soldiers (non-officers), warehousemen, fishermen, farmers, shop assistants to: tailors, butchers, bakers, drapers etc.

UNSKILLED WORKING CLASS

Servants.

OTHERS

People difficult to classify, e.g. artists, butlers, comedians, equestrians.

Merchants presented a slight problem. Following Armstrong, who gave them an initial classification of upper middle class, they were sometimes downgraded after consulting postal directories to lower middle class, if they did not live in affluent areas. Some other occupations were treated similarly. For instance, Conrad Jockel at St Thomas's in 1854 is listed in the baptismal register as 'butcher' residing at 59, Frederick Street. Butchers would normally be placed in the skilled working-class group, but Jockel's address in the prosperous New Town of Edinburgh suggested that he was probably more likely to have been lower middle class. Instances such as this for Edinburgh were easily corroborated in a useful document in the Edinburgh Public Library, George IV Bridge, which consisted of a summary of the census records for 1851 for Edinburgh. Jockel turned out to be the owner of the shop in Frederick Street and employed four men, and so was, indeed, a member of the lower middle class.

---

[21] W. A. Armstrong, 'The Use of Information about Occupation', pp. 215-223, in E. A. Wrigley, *Nineteenth Century Society: Essays in the Use of Quantitative Methods for the Study of Social Data* (London, 1972), pp. 191-252.

Social Class

Again, if the occupation of an individual was not listed in the baptismal record, it was sometimes possible to find it from the postal directory. This was carried out for people in Glasgow, Aberdeen and Edinburgh. Alternatively, trade directories frequently showed that people with unrecorded occupations in the baptismal record, or inadequate descriptions in the postal directory, were factory or company owners. For instance, at St Silas's, Glasgow, Thomas Armstrong, 'Iron Merchant', with no address in the baptismal register, was found to be the owner of F. Armstrong and Co., Iron Merchant, while Richard Barnwell, 'Shipbuilder', was a director of Fairfields, Shipbuilders. If these methods yielded no fruit, a person sometimes had to be classified as 'unidentified'. But, examination of the numbers of such persons in the following tables shows that they did not usually make the sample too unreliable, and that there were normally enough recognised people to enable conclusions to be drawn. Postal and trade directories were useful tools for classifying the social class of individuals.

Tables 3.4-14 and Graphs 3.1-11[22] show the results of the investigation. They record the total numbers and percentages of baptisms of children from upper middle-, lower middle-, skilled working- and unskilled working-class families in various urban Evangelical Episcopal chapels over a period of years. They are mainly representative of the English Episcopal movement, but also contain data for the Edinburgh Scottish Episcopal churches of St James's and St Paul's, Carrubber's Close.[23] Where possible it was decided to present the results in ten-year periods, since yearly analysis would have given too small a number of baptisms for trends to be shown reasonably accurately. The tables show that there was sometimes difficulty in arranging the results for the different churches in similar time blocks. This was because entries in registers were often erratic. St Thomas's, Edinburgh, was a prime example with no records from 1856 to 1863, many missing entries in the period 1863 to 1869, followed by a further gap from 1869 to 1874.[24] Figures for single years only are recorded for St Jude's, Glasgow, since the number of baptisms was very large. This was considered to be justified since spot checks of mid-decade baptisms revealed similar trends to the years chosen.

Nevertheless, it was sometimes useful to record the numbers of baptisms for shorter periods. Thus at St Thomas's the period 1874 to 1875 was isolated because it covered the years when there was a serious dispute between its incumbent, D. T. K. Drummond, and his assistant, W. S.

---

[22] See Chapter 3, pp. 93-115.

[23] Records of rural congregations were not available.

[24] Heads of families with voting rights at St Peter's, Montrose, were available for only 1842 and 1886. St Paul's, Carrubber's Close, Edinburgh, had 76 unidentifiable entries, making the sample unreliable.

Moncrieff, resulting in the resignation of both.[25] Again, the years surrounding the revivals of 1859 to 1860 and 1874 were treated likewise where possible in order to ascertain any resulting changes in the congregations and to compare the evidence with recent work produced by K. S. Jeffrey.[26] While ten-year samples, usually providing close to one hundred baptisms, were considered large enough to ignore random variations, it was sometimes justified to look at shorter time scales.

St Paul's, Aberdeen

St Paul's, situated in the Gallowgate of Aberdeen, where many poor people lived by mid-century,[27] might be expected to have been home to a noticeable unskilled working-class element. But the investigation here shows that this was not the case. Table 3.4 and Graph 3.1 record the membership figures for St Paul's from 1860 to 1889 where it can be seen that the upper middle class, who made up 51.8%, 50.6% and 57.7% of the entries, dominated the rolls. The skilled working class was the next most numerous group at 28.9%, 34.4%, and 21.1%, followed by the lower middle class at 18.0%, 14.5%, and 18.7%. The unskilled working class never accounted for more than 2.4% of the list. Membership at St Paul's was noticeably the province of the upper middle class, although the skilled working class was the second largest group.

Baptismal figures for 1870 to 1900 are recorded in Table 3.5 and Graph 3.2. The sample for the years 1873, 1874, and 1875, straddling the Moody and Sankey revival, was too small to enable conclusions to be drawn. It is evident, however, that skilled working-class baptisms rose from 35.0% (1870-1879), to 51.1% (1880-1889) and to 73.2% (1890-1900), figures considerably higher than the membership data presumably because of the monetary constraints faced by working-class people on taking up membership.[28] The upper middle class dropped correspondingly from 36.4% to 24.7% and 13.7% mirrored by the lower middle class at 22.3%, 14.7% and 5.9%. While the combined upper and lower middle-class figure of 58.7% in 1870 to 1879, suggests that the group made up the bulk of the congregation, thereafter it appears to have been overtaken by the skilled working class. The unskilled working-class baptismal level was, like its membership representation, low, never rising above 10%. No unmarried women presented children for baptism, but two widows did so. While

---

[25] See Chapter 10, pp. 339-351.
[26] K. S. Jeffrey, 'The 1858 to 1862 Revival in the North-East of Scotland' (Stirling University Ph. D. thesis, 2000). See also Chapter 4, pp. 122-125.
[27] MacLaren, *Religion and Social Class*, p. 190.
[28] See Chapter 3, pp. 70-72.

Social Class

skilled working-class people attended St Paul's, the unskilled poor living in its location were not reached.

St Peter's, Montrose

Only membership details, which were specified in the minute book of the church as heads of families with voting rights, were available for St Peter's.[29] Table 3.6 and Graph 3.3 show that the skilled working class dominated the membership at 74.6% in 1842 and 70.8% in 1886. The upper middle-class level at 13.2% and 16.7% for these years was higher than the lower middle-class figures at 10.5% and 4.2%. The unskilled working-class level was only 1.8% in 1842, but rose above the lower middle-class by 1886 to 8.3%. The high skilled working-class membership figure of over 70% at both dates, indicates that the group was the largest sector in the church which was, however, relatively ineffective in reaching unskilled people.

The data for the managers, who appear to have been the equivalent of vestry members in other churches, taking spiritual and practical decisions on behalf of the congregation,[30] provide a different picture. Of those who could be identified in 1886, three were upper middle-class and three were lower middle-class, with one, or possibly two, skilled working-class. The dominance of the combined middle classes as managers, even allowing that Melville, Velly and Lyall might have been working-class, is to be expected since they would have had the spare time and expertise to enable them to attend to matters at the church. While the skilled working class made up the majority of the congregation, the management of the church was in the hands of the middle classes.

St James's, Edinburgh

St James's was situated in Broughton Street, an area of mixed social tone, on the edge of the prosperous New Town of Edinburgh.[31] Table 3.7 and Graph 3.4 show the baptismal figures when the church was clearly Evangelical from 1820 to 1846, and for the years 1847 to 1890 when it lost this status.

From 1820 to 1846 the upper middle class dominated the baptismal roll with figures of 59.2%, 66.7% and 66.1% of presentations. The skilled working class was the next largest group, accounting for 25.2% initially and

---

[29] St Peter's Minute Book, 22 March 1842, pp. 81-85, 22 March 1886, p. 497, St Peter's Church, Montrose, Archives.

[30] *Ibid., passim.*

[31] James Grant, *Cassell's Old and New Edinburgh, Volume II* (London, n.d.) pp. 178-184.

dropping to 14.3% by 1846. While the lower middle class rose steadily from 5.8% in 1820 to 14.3% by 1846, the unskilled working class reached only 3.6% by that date. Thus at this time the high upper middle-class baptismal figures indicate that the group was probably numerically dominant.

After 1857 the picture changed completely with figures of 8.0% for the upper middle class and 76.0% for the skilled working class by the end of the century. However, St James's continued to fail to reach unskilled working-class people, who maintained a baptismal figure of only around 4% to 5%. The period after 1858 was marked by the presentation of children for baptism by three single women.

St James's took no part in the revivals of 1859 to 1860 and 1874, having lost its Evangelical status by those dates.

St Thomas's, Edinburgh

St Thomas's was situated in the wealthy West End of Edinburgh, on the edge of the New Town. The results of the baptismal investigation are recorded in Table 3.8 and Graph 3.5. Baptismal entries for the early years from 1842 to 1853 are unavailable, and those for 1863 to 1869 are unreliable since the register is full of gaps. Although the sample for 1854 to 1855 should be analysed with caution, since it represents only one year which might have been exceptional, this period indicates congregational dominance by the upper middle class with baptismal presentations of 40.8%. The lower middle-class level, at 24.5%, matched that of the skilled working class. The unskilled working-class accounted for only 10.2% of the baptisms during the year. Thus St Thomas's appears to have been dominated by the middle classes in the year 1854 to 1855.

The years 1874 to 1900 saw a diminution of upper middle-class baptisms from 38.5% to 27.8%, and a corresponding rise of those of the skilled working class to around 45%. Table 3.8 and Graph 3.5 show that at the time of the Moody and Sankey revival of 1874 there was a marked increase in skilled working-class and unskilled working-class baptisms to 42.3% and 7.7% respectively.

The lower middle-class figure also dropped by the end of the century to 16.5%. Butlers were a noticeable group, numbering two in 1874 to 1875, fourteen in 1876 to 1886 and seven in 1887 to 1890. One single woman presented in 1874 and in the 1887 to 1900 period.

The combined figures of 36.6% to 44.3% for the upper and lower middle class after 1876 are probably not low enough to suggest that the congregation lost its middle-class dominance. But the rise of the skilled working class over the years indicates a gradual change of balance between the social groups at the church.

St James's, Aberdeen

St James's, Aberdeen, built in Crown Street, was situated in the wealthy West End of the city. Table 3.9 and Graph 3.6 show that, from the time of foundation in 1854 to 1858, the upper middle class accounted for the majority of baptisms at St James's at 42.5%.

At the time of the revival of 1859 to 1860 there was a marked increase in skilled working-class baptisms which reached 51.7%. The unskilled working-class proportion also rose slightly to 15.5%, and there was a significant representation of women presenters at 20.7%. At the same time the upper middle-class and lower middle-class baptisms dropped dramatically to 8.6% and 1.7% respectively.

From 1861 to 1862 the situation reverted closer to the earlier pattern of upper middle-class dominance, but at a lower level of 25%. However, in 1863 to 1871 there was another increase in skilled and unskilled working-class baptisms to 46.2% and 29.2% respectively, and an influx of women presenters at 10.6%.

With the exception of Partick, St James's consistently had the lowest number of lower middle-class baptisms after 1858, never exceeding 3.8%. Overall, the church appears to have been one of the most successful in reaching a wider social group than that of its immediate location.

St Vincent's, Edinburgh

St Vincent's stood in the heart of Edinburgh's New Town, near Royal Circus. The Post Office directories for the city indicate that the area was home to a myriad of middle-class and skilled working-class people. In 1874 only two baptisms were recorded, both with unidentified occupations. Thus it is impossible to judge the impact of the Moody and Sankey Revival.

Table 3.10 and Graph 3.7 show that from 1859 to 1868 the skilled working class dominated the baptismal presentations at 52.7%, was overtaken by the upper middle class at 40.5% from 1869 to 1878, and reverted to dominance from 1879 to 1898 at 44.9% and 53.2 %. St Vincent's thus appears to have been representative of its location.

The unskilled working-class sector was poorly represented up to 1889, although it reached 15.8% by the end of the century, higher than the upper middle-class representation at that time.

St Silas's, Glasgow

St Silas's was situated at the Eldon Street Park Road junction, overlooking Kelvingrove Park at the prosperous West End of Glasgow.[32] The year 1864 to 1865 was isolated as being the nearest to the foundation of St Silas's in 1863. The 1874 list showed very little change in baptismal presentations compared to 1873 for any of the social groups, indicating no significant change resulting from the Moody and Sankey revival of 1874.

Table 3.11 and Graph 3.8 show that the upper middle-class baptismal level was 68.4% at the foundation of St Silas's, dropping thereafter to around 50%. Thus it probably had the most predominantly upper middle-class congregation of all the churches. The lower middle-class figure was, by contrast, below 10% until 1876 to 1900 when it reached 14.9% to 16.9%. The skilled working-class entries, ranging from 15.8% in 1864 to 27.1% in 1887 to 1900, were never high enough to suggest dominance in the congregation. Unskilled working-class levels remained below 10%. The higher skilled and unskilled working-class presence in 1866 to 1875 was due, partly, to representation from Partick.

St Jude's, Glasgow

St Jude's, Glasgow, built in 1838 in West George Street, stood in a mixed social area.[33] There are no early baptismal records for the church when it was reported to be composed mainly of the upper classes.[34] The only records available were for 1869 to 1889.

Table 3.12 and Graph 3.9 show that the upper middle-class baptismal levels were consistently low ranging from 14.5% in 1873 to 0% in 1889. The lower middle-class level never rose above 13.3% in 1873 and in 1869 was only 2.4%. The dominant group in the congregation appears to have been the skilled working class which was representative of 73.3% of the baptismal presenters in 1889. St Jude's also had success in attracting the unskilled working class with baptismal levels of 26.8% in 1869, falling to 13.3% in 1889.

The years 1874 and 1875, around the Moody and Sankey Revival, indicate an increase in the proportion of skilled and unskilled working-class people in the congregation. The former at 53.2% and 60.9%, and the latter at 23.4% and 14.1%, represented a substantial rise from 49.4% and 10.8% respectively in 1873.

---

[32] Elizabeth Williamson, Anne Riches and Malcolm Higg, *The Buildings of Scotland, Glasgow* (Harmondsworth, 1990), p. 275.

[33] *Ibid.*, pp. 278-282.

[34] See Chapter 3, p. 69.

Social Class 83

Single women regularly presented children for baptism with a maximum of 7.2% in 1873.

St Silas's Partick Mission, Govan, Glasgow

This church, situated in the run-down district of Govan, attracted the highest numbers of unskilled working-class people, so fulfilling its purpose as a mission. As indicated in Table 3.13 and Graph 3.10, there was a complete absence of upper middle-class people and only two lower middle-class individuals on the baptismal lists from 1887 to 1889. The unskilled working-class was the largest group, at around 62%, from 1887 to 1899. The skilled working-class baptismal representation rose from 32.9% in 1887 to 37.2% by 1899, mirroring the rise of the group in the national statistics. Figures are not available for St Thomas's Canongate Mission, but they would be expected to be similar to those of Partick.

St Paul's, Carrubber's Close, Edinburgh

Carrubber's Close was a poor area of the Old Town in Edinburgh. The social class of the fathers of children on the baptismal roll, when D. T. K. Drummond conducted a clearly Evangelical ministry between 1832 and 1836, are shown in Table 3.14 and Graph 3.11. Seventy-six out of one hundred and forty-four entries were unidentifiable, possibly because they were of the unskilled working-class group. The sample is thus unreliable, and all that can be said with certainty is that upper middle-class and skilled working-class people attended the church, although it is also possible that around 50% of the congregation was unskilled people.

Analysis

The results of the foregoing investigation can be compared with those of Hillis (who analysed nine congregations) and Brown (who considered one congregation) concerning the Presbyterian churches of Glasgow from 1845 to 1865, recorded in Table 3.15.

Table 3.15 Class Distribution in the Presbyterian Churches of Glasgow, 1845-1865

Church	Upper Middle Class	Lower Middle Class	Skilled Working Class	Unskilled Working Class
Non-Established 1845-65	17.2%	18.6%	43.2%	11.0%

| Established 1855-65 | 12.2% | 8.6% | 54.2% | 24.5% |

Adapted from, P. L. M. Hillis, 'Presbyterianism and Social Class in Mid-Nineteenth Century Glasgow: A Study of Nine Churches', *Journal of Ecclesiastical History* 32, (1981), pp. 54-55.

	Upper Middle Class	Lower Middle Class	Skilled Working Class	Unskilled Working Class
John Street Relief/United Presbyterian Church, Glasgow, 1853-57	10%	27%	50%	13%

Source: C. G. Brown, *Religion and Society in Scotland since 1707* (Edinburgh, 1997), p. 108.

Here it is evident that, from 1845 to 1865, the working classes were represented in all the Presbyterian congregations, with the skilled sector accounting for 43.2%, 50.0% and 54.2% of the total baptisms. The unskilled workers in the established church amounted to 24.5% of the sample, while in the non-established churches they totalled only 11% to 13%. The upper middle-class baptismal levels were below 20% in all the churches, but the non-established churches attracted more than twice as many lower middle-class people than the established churches. Thus it can be assumed that the congregations of established and non-established churches in Glasgow between 1845 and 1865 were composed of all classes, with the skilled working class probably being the largest group of attenders.

Skilled Working Class in Evangelical Episcopal Churches

The investigation conducted in this chapter also shows that the skilled working class was not absent from the Evangelical Episcopal churches in nineteenth-century Scotland. However, near the times of foundation of the churches, it was only at St Vincent's, Edinburgh, that skilled working-class representation (52.7%) was equivalent to that of the Presbyterian churches studied by Hillis and Brown (43.2%, 54.2%, 50%). This was possibly a factor of its unusual circumstances as a breakaway church from St Thomas's where most of the middle-class people probably chose to stay, leaving the way open for skilled working-class recruitment at St Vincent's from its neighbourhood.[35] At St James's, Edinburgh (14.3%), St Thomas's, Edinburgh (24.5%), St James's, Aberdeen (25%), and St Silas's, Glasgow

---

[35] See Chapter 9, pp. 303-305.

(15.8%), the skilled working-class baptismal presentations were considerably lower. But by the later decades of the century the skilled working-class proportions rose in all the congregations. At this time the group probably composed the largest sector of the congregations except at St Silas's, Glasgow, and St Thomas's, Edinburgh, where the middle classes still retained superiority. This pattern was different from that noted by C. G. Brown for many dissenting denominations, especially the United Presbyterian churches, where a trend towards middle-class dominance flourished by the end of the century.[36]

There could be several reasons for the rise in the skilled working class over the century in the Evangelical Episcopal churches. The involvement of clergy like Drummond in Young Men's Associations, temperance and sabbatarian societies,[37] together with the desire of the group for respectability and self-improvement,[38] might have helped the process. Again, some churches, once firmly settled, probably sought to broaden their scope by actively encouraging a wider congregation which enjoyed the ministry offered. The revival movements of 1859 to 1860 and 1874 appear, importantly, to have been a possible reason for the increased representation of the group at St James's, Aberdeen, St Thomas's, Edinburgh and St Jude's, Galsgow. For instance, at St James's there were sixteen baptisms for the group in 1860, 87.5% of which were for new presenters. This finding is contrary to that of K. S. Jeffrey who has suggested that St James's, Aberdeen, was unaffected by the 1859 to 1860 revival.[39] Material for similar dates at St Thomas's is missing, but at the time of the Moody and Sankey revival baptisms rose from four in 1874 to seven in 1875, all of which were for new families and, in 1876, 71.5 % of the seven baptisms were for new presenters albeit representing only small numbers. Similarly, at St Jude's, Glasgow, in 1875, out of 56 skilled working-class baptismal presenters 57.6% were new people. There seems to have been a specific successful attempt to reach the skilled working class again at St James's, Aberdeen, in 1863. At this time 92.3% of the baptisms were for new families, rising to 100% in 1864. Some churches, as a result of revival movements and special outreach, thus probably reached the skilled working class.

---

[36] Hillis, 'Presbyterianism and Social Class', pp. 55-56. Brown, *Religion and Society*, pp. 109-110.

[37] See Chapter 5, pp. 169-175. D. T. K. Drummond, 'Lecture Notes' (n.d.), DRO, D5550/3/5/9.

[38] Hillis, 'Social Class', p. 63.

[39] Jeffrey, 'Revival in the North-East of Scotland', p. 113. Part of the discrepancy may be because Jeffrey based his assumption on the number of seats let. As has been pointed out here, many working-class people would not have been able to afford to buy seats, but were, nonetheless, regular attenders. See Chapter 3, pp. 70-72.

From the collected data, it is also evident that the skilled working-class baptismal levels rose at all the churches at the same time as the upper middle-class presentations dropped. It might be supposed, taking the line suggested by Strong, that the former group began to attend the churches when it saw more opportunity to contribute to congregations in which the upper middle class no longer dominated. But perusal of the minute books of St Thomas's, Edinburgh, for example, casts doubt on this supposition because the vestry and trustees, responsible for the running of the church, were always firmly upper middle-class with no lower status representatives whatsoever. St Peter's, Montrose, was unusual in having skilled working-class people among its managers, seemingly, like St Vincent's, Edinburgh, a reflection of its social milieu.[40] Overall, the skilled working class was well represented at the Evangelical Episcopal churches in the nineteenth century, regardless of the extent of its influence over affairs.

The location of the homes of skilled working-class people attending St Thomas's and St Vincent's, Edinburgh, St Paul's and St James's, Aberdeen, and St Silas's, Glasgow, in the latter half of the nineteenth century, shown on Maps 3.1, 3.2 and 3.6, and extends the foregoing analysis.[41] It is evident from Post Office directories that the group constituted a shifting population, since many individuals appear to have had no fixed address. Thus those who attended the churches often did not stay long enough to make their presence felt. However, the maps help to elucidate the more permanent skilled working-class attendance at these churches. Map 3.1 shows that St Vincent's catered for its immediate area in the New Town. The absence of the middle classes from St Vincent's was thus compensated for by the appeal of the church to its local community which was home to a number from the skilled working classes. St Thomas's, however, served the whole city and outlying areas, attracting people from the north and east as far as Kirkcaldy and Leith, and from the south, stretching beyond Newington to Dalkeith. One skilled working-class baptismal presenter at St Thomas's was from South America. The reputation of St Thomas's as the leading English Episcopalian congregation probably contributed to its wide popularity. St Paul's, Aberdeen, by contrast, attracted few skilled workers from its own area although the militia attended, possibly a tradition carried on from the days when the

---

[40] See Chapter 2, p. 40.

[41] As with all the map work, care has been taken to record only home addresses rather than places of work, but there may be some inaccuracies among the working classes who sometimes appear to have given their place of work as their address. This may explain some of the city centre entries for St Silas's, Glasgow, but it is impossible to be certain.

Social Class

church had qualified status.[42] St James's was far more successful in reaching skilled working people, and served a large area around St Paul's, as well as its own location. St Silas's drew mainly from its own area and Partick, the latter probably contacted through its mission church. Thus the reputation of a church and specific outreach ventures drew in skilled working-class people.

Examination of the surnames gives an idea of the probable nationality of members of the group. At St Thomas's, Edinburgh, in 1854 around 50% appear to have been Scottish, and similar levels were maintained from 1874 to 1899, rising as high as 88% and 80% in 1876 and 1880 respectively. St James's, Aberdeen, in the years 1854 to 1871, had around 74% with Scottish names. While the picture was probably different in Glasgow where there was a high Irish population, Evangelical Episcopalianism seemed to appeal to the Scottish skilled working class. This was possibly because of the affinity of its teaching with Presbyterian doctrine and also, as reported for St Thomas's, Edinburgh, where, although services were liturgical, there was 'no fear of anything at all high'.[43] Rowan Strong's suggestion that working-class attenders were mainly English and Irish was probably not always the case.

Unskilled Working Class in Evangelical Episcopal Churches

As with the non-established Presbyterian congregations studied by Hillis and Brown, those of the Evangelical Episcopalians, apart from Partick, contained very few unskilled working-class people. Only St James's, Aberdeen, in 1863 to 1871 and St Jude's, Glasgow, were comparable to the established churches studied by Hillis, the former recruiting at the time of the 1859-1860 Revival, and the latter during the 1874 Moody and Sankey event. But even these levels of attendance by the lowest social group were small considering its numbers within Scottish society. Many reasons for the absence of the unskilled working class at church have been suggested. Pew rents were a problem. The letting of pews in nineteenth century-Britain was normal practice, and it helped to augment church funds. For instance, apart from some free seats in Glasgow, the most common rents there in 1870

---

[42] The numbers of skilled working-class people at St Paul's appear low on the map. This is because the people on the membership list altered very little over the years in question, and they have been plotted only once on the map. Additionally, only 42 out of a total of 76 on the baptismal register could be assigned to addresses after consultation of the Post Office directory for Aberdeen.

[43] *Perthshire Constitutional*, 13 June 1877.

were from fourteen shillings to nine shillings a year.[44] The rents at St James's, Aberdeen, in 1854 varied from twelve shillings to fifteen shillings a year.[45] At St Thomas's, Edinburgh, in 1877, the total income from eight hundred pew rents was £556.1.6, which works out at around fourteen shillings a seat on average.[46] The unskilled working-class man, with a family of perhaps five children and an average wage of 15 shillings a week,[47] would have been hard pressed to afford such prices. But, as S. J. D. Green points out, pew rents were probably not a major deterrent to poor people attending church. Often seats, which were vacant five minutes before the start of a service, were given free to those who were considered deserving. Again, by the end of the century, when pew letting had been discontinued in favour of weekly collections, there was no apparent rise in the level of unskilled people in church.[48] Other reasons have to be investigated to explain the absence of the unskilled working class from church.

The strict views of Evangelicals on drunkenness and sexual morality[49] possibly alienated some of the unskilled working class. But the high level of the group at the Partick Mission, which would have upheld similar standards, suggests other factors played a part. General unease about mixing with people of higher social status was a probable factor, as is indicated by the rise of unskilled working people at St Jude's, Glasgow, where the upper middle-class level dropped to zero in 1869. Inability to contribute money towards special church events, concern over the need to appear in church in smart clothes, difficulty in following sermons and services designed for those of higher educational standards and exhaustion after a week at work were also likely to have been a deterrent to church commitment. A multitude of factors probably contributed to the absence of the unskilled working class from church.

The relative success of St James's, Aberdeen, in reaching the unskilled working class is clarified by reference to Map 3.3, showing the locations of those appearing on the baptismal list, 1854-1871. Not surprisingly, some were clustered around St James's in the Crown Street area. But the majority were concentrated in the market district of the Green, and south of the

---

[44] C. G. Brown, 'The Cost of Pew-renting: Church Management, Church-going and Social Class in Nineteenth-century Glasgow', *Journal of Ecclesiastical History*, Vol. 38, No. 3, July 1987, pp. 347-359.

[45] St James's Minute Book, May 1854. St James's Church, Aberdeen, Archives.

[46] St Thomas's Minute Book, 24 January 1878. St Thomas's Church, Edinburgh, Archives.

[47] Adapted from, Smout, *Scottish People*, p. 111.

[48] S. J. D. Green, 'The Death of Pew Rents, The Rise of Bazaars, and the End of the Traditional Political Economy of Voluntary Religious Organisations: the Case of the West Riding of Yorkshire, c. 1870-1914', *Northern History*, Vol. XXVII (1991).

[49] See Chapter 5, pp. 174-176.

Gallowgate between King Street and West North Street, areas which also housed a number of the single mother presenters. While unskilled working-class attendance at St James's might have been due to personal contact between the people themselves, it would certainly have been easier for the West North Street group to attend St Paul's in the Gallowgate. Their adherence to St James's appears to suggest some sort of successful outreach venture, possibly in conjunction with the revival meetings of the period or with philanthropy. This proposition is substantiated since, at the time of the 1859 to 1860 revival, baptisms for the group rose from two in 1859 to five in 1860, all of which were for new families. In 1863, out of eleven entries 99% were new presenters and, in 1864, the figure was 89% out of nine baptisms. The unskilled attenders at St James's, Aberdeen, appear to have been contacted through the revival movement or special endeavour.

Map 3.1 shows that St Vincent's, Edinburgh, attracted its few unskilled baptismal presenters from around its own area, while St Thomas's drew from the western edges of Edinburgh and from the Canongate where its mission was situated. Table 3.11 and Map 3.6 show that, similarly, St Silas's attracted the unskilled from its Partick Mission in the 1860s, and also picked up a few from outlying areas. Thus although unskilled workers attended some of the Evangelical Episcopal churches it appears that a particular effort was required if they were to be attracted in any numbers.

The missions of St Thomas's in the Canongate and St Silas's in Partick achieved by far the most significant inroads into the unskilled working class. The former, founded in 1845,[50] was possibly a response to a call in 1844 from Thomas Chalmers to all Protestant churches, urging them to reclaim deprived urban areas by setting up working-class territorial churches, starting with sixty in Edinburgh.[51] Unfortunately no congregational records remain of the work in the Canongate, but a few details survive. In April 1844, St Thomas's leased an area of land seventy feet long by twenty feet broad in the poverty-stricken area of Gibb's Close on which it built a 'preaching station'. A schoolmaster and a missioner from the Edinburgh City Mission were employed to deal with the educational and spiritual sides of the venture. The congregation, which was composed entirely of the inhabitants of the area, met in a hall rather than a church. Services were non-liturgical, presumably because they proved more popular than the set liturgy for those of limited education. Drummond and members of St Thomas's helped with the preaching and visiting, and some of the women of the congregation were engaged in a sewing society which worked with poor females resident in the Canongate. It is not clear whether

---

[50] David Bertie is mistaken in recording the Canongate mission as opening in only 1883. See D. M. Bertie, *Scottish Episcopal Clergy 1689-2000* (Edinburgh, 2000), p. 657.

[51] S. J. Brown, *Thomas Chalmers* (Oxford, 1982), pp. 350-351.

the mission was designed to be eventually self-supporting, but it, like Chalmers's West Port venture, never was and always relied on financial support from the congregation at St Thomas's.[52] When St Silas's, under the incumbency of J. M. Maynard, opened a mission between 1865 and 1871 in Hayburn Street, Partick, it ran on the lines of its Canongate predecessor and consisted of a mission hall and Sunday School.[53] The success of such schemes is evident from the data for the Partick Mission which, as shown on Table 3.11, attracted far greater numbers of unskilled working-class people than any other church investigated here.[54]

There had been previous Scottish Episcopal efforts to reach the unskilled working-class city dwellers, but they did not achieve the success of missions like Canongate and Partick. David Aitchison had congregations of four and five hundred, composed mostly of handloom weavers, at his two mission halls at Bridgetown, near Glasgow, in 1834. These people were skilled workers who had become destitute when machinery robbed them of their jobs. But when Christ Church was built to replace the halls in 1835, middle-class attenders increasingly dominated the congregation, and the weavers left. In 1846, A. J. D. D'Orsey opened a mission in a hall at Anderston, near Glasgow, again in an attempt to reach handloom weavers. When St John's was erected there in 1850, the congregation, like Aitchison's before it, attracted middle-class people, and the poorer members departed.[55] However, when John Comper, in 1867, set up an Anglo-Catholic Episcopal mission in the Gallowgate, Aberdeen, a more lasting provision for the urban unskilled working class developed. Comper introduced the Sisters of Mercy to work with him in the mission. The

---

[52] Details of the Canongate Mission are recorded in, 'Lease betwixt the Right Honourable the Earl of Airlie and James Walker, W. S. and Captain Francis Grove R. N. for behoof within mentioned', 21 April 1845. See also Sewing Guild Account Book. St Thomas's Minute Book, 1877-1900, *passim*. St Thomas's Church, Edinburgh, Archives. *Memoir*, pp. liv-lv, cxxxii. For the West Port scheme see S. J. Brown, 'Thomas Chalmers and the Communal Ideal in Victorian Scotland', T. C. Smout (ed.), *Victorian Values* (Oxford, 1992), p. 68.

[53] 'A Short History of the English Episcopal Church of St Silas', pp. 9-10. St Silas's Church, Glasgow, Archives. The changing social pattern after the Second World War led to the closure of the Partick mission in 1951. *Ibid*. Similarly, it led to the closure of the Canongate mission in 1947. St Thomas's Church Minute Book, 14 July 1947, St Thomas's Church, Edinburgh, Archives.

[54] Thomas Chalmers's West Port scheme similarly attracted a working-class congregation. See Brown, 'Chalmers and the Communal Ideal', p. 68.

[55] Strong, *Episcopalianism*, pp. 169-195. John Alexander, incumbent of St Columba's, Edinburgh, 1846-1869, was also an assiduous worker among the poor of the Old Town, offering both material and spiritual help, but it is not clear how successful he was in attracting such people to his church. *Ibid*., pp. 236-238.

Social Class

Sisters lived in the Gallowgate, ran services, and worked among the poor.[56] While it is not clear where the missioner for the Canongate venture lived, it is evident that the mission, like Comper's later contribution, was run purely for the local people without any intrusion from the middle classes who supplied the funds. Anglo-Catholic and Evangelical missions thus operated on similar successful lines.

An indication of the contribution made by the Canongate and Partick missions in reaching the lowest classes can be obtained by reference to the baptismal figures, displayed in Table 3.16, for St Andrew's Episcopal Chapel, Back of Castle, Edinburgh, situated close to the Old Town slum area, and under the mild Evangelical incumbency of C. R. Teape.[57]

Table 3.16 Baptismal Record of St Andrew's, Back of Castle, Edinburgh, 1857-1862

1857-1862 Total 306 Unidentified 0	Upper Middle Class	Lower Middle Class	Skilled Working Class	Unskilled Working Class	Others
Nos	3	7	254	39	3
%	1	2.3	83.8	12.9	1

Source: St Andrew's Back of Castle Baptismal Register, NAS, CH12/48/7.

It is evident that, while St Andrews was successful in reaching the skilled working class, it did not match the Canongate and Partick Missions in reaching the unskilled group. Providing an informal, local meeting place, not infiltrated by the higher social strata, seems to have been the most successful way of attracting the unskilled. The contribution of St Thomas's and St Silas's to work among the poorest members of Scottish society has been demonstrated to have been substantial.

Upper Middle Class in Evangelical Episcopal Churches

Scottish Episcopalianism was traditionally the home of the gentry and the upper middle class.[58] This is reflected in the baptismal lists for the Evangelical Episcopal churches studied here which often record levels of over 20% for the group – higher than the 10% to 17.2% in the Presbyterian churches studied by Hillis and Brown. At the time of foundation of St James's, Edinburgh, St Thomas's, Edinburgh, St James's, Aberdeen, and St Silas's, Glasgow, the group probably dominated the congregation with baptismal levels of 59.2%, 40.8%, 42.5% and 68.4% respectively. The

---

[56] MacLaren, *Religion and Social Class*, pp. 189-190.
[57] See Chapter 1, p. 21.
[58] Lawson, *Scottish Episcopal Church*, pp. 432-433.

money it provided would have been important when the churches were founded, paying for buildings and stipends. The high representation was possibly because only the élite had enough social stature to give the confidence to attend initially, with the balance changing when congregations became established.

However, particular circumstances could lead to a diminution of the upper middle-class group. At St Thomas's, Edinburgh, the years 1875 and 1888 were ones of uncertainty over the issue of joining the Scottish Episcopal Church. The drop in upper middle-class figures at these times possibly reflects this dilemma with some people joining other churches.[59] Again, the very low entry of 4% and 0% at St Jude's, Glasgow, from 1869 to 1889, was a likely product of high status migration to St Silas's, set up in 1863 and pledged by its founders to uphold a strong Evangelical stance.[60] The diminution of the upper middle-class baptismal figures to 9.7% at St James's, Aberdeen, around 1863 corresponds to the time when the Scottish Communion Office was demoted from being the official liturgy of the Scottish Episcopal Church, and when T. G. S. Suther, Bishop of Aberdeen, tried to encourage St James's into the Church.[61] At St Vincent's, Edinburgh, the drop in upper-class figures, in 1889, to 6.8% coincided with the retirement of T. K. Talon who had conducted a clearly Evangelical ministry there from 1867. Under Talon's incumbency, St Vincent's had joined the Scottish Episcopal Church in 1882.[62] The sharp decline in the upper and lower middle classes after he left possibly indicates that many had remained at the church through loyalty to him while not being altogether supportive of the new position. Upper middle-class levels often dropped in response to dispute and uncertainty.

The distribution of upper middle-class people attending the Edinburgh, Aberdeen and Glasgow English Episcopal churches is shown in Maps 3.4, 3.5 and 3.6. St Vincent's, Edinburgh, St Paul's, Aberdeen, and St Silas's, Glasgow, attracted mainly from their own areas. St Thomas's, Edinburgh, and St James's, Aberdeen, however, drew also from further afield. St Thomas's was particularly noteworthy and, with some of its baptismal addresses being as far away as England and abroad, it thus exerted a very important influence in gathering support for the English Episcopal movement.

---

[59] See Chapter 10, pp. 340, 348-351.
[60] See Chapter 9, pp. 305-306.
[61] See Chapter 10, p. 336.
[62] *Ibid.*, p. 355.

Lower Middle Class in Evangelical Episcopal Churches

Lower middle-class data is rather confusing. Sometimes the proportion of the group was low if the upper middle-class representation was high. This was the case at St James's, Edinburgh (1820-1846), St Silas's, Glasgow (1864-1880) and St Thomas's, Edinburgh, (1876-1900). It was also particularly noticeable in the membership of St Paul's, Aberdeen (1860-1889). Absenteeism of the lower middle class was possibly because members of the group considered that the upper middle class would block their election to leadership roles. But in other churches with a high upper middle-class level, the lower middle-class figure was also fairly substantial and similar to that in the non-Established churches of Hillis and Brown. This was apparent at St Thomas's, Edinburgh (1854-1855), and St Vincent's, Edinburgh (1869-1888), possibly merely because the group enjoyed the ministry offered. At other churches the picture was different again. St Jude's, Glasgow, had few upper middle-class baptisms after 1869, St Vincent's, Edinburgh, only 7.0% in 1889, and St James's, Aberdeen, 9.7% in 1863 to 1871. But in these churches, lower middle-class people stayed away even though they could have taken on leadership positions, and the explanation here might be that they felt swamped by the inferior skilled working class. Lower middle-class attendance seems to have been somewhat variable.

Conclusion

Working-class people were never absent from the Evangelical Episcopal churches in the nineteenth century. While St Thomas's, Edinburgh, St James's, Aberdeen, and St Jude's, Glasgow, appear to have recruited from the revival movements, skilled working-class numbers increased in all of the congregations by the end of the century while upper middle-class levels dropped. The skilled working class thus became the dominant group, with only St Silas's, Glasgow, and possibly St Thomas's, Edinburgh, retaining middle-class superiority. This pattern was different from the dissenting congregations studied by Brown and from the situation in many Scottish Episcopal urban congregations suggested by Strong. Overall it was possibly the result of a concerted effort to reach a wider social group which subsequently enjoyed the ministry offered. Moreover, there is evidence that the group contained many of Scottish nationality who empathised with the doctrinal basis of the churches and the form of worship offered.

St James's, Aberdeen, was fairly successful in reaching the unskilled working class between 1854 and 1871, appearing to draw from the 1859 to 1860 revival, or on special outreach endeavours. Similarly, St Jude's, Glasgow, and St Thomas's, Edinburgh, possibly recruited from the 1874 Revival. But the most significant inroads into this group were by St

Thomas's Canongate Mission from 1845 to 1900, and St Silas's Partick Mission from the mid-sixties onwards. These churches, which were not infiltrated by higher social groupings, met informally in halls, and appear to have been particularly attractive to unskilled people who usually did not attend churches serving more fashionable areas.

Apart from St Vincent's, Edinburgh, the upper middle class made up the bulk of the baptismal lists at the time of foundation. This was higher than in the Presbyterian data collected by Hillis and Brown, possibly because the social élitism of the group provided it with the self-confidence required to join congregations which represented only a minority group in Episcopal Scotland. Lower middle-class levels were somewhat variable and it is difficult to make reliable comment on them. Certainly there is some evidence to suggest that the lower middle class was absent in congregations where the upper middle class dominated leadership positions, but this was not always the case. It is probable therefore that the group attended when the ministry attracted them, in a similar manner to the skilled working class. Most of the churches recorded baptisms of children of single mothers, indicating a desire to welcome them to the congregations if an appropriate lifestyle were adopted.

Hillis and Brown, contrary to MacLaren's proposition, indicated that working-class people were not absent from Presbyterian churches in nineteenth-century Scotland. From the data presented in this chapter, it would seem that, overall, Evangelical Episcopal churches also enjoyed a measure of success in attracting the working classes.

Table 3.4 Members, St Paul's, Aberdeen

	Upper Middle Class	Lower Middle Class	Skilled Working Class	Unskilled Working Class	Others	Women
1860-1869 1862 and 1866 missing						
Nos	299	104	167	7	-	-
%	51.8	18.0	28.9	1.2	-	-
Total 577 Unidentified 67						
1870-1879						
Nos	478	137	325	4	-	-
%	50.6	14.5	34.4	0.4	-	-
Total 944 Unidentified 212						
1880-1889 1881-1888 missing *Unreliable sample*						
Nos	71	23	26	3	-	-
%	57.7	18.7	21.1	2.4	-	-
Total 123 Unidentified 20						

Source: Roll of Constituent Members, St Paul's Church, Aberdeen, Aberdeen University Library, MS 3320/8.

Table 3.5 Baptismal Presenters, St Paul's, Aberdeen

	Upper Middle Class	Lower Middle Class	Skilled Working Class	Unskilled Working Class	Others	Women
1870-1879 Nos % Total 206 Unidentified 44	75 36.4	46 22.3	72 35.0	12 5.8	- -	1 widow 0.5
1880-1889 Nos % Total 170 Unidentified 13	42 24.7	25 14.7	87 51.1	16 9.4	- -	
1890-1900 Nos % Total 205 Unidentified 6	28 13.7	12 5.9	150 73.2	14 6.8	- -	1 widow 0.5

Source: Baptismal Register, St Paul's Church Aberdeen, Aberdeen University Library, MS 3320/8.

Table 3.6 Heads of Families with Voting Rights, St Peter's, Montrose

	Upper Middle Class	Lower Middle Class	Skilled Working Class	Unskilled Working Class	Others	Women
1842 Nos	15	12	85	2	-	-
%	13.2	10.5	74.6	1.8	-	-
Total 114 Unidentified 10						
1886 Nos	4	1	17	2	-	-
%	16.7	4.2	70.8	8.3	-	-
Total 24 Unidentified 11						

Managers 1886

James Low, ship builder, upper middle class
Alex. Lyall, solicitor, upper middle class
Edward Millar, wood merchant, upper middle class
George Gray, clerk, lower middle class
John Heckford, hotel keeper, lower middle class
W. S. Mitchell, mill foreman, lower middle class
David Lyall, hatter, skilled working class
John Low, fish dealer or cooper, lower middle or skilled working class
A. Melville, unidentified,
J. D. Velly, unidentified
Robert Lyall, unidentified
Source: Minute Book, St Peter's, Montrose, Montrose Public Library, MS 549/3.

Table 3.7 Baptismal Presenters, St James's, Edinburgh

	Upper Middle Class	Lower Middle Class	Skilled Working Class	Unskilled Working Class	Others	Women
1820-1830 Nos	61	6	26	10	-	
%	59.2	5.8	25.2	9.7	-	
Total 103 Unidentified 25						
1832-1835 Nos	24	3	8	1	-	
%	66.7	8.3	22.2	2.8	-	
Total 36 Unidentified 10						
1839-1846 Nos	37	8	8	2	1	
%	66.1	14.3	14.3	3.6	1.8	
Total 56 Unidentified 6						
1847-1857 Nos	109	22	64	11	1	
%	52.7	10.6	30.9	5.3	0.5	
Total 207 Unidentified 0						
1858-1868 Nos	40	49	111	10	1	2
%	18.8	23.0	52.1	4.7	0.5	0.9
Total 213 Unidentified 1						
1869-1879 Nos	33	35	122	9	3	1
%	16.3	17.2	60.1	4.4	1.5	0.5
Total 203 Unidentified 12						
1880-1890 Nos	2	4	19	-	-	
%	8.0	16.0	76.0	-	-	
Total 25 Unidentified 0						

Source: Minute Book, St James's Church, Edinburgh, Archives.

Table 3.8 Baptismal Presenters, St Thomas's, Edinburgh

	Upper Middle Class	Lower Middle Class	Skilled Working Class	Unskilled Working Class	Others	Women
1854-1855 Nos	20	12	12	5	-	
%	40.8	24.5	24.5	10.2	-	
Total 49 Unidentified 7						
1863-1869 Nos	13	-	2	-	-	
%	86.7	-	13.3	-	-	
Total 15 Unidentified 1 1865, 1868 missing 14 gaps in 1869 Unreliable Sample.						
1874-1875 Nos	10	-	11	2	2	1 washer-woman
%	38.5	-	42.3	7.7	7.7	3.8
Total 26 Unidentified 0					(2 butlers)	
1876-1886 Nos	50	15	82	15	16	
%	28.1	8.5	46.1	8.4	9.0	
Total 178 Unidentified 1					(14 butlers)	
1887-1900 Nos	37	22	59	6	8	1 single woman
%	27.8	16.5	44.4	4.5	6.0	0.8
Total 133 Unidentified 0					(7 butlers)	

Source: Baptismal Register, St Thomas's Church, Edinburgh, Archives.

Table 3.9 Baptismal Presenters, St James's, Aberdeen

	Upper Middle Class	Lower Middle Class	Skilled Working Class	Unskilled Working Class	Others	Women
1854-1858						
Nos	17	5	10	5	1	2
%	42.5	12.5	25	12.5	2.5	5
Total 40 Unidentified 1						
1859-1860						
Nos	5	1	30	9	1	12
%	8.6	1.7	51.7	15.5	1.7	20.7
Total 58 Unidentified 1						
1861-62						
Nos	3	0	4	2	0	3
%	25	0	33.3	16.7	0	25
Total 12 Unidentified 0						
1863-1871						
Nos	23	9	109	69	1	25
%	9.7	3.8	46.2	29.2	0.4	10.6
Total 236 Unaccounted 33						

Source: Baptismal Register, St James's Church, Aberdeen, Aberdeen City Archives, MS DD 15/3.

Table 3.10 Baptismal Presenters, St Vincent's, Edinburgh

	Upper Middle Class	Lower Middle Class	Skilled Working Class	Unskilled Working Class	Others	Women
1859-1868 Nos	11	5	29	6	2	2
%	20	9.1	52.7	10.9	3.6	3.6
Total 55 Unidentified 4						
1869-1878 Nos	17	12	10	3	-	
%	40.5	28.6	23.8	7.1	-	
Total 42 Unidentified 22						
1879-1888 Nos	20	20	44	13	-	1
%	20.4	20.4	44.9	13.3	-	1.0
Total 98 Unidentified 1						
1889-1898 Nos	11	34	84	25	1	3
%	7.0	21.5	53.2	15.8	0.6	1.9
Total 158 Unidentified 1						

Source: Baptismal Register, St Vincent's Church, Edinburgh, Archives.

Table 3.11 Baptismal Presenters, St Silas's, Glasgow

	Upper Middle Class	Lower Middle Class	Skilled Working Class	Unskilled Working Class	Others	Women
1864-65 Nos	26	3	6	3	-	-
%	68.4	7.9	15.8	7.9	-	-
Total 38 Unidentified 2						
1866-1875 Nos	157	32	121	32	5	-
%	45.2	9.2	34.9	9.2	1.4	-
Total 347 Unidentified 0			(33 from Partick)	(14 from Partick)		
1876-1887 Nos	108	31	63	4	2	-
%	51.9	14.9	30.3	1.9	1.0	-
Total 208 Unidentified 1			(3 from Partick)	(1 from Partick)		
1888-1900 Nos	56	20	32	10		
%	47.5	16.9	27.1	8.5		
Total 118 Unidentified 8						

Source: Baptismal Register, St Silas's Church, Glasgow, Mitchell Library, Glasgow, MS TD 1250/3, 6.

Table 3.12 Baptismal Presenters, St Jude's, Glasgow

	Upper Middle Class	Lower Middle Class	Skilled Working Class	Unskilled Working Class	Others	Women
1869						
Nos	5	3	82	33	-	-
%	4.1	2.4	66.7	26.8	-	-
Total 123						
Unidentified 9						
1873						
Nos	12	11	41	9	4	6
%	14.5	13.3	49.4	10.8	4.8	7.2
Total 83						
Unidentified 0						
1874						
Nos	7	9	41	18	-	2
%	9.1	11.7	53.2	23.4	-	2.6
Total 77						
Unidentified 0						
1875						
Nos	8	10	56	13	1	4
%	8.7	10.9	60.9	14.1	1.1	4.3
Total 92						
Unidentified 0						
1879						
Nos	1	7	39	11	1	1
%	1.7	11.7	65.0	18.3	1.7	1.7
Total 60						
Unidentified 1						
1889						
Nos	-	5	33	6	-	1
%	-	11.1	73.3	13.3	-	2.2
Total 45						
Unidentified 1						

Source: Baptismal Register, St Jude's Church, Glasgow, Mitchell Library, Glasgow, MS TD 66/1/1.

Table 3.13 Baptismal Presenters, Partick Mission, Govan, Glasgow

	Upper Middle Class	Lower Middle Class	Skilled Working Class	Unskilled Working Class	Others	Women
1887-1889 Nos	-	2	77	155	-	-
%	-	0.9	32.9	62.2	-	-
Total 234 Unidentified 0						
1893 Nos	-	-	34	63	-	-
%	-	-	35.0	64.0	-	-
Total 97 Unidentified 0						
1899 Nos	-	-	29	49	-	-
%	-	-	37.2	62.0	-	-
Total 78 Unidentified 0						

Source: Baptismal Register, Partick Mission, Mitchell Library, Glasgow, MS TD 1250/4,5.

Table 3.14 Baptismal Presenters, St Paul's, Carrubber's Close, Edinburgh

	Upper Middle Class	Lower Middle Class	Skilled Working Class	Unskilled Working Class	Others	Women
1832-1837 Nos	37	8	23	0	-	-
%	54.4	11.8	33.8	0	-	-
Total 144 Identified 68 Unidentified 76 *Unreliable Sample*						

Source: Baptismal Register, St Paul's, Carrubber's Close, Edinburgh, Edinburgh City Archives, MS ED 10.

Social Class

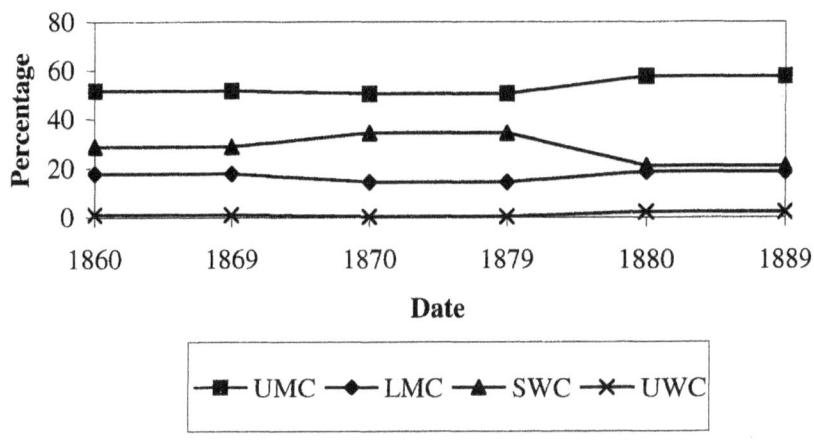

Graph 3.1 Members, St Paul's, Aberdeen

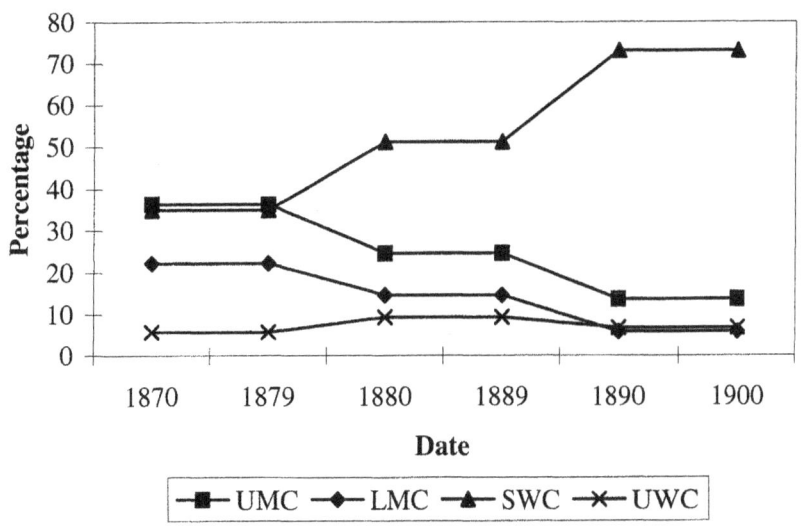

Graph 3.2 Baptismal Presenters, St Paul's, Aberdeen

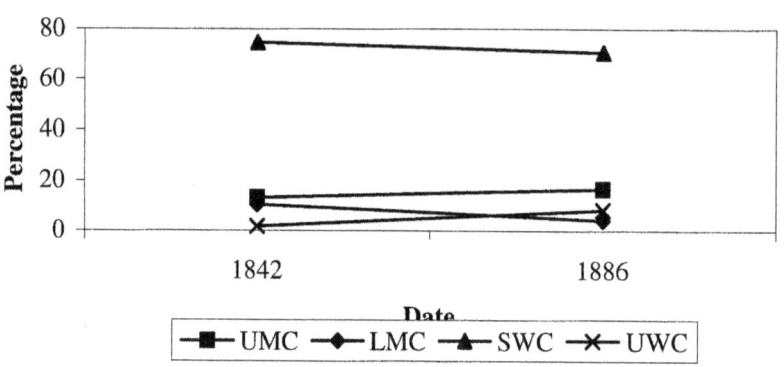

Graph 3.3 Heads of Families with Voting Rights, St Peter's, Montrose

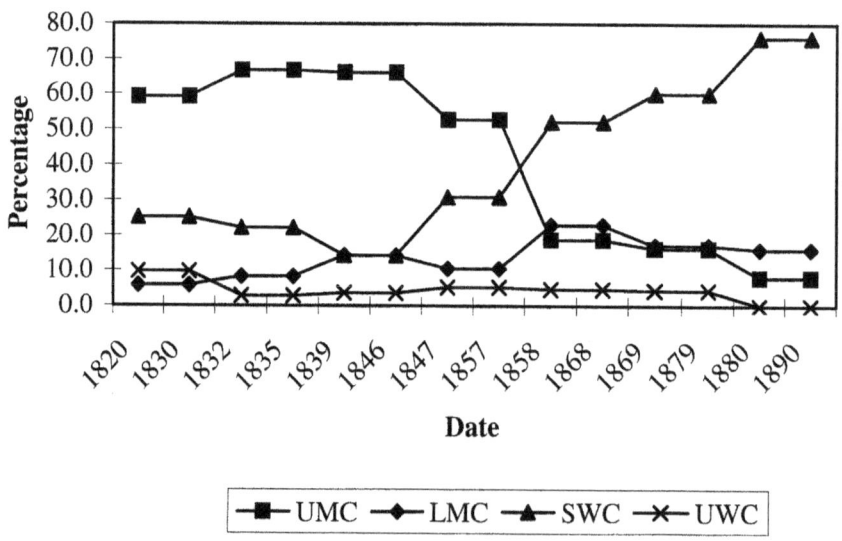

Graph 3.4 Baptismal Presenters, St James's, Edinburgh

Graph 3.5 Baptismal Presenters, St Thomas's, Edinburgh

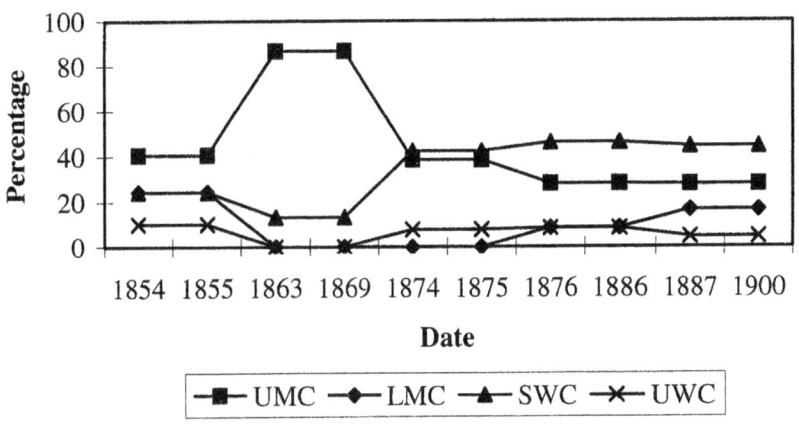

Graph 3.6 Baptismal Presenters, St James's, Aberdeen

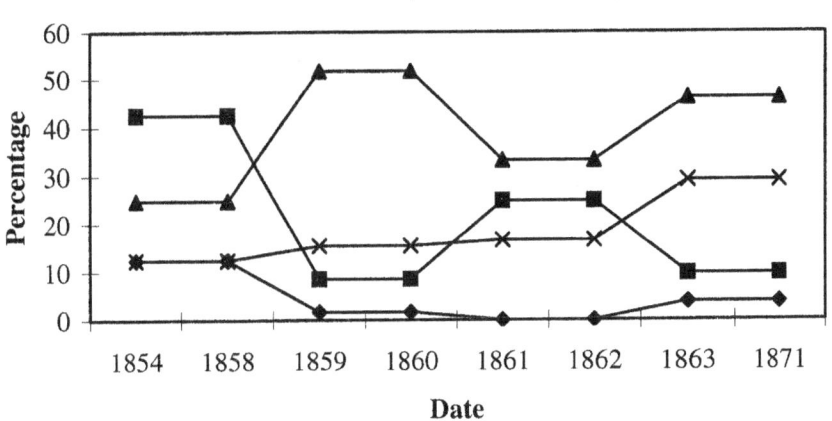

108 *Conscience and Compromise*

Graph 3.7 Baptismal Presenters, St Vincent's, Edinburgh

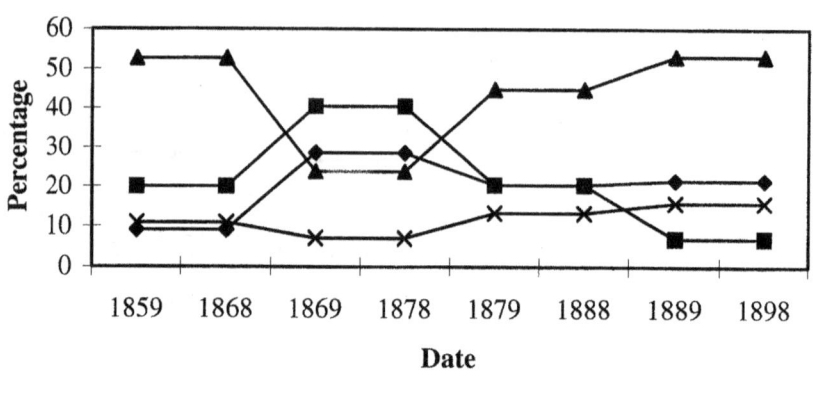

Graph 3.8 Baptismal Presenters, St Silas's, Glasgow

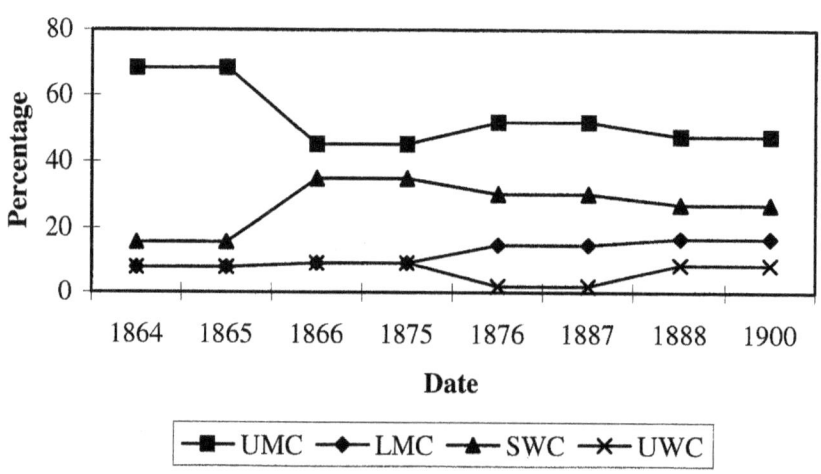

Social Class 109

Graph 3.9 Baptismal Presenters, St Jude's, Glasgow

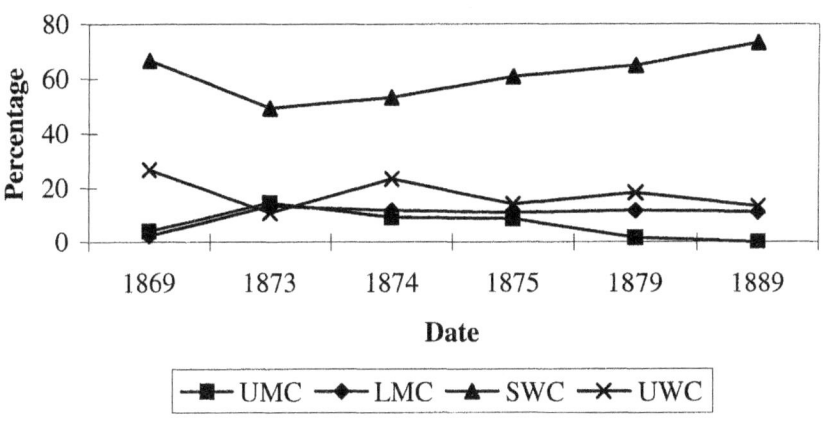

Graph 3.10 Baptismal Presenters, Partick Mission, Govan, Glasgow

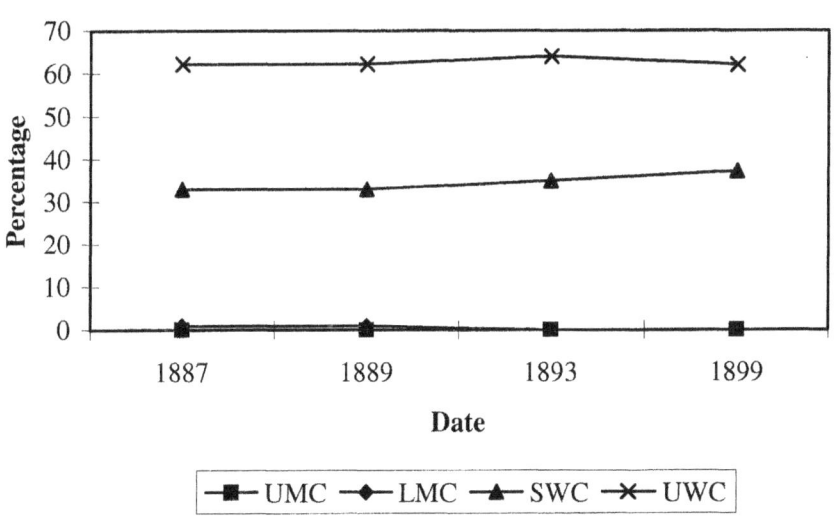

Graph 3.11 Baptisms, St Paul's, Carrubber's Close, Edinburgh

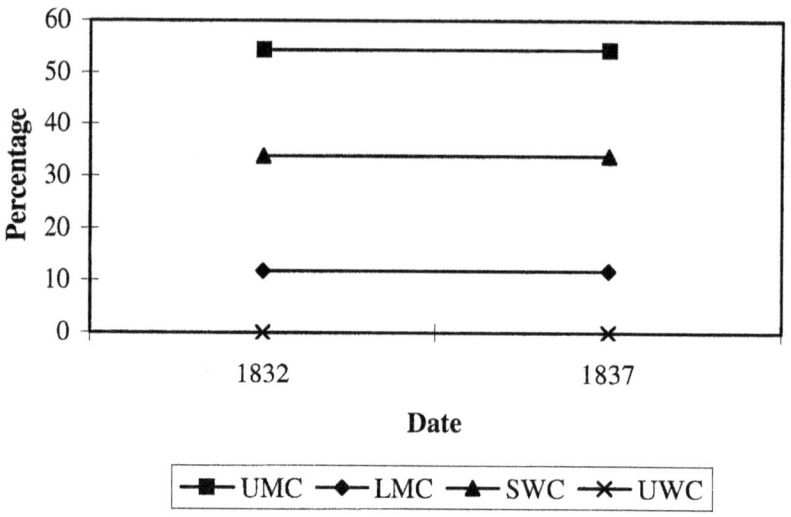

Map 3.1 Skilled and Unskilled Working Class, St Thomas's and St Vincent's, Edinburgh, 1869-1900

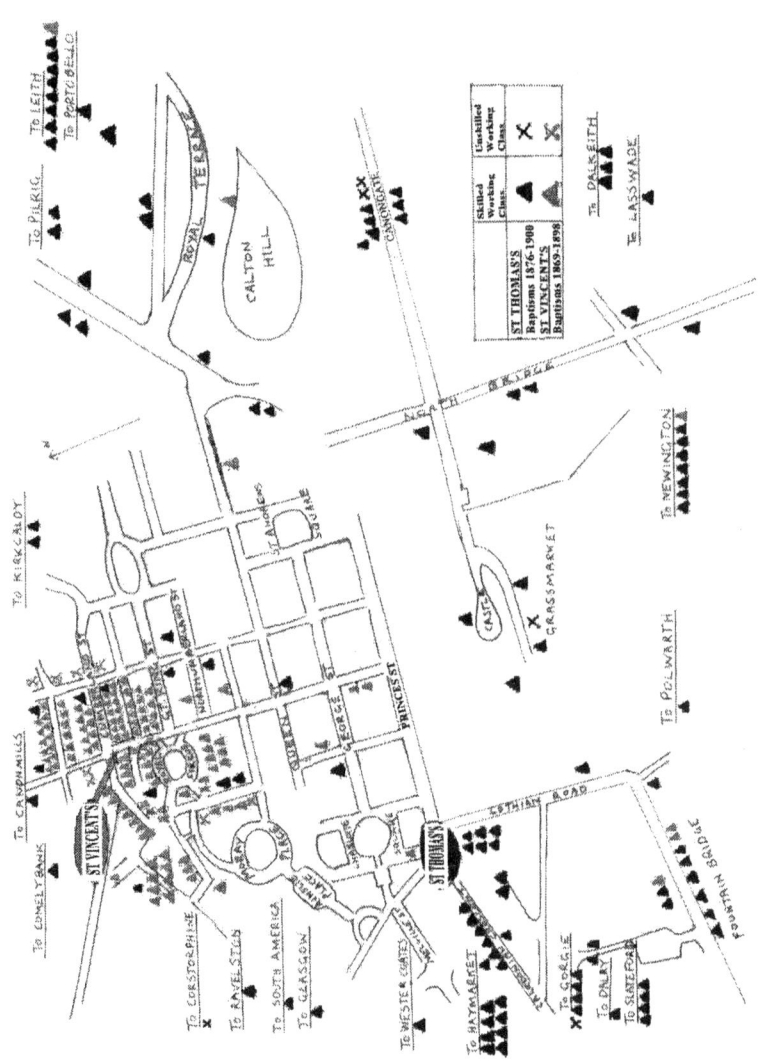

Map 3.2 Skilled Working Class, St James's and St Paul's, Aberdeen, 1854-1879

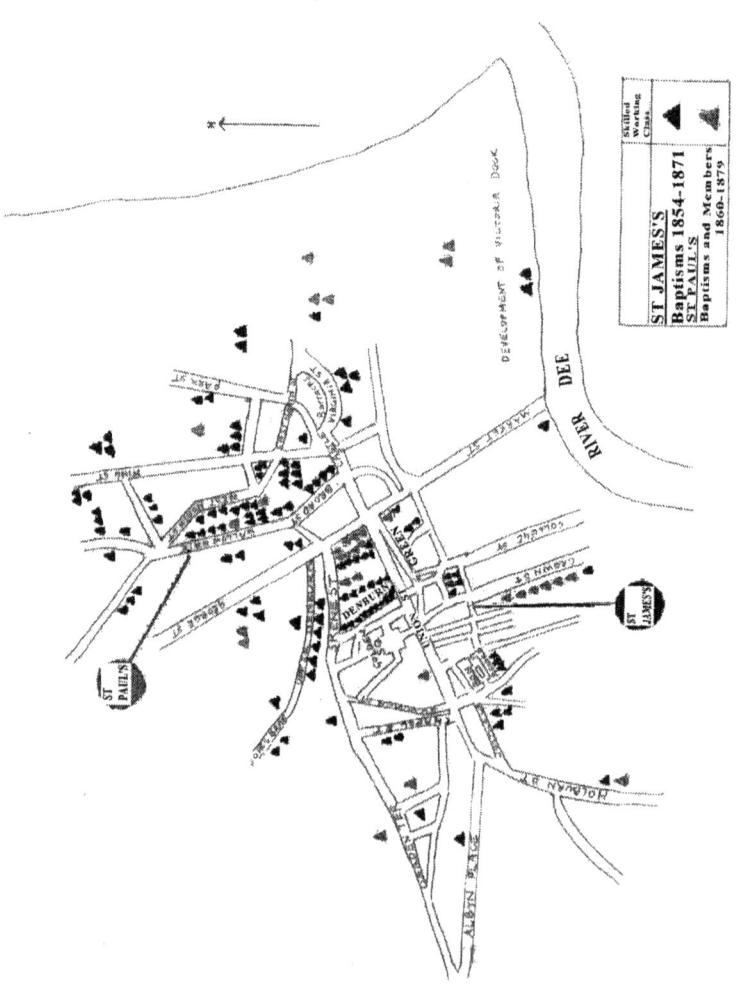

Map 3.3 Unskilled Working Class and Single Mothers, St James's, Aberdeen, 1854-1871

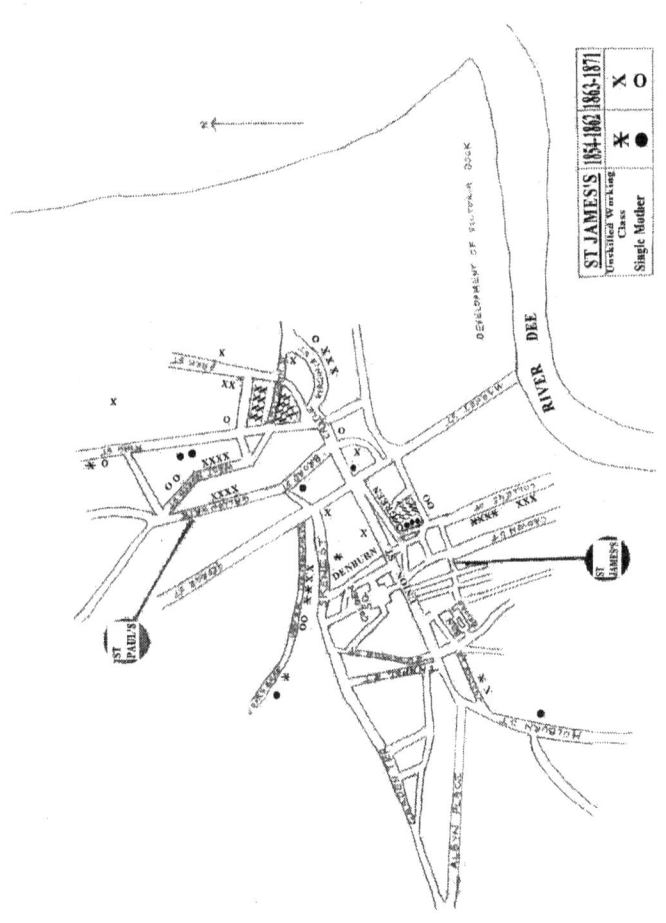

Map 3.4 Upper and Lower Middle Class, St Thomas's and St Vincent's, Edinburgh, 1869-1900

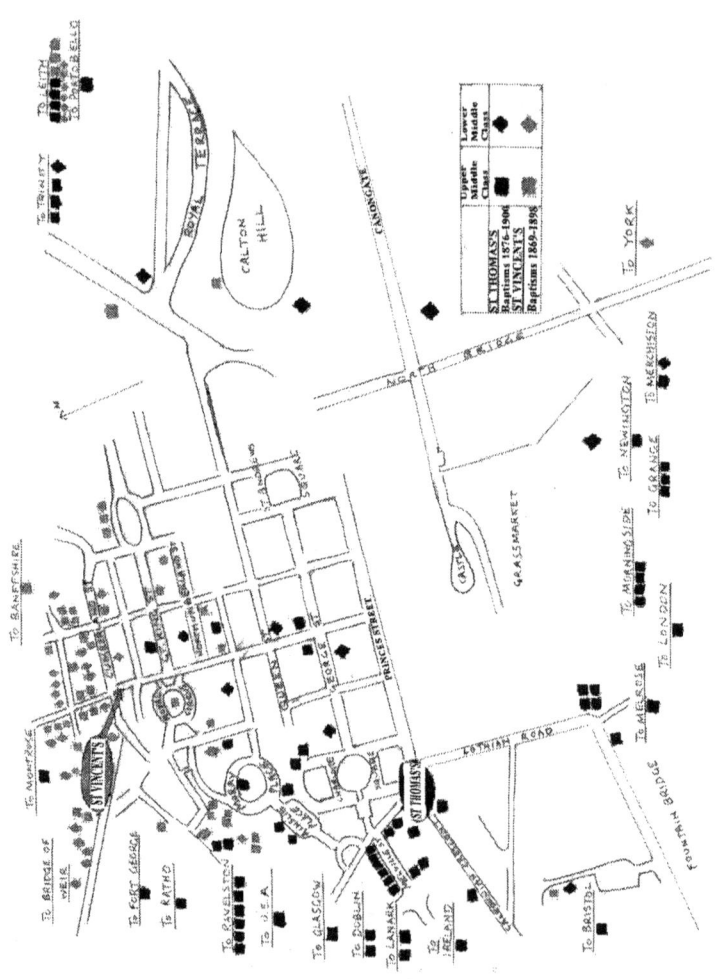

Social Class

Map 3.5 Upper and Lower Middle Class, St James's and St Paul's, Aberdeen, 1854-1879

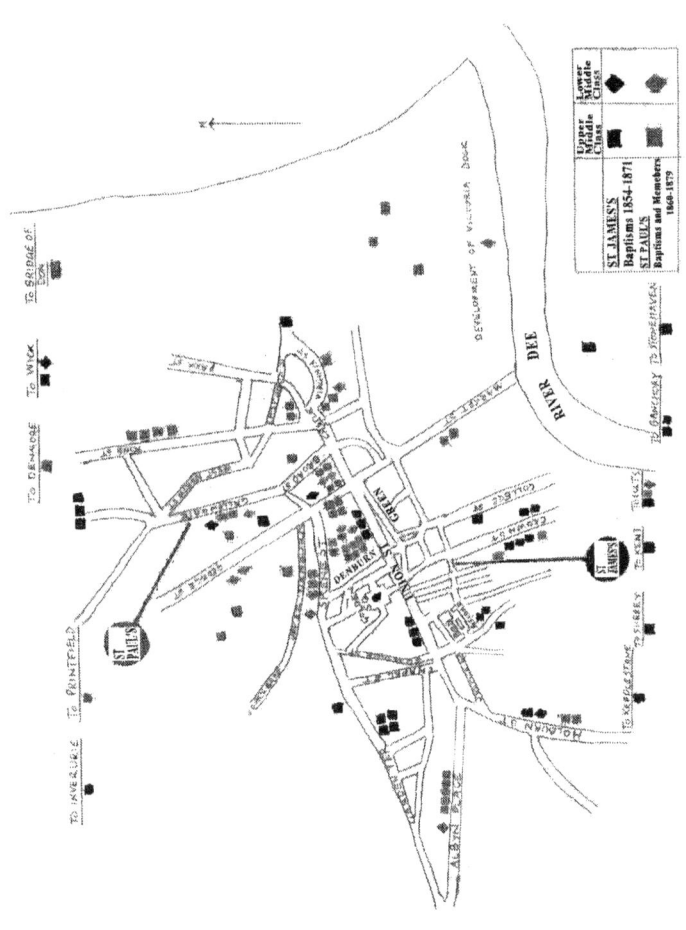

Map 3.6 Class Distribution, St Silas's, Glasgow, 1864-1900

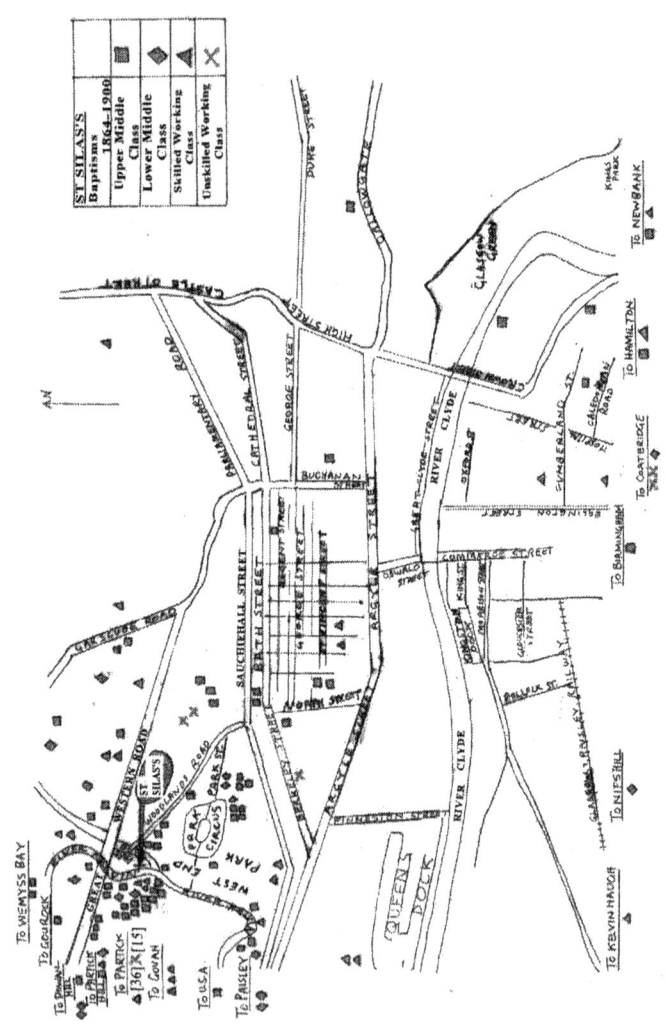

Chapter 4

Theology

The four hallmarks of Evangelicalism discussed in Chapter 1 were: a strong adherence to the doctrine of conversion, a resulting desire to proselytise, the belief in the centrality of Christ's death on the cross as the means of salvation, and a concern that the Bible was supremely the revelation of spiritual truth.[1] This chapter will show how the theology of those nineteenth-century Scottish Evangelical Episcopalians whose writings have survived matched this pattern. Additionally, other wider, important aspects of belief which had affinities with High Churchmanship, Tractarianism and Presbyterianism, and which were also subject to influences from the culture of the time, such as liberal theology and Romanticism, will be examined. A theological profile of Scottish Evangelical Episcopalianism will thus become clear.

Core Theology

Conversionism

The Evangelical belief in conversion stemmed from an understanding of original sin. In 1819, Edward Craig, at St Paul's, Carrubber's Close, Edinburgh, preached that 'we are conceived in sin and shapen in iniquity...we cannot bring a clean thing out of an unclean'.[2] The doctrine that human nature was seriously flawed was based on the first chapters of Genesis where Adam sinned by disobeying God. But Evangelicals also stressed that all were seminally present in Adam when he sinned, and therefore all sinned in him. As C. P. Miles, of St Jude's, Glasgow, expressed it in 1844: 'Adam...was a common representative and a public person; and, therefore, not only he, but we, by eating of the forbidden fruit, sinned and fell'.[3] Everyone was thus equally unacceptable to God – the very best stood on the same ground as the worst. This was the Calvinistic

---

[1] See Chapter 1, p. 1.
[2] Edward Craig, *The Religious Instruction of the Poor, The Duty of the Rich* (Edinburgh, 1819), p. 7.
[3] C. P. Miles, *The Voice of the Glorious Reformation*, Second Edition, (London, 1844), pp. 160-161.

doctrine of the total depravity of mankind, enshrined in Article IX of the Church of England and in the Westminster Confession.

Evangelicals believed that the Bible taught that nothing but a radical cure could obliterate original sin.[4] People needed to recognise their natural state of sinfulness and turn by an act of repentance and faith to God. Robert Montgomery, of St Jude's, Glasgow, showed this process of conversion, or being born again, to be strikingly profound in its effects since 'the whole nature of man must experience this transformation'.[5] Such an event was unlikely to go unnoticed by the recipient and, therefore, many Evangelicals could identify a specific time when they had been converted. But conversion was not necessarily sudden; it could be gradual. D. T. K. Drummond of St Thomas's, Edinburgh, described both processes in an exposition of Psalm 33:

> When you look back dear friends, on that day in the past, when after long years of wandering upon the dark mountains the Good Shepherd found you at last, poor wandering sheep, and brought you back to the fold rejoicing; when the scales fell off at last from your blinded eyes, and you were enabled to see Christ as your Saviour, suffering, bleeding, dying for you; did He not then put a 'new song' into your mouth? Did you not then realise that the earth indeed is full of the goodness of the Lord? Or if it was a more gradual work; from day to day the light growing imperceptibly as He led you on step by step to the measure of the fullness of Christ, and the darkness at last fled away, and the true light shone in your heart...[6]

This extract illustrates the steps believed to occur in all conversions: the initial lost state of the human being; the realisation that Christ died personally for the sinner; and a feeling of translation from one state to another. But Drummond also taught, with copious scriptural evidence, that conversion was not a stereotyped event, that 'beyond this each has an experience peculiarly his own'.[7] The Evangelical doctrine of conversion, with all its miraculous and emotional aspects, was clearly based on individual knowledge and was felt as a distinct change in the life of the recipient.

High Churchmen also believed in the doctrine of original sin but there were some variations as to its exact nature. For instance Bishop George Gleig of Brechin, in his Charge of 1819, expressed almost semi-Pelagian

---

[4] For examples of parts of the Bible claimed by Evangelicals to teach conversion, see Daniel Bagot, *A Catechism Explanatory of the Leading Truths of the Gospel* (Edinburgh, 1839), pp. 6-7.

[5] Robert Montgomery, *The Gospel Before the Age* (London, 1844), p. 64.

[6] D. T .K. Drummond, *Sparkling Rills by the Wayside*, ed. Harriet Drummond (Edinburgh, 1879), p. 248.

[7] D. T. K. Drummond, Sermon notes (n.d.), DRO, D/5550/3/5/9.

Theology

views. While he accepted that human nature may be depraved as a result of the fall of Adam, rendering people 'much more prone...to the commission of actual sin', he regarded contemporary Evangelical theology as 'heresy', and held that 'we cannot be considered as *sharers* in the *guilt* of our first parents'.[8] Thus Gleig, while admitting the Adamic connection, did not believe like Miles that all were equally responsible along with Adam for the fall of mankind. However, other Scottish Churchmen were more in line with Evangelical opinion on the topic. Drummond testified that E. B. Ramsay of St John's, Edinburgh, had 'from the very first preached distinctly...the great doctrines of the fall of man, his utter depravity'.[9] Variations of belief concerning original sin marked non-Evangelical theology in the Scottish Episcopal Church.

Unlike Evangelicals, High Churchmen taught that God dealt with original sin in the sacrament of baptism which provided an infusion of righteousness into the soul. Thereafter they believed that, if a person fell into sin and drifted away from God, faith was renewed by a type of conversion that was the fruit of baptism.[10] But for Evangelicals this was a misconception. As J. S. S. Robertson, incumbent of Dunblane in 1844 explained, 'being born again is as necessary to us who have been baptized in infancy, as it is to the pagans in the heathen nations'.[11] Thus Scottish Evangelical Episcopalians and High Churchmen interpreted the Bible differently on the topic of conversion from man's sinful nature.

Evangelical sermons regularly featured the doctrine of conversion. Sir William Dunbar, of St Paul's, Aberdeen, urged the unconverted in his congregation to 'come and learn of the pardon which is offered...others have accepted it and have been thereupon forgiven'.[12] The numbers affected by such preaching are unknown, but W. S. Moncrieff, on leaving St Thomas's, Edinburgh, in 1875 made reference to Drummond 'who for forty years has preached the Gospel, and has been honoured by our Lord in binding up many a bleeding heart, and winning souls to Him'.[13] Some Scottish Evangelicals composed hymns on the topic as exemplified by R. K. Greville, a layman of St Thomas's, Edinburgh, in his 'A lost and sinful

---

[8] *Scottish Episcopal Review and Magazine*, February 1820, p. 74. William Walker, *Memoirs of Bishops Jolly and Gleig* (Edinburgh, 1878), pp. 245-247.

[9] Charles Rogers, *Memorial Recollections of the Very Reverend Edward Bannerman Ramsay* (London, 1873), pp. 58-59.

[10] See Chapter 6, pp. 194.

[11] J. S. S. Robertson, *Lectures on the Philippians* (London, 1849), p. 8.

[12] Sir William Dunbar, *Pulpit Recollections or Miscellaneous Sermons* (London, 1841), p. 93.

[13] D. T. K. Drummond, *Letter to the Very Rev. the Dean of Carlisle* (Edinburgh, 1875), p. 20.

world to save, in human form the Saviour came'.[14] Poems were a popular way of expressing the doctrine. Drummond's daughter, Harriet, versified the conversion experience as a response to 'the voice of my Beloved [who] whispered come with me',[15] and E. C. Wrenford, of Nairn English Episcopal Church, bore testimony to spiritual new birth in writings such as 'We were lost...but he hath washed...us'.[16] The doctrine of conversion was prominent in the teaching, worship and writings of Evangelical Episcopalians in Scotland.

Conversion theology was deeply rooted in the Reformation doctrine of justification by faith alone. The total depravity of mankind and justification by faith were inextricably linked in the Evangelical mind. Since the former declared that even the very best of human beings was flawed by a propensity to sin, it was believed that there was no way in which anyone could please a holy God – people were just too sinful. Access to God could be gained only through Christ whose death had paid the price of man's sinfulness. When people accepted this, by faith at conversion, they were justified in God's eyes. J. D. Hull, the incumbent of Huntly English Episcopal Church summed it up as follows:

> Jesus Christ, has...satisfied the Divine justice for our disobedience...Once let us by faith avail ourselves of His propitiation, and the flaming sword of vengeance, which previously was suspended over our heads, is exchanged for the overshadowing wings of everlasting love.[17]

The doctrine of justification by faith alone sought to focus the whole process of man's redemption on God. At the Reformation, Martin Luther had pressed it in reaction to the contemporary belief that righteousness was obtainable by man's own efforts and good works. By contrast he preached that God was supremely eminent and that man could contribute nothing towards his salvation. Drummond encapsulated the teaching as follows: 'the robe of His righteousness [was] woven by the Great King Himself, and by Him pronounced entirely and forever sufficient to cover all our sins'.[18] The work of justification was God's entirely.

In the post-Reformation era some Churchmen, such as Jeremy Taylor and George Bull, reacted against the doctrine of justification by faith alone.

---

[14] D. T. K. Drummond and Robert Kaye Greville, *The Church of England Hymn Book* (Edinburgh, 1838). R. K. Greville, 1730-1860. His private fortune allowed him to pursue a career as a botanist and illustrator. Vice President of the Anti-Slavery Convention, 1840. Joined St Thomas's Church, Edinburgh, 1842. D. M. Lewis (ed.), *The Blackwell Dictionary of Evangelical Biography*, Vol. I (Oxford, 1995), p. 475.

[15] Drummond, *Rills*, pp. 265-267.

[16] Edwin Wrenford, *First Fruits of Sacred Song* (London, 1876), p. 66.

[17] J. D. Hull, *The Cluster Crushed* (London, 1867), p. 20.

[18] Drummond, *Rills*, p. 241.

Theology 121

They considered that the importance of good works had been neglected, and argued that faith without them was non-existent. But, in the eighteenth century, George Whitefield and the Calvinistic Methodists re-emphasised justification by faith alone, causing some High Churchmen to label Evangelicals as antinomian and to claim that they preached justifying faith as releasing people from the Mosaic law.[19] High Churchmen through to the nineteenth century, following the teaching of Taylor and Bull, continued to stress that faith should be expressed in good works and moral behaviour, that these were a necessary adjunct to baptism if salvation were to be certain. For instance Gleig, in 1820, argued that even if Evangelicals claimed that faith was 'the sole condition of what has been called our first justification, good works...shall certainly be the condition of our last'.[20] Evangelicals, by contrast, emphasised that faith alone was the qualification for salvation.

But it was not the case that Evangelicals disregarded good works. They taught what most converted people testified to, that after conversion the individual, having a new nature implanted by God, wanted to behave in a way pleasing to him. It was not that the converted never sinned again, but it was evident that they had different priorities. Drummond preached, 'The soul of the sinner, when taken possession of by Christ, is not left as an empty habitation...it is also filled with consecrated things ... inscribed on every affection, and stimulating every energy'.[21] Evangelicals did not undervalue good works; they believed them to be the natural fruit of conversion.

During the Evangelical Revival the doctrine of assurance became closely associated with that of conversion. While High Churchmen preached that the grace of baptism could be lost, the revivalists taught that, on conversion, there was immediate assurance of salvation. This view was different from the Calvinistic tradition where certainty of being in a state of grace was by no means guaranteed. Rather, the believer would be constantly introspective, wrestling with sin and imperfection. Anglican Evangelicals took up the Weslyan idea although admitting that faith could waver. By contrast, in Scotland, the old Calvinist understanding hung on, changing only gradually.[22] Among Episcopal Evangelicals in Scotland Drummond was typical of his Anglican counterparts. In the late 1830s he encouraged believers who were afraid 'lest the little life you have may altogether fail' that their souls 'were in the safe keeping of the living God...safe from the

---

[19] P. B. Nockles, *The Oxford Movement in Context* (Cambridge, 1994), pp. 256-261.
[20] *Scottish Episcopal Review and Magazine*, February 1820.
[21] D. T. K. Drummond, *Last Scenes in the Life of our Lord and Saviour* (London, 1850), p. 151.
[22] D. W. Bebbington, *Holiness in Nineteenth-Century England* (Carlisle, 2000), p. 36. D. W. Bebbington, *Evangelicalism in Modern Britain* (London, 1993), pp. 44-45.

asault of every foe'[23] Similarly, in 1849 J. S. S. Robertson preached that 'once a man is converted to God he is introduced to a state of safety from which...he should never after...fall away'.[24] Such Evangelicals, assured that God was a constant presence in their lives from the moment of conversion, were certain that, even if they made mistakes, God would not relinquish them.

Early in the nineteenth century the High Churchman, John Skinner of Linshart found the doctrine of conversion distasteful. He claimed that all Evangelicals believed that 'without them there would be no more Gospel in Britain than amongst the wildest Indians'.[25] Certainly Scottish Evangelical Episcopalians preached it enthusiastically, seeking to bring the experience to others. They regarded it as vivifying, the gateway to true faith, because it was experienced as a personal relationship with Christ. E. F. D. Hutton of St Silas's Church, Glasgow, thus encouraged doubters 'if [Christ] be your Saviour...then you can say He is mine'.[26] The doctrine of conversion clearly separated Scottish Evangelical Episcopalians from their High Church colleagues.[27]

Activism

The converted person had an overwhelming urgency to pass the experience on to as many others as possible. Thus Evangelicals were characteristically imbued with a vigorous missionary outlook, both at home and abroad, which may be defined as their activism. It is true that there were High Churchmen in Scotland in the nineteenth century who were anxious to spread the gospel, as was evident in the ministries of David Aitchison in the 1830s and A. J. D. D'Orsey in the 1840s. Working respectively among the poor of the Calton and Anderston districts of Glasgow, they were untiring in their efforts.[28] Again some Tractarians, such as A. P. Forbes, Bishop of Brechin, showed dedicated and vibrant ministries.[29] But Aitchison, in 1857, criticised the overall non-aggressiveness of the Scottish Episcopal Church

---

[23] *Last Scenes*, pp. 119-120.

[24] Robertson, *Philippians*, p. 27.

[25] William Walker, *The Life and Times of the Rev John Skinner of Linshart, Longside* (London, 1883), p. 141.

[26] E. D. Hutton, *Burning Questions of the Day* (London, 1882), p. 33.

[27] See also W. P. McFarquhar, *Sermons* (Edinburgh, 1844), pp. 47-48: 'It is not enough that mercy has been offered, it must be accepted as well...if we do not come to Jesus in this penitent and believing manner...he cannot be Saviour to us...we must perish everlastingly'. Similarly, McFarquhar, *Sermons*, pp. 325-327, gives further examples.

[28] See Chapter 3, p. 90.

[29] Rowan Strong, *Episcopalianism in Nineteenth-Century Scotland* (Oxford, 2002), p. 160. Rowan Strong, *Alexander Forbes of Brechin* (Oxford, 1995), pp. 59-60.

Theology

in conveying faith. Commenting on a quality of disengagement in such matters he spoke of it as a 'quiet, orderly, aristocratic society, very punctilious'.[30] From within their own ranks, High Church Scottish Episcopalians were criticised for lack of evangelistic fervour.

By contrast Evangelicals tended to be burdened with an overwhelming desire to pass on their particular brand of faith. As Sir William Dunbar put it, 'a faithful Christian minister...carried from his dying pillow...would he not urge once more upon his people to dedicate themselves to the Lord in a perpetual covenant never to be forgotten?'[31] Similarly, when St Thomas's, Edinburgh, was set up in 1842, its founders ensured that 'the work of evangelisation went on vigorously'.[32] Schemes such as the Canongate Mission, Edinburgh, started in 1845, financed by St Thomas's, and the Partick Mission, begun in 1865 by St Silas's, Glasgow, provided outlets for activism in the poor areas of the cities.[33] On a smaller scale, D. T. K. Drummond evangelised the fishermen of Usan, near Montrose, in the 1830s,[34] and, from the mid 1830s to 1840s, he was involved in holding special, informal evangelistic meetings in Edinburgh with the purpose of bringing people to the point of conversion.[35] Public lectures were another field of opportunity. E. F. D. Hutton, while incumbent of St Columba's, Crieff, gave a series on Bunyan's *Pilgrim's Progress* in which he preached 'great truths with plainness, earnestness and effect'. Hutton considered the events to be of such importance that he offered them free of charge in order to attract a large audience.[36] Even on vacation Evangelicals were active. The Drummonds' daughter, Harriet, during family holidays at St Fillans, in Perthshire, was reported as taking, from an early age, a 'very great interest in seeing to the spiritual welfare of the young' of the village. She started a Sabbath school class for the purpose and 'continued to conduct it with unabated assiduity and zeal' until the Sunday before her wedding in 1871.[37] Evangelical activism was expressed in a myriad of ways.

On a larger scale revivalism, a spiritual movement of unusual power resulting in large numbers of conversions, was notable by the 1850s. The dimension of spontaneous revivalism of earlier years was supplemented by more organised events, backed by careful planning and prayer, and culminating in special services. A movement, emanating from America,

---

[30] Strong, *Episcopalianism*, p. 194.
[31] Sir William Dunbar, Bart., *A Sermon Preached in Kew Church, 21 June 1863* (Private, 1863), p. 6.
[32] *Memoir*, p. xlviii.
[33] See Chapter 3, pp. 89-90.
[34] See Chapter 8, p. 251.
[35] *Ibid.*, p. 250, 259-260.
[36] *Crieff Journal*, 17 November, 15 December, 22 December 1866.
[37] *Strathearn Herald*, 14 October 1871.

started in Ulster in 1859. Anglican Evangelicals were largely, but not universally, wary of involvement, especially in the context of the reported physical manifestations, and in England the revival was confined mainly to Cornwall and north Devon.[38] Those Anglicans who contributed were often subsequently influenced by the perfection doctrine of Robert and Hannah Pearsall Smith.[39] As discussed later,[40] Scottish Evangelical Episcopalians were largely unaffected by that particular teaching, but some of them were, nevertheless, involved in revivals north of the border from 1859 to 1860. This was partly because those involved were all from the English Episcopal movement. Their close ties with the Free Church, which was the main organiser of events,[41] and their large contingent of Irish clergy and lay people[42] with first-hand knowledge of the Ulster revival would have encouraged participation.[43]

Events in Scotland typically illustrated the ways in which Evangelical activism was expressed. Preparation began at an early stage with 'fervent weekly prayer for religious awakening' such as the Edinburgh Union Prayer Meeting in April 1858, attended by J. H. Balfour, a layman from St Thomas's, Edinburgh.[44] On 15 March 1860 'special services for united prayer were held...when ministers and members of the various Evangelical Churches united in supplication for the outpouring of the Holy Spirit and the revival of religion'. Drummond officiated at one of these in Queen Street Hall in Edinburgh.[45] The revival itself revolved around numerous public evangelistic events. In Edinburgh various clergy and laypeople from Scotland took part and 'appeared to produce a deep impression' with 'crowded meetings in Queen Street Hall'.[46] Drummond spoke on several occasions, and also gave an educational address in Edinburgh on Home Evangelization in October 1860.[47] In Glasgow, G. K. Flindt, of St Jude's, led a Children's Prayer Meeting at the Free Gaelic Church when 'young people who were anxious about their souls were invited to meet...in the

---

[38] Bebbington, *Evangelicalism in Modern Britain* pp. 114-117.

[39] Anne Bentley, 'Transformation of the Evangelical Party in the Church of England in the Late Nineteenth Century', (Durham University Ph. D. thesis, 1971), p. 344.

[40] See Chapter 4, p. 139.

[41] See Chapters 8 and 9, *passim*.

[42] See Chapter 1, pp.11-14. Chapter 9, *passim*.

[43] *Cf.* K. S. Jeffrey, 'The 1858-1862 Revival in the North-East of Scotland' (Stirling University Ph. D. thesis, 2000), pp. 112-114 which suggests that St Paul's and St James's, Aberdeen, were not involved with the Scottish revival. See also Chapter 3, pp. 78, 81, 84-87.

[44] *United Presbyterian Magazine*, Vol. IV, 1860, p. 82.

[45] *Scottish Guardian*, 15 March 1860.

[46] *United Presbyterian Magazine*, Volume IV, 1860, p. 522.

[47] *Scottish Guardian*, 6 October 1860.

adjoining session house'.[48] The Duchess of Gordon, who offered hospitality at Huntly to the members of the revival conference there, gave practical support.[49] After the meetings those who had professed conversion were monitored to ensure that their commitment was reliable. For instance, several prostitutes in Edinburgh were reported as showing signs of 'dramatic and sincere transformation'.[50] The 1860 revival in Scotland was imbued with Evangelical English Episcopal support.

Revival prayer meetings continued into the 1860s when further ventures were considered. In 1863 Drummond attended such a gathering in Perth along with Free Church colleagues.[51] The culmination of such preparation came with the Moody and Sankey meetings in January to February 1874. Although the Scottish Episcopal Church took no official part, probably because it was wary of the overtly evangelistic nature of the event, there was heavy involvement of the Free Church, along with other Presbyterian churches,[52] and English Episcopalian clerical and lay involvement was again evident. W. S. Moncrieff, assistant at St Thomas's, Edinburgh, and Balfour represented Drummond who was seriously ill and unable to attend. T. K. Talon, incumbent of St Vincent's, Edinburgh, also took part in various meetings and, in Glasgow, John Burns of Castle Wemyss and St Silas's presided on the platform when Moody preached there.[53] English Episcopalians were notable supporters of Moody and Sankey.

Evangelism also took place in the private sphere. One particular concern was to reach the dying in order to secure their salvation. Two records illustrate such events in Edinburgh. A young Edinburgh boy, David Tod, with his family, was a member of the Free Church, St John's, under the ministry of Thomas Guthrie. In 1845 S. C. Baker, a curate at St Thomas's, Edinburgh, was asked to visit the boy who was ill with consumption because, although he 'attended with the utmost earnestness to his religious duties, he was taught to pray to God and read his Bible...to repeat a grace before taking food...there was...no decided evidence of a change of heart'. Baker, although endeavouring 'to show him the wickedness and guilt of his own heart', was sympathetic to his age and health. Feeling 'that comfortable words would better suit the weak state of his body' he 'spoke not in the way of reproach...but to show him how much he needed Christ,

---

[48] *Ibid.*, 11 September 1860.
[49] *United Presbyterian Magazine*, Volume IV, 1860, p. 83.
[50] J. E. Orr, *The Second Evangelical Awakening in Britain* (London, 1953), pp. 73-74.
[51] *Record*, 9 September 1863.
[52] *Ibid.*, 1 February 1875. Mrs Robert Peddie (ed.), *A Consecutive Narrative of the Remarkable Awakening in Edinburgh* (London, 1874), *passim*.
[53] Peddie, *Remarkable Awakening*, pp. 51-52. *Record*, 26, November 1873, 19 January 1874, 18 March 1874.

and that he had nothing to bring to Christ'. Various portions of scripture were used to convey the message of 'human guilt and depravity', and the boy was thus 'led to know his full need before he received the all-sufficient remedy'. When he died, on the day of the opening of Guthrie's new church in Edinburgh, Baker was sure that he had 'passed into the general assembly and church of the first-born above'.[54] The other episode concerns the second wife, 'Mousie', of Thomas Ogilvy who founded the English Episcopal chapel at Corrimony, Ross and Cromarty. When not at their country home, the Ogilvies attended St Thomas's, Edinburgh. In 1850 'Mousie' became terminally ill and Ogilvy, regretting that he himself had not been able to speak to her freely and easily about Christ, asked Drummond to call and tell her the gospel. Ogilvy records that 'Mousie was delighted with his two visits…and with a book he lent her, and requested his return at as early a day as she could be permitted to see him'.[55] The accounts show various aspects of Evangelical concern in passing on the gospel. Scripture and Christian literature, not human reason, were appealed to in conveying the message. The urgency with which Evangelicals viewed their task, and the relief felt when the teaching was accepted, was evident. Although it has been impossible to find further data, the excerpts above provide a striking contrast particularly to the accounts of youthful deathbed scenes where 'the business of frightening little children into being Evangelical little children' was exemplified by the ministry of the Calvinist, William Carus Wilson, founder of the school for clergy daughters at Cowan Bridge, Yorkshire.[56] The Scottish Evangelical Episcopalians discussed here conducted evangelism with sensitivity.

The burden to tell the gospel was acutely felt in the sphere of foreign mission. Impetus was given initially by the postmillennial viewpoint of many Evangelicals who believed Christ would return when the whole world had been converted to Christianity. When, by the 1840s, many Anglican Evangelicals became premillennialists, the urgent need to reach as many people as possible with the gospel before Christ returned was acutely felt and involvement with missionary societies thrived. In particular, interest in Jewish evangelism grew since, as the premillennial view took hold, some Evangelicals believed the Bible to prophesy the return of the Jews to Palestine as a sign of Christ's Second Coming.[57] Taking the gospel to the

---

[54] S. C. Baker, *Early Grace Illustrated in the Memoir of David Tod* (Edinburgh, 1846), pp. 23, 30, 31, 74.

[55] Thomas Ogilvy, *Dying Scenes in My Own Family* (privately printed, 1854), pp. 39-46.

[56] Ford K. Brown, *Fathers of the Victorians: The Age of Wilberforce* (Cambridge, 1961), pp. 461-463.

[57] Napoleon I in 1798, fighting in Palestine against the Turks, issued a proclamation to Jews of Asia and Africa to cooperate with the French army and promising to re-

Theology

Jews was regarded as a biblical demand and failure to obey would result in God's judgement on the church. Thus Drummond, quoting Psalm 22.6, urged his congregation to 'pray for the peace of Jerusalem. They shall prosper that love thee'.[58] The Jews' Society, founded in 1809, and its Anglican successor, became the focus for reaching Jewish people with the Evangelical message. It was a prime concern of St Thomas's, Edinburgh,[59] St Silas's, Glasgow, and Wemyss Bay under the oversight of George Burns.[60]

Similarly, the Church Missionary Society was an area of interest. Edward Craig at St James's, Edinburgh, organised Scottish support in the 1820s. When he became disheartened with the society in the 1830s, Drummond took over the directorship[61] and interest flourished again. Evangelicals filled most of the main administrative posts on the local committees by the 1840s and, after 1842, the English Episcopal movement was the driving force behind operations.[62] The intensity of its involvement was evidenced in the recurring pseudonyms, 'I am a debtor for Africa and China' and 'peace offering', adopted by donators at St Thomas's, Edinburgh.[63] Evangelical Episcopalians in Scotland provided outstanding contribution to CMS, with its work in Africa, India and North America.

The Church of England Colonial Society, later to become the Colonial and Continental Society in 1851, the Italian Evangelization Society and the Scripture Readers' Society of Ireland were further concerns of St Thomas's, Edinburgh.[64] In addition Drummond had an early interest in the Waldensian Church.[65] John Burns assisted in establishing the Cumbelana training ship

---

establish the Jewish State. Sir Moses Montefiore, Chairman of Board of Deputies of British Jews, 1835-1874, visited the Holy Land and esblished agricultural settlements. Mordecai Manuel Noah, an American Jew, pleaded for the resettlement of Jews in Palestine in 1844. Political Zionism took root by 1862 under Moses Hess and later with Theodore Herzl and Leon Pinnsher. See Max Wurmbrand and Cecil Roth, *The Jewish People: 4000 Years of Survival* (Jerusalem, 1966), pp. 331, 342, 378-380. See also Chapter 3, pp. 143-147. Bebbington, *Evangelicalism*, pp. 82-83.

[58] *Memoir*, p. lv.
[59] *Ibid.*
[60] Edwin Hodder, *Sir George Burns, Bart.* (London, 1892), p. 230.
[61] CMS Archive, Birmingham University, MS G/AC/3. CMS was increasingly criticised for inter-party involvement by some Evangelicals who were concerned about doctrinal laxity and liberalism in the 1820s and 1830s. W. J. C. Ervine, 'Doctrine and Diplomacy: Some Aspects of the Life and Thought of Anglican Evangelical Clergy 1797-1837' (Cambridge University Ph. D., 1979), pp. 274-276.
[62] *Proceedings of the Church Missionary Society* (London, 1840-1899), *passim*.
[63] *Ibid.*, 1842-1874.
[64] *Memoir*, p. cx.
[65] *Ibid.*, p. lxxiv.

for Street Arabs.[66] His father, George Burns, was on the committee of the Glasgow Auxiliary to the Moravian Missions. He, with his wife, set up the Lebanon Schools scheme, eventually taken on by the Free Church, and supported the Pilgrim Mission of St Chrischona, Basle, established in 1840 by C. F. Spittler to train young artisans as missionaries.[67] J. H. Balfour took on the establishment of a Juvenile Missionary Association at St Thomas's, Edinburgh, and in the Canongate Mission, to encourage and inform young people in the congregations about mission.[68] Overseas missionary work was very much part of English Episcopal life.

Some Evangelical Episcopalians in Scotland became, or had been, missionaries themselves. J. S. S. Robertson worked for CMS in India from 1839.[69] Among the English Episcopalians, C. B. Gribble, assistant at St Jude's from 1846 to 1847, served in Canada on Lake Erie.[70] Sholto Douglas, incumbent at St Silas's, Glasgow, in 1886, had been a missionary in Madras in 1875.[71] Several members of St Thomas's congregation devoted themselves to missionary work, in particular in India and New Zealand. Among these, the Drummonds' adopted daughter, Ellen Sherwood, was notable for her work in the former with CMS.[72] Home support for the missionaries was a time-consuming lay occupation. Women acted as collectors and treasurers of funds for missionary societies, visiting numerous households in the process.[73] Prayer support was regarded as vital. For Drummond it took on the nature of a military operation and he urged his congregation to 'come to the help of the Lord against the mighty' at the monthly prayer meetings for 'Home, Foreign and Jewish' missions.[74] There was no excuse for non-involvement; those remaining at home could be just as active as the missionaries. Evangelical commitment to overseas mission was thus almost universal.

Non-Evangelical Scottish Episcopalians were also involved in mission, as is evident in the records of the Church Missionary Society.[75] Similarly, in 1871, the Church accepted responsibility for the existing Anglican Mission in Chandra, India, and, in 1873, consecrated Henry Callaway as bishop to a similar mission in Kaffraria, southern Africa, at the request of

---

[66] Hodder, *Burns*, p. 62.

[67] *Ibid.*, pp. 62, 230.

[68] *Memoir*, p. lvii.

[69] See Chapter 1, p. 9.

[70] Hodder, *Burns*, p. 170.

[71] *Record*, 19 March 1875.

[72] *Memoir*, p. lviii.

[73] Harriet Drummond, *Emily Vernon or Filial Piety Exemplified* (New York, 1855), pp. 110-131.

[74] *Memoir*, pp. lii, lv.

[75] Chapter 2, pp. 46-53.

Theology

the Church of South Africa.[76] But it is fair to say that the input of Evangelicals to mission was far more dynamic, driven as it was by their desire for conversions.

Rowan Strong remarks on the relative conservatism and caution of Scottish Episcopalians towards matters of outreach, particularly among the underprivileged at home, in the early decades of the nineteenth century. It was exemplified in a sermon by James Walker of Edinburgh, at the consecration of Daniel Sandford in 1806, specifically eschewing the desire to proselytise. Strong suggests that this was 'to be expected in a church that had newly raised its head from the trench of illegality [since] it was at pains to stress [its] political innocuousness'.[77] However, this study has shown that, in the first part of the nineteenth century, Scottish Evangelical Episcopalians were outstandingly active not only in foreign mission support but also in home evangelization. Strong goes on to suggest that, because the Scottish Episcopal Church began to develop a secure public infrastructure only at the start of the nineteenth century, it took time to build up sufficient funds and support to enable outreach.[78] However, St Thomas's, Edinburgh, indicates that the position was not quite as clear-cut. It was a small, independent body in 1842 with little support from outside and with only limited funds, and regarded as being in an illegal position by many. But, from the outset, it contributed large sums to foreign mission, set up its own urban mission in the Canongate, and worked and preached for conversions at home. Its example is indicative that Evangelical activism sprang from an overwhelming desire to pass on the doctrine of conversion which had been personally experienced by its adherents.

Crucicentrism

The crucifixion of Christ was central to Evangelical theology. Original sin, the cause of all suffering and death, required an appeasement. In the Old Testament the High Priest offered a sacrifice to God on the Day of Great Atonement for the sins, conscious and unconscious, of the nation of Israel. Evangelicals believed that, in the New Testament, Christ himself became the sin offering by his death on the cross. Christ, being sinless, was not bound by death but, on the cross, the guilt and subsequent punishment due to sinful humanity were imputed to him. Typically, in 1873 James McCann, formerly of St Jude's, Glasgow, preached 'it is to His death, His blood, His cross, that we are pointed as the means by which we are reconciled to

---

[76] Frederick Goldie, *A Short History of the Episcopal Church in Scotland* (Edinburgh, 1976), p. 93. Strong, *Episcopalianism*, p. 31.

[77] Strong, *Episcopalianism*, p. 153.

[78] *Ibid.*, pp. 154-165.

God'.[79] Moreover it was a unique, once-for-all event. As W. T. Turpin of St Silas's, Glasgow, explained in 1883 'it is a finished work for it can never, nor need ever, be repeated'.[80] Christ's death was the substitutionary, or vicarious, atonement for the sins of the whole world for all time. The sinner was made acceptable to God only through the cross.

This was strikingly different from the belief of the Nonjuring clergy in the Scottish Episcopal Church. They believed that Christ offered his body and blood under the symbols of bread and wine at the Last Supper, and commanded an offering of the elements thereafter at all eucharistic celebrations. As Bishop Alexander Jolly, of Moray, taught in 1829, Christ did not 'offer the sacrifice of Himself upon the cross...it was slain on the cross but it was offered at the institution of the eucharist'.[81] Again, even the more orthodox Alexander Ewing, Bishop of Argyll and the Isles, showed, in the 1860s, one of the most striking examples of the downgrading of the Evangelical doctrine of vicarious atonement. While holding standard Protestant views on justification by faith and many other doctrines, he seemed to react against the Evangelical understanding of the atonement believing that 'penal offering by another...must be thrown to the moles and the bats'.[82] Although by the 1880s some liberal Evangelicals like J. J. Lias of St Edward's, Cambridge, veered towards Christ's life as the focus of the atonement,[83] the traditional emphasis on the cross remained the dominant view as exemplified by the Scottish Evangelical Episcopalians discussed above.

Preaching the doctrine of the cross was a way of opening up the invitation to conversion. Edward Craig explained that 'the Lamb of God, the victim whose life-blood has been shed for sin, taketh away the sin of the world...it remains only for man to comply with the gracious terms of the message and by faith made one with Christ'.[84] Accordingly, as with the doctrine of conversion, Evangelicals applied their teaching on the cross in a very personal manner. D. T. K. Drummond was typical: 'Look at Him...dying for you... willing to give His life a ransom for many, that all who believe in Him might be saved.'[85] High Churchmen, believing that all who had been baptised were regenerate, tended towards a less intense

---

[79] James McCann, *Salvation* (Glasgow, 1873), p. 45.

[80] W. T. Turpin, *Gospel Papers* (London, 1883), p. 152.

[81] Quoted in D. T. K. Drummond, *Sketch of Episcopacy* (Edinburgh, 1844), pp. 143, 145. See Chapter 7 for the eucharistic beliefs of Nonjurors.

[82] A. J. Ross, *Memoir of Alexander Ewing* (London, 1877), pp. 318-319.

[83] J. J. Lias, *The Atonement Viewed in the Light of Certain Modern Difficulties: the Hulsean Lectures for 1883, 1884* (Cambridge, 1884), Lectures I, II. Quoted in, E. M. Culbertson, 'Evangelical Theology 1857-1900', (King's College, London, Ph. D. thesis, 1991), pp. 258-263.

[84] Edward Craig, *The Gospel Message Plainly Stated* (Edinburgh, 1830), p. 6.

[85] Drummond, *Rills*, p. 608.

personal recognition of Christ's atonement and criticised Evangelicals for a lack of awe on the subject. In 1837, *Stephen's Episcopal Magazine and Ecclesiastical Journal* commented, 'they speak with too much familiarity...of the atonement of our Saviour'.[86] For Evangelicals, however, Christ's suffering on the cross was personally felt. The three strands of the doctrine of the cross discussed here – its absolute centrality, its uniqueness in human history and the fervency with which it was preached – marked Evangelicals out from other Churchmen in the nineteenth century. They were typically cross-centred.

Biblicism

Nineteenth-century Evangelicals understood the Bible to be the inspired word of God. While the implications of inspiration varied over the century,[87] Evangelicals always believed that the Bible contained a clear revelation of the way of salvation as expressed in their particular doctrines of conversion and the cross. In 1819 Craig preached, 'that sacred and inspired record contains all that is necessary to salvation...the traditions and inventions of men can add nothing to its truths'.[88] With such beliefs, Craig and Drummond were both active in the 1830s in the Edinburgh Auxiliary of the Naval and Military Bible Society, set up to distribute Bibles among seamen,[89] and Drummond served on the committee of the National Bible Society of Scotland for several years.[90] Encouragement to read the Bible was a way of conveying the Evangelical message of conversion.

The Bible also opened the way for Evangelicals to obtain guidance and teaching for everyday life. In 1860, S. C. Baker preached that 'God has provided us with a treasury and storehouse of riches...for the wants of our minds, our souls, our hearts'.[91] In Evangelical households like the Drummonds', therefore, there was the twice-daily observance of family prayers and Bible reading which servants also attended.[92] Likewise, when St Thomas's, Edinburgh, was set up in 1842, it ran, each month, three different Bible classes for children of various ages and a fortnightly class for older people.[93] The Bible, for Evangelicals, was the primary means by which God spoke.

---

[86] *Stephen's Episcopal Magazine and Ecclesiastical Journal*, December, 1837.
[87] See Chapter 4 pp. 147-151.
[88] Craig, *Religious Instruction of the Poor*, p. 10.
[89] *Edinburgh Almanack*, (Edinburgh, 1835).
[90] *Memoir*, p. clxx.
[91] S. C. Baker, *Hope Founded on the Word* (London, 1860), p. 8.
[92] *Memoir*, pp. xiv, cxxi.
[93] *Ibid.*, p. liv.

Evangelicals did not consider that either age or lack of education prevented anyone from gaining help from the Bible; the Holy Spirit was believed to illuminate all minds. Children were thus encouraged to read the Bible for themselves. In Harriet Drummond's novel, *Lucy Seymour*, a father gave his nine-year-old daughter a Bible for her birthday, describing it as 'the best gift I can bestow on my child'.[94] Concerning education and the Bible, Drummond remarked in the 1830s that 'the poor illiterate man, guided by the Spirit of God, draws as much sweetness, refreshment and comfort from its everlasting truths as the true Christian philosopher can do'.[95] That the Scriptures were to be open to all classes in their entirety was evident in the enthusiasm with which Evangelicals distributed Bibles personally among the poor. In 1898, St Thomas's employed a Bible Woman, Mrs Main, not highly educated herself, to work in its mission among the poor in the Canongate.[96] The Gaelic Episcopal Society, set up in the 1830s to take the Scriptures to impoverished Gaelic speakers, recorded Craig and Drummond as committee members in 1837.[97] Similar concerns were shown later in the association of St Thomas's with the Scripture Readers' Society of Ireland and the Gaelic School Society.[98] Accordingly, Evangelicals denounced the Roman and Anglo-Catholic doctrine of 'Reserve' by which only partial teaching of scripture was conveyed to the uneducated and the young. Daniel Bagot of St James's, Edinburgh, was typical in 1836, proclaiming, 'we protest against the restriction of Scripture'.[99] Evangelicals believed that the whole Bible should be available to everyone.

While High Churchmen also upheld the supremacy of scripture, and showed similar concerns to Evangelicals, they looked to the early Fathers as arbiters on certain issues. In fact, however, it was not until the Tractarians began to elevate the Fathers, notably with John Keble's *Primitive Tradition Recognised in Holy Scripture* in 1836 and J. H. Newman's *Lectures on the Prophetical Office of the Church* in 1837, that Evangelicals became more inclined to the idea of disregarding them. Even then, however, Edward Bickersteth, of Watton, Hertfordshire, answering critics of the *Tracts* on patristic writings, maintained 'because they have been overvalued...we must not undervalue them...in assisting us to a fuller

---

[94] Harriet Drummond, *Lucy Seymour* (Edinburgh, 1847), p. 83.

[95] Drummond, *Last Scenes*, pp. 212-213.

[96] St Thomas's Minute Book, 6 April 1898 and 26 December 1899, St Thomas's Church, Edinburgh, Archives.

[97] *Stephen's Episcopal Magazine*, May 1837.

[98] *Memoir*, pp. cxxxiii, lv.

[99] Daniel Bagot, *A Protestant Catechism* (Edinburgh, 1836), p. 1.

understanding of the sacred volume'.[100] Evangelicals were not totally opposed to recourse to the early Fathers.

The information regarding the reaction of the Scottish Evangelicals to Tractarian teaching revolves around C. P. Miles's *The Voice of the Glorious Reformation*, written in 1844. For Miles, 'Holy Scripture is sufficient as a guide to salvation irrespective of traditions'.[101] He warned that human writings were likely to lead to 'pernicious consequences' and preferred receiving 'doctrinal views from the exclusive teaching of the Scriptures'.[102] In contrast, the Scottish Episcopal Church, in Canon XIII, recommended its clergy 'to apply diligently to the study not only of the Holy Scriptures but also to the writings of the ancient Fathers', a practice that the English Episcopalian, J. D. Miller of St Paul's, Aberdeen, regarded as representative of 'Popish super additions'.[103] After the impact of Tractarianism some English Episcopalians shunned patristic writings.

Thus for Drummond's daughter, Harriet, in 1871, the Bible was 'the Father's own loving gift to His little flock' and was, moreover, 'the only Light which, by God's Holy Spirit, can guide...through the dangers and trials of Earth'.[104] Adherence to its teaching as the exclusive rule of faith and practice was a cornerstone of Scottish Evangelical Episcopalian belief.

Wider Evangelical Theology

Incarnation Theology

Many High Churchmen were keen exponents of incarnation theology, examining the implications of Christ's assumed human nature as the means of atonement. Lancelot Andrewes, the sixteenth-century Bishop of Winchester, the Nonjuror, William Law, in the eighteenth century and the members of the early nineteenth-century Hackney Phalanx were notable examples.[105] The Tractarians developed the tradition. H. E. Manning

---

[100] P. B. Nockles, *The Oxford Movemen in Context* (Cambridge, 1994), pp. 106-107. Peter Toon, *Evangelical Theology, 1833-1856* (London, 1977), p. 30.

[101] C. P. Miles, *Voice of the Glorious Reformation* (London, 1844), p. 48.

[102] *Ibid.*, p. 412.

[103] [J. D. Miller], 'Justitia', *Peculiarities of the Scottish Episcopal Church* (Aberdeen, 1847), pp. 18-19.

[104] Harriet Drummond to the congregation of St Thomas's Church, Edinburgh, 1871, on the occasion of her marriage to C. T. Moor, DRO, D5550/3/3/4.

[105] Kenneth Hylson-Smith, *High Churchmanship in the Church of England* (Edinburgh, 1993), pp. 22, 92-93, 101-120. Although members of Hackney Phalanx, for example Charles Daubeny of North Bradley, Wiltshire, were often wary of Evangelical enthusiasm, many were deeply devotional, drawing on Nonjuring spirituality. *Ibid.*, pp. 105-106.

typically taught, in 1850, that 'the incarnation is the channel of [Christ's] influence, of His presence'.[106] By 1889 *Lux Mundi*, under the editorship of Charles Gore, principal of Pusey House, Oxford, examined modern intellectual and moral critiques of scripture in the light of Christ's humanity.[107] Incarnation theology was an established facet of Anglican High Church teaching.

However, many nineteenth-century Evangelicals tended to concentrate on the atonement and the need for conversion. In reaction to Tractarian teaching from the 1830s, with its greater emphasis on sacramental grace, this trend was sometimes magnified. It led the Quaker, John Bright, in mid-century to remark, 'The atonement, always the atonement! Have they nothing else to say?'[108] But some Evangelicals did recommend preaching on the incarnation as giving more depth to understanding the scope of Christ's work, while not detracting from atonement theology. It was a Romantic trend in some respects, bringing Christ into focus both as human and as God. Henry Budd, rector of White Roothing, Essex, in 1827, typically preached that Christ 'had a human nature, a local habitation: He lives, He feels, He acts, He thinks as we do, yet without sin'.[109] Edward Irving of the Church of Scotland went further. In 1828 he propounded that Christ was so much a man that he took on human sinful nature,[110] and although Irving maintained that the Holy Spirit kept Christ from sin, he was dismissed from his ministry for unsound views.[111]

Information concerning the teaching of Scottish Evangelical Episcopalians is not extensive. Around 1820, G. T. Noel's sermons can be compared with those of Edward Craig. Noel preached on the atonement, but urged that understanding about Christ's humanity opened the way to deeper faith: 'The mystery of the Gospel is this...the Godhead uniting itself to the nature of man, in order that the nature of man might be raised to the nature of God'.[112] Craig, by contrast, appeared more focused on atonement

---

[106] H. E. Manning, *Sermons III* (London, 1850), p. 164. Quoted in Geoffrey Rowell, *The Vision Glorious* (Oxford, 1983), p. 20.

[107] Smith, *High Churchmanship*, p. 186. See also B. F. Westcott, Bishop of Durham in: *The Incarnation: A Revelation of Human Duties* (London, 1892). *The Incarnation and Common Life* (London, 1893).

[108] A. J. Davidson (ed.), *The Autobiography of Samuel Davidson, D.D. LL.D.* (Edinburgh, 1899), p. 64. Quoted in Bebbington, *Evangelicalism*, p. 14.

[109] Henry Budd, *A Sermon Preached Before C. M. S. 30 April 1827* (London, 1827), p. 21. Quoted in Ervine, 'Doctrine and Diplomacy', p. 239.

[110] Edward Irving, *The Orthodox and Catholic Doctrine of Our Lord's Human Nature* (London, 1830), p. vii. Quoted in Bebbington, *Evangelicalism*, p. 93.

[111] Nigel M. de S. Cameron (ed.), *Dictionary of Scottish Church History and Theology* (Edinburgh, 1993), p. 436.

[112] G. T. Noel, *The Gospel: A Revelation of Mercy to the Guilty* (Edinburgh, 1818), p. 18. *Cf.* Ervine, 'Doctrine and Diplomacy', p. 238.

theology.¹¹³ However, in the late 1830s to early 1840s, D. T. K. Drummond's preaching revealed many examples of incarnational theology alongside teaching on the atonement. Having explained that Christ resolved to become 'our brother; bone of our bone...to tabernacle with man',¹¹⁴ he showed what this meant in everyday life. Referring to the gospel account of the Garden of Gethsemane, Drummond preached that Christ's 'human nature shrunk from suffering'. The full impact of the incarnation for Drummond was that Christ became formally identified with humanity and all its problems. On a practical level this meant that 'God does not expect his children to manifest no feeling, no shrinking from trial; nor does he require that they should, with callous stoicism, strive to steel the heart against the entrance of natural grief'. Rather, through Christ's example people could understand that their 'portion here is one of trial' although they could mirror Christ in '*wishing* the removal of the trial, but *preferring* the fulfilment of God's will'.¹¹⁵ In the 1850s Drummond included the idea of Christ experiencing 'the accumulated joy...as if it were his own, of all his ransomed children' when they came to authentic faith.¹¹⁶ Again, his later sermons showed that Christ 'alongside of us is entering into all our afflictions...he is feeling with us as well as for us'.¹¹⁷ Thus from the 1830s to the 1870s Drummond preached on incarnational themes.

W. J. C. Ervine suggests why some Evangelicals went beyond the subject of the atonement into incarnational theology. Wider reading of eighteenth-century divines such as William Law's *A Serious Call to a Devout and Holy Life* written in 1728 might have influenced them. Again, those who taught gradual, rather than sudden, conversion were likely to develop the less urgent incarnation themes.¹¹⁸ But these propositions are not entirely satisfactory. For example, there is no reason to suppose that Craig was less well read than others with whom he shared similar university training, and Drummond taught both types of conversion.¹¹⁹ On a practical level, it may be the case that incarnational theology was more widely preached than realised. While many existing sermons, such as Craig's, often focus on the atonement, this may be because clergy published them hoping to reach a wider audience with conversion theology, leaving

---

¹¹³ See Edward Craig, *Pastoral Addresses on Regeneration* (Edinburgh, 1823), *Religious Instruction of the Poor, Gospel Message Plainly Stated, Christian Circumspection* (Edinburgh, 1832).

¹¹⁴ Drummond, *Last Scenes*, p. 13.

¹¹⁵ *Ibid.*, p. 301.

¹¹⁶ D. T. K. Drummond, *The Engravings of the New Testament* (Edinburgh, 1855), p. 214.

¹¹⁷ *Memoir*, pp. clx-clxi.

¹¹⁸ Ervine, 'Doctrine and Diplomacy', pp. 238-241.

¹¹⁹ See Chapter 3, p. 118.

incarnational sermons for the weekly teaching of the committed in church. Again, it is likely that some clergy were drawn to the pastoral as well as the evangelistic side of ministry, while others would have classed themselves purely as evangelists. The former would have developed incarnational themes in order to help people with problems. J. H. Balfour, testifying to Drummond's pastoral gifts, remarked, 'he would gently lead the mourners to look at [Christ]...this had something to do with the remarkable way in which his ministrations were sought often in times of sorrow. Nor was his sympathy less in times of joy'.[120] Pastoral concern would have led clergy like Drummond to develop the wider teaching discussed here.

However, Drummond's incarnational preaching never superseded his teaching on the cross as the way of salvation. Whereas in 1884 the liberal Evangelical, J. J. Lias, vicar of St Edward's, Cambridge, leaned towards teaching that redemption came through Christ's spotless life, not his death,[121] Drummond declared in 1875, 'the gospel which I preached when I first came to Edinburgh, I preach still: Jesus Christ and him crucified'.[122] Drummond was typical of mainstream Evangelicalism.

Sanctification

Sanctification, the development of individual holiness, was another recurring theme of Anglican spirituality. High Churchmen of the late eighteenth and nineteenth centuries drew on the teaching of earlier divines such as Jeremy Taylor, Bishop of Down and Connor in the seventeenth century and Thomas Secker, the eighteenth-century Archbishop of Canterbury. Their religiosity was undemonstrative, aiming at a practical spirituality based on good works, nourished by sacramental grace and devotional reading. In Scotland, some Nonjuring clergy again encouraged their congregations in habits of personal meditation, study of sermons and the scrupulous use of time. Alexander Jolly, Bishop of Moray, was notable for his habit of constant prayer including sudden, short, public petitions for people and events.[123] The advent of the Oxford Movement in the 1830s breathed new life into orthodox High Churchmanship. While continuing to exalt the sacraments as the means of sanctification, the Tractarians vivified the process by an emphasis on intuition, mystery and beauty in worship.[124] An evolving aesthetic strain led them into self-denial and the settting up of

---

[120] *Memoir*, p. cxxvi.

[121] Culbertson, 'Evangelical Theology', pp. 258-259. For J. J. Lias see also p. 85, n. 82 above.

[122] *Memoir*, p. cxxx.

[123] Strong, *Episcopalianism*, pp. 56-58. William Walker, *The Life of the Right Reverend Alexander Jolly* (Edinburgh, 1878), pp. 51, 160.

[124] Bebbington, *Holiness*, pp. 7-28.

Theology

religious communities as a way of developing personal holiness. The establishment of the Community of St Mary the Virgin and St Modwenna, Dundee, by A. P. Forbes, Bishop of Brechin, in 1871, was an example of such concern.[125] But whether in this sphere or less cloistered settings, E. B. Pusey spoke for those High Churchmen who longed for 'a tingling closeness of God'.[126] Sanctification was valued by various strands of High Churchmanship.

Holiness was also a theme of the Calvinist tradition. The Puritans had advocated intense exercises of the soul as a means of growing close to Christ. Although in the early years of the nineteenth century a few Anglican hyper-Calvinists, like Robert Hawker of Plymouth, taught that believers were secure in a fixed state of eternal sanctification and refused to preach on the cultivation of a holy lifestyle, Charles Simeon, vicar of Holy Trinity, Cambridge, influenced by the eighteenth-century teaching of Jonathan Edwards in America, repudiated such ideas. He feared they left the way open to High Church antinomian accusations and, with similarly moderate but firm, Evangelicals like Edward Bickersteth in the 1820s, taught, instead, that the Holy Spirit, entering individual lives at conversion, gradually renewed human nature into the image of God, enabling the performance of good works.[127] It complemented, like incarnational theology, the rather stark statements of justification by faith alone. However, W. J. C. Ervine suggests that, in reaction to Tractarianism, Evangelical theology from the late 1830s ceased to emphasise sanctification teaching.[128] This section will trace the thought of some Scottish Evangelical Episcopalians on the topic.

The life-long nature of sanctification was emphasised by J. D. Hull in 1840, explaining that it was like 'needlework...a gradual, progressive accomplishment'.[129] Daniel Bagot wrote in 1839 that 'sanctification...commences when a sinner is converted and advances as he grows in grace and in the knowledge of Christ'.[130] As with justification, the believer could offer nothing of his own; Bagot continued that 'it is

---

[125] Nigel Yates, *Anglican Ritualism in Victorian Britain 1830-1910* (Oxford, 1999), pp. 136-137. The following communities in Scotland have been noted by Yates: Society of St Margaret, 1864, Aberdeen. Community of St Andrew, Edinburgh, 1864. The Scottish Society of Reparation, Perth and Cove, 1870. The Society of the Holy Cross, Aberdeen, Dundee, Edinburgh, 1872. *Ibid.*

[126] E. B. Pusey, *Parochial and Cathedral Sermons* (Oxford, 1882), pp. 476-477. Quoted in Rowell, *Vision Glorious*, p. 15.

[127] Bebbington, *Holiness*, pp. 29-33. Ervine, 'Doctrine and Diplomacy', p. 244.

[128] *Ibid.*, pp. 243-246.

[129] J. D. Hull, *The Church of God; A Book for the Age* (London, 1840), pp. 79-80.

[130] Daniel Bagot, *A Catechism Explanatory of the Leading Truths of the Gospel* (Edinburgh, 1839) p. 9.

throughout the work of God'.[131] This view of sanctification differed from Wesleyan teaching which taught that the believer could obtain perfect holiness through a crisis experience, usually subsequent to conversion, which, while it might be lost, could then be regained.[132] The ideas of progressive holiness, by contrast, were typical of Calvinistic Evangelicalism.

But Evangelicals recognised that a holy life-style could be neglected. D. T. K. Drummond, in 1841, while at Holy Trinity, Edinburgh, challenged his congregation 'What! The friends of God, and yet living in daily neglect of his commands, and opposition to his will?'[133] Thus holiness required nourishment. While upholding the communion service as a 'Feast of Good Things', Drummond and his wife taught, in contrast to sacramental High Church belief, that such blessing was not automatic but depended on the believer 'taking [Christ's] presence with him to the feast, not finding it in the bread and wine'.[134] To cultivate such closeness to God, stress was placed on Bible reading as a means of sanctification. Bagot, in 1839, wrote that 'Christians...are sanctified only in proportion as they are acquainted with the Word'.[135] S. C. Baker, in 1860, taught that the Bible 'alone forms our character after the mould of Jesus',[136] and Drummond, in 1841, highlighted that when such reading was 'applied inwardly and powerfully by the Spirit of God; – then Christ is formed within'.[137] Familiarity with the Bible aided sanctification.

Prayer was another means. In 1818 Edward Bickersteth emphasised the family union achieved when the believer approached God both as parent and king through Christ.[138] Similar teaching was evident among Scottish Evangelicals. In 1866 T. K. Talon preached 'Go as a little child unreservedly pours out its wants into the loving mother's willing ear...pour out your hearts to Him'.[139] In 1841 Drummond illustrated that prayer 'is the children with their elder brother, speaking to their heavenly Father...from such union the prayers of God's saints ascend up as incense...and God

---

[131] *Ibid.*, p. 10.

[132] This teaching was modified by James Caughey, the American revivalist, in the 1860s. He taught that there was no need to wait to be sanctified and that no confirming awareness of the event was required. A deliberate act of believing was enough to guarantee that holiness had come into a person's life. See Bebbington, *Holiness*, pp. 65-70.

[133] Drummond, *Last Scenes*, p. 167.

[134] Harriet Drummond, *The Upper Room Furnished: A Help to the Christian at the Lord's Supper* (Edinburgh, 1875), pp. v, ix.

[135] Bagot, *Catechism*, pp. 10-11.

[136] Baker, *Hope Founded*, p. 7.

[137] Drummond, *Last Scenes*, p. 276.

[138] Ervine, 'Doctrine and Diplomacy', p. 245.

[139] T. K. Talon, *Sermons* (London, 1866), p. 122.

bows down...graciously to bless'.[140] Some testified that embracing such teaching led to personal communion with Christ. Drummond's daughter, Harriet, wrote of the voice of Christ bringing her companionship, comfort, spiritual treasure, and peace in prayer. Her sister, Ellen, was aware of Christ's presence as a 'radiancy divine, filling the room of prayer'.[141] Edwin Wrenford wrote a poem in 1876 expressing that in prayer he heard 'Jesus full of tenderness as in the days of old'.[142] Drawing close to Christ in prayer in this manner resulted in becoming more like him. Hull, in 1834, urged 'oft on his glory gaze...till on our hearts his image be imprest'.[143] Drummond, in 1846, preached that 'prayer will give us the inward adorning of Christ'[144] and, in 1877, exhorted his congregation to pray 'if I could only get a little nearer...only get into that which is pure, lovely and of good report', assuring them that 'God gives his child everything he asks'.[145] Prayer, like Bible reading, was taught and experienced as a way in which God sanctified his people.

Ideas of progressive sanctification were sometimes supplanted in the 1870s with those of holiness resulting from a second, sudden spiritual experience after conversion when sin was repressed, rather than eradicated as in earlier Wesleyan teaching. This was the central teaching of the Pearsall Smiths from America who held meetings at Keswick in 1875, attended by large numbers of Evangelical Anglicans.[146] But there is no evidence that these views were taken up by the clergy discussed here. Neither does the group appear to have reacted against Tractarianism by ceasing to preach sanctification theology as indicated by Ervine. Its members were assiduous, throughout the century, in recommending the theme of a holy life-style attained through Bible reading and prayer.

Election

Although Calvinism and Arminianism are often presented as opposing Evangelical doctrines, it was only on a few points that they differed substantially. One of these was the Calvinistic teaching of limited atonement, the idea that God chose some people before the creation of the world to whom alone salvation was possible. It was understood by strict Calvinists to express the idea of God's sovereignty, that God had total

---

[140] Drummond, *Last Scenes*, p. 239.
[141] Drummond, *Rills*, pp. 265-267, 554-555. The poems were probably written in the 1850s.
[142] Edwin Wrenford, *Carminia Regia* (London, 1878), p. 245.
[143] *Christian Lady's Magazine*, July–December 1834, p. 273.
[144] *Memoir*, p. lii.
[145] *Memoir*, p. cxlvii.
[146] Bebbington, *Holiness*, p. 83. Bebbington, *Evangelicalism*, pp. 151-152.

control of the fate of mankind. Arminians believed, in contrast, that salvation was open to all and that any person could turn to God in faith.

Expression of such views differed in England and Scotland at the beginning of the nineteenth century. Anglican Evangelicals were only mildly Calvinistic. Their moderate temperament was typical of the Enlightenment era from which they had emerged with its stress on reason and non-extremism.[147] In tune with the early nineteenth-century mood, and despite a clear statement of election in Article XVII, Charles Simeon, of Holy Trinity, Cambridge, and G. S. Faber of Durham, both advocated the idea that Christ's death had been for all people, not just for the elect.[148] However, there were exceptions such as Robert Hawker of Plymouth who clung robustly to the old ideas of limited atonement.[149] By 1816 the pendulum had begun to swing in the direction of Hawker, initially under the influence of Robert Haldane, a Scottish Evangelical who eventually became a Baptist in 1808, and the Scottish born English banker, Henry Drummond. Both, speaking out against Socinian theology[150] in the Genevan Church, stimulated a resurgence of high Calvinism and the doctrine of election in Anglican Evangelicalism which reached a climax under the ministry of Henry Bulteel at St Ebbe's, Oxford, from 1826. Such ideas were aided by the growing culture of Romanticism in the late 1820s, with its desire to look to the past, by the uncertainty resulting from the French Revolution and the increasing Roman Catholic presence in Britain,[151] and by the pessimism of Evangelicals like Edward Irving and Hugh McNeile, the future Dean of Ripon, who remarked on the shallowness of Evangelicalism in the late 1820s.[152]

In Scotland the situation was different. The Scottish Episcopal Church was almost without exception made up of non-Calvinistic High Churchmen who upheld ideas of sacramental grace open to all, and who eschewed the doctrine of election.[153] In the Church of Scotland, however, there was a split between moderates and Evangelicals. Whereas most of the latter were loyal to a strict interpretation of the Calvinism of the Westminster

---

[147] Bebbington, *Evangelicalism*, pp. 50-59.

[148] Ervine, 'Doctrine and Diplomacy', pp. 234-235.

[149] *Ibid.*, pp. 32-33. Bebbington, *Evangelicalism*, pp. 63-64, 77.

[150] Socians were anti-Trinitarians, denying not only the deity of Christ but also predestination and original sin. They laid the foundation for the later Unitarian movement. Elwell, *Evangelical Dictionary of Theology*, p. 1031.

[151] Bebbington, *Evangelicalism*, pp. 77-78, 84. Ervine, 'Doctrine and Diplomacy', p. 282.

[152] Edward Irving, *Babylon and Infidelity Foredoomed* (Glasgow, 1828), p. 313. Hugh McNeile, *Sermon Preached Before the London Society for the Propagation of Christianity Among the Jews* (London, 1826), pp. 23-23. Quoted in Ervine, 'Doctrine and Diplomacy', pp. 278-288.

[153] See Chapter 1 p. 4.

Theology

Confession and predestination, the former often paid only lip service to it.[154] Many Anglican and Scottish Presbyterian Evangelicals thus tended to hold varying views on election in the early nineteenth century.

It is possible to set the early stance of some of the Scottish Evangelical Episcopalians against this background. They appear to have represented only moderate Calvinism in the years around 1820, uninfluenced by the ideas of Haldane, Henry Drummond and Evangelical Scottish Presbyterianism. In 1818, G. T. Noel preached that 'God willeth not the death of...one sinner',[155] and in 1819 Edward Craig pronounced that 'there is not a human being to whom the Gospel may come but he is warranted to make it...his own in all its riches'.[156] Noel and Craig did not represent high Calvinist views on election.

By the 1830s there was again a shift of opinion against high Calvinism. This was not so much a reaction against the Romanticism which had nurtured it in the 1820s, but rather a response to emerging theology concerning the unity of mankind in Christ.[157] The trend was established by the publication, in 1828, of *The Unconditional Freeness of the Gospel* by Thomas Erskine,[158] a Scottish Congregationalist and trustee of Edward Craig's church, St James's, Edinburgh. Erskine argued that God had pardoned, in Christ, the sins of the whole human race. Presbyterian churches, however, threw off the teaching of election only slowly, although isolated clergy became less rigid. For instance, in 1831, John Macleod Campbell, who had convinced Edward Irving of the new views in 1828,

---

[154] S. J. Brown, *Thomas Chalmers and the Godly Commonwealth* (Oxford, 1982), pp. 44, 47. Strict Calvinism was rejected by John Simson, Professor of Divinity, University of Glasgow, in 1714. Cameron, *Dictionary*, p. 775. Again, when Alexander Gillies was licensed by the Presbytery of Stranraer on 1 January 1766 he signed the Confession of Faith '*errobis exceptis*' and was accepted on this basis. Even the Marrowman James Hog, the Evangelical minister of Carnock, Fife (1699-1734) upheld universal redemption, in contrast to the other Marrow Brethren. *Ibid.*, p. 547. Thomas Chalmers, also, did not adhere strictly to the Calvinism of the Westminster Confession. His sermons emphasised non-election theology. Brown, *Chalmers*, p. 216. But opinion as to the extent of conformity to the doctrine of election is somewhat divided. A. L Drummond and James Bulloch claim that most moderates and many Evangelicals rejected it. See A. L. Drummond and James Bulloch, *The Scottish Church 1688-1843* (Edinburgh, 1973), p. 110. However, A. C. Cheyne in *The Transforming of the Kirk* (Edinburgh, 1983), p. 11 takes the opposite view positing that the doctrine was largely intact in 1800 and, although allowing that it was held sometimes reluctantly, maintains that adherence was more often eager and whole-hearted.

[155] Noel, *Revelation of Mercy*, p. 30.

[156] Craig, *Religious Instruction of the Poor*, p. 18.

[157] This teaching was to become well known through F. D. Maurice, the leading Broad Church theologian, in the 1850s. Bebbington, *Evangelicalism*, pp. 92-93.

[158] *Ibid.* Cameron, *Dictionary*, pp. 302-303.

was debarred by the Church of Scotland for upholding the doctrine of non-election.[159] Again, from 1841 to 1845, the Atonement Controversy rocked the United Secession Church, resulting in the expulsion of James Morrison and the investigation of Robert Balmer and John Brown for upholding unsound doctrine.[160] Similarly, dispute ensued in the Free Church in 1889 when A. B. Bruce rejected the Calvinist thesis.[161] It was not until the United Presbyterian Church produced its Declaratory Statement in 1878, followed by the Free Church in 1892 and the Church of Scotland in 1910 that allowance was made for a freer interpretation of the Confession.[162]

Scottish Evangelical Episcopalians by contrast continued in the mild Calvinistic mould of the majority of their Anglican counterparts. Craig preached in 1830 that 'the grace of Christ is free, full and accessible to all'.[163] Again, in 1841, D. T. K. Drummond offered a softened view of predestination, which at the same time attempted to preserve God's sovereignty. In dealing with the treachery of Judas Iscariot he touched on the problem of free will in the strict Calvinist system, stressing that Judas was 'not lost, *because* the scripture had foretold it, but because, having sold himself to work wickedness the omniscience of God descried this afar off'.[164] In Drummond's teaching God, as sovereign, knew in advance that Judas would betray Christ, not because Judas acted in a predetermined way but, rather, as the result of freedom of choice. Daniel Bagot's catechism of 1839 did not even mention election, and instead used several biblical references to concentrate on God's grace being the chosen means of general salvation.[165] In 1866, T. K. Talon preached that God's call was 'not to a special favoured class of mankind...Is it not to all men universally?'[166] Only C. P. Miles seemed to hold strict Calvinist views, remaining loyal to Article XVII.[167] In 1844 he wrote:

> There is predetermined a certain number of predestinate, which can neither be augmented nor diminished. Those who are not predestinated to salvation shall necessarily be damned for their sins.[168]

---

[159] Cameron, *Dictionary*, p. 129. Bebbington, *Evangelicalism*, pp. 92-93. For Edward Irving see p. 90 above.

[160] Cameron, *Dictionary*, pp. 43-44, 54-55, 100-101. Cheyne, *Transforming of the Kirk*, pp. 60-66.

[161] Cheyne, *Transforming of the Kirk*, p. 53.

[162] *Ibid.*, pp. 83-85.

[163] Craig, *Gospel Message Freely Stated*, p. 37.

[164] Drummond, *Last Scenes*, p. 251.

[165] Bagot, *Catechism*, p. 17.

[166] Talon, *Sermons*, p. 25.

[167] Miles, *Voice of Reformation*, pp. 516-517. Article XVII speaks of 'predestination to life' of those God 'hath chosen in Christ out of mankind'.

[168] *Ibid.*, p. 522.

Theology

However, Miles seems to have been unusual among Scottish Evangelical Episcopalians who were not, generally, predestinarian. The group was representative of mainstream, non-extreme Anglican views, uninfluenced by strict Scottish Presbyterianism.

Millenarianism

Nineteenth-century Evangelicals understood that the Bible, in Revelation 20, taught of a future state of happiness on earth when Satan would be bound and cast into a bottomless pit for one thousand years. At the end of that time he would be released for a short period of tribulation before the Final Judgement of humankind.

In connection with millenarianism, there were two views concerning the timing of Christ's return to earth, his second coming. Postmillennialists believed it would happen at the end of the millennium, while premillennialists placed it at the beginning. In the early nineteenth century, when most Evangelicals were optimistic that the world was improving and that, given more time, missionary work would show its fruits, postmillennialism held sway. However, the balance began to tilt to premillennialism by the 1820s for similar reasons to those surrounding the resurgence of high Calvinism.[169] Premillennialism was, typically, a product of a Romantic and uncertain age.

Early premillennialists such as William Cuninghame of Lainshaw, in 1813 understood that Christ's return would be metaphorical, not bodily, evident in an unusual outpouring of his power. However, in 1827, there was a turning point when Edward Irving, in *The Coming of Messiah in Glory and Majesty*, concluded that Christ would actually return in person. Those interested in Jewish mission, such as Lewis Way of the Anglican Jews' Society, noting the biblical connection between Christ's second coming and the conversion of the Jews, readily supported his beliefs. However, the majority of Anglican Evangelicals did not accept premillennialism in the 1830s and 1840s.[170] It was embraced more enthusiastically by the young who, willing to throw off the old Enlightenment ideas of confidence in progress, were influenced by the exciting ideas of Romanticism. But the ageing Charles Simeon of Holy Trinity, Cambridge, still held to the

---

[169] See Chapter 3, pp. 139-141.

[170] William Cuninghame of Lainshaw was a Scottish Presbyterian who later founded a Congregational church at Stewarton after his views on the universality of the atonement were criticised. He published a premillennialist view in *A Dissertation on the Seals and Trumpets of the Apocalypse*, (London, 1813) followed by similar writings through to the early 1840s. In 1815 James Hatley Frere argued similarly in *A Combined View of the Prophecies of Daniel, Esdras, and St John*. See Bebbington, *Evangelicalism*, pp. 82-84.

postmillennial view and spoke for the majority who feared that the new ideas detracted from the Evangelical message of 'Christ crucified'.[171] It was not until the mid 1850s that premillennialism, with a concentration on a personal second advent of Christ, became widespread among Anglican Evangelicals.[172] But even then there was a considerable number still adhering to the postmillennial view.[173] However, in Scottish Presbyterianism postmillennialism remained the dominant view although the Free Churchmen, Andrew and Horatius Bonar, in their *Quarterly Journal of Prophecy*, propagated premillennialism from the 1840s onwards.[174] Overall, then, premillennialism was more the province of Evangelical Anglicanism than of Scottish Presbyterianism.

Within premillennialism there were historicist and futurist views. Historicists believed that major contemporary events were clearly predicted in the Bible. The French Revolution in 1789, the cholera epidemics in 1832 and 1849 and revolutions in Europe in 1830 and 1848 were signs to them that Christ's second coming was imminent. Prior to this, however, historicists understood that the Bible predicted, in 2 Thessalonians 2-3, that sin and evil would continue to increase under the influence of the Antichrist, a satanically inspired person or organisation connected in some way with both the Church and a political power. Thus they held that it was vitally important for true believers to be uncontaminated, making a sacrificial stand if necessary.[175] Identification of the contemporary Antichrist became focused on the Roman Catholic Church and often on the Pope himself, leading to an upsurge of violent anti-Catholicism.[176] The historicists were the most numerous premillennialists within the Anglican Evangelical party by the 1850s, nourished by the Prophecy Investigation Society, under H. M. Villiers, at St George's, Bloomsbury, in London.[177] By 1836 they included Edward Bickersteth, regarded as a moderate but firm Evangelical, who became an outspoken critic of Roman Catholicism.[178]

---

[171] Ervine, 'Doctrine and Diplomacy', p. 282.

[172] *British and Foreign Evangelical Review,* vol. 4, no. 14 (1855), p. 698. Quoted in Bebbington, *Evangelicalism*, p. 85.

[173] G. R. Balleine, *A History of the Evangelical Party in the Church of England* (London, 1951). p. 165.

[174] Cameron, *Dictionary*, pp. 83-85, 563. David Brown, Principal of the Free Church College, Aberdeen, wrote *Christ's Second Coming: Will it be Premillennial?* (Edinburgh, 1846) as a polemic against premillennialism. *Ibid.*, pp. 97, 563.

[175] John Wolffe, *Evangelicals, Women and Community*, Open University Study Guide, (Milton Keynes, 1994), p. 37.

[176] See Chapter 6, pp. 183-193.

[177] Bebbington, *Evangelicalism*, p. 85.

[178] John Wolffe, *The Protestant Crusade in Great Britain 1829-1860* (Oxford, 1991), pp. 113-114. See also Chapter 4, p. 137.

Theology

Futurists, by contrast, believed that many more prophecies had to be fulfilled before Christ returned. Therefore, because they were not constrained by such a pressing time scale as historicists, they might be expected to have taken less of a stand on issues. But the position was not clear-cut. For instance, Hugh McNeile, a futurist, was an ardent evangelist, and an avid supporter of the anti-Catholic movement.[179] The futurist position was taken further by J. N. Darby of the Brethren who believed that the prophecies of Revelation would be fulfilled only after Christ had secretly removed the invisible church of true believers to the spiritual realm in a 'rapture'.[180]

The views of the Scottish Evangelicals in the first decades of the nineteenth century are not apparent, apart from those of G. T. Noel in 1828. He took a premillennial stance which led him to believe that Christ would 'return to earth to establish a visible and personal kingdom' before which the Jews would reclaim their own land and play a significant role in the new creation. From a study of Daniel 7 he concluded that Christ would return in the 1860s.[181] Edward Craig was pessimistic in the early 1830s over the gathering strength of Roman Catholicism in Britain, possibly indicating that he, too, held historicist views by that time,[182] but there is no proof.

J. D. Hull made a detailed analysis in 1840. Expounding Revelation 16 and other biblical passages from a historicist standpoint, he pointed to a myriad of signs of the time indicating that Christ's return was near: 'novel opinions in religion, worldliness, sensuality and abounding iniquity the almost universal revolutionary spirit abroad; the portentous movements in the East; the gradual decay of the Mohammedan empire; the signs in the heavens – hurricanes, eclipses, inclemency of seasons; plagues, fevers, earthquakes'.[183] By 1867 he warned that history had reached 'an epoch to which the lines of many prophecies converge' and predicted 'the Lord is coming out of His place'.[184] However, D. T. K. Drummond's premillennial views seem to have become concrete only in 1844 or 1845 when he read *Horae Apocalypticae*, a historicist and scholarly analysis in four volumes written by his friend E. B. Elliott, a fellow of Trinity College, Cambridge, which predicted that the millennium would start around 1866. Elliott testified that Drummond gave one of the first commendations for his work,

---

[179] *Ibid.*, p. 116. Balleine, *Evangelical Party*, pp.159-160. Chapter 6, p. 183-193.

[180] Bebbington, *Evangelicalism*, p. 86.

[181] G. T. Noel, *A Brief Inquiry into the Prospects of the Church of Christ in Connexion with the Second Advent of our Lord Jesus Christ* (London, 1828), pp. 34-35, 240-252. Ervine, 'Doctrine and Diplomacy', pp. 285-288.

[182] See Chapter 6 pp. 184-185.

[183] Hull, *Church of God*, pp. 192-195.

[184] Hull, *Cluster Crushed*, pp. 186-187.

telling him 'I now feel I possess the Apocalypse'.[185] Drummond, however, if he believed Elliott's prediction, did not seem to preach it openly. Although taking the premillennial view in 1855 that the Bible foretold the world would not become 'better...but every day more hostile to God', his prime concerns were to advise a 'quiet, steady waiting...for ye know neither the day nor the hour'. He drew attention to the joyousness and certainty of the event, quoting Christ's words from scripture, 'I will see you again, and your heart shall rejoice, and your joy no man taketh from you'.[186] As such it complemented his sanctification themes, preparing his congregation to meet with Christ. Thus premillennial ideas, taking hold among some Scottish Evangelical Episcopalians in the 1840s, predated the trend in mainstream Anglicanism.

By 1860 premillennialism was vindicated in a series of four sermons by H. J. Marshall, the incumbent of St Peter's, Montrose.[187] In 1878, John Bennett of St Jude's, Glasgow, after confidently assuring his readers that 'the Lord's return will precede the millennium',[188] like Hull suggested that the infidelity of the Church and the general unrest in the world heralded the millennium. But he was less certain as to its imminence and considered that it could be a lengthy process, the result 'of a long toil'.[189] His analysis shows an emphasis towards exploring the details of the millennial world – that it 'is not perfect...Evil is not wholly abolished. The millennium terminates in open apostasy', rather than looking to an exact date.[190] Among the laity, George Burns also held premillennial beliefs, possibly of the type held by Bennett. When he died, in 1890, he 'believed in a millennial glory, then a falling away and then the end...but not today or any present day'.[191] From the 1870s it appears that some Scottish Evangelicals, had become less certain of the imminence of Christ's return, and turned instead to scrutinising their Bibles to discover the characteristics of Christ's new kingdom.

Other aspects of premillennialism are evident in the writings of Hull, Drummond and Bennett. In 1840 Hull pinpointed the Pope as the Antichrist, 'the Beast of Revelation 17. 13'.[192] Drummond was similarly outspoken in 1852 referring to the succession of popes as the 'Antichrist who has so long had his seat on the seven hills'.[193] However, Bennett, in

---

[185] *The Rock*, 15 June 1877, p. 506.
[186] Drummond, *Engravings*, pp. 509, 510, 512, 521.
[187] *Montrose Review*, 3 February 1860. I thank D. W. Bebbington for this reference.
[188] John Bennett, *The Second Advent* (London, 1878), p. 38.
[189] *Ibid.*, pp. 20-34, 190.
[190] *Ibid.*, p. 151.
[191] Hodder, *George Burns*, p. 230.
[192] Hull, *Church of God*, p. 246.
[193] *Memoir*, p. lxxxiii.

Theology

1878, put forward the opinion that the threat of Roman Catholicism had been removed because of the success of the *Risorgimento* in 1870 and that 'giant pope may mutter at the passing pilgrim but he can hardly, from lack of power, not will, do more'. He looked for a new Antichrist, proposing a person possessing miraculous powers arising from Greece, Egypt, Syria or Turkey.[194] Whether Bennett's views were widely held is not clear. Possibly not, since many would have been alarmed when the Roman Catholic Church declared the Pope to be infallible in 1871, but Evangelical historicists clearly expected a personal Antichrist. Again, premillennialism encouraged evangelism. In 1867 Hull warned that 'all things indicate a speedy and universal restoration' and urged 'will you live on, regardless and apathetic, as though the petty trivialities of this life demanded a moment's attention?'[195] It was thus imperative that people should come to Christ before his personal return in order to ensure a place in heaven.

Thus Noel, Hull and Drummond represented an early adherence to premillennialism among Anglicans. Belief in an imminent, personal meeting with Christ possibly enhanced the exposition of sanctification theology by Evangelicals such as Drummond and Hull. Again, it would probably have made them careful to adhere to their understanding of doctrinal purity, and have given impetus to their stand against the Scottish Episcopal Church in the 1840s.

Inspiration of Scripture

Most early nineteenth-century Evangelicals believed that the different parts of the Bible were unequally inspired. In 1800 John Venn, of Clapham, distinguished between the prophetical books of the Bible as the totally reliable, exact words of God, and the historical books where God had simply superintended the writing, which accounted for some of the apparent inaccuracies. Henry Foster of Long Acre Chapel, London, was exceptional in the early nineteenth century in holding that the Bible contained the actual words of the Holy Spirit, that it was verbally inspired.[196]

Counter-reaction came in 1816, from Robert Haldane. After visiting Geneva, where ideas of interpreting scripture in the same way as poetry were popular, he pressed for uniform inspiration in his *Evidence and Authority of Divine Revelation*.[197] Such ideas gained further impetus in

---

[194] Bennett, *Second Advent*, pp. 75-76.
[195] Hull, *Cluster Crushed*, p. 187.
[196] Bebbington, *Evangelicalism*, p. 87. Ervine, 'Doctrine and Diplomacy', p. 144.
[197] Haldane's ideas became more widespread in response to the Apocrypha crisis which rocked the British and Foreign Bible Society in the 1820s. He and notable Evangelicals in Edinburgh and Glasgow criticised the society for distributing Bibles

1841 when Louis Gaussen, Professor of Theology at Geneva, in *Theopneustia*, argued for verbal inspiration and the inerrancy of the whole Bible. While saying that the actual mode of inspiration 'is unknown, and indifferent to me',[198] he suggested that God spoke through the biblical authors in a way whereby his words were theirs simultaneously. This was not divine dictation, but was a mingling of the Holy Spirit with the consciousness of the authors to produce a totally reliable text. Within it there would be figurative and poetic language, not to be taken literally, but the overall result was that the Bible was inerrant. The *Record* backed Gaussen in 1850, but at a meeting in 1861 the majority of Anglican Evangelicals retained the view that the Bible might contain inaccuracies on non-religious topics.[199] In the later 1860s, however, in response to the liberal theology of *Essays and Reviews*, there was a dogmatic reaction from many Anglican Evangelicals pushing for verbal inspiration and inerrancy. By the end of the century, J. C. Ryle, Bishop of Liverpool, represented most Evangelical Anglicans in declaring his belief in verbal inspiration although some, like Henry Wace, Principal of King's College, London, admitted there might be unimportant errors in the text.[200]

In Scottish Presbyterianism the pattern was different. A strong view of inspiration of the whole Bible held from an early date. In 1828, Marcus Dods, senior, the Church of Scotland incumbent of Belford, criticised the idea that 'civil and domestic' matters in the Bible were not inspired in the same way as moral and religious ideas.[201] By the 1840s William Cunningham, John Duncan and Alexander Black of the Free Church were committed to Gaussen.[202] However there were exceptions to the rule. In the 1840s George Hill, a Church of Scotland moderate, and John Dick of the United Secession Church did not regard the whole Bible as equally inspired, and the Congregationalist, Thomas Erskine, had rejected verbal infallibility before 1865.[203] When A. B. Davidson in the 1860s and William Robertson Smith in the late 1870s, both of the Free Church, took on ideas of biblical criticism, Marcus Dods, junior, and J. S. Candlish supported

---

containing the Apocrypha, viewing this as a contamination of scripture with uninspired writing. It is not clear whether Edward Craig was involved. Bebbington, *Evangelicalism*, pp. 86-88. Cameron, *Dictionary*, p. 19. The premillennialist literal interpretation of the personal second coming of Christ, and the belief that the prophecies in the Old Testament and Romans concerning the Jews could be taken literally, also hardened the trend towards verbal inspiration. Bebbington, *Evangelicalism*, pp. 88-89.

[198] *Record*, 24 October 1850.
[199] Bebbington, *Evangelicalism*, pp. 88-91.
[200] *Ibid.*, pp. 188-190.
[201] Quoted in Cheyne, *Transforming of the Kirk*, p. 6.
[202] *Ibid.*, pp. 8-9. A. L. Drummond and James Bulloch, *The Victorian Church in Scotland 1843-1874* (Edinburgh, 1975), p. 252.
[203] *Ibid.*, pp. 253-254.

Theology

them. But although Scottish Presbyterianism witnessed a swing against conservative views during the nineteenth century, many remained firm.[204]

Early opinions of the Evangelical Scottish Episcopalians are unclear, although Noel's literal interpretation of Jewish prophecies indicates an adherence to Haldane and infallibility in 1828. In 1819 Edward Craig appeared to preach the standard early nineteenth-century view that the Bible had 'the blessing and instruction of Him by whose inspiration it was written'.[205] By the late 1830s, D. T. K. Drummond was at pains to show that there were no inaccuracies in the text of John 20 concerning the numbers of angels recorded at the empty tomb of Christ and, in 1840, J. D. Hull preached that 'by [God's] inspiration all Scripture was given'.[206] But it is not totally clear whether Craig, Drummond and Hull reflected Haldane's position at this time.

However, after 1844, some Scottish Evangelical Episcopalians seem to have been clearly in line with Gaussen. In 1844, Robert Montgomery pronounced that 'all scripture is given by inspiration from God...not in general, but in the inspiration of scriptural words in particular'.[207] J. S. S. Robertson, in 1849, maintained that if any statement in the Bible seemed imperfect it was because of his own 'inability to grasp the fullness of meaning which the Holy Spirit hath imparted'.[208] Similarly, in 1857 Joshua Kirkman of St James's, Aberdeen, declared, 'there is a volume of books which holy men of God spake or wrote as they were moved by the Holy Ghost'.[209] By mid-century, and contrary to the general opinion among their English counterparts, Scottish Evangelical Episcopalians could number some who clearly held the inerrancy and verbal inspiration of scripture. They were similar to the bulk of Free Church theologians at this time, and unlike mainstream Evangelical Anglicans.

After the production of *Essays and Reviews* in 1860, the separatist English Episcopalians in Scotland held conservative views on inspiration. The layman, J. H. Balfour, wrote in 1866 that 'unless we have verbal inspiration we have nothing...[the Bible] not merely contains a revelation from God, but it is in its words and minutest details, even to the very plants, given by Him'.[210] Similarly, in 1865, Drummond was confident that the Bible was 'not partially but fully inspired...from the first verse of Genesis to the last of Revelation'.[211] T. K. Talon, taking issue, in 1866, with

---

[204] Cheyne, *Transforming of Kirk*, pp. 37-60.
[205] Craig, *Religious Instruction of the Poor*, p. 11.
[206] Drummond, *Last Scenes*, pp. 374-379. Hull *Church of God*, p. 224.
[207] Montgomery, *Gospel Before the Age*, p. 6.
[208] Robertson, *Philippians*, pp. 117-118.
[209] Joshua Kirkman, *The Scriptures the only Rule of Faith* (Aberdeen, 1857), p. 8.
[210] J. H. Balfour, *The Plants of the Bible* (London, 1866), pp. 187-188.
[211] *Memoir*, pp. lxx-lxxi.

Rowland Williams who had posited in *The Pentateuch Critically Examined* that Exodus was not historically true, argued instead that, since Christ had testified to the veracity of the Old Testament, it must be totally reliable.[212] By 1900 W. L. Holland, of St Thomas's, Edinburgh, proclaimed that God had used writers of the Bible 'as passive instruments in His hands'.[213] From the 1860s, like most of their Anglican counterparts, these Evangelicals were strong upholders of verbal inspiration.

The doctrine of eternal punishment in hell was an area of interpretation examined in *Essays and Reviews*. When H. B. Wilson, one of its contributors, argued against its morality, he suggested, instead, that there might be some sort of remedial process after death enabling people to have a second chance.[214] Evangelicals along with High Churchmen in Scotland condemned the proposition. In 1866 Talon maintained that hell was 'eternity...in endless doom...for ever fixed',[215] and W. J. Trower, the former Bishop of Argyll and the Isles, encouraged A. P. Forbes, Bishop of Brechin, to write a critique of *Essays and Reviews*.[216] The issue came to a head for Evangelicals in 1867 when T. R. Birks, the honorary secretary of the Evangelical Alliance, propounded, in his *Victory of Divine Goodness*, a view of Mark 14.21 whereby the wicked would be punished in hell everlastingly but enjoy, also, the passive contemplation of God's goodness.[217] Drummond and Balfour, together with the Free Churchman R. S. Candlish, resigned from the Alliance, protesting that Birks had propagated unscriptural views.[218] While not necessarily believing a literal interpretation of physical torture in hell they, nevertheless, represented a strong conservative stance on verbal inspiration.

Emerging scientific theories also challenged verbal inspiration. Concerning Charles Darwin's evolutionary claims, Drummond, a member of the Royal Society of Edinburgh and an amateur geologist,[219] certainly remarked in 1865 that there were 'difficulties of interpretation' in the Bible. However, he was totally wedded to its inerrancy, putting the problem down to 'ignorance in us', and was convinced that scripture would 'eventually be found to be in harmony with all that is true in Philosophy, History and Science'.[220] Similarly, in 1878, Daniel Bagot was confident that the

---

[212] Talon, *Sermons*, p. 255.

[213] W. L. Holland, *Bunyan's Sabbatic Blunders* (London, 1900), p. 121.

[214] Geoffrey Rowell, *Hell and the Victorians* (Oxford, 1874), pp. 116-117.

[215] Talon, *Sermons*, p. 317.

[216] Strong, *Alexander Forbes*, pp. 116-117.

[217] Rowell, *Hell*, pp. 123-129. Culbertson, 'Evangelical Theology 1857-1900', p. 138.

[218] *Record*, 30 May 1870.

[219] *Memoir*, p. cxix.

[220] *Ibid.*, pp. lxx-lxxi.

Theology

'discoveries of geology will ultimately be found to correspond with the statements of Genesis'.[221] T. H. Huxley's claim that everything was determined by physical consequences and that man 'is nothing but matter', was combated by James McCann. In a paper delivered to the British Association for the Advancement of Science in 1869 McCann put forward a philosophical argument calling for the recognition of the human spirit which could not have evolved from material substances.[222] While not adding to the debate on the inspiration of scripture directly McCann, who was a member of the Victoria Institute, a Doctor of Divinity, and a Fellow of the Geological Society, gave an academic contribution upholding the biblical account of the human soul. The reaction to new scientific knowledge was, in the case of Drummond, Bagot and McCann, to defend the inerrancy of the Bible.

Conclusion

Unavailability of writings has made it impossible to trace the beliefs of all the nineteenth-century Episcopal Evangelicals in Scotland, but those identified here were strong advocates of the core Evangelical theology of conversionism, activism, crucicentrism and biblicism. Like most Evangelical Anglicans, they were Calvinistic, stressing the sovereignty of God in the process of redemption, that man could do nothing to earn his own salvation, and that justification was by faith alone. Their experience of assured faith gave confidence that, even if they made mistakes, God would never relinquish them and possibly this reinforced the decision of the English Episcopalians to leave the Scottish Episcopal Church after 1842.

Wider theology was subject to various influences. There were affinities with High Churchmen and Tractarians among those who taught incarnational and sanctification themes. But the centrality of the cross as the means of salvation was not downgraded. Most were typically Anglican in eschewing election. Romanticism contributed to their historicist premillennialism, which was evident earlier than among many Anglican Evangelicals possibly due to the influence of Noel and, in the case of Drummond, to Elliot. Early adherence to biblical inerrancy and verbal inspiration in the 1840s showed an affinity with Scottish Presbyterianism. The group exhibited a typically strong backlash against liberal views surrounding *Essays and Reviews* and emerging scientific knowledge in the 1860s. Overall, we may conclude that the theology of the group was representative of mainstream Anglican Evangelicalism, together with some Scottish Presbyterin influences.

---

[221] Daniel Bagot, *The Inspiration of Holy Scripture* (London, 1878), p. 55.

[222] James McCann, *Anti-Darwinism* (Glasgow, 1869), pp. 10-11.

Chapter 5

Lifestyle

Evangelical doctrine, centred on the need for a conversion experience when individuals came to know Christ in a new and personal way, was held to lead to transformed lives and values. Whether based on a gradual or more dramatic event, such belief was expected to impact upon conduct, social concern and leisure activities, imbuing them with the particular character and values of new spiritual life. Most Evangelicals pointed to good works and self-denial as evidence of true faith. In 1832 at St James's, Edinburgh, Edward Craig preached that 'your habits of dress and household decoration and expenditure [should] be rather below than above the usual standards'.[1] J. D. Hull, future incumbent of Huntly, in 1834, warned that 'several of my friends, making a high, and I cannot doubt, a sincere profession of vital godliness, come rolling in carriages to the church-door, from distances too short to excuse it'.[2] High Churchmen often exhorted similarly. G. H. Wilkinson, Bishop of St Andrews, Dunkeld and Dunblane in 1893, had recommended his hearers to 'sell that diamond cross which you carry with you into the sin-polluted atmosphere of the Opera, and give the proceeds to feed the poor'.[3] A. P. Forbes, Bishop of Brechin from 1847 to 1875, gave much of his money to the destitute, along with supplies of food and wine.[4] Lifestyle and faith were inextricably linked.

However, as in areas of theology, individuals engaged with culture in different ways. For instance, what was family practice for one household would not necessarily have been so in others, and so it is impossible to make blanket conclusions concerning the manner in which Churchmen conducted their daily lives. In particular, the lifestyle of some nineteenth-century Evangelicals has come under criticism. They were accused of hypocrisy by commentators of their own time, such as Dickens when writing, for example, of Chadband in *Bleak House*, and modern historians have concluded that some Evangelicals were negative and life-denying, rather than life-affirming.[5] In terms of learning and aestheticism

---

[1] Craig, *Christian Circumspection*, p. 60.
[2] *Christian Lady's Magazine*, July-December 1834, p. 452.
[3] Quoted in Marion Lochhead, *Episcopal Scotland in the Nineteenth Century* (London, 1966), p. 231.
[4] *Ibid.*, p. 114.
[5] Ian Bradley, *The Call to Seriousness* (London, 1976), p. 28. D. M. Rosman, *Evangelicals and Culture*, (London, 1984), p. 79.

Evangelicals have been described as barren, a sentiment epitomised in 1905 by the scathing comment of A. V. Dicey, Vinerian Professor of English at Oxford, that the High Church movement 'was a revolt against [Evangelical] under-estimate of taste'.[6] This chapter will explore some standards and concerns within Evangelical Episcopalianism in nineteenth-century Scotland. The evidence is not extensive, and centres mainly on D. T. K. Drummond, the incumbent of St Thomas's, Edinburgh, from 1842 to 1875. But given that he was the acknowledged leader of the substantial group of English Episcopalians, it is informative to understand the way in which his religious beliefs influenced his daily life and wider interests. A further limitation in this study is that it is centred on upper- and middle-class people alone. There is no data for working-class Evangelical Episcopalians, and so the picture presented is incomplete.

Femininity and Masculinity

The conventional role of women in the nineteenth century was one of deference to men. Both in working-class circles, where women were employed in paid jobs, and in other strata of society, economic independence was lost on marriage when all property and earnings were transferred to the husband. This, together with lack of enfranchisement, led to a society where male dominance was a marked feature. Within Evangelicalism, endorsement for such a role could be found in the Bible. The creation of Eve as a companion for Adam, the subsequent part she played in the fall of humankind and the apostle Paul's teaching in Corinthians 14 that women should be submissive in daily life and keep silent in church, were understood to give a biblical model of women as subordinate helpmeets for men. Therefore, while many Evangelical women engaged in writing, teaching, philanthropic work and, if within a clerical family, assisting clergymen behind the scenes, the centre of female activity was the home. Whether as single women, wives, or mothers, they contributed to society by helping to create a community based on the values of family life which they believed the Bible to inculcate. But subordination did not necessarily mean inferiority because Evangelicals also held that the Bible placed men and women as spiritual equals before God. However, although Evangelicals did not regard women as necessarily of less importance than men, they understood that their sphere of influence and action was, nonetheless, quite different.[7]

---

[6] A. V. Dicey, *Lectures on the Relation between Law and Public Opinion in England* (1905), p. 404, quoted in Rosman, *Evangelicals and Culture*, p. 4. See Rosman, *Evangelicals and Culture*, pp. 1-7 for other examples of criticism of Evangelicals.

[7] Leonore Davidoff and Catherine Hall, 'Ye are all one in Christ Jesus', *Family Fortunes: Men and Women of the English Middle Class 1780-1850* (London, 1987), pp.

Lifestyle 155

At the same time, Evangelicals believed the Bible to teach that men had an important role in ensuring that good order prevailed in the family circle. They were to provide a model of leadership and authority which would support the efforts of women. But, adhering to such texts as Colossians 3, Evangelicals often emphasised that this was to be performed with gentleness and sensitivity, attributes normally associated with women in the nineteenth century.[8] Thus Evangelicals not only highlighted the differences between men and women, but they also pointed to their similarities. While Evangelical women had prescribed roles of authority within the private family sphere, men took on the more public duties but, at the same time, were encouraged to be less hearty and aggressive than the traditional male. Such beliefs were the result of a particular understanding of the Bible, and reflected the general tenet of Evangelicalism that all truth was to be found in its pages.

There was more flexibility for aristocratic women. Elisabeth Brodie, the Duchess of Gordon, with her husband, provided the funds to build the Episcopal church and infant school at Fochabers in 1834. Since the Duke was a member of the Church of Scotland, the Duchess was left in sole control of affairs. She imbued the congregation with her Evangelicalism over the next ten years, up to the time when she joined the Free Church, by appointing clergy of only her own party and opposing the use of the Scottish Communion Office.[9] At the highest levels of society, Evangelical women could wield considerable ecclesiastical power.

Upper- and middle-class Evangelical Episcopalians in nineteenth-century Scotland shed interesting light on the role of women. While Drummond was responsible for the 'serious realities of life with which a minister must be conversant',[10] his wife, Harriet, like other married women and a host of spinsters, took a subordinate role in assisting him 'in all pastoral and charitable duties'.[11] The production of goods to be sold for missionary funds was a particular province of women. At St Thomas's, Edinburgh, in December 1875, 'Miss Simpson, Fanny Holmes and Lady Scott' sent 'beautifully worked things all done at home', to be sold as a contribution towards outreach,[12] and the women's sewing circle at St Thomas's raised

---

114-118. F. K. Prochaska, *Women and Philanthropy in Nineteenth-century England* (Oxford, 1980), pp. 3-4.

[8] Davidoff and Hall, 'All one in Christ Jesus', pp. 108-113. Colossians 3 emphasizes loving relationships.

[9] See Chapter 9, pp. 298-299.

[10] D. T. K. Drummond to Harriet Drummond, 30 May 1831, *Memoir*, p. clxxxix.

[11] D. T. K. Drummond to Harriet Drummond, 30 May 1830, *Memoir*, p. clxxxvii. For examples of charitable work involving Evangelical Episcopalian women in Scotland, see Chapter 5, pp. 162-168, and also Chapter 3.

[12] D. T. K. Drummond to Harriet Moor, 19 December 1875, DRO, D5550/3/3/5.

money for its Canongate Mission among the poor of Edinburgh.[13] Again, individual women were often the prime fund-raisers and collectors of money for religious societies as shown by the records of the Church Missionary Society for Scotland.[14] But separation of roles did not necessarily mean that women had no interest in more public matters of doctrine, or that their husbands failed to value their opinions. In 1850, while away from Edinburgh, Harriet Drummond wrote to her husband concerning the Gorham baptismal crisis in the Church of England.[15] As a result of what she considered to be an inevitable split 'when all the Evangelical clergy will be driven out of the Church of England by the authoritative declaration that baptismal regeneration is the doctrine of the Church', she questioned Drummond's desire for an official link between the English Episcopalians and the Anglican community.[16] Working in a subordinate role in church did not mean that women had no input or interest in discussions and decision-making, albeit normally behind the scenes.

In the public arena, Harriet Drummond was able, like many other Evangelical women, to establish herself as a well regarded writer of children's books, an occupation which was generally acceptable because it did not usurp the preaching activities of men. From 1847 to 1870 she wrote five such novels, some of which were republished two or three times, with *Emily Vernon* also seeing print in America in 1855. Reviews in the *British Mothers' Magazine*, the *Commonwealth*, the *Christian Times*, the *Evangelical Magazine*, and the *Bible Class Magazine* all applauded them for their high literary standard and beneficial sentiments.[17] But whereas many women confined themselves to this genre, along with poetry and hymn writing, Harriet branched out into more controversial fields. Although she contributed devotional books such as *The Christian Anchor* in 1851, her subsequent production, *The Upper Room Furnished; or a Help to the Christian at the Lord's Table*, published in 1853 and 1875, had the intention of directing thought away from a high sacramental understanding

---

[13] See Chapter 3, p. 89-90.

[14] For an example, see *Proceedings of the Church Missionary Society for Africa and the East* (London, 1842), ANXLIII.

[15] See Chapter 6, pp. 204-204.

[16] Harriet Drummond to D. T. K. Drummond, 1850, DRO, D5550/3/5/26.

[17] End Plate in D. T. K. Drummond, *The Engravings of the New Testament or the Parabolic Teaching of Christ* (Edinburgh, 1855). Harriet Drummond's books for children are: *Lucy Seymour: or, It is more Blessed to Give than to Receive* (Edinburgh, 1847, 1849. London, 1870). *Wilmot Family: or, 'They that Deal Truly are His delight'* (Edinburgh, 1848. London, 1870). *Emily Vernon, or, Filial Piety Exemplified* (Edinburgh, 1855. New York, 1855). *Glen Isla, or, 'The Good and Joyful Thing'* (London, 1870). *Louisa Morton, or, Children Obey your Parents in All Things* (London, 1871).

of the service for Holy Communion.[18] Coming, as the books did, at times of intense controversy between English and Scottish Episcopalians on the doctrine of the communion service, they represented a public declaration of her opinions. Drummond's endorsement of the book in his prefatory remarks, while no doubt illustrative of his gratitude for her support, indicated the degree of value he placed on the role of informed women in church life. Indeed, Harriet herself testified in 1877 that he had sought her advice on many matters and 'never seemed happy in any difficulty or perplexity unless my judgement coincided with his own',[19] and Drummond referred to her as his 'true yokefellow' in the ministry.[20] While appreciating his wife's accepted womanly attributes of 'loving sympathy, tender thoughtfulness, and gentle firmness', Drummond also sought her 'wise counsel'.[21] The Drummond marriage therefore not only exemplified what was understood by Evangelicals to be the biblical model of separate spheres of ministry, but also showed that there was freedom within this relationship for Harriet to express her own views and exert a degree of influence publicly as well as privately.

Additionally, the Drummond family shows that women were not necessarily excluded from scientific and other pursuits which might be expected to have been the province of men. While Drummond's view of femininity included sending a present of 'collar and cuffs', chosen by himself, to his daughter, Harriet Moor, on her thirty-third birthday,[22] he also wrote to her, when she was on the point of giving birth to her first child in August 1875, concerning 'a large slab of rock having the distinct marks of the flow of a glacier' which he had photographed for the Royal Society of Edinburgh.[23] Harriet Moor's education, pursued at home under the direction of her parents and governesses, was described as 'rich, varied and refined', by the *Strathearn Herald* on the occasion of her marriage in 1871.[24] Her private papers reveal that, at the age of sixteen she was able to translate several poems, such as *Der Erle-König*, from German[25] which, together with her mother's description of teaching girls French, Italian, drawing, bookkeeping, sewing and 'fancy-work',[26] indicates that some Evangelical women were quite widely educated.

---

[18] Harriet Drummond, *The Upper Room Furnished, or, a Help to the Christian at the Lord's Table* (Edinburgh, 1875), pp v-vi. See also, Chapter 7.

[19] *Memoir*, p. cxx.

[20] D. T. K. Drummond to Harriet Drummond, 30 May 1870, *Memoir*, p. cci.

[21] *Ibid.*, p. ccii.

[22] D. T. K. Drummond to Harriet Moor, 19 December 1873, DRO, D5550/3/3/5.

[23] D. T. K. Drummond to Harriet Moor, 28 August 1875, DRO, D5550/3/4/9.

[24] *Strathearn Herald*, 14 October 1871, p. 3.

[25] DRO, D5550/3/3.

[26] Harriet Drummond, *Emily Vernon*, p. 113.

However, running the home was the focus of female attention. Drummond himself valued the task in the biblical terms of beginning 'there to build the temple of Christ'.[27] While child rearing will be dealt with later in this chapter,[28] there were many other domestic duties which were understood to be endorsed by scripture. Harriet Drummond regarded 'supineness, indolence and carelessness' as incompatible with the demands laid down in the Bible for a disciplined life.[29] Accordingly she recommended women to make clothes for 'the whole family', seeing this as 'good, plain, useful work' and, although she had servants, did not 'think there is anything very shocking in a lady making a pie or a pudding'.[30] Supervision of domestic staff required the exercise of both authority and understanding if biblical standards of compassion and care were to be recognised. The complexities of such work were evident in a letter from Harriet to her daughter, Harriet Moor, who had dismissed a maid for reading her private letters. While admitting that the girl had 'provoked' her daughter, Harriet reminded her that 'you know I wanted you to give her a warning long ago' and regretted 'the way it has been done at last as it appears hard, and so much against her prospects'.[31] Evangelical women believed that useful daily work in the home, Christian compassion and the maintenance of professional standards in dealings with staff were based on biblical principles.

Nonetheless, domestic roles could sometimes be reversed. On the event of the birth of his grandchild in 1875, Drummond was responsible for buying baby clothes since his wife was suffering the ravages of varicose veins. In a letter to his daughter he displayed an understanding of such matters which modern commentators do not usually associate with nineteenth-century men: 'I have done what I can about the cape for the *wee wee*, but there is nothing of a light, lace, fly away character'. Instead Drummond chose 'a nice white cloak'. Although he was obviously not totally conversant with the task, advising his daughter that, if his choice was 'not according to good taste and manners – just stick a label upon it, and say *grandfather's mistake*',[32] the incident does reveal that, among some Evangelical Episcopalians, there could be an overlapping of the roles of men and women in the domestic sphere.

Polite behaviour within marriage was also based on biblical tenets. J. D. Hull, chaplain to the Duchess of Gordon in 1840, used Psalm 45 to recommend a code of conduct between spouses. He advised the biblical

---

[27] *Memoir*, p. cliv.
[28] See Chapter 5, pp. 159-164.
[29] Harriet Drummond, *Louisa Morton*, p. 5.
[30] Harriet Drummond, *Emily Vernon*, pp. 157, 159.
[31] Harriet Drummond to Harriet Moor, 26 September 1875, DRO, D5550/3/4/8.
[32] D. T. K. Drummond to Harriet Moor, Edinburgh 1875, DRO, D5550/3/4/8.

Lifestyle

model: 'never speak when angry...endeavour to be...pitiful and courteous, having compassion on one another...frequently pray together'.[33] Romantic love was also often expressed in scriptural terms. For Drummond it was a reflection of 'the more wondrous love...between Christ and the Lamb's wife'.[34] But such biblical expression did not hamper a very warm relationship between the Drummonds which was to endure throughout the fifty years of their marriage. When newly wed, Drummond gave his wife the title 'my Queen of May' on her birthday, sealing his love with a crown of fresh flowers. The name remained and in old age Drummond continually referred to Harriet as 'my own darling wife' or 'my precious one', and delighted 'that our love has always been coming and never going'.[35] Harriet responded in like manner. Aged fifty, and away from Edinburgh tending her sick mother in Essex, she was excited to know that Drummond would soon be joining her. Writing to 'my own darling', she confided to him that 'my heart goes pit a pat...when I think that I may hope to see you so soon', and she assured him of the joy which would result from 'seeing your own dearly loved face'.[36] Again, George Burns, of Wemyss Chapel, testified to 'sixty years of fervent love' during his marriage to Jeannie Cleland.[37] Although some Evangelical marriages were depicted in nineteenth-century literature as formal and unloving, with romantic love sublimated in religious language and emotion,[38] in reality others were the opposite.

The study of masculine and feminine roles among Evangelical Episcopalians in Scotland shows that beliefs in these matters were based on a particular understanding of the Bible. Although women were subordinate, their role was not necessarily regarded as less valuable than that of men, and there was flexibility of action within the separate spheres. In marriage human love was often expressed in spiritual terms, but there is also evidence that affection and romance were not inhibited.

Children

The desire among Evangelicals for the conversion of their children to their own brand of Christianity and to see its fruition was of paramount

---

[33] J. D. Hull, *The Church of God. A Book for the Age* (London, 1840), pp. 43-44.

[34] D. T. K. Drummond to Harriet Drummond, 30 May 1870, *Memoir*, p. cci.

[35] D. T. K. Drummond to Harriet Drummond. 30 May 1870, *Memoir*, p. cci. 'Birthday Letters', *passim, Memoir*, pp. clxxxviii-ccv.

[36] Harriet Drummond to D. T. K. Drummond, 1850, DRO, D5550/3/5/26.

[37] Edwin Hodder, *Sir George Burns Bart: His Times and Friends* (London, 1892), p. 317.

[38] St John in Charlotte Brontë's *Jane Eyre* is an example. See also, Pat Jalland and John Hooper (eds.) *Women from Birth to Death: the Female Life Cycle in Britain, 1830-1914* (Brighton, 1986), pp. 121-131, for discussion of female ignorance of pregnancy and sex in the nineteenth century which contributed to such problems.

importance, particularly for those holding premillennial views and an interpretation of hell as a place of everlasting punishment.[39] Ian Bradley points to some parents subjecting their children to lurid descriptions of their fate if they did not turn to God, and to the sadistic sufferings sometimes inflicted in an attempt to inculcate a disciplined and self-sacrificing lifestyle.[40] Ford K. Brown highlights that the message conveyed in some children's literature had the 'explicit end of terrifying with the threats of a vengeful God'.[41] There is thus some evidence pointing to Evangelicals using extreme methods in an attempt to procure the conversion of children, and this does not marry well with Churchmen professing a personal relationship with God and cultivating a sanctified lifestyle.

In dealing with Episcopal Evangelicals in Scotland in the nineteenth century, there is only limited information. Based as it is on upper- and middle-class people, it has little bearing on the conduct of poor working-class families where children often had to labour and where living conditions were difficult. Additionally, all the data is supplied by adults who might have presented rather idealised accounts of their formative years. However, the material is a valuable palliative to the more horrendous examples of Evangelical behaviour uncovered by some historians.

There is no doubt that the Episcopal Evangelicals in Scotland were assiduous in seeking the conversion of their children. W. E. Gladstone's mother, Anne,[42] is reported to have taught her children the daily habit of self-scrutiny in order to expose sins, both open and hidden, and to seek God's forgiveness. She encouraged them to write accounts of deathbed scenes with the purpose of implanting in them a sense of the importance of entering the afterlife in a fit spiritual state.[43] Montague Stanley, a renowned actor who had given up the stage when he was converted, joined St Thomas's, Edinburgh, in the 1840s. He was particularly forthright in 1844 when writing to his eldest son, Mont. While referring to him as 'my own little boy', he warned in vivid terms 'if you do not love the Lord your God...you will be in misery hereafter in the place where all the wicked go – where there is wailing and gnashing of teeth'.[44] D. T. K. Drummond, in less severe but equally watchful tones, wrote to his wife in 1853 concerning their daughters, aged twenty-two and thirteen, that he was 'encouraged on the whole regarding our beloved children. Much yet to be done...but there

---

[39] See Chapter 4, pp. 143-147, 150-150.

[40] Bradley, *Call to Seriousness*, pp. 186-189.

[41] Ford K. Brown, *Fathers of the Victorians* (Cambridge, 1961), pp. 462-467.

[42] See Chapter 1, p. 23.

[43] S. G. Checkland, *The Gladstones. A Family Biography 1764-1851* (Cambridge, 1971), p. 85.

[44] D. T. K. Drummond, *Memoir of Montague Stanley A. R. S. A.* (Edinburgh, 1848), p. 73.

Lifestyle 161

are some indications of hearts being touched'.[45] The desire of Scottish Evangelical Episcopalians to see the gospel message received by their children was typically intense.

But such activity did not necessarily mean that parents were harsh towards their offspring. As in the marriage relationship, biblical standards were applied. Given that Christ had 'consecrated home' by his own inclusion in a human family,[46] Drummond urged, in 1877, that 'the earthly home may be a foretaste and pledge of the gathered family of Adam' and he encouraged his congregation to 'promote Christ's kingdom in your own families...take care of your children...your servants'.[47] Such sentiments required that fathers were to be representative of the fatherhood of God. Harriet Drummond warned 'how can we hope that the image called up in the child's mind by addressing God as Father will be of a loving, tender, endearing character if that child has been accustomed to associate all that is harsh, and stern and repelling with the name Father?'[48] Drummond saw his wife's duties to their two daughters as a reflection of Christ's dealings with believers: 'may you be a faithful friend, and a sweet counsellor, and a loving guide to them'.[49] Boys also required gentle handling. Drummond recommended that they be 'watched over with a mother's prayerful tenderness and a father's loving protection [and] be surrounded by domestic happiness...uncontaminated by the evil and corrupt habits of the world'.[50] It is not surprising, therefore, that Evangelical parents often showed much affection for their children. Drummond, when absent from home, continually asked his wife to 'kiss our dear little pet, our darling boy'.[51] R. K. Greville, a member of St Thomas's, Edinburgh, and a close personal friend of Drummond's,[52] wrote approvingly in his novel, *Waifs of Fair Edina*, of a mother who consistently caressed and kissed her adopted sons.[53] Evangelical families were often places of love and tenderness.

The available evidence surrounding Drummond and his wife suggests that they achieved much of what they recommended. Of their four children, the first, born in 1831, died at birth,[54] followed by a son, Henry, aged two, in 1835. Two daughters survived to adulthood: Ellen, who was adopted in

---

[45] D. T. K. Drummond to Harriet Drummond, 30 May 1853, *Memoir*, p. cc.

[46] D. T. K. Drummond, 'Sermon Notes' (n.d.), DRO, D5550/3/9/5.

[47] D. T. K. Drummond, Sermon, 3 June 1877 at St Vincent's Church, Edinburgh, *Memoir*, p. cliv.

[48] Harriet Drummond, *Emily Vernon*, p. 192.

[49] D. T. K. Drummond to Harriet Drummond, 30 May 1845, *Memoir*, p. cxcix.

[50] D. T. K. Drummond, 'Sermon Notes' (n.d.), DRO, D5550/3/9/5.

[51] D. T. K. Drummond to Harriet Drummond, September 1834, *Memoir*, p. xxxiii.

[52] See Chapter 4, n. 14 for R. K. Greville.

[53] R. K. Greville, *Waifs of Fair Edina* (Edinburgh, 1898), pp. 12-14. This was probably written in the 1840s.

[54] Letters of Condolence, DRO, D5550/3/5/25.

1835 at the age of four, and Harriet, born in 1841.[55] At Drummond's memorial service, C. T. Astley, incumbent of Gillingham, Kent, referred to the home of the deceased minister as 'the beau-ideal' of Christian family life.[56] Harriet paid tribute to her father after his death, drawing attention to the biblical picture of parenthood that he had fulfilled for her: 'I thank God for having given me in the love of my earthly father, such bright and holy teaching regarding the heavenly Father'. In practical terms it meant that he was 'ready in a moment to throw aside everything, and give his whole heart to help or comfort me...so strong was the instinct of his loving sympathy...I do not think I ever had a thought or a feeling which I could not tell him'.[57] Even in her adult life, Drummond sent Harriet his 'loving, loving, loving wishes' on her thirty-third birthday, assuring her that she became 'more precious every year as it passes away'.[58] There are no surviving letters from Ellen, apart from one, reflecting similar feelings of family love, written to her parents in 1859 regarding her decision to serve with the Church Missionary Society in India. Writing to her 'beloved parents', she assured them 'that we must not think of sundered ties and separation. No! We are bound together more sweetly and closely than ever'.[59] There is no evidence of fear or coldness in the relationship between children and parents in the Drummond household.

However, children were expected to learn scriptural modes of behaviour. As Christ had been subject to his parents, children were exhorted to be obedient. Correction was necessary for children since, as Drummond's wife pointed out, the Bible taught that 'a child left to himself bringeth his mother to shame'.[60] But, again, the parents appear to have been mild in their treatment of wrongdoing. Drummond's daughter, Harriet, wrote that her father's 'reproof was sweeter than the approbation of others would have been. There was so much of the tenderness of the heavenly Father, so much of the gentleness of Christ, that those who heard could not but testify that he had been with Jesus'.[61] Lessons in self-sacrifice were, likewise, lovingly administered. Drummond's wife described a model for parents in her novel, *Lucy Seymour*. The child whose birthday was celebrated certainly shared her party with the village children, who ate the 'buns, cake, and strawberries', joined in the games and 'magic lantern show' arranged by father, and received presents of books and clothing. But all this took place

---

[55] *Memoir*, p. xxxix.

[56] *Memoir*, p. clxxix.

[57] *Ibid.*, pp. cxxii-cxxiii.

[58] D. T. K. Drummond to Harriet Moor, 19 December 1873, DRO, D5550/3/3/5.

[59] Ellen Sherwood to D. T. K. and Harriet Drummond, 27 April 1859, DRO, D5550/3/5/27/13.

[60] Harriet Drummond, *Louisa Moreton*, p. 4.

[61] *Memoir*, p. cxxii.

Lifestyle 163

in the context of a day begun with the young heroine running to her parents' room where they all knelt in prayer as she listened to them 'fervently and earnestly imploring the blessing of their heavenly Father upon their child'. Afterwards she was presented with a 'beautiful waxen doll with blue eyes and flaxen locks', a 'rosewood workbox' and a Bible.[62] The Drummond parents thus advocated rearing children in a manner which reflected their own experience of God as both loving and giving.

Fun and recreation were not excluded from Evangelical family life. John Burns, when a boy, joked with his father 'you *know* what I want, and hoping you will *do* what I want' concerning provision of money to buy a 'powerful magnet'.[63] The Gladstone children in the 1820s were enthusiastic sketchers, musicians and readers. They made toy theatres and played card games,[64] pastimes which in future years would be frowned upon by others for conscientious reasons.[65] While Harriet Drummond's books therefore omit all mention of these, she nonetheless recommended the provision of simple toys such as bricks and puzzles, together with the cultivation of gardens, care of pets, botanic rambles and classification of plants and shells as hobbies. Added to these was the thrill of family picnics, involving everyone in the preparation of food and plans for the day.[66] Again, Greville openly criticised some Evangelical parents and governesses whom he considered to be of 'the Gradgrind school', where fun was sacrificed for learning, and where frivolities were discouraged. In *Waifs of Fair Edina* 'Miss Orlop' was deplored for conducting a regime where 'no daisy chains were ever allowed to be threaded' and 'the innocent offender [told] that such was the commencement of pride and vanity, both of which were hateful to God, and that He would punish them accordingly'. Greville noted sadly that Miss Orlop 'took no notice of hedgerows, nor the songs of birds…nor did she know that every rippling rill, every tree, plant, flower and stone bears the impression of Jehovah…for the enjoyment of His creatures'.[67] Episcopal Evangelicals in Scotland seem to have encouraged a positive attitude to family enjoyment.

The Drummond daughters were obviously not ill at ease with their upbringing because both married Evangelical clergymen, and it seems that

---

[62] Harriet Drummond, *Lucy Seymour*, pp. 84-90.
[63] John Burns to Gerorge Burns, 30 March 1843. Hodder, *Burns*, pp. 150-151.
[64] Checkland, *Gladstones*, p. 87.
[65] See Chapter 5, pp. 177-178.
[66] Harriet Drummond, *Wilmott Family*, pp. 145-146.
[67] Greville, *Waifs*, pp. 27-28. The publication of *Waifs* in 1898 must have been several years after its initial writing, which probably coincided with Charles Dickens's *Hard Times* (1854) with its discussion of Gradgrindism.

they fully embraced their parents' faith.[68] The account given here helps to put into context the rather sombre letter of Montague Stanley to his son, discussed at the beginning of this section. Drummond himself 'knew [Stanley] intimately and loved him dearly'.[69] It is unlikely, therefore, that Stanley was overly stern or harsh with his children. His description of hell can be understood as a solemn warning of perceived danger from a father who was loved and trusted by his offspring. Evangelical Episcopalians in Scotland were certainly active in working for the conversion of their children to their own brand of faith, but it has been shown that this was often carried out within affectionate and disciplined family lives, following biblical teaching.

Philanthropy

While Churchmen of all persuasions undertook charitable work in the nineteenth century, the contribution of Evangelicals was considerable. Various historians have argued that such philanthropy was the product of a paternalist desire to control the poor by infusing them with the values of Evangelicalism which would, in turn, lead them into better ways of life based on useful employment and improved behaviour.[70] Others have countered this, suggesting that the primary concern of Evangelicals in caring for the poor was a humane one springing up from a form of religion which spurred its members on to perform good works as laid out in the Bible.[71] This section will present evidence supporting the latter view showing that, while Scottish Evangelical Episcopalians were driven by the desire to pass on their faith, their concern to help the poor sprang primarily from an adherence to biblical principles of caring for the disadvantaged.

Certainly Evangelicals hoped that their philanthropic enterprises would lead to the embracing of faith by the poor. While visiting Edinburgh in 1818, G. T. Noel declared in a sermon that the Magdalene Asylum in the city had been set up in 1797 'to shew mercy to single mothers and female

---

[68] Ellen married a fellow missionary, Rev Brocklesby Davis, 28 May 1861, and Harriet married Rev C. T. Moor, future incumbent of Cally English Episcopal Church, on 4 October 1871. After Moor's death in 1877, Harriet married another Evangelical, J. S. Owen, in 1879, incumbent of St Paul's, Sheerness, later of St Alkymund's, Derby, a widower with four children.

[69] Harriet Drummond, *Christian Experience Being the Second Series of Peace For the Dying Christian* (Edinburgh, 1855), p. 350.

[70] F. K. Brown, *Fathers of the Victorians* (Cambridge, 1961), pp. 1-11. Victor Kiernan, 'Evangelicalism and the French Revolution', *Past and Present*, no. 1, (1952). R. J. Morris *Class, Sect and Party: The Making of the Middle Class, Leeds* (Manchester, 1990), p. 321.

[71] Brian Dickey, 'Evangelicals and Poverty', in John Wolffe, (ed.), *Evangelical Faith and Public Zeal* (London, 1995), p. 50.

Lifestyle

criminals', but he also trusted that the residents would be led 'to bend their knees in prayer to God'.[72] D. T. K. Drummond likewise remarked that personal involvement with the poor would lead to success 'in engaging the sympathies of our more distressed brethren'.[73] Philanthropy and preaching the gospel went hand-in-hand for Evangelicals.

But while conversion was a hoped-for product of social provision, it cannot be said that the latter was undertaken with the sole purpose of preaching the message of Evangelicalism. Rather, philanthropy resulted from the belief that good works were an outward demonstration of faith and were commended by the Bible. In 1851, Richard Hibbs, curate at St Thomas's, Edinburgh, from 1852 to 1854, and later incumbent of St Vincent's, Edinburgh, from 1857 to 1860, expressed the scriptural basis for the necessity of helping the poor in material ways. Pointing to Matthew 25, verses 31-43, he warned of 'God's terrible judgement' against 'those who, while enjoying the good things which God had given them...had neglected to search out the poor and destitute, and to administer to their necessities'.[74] Likewise Drummond, at St Thomas's, Edinburgh, pointed his congregation to Proverbs 19, verse 17, 'he that hath pity on the poor, lendeth unto the Lord', in an appeal for relief of destitution in the Highlands.[75] Such sentiments appear to have been uppermost in his mind when, as joint incumbent of Trinity Chapel, Edinburgh, in 1842, he set up a school for the impoverished community living beside the Water of Leith. When asking Thomas Chalmers, the future leader of the Free Church, to be its patron, he wrote that the school 'will form an incalculable blessing to many families whose young children, if not at school, must be left to run wild in the streets and drink [the polluted] water'.[76] Drummond and Hibbs were typical of Evangelicals who pointed to the Bible as enjoining philanthropy.

However, there was some discrepancy among Evangelicals in the mid-nineteenth century concerning the best method for tackling social deprivation. Some followed Thomas Chalmers who was committed to *laissez-faire* social policy and the undesirability of state intervention, preferring, rather, to focus on private charity as the means of relieving poverty. J. B. Sumner, the future Archbishop of Canterbury, held similar

---

[72] G. T. Noel, *The Gospel. A Revelation of Mercy to the Guilty. A Sermon Delivered at Charlotte Episcopal Chapel, January 22 1818* (Edinburgh, 1818), pp. 29, 33.

[73] D. T. K. Drummond, *Last Scenes in the Life of our Lord and Saviour*, (London, 18750), pp. 32.

[74] Richard Hibbs, *God's Plea for the Poor Concerning the Poor and the New Poor Law* (London, 1851), p. 47.

[75] D. T. K. Drummond, *Destitution in the Highlands of Scotland. A Sermon preached in aid of the Fund for the Destitute Highlanders* (Edinburgh, 1847), p. 22.

[76] D. T. K. Drummond to Thomas Chalmers, 22 July 1842. New College, Edinburgh, CHA 94.303.15.

views, although he eventually accepted Edwin Chadwick's thesis for administrative action which led to the Poor Law Amendment Act of 1834. By contrast Lord Shaftesbury advocated aid from state legislation. The restriction of child labour to eight hours a day in 1833 and further social reforms throughout following decades, owed much to him.[77]

There is not extensive evidence about Evangelical Episcopalian thought in Scotland on these matters. An early example of pressing for government action in removing injustice comes with Edward Craig of St James's, Edinburgh, in 1831 in his capacity as Vice-President of the Edinburgh Society for the Abolition of Negro Slavery.[78] R. K. Greville, a future member of St Thomas's, Edinburgh, was also active in this field, publishing *The Negro's Appeal*, a poem, in 1832,[79] and becoming Vice-President of the international Anti-Slavery Convention in 1840.[80] Such involvement would have contributed to the movement to eradicate slavery in the West Indies in 1833, spearheaded by T. F. Buxton, M. P. for Weymouth, and to his continuing campaign.[81] Drummond appears to have followed Shaftesbury's lead in 1853, by urging his congregation to help the impoverished by seeking 'every means within our power' to improve their dwellings, 'to limit the numbers who now throng them', and to ameliorate 'the existing conditions of sanitation, food and clothing'.[82] But state intervention was criticised fiercely if Evangelicals saw that it failed the underprivileged. Hibbs, while resident in England in 1851, was scathing in his attack on the Poor Law Amendment Act of 1834. He accused its administrators of 'regarding every application for relief as a person of doubtful character', and of providing food and clothing in workhouses 'worse than in prisons', in its attempt to limit spending on paupers. As an alternative he pressed that 'pauperism would scarce exist if a fair day's wages [were paid] for a fair day's work'.[83] Clergy like Drummond and Hibbs brought the plight of the working population before their congregations, and pressed that improvements should be made.

---

[77] J. F. McCaffrey, 'Thomas Chalmers and Social Change', *The Scottish Historical Review*, Volume 60, (1981), pp. 32-60. J. F. McCaffrey, 'The Life of Thomas Chalmers', in A. C. Cheyne (ed.), *The Practical and the Pious* (Edinburgh, 1985), pp. 31-64. Boyd Hilton, 'The Role of Providence in Evangelical Social Thought', in Derek Beales and Geoffrey Best (eds.), *History and Society and the Churches* (Cambridge, 1985), pp. 215-233. Dickey, 'Evangelicals and Poverty', pp. 43-47.

[78] *Edinburgh Almanack*, (Edinburgh, 1831), p. 386.

[79] Richard Huie and Robert Kaye Greville, *The Amethyst* (Edinburgh, 1832), pp. 260-261.

[80] Lewis, *Dictionary of Evangelical Biography*, Volume I, p. 475.

[81] G. R. Balleine, *The Evangelical Party in the Church of England* (London, 1951), pp. 148-150.

[82] D. T. K. Drummond, *The Three Voices* (Edinburgh, 1853), pp. 7-8.

[83] Hibbs, *God's Plea*, pp. 4, 14, 22, 24.

Lifestyle

However, Evangelicals were anxious that state provision should not preclude the responsibility of individual awareness of the plight of the poor. In 1838 Drummond pointed to the gospel account of the Good Samaritan as the example to follow when dealing with the afflicted. He deplored all 'cold calculation' which might arise from organised aid and the effect it could have in preventing the rich from seeing 'the abject misery of many at their door', thus hindering 'that unity and sympathy which ought to exist between the different classes in our land'. His idea was that the biblical model gave the mode of practice for all Christians, one in which even the poor could help those less fortunate than themselves by giving 'out of their deep poverty'. As little as a 'cup of cold water' would improve the tone of society.[84] George Burns had worked with Thomas Chalmers on the St John's scheme in Glasgow, dating from 1817,[85] where the idea of private philanthropy as central to the aid provided for the destitute was a priority.[86] Again, Mrs George Burns's 'greatest work' was reported by the *Glasgow Herald* to be her 'unsparing bounty' to the individual poor of Glasgow,[87] and Drummond was happy to hear of his daughter, Harriet Moor, running a 'Dorcas' group at her home at Cally, Kirkcudbrightshire, consisting of women engaged in sewing for the poor.[88] Similarly, Harriet Drummond's books are full of examples of aiding the less fortunate. In *The Wilmott Family*, children were involved on Saturdays in making necessities to help the poor. Girls provided hand-sewn clothing, boys made nets for fruit trees, and together they knitted socks. Although it was advocated that the poor purchase 'in part, in order that they might be stimulated to habits of carefulness',[89] Harriet Drummond's books abound with examples of benevolence. Evangelical Episcopalians in Scotland were assiduous in their provision of help for the individual poor.

With similar concerns individual charities still catered for deprived people after the Scottish Poor Law Amendment Act of 1845 introduced a statutory obligation to care for the poor, removing it from the province of the parochial system. Evangelical Episcopalians were involved with a variety of such enterprises. Some were set up to help only the deserving poor, a principle applauded by Evangelicals who tended to fear that indiscriminate help would encourage greed and laziness. Typical of these ventures was the Society in Edinburgh for Clothing the Industrious Poor. Drummond served as a patron from 1841 to the 1850s, along with George

---

[84] Drummond, *Last Scenes*, pp. 30-34.
[85] Lewis, *Dictionary of Evangelical Biography*, p. 172.
[86] A. L. Drummond and James Bulloch, *The Scottish Church 1688-1843* (Edinburgh, 1973), pp. 172-175.
[87] *Glasgow Herald*, 2 July 1877.
[88] D. T. K. Drummond to Harriet Moor, 19 December 1873, DRO, D5550/3/3/5.
[89] Harriet Drummond, *Wilmott Family*, pp. 96-98.

Coventry of Trinity chapel. Drummond's wife, Harriet, was on the Ladies' Committee, and Greville served on the assisting committee.[90] St Thomas's Canongate Mission, begun in 1845, while providing the poor of the area with a meetinghouse for church services, also cared for the 'temporal benefit' of the people, and Drummond urged his congregation to give generously in order that such provision might continue.[91] The Edinburgh City Mission, founded in 1832 by David Nasmith, was primarily an evangelistic society, employing lay missionaries to work in the poorest areas of the city. There is no detailed information regarding the mission but, like the London City Mission, it probably combined spiritual concerns with active campaigning for state action to improve the conditions in factories and slums.[92] Edward Craig, served as an examiner of missionaries from 1833, followed by Daniel Bagot, his successor at St James's, Edinburgh, from 1837 and Drummond from 1842. By the 1860s, Daniel Ainslie and James Mylne, two laymen from St Thomas's, Edinburgh, served as directors.[93] Mrs George Burns, of St Jude's, St Silas's, Glasgow, and Wemyss Bay English Episcopal churches, was Lady President of the Glasgow City Mission from the early 1850s. Her position there gave her first-hand knowledge of the long working hours of cabmen, for whom she successfully obtained 'rests', along with provision for 'spiritual interests'.[94] Thomas Guthrie's Ragged Schools, set up in Edinburgh in 1847 to provide religious instruction along with free food, clothing and vocational training, caught the imagination of Drummond early on, and of Greville, who was appointed to the committee in the 1860s.[95] Church Schools, such as Edward

---

[90] *Edinburgh Almanack* (Edinburgh, 1851), p. 568. Evangelicals were not the only participants in charitable societies. For instance, Bishop C. H. Terrot also served on this society.

[91] Drummond, *Three Voices*, p. 19. See Chapter 3, pp. 87-90 for the Canongate mission and the similar venture set up by St Silas's, Glasgow, in Partick. There is no evidence to indicate how successful the Canongate mission was in improving the social tone of the area. Critics argued that Thomas Chalmers's nearby West Port scheme in the Old Town of Edinburgh did little to transform the hardship and conditions experienced by the members of the congregation of his church there. See S. J. Brown, 'Thomas Chalmers and the Communal Ideal in Victorian Scotland', T. C. Smout (ed.), *Victorian Values* (Oxford, 1992), p. 68.

[92] D. M. Lewis, *Lighten Their Darkness: The Evangelical Mission to the Working-Class of London, 1820-1860* (New York, 2001), pp. 119-149, 164-175. Ian Bradley, *The Call to Seriousness* (London, 1976), pp. 122, 126.

[93] *Edinburgh Almanack* (Edinburgh, 1833), p. 374, (1837), p. 362, (1842), p. 477, (1851), p. 550, (1861), p. 800, (1871), p. 881.

[94] *Glasgow Herald*, 'Obituary Notice', 2 July 1877.

[95] See Chapter 6, p. 192. *Edinburgh Almanack* (Edinburgh, 1861), p. 810. Cameron, *Dictionary*, p. 689.

Lifestyle

Craig's Episcopal Free School, set up in 1817,[96] also catered for both spiritual and material needs. Again, Drummond was a founder of the Edinburgh Christian Institute for Young Men.[97] He drew attention to its purpose of presenting 'a clear and explicit recognition of the whole Truth of God', while also providing young newcomers to the city with 'influences at once pure and invigorating', and lodgings with devout families to avoid exposure 'to the blighty effects of immoral example'.[98] In charities such as these, set up to augment state provision, preaching of the gospel and social concern were interwoven.

But other organisations, which were not overtly religious in character, also drew the allegiance of Evangelicals. Philanthropy alone appears to have been the main concern in such participation, and members of St Thomas's exemplify those Evangelicals who contributed to a myriad of such charitable projects. From 1841 onwards Drummond, Greville and Captain Francis Grove were on the board of directors of the House of Refuge and Night Refuge at Queensberry Lodge, set up in Edinburgh's Canongate to provide shelter for paupers.[99] Medical enterprises were of particular interest. The New Town Dispensary was served by Professor J. H. Balfour, Daniel Ainslie and John Buckle.[100] Drummond was on the boards of the Royal Maternity Hospital of Edinburgh and the Midwifery Dispensary and Lying-in Hospital in the 1850s, medical institutions providing women with help in childbirth.[101] In the 1860s, Balfour was a manager of the Royal Edinburgh Asylum for the Insane, regarded as one of the most efficient hospitals of its type in Scotland, and John Don Wauchope was Vice-President of the Royal Edinburgh Hospital for Sick Children in 1891.[102] Mrs George Burns was involved with the Cottage for Incurables at Maryhill, the Outdoor Blind Society, and the House of Shelter for paupers in Glasgow.[103] At St Mark's, Portobello, G. M. Drummond, incumbent from 1828 to 1839, was noted as 'taking much interest in the welfare of the poor', especially in his capacity of secretary of the Destitute Sick

---

[96] *Edinburgh Almanack* (Edinburgh, 1831), p. 376.

[97] This was probably an offshoot of David Nasmith's *Glasgow Young Men's Society for Religious Improvement* founded in 1824, with the purpose of preaching the gospel to young working men. Nigel M. de S. Cameron (ed.), *Dictionary of Scottish Church History and Theology* (Edinburgh, 1993), p. 902.

[98] D. T. K. Drummond, 'Lecture Notes' (n.d.), DRO, D5550/3/9/5.

[99] *Edinburgh Almanack* (Edinburgh, 1841), p. 490. James Grant, *Cassell's Old and New Edinburgh*, Volume II, (London, 1882), p. 38.

[100] *Edinburgh Almanack* (Edinburgh, 1851), p. 571.

[101] *Ibid.*, pp. 571-572.

[102] *Edinburgh Almanack* (Edinburgh, 1861), p. 828, (1891), p. 1094. Grant, *Cassell's*, p. 39.

[103] *Glasgow Herald*, 2 July 1877.

Society.[104] In the wider field, W. F. Burnley was a committee member of the Society for Giving Higher Education to the Blind of Scotland, a charity which paid particular attention to training piano tuners.[105] The contribution of Evangelical Episcopalians in Scotland to voluntary charitable societies, both religious and secular, was thus most significant. It is evident from this discussion that while Evangelicals hoped that the poor would be successfully evangelised through public and private philanthropy, they were equally concerned to alleviate hardship by following the biblical model.

Sabbatarianism

Sabbatarianism, the belief that the Christian Sunday should be free from labour and set apart as a day devoted to the public and private worship of God, was based on the fourth commandment given to Moses, as recorded in Exodus Chapter 20: 'Remember the Sabbath day by keeping it holy'. In nineteenth-century Scotland, as elsewhere, it was a view held by Evangelicals in all denominations. Sir Andrew Agnew, later a prominent Free Churchman, was active in the Lord's Day Observance Society from 1839, and the most outspoken defenders of the Sabbath among Episcopalians were D. T. K. Drummond and R. K. Greville.

In 1862, in response to a move to open the Botanic Garden of Edinburgh on Sundays, Drummond wrote a fifty-two page biblical exposition of his view of the Sabbath, entitled *The Jewish Sabbath. What it was not, and what it was*. Distinguishing between the weekly ordinance and other Jewish sabbaths, Drummond strongly upheld that Christians were still enjoined to observe the Sabbath by resting from work and focusing on God. His argument was based on the interpretation that the Pharisees of Christ's day had distorted the Sabbath into a series of burdensome demands, resulting in a day of austerity and strictness which Christ had challenged and overthrown. The restoration of the original Jewish Sabbath by Christ to the church was a gift 'fragrant with His love',[106] a time to 'drink deeper from the wells of salvation' when God would, in the words of Isaiah 58.13, bring the believer 'to ride upon the high places of the earth, and feed on the inheritance of Jacob'.[107] Thus Drummond claimed that the Christian Sabbath, like its Jewish predecessor, was to be 'a high and happy day – a day of rest – of soothing joys – of gentle communings – a day of love and charity – a day of prayer – of thanksgiving and the voice of melody – a day

---

[104] William Baird, *Annals of Duddingstone and Portobello* (Edinburgh, 1898), p. 460.

[105] *Edinburgh Almanack* (Edinburgh, 1891), p. 1086.

[106] D. T. K. Drummond, *The Jewish Sabbath. What it was not, and what it was* (Edinburgh, 1862), p. 29.

[107] *Ibid.*, pp. 42-44.

of serenity and peace'.[108] The Sabbath for Drummond was to be a spiritual 'delight'[109] and his teaching aimed at a positive outlook based on scriptural evidence.

Drummond's view was thus far removed from the doom-laden experience of some nineteenth-century Churchmen. Robert Wallace, Professor of Ecclesiastical History at Edinburgh University, speaking of the Sabbaths of his childhood in the 1830s, remarked of Sunday that 'to me the day was a terror' with endless sermons, religious conversations, and the reading of literature with only biblical themes.[110] Such practice probably emanated from a strict adherence to the Westminster Confession which discouraged worldly employments which were lawful on other days. By contrast Drummond, although insistent that the Sabbath was a day of spiritual refreshment, was not unduly restrictive. He allowed that simple amusements like walking in a garden were quite permissible[111] and, in 1829, when newly married but living in Oxford away from his wife, he did not desist from writing to her on Sundays, albeit with some restraint. While assuring her that 'I cannot suffer this sacred day to pass without a little word with you', he added 'but let it be as becometh the day on which we are enjoined...to give ourselves up entirely to him who has so greatly favoured us'.[112] Again in 1855 he wrote from La Tour, Switzerland, 'I must have a little chat with you today', but once more in the context that she, their children, servants and the congregation at St Thomas's 'may all feel a sweet hope, that the one Sabbath day does not run its course without leaving us a little further on in our heavenly journey'.[113] Given that Drummond's daughter, Harriet Moor, also emphasised that her father 'seemed to brighten all he touched, and to give a zest and joy to things which would have otherwise been commonplace',[114] it is difficult to conclude that Sundays in all Evangelical Episcopal households were necessarily dull and boring.

There were critics of sabbatarianism, both within and without the church. Charles Dickens wrote in *Little Dorrit*, in 1855, that sabbatarians produced a situation where there was 'nothing for the spent toiler to do but to compare the monotony of his six days with the monotony of the seventh'.[115]

---

[108] *Ibid.*, p. 45.

[109] *Ibid.*, pp. 43-44.

[110] J. C. Smith and W. Wallace (eds.), *Robert Wallace: Life and Last Leaves* (London, 1903), pp. 48-49, 59. Quoted in A. C. Cheyne, *The Transforming of the Kirk* (Edinburgh, 1983), p. 30.

[111] Drummond, *Jewish Sabbath*, p. 51.

[112] D. T. K. Drummond to Harriet Drummond, Sunday evening 1829, *Memoir*, p. xxii.

[113] D. T. K. Drummond to Harriet Drummond, 2 September 1855, *Memoir*, p. cviii.

[114] *Memoir*, p. cxxiii.

[115] *Little Dorrit*, Chapter 3. Quoted in Bradley, *Seriousness*, pp. 105-106.

Likewise, Dickens opposed closure of bakers' shops on Sundays because it removed the valuable service of cooking a hot meal for the poor who had no ovens of their own.[116] Within the churches, although Scottish Episcopalians, apart from Evangelicals, appear to have made little contribution to such debate, Norman MacLeod of the Church of Scotland and W. C. Smith of the Free Church argued in 1865 that the New Testament had introduced a different aspect of the Lord's Day from that laid down in Exodus. When regular Sunday passenger services were introduced in that year on some Scottish rail timetables, they supported the move, proposing that Christians had freedom to take part in pleasures and relaxing activities, alongside the religious aspects of Sunday worship. The fact that MacLeod was not condemned by any church court and that Smith escaped a heresy trial, although narrowly, showed the widely differing views among Churchmen on the topic as the century progressed.[117] However, Evangelical Episcopalians in Scotland have been shown to have exhibited firm sabbatarian views.

But, although spiritual concerns were of prime importance to strict sabbatarians, other issues were involved. Rest from daily labour was understood to be a reflection of God's own repose from the work of creation and redemption on the seventh day.[118] A number of working people themselves took up this theme. Referring to one thousand essays from Scottish workmen in 1847, extolling Sunday as a day of refreshment, Greville wrote, 'nobly has the British operative...proclaimed to the world how dear to him is the sacred day of rest'.[119] Again, on the proposed Sunday opening of the Botanic Garden in Edinburgh in 1862, twenty-three superintendent gardeners and workmen sent a memorial to the Lords Commissioners of the Treasury asking for protection against 'the attempt to rob them of their divine right to entire rest on the Sabbath'.[120] Drummond supported their petition, regarding the opening of the garden as undesirable because it deprived labourers of God-ordained rest and time spent with their families merely in order to supply pleasure to others.[121] For Drummond, Sabbath desecration 'inevitably issues in the oppression of the weak by the strong, the poor by the rich, the employed by the employer'.[122] Likewise Greville, in 1850, criticised the Sabbath employment of fifteen thousand people in the Post Office because it reduced them to 'a condition of almost

---

[116] Bradley, *Seriousness*, pp. 104-105.

[117] Cheyne, *Transforming of Kirk*, pp. 161-162

[118] Drummond, *Jewish Sabbath*, p. 38.

[119] R. K. Greville, *A Letter to the Marquis of Clanricarde, Post Master-General, on the Desecration of the Lord's day in the Post Office* (Edinburgh, 1850), p. 24.

[120] Drummond, *Jewish Sabbath*, p. 52.

[121] *Ibid.*, pp. 49-50.

[122] D. T. K. Drummond, 'Lecture Notes' (n.d.), DRO, D5550/3/9/5.

Lifestyle 173

positive slavery'.[123] Such sabbatarians were assiduous in defending what they saw to be the rights of the underprivileged, sentiments often endorsed by labourers themselves.

Far reaching destruction of the social fabric was also seen to be a product of Sabbath desecration. Drummond warned that if people were kept away from church they were often led instead 'into an abyss of sin and misery, never to be recovered'.[124] Greville elaborated the argument, seeing the Sunday timetables for trains and steamers on the Thames as the tool of increased drunkenness: 'heartbroken wives and starving children' were, for Greville, the innocent victims of Sabbath desecration.[125] While Drummond allowed that it was wise 'to keep the police force on duty' on Sunday,[126] he was concerned that other employees were being forced to break the Sabbath in order to preserve their jobs, and he urged the government to stop such practices.[127] Both spiritual and social concerns were at the heart of sabbatarianism.

Such priorities led Scottish Evangelical Episcopalians into several public campaigns. On 1 November 1847 Greville convened and acted as secretary of the Sabbath Alliance, set up in Edinburgh and Glasgow to co-ordinate the Scottish campaign against government plans to introduce Sunday mail trains. Almost three thousand Evangelical churches of many denominations were involved, as evidenced by the support of R. S. Candlish and Robert Rainy of the Free Church. Drummond, along with the laymen Thomas Buckmaster, Captain Francis Grove, J. H. Balfour, Alex Stuart, Daniel Ainslie and W. F. Burnley from St Thomas's, Edinburgh, were all subscribers. George and John Burns from St Jude's English Episcopal chapel in Glasgow joined them, along with William Macdonald Macdonald of Montrose qualified church. The considerable measure of enthusiasm among English Episcopalians was obvious from the generous subscriptions of £10.0.0, £5.0.0, £4.4.0 and £3.0.0 from Macdonald, Ainslie, Captain Grove, and the two Burns respectively.[128] Such financial backing enabled the society to spearhead Scottish sabbatarian views for several decades, notably when it played a part in Shaftesbury's partially successful campaign to reduce Sunday working hours at the Post Office and to limit deliveries and collections in 1850. Scottish signatures were added to

---

[123] Greville, *A Letter to the Post Master-General*, p. 9.

[124] Drummond, *Three Voices*, p. 8.

[125] Greville, *Letter to the Post-Master General*, pp. 7-8.

[126] Drummond, *Jewish Sabbath*, p. 50.

[127] *Ibid.*, pp. 49-50.

[128] R. K. Greville, *Statement and Proceedings of the Sabbath Alliance from its formation November 1 1847 to March 31 1848* (Edinburgh, 1848), pp. 1-3. The *Dictionary of Evangelical Biography*, Volume I (Oxford, 1995), p. 475, notes Greville's secretaryship of the *Sabbath Alliance* as starting only in 1850.

petitions and Greville wrote a protest to the Marquis of Clanricarde, the Post Master-General.[129] By 1853 Greville again joined the effective protest against the opening of the Crystal Palace on Sundays.[130] Evangelical Episcopalians in Scotland were thus at the forefront of the sabbatarian campaign.

The concerns for the Sabbath among Evangelical Episcopalians in Scotland rested on both biblical and social grounds. While some might have criticised that they sought to impose their views on others who did not hold the same religious beliefs, their expression of the Sabbath was neither unattractive nor bound exclusively by prohibitions.[131]

Temperance

With an average annual consumption of 2.55 gallons of spirits per head of the Scottish population in the 1830s, the problem of drunkenness was a concern for many in the country.[132] Whereas Presbyterians like Thomas Chalmers in the Church of Scotland initially held aloof from early temperance movements, concerned that their teaching implied that people could save their souls by refusing drink, and Anglicans generally were also slow to join, some Scottish Evangelical Episcopalians were active from an early stage.[133] Possibly influenced by the lecturing campaigns from 1829 of John Dunlop, a magistrate from Greenock, and William Collins, the Glasgow Evangelical publisher, R. K. Greville was Vice-President of the Edinburgh Temperance Society in 1834 which had five hundred members from different religious denominations, including Baptists and

---

[129] R. K. Greville, *A Letter to the Most Hon. The Marquis of Clanricarde, Post Master-General on the Desecration of the Lord's Day in the Post-Office Establishment* (Edinburgh, 1850).

[130] R. K. Greville, *Letter on the Opening of the Crystal Palace on Sundays* (Edinburgh, 1853).

[131] *Cf.* Cheyne, *Transforming of Kirk*, pp. 32-34, where a similar proposition is made concerning Sabbath observance in the Church of Scotland in the 1820s.

[132] T. C. Smout, *A Century of the Scottish People 1830-1950* (London, 1987), p. 135.

[133] In Scotland Thomas Guthrie was one of the first among Presbyterian supporters of teetotal societies. In 1853 the United Presbyterians had about 150 ministers who were abstainers, the Free Church over 100, but the Church of Scotland only about 20. *The Abstainers Journal* (Glasgow, 1853), pp. 28-29, 166-168. Quoted in Smout, *Century of the Scottish People*, p. 141. In 1837 the membership of English teetotal societies was composed of only 5% Anglicans, and 4% in 1848, compared to Congregationalists who represented by 25% of the membership at both dates, Baptists at 21% and 15%, Primitive Methodists at 4% and 19%, and Calvinistic Methodists at 26% and 12% of the membership at the two dates respectively. See Brian Harrison, *Drink and the Victorians: The Temperance Question* (London, 1971), p. 179.

Lifestyle 175

Congregationalists.[134] Initially, concern was directed at abstinence from spirits but by the late 1830s teetotalism, with a pledge to renounce all alcohol and often a refusal to offer it to others, was the aim.[135] Accordingly, Greville and D. T. K. Drummond acted as Vice-Presidents of the Edinburgh Society for Suppressing Intemperance in 1841, and Captain Francis Grove, at that time a member of St James's, Edinburgh, was part of the committee.[136] While Presbyterian support blossomed during the 1840s, leading to the formation of the Free Church Temperance Society in 1849,[137] Scottish Evangelical Episcopalian concern over drunkenness was evident from an early date.

The demands of such societies were, according to Greville and Drummond, entirely scriptural. Both pointed to 1 Corinthians 6.10 with its warning that drunkards would not inherit the kingdom of God.[138] Therefore it was, according to Greville in 1834, imperative that Christians, in obedience to Romans 14.21, should exercise 'self-denial for the good of ourselves and our fellow-creatures'.[139] But social concern also played a large part in the crusade. Drummond warned in 1853 that drinking tended to 'induce disease, impair all moral feeling, and influence every bad passion', and that because the problem existed among both rich and poor, 'profligacy is the rule and not the exception' in society.[140] Greville highlighted a survey showing that alcohol was responsible for nearly all the crimes in the army and that petty theft in Edinburgh from 1832 to 1834 was 'directly or indirectly connected with drinking'.[141] Poverty as a result of intemperance was a further problem. Greville pointed to £6,300,000 spent on spirits in Ireland annually which could have been used for 'food, clothes, wages, schoolmasters, supporting the aged and infirm, charities, employing people'.[142] With similar concerns in 1853, Drummond called for some arrangement in the payment of wages to labourers, among whom drunkenness was particularly prevalent, 'at a time, and in a way, as to be suitable for the well being of their families, instead of supplying a temptation for the sin we deplore'.[143] As with the sabbatarian crusade,

---

[134] R. K. Greville, *Facts Illustrative of Drunkenness in Scotland* (Edinburgh, 1834), pp. 1, 16.

[135] Nigel M. S. de Cameron (ed.), *Dictionary of Scottish Church History and Theology* (Edinburgh, 1993), p. 815.

[136] *Edinburgh Almanack* (1841), p. 502.

[137] Cameron, *Dictionary*, p. 815. A. L. Drummond and James Bulloch, *The Church in Victorian Scotland, 1834-1874* (Edinburgh, 1975), pp. 25-27.

[138] Greville, *Facts Illustrative*, p. 6. Drummond, *Three Voices*, p.7.

[139] Greville, *Facts Illustrative*, p. 3.

[140] Drummond, *Three Voices*, p.8.

[141] Greville, *Facts Illustrative*, pp. 5-7.

[142] *Ibid.*, p. 14.

[143] Drummond, *Three Voices*, p. 7.

biblical standards along with social concern were the driving factors in the Scottish Evangelical response to intemperance.

In order to entice people away from public houses and provide for those who had abandoned drinking alcohol, Evangelicals ran temperance meetings and clubs. Typical of these was the Gatehouse Total Abstinence Society under the auspices of C. T. Moor, Drummond's son-in-law and incumbent of Cally English Episcopal Church. A meeting in 1872 involved the provision of 'tea, cake and fruit' along with contemporary musical entertainment, the star attraction being a rendering of the song *Roger Tichborne*, 'the great rage at present'.[144] Although Moor pronounced a benediction, there appears to have been little overt evangelism. Temperance societies thus endeavoured to provide attractive centres of friendship and support in comfortable surroundings, free from alcohol.

Some social commentators have considered that such ventures failed, suggesting that the diversions offered could not compete successfully with those of public houses which were open daily and provided a focus for the neighbourhood. Again, the demands of the movement have been highlighted as too stringent in calling for total abstinence rather than disciplined control.[145] By contrast, legislation, often supported by Evangelicals, is considered by many as having been a more effective deterrent. For instance, the Forbes-Mackenzie Act of 1853, which closed Scottish public houses on Sundays and introduced 11 pm closing on weekdays, appeared to be instrumental in achieving a drop in annual spirit consumption to 1.61 gallons per head per year by the 1860s.[146] However, other historians have suggested that the temperance movement played an important part and that without it the problem of drunkenness would have been more serious. Certainly the Evangelicals discussed here extended the area of human compassion to the drunkard in local ventures such as Moor's at Cally[147] and, together with their work in pressing for better social conditions for the poor, they did look towards alleviating the causes of intemperance. Their work can probably be regarded as an important contribution to the general campaign against drunkenness in nineteenth-century Scotland.

---

[144] *Dumfries and Galloway Courier*, 24 December 1872.

[145] *Cf.* John Kent, *Holding the Fort: Studies in Victorian Revivalism* (London, 1978), p. 93.

[146] Smout, *Scottish People, 1830-1950*, pp. 143-145. William MacDonald MacDonald, a manager of St Peter's, Montrose, supported the Forbes-Mackenzie Act, and provided a coffee room for Montrose in 1857. See Andrew Douglas, *A History of Ferryden* (Montrose, 1857), p. 55. I thank D. W. Bebbington for this reference. It is not clear which other Scottish Evangelicals supported the Forbes-Mackenzie Act.

[147] Harrison, *Drink and the Victorians*, pp. 354-355, 365.

Recreation

Evangelicals were assiduous in examining hobbies lest they be dishonouring to biblical standards. Mid-century Anglican Evangelicals, touched by premillennialism, were particularly watchful that time was not wasted on mere pleasure when it could be used for preaching the gospel to the unconverted, and they tended to have a more rigid outlook on such matters than some of their forebears.[148]

The theatre was an area of particular concern. It was not that Evangelicals necessarily condemned the content of all plays. They were well used to the Old Testament accounts of violence and human passion, but they tended to condone only those works which, like the Bible, made moral comment on the condition of mankind. Thus while it is true that some Evangelical correspondents to the *Christian Observer* in the early decades of the nineteenth century could see no moral content in Shakespeare's work,[149] William Wilberforce and Hannah More read his plays, the latter declaring in the 1830s, 'did Virgil ever weep, like good King Lear, that he a daughter had?'[150] Likewise, D. T. K. Drummond's inaugural address to the Institute for Young Men included quotes from *As You Like It* and *Macbeth*, indicating familiarity with some texts.[151] Evangelicals were not necessarily opposed to reading plays containing what they understood to be salutary teaching on human life.

But while some Evangelicals were content to engage with such plays in the privacy of their own homes, visual presentation on stage was a problem. R. K. Greville, in 1830, deplored that some modern drama was 'replete with indecency', allowing 'language and gesture...that would never be tolerated in private society'. He proceeded to show that the contemporary theatre upheld profaneness, impurity, drunkenness, irreverence for the old along with caricatures of religion. Referring to almost thirty biblical texts on such matters, he challenged Evangelicals to boycott the theatre. Montague Stanley, a member of St Thomas's, Edinburgh, who was converted in 1837, gave up a glittering stage career in that year because of 'the false sensibilities' it engendered and that it 'was calculated to deaden spirituality'.[152] Although such resistance was beginning to diminish by 1883, as shown by a United Presbyterian minister who declared the theatre

---

[148] D. W. Bebbington, *Evangelicalism in Modern Britain* (London, 1993), p. 130.

[149] See Rosman, *Evangelicals and Culture*, pp 176-177 for examples from correspondents in the *Christian Observer* condemning Shakespeare.

[150] Henry Thompson, *The Life of Hannah More*, (London, 1838), p. 372. Quoted in Rosman, *Evangelicals and Culture*, p. 177.

[151] D. T. K. Drummond, 'Lecture to the Institute for Young Men', (n.d.), DRO, D5550/3/5/9.

[152] D. T. K. Drummond, *Memoir of Montague Stanley A. R. S. A.* (Edinburgh, 1848), pp. 27, 31.

to be educative,[153] Drummond continued in similar vein to Greville in 1876 condemning modern plays which 'owe much of their attractiveness to the open or covert representation of what is criminal and sinful'.[154] Some Evangelical Episcopalians in Scotland thus found the theatre of their day to be graphically immoral.

Other aspects of social concern played a part in the protest. Actors and actresses were often of low moral reputation: 'many of the women...are of the worst principles and conduct, and many of the men are insolent and depraved to an excess', quoted Drummond in 1848.[155] A further problem lay within the audiences themselves where prostitutes were 'provided with special accommodation and...unblushingly declare their shame'. Drummond thus challenged 'men of professedly moral character willing to allow their daughters to sit for a whole evening within the gaze of the most abandoned of their sex'.[156] Evangelicals opposed theatres as centres of vice.

Drummond also called attention to the exploitation of child actors. Referring to Christmas pantomimes in 1876, he criticised Evangelical parents who took their families to performances and pointed out the 'cost to many other children'. He gave particular attention to the small sum of £1 being paid to 'one little girl...for the whole run of the pantomime' whose home was 'cold, dark and cheerless' and in need of generous help.[157] While there is no evidence from other Evangelical Episcopalians in Scotland, Greville and Drummond represent a strong condemnation of the theatre on moral and social grounds which persisted into the latter decades of the nineteenth century.

Novel reading was also scrutinised by Evangelicals on several counts. Sir Walter Scott's books had been criticised by the Nonconformist *Eclectic Review* in the early decades of the century for 'absence of moral or religious object', although it did not regard his writing as depraved and applauded his literary style.[158] A further problem for some was that the fictitious character of novels tended to produce characters who were impossible to emulate. Such concerns possibly worried Drummond who, while possessing Scott's historical *Tales of a Grandfather*, and E. C. G. Murray's satirical comment on life, *Strange Tales from Vanity Fair, by Silly Billy*, seemingly owned no novels.[159] But consternation among some

---

[153] Bebbington, *Evangelicalism*, p. 131.
[154] D. T. K. Drummond, *A Serious Inquiry into the Nature of the Stage* (Edinburgh, 1876), p. xi.
[155] Drummond, *Montague Stanley*, p. 39.
[156] *Ibid.*, pp. 47-48.
[157] Drummond, *Serious Inquiry*, p. xxi.
[158] Rosman, *Evangelicals and Culture*, pp. 186-188.
[159] *Catalogue of the General and Theological Library of the late D. T. K. Drummond 5 February 1878* (Messrs. T. Chapman and Son, Edinburgh, 1878). Murray's book,

Lifestyle

Evangelicals reached a peak by the 1870s when a different genre appeared. This was the era of what Drummond termed 'sensational writing', epitomised by Wilkie Collins, George Eliot and Anthony Trollope. While Harriet Drummond's *Emily Vernon* had included a cautionary tale about an elopement resulting in a disastrous marriage and the abandonment of a young wife and her baby, no intimate details were included.[160] By contrast, Drummond regarded the new novels as 'vice set forth clothed in gross [and] euphonious terms' which could only 'blight and stifle...corrupt and...destroy'.[161] He applauded the *Saturday Review* for its comment: 'things are introduced which our grandmothers went down to the grave without knowing...and discussed in unmistakeable terms before our unmarried girls', and he condemned the novels because they caused 'all the feminine qualities, shame, delicacy and reticence [to be] discarded'.[162] By the later decades of the nineteenth century, some Scottish Evangelical Episcopalians castigated novels that sensationalised low morality rather than teaching its danger.

Poetry, however, was popular with Evangelicals. Its language tended to be regarded as less direct in its depiction of human shortcomings and emotions than that of novels, and its perusal in private gave opportunity for reflection and intellectual expertise. Religious poetry was particularly applauded. Robert Montgomery of St Jude's, Glasgow, from 1837 to 1843, was prolific in the field, his most famous poem being *Satan, or the Intellect without God*, written in 1830. He received much praise in the press, despite being roundly criticised for his style by T. B. Macaulay, the historian and poet, who additionally accused him of plagiarism.[163] E. C. Wrenford, of Nairn English Episcopal Church, also published within the genre, notably *Carmina Regia and Other Sacred Songs of the Heart* dedicated to Queen Victoria in 1878. The Drummond daughters were enthusiastic poets. Although largely unpublished, they wrote compositions, both religious and secular, from an early age.[164] Drummond, too, delighted in poetry. Among the books catalogued in his library sale after his death were works by

---

published in 1875, offered shrewd observations on contemporary affairs, sometimes flippant. See Ian Ousby, *The Cambridge Guide to Literature in English* (Cambridge, 1993), p. 975. J. F. Kirk, *Supplement to Allibone's Critical Dictionary of English Literature and British and American Authors* (Philadelphia, 1891), p. 1159.

[160] Harriet Drummond, *Emily Vernon*, pp. 270-292.

[161] Drummond, *Serious Inquiry*, p. xviii.

[162] *Ibid.*, p. xxix.

[163] Lewis (ed.), *Dictionary*, Vol. II, p. 785.

[164] D. T. K. Drummond, *Sparkling Rills by the Wayside or Thoughts from the Book of Psalms* (London, 1878), pp. 265, 527, 550, 639. Ellen Sherwood, 'All hail', 'The River Side', DRO, D5550/3/5/27/10,14. H. E. B. Drummond, 'Sacred Poetry', DRO, D5550/3/3.'The Billow', 'The Waterfall', 'The Wind' in 'Book of Poems written when aged sixteen', DRO, D5550/3/3.

Goldsmith and Shelley, together with Scott's *Minstrelsy of the Scottish Borders*, George Herbert's *Sacred Poems*, as well as a volume of *Select Poetry*.[165] He was also conversant with the texts of Milton and Byron, the latter of whom was admired by many Evangelicals for his work rather than his life-style,[166] and quoted them in his public lectures.[167] Although Drummond does not appear to have written any poems, his letters and published sermons often resonate with powerful poetic imagery and language.[168] Poetry was popular among Episcopal Evangelicals in Scotland.

While Evangelical Episcopalians in Scotland opposed any undue decoration in churches, they often accepted it in a non-ecclesiastical setting. Drummond showed an acute interest in the topic. He possessed several art books,[169] and part of his farewell gift from St Thomas's in 1877 was a folio edition of the *Turner Gallery Engravings* and David Roberts's *Sketches of the Holy Land*. When in Milan in 1853, his aesthetic pleasure in Leonardo da Vinci's *Last Supper* was evident in a letter to St Thomas's congregation where he described its 'power' to enlarge feeling. Milan Cathedral captivated him with 'the infinite number of lines and the gorgeous ornaments...those wonderful pinnacles, shooting up into the air, so slight, so sharp...and inside the soft, mellow light streaming through the brilliant windows'.[170] Some Scottish Evangelical Episcopalians, knowledgeable about art, thus exemplified the sentiments of the *Eclectic Review* in the

---

[165] *Catalogue of Library 1878*.

[166] Rosman, *Evangelicals and Culture*, pp. 181-182.

[167] *Record*, 16 December 1872, 'Meeting of the Church Association at Exeter Hall'. D. T. K. Drummond, 'Lecture Notes' (n.d.), DRO, D5550/3/5/9. Among those quoted were Milton's *Paradise Lost*; Scott's *Marmion* and *The Lay of the Last Minstrel*; Byron's *The Destruction of Sennacherib* and *Oh! Weep for those*. See Rosman, *Evangelicals and Culture*, p. 183. Cf. M. J. Quinlan, *Victorian Prelude* (New York, 1941), p. 80.

[168] The following lines, written in a letter to his wife concerning their baby daughter in 1842, are typical of Drummond's skill: 'True she often gives memory wings to flit back among the withered branches of departed joys, and draws forth the tear as she hurries us back to the grave of our first-born – our sweet, gentle boy; yet soon as she gives birth to thoughts which seemed fixed in the sepulchre, the sleep of the past, she robs them of their pain, dries up the fount of sadness, and wipes away the tears.' *Memoir*, p. cxcvi.

[169] Typical were: *Finden's Landscape and Portrait Illustrations to Byron's Works; Mitchell's Sketches After Van Dyke; The Art Journal*, 1867-1868; *Burnet on Light and Shade in Painting; Landscape Illustrations of the Bible*. See *Catalogue Sale*. See *Catalogue of Library 1878*

[170] D. T. K. Drummond, *Scenes and Impressions in Switzerland and the North of Italy* (Edinburgh, 1853), pp. 83-84, 89-90.

Lifestyle

1820s which condoned it for the way in which it could 'elevate and expand' and improve the mind.[171]

However, once involved with a hobby, Evangelicals were stringent in examining its effects on their lives, anxious that nothing should deprive them of time which could be spent more usefully on religious duties. Drummond gave up gardening when newly ordained in order to do more parish visiting.[172] But once reassured, they saw leisure as a gift from God. When testifying publicly to the Photographic Society of Scotland in 1864, Drummond remarked that 'it is impossible to say how much, under God, I owe both in mind and body to photography in my hours of leisure'.[173] Acknowledged as one of the best amateurs in the field by Vernon Heath, the renowned English photographer,[174] Drummond became Vice President of the society from 1864 to 1867. He had been interested in experimental chemistry since childhood,[175] a hobby which enabled him to perfect his highly acclaimed dry malt process with which he obtained photographs comparable in detail and colour with the more cumbersome wet collodion method.[176] But Drummond was careful to give the proceeds of his photographic sales to missionary work,[177] an indication of the way in which Evangelicals dedicated all interests and skills to God. Evangelical faith penetrated leisure time.

Nineteenth-century Evangelicals have been described as deeply serious people, always conscious of their great responsibility and duty to win souls for God.[178] The way in which they conducted their lives has been shown here to endorse this comment. Yet among Evangelical Episcopalians in Scotland there was much fun. George Burns, of Wemyss Bay English Episcopal chapel, was 'always a humorist'. His *Gaiter Club* organised walking tours in Scotland, for appropriately shod participants, with an annual dinner complete with comical speeches.[179] The Drummond family correspondence abounds with touches of humour. Drummond loved his son-in-law, C. T. Moor as 'dear and good and Christlike',[180] but this did not prevent a cheerful camaraderie between them. When Moor telegrammed

---

[171] Rosman, *Evangelicals and Culture*, pp. 149-150.

[172] *Memoir*, p. cxviii.

[173] D. T. K. Drummond, 'Some Remarks on the Malt Process', *Photographic News*, 22 January, 1864, p. 42.

[174] Vernon Heath, *Recollections* (London, 1892), pp. 117-119.

[175] *Memoir*, p. cxviii-cxix.

[176] Sara Stevenson, *Scottish Photography*, Bulletein 2 (Edinburgh, 1992), pp. 3-10. Drummond, 'Malt Process', p. 42.

[177] *Memoir*, p. cxix.

[178] Bradley, *Call to Seriousness*, p. 202.

[179] Edwin Hodder, *Sir George Burns Bart. His Times, His Friends* (London, 1892), p. 230.

[180] D. T. K. Drummond to Harriet Moor, 19 December 1873, DRO, D5550/3/3/5.

the Drummonds on the birth of his daughter, he carefully concealed the news amongst a discussion on plants. Drummond replied: 'I opened [your telegram] with my heart in my mouth and was disposed to throw it down with a 'pshaw', when the words 'ferns' caught my eye, but your sauce soon appeared when you added – also a granddaughter'.[181] Again, when Harriet Moor gave birth to her child, her mother, Harriet Drummond, was amused to tell Charles Moor that the verger at St Thomas's had announced the event to the congregation as *'Miss* Harrie has got a *bairn'*.[182] Evangelical Episcopalians in Scotland were certainly serious about the outworking of their faith, but there was laughter as well.

Conclusion

It has been shown that, in areas of lifestyle such as marriage, family, philanthropy, sabbatarianism, temperance and recreation, Scottish Evangelical Episcopalians were guided by both biblical standards and social concern. If a practice was not endorsed by scripture, or resulted in hardship for others, it was avoided. Thus the charge of hypocrisy levelled by Dickens, quoted at the beginning of this chapter, cannot be endorsed. While Evangelicals certainly hoped that people would be converted in the process of their campaigns, their concerns were equally those of a humanitarian nature. Neither were all Evangelicals life-denying. While their demands were, maybe, unrealistic and not open to negotiation, their intervention in the cause of sabbatarianism and temperance, for instance, was always focused on providing wholesome alternatives to what they considered to be harmful to society. Likewise, philistinism has been shown not to have applied to Scottish Evangelical Episcopalianism, whose adherents were often knowledgeable devotees of the arts. Lastly, as in the public sphere, they were not killjoys in their private lives, but exhibited attractive geniality among family and friends. That people rejected Evangelicalism was probably due as much to its theological demands as to its lifestyle.

---

[181] D. T. K. Drummond to Charles Moor, 1975, DRO, D5550/3/4/9.
[182] Harriet Drummond to Charles Moor (n.d.), DRO, D5550/3/4/9.

Chapter 6

Doctrinal and Practical Issues

Evangelicals faced various issues in the nineteenth century. The impact of liberal views of scripture has been considered previously.[1] There were doctrinal skirmishes with orthodox High Churchmen, particularly concerning the sacraments, and sustained opposition to Tractarianism in the 1830s together with Ritualism in the 1860s. The response of Evangelicals was never uniform, and factions of conservatives, liberals and those who adopted High Church nuances evolved amongst them. Within Scotland such matters often took on a characteristic complexion, affected as they were not only by British affairs in general but also by concerns which held particular sway north of the border. This chapter will consider some emerging characteristics of Scottish Evangelical Episcopalians as they formulated their beliefs in response to High Church views concerning baptism, church architecture and worship. Much of the difference of opinion was, at heart, a mounting antipathy to the Roman Catholic Church which was growing in confidence and influence during the nineteenth century, and so a discussion of that theme will be undertaken first.

Anti-Catholicism

Scotland had been host to outbreaks of anti-Catholicism in the eighteenth century such as the serious mob riot in Edinburgh in 1779 in response towards moves to abolish penal restrictions from Catholics.[2] By the 1820s there was a growing anti-Catholic feeling in Britain generally that was to last throughout much of the rest of the century. Various factors were contributory. The public debate leading up to the emancipation of Roman Catholics in 1829 fostered the fear that a Catholic presence in Parliament would alter the Protestant constitution of Britain.[3] Added to the political rumpus there was concern over the increasing numbers of poor Irish immigrants to the mainland in the 1820s.[4] In Edinburgh, for instance, they

---

[1] See Chapter 4, p. 150.
[2] A. L. Drummond and James Bulloch, *The Scottish Church 1688-1843* (Edinburgh, 1973), p. 138. Nigel M. de S. Cameron, *Dictionary of Scottish Church History* (Edinburgh, 1993), p. 149.
[3] John Wolffe, *The Protestant Crusade in Great Britain 1829-1860* (Oxford, 1991), pp. 22-23.
[4] See Chapter 2, pp. 39-40.

were commonly employed as labourers, porters, carters and scavengers, and were to be found clustered in the most menial of dwellings of the Old Town, often with two or more families occupying a single room.[5] Parallels drawn between the poverty and lack of skills of many of the immigrants and the reported backwardness of the Papal States tended to exacerbate anti-Catholic feeling. Again, the growing premillennial mood of the late 1820s and 1830s, which linked Rome with the Antichrist, was reinforced by incidents such as the discovery of prayers for the conversion of England to the Catholic faith together with the circulation of tracts by the Catholic Institute in 1835.[6] Anti-Catholicism was increasingly entrenched by the 1830s.

For Churchmen, such events brought the theological matters that lay at the heart of their concerns into focus. Evangelicals and High Churchmen alike were antagonistic to the Roman Catholic belief in transubstantiation and the sacrificial role of the priest in the mass. Charles Wordsworth, Bishop of St Andrews, Dunkeld and Dunblane, spoke for many Scottish High Churchmen when he wrote in 1853, 'no man can be more prepared than I am to protest...against the error and corruptions of the Church of Rome'.[7] But it was probably in Evangelical circles that the most marked antipathy to Roman Catholic theology was expressed. *The Protestant*, begun in 1818 under the editorship of the Glasgow layman William McGavin, advertised itself as 'a weekly paper on the principle points of controversy between the Church of Rome and the Reformed'.[8] In 1831, possibly in response to fears that the proposed Reform Bill would enfranchise some Irish immigrants, Edward Craig of St James's, Edinburgh, preached on the differences between Evangelical and Roman Catholic doctrine. Craig's emphasis on conversion as the means of drawing close to God was shown to contrast sharply with Catholic doctrines of sacramental grace, invocation of the saints and veneration of the Virgin Mary. Highlighting the Catholic belief in purgatory, papal supremacy, and the practice of withholding parts of scripture from common use, Craig denounced the Roman Catholic Church as 'superstitious and unscriptural' and called for its reform.[9] Other Evangelicals criticised the ceremonial aspects of Catholic worship. D. T. K. Drummond, of Trinity Chapel,

---

[5] J. E. Handley, *The Irish in Modern Scotland* (Cork, 1847), pp. 37, 44.

[6] Wolffe, *Protestant Crusade*, pp. 116, 120-121.

[7] Berkeley Addison, *Remarks on Bishop Wordsworth's Recent Letter Reprobating the Author's Conduct for Taking Part in the Public Meetings of the Scottish Reformation Society* (Edinburgh, 1853), p. 6.

[8] *The Protestant* (Glasgow, 1819).

[9] Edward Craig, *A Friendly Address to Roman Catholics occasioned by an Introductory Address from the Rev Mr M'Kay to the Congregation of St James's Episcopal Chapel* (Edinburgh, 1831), pp. 3-23.

Doctrinal and Practical Issues

Edinburgh, teaching his congregation in the late 1830s to follow Christ's example by displaying 'a mind full of meekness, and humility', went on to criticise the Pope's public ceremony of washing the feet of the poor using 'a silver bason, and having attendants around bearing the most costly materials'. Comparing this with Christ's humility when bathing the feet of the disciples in a private room away from public view, he understood that the Catholic practice would lead to 'the pride of being the greatest...the canker which eats out the spirit of the Gospel'.[10] The distinctive theology and practice of Evangelicals and Catholics separated them uncompromisingly.

Scottish Evangelical Episcopalians were prolific in publishing pamphlets and articles on Roman Catholicism. Theology was, again, the predominant concern. Daniel Bagot, of St James's, Edinburgh, wrote a catechism refuting 'all the leading errors of the Church of Rome', ending with a plea 'to pray earnestly' for the conversion of Catholics.[11] Drummond included a critique of Roman Catholicism in Italy as part of a travel journal, labelling the Papacy as 'a monstrous combination [of] deadly principles...with some of the verities of the Christian faith'.[12] In 1868, T. K. Talon of St Vincent's, Edinburgh, opposed the disestablishment of the Church of Ireland because he believed it would hand the people over 'to the cruel and iron bondage of Rome...the mother of the superstition she blindly inculcates'.[13] W. L. Holland, of St Thomas's, Edinburgh, in 1895, strayed from the theological into the realm of lobbying parliament to authorise the inspection of convents after reports of ill treatment of nuns.[14] Theological and practical concerns formed the base of Evangelical protest.

However, Evangelicals were assiduous in claiming that their attitude to Catholicism was marked by no hostility towards individuals. J. D. Hull, of Huntly English Episcopal Church, was typical in entreating 'Hate their errors as much as you please, but oh, love, love, their persons'.[15] In a similar manner Craig declared, 'We abhor the religion...but we love them, we pity them, we pray for them'.[16] Individual Roman Catholics were sometimes praised. After staying at a hospice in Switzerland, Drummond commented on the 'real and useful devotedness' of the monks who offered

---

[10] D. T. K. Drummond, *Last Scenes in the Life of our Lord and Saviour* (London, 1850), pp. 27-28. See also, Wolffe, *Protestant Crusade*, pp. 118-119, for similar examples.

[11] Daniel Bagot, *A Protestant Catechism* (Edinburgh, 1836), p. 62.

[12] D. T. K.Drummond, *Scenes and Impressions in Switzerland and the North of Italy* (Edinburgh, 1853), p. 10.

[13] T. K. Talon, *The Established Church in Ireland, being the Substance of a Lecture delivered in Edinburgh on May 1868* (Edinburgh, 1868), pp. 33-34.

[14] W. L. Holland, *Walled Up Nuns and Nuns Walled Up* (Edinburgh, 1895).

[15] J. D. Hull, *The Church of God, A Book for the Age* (London, 1840), p. 225.

[16] *Scotsman*, 6 October 1835.

him lodging, adding 'were all monkery like this I should have no objection to it, with the exception of the blind, superstitious Popery with which it has ever been allied'.[17] Scottish Evangelical Episcopalians opposed the system of Roman Catholicism, but not necessarily its individual adherents.

Various Protestant societies emerged against this background with the object of halting Roman Catholic advance in Britain. James Edward Gordon, a Scot,[18] aiming to disseminate information about Catholic doctrinal error, founded the London Reformation Society in 1827.[19] Growing apprehension over political developments in the late 1820s and early 1830s led the society to widen its membership. Craig, along with Thomas Chalmers of the Church of Scotland, was present at meetings in Edinburgh on 16 and 23 April 1830 to form a Scottish auxiliary of which he was secretary by 1831.[20] Unfortunately, the records of the Reformation Society are no longer available for consultation and it is impossible to know if Episcopal High Churchmen were involved. But despite the small numbers of Evangelical Episcopalians in Scotland, Craig's early position in the Reformation Society was an important contribution.

A politicised approach was heralded when Gordon founded the Protestant Association in 1835 in response to the Irish Church Bill of 1833[21] and the ongoing parliamentary arguments surrounding the grant to the Catholic seminary at Maynooth. The ultimate aim of the society was to press for repeal of the Catholic Emancipation Act.[22] From October 1835 to early 1836, the Protestant Association held large meetings in Edinburgh, Glasgow, Perth and Aberdeen. On 6 October a preliminary event was held in Edinburgh for 'all those favourable to the principles of the Established

---

[17] D. T. K. Drummond, *Scenes and Impressions in Switzerland and the North of Italy* (Edinburgh, 1853), p. 27.

[18] J. E. Gordon, an Evangelical, toured Ireland for the Hibernian Bible Society with Baptist Noel in 1824. He was a friend of Thomas Chalmers of the Church of Scotland. Wolffe, *Protestant Crusade*, pp. 34-35.

[19] Wolffe, *Protestant Crusade*, pp. 36-37.

[20] *Record*, 24 April 1830.

[21] The Irish Church Bill abolished two of the four archbishoprics of the Church of Ireland and eight of the bishoprics. Some clergy stipends were amalgamated or removed. The money saved was to be used to help poor clergy and to repair churches, but many feared that the surplus would contribute to the building of Catholic schools or even towards paying priests. The ferment was particularly great among High Churchmen who felt that a dangerous erastianism, which included much Dissenting influence, had been established and which might well have repercussions against the Church of England. John Keble's assize sermon at Oxford on the interference of the state in the affairs of the Irish Church, was popular with High Churchmen, and came to mark the beginning of the Oxford Movement. See Owen Chadwick, *The Victorian Church: Part I 1829-1859* (London, 1992), pp. 56-58, 86-90.

[22] Wolffe, *Protestant Crusade*, p. 88.

Doctrinal and Practical Issues

Church for the purpose of passing resolutions declaratory of their detestation of popery'.[23] The attendance was mainly from the Church of Scotland, but Craig was an invited speaker. Drummond, then incumbent of St Paul's, Carrubber's Close, and the Edinburgh High Churchmen G. A. Poole, of St John's, John Sinclair of St Paul's, York Place, and George Rose of St Peter's were present. By 23 December the Edinburgh Protestant Association was formed. Presbyterians again dominated with the future Free Churchmen, R. S. Candlish and William Cunningham, being prominent. Evangelical Episcopal support came from Drummond, R. K. Greville and Captain Francis Grove. At a further Edinburgh meeting in 1839 Drummond and Greville were reported as committee members, and George Coventry, of Trinity Chapel, Edinburgh, and J. W. Ferguson[24] of St Peter's, Edinburgh, both Evangelical sympathisers, attended. In 1851 C. P. Miles and Sir Archibald Campbell of Blythswood, of St Jude's, Glasgow, were noted as members.[25] Thus, Evangelical Episcopalians played a particularly prominent part in the Protestant Association along with Church of Scotland clergy.

Theological matters were the motor for the political aims of the Protestant Association. At the Edinburgh meeting in October 1835 Craig, drawing attention to a Roman Catholic catechism published in 1834, denounced its sacerdotalism whereby priests could 'change eternal to temporal punishment by penance' and implement the system of indulgences.[26] At the December gathering Greville actually distanced himself from politics. His doctrinal concerns were 'to leaven [Roman Catholics] with true Protestantism and Evangelical religion'.[27] Again at Edinburgh, in 1839, the invited speaker, Hugh McNeile of Liverpool, maintained that 'the Papal system entirely demolishes the atonement' by its declaration of the sacrifice of the mass, and on this basis he made it clear that the Association would press the government for abolition of the

---

[23] *Scotsman*, 6 October 1835.

[24] J. W. Ferguson was not an Evangelical although he was sympathetic to the party, eventually becoming incumbent of St James's, Edinburgh, from 1846-1854. See Chapter 1, p. 18, Chapter 6, p. 190.

[25] *Scotsman, 6 October 1835. Record,* 8 October 1835. *Reports on Speeches delivered at a meeting on Wednesday December 23 1835 for the Purpose of forming a Protestant Society for that City and its Vicinity* (Edinburgh, 1835), p. 3. *Reports of the Proceedings of the Edinburgh Protestant Association read at a Public Meeting of the Association and those friendly to its objects, held in the West Church on Friday 6 December 1839, with an appendix containing the speeches of the Rev H.McNeile of Liverpool* (Edinburgh, 1839), pp. 2, 14. *Address from the Protestant Association of the Members of the United Church of England and Ireland in Scotland* (Glasgow, 1851).

[26] *Scotsman*, 6 October 1835.

[27] *Reports on December 23 1835*, p. 31.

Maynooth grant.[28] Although McNeile strongly stated the Association's political programme, his speech, together with those of Craig and Greville, showed that spiritual concerns were at the heart of the work.

Following an increase in the Maynooth grant in 1845, John Hope, a lay member of the Church of Scotland, set up the Edinburgh Protestant Society in protest. But, despite the support of the Kirk, Hope's initiative was not universally welcomed. The Edinburgh Congregationalist, W. L. Alexander, declined to join the society, objecting to joint ventures with the Established Church while Nonconformist disabilities remained.[29] Again, the disruptions in the Scottish Episcopal Church and the Church of Scotland in the early 1840s alienated others. Many Free Churchmen were wary of joining a venture headed by the Kirk.[30] Similarly Drummond, by this time an English Episcopalian, although assuring Hope of a 'cordial desire to co-operate with you in your most praiseworthy efforts against Romanism', felt that after the upheaval of leaving the Scottish Episcopal Church it would not be 'prudent to involve [my congregation] in another controversy'. But he withdrew even this guarded support on hearing that Hope had invited John Alexander, incumbent of St Paul's, Carrubber's Close, Edinburgh, an admirer of the Scottish Communion Office, to join. Drummond's antipathy to the Scottish rite led him to brand Alexander with 'a zeal which tended to popery and not from it', adding, 'I would rather put my hand in the fire than co-operate with such men'.[31] In fact, Alexander himself refused to join Hope's society on similar grounds to Drummond, but for opposing reasons, since although he was 'anxious enough to overthrow Romanism...those who endeavour to do so should first be at unity among themselves'.[32] Later the Scottish Episcopal Church took an official line to decline membership because, as C. H. Terrot, Bishop of Edinburgh, put it, 'co-operation of the Scottish Episcopal Church in religious matters with those with whom we differ makes it difficult'.[33] Inter-church tensions in Scotland by 1845 hampered the Edinburgh Protestant Society.

---

[28] *Proceedings of the Edinburgh Protestant Association 6 December 1839*, pp. 18, 21.

[29] W. L. Alexander to John Hope, 25 November 1845, NAS, Hope MSS GD 253/28/11/12.

[30] Wolffe, *Protestant Crusade*, p. 138.

[31] D. T. K. Drummond to John Hope, 26 November 1845, NAS, Hope MS GD 253/28/11/6. D. T. K. Drummond to John Hope, 4 February 1846, NAS, Hope MS GD 253/28/14/73.

Note: in Wolffe, *Protestant Crusade*, p. 138, there is an error in supposing that Drummond's objection was to W. L. Alexander in the above letter.

[32] John Alexander to John Hope, 2 December 1845, NAS, Hope MS GD 253/28/12/24.

[33] Letter from Charles Terrot to John Hope, 16 December 1845, NAS, Hope MS GD 253/28/12/60.

Doctrinal and Practical Issues

But when Pope Pius IX restored the Roman Catholic hierarchy to England and Wales in 1850, a huge Protestant demonstration was held in Edinburgh in December of that year. Clergy and laymen of most denominations were present, among whom were Drummond and two of his congregation from St Thomas's, Edinburgh, Greville and John Wauchope. George Coventry, of Trinity Chapel, Edinburgh, and all the bishops of the Scottish Episcopal Church, apart from David Low of Ross and Argyll, joined in the opposition.[34] A distinct political agenda was formulated with a resolution to encourage the government to withdraw all aid to the Roman Catholic Church.[35] Out of this meeting the Free Churchmen, headed by William Cunningham, R. S. Candlish and James Begg, formed the Scottish Reformation Society in January 1851. Operative throughout Scotland, except in Glasgow where the Protestant Layman's Society was active,[36] it drew on the success of the 1850 meeting, aiming to be an inter-church society.

English Episcopalians were prominent in the Scottish Reformation Society as shown in Table 6.1. Additionally, Drummond served on the editorial board of the society's journal, *The Bulwark*, from an early stage.[37] The exact dates of service are not clear from the data available, but it can be seen that the representation of clergy and laity from St Thomas's, Edinburgh, was large, probably because of their close association with Cunningham, Candlish and Begg who were all resident in the city. Some Scottish Episcopal High Churchmen, like Charles Wordsworth, Bishop of St Andrews, Dunkeld and Dunblane, who held strong views on the unity of the Church, could not approve of any co-operation with Presbyterians because of 'the false position' of their separation from Episcopacy.[38] But Berkeley Addison had no such scruples and was followed by Ferguson and Coventry, and the mild Evangelical C. R. Teape, in 1883.[39] The mixed churchmanship of the society, of which English Episcopalians formed a substantial group, probably helped in its perpetuation until the end of the century.

---

[34] Peter Nockles, 'The Scottish Episcopal Church and the Oxford Movement', *Journal of Ecclesiastical History (47)* (1996), p. 673. *Scotsman*, 7 December 1850.

[35] *Scotsman*, 7 December 1850. *Inverness Courier*, 12 December 1850.

[36] Wolffe, *Protestant Crusade*, p. 160.

[37] *The Bulwark, passim*.

[38] Berkeley Addison, *Remarks on Wordsworth's Recent Letter Reprobating the Author's Conduct for Taking Part in Public Meetings of the Scottish Reformation Society* (Edinburgh, 1853), p. 6. *Record*, 20 February 1854.

[39] Scottish Reformation Society Minute Books, 1853-1884. *The Bulwark*, 1852-1853. Note: Berkeley Addison, although not an Evangelical in the 1840s, did seem to have some sympathy with Evangelicals by 1853, declaring himself to be a premillennialist at that time. See Addison, *Remarks on Wordsworth's Recent Letter*, pp. 9-10.

Table 6.1 Episcopal Committee Members of the Scottish Reformation Society, 1851-1880

ENGLISH EPISCOPAL CLERGY	CHURCH	ENGLISH EPISCOPAL LAITY	CHURCH	SCOTTISH EPISCOPAL CLERGY	CHURCH
D. T. K. Drummond	St Thomas's, Edinburgh	Daniel Ainslie	St Thomas's, Edinburgh	George Coventry	Trinity Chapel, Edinburgh
Richard Hibbs	St Vincent's, Edinburgh	J. H. Balfour	St Thomas's, Edinburgh	J. W. Ferguson	St James's, Edinburgh
J. D. Miller	St James's, Aberdeen	Mrs Buckle	St Thomas's, Edinburgh	Berkeley Addison	St John's, Edinburgh
G. W. Butler	St Thomas's, Edinburgh	W. F. Burnley	St Silas's, Glasgow	C. R. Teape	St Andrew's Back of Castle, Edinburgh
E. C. Dawson	St Thomas's Edinburgh	George Burns	St Silas's, Glasgow and Wemyss Bay		
		John Murray of Philiphaugh	Selkirk		
		Thomas Ogilvy	St Thomas's, Edinburgh		
		John Wauchope	St Thomas's, Edinburgh		

Source: Scottish Reformation Minute Books, 1853-1884; J. D. Miller, *A Lecture Delivered at the Request of the Aberdeen Reformation Society* (Aberdeen, 1858); Chapters 7, 8.

As in the Protestant Association, theological matters underpinned the concerns of the Scottish Reformation Society. Its founders declared their aims to rest on the basis of the Reformation and they sought to stand 'in opposition to a system which aims the overthrow of every form of Protestantism'. Tractarianism, which they feared contained 'disguised

Doctrinal and Practical Issues

Papists...pioneering the way to Rome', was also vigorously condemned.[40] Titles such as 'God's Word Regarding Twelve Leading Errors of Rome' and 'The Tractarian Heresy' appeared regularly in *The Bulwark*.[41] In 1860 the society set up the Protestant Institute which held regular lectures on theology and trained missionaries to work among Roman Catholics.[42] Theological matters lay at the heart of the work of the Scottish Reformation Society.

Although not seeking abolition of the Emancipation Bill, the society was active in petitioning Parliament to halt any assistance given to the Roman Catholic Church and was applauded by the moderate Evangelical newspaper, the *Christian Guardian*, as 'manned by vigilant sentinels'.[43] The society feared that, since the introduction of Roman Catholic bishoprics to England in 1851, 'the entire power and policy of Rome is being directed against Britain, with a view to its being subjected again to the degrading slavery of the Vatican'.[44] Accordingly, *The Bulwark* regularly informed its readers of the voting patterns of Members of Parliament on Catholic measures, so that electors could bring 'their influence to bear on wavering representatives'.[45] Mixed results ensued. On 16 December 1853 the society challenged the provision of Roman Catholic prison and army chaplains, believing that this hindered evangelism of Catholics, but without success.[46] Again, campaigns organised in 1855 for the repeal of the Maynooth grant were unfruitful.[47] But the society did obtain the support of Lord Clarendon, Lord Lieutenant of Ireland, for securing liberty of Protestants in Catholic countries to profess their faith.[48] Opposition to British money being paid to Catholic causes was high on the agenda, sometimes causing the society to appear heartless. In 1863 it opposed the reduction of the residency qualification from five years to six months which would have enabled earlier implementation of relief from the poor fund, fearing that this would increase Irish immigration with its attendant social problems. A nationwide protest was organised and Parliament was petitioned to consider the alternatives of maintaining the Irish poor, both in Britain and Ireland, by their own landlords, and

---

[40] Scottish Reformation Society Archives, 'Declaration of Principles of the Scottish Reformation Society'. R. S.Candlish, *The Aims and Principles of the Work of the Scottish Reformation Society* (Edinburgh, 1891), p. 2.

[41] *The Bulwark*, Volume 2 1852-1853, p. 167, 1853-1854, pp. 248-249.

[42] Wolffe, *Protestant Crusade*, p. 162.

[43] *Christian Guardian*, December 1853, p. 367.

[44] *The Bulwark*, Volume 1, 1851-1852, p. 1.

[45] *Ibid.*, p. 46.

[46] Scottish Reformation Society Minute Book, 16 December 1853 and 26 March 1855.

[47] *Ibid.*, 26 March 1855.

[48] *Ibid.*, 9 April 1854.

increasing facilities for returning Irish paupers to their own land. It is unclear whether these ideas were considered by the British government, but public outcry against the bill was considerable, leading to its defeat in 1863.[49] Reduction of financial support to a Church considered to be in error was an important facet of the work of the Scottish Reformation Society.

The premillennial theology of Evangelicals, which led them to believe that they were engaged with God in a battle to defeat the Antichrist situated in Rome, serves to put the events of 1863 into context.[50] It resulted in Evangelicals vigorously branding help given by the State to Catholic causes as national apostasy.[51] But this did not preclude them from engaging in their own philanthropic work among Catholics. For instance, the purpose of the Canongate Mission, Edinburgh, run by St Thomas's Church from the mid-1840s, was to bring material relief, education and evangelism to the poor of the area.[52] Table 6.2 illustrates the nationalities of the population of the Canongate in 1841 and 1851.

Table 6.2 Residents living 1/2 Mile from St Thomas's Canongate Mission, Edinburgh, 1841-1851

	Scottish	Irish	English	Other
1841	8,142	276	470	56
1851	9,648	567	230	14

Source: Enumerator's Schedule, Census Returns for Edinburgh, 1841, 1851. Stored in Edinburgh Room, Edinburgh City Library.

It is apparent that, while native Scots were the most numerous group in the Canongate, there were growing numbers of Irish-born residents. There is no evidence to suggest that the mission withheld material help and religious instruction from them. Rather, it would probably have aligned itself with most Evangelicals who regarded such efforts, linked to evangelism, as justifiable Christian charity. But they strongly opposed government initiatives involving public money as national capitulation to heresy.[53]

An attempt by Lord Murray in 1847 to provide separate education for Roman Catholic children in Thomas Guthrie's Ragged Schools sheds

---

[49] *The Position of Popery in Great Britain and the Means in Scotland for Resisting it, being the Report of the Operations of the Scottish Reformation Society for the Year 1863* (Edinburgh, 1864), pp.16-23.

[50] See Chapter 4, pp. 143-147.

[51] *Cf.* G. F. A. Best, *Shaftesbury* (London, 1964), p. 61.

[52] See Chapter 5.

[53] Philanthropy and proselytism of Roman Catholics frequently went hand-in-hand. At the Canongate poorhouse in Edinburgh in 1869 Catholics attended morning prayers compiled by the United Presbyterian Church and evening prayers read by a Protestant. Handley, *Irish in Modern Scotland*, pp. 256-258.

Doctrinal and Practical Issues 193

further light on Evangelical attitudes. At a public meeting on 2 July 1847 Guthrie objected to Murray's proposal, and Drummond secured a motion that the school should deliver 'the free and unrestricted use of the authorised version of the word of God'. Murray argued that the committee had no 'right to force the authorised version of the Bible' on Catholics,[54] and modern commentators have, likewise, referred to the policy as reprehensible.[55] But Guthrie believed that his brand of 'religious instruction was the very essence and element of those Ragged Schools'.[56] His philanthropy was informed by his religious conviction that Catholics were without authentic faith and were part of the Evangelical mission field.

At heart, the motives of the Scottish Evangelical Episcopalians considered here were driven by strong theological differences with the Roman Catholic Church, and with the belief that the Pope was the Antichrist. They manned Protestant societies and frequently lobbied Parliament to prevent concessions to Catholics. But they claimed no hatred of individuals to whom they provided philanthropic provision, admittedly alongside evangelism. However, Scottish Evangelical Episcopalians were not an isolated voice and worked with Presbyterians and High Churchmen in an effort to halt Catholic advance. Anti-Catholicism was a widespread movement.

Baptism

In Chapter 4 a preliminary investigation showed that Evangelicals and High Churchmen interpreted the effects of infant baptism quite differently. The problem revolved around what was meant by the word 'regeneration' at the end of the Anglican service. Did it imply, as High Churchmen believed, that God's grace was exhibited in baptism by the planting of his Spirit in the soul of the candidate, or did this occur, as Evangelicals contended, at conversion? The divergence of opinion was to lead to dispute. From 1800 to 1850 there were at least forty-two secessions from the Church of England to the Baptist churches[57] and Episcopal Scotland was rocked with controversy.

William Humphrey, a Roman Catholic who had been the incumbent of St Mary Magdalene, Dundee, in the late 1860s, commented of the numerically dominant High Churchmen in Scotland at the time that their

---

[54] *Report of a Discussion Regarding Ragged Schools, July 2 1847* (Edinburgh, 1847), pp. 45-46.
[55] Handley, *Irish in Modern Scotland*, pp. 198-201.
[56] *Report Regarding Ragged Schools*, p. 31.
[57] Grayson Carter, *Anglican Evangelicals: Protestant Secessions from the Via Media 1800-1850* (Oxford, 2001), pp. 399-402.

'strong point was Baptismal Regeneration'.[58] Typically, Daniel Sandford, Bishop of Edinburgh in 1821, preached that 'the baptised person is regenerated, or born again',[59] and Berkeley Addison of St John's, Edinburgh, in 1843, pronounced, 'I thought Baptism was the gate of heaven...the grace freely flowing through the blessed sacrament'.[60] Alexander Jolly, Bishop of Moray, Ross and Caithness, in 1826, continued by expounding the classic High Church understanding that 'the baptismal gift...may lie for ever dormant, or it may bloom into the most vigorous life of God', this being accomplished when 'the Church, through her ordinances, supplies the means of gradually unfolding and maturing the germ of life thus breathed into the soul'.[61] The dominant High Church sector of Scottish Episcopalianism taught that regeneration accompanied baptism.

In 1815, Richard Mant, the future Bishop of Down and Connor, elucidated High Church doctrine. He did not say that baptism guaranteed salvation. It could be forfeited because of lack of instruction from the Church, or from unbelief and disobedience. If this occurred there would be a need for a personal rededication, a type of conversion experience. But he criticised Evangelicals for dismissing baptismal regeneration and treating the rite as a mere sign. At the time, Mant's view was taken as the accepted High Church line,[62] and was adhered to by the Tractarians in the 1830s. For instance, in 1835, although E. B. Pusey, in *Tract 67*, called for more evidence of spiritual renewal in baptised people, causing Bishop Henry Phillpotts of Exeter to accuse him of downgrading the efficacy of the sacrament,[63] he never relinquished the traditional view. For Pusey, God 'washed away...sins in Baptism' and the sacrament was 'a living seal bearing with it the impress of Divine Nature'.[64] High Churchmen in nineteenth-century Britain emphasised the spiritually regenerative nature of baptismal grace, while admitting that mature faith resulted from spiritual nurturing.

---

[58] William Humphrey, *Recollections of Scottish Episcopalianism* (London, 1896), p. 4.

[59] *Scottish Episcopal Review and Magazine*, June 1821.

[60] Berkeley Addison, *An Earnest and Solemn Remonstrance Addressed to the Rev D. T. K. Drummond* (Edinburgh, 1843), p. 8.

[61] William Walker, *The Life of the Right Reverend Alexander Jolly DD* (Edinburgh, 1878), pp. 125-126.

[62] W. J. C. Ervine, 'Doctrine and Diplomacy: Some Aspects of the life and thought of Anglican Evangelical Clergy 1797-1837' (Cambridge University Ph. D. thesis, 1979), p. 64.

[63] Nockles, *Oxford Movement*, p. 232.

[64] E. B. Pusey, *Tract 67*, pp. 173-176. Quoted in Geoffrey Rowell, *The Vision Glorious* (Oxford, 1983), pp. 75-76.

Doctrinal and Practical Issues

Evangelicals opposed these ideas as diminishing the role of faith in the decision to embrace Christianity and as redolent of Roman Catholicism.[65] But, although they linked regeneration to conversion alone, they did, in fact, display a range of understanding of the term regeneration. The very variety of their views was indicative of their problem with the Anglican rite. In the early years some, like Basil Woodd of Bentinck Chapel, London, and Thomas Scott of Aston Sandford, Buckinghamshire, veered slightly towards High Church beliefs, holding that some sort of special grace, but not regeneration, resulted from baptism. However, although the respected Charles Simeon of Cambridge also took this position, Henry Foster of Long Acre Chapel probably spoke for most when he described the baptismal service as 'unhappily drawn up' and inexpressive of the need for conversion.[66] When Mant, in 1812, criticised Evangelicals for holding such divergent views, a spectrum of responses was displayed. Some Evangelicals rallied to Woodd and Scott. For example J. B. Sumner, who was to become Archbishop of Canterbury in 1848, took a moderate stance in 1815, pressing that something spiritual was apparent in baptism, while at the same time allowing that actual regeneration could often be separated from it.[67] Henry Budd, the clerical secretary of the Prayer Book and Homily Society, in 1827, took matters further, urging Evangelicals to take baptism seriously. He criticised believing parents who brought their children up in the assumption that they were pagans and not the adopted children of God through baptism. In contrast Budd believed that, through the infant rite, such children were incorporated into the mystical 'Body of Christ' immediately after the prayers of the sponsors and would come personally to profess a faith which was already theirs.[68] However, most Evangelicals followed T. T. Biddulph, of Bristol, and John Scott, of North Ferriby, understanding that baptism of believers' children procured entry to only the visible church, similar to Presbyterian belief.[69] Although not entirely

---

[65] Ervine, 'Doctrine and Diplomacy', p. 64.

[66] *Ibid.*, p. 55.

[67] J. B. Sumner, *Apostolical Preaching Considered, in an Examination of St Paul's Epistles* (London, 1815), p. 137 n. Quoted in D. W. Bebbington, *Evangelicalism in Modern Britain*, (London, 1993), p. 9.

[68] Bebbington, *Evangelicalism,* pp. 78-82. Nockles, *Oxford Movement*, p. 230.

[69] A. C. Cheyne, *The Transforming of the Kirk* (Edinburgh, 1983), p. 105. By 1894 the United Presbyterian Church in *Presbyterian Forms of Service* plainly declared baptised children as 'members of the visible Church'. *Presbyterian Forms of Service Issued by the Devotional Service Association in Connection with the United Presbyterian Church* (Edinburgh, 1894), p. 115. In 1898, the Free Church published *A New Directory for the Public Worship of God* which again stressed that baptised infants were given a right to all the privileges of the Church 'so far as their age allows'. *A New Directory for the Public Worship of God* (Edinburgh, 1898), p. 123. Only the Church of Scotland in its *Euchologion* in 1867 was marginally less succinct, praying that, in

denying the possibility that some germs of piety might result from baptism, they emphasised that the future conversion of the child would be needed to ensure its salvation. In this thinking baptism was viewed as a parallel to the Jewish rite of circumcision, a signing-up contract into a society where privileges were enjoyed until the person chose to opt out of the system. But even this interpretation was unsatisfactory for George Bugg of Lutterworth, and George Nicholson of Little Budworth, who represented a militant wing dismissing baptismal regeneration entirely.[70] The situation became so uneasy that a group of clergy in the west of England seceded from the Church in 1815, pointing to the service of infant baptism as one of its concerns.[71] Thus, in the first two decades of the nineteenth century, various Evangelicals allowed that something spiritual happened at baptism while others viewed the service as an initiation only, with conversion at a later date resulting in true regeneration.

Over the 1830s and 1840s the situation remained largely unchanged. In 1844 S. C. Wilks, the editor of the *Christian Observer*, identified the majority of Evangelicals as followers of Biddulph. There were, also, representatives of Budd's point of view, notably Edward Bickersteth of Watton, and others with strong Calvinist beliefs, who understood that the elect were regenerated in baptism.[72] However in 1848, when the High Churchman, Henry Phillpotts, Bishop of Exeter, refused to appoint the Evangelical, G. C. Gorham, because he did not hold that regeneration always accompanied infant baptism, a new mood was heralded among Evangelicals. When Gorham appealed to the Privy Council[73] it concluded that the Church of England service was unclear, and that there was room for divergent views on the topic. As a result, most Evangelicals felt their beliefs had been vindicated. In some cases this led them to soften their stance and to concede that baptism did, indeed, mark at least the first stage of Christian life. Henry Melvill, of Brighton, even went as far as to be favourable to the doctrine of baptismal regeneration, while the *Christian Observer*, in 1868, took a middle path, denouncing on the one hand the view that regeneration never accompanied baptism, and, on the other, the

---

baptism, children 'ingrafted into Christ the true vine' should in due time renew their baptismal vows. *Euchologion: A Book of Common Order Being Forms of Worship Issued by the Church Service Society* (Edinburgh, 1867), p. 15.

[70] Ervine, 'Doctrine and Diplomacy', pp. 69-70.

[71] *Ibid.*, pp 69-86. Carter, *Anglican Evangelicals*, pp. 105-151. Nockles, *Oxford Movement*, pp. 229-232.

[72] Peter Toon, *Evangelical Theology 1833-1856* (London, 1977), pp. 190-191.

[73] Gorham had applied to the Court of Arches in 1849 to compel Phillpotts to institute him, but it ruled in favour of the Bishop's belief that the Anglican service taught that infants were regenerated at baptism. Kenneth Hylson-Smith, *Evangelicals in the Church of England 1734-1984* (Edinburgh, 1989), pp. 123-125.

Doctrinal and Practical Issues

belief that it invariably did.[74] Throughout the nineteenth century there was thus a range of views among Evangelicals on the rite of infant baptism. Some accommodated aspects of High Church belief, while others rejected it totally.

Although views are sometimes unclear, it would appear from the existing literature that Scottish Evangelical Episcopalians also held a mixture of views in the nineteenth century. Some followed Biddulph, or Bugg and Nicholson, believing that regeneration in baptism could be defined as entry only to the visible church. While it is not always apparent whether they conceded, along with Biddulph, that germs of piety resulted from baptism, the overriding emphasis of this group was that regeneration occurred at conversion. In this respect they were typical of mainstream Anglican Evangelicalism. For instance, in 1826, Edward Craig, of St James's, Edinburgh, like Biddulph, allowed that baptism might confer 'the inchoation of grace – the initial blessing which in after life is to be developed',[75] but declared 'I am not prepared to say...all men in a Christian country, who have been baptised...have actually been grafted into Christ's mystical body'.[76] Again, Richard Hibbs, of St Thomas's, Edinburgh, argued in 1848 against 'holding that all who are baptised in their infancy are necessarily Christ's'.[77] But C. P. Miles, of St Jude's, Glasgow, is somewhat difficult to pin down. In 1844, seemingly along the lines of Craig and Hibbs, he asked, 'Are we then to conclude that every baptized child is regenerated?' and answered, 'assuredly not',[78] illustrating his point by adding 'the baptized community...not excluding the ecclesiastics themselves...are wrapped in darkness'.[79] But then he appeared, possibly, to veer towards Budd, implying that the regeneration of baptism was 'in its proper and highest sense...new birth' adding, however, similar to Biddulph again, that this operated in the child of believing Christians only until 'of age to take it upon himself'.[80] For Miles baptism resulted in God looking on the child as if he or she were a true believer until the age of accountability. At that time the gift could be jettisoned or appropriated by a definite decision allied to a conversion experience. Craig, Hibbs and Miles, holding views similar to Biddulph, Bugg and Nicholson, and, sometimes, Budd,

---

[74] Eric Culbertson, 'Evangelical Theology 1857-1900' (London University Ph. D. thesis, 1991), pp. 154-157.

[75] Edward Craig, *A Reply to the Rev. James Walker M.A. Rendered Necessary by his Serious Expostulation on the Subject of Baptismal Regeneration* (London, 1826), p. 21.

[76] Craig, *Reply*, p. 62.

[77] Richard Hibbs, *The Substance of a Series of Discourses on Baptism, Preached Prior to a General Confirmation, in which it is shown that the teaching of the Church of England on the subject is consentient with Holy Scripture* (London, 1848), pp. 21-22.

[78] C. P. Miles, *Voice of the Glorious Reformation* (London, 1844), pp. 498-499.

[79] *Ibid.*, p. 504.

[80] *Ibid.*, pp. 445, 498.

were representative of the different emphases in nineteenth-century Evangelicalism.

However, Craig, Hibbs and Miles, unlike High Churchmen, all believed that baptism did not convey God's grace universally and they claimed that this was the doctrine held by the Church of England. They pointed to Article XXVII as demonstrating that 'faith is confirmed...by virtue of prayer' rather than by an automatic result of baptism.[81] Looking at the service itself, they considered that it implied only a charitable assumption, not a guaranteed promise, that new life would be granted.[82] Miles referred to the writings of several Reformers, showing that the sixteenth-century Articles and service they had drawn up reflected the belief that regeneration was not tied to baptism. Thomas Cranmer, the framer of the Prayer Book service, was quoted as saying, 'those that come feignedly, and those that come unfeignedly, both be washed in sacramental water, but both be not washed with the Holy Ghost, and clothed with Christ'. Hugh Latimer, Bishop of Worcester from 1535 to 1555, who had written, 'what is this regeneration? It is not to be christened in water as the Papist firebrands expound it', and James Ussher, Archbishop of Armagh from 1625 to 1656, whose words 'Are all they then that are partakers of the outward washing of baptism, partakers also of the inward washing of the Spirit?...surely no', were among eighteen Anglican divines quoted by Miles in identifying the Evangelical position with that of the Church of England.[83] But Miles epitomised Evangelical uneasiness with the Anglican service when he took refuge in the writings of the Archbishop of Canterbury, Edmund Grindal, and Bishop Robert Horne of Winchester in 1567, who admitted that 'we tolerate until the Lord shall give us better times the interrogations to infants'.[84] While Scottish Evangelical Episcopalians argued insistently that the word regeneration used in the baptismal service did not imply unrestricted grace, the rite did present difficulties for them.

After the Gorham judgement the available evidence suggests that none of the Scottish Evangelical Episcopalians adopted the accommodating lines conceded by some Anglicans. Seemingly reacting against the High Churchmanship of Scottish Episcopalianism, they retained Biddulph's position that baptism procured only formal entry to the Church. For instance D. T. K. Drummond of St Thomas's, Edinburgh, in 1855

---

[81] *Ibid.*, p. 495. See also Hibbs, *Discourses on Baptism*, pp. 38-39. Edward Craig, *A Respectful Remonstrance Addressed to the Rev James Walker M. A. on the Subject of a Sermon Preached before the Bishop and Clergy of the United Diocese of Edinburgh and Fife and Glasgow in St John's Chapel on 22nd June 1825* (Edinburgh, 1825), pp. 22-23.

[82] Craig, *Respectful Remonstrance*, pp. 22-23. Miles, *Glorious Reformation*, pp. 496-497.

[83] Miles, *Glorious Reformation*, pp. 435-492.

[84] *Ibid.*, p. 502.

denounced any clergyman 'who stands by the baptismal font and dogmatically proclaims that everyone therein is really and truly changed by the operation of the Holy Spirit on his heart'.[85] In the same year his wife described infant baptism as a reception 'into the outward and visible Church'.[86] The views of A. H. R. Hebden, curate at St Thomas's from 1864 to 1865, had actually hardened by 1874 when he admitted that 'I am unable to persuade myself that [infant baptism] rests on scriptural authority'.[87] T. K. Talon, of St Vincent's, Edinburgh, possibly exhibited more moderate views. In 1866 he wrote, 'everyone that is admitted by baptism into the fellowship of Christ's religion, is thereby made a "member of Christ"...numbered among God's elect children'.[88] But it is not entirely clear whether he was referring to only the adult rite or to baptism in general, and so no definite conclusion can be postulated. Apart, possibly, from Talon, the clergy discussed here were representative of strict Anglican Evangelicalism after the Gorham judgement.

However, Scottish Evangelical Episcopalians took a benevolent view of the fate of children dying in infancy. Craig made it clear in 1826 that 'we would believe that even the children of unbelieving parents and of the actual heathen are, if removed before the age of responsibility, sanctified by the Redeemer's merits'.[89] Craig, who did not hold strong Calvinist sentiments on election, thus understood the bounds of God's grace to be limitless. But Miles, a predestinarian, concurred, presumably because he understood all such children to be among the elect.[90] Commenting on the subject in 1840, Miles quoted the teaching of the early Reformer John Wyclif, 'those are fools and presumptuous which affirm such infants not to be saved which die without baptism'.[91] The beliefs of Scottish High Churchmen are unavailable, but strict and moderate Calvinist Evangelicals alike held a charitable understanding of the eternal destination of the souls of infants.

The divergent baptismal views of Scottish Evangelicals and High Churchmen led to controversy in the nineteenth century. From 1825 to 1826 Craig had a serious dispute concerning a sermon on baptismal regeneration preached by James Walker, incumbent of St Peter's, Edinburgh. Several points of major disagreement between the parties were

---

[85] D. T. K. Drummond, *Engravings of the New Testament* (Edinburgh, 1855), p. 291.

[86] Harriet Drummond, *Emily Vernon or Filial Piety Exemplified* (Edinburgh, 1855), p. 243.

[87] A. H. R. Hebden, *Baptism: Are We Right?* (London, 1874), p. 3. Hebden, however, does not appear to have seceded from the Church of England.

[88] T. K. Talon, *Sermons* (London, 1871), p. 117.

[89] Craig, *Reply*, p. 37.

[90] See Chapter 4, p. 142.

[91] Miles, *Glorious Reformation*, p. 505.

evident, illustrating the difficulty in reaching a working relationship. The theological gulf between Craig and Walker was vast. Fundamental beliefs which Craig expressed as 'the way in which the Almighty resumes his legitimate throne in the heart of his rebel creature' were involved.[92] Craig disagreed with Walker that both scripture and the early church taught that regeneration, 'a spiritual grace imparted to the soul', always occurred at baptism 'without exception', even in babies.[93] Craig's understanding of the Bible was that there was no evidence 'of a single instance in which baptism and regeneration are stated to be synchronical'.[94] Although Craig, in the manner of Biddulph, accepted that the children of believing parents often, but not always, received some sort of spiritual benefit at baptism, he pressed Walker to accept that others who were 'brought to the baptismal font...and regularly baptized' were not regenerate. He maintained that in such cases the service had been 'merely an outward ceremony' and, consequently, it was the duty of clergy to preach the doctrine of conversion.[95] The problem was thus concerned with biblical interpretation. Walker believed the Bible taught that God's grace was transmitted universally at baptism whereas Craig, although not dismissing the occasional imparting of grace, understood it to happen generally at conversion.

Walker replied by striking at the heart of Evangelical theology. Objecting to clergy 'telling their people that some are not yet regenerate',[96] he understood the Evangelical doctrine of conversion as 'the consequence of absolute delusion...mere animal excitement',[97] and that the preaching was 'altogether unnecessary and improper'.[98] Craig, likewise, questioned the *raison d'être* of Walker's theology. He argued that it offered, with its stress on post-baptismal discipline and church attendance, a distorted view as to the way of obtaining what he understood to be real faith. For Craig, 'true conversion is not so slight a work...the outward change of some bad customs. It is a new birth and being'.[99] He maintained that many baptised people, if challenged, would realise that they were in a state of separation from God, that if we 'would not study to cozen ourselves, the discovery whether we are or not [a new creation] would not be so hard', and accused Walker that his sermon was 'likely to lull the souls of men into a state of

---

[92] Craig, *Reply*, p. 3.
[93] *Ibid.*, pp. 7-8.
[94] Craig, *Respectful Remonstrance*, pp. 15-16.
[95] Craig, *Reply*, pp. 15-17.
[96] *Ibid.*, p. 17.
[97] Walker, *Sermon*, p. 30.
[98] Craig, *Reply*, p. 17.
[99] *Ibid.*, p. 57.

Doctrinal and Practical Issues

religious indifference'.[100] The theological dispute thus widened into one where each clergyman challenged the other to justify his doctrine and thus his function within the Christian community.

Other important points of theology came to light during the conflict. Craig's Calvinistic Evangelicalism taught the doctrine of the perseverance of the saints, that true believers remained so despite sin. It was irreconcilable with Walker's teaching that the grace of baptism could be lost. While Wesleyan Arminianism had something in common with High Church dogma, teaching that faith could be relinquished as a result of sin,[101] Craig, by contrast, believed that, 'if baptism is absolutely regeneration, then the subsequent conduct of the individual cannot make it not so'.[102] There was also a fundamental disagreement as to the value of preaching in nourishing faith. Walker had affirmed 'that the sacraments are the ordinary means by which the Christian life is conferred, formed, fed and brought to maturity'.[103] But Craig understood this to be close to Roman Catholic teaching, and denounced it as 'Popery'. While not dismissing the benefits of the sacraments, Craig believed that 'an enlightened, judicious, and copious administration of God's word, by full and frequent preaching, is the life of true religion'.[104] Calvinistic Evangelicalism did not meld with Scottish Episcopal High Church doctrine.

Because of such obvious and serious differences, each of the disputants tried to show that the Church of England upheld his beliefs. Craig quoted Article XXVII that baptism is 'a sign of Regeneration...whereby, as an Instrument, they that receive Baptism rightly are grafted into the Church'[105] as according with his beliefs. He understood the Prayer Book service, when used by believing parents and sponsors, merely prayed that 'with the outward sign, the inward and spiritual grace may be communicated' at some time to the child.[106] Walker agreed that the service was intended for believers only, that 'baptism of prayerless and vicious parents' was a 'perversion'.[107] But he nevertheless understood that 'the church hath ever believed' that baptism conferred regeneration[108] of which 'the sense of our

---

[100] *Ibid.*, pp. 57, 62.
[101] Bebbington, *Evangelicalism*, p. 28.
[102] Craig, *Reply*, p. 30. See also Chapter 4, p. 119.
[103] Craig, *Reply*, p. 10.
[104] *Ibid.*, p. 41.
[105] Craig, *Respectful Remonstrance*, p. 22.
[106] *Ibid.*, pp. 22-25.
[107] *Ibid.*, p. 25.
[108] James Walker, *A Serious Expostulation with the Rev. Edward Craig, M. A., in Reference to the Doctrine Falsely Attributed (in a remonstrance addressed) to the Rev James Walker, Humbly submitted to the Judgement of the Bishops and Clergy and Earnestly tendered to the consideration of the Laity of the Episcopal Communion in Scotland* (Edinburgh, 1826), p. 5.

liturgy admits not a moment's hesitation'.[109] Each, therefore, believed that the Church of England upheld his own particular theology.

The dispute led to distrust among Churchmen. Craig accused those who taught baptismal regeneration to be 'notoriously light-minded and frivolous men...who wanted the exemption from diligent pastoral labour', and whose parishes exhibited 'practical religion at a low ebb'. He pointed to what he saw to be the contrast with Evangelical clergy who 'laboured to win souls'.[110] Walker, for his part, highlighted the activism of Evangelicals as leading to the formation of 'those busy associations of ignorant men and of prejudiced women',[111] with their 'total want of charity, and the insulting activity of opposition...[as] proof that...they are now profoundly ignorant of the truth as it is in Jesus, at least as it is calculated to affect the heart'.[112] The lines of the dispute produced a deep antagonism between the parties.

In contrast to Craig's antipathy to the High Church doctrine, his empathy with Scottish Presbyterian teaching on baptismal regeneration was marked. Walker had criticised the Westminster Confession for admitting that there could be exceptions to baptismal regeneration as a 'serious error'. Craig, however, aligned himself with the Confession by seeing the issue of exceptions as 'the grand point of difference between you and me'.[113] Moreover, Craig remarked that there were 'several clergy in the Edinburgh diocese' to whom Walker's sermon would have been 'controversial'.[114] It is not clear from existing literature who these were, but Walker himself commanded loyalty from High Churchmen throughout Scotland. William Rulerson, Dean of Argyll, Charles Fyvie of Inverness, Donald McColl of Appin, Duncan MacKenzie of Dingwall and John MacMillan of Arpafilie, near Inverness, sent a written statement in January 1826 to the Scottish bishops supporting the doctrine of baptismal regeneration, and described Craig's views as an 'enthusiastic novelty of doctrine'.[115] Bishop Patrick Torry of St Andrews, Dunkeld and Dunblane also wrote to Walker on 14 February 1826, thanking him for the sermon as being of 'vital importance to the preservation of Christian truth, and to the purity as well as the existence of the Christian life'.[116] Bishop Daniel Sandford of Edinburgh communicated to Torry that he had 'received an official requisition' from

---

[109] James Walker, *A Sermon Preached in St John's Episcopal Chapel on Wednesday June 22 1825* (Edinburgh, 1826), p. 21.

[110] Craig, *Respectful Remonstrance*, pp. 34-39.

[111] Walker, *Sermon*, p. 23.

[112] *Ibid.*, p. 57.

[113] Craig, *Reply*, pp. 12-13.

[114] *Ibid.*, p. 4.

[115] 'Protests by Clergy to Bishops on the Rev E. Craig's statement', 3 January 1826, NAS, CH12/12/219.

[116] J. M. Neale, *The Life and Times of Patrick Torry* (London, 1856), p. 140.

Doctrinal and Practical Issues

another bishop asking that Craig be officially disciplined.[117] But despite this large body of opinion against Craig it was decided, at a meeting of the bishops on 9 August 1826, to take the matter no further for fear that he might use it 'to his own advantage'.[118] By August 1826, the only official counter-measure against Craig's views was the production by Alexander Jolly, Bishop of Moray, of *A Friendly Address on Baptismal Regeneration* at the request of 'Walker and other influential Churchmen in the south'.[119] In 1826 High Churchmen feared that Craig's doctrine of baptism was capable of causing a major disturbance in the Scottish Episcopal Church.

A similar disagreement arose in 1836 following the publication of a *Catechism*[120] by Daniel Bagot of St James's, Edinburgh. *Stephen's Episcopal Magazine* was critical that Bagot had 'omitted all mention of baptismal regeneration'.[121] A vigorous correspondence on the subject ensued during the second half of 1836, with the editor maintaining the orthodox High Church line that if a person 'fall into sin after baptism, he cannot again be regenerated; but he may and must be converted before he can enter the kingdom of God'.[122] The argument followed the lines of the previous one between Craig and Walker, with Drummond now contributing to the debate and maintaining that the High Church doctrine was 'unscriptural and dangerous' because it hindered people coming to authentic faith.[123] Evangelicals considered the matter of such importance that Bagot, Drummond and 'some others of [their] Edinburgh brethren' withdrew their subscriptions from *Stephen's Episcopal Magazine*. Tempers were frayed, and Bagot was accused of communicating to the editor 'in a style and language very unbecoming to a clergyman'.[124] The working relationship between Evangelicals and High Churchmen again broke down over the issue of infant baptism.

The seriousness with which Scottish Evangelical Episcopalians and High Churchmen approached the topic of baptism was seen in petitions brought to the highest authorities in Britain. By 1839, some Evangelicals were calling for a revision of the Anglican Prayer Book which would remove ambiguous phrases from various services, including the one for baptism. This was supported by J. D. Hull, later of Huntly Chapel, in a pamphlet

---

[117] *Ibid.*, p. 142.

[118] *Ibid.*, p. 147.

[119] Walker, *Alexander Jolly*, pp. 124-125.

[120] Daniel Bagot, *A Catechism Explanatory of the Leading Truths of the Gospel* (Edinburgh, 1939).

[121] *Stephen's Episcopal Magazine* (1836), pp. 172-176.

[122] *Ibid.*, p. 344.

[123] T. Stephen to D. T. K. Drummond, December 1836, LPL, MS 1537 f. 12.

[124] *Ibid.* It has not been possible to identify the other clergy.

published in 1840.[125] Similarly, official pronouncements from both Evangelicals and High Churchmen followed the decision of the Privy Council on the Gorham case. When the High Church Bishop of London, C. J. Blomfield, opposed the Privy Council ruling on 8 March 1850, the Scottish bishops William Skinner of Aberdeen and Primus, Patrick Torry of St Andrews, Dunkeld and Dunblane, A. P. Forbes of Brechin, and W. J. Trower of Glasgow and Galloway, wrote to thank him 'for refusing to concur in a decision whereby it is propounded that the regeneration of infants in holy baptism is not the clear doctrine of the Church of England'.[126] The Scottish Episcopal Synod, meeting in Aberdeen on 19 March, obtained a unanimous vote declaring that the Gorham judgement had no legal authority in Scotland.[127] A group of eighty Evangelical Episcopalians in Scotland, led by Drummond, responded by sending a letter, in May 1850, to the Archbishop of Canterbury, J. B. Sumner, severing themselves from the teaching of the Scottish bishops which enjoined 'that then and there in the sacrament of baptism every child is regenerate and grafted into the body of Christ's Church'.[128] The Gorham judgement thus perpetuated controversy in Scotland.

It has been impossible to locate Scottish Evangelical Episcopal baptismal views after 1860, apart from those of Talon,[129] but this discussion has revealed that earlier on Craig, Drummond, Hibbs and Hull were typical of mainstream Anglican Evangelicalism in stressing that baptism marked entry only to the visible church. Miles, however, possibly, acknowledged a type of baptismal regeneration which was something less decisive than conversion. In this respect he was marginally closer to High Churchmen than the others. But all denied the universality of baptismal grace, understanding it as stepping close to Roman Catholic doctrine.

Baptismal doctrine has been shown to have had the potential of escalating into a serious division between Evangelicals and High Churchmen in Scotland as each challenged the other to substantiate their claim to be the legitimate representatives of Anglicanism. That this did not happen can be attributed to the fact that both parties, as was also the case in England, found it possible to read the service in a manner consonant with

---

[125] J. D. Hull and William Winstanley Hull, *Observations on a Petition for the Revision of the Liturgy of the United Church of England and Ireland in a report of the discussion in the House of Lords*, Second Edition (London, 1840).

[126] *Record*, 28 March 1850.

[127] A. J. Ross, *Memoir of Alexander Ewing* (London, 1877), p. 173. Bishop Alexander Ewing of Argyll and the Isles, who was not as overtly High Church in his beliefs, gave only guarded support for the decision in an attempt to prevent a future general synod laying down 'some formula on Baptism which might have been the cause of severing our connection with the Church of England'.

[128] *Record*, 27 June 1850.

[129] See Chapter 6, p. 199.

Doctrinal and Practical Issues

their own theology. However, when this variety of understandings was eventually endorsed by the Gorham judgement of 1850 Scottish Evangelical Episcopalians, unlike some of their counterparts in England, did not soften their views on baptism at all. This can be attributed, partly, to their interaction with Evangelicals in the Presbyterian denominations and to a reaction to the dominant High Church teaching in the Scottish Episcopal Church. Baptismal doctrine was a matter of serious division between Evangelicals and High Churchmen in nineteenth-century Scotland. It certainly soured working relationships but, of itself, did not lead to a major disruption.

Architecture

The architecture of a newly erected church is probably one of the most obvious declarations of its heritage, beliefs and worship. For instance, the often plain design of Scottish Episcopal churches in the eighteenth and early nineteenth centuries arose, in part, out of their history. Qualified congregations, allowed to meet unhindered after the Act of Toleration in 1712,[130] were anxious not to aggravate their position and chose to adopt simple buildings similar to those of Scottish Presbyterianism.[131] After the incorporation of the Nonjuring congregations in 1792, the Church was in no financial position to embark on a major building programme, and buildings usually remained plain. But early in nineteenth-century Britain an interest in antiquity and national heritage developed, extending into the realm of church architecture. In Edinburgh, for example, St John's and St Paul's, both built in 1818, were of Gothic design, St John's having an elaborate fan-vaulted plaster ceiling.[132] Scottish Episcopalian architecture in the early nineteenth century reflected past and current trends.

Against this background Evangelical Scottish Episcopalians built churches reflecting their religious beliefs, often rebelling against current fashions. St James's, Broughton Place, Edinburgh, erected in 1820, was part of a plain tenement block, scarcely recognisable as a church. It made a striking contrast to the nearby ornate St John's and St George's. Although St James's cost only £4,000, compared to the £18,000 for St John's, its total lack of any adornment seemed to express the Evangelical conviction that heartfelt response, rather than outward form, was at the centre of Christian

---

[130] See Chapter 1, p. 29.

[131] Pulpits were placed against one of the long walls of simple rectangular churches, with a plain wooden altar positioned inconspicuously beneath, and baptismal basins were used rather than fonts. F. C. Eeles, *Alcuin Club Collection XVII: Traditional Ceremonial and Customs Connected with the Scottish Liturgy* (London, 1910), p. 14.

[132] George Hay, *The Architecture of Scottish Post-Reformation Churches* (Oxford, 1957), p. 149.

experience.¹³³ The chosen design was probably influenced, too, by the acrimonious argument between its incumbent, Edward Craig, and Bishop George Gleig of Brechin,¹³⁴ leading to a clear statement of Craig's beliefs in the style of the façade of the chapel. Again, the interior design of St James's, which was like a 'plain courtroom...uncompromising' with no decoration whatsoever,¹³⁵ was expressive of the Evangelical desire to focus the mind of the worshipper on God, by encouraging attention to the spoken word rather than the visual experience. St Jude's, West George Street, Glasgow, which was not at the centre of great controversy when it was built in 1838, adopted the more customary style of a Greek temple. But it was, again, severely plain with undecorated pillars, apart from those in the outside porches.¹³⁶ The simple design of Evangelical Scottish Episcopal chapels in the early decades of the nineteenth century was expressive of the theology of their founders.

John Mason Neale, a High Churchman who in 1839 founded the Cambridge Camden Society, later known as the Ecclesiological Society, was concerned to guide taste in church architecture. His ideal was the pre-Reformation, Gothic style with tall spires and an overall height which would dominate the skyline, so reminding people of their faith and heritage. Chancels, which had previously often been used as storehouses or schoolrooms, were now to be raised and occupied by surpliced choirs; open pews were to replace the old high box variety; and prominent fonts, placed at the doors of churches, rather than the small basins which had traditionally been attached to pulpits, were recommended. The altar, often made of stone and embellished with a cross, was given pride of place, with pulpits and lecterns removed to the side of the nave. Stencilling, stained glass, colourful encaustic tiles, and altars vested with liturgical colours were regarded as vehicles for enhancing devotion. In short, parish churches were to become like mini cathedrals or college chapels.¹³⁷

In 1843, Scottish Episcopal chapels in the ecclesiological idiom were erected at Cruden and Fyvie, Aberdeenshire.¹³⁸ Tractarians, such as the

---

[133] St James's Minute Book, 30 October 1835. St James's Church, Aberdeen, Archives. Gilbert Cole, *A Church for Golden Acre* (Edinburgh, 1988), pp. 18-20. John Gifford, Colin MacWilliam, David Walker, *The Buildings of Scotland* (London, 1984), pp. 277-278.

[134] See Chapter 8, p. 248.

[135] Charles Jenkins, *Cathedral Monthly Paper* (Edinburgh, 1895). Quoted in Cole, *Church in Golden Acre*, pp. 20-21.

[136] Elizabeth Williamson, Anne Riches, Malcolm Higg, *The Buildings of Scotland: Glasgow* (1990), p. 60.

[137] J. F. White, *The Cambridge Movement: The Ecclesiologists and the Gothic Revival* (Cambridge, 1962), pp. 1-24, 178-197, 231-236, 256-258.

[138] Scottish Roman Catholics had little money to spend on architectural innovations before 1850. But for Scottish Episcopalians Aberdeenshire continued to lead the way

Marchioness of Lothian, were involved in the movement. She organised the building of St John's, Jedburgh, in 1844 to accord with her own newly found Oxford Movement convictions, incorporating the current medieval principles of architecture.[139] Presbyterian churches also adopted some architectural novelties. While simple, rectangular construction remained common, particularly in rural areas,[140] the extension to Dunfermline Abbey and the alterations to St Nicholas, Aberdeen, were surprisingly Gothic Revival.[141] Similar trends were pursued by Evangelicals in the Church of England, illustrated in buildings such as Christ Church, West Hartlepool, built in 1854.[142] Ecclesiological influence increased nationwide by the mid-nineteenth century.

When the English Episcopal Evangelicals built churches they exhibited varying responses depending on their circumstances. St Thomas's, Rutland Place, Edinburgh, erected in 1842, showed some affinity with new ideas for beauty in architecture by using part of the £4,200 collected for its construction on a richly carved exterior. But it was distinctly neo-Norman rather than Gothic, allying itself with an age when papal reform movements looked to re-energise the pre-Reformation Church. Standing with its back to St John's, Princes Street, it made a clear statement that it had relinquished its links with the Scottish Episcopal Church and looked to a vigorous

---

with St John's, Aberdeen (1850), St Drostan's, Deer (1851), St Ternan's, Banchory (1851), St John's, Longside (1854) – all with stained glass and encaustic tiles. A writer in the *Ecclesiologist* remarked favourably of the 'improvement in the style…and the increased order and zeal among the worshippers'. P. F. Anson, *Fashions in Church Furnishings 1840-1940* (London, 1960), pp. 104-106. However, it is also true that some Episcopal chapels remained simple until the mid-nineteenth century and beyond. St John's, Dumfries, and Muthill Chapel, Perthshire, resisted architectural innovations until 1867 and 1904 respectively. Rowan Strong, *Episcopalianism in Nineteenth-Century Scotland* (Oxford, 2002), pp. 258-261.

[139] St Ninian's Cathedral, Perth (1850), was also of Gothic design, again with stone altar, a jewelled cross, a choir screen of wrought iron, a throne for the bishop, and an east end hung with silk. Two Tractarian laymen, Horace Courtney (later Lord) Forbes, and George Frederick Boyle (later the sixth Earl of Glasgow), directed the building operations, and its first canons, S. C. Chambers, Henry Humble and Joseph Haskoll, were all advanced Tractarians. Trinity College, Glenalmond (1847) and the new foundation at Cumbrae (1849) were designed by William Butterfield, a favourite architect of the Tractarians. Gavin White, *The Scottish Episcopal Church: A New History* (Edinburgh, 1998), p. 48. Strong, *Episcopalianism*, p. 249.

[140] Hay, *Post Reformation Churches*, pp. 75-86.

[141] Ibid., pp. 114-116. When Greyfriars Kirk, Edinburgh, burned to the ground in 1857, its incumbent, Robert Lee, rebuilt it with stained glass windows. A. C. Cheyne, *The Transforming of the Kirk* (Edinburgh, 1983), p. 93.

[142] Gerald Parsons, *Religion in Victorian Britain Study Guide 2*, (Manchester, 1988), p. 21.

future.[143] However, St James's, in Crown Street, Aberdeen, built in 1854, declared its Evangelicalism by being severely plain,[144] probably because its owners considered that anything more ostentatious would be unsuitable after their acrimonious split from St Paul's, Aberdeen. Again, in rural areas, chapels were almost identical to simple, stone Presbyterian kirks with small bell towers. Evangelicals in these areas were anxious to show that they shared their core theology with Presbyterians, many of whom attended their services and contributed money to their cause. Typical of these buildings were those at Huntly (1843) and Nairn (1845). The design of the latter was deemed to be so appropriate for Presbyterian worship that it was dismantled stone by stone and rebuilt as a faithful replica at Lochinver, Sutherland, at the end of the century, to serve the Church of Scotland parish.[145] However, as the English Episcopal movement became established more firmly, some Gothic churches were erected. While St Silas's, 1864, positioned at Eldon Street Junction, Glasgow, was of 'muscular' design,[146] William Forbes Skene, historiographer Royal for Scotland, accepted plans for St Vincent's, of which he was the benefactor, to be built as a simple Gothic church in the New Town of Edinburgh in 1857. St Silas's Mission in Partick, 1874, and Wemyss Bay chapel, rebuilt in 1877, followed similarly. The latter even had a one-hundred-foot spire.[147] Aspects of ecclesiological architecture were evident in the exterior design of English Episcopal buildings as the century progressed.

But whereas exteriors were sometimes embellished, the unencumbered interior impression of English Episcopal churches aimed to focus attention on the spoken word rather than any visual display. For instance, St Thomas's, Edinburgh, was 'very simple, without decoration',[148] and the chapel at Wemyss had 'no decoration...no angels or saints'.[149] To the same end, the visual impact of the pulpit was always evident, exemplified by the one at St Thomas's which was a 'great wooden tower'.[150] Evangelical, non-sacrificial, eucharistic theology affected design. Chancels were non-structural with plain, wooden, moveable tables. At St Thomas's the table was probably placed significantly at the west end of the church, rather than

---

[143] 'Memo as to the History of St Thomas's English Episcopal Chapel or Church as Disclosed in its Minute Books' (1907), St Thomas's Church, Edinburgh, Archives. Gifford, *Buildings of Scotland*, p. 367.

[144] Alexander Gammie, *Churches of Aberdeen: Historical and Descriptive* (Aberdeen, 1909), pp. 290-291.

[145] Alan Banon, *Old Nairn* (Nairn, 1999), p. 15.

[146] Williamson, *Buildings (Glasgow)*, p. 275.

[147] *Ibid.* Edwin Hodder, *Sir George Burns Bart* (London, 1892), p. 321.

[148] *Memoir*, p. xlviii.

[149] Hodder, *George Burns*, p. 320.

[150] W. H. B. Proby, *Annals of the Low Church Party*, Vol. I (London, 1888), p. 494.

Doctrinal and Practical Issues

at the east,[151] and even the presence of a simple cross behind it was still objected to in 1894.[152] Drummond explained such concerns in 1860 when lecturing on the Czech Reformer, Jan Hus, executed in 1415:

> He was turned to the east upon which, certain bigots cried out that he should not look to the east for he was a heretic, so he was turned towards the west. It is indeed a matter of surprise, that a foolish and superstitious practice could outlive such a scene as this! Who would not rather turn with Hus to the west, than with his persecutors to the east?[153]

The interior design of these Evangelical English Episcopal churches was thus a statement of the theology of their congregations.

However, as with external design, some internal features of Evangelical chapels changed during the century in accord with modern fashion. In 1882, a granite font replaced the baptismal bowl which had been housed in the rail in front of the communion table at St Thomas's.[154] Similarly, pulpits became more ornate, although alterations were carefully regulated so as not to conflict with doctrine. While the pulpit at St Silas's in 1864 had carved leaf capitals, and the new one at St Thomas's in 1882 was 'richly carved with dove grey marble inlaid', they both remained prominent features in the churches.[155] Again, coloured glass was introduced at St Vincent's, St Thomas's, St Silas's and Wemyss in the late 1870s to 1880s. But the large window above the Lord's Table at St Vincent's was loyal to Evangelicalism carrying the words 'Except ye be converted, and become as little children, ye shall not enter the kingdom of heaven', and the design at Wemyss was of 'shapes only, and the shield, sword, and helmet of the armour of God'.[156] Innovations were acceptable only if they did not contradict Evangelical belief.

Nevertheless, change often brought conflict. In 1882, a tremendous row broke out at St Thomas's when an innovatory reredos showed a painted image of Christ rather than the previously planned Ten Commandments and Creed emphasising Evangelical loyalty to the Bible and allegiance to the Protestant basis of Anglicanism. Many criticised it as encouraging adoration of an image and sacrificial eucharistic theology. Feelings ran so

---

[151] Proby, *Annals*, Vol. I, p. 494.

[152] Hodder, *George Burns*, p. 320. St Thomas's Minute Book, 23 April 1894, p. 306, St Thomas's Church, Edinburgh, Archives.

[153] Scottish Reformation Society, *The Truth of God against the Papacy* (Edinburgh, 1860), p. 32.

[154] Proby, *Annals*, p. 494. *Edinburgh Evening Express*, 11 December 1882, 'The Edinburgh Kirks'.

[155] McWilliam, *Buildings (Glasgow)*, p275. *Edinburgh Evening Express*, 11 December 1882, 'The Edinburgh Kirks'.

[156] The window is still in place at St Vincent's Church, Edinburgh. Hodder, *George Burns*, p. 320.

high that one member of the vestry threatened the new incumbent, E. C. Dawson, with pulling 'the Reredos down about my ears'.[157] T. K. Talon of St Vincent's also expressed caution: 'I would not have been on the side of those who desired to set up the Reredos'.[158] Others showed more accommodation exemplified by one member who found the reredos 'most harmless'.[159] But the structure was dismantled and the Ten Commandments and Creed reinstated. Thus, among English Episcopalians, while some countenanced a few innovations towards the end of the century, the general mood was conservative.

Ritualism

After the repeal of the Penal Laws in 1792, the descendants of the Scottish Nonjurors retained certain rituals not common to Anglicanism. The mixed chalice, reservation of the eucharist and the sign of the cross at the communion and confirmation services were typical.[160] However, the clergy, as in the Presbyterian Churches, wore the black gown for all ministrations until 1811, when the General Synod recommended that it was more suitable 'for ministers of the Prince of peace and purity' to wear the surplice except for preaching – predating the practice in the Anglican Church where it was introduced only gradually from mid-century.[161] Again as early as 1853, aspects of the Ritualist movement became apparent in some Scottish Episcopal churches. Lighted candles, incense and linen vestments were among the practices introduced to enhance congregational devotion,[162] and by the 1870s even the more orthodox High Church clergy of St John's, Edinburgh, had taken on ideas such as flower services.[163] Ritualism increased in the Scottish Episcopal Church during the later nineteenth century.

Evangelicals understood the devices adopted by Ritualists to be similar to those of Roman Catholicism. S. C. Baker, curate at St Thomas's in 1843 to 1844, described them in 1868 as 'empty show...Popery diluted and

---

[157] E. C. Dawson to Bishop John Dowden, 9 February 1892, DC.

[158] T. K. Talon to E. C. Dawson (n.d.), DC.

[159] A Churchman to Lancelot Holland, October 1891, DC.

[160] Eeles, *Traditional Ceremonial*, p. 34. [J. D. Miller]. 'Justitia', *Peculiarities of the Scottish Episcopal Church* (Aberdeen, 1844), pp. 1-8.

[161] George Grubb, *An Ecclesiastical History of Scotland*, Vol. IV (Edinburgh, 1861), p. 134. Bebbington, *Evangelicalism*, p. 149.

[162] Chapter 10, pp. 335-336, 345-347 gives lists of Ritualist churches in Scotland together with the ritual used.

[163] D. T. K. Drummond, *Letter to the Very Rev the Dean of Carlisle* (Edinburgh, 1876), p. 15.

Doctrinal and Practical Issues

Protestantism defiled'.[164] C. R. Teape, of St Andrew's-back-of-Castle, Edinburgh, feared that undue ceremony was 'rather to be seen by the eye, than felt by the heart, mind and soul'.[165] Drummond described it as 'the theatre transferred to the church', and dismissed 'altars gloriously decked, and priests beautifully arrayed in cope and stole...and the ever-changing ornamentation of flowers' as 'histrionic'.[166] Rather, Evangelicals strove to engage the minds of their congregations by keeping the impact of the sensual to a minimum. Baker spoke for them, understanding that 'spiritual worship when unadorned is adorned the most, and needs no tawdry dressing up to set it off'.[167] But this did not mean that Evangelical worship was necessarily lacking in warmth. In 1872 Drummond extolled the Anglican Prayer Book as a superior tool for eliciting heartfelt devotion in a congregation. In contrast he found that 'of Scotch Presbyterianism it might be said...as Byron had said of the moon, Clear, but oh! how cold!'.[168] Given such sentiments, Drummond doubtless strove to make the liturgy a living celebration of faith. Expressiveness of speech, variation of the pitch of the voice and emotion would probably have been the devices used by many Evangelicals who were as anxious as Ritualists to enhance the devotional aspects of worship, but approached the matter quite differently.

But as with architecture there was some accommodation of ritual even among the Evangelical English Episcopalians towards the end of the century, although this was by no means uniform. The available information comes from St Thomas's, Edinburgh. While Sir John Don Wauchope and his wife were 'very glad the evergreens were desirable' at the Christmas services in 1889, the new incumbent, W. L. Holland, in 1891, objected to their use.[169] Wearing the surplice for preaching, upheld by the Oxford Movement in the 1840s, also caused mixed responses. When E. C. Dawson adopted the custom in 1887, a long-standing vestry member, Daniel Ainslie, accused him of 'threatening the spiritual integrity of St Thomas's'.[170] Similarly, *The Rock* reporting that E. H. Beckles, Bishop to

---

[164] S. C. Baker, *A Pastor's Word against Ritualistic Innovations* (London, 1868), pp. 23-24. In the Roman Catholic Church innovations had increased since the beginning of the nineteenth century. See Nigel M. de S. Cameron (ed.), *Dictionary of Scottish Church History and Theology* (Edinburgh, 1993), pp. 898-899 for development of Roman Catholic worship and devotion in the nineteenth century.

[165] C. R. Teape, *Effect of Ritualism in Clergy and Laity* (Edinburgh, 1882), p. 40.

[166] John Witherspoon, *A Serious Inquiry into the Nature of the Stage with a Preface by D. T. K. Drummond* (Edinburgh, 1876), pp. xix-xx.

[167] Baker, *Ritualistic Innovations*, p. 23.

[168] *Record*, 16 December 1872 and 27 December 1872.

[169] E. H. Don Wauchope to E. C. Dawson, 27 December 1889, DC. St Thomas's Minute Book, 18 December 1891, St Thomas's Church, Edinburgh, Archives.

[170] Daniel Ainslie to E. C. Dawson, 2 February 1887, DC.

the English Episcopalians in 1877,[171] had preached in a surplice and had a vested choir in London, declared the news as 'circumstances which detract somewhat from our satisfaction'.[172] It is not clear how many took up these new fashions, but judging by the reaction at St Thomas's, it is likely that there was resistance to them. The group was probably representative of conservative opinions on such matters, influenced by Scottish Presbyterianism in reaction to developing practices in the Scottish Episcopal Church.

But unlike Scottish Presbyterians, English Episcopalians were typically Anglican in their devotion to musical services. Drummond produced a hymn-book in 1838.[173] An organ was installed at St Thomas's, Edinburgh, in 1847, having been rejected in 1844 only because of lack of money.[174] The congregation of St Silas's, Glasgow, purchased one in 1864, as soon as the church was built.[175] However, although organ music was appreciated at St Thomas's, as evidenced by the annual salary of £70 to the organist in 1878,[176] it was used only as an aid to help worshippers concentrate on the words of the hymns and psalms. Thus in 1899, the organist was asked to play more quietly so as not to disturb the meditations of the congregation.[177] Again, innovations veering towards Ritualist and Catholic practice were vigorously opposed. When E. C. Dawson introduced singing of the 'Amens' and the responses to the Ten Commandments, at St Thomas's in 1882, one long-standing member referred to it as 'most revolting to a great many', and looked back to the days 'of simple worship'. Even the chanting of psalms was resisted until 1895 at St Thomas's, placing it more in line with Presbyterian worship.[178] English Episcopalians tended to be conservative in musical taste.

Conclusion

In Scotland, Evangelical Episcopalians were typical of mainstream Evangelical Anglicanism in many respects. Like their colleagues south of the border they were active opponents of Roman Catholic advances from

---

[171] See Chapter 10, p. 352.

[172] *The Rock*, 23 February 1877.

[173] D. T. K. Drummond and R. K. Greville, *The Church of England Hymn-Book* (Edinburgh, 1838).

[174] 'Memo as to the History of St Thomas's', 11 October 1844, 14 October 1847, St Thomas's Church, Edinburgh, Archives.

[175] 'A Short History of the English Episcopal Church of St Silas', p. 5. St Silas's Church, Glasgow, Archives.

[176] St Thomas's Minute Book, 5 December 1878, St Thomas's Church, Edinburgh, Archives.

[177] *Ibid.*, 28 April 1899.

[178] *Ibid.*, 4 October 1895.

Doctrinal and Practical Issues

the late 1820s to the 1870s, although orthodox High Churchmen were also prominent in this field. Their objections were based on theological differences, and on their belief that the Catholic Church was the Antichrist. Thus they opposed any concessions made to Catholicism in Britain, fearing it to be a threat to the Protestant basis of the country.

Objections to Roman Catholicism caused Evangelicals to reject vigorously anything reminiscent of it. In Scotland this reaction was often stronger, probably because of close interaction with Scottish Presbyterianism and the vastly dominant High Churchmanship of the Scottish Episcopal Church. Thus the English Episcopal movement in particular retained very conservative views on baptism throughout the century. It expressed its Evangelical conviction in the architecture of its churches, although it adopted, like Anglican and Presbyterian Evangelicals, some Gothic influences by mid-century. Again, like strict Evangelicals in England and Scottish Presbyterians, the group resisted many ritualistic innovations, and in music even slight alterations to the cherished mode of services were opposed. On these matters, the Episcopal Evangelicals considered here, because of their position in Scotland were, overall, representatives of a stricter form of Anglican Evangelicalism.

Chapter 7

The Doctrine of the Scottish Communion Office

While Anglicans disagreed over the meaning of regeneration in the baptismal service, they also held different interpretations of the Order for Holy Communion. One issue was of particular importance: how was Christ present at the service? Was his presence connected in some way to the elements, or was he to be found only in the hearts of the faithful? The differing understandings can be traced back to the Reformation. While Martin Luther, Huldrych Zwingli and John Calvin rejected as unscriptural the idea of the priest making an offering or sacrifice on behalf of the people, there was no such consensus on the eucharistic presence. Luther eschewed the Roman Catholic idea of transubstantiation but held the doctrine of consubstantiation whereby the elements after consecration coexisted with the actual body and blood of Christ. Zwingli took a different view. He understood the service as a commemoration of Christ's death in which there was no alteration whatsoever in the elements. The recipient was fed, spiritually, but this resulted from the powerful reminder the service gave of Christ's passion and death. Calvin sought a middle way. He agreed with Zwingli that the bread and wine remained unaltered, but he maintained that, on reception, the communicant simultaneously received Christ's flesh and blood through the action of the Holy Spirit. As a result, virtue diffused through the believer.[1]

The English Book of Common Prayer of 1662 bore, clearly, the marks of compromise on the topic, showing the influence of Luther, Zwingli and Calvin. Evolving as the service did from the 1559 version, when the complexities of politics had made it necessary to accommodate varying religious views, it contained examples of the developing thought of Thomas Cranmer, Archbishop of Canterbury from 1533 to 1556. This is evident in its words of administration: 'The Body of our Lord Jesus Christ which was given for thee, preserve thy body and soul unto everlasting life. Take and eat this in remembrance that Christ died for thee, and feed on Him in thy heart by faith with thanksgiving.' The first sentence was expressive of the Lutheran sentiments of Cranmer's Prayer Book of 1549. The second phrase was plainly Zwinglian, taken from the version of 1552. Thus the statement

---

[1] A. E. McGrath, *Reformation Thought* (Oxford, 1999), pp. 174-194. John Calvin, *Tracts Relating to the Reformation*, Vol. II, Translated by H. Beveridge, p. 577, quoted in W. A. Elwell, *Evangelical Dictionary of Theology* (Grand Rapids, 1999), p. 656.

of 1662 contained a range of understanding as to the manner of Christ's presence.² The Black Rubric at the end of the service was similarly unclear, denying only the carnal presence of Christ in the elements. However, the Catechism, retained since 1604 at the request of the Puritans, was more Zwinglian. While teaching 'that the Body and Blood of Christ...are verily and indeed taken and received by the faithful', it qualified this by explaining that the elements were only signifiers, or representations, of Christ's human body.³ Even the Thirty-Nine Articles, produced in 1571, were not devoid of double meaning. Article XXVIII, like Cranmer's original one of 1553, denied transubstantiation, but allowed that 'the body of Christ is given and eaten in the supper only after a heavenly and spiritual manner. And the means whereby the body of Christ is received and eaten...is faith.' In 1841, J. H. Newman's *Tract 90* interpreted the Article as indicating some sort of presence of Christ in the elements.⁴ The English communion service and formularies thus opened up different schools of thought on the matter of Christ's presence.

By the late eighteenth century there were three main bodies of Anglican understanding on the topic. Firstly, there was the Memorialist position, influenced by Zwingliansm, propounded by Benjamin Hoadly, Bishop of Winchester. In 1735 he taught that the communion service was a public acknowledgement of faith. The bread and wine were purely commemorative representations of the body and blood of Christ, and as such led 'by their peculiar tendency to all such thoughts and practices as are indeed the improvement and health of our souls'.⁵ The emphasis was on remembering Christ's death rather than on expecting an event of particular blessing. In contrast there was the Virtualist opinion of the High Churchman, John Johnson, Vicar of Cranbrook. In his treatise, *The Unbloody Sacrifice* (1714-1718), Johnson rejected the Roman Catholic idea of transubstantiation. But in order to explain how Christ was present at the service he tried to express the idea of the bread and wine as Christ's 'spiritual body and blood'. For Johnson the elements were a 'middle way' between being mere emblems on one hand and the transubstantiated body of Christ on the other. Instead, at consecration, they took on the character of 'the mysterious Body and Blood of Christ by the secret power of the Spirit',

---

[2] McGrath, *Reformation Thought*, p. 259.

[3] D. T. K. Drummond, *The Scottish Communion Office Examined and Proved to be Repugnant to Scripture and Opposed to the Articles, Liturgy and Homilies of the Church of England* (Edinburgh, 1842), p. 33. See also Alf Härdelin, *Tractarian Understanding of the Eucharist* (Uppsala, 1965), pp. 124-125.

[4] Härdelin, *Tractarian Understanding of Eucharist*, pp. 56, 191-192.

[5] Benjamin Hoadly, *The Works of Benjamin Hoadly Published by his Son, John Hoadly*, Volume III (London, 1773), p. 894, quoted in C. W. Dugmore, *Eucharistic Doctrine from Hooker to Waterland* (London, 1942), p. 160.

whereby they 'are made as powerful and effectual...as the natural body itself could be if it was present'. Thus although there was not a substantial presence of Christ connected specifically to the elements, they were, however, 'made to be in energy and effect the very Body and Blood Which they represent',[6] and thus were capable of conveying God's grace. In 1737, Daniel Waterland, Archdeacon of Middlesex, in *A Review of the Doctrine of the Eucharist*, suggested an intermediate path between the ideas of Hoadly and Johnson. Waterland agreed with Hoadly that the presence of Christ was not to be found in the elements but in the worthy receiver. But he considered Hoadly's ideas as an insufficient exposition of the unique spiritual feeding provided by the service. Johnson's teaching was regarded as misplaced because Waterland understood the 'union of the Spirit with the elements rather than the persons' to be a 'gross notion, groundless...a kind of impanation [inclusion] of the Spirit'. He felt this would lead to Christ's body being received by the 'unworthy as well as the worthy'. Waterland's developed theory, termed Receptionism in the mid-nineteenth century, was that God had appointed the consecrated bread and wine as efficacious signs of the natural body of Christ to the believer. As such they would effect a mystical union of the worthy with Christ, described by Waterland as 'adhering inseparably to him'.[7] The recipient was thus made one with Christ without Calvin's idea of the transference of the actual body and blood of Christ or Johnson's notion of the infused elements conveying Christ.

The three theories were represented in early nineteenth-century Anglicanism. Edward Bickersteth, incumbent of Watton, Hertfordshire, noted the near Hoadlyism, or Zwinglianism, of some of his fellow Evangelicals,[8] and Waterland's Receptionism also found expression among them as among High Churchmen.[9] But ultra-High Churchmen, by the

---

[6] John Johnson, *The Unbloody Sacrifice*, Volume I (London, 1714-1718), pp. 266, 268, quoted in Dugmore, *Eucharistic Doctrine*, pp. 144-145.

[7] Daniel Waterland, *A Review of the Doctrine of the* Eucharist (Oxford, 1896), p. 149, quoted in Dugmore, *Eucharistic Doctrine*, pp. 177,179. See also, William Goode, *The Nature of Christ's Presence in the Eucharist*, Vol. II (London, 1856), p. 971 William Van Mildert, *The Works of the Rev. Daniel Waterland D. D.*, Vol. VII (Oxford, 1823), pp. 149-150.

[8] W. J. C. Ervine, 'Doctrine and Diplomacy: Some Aspects of the Life and Thought of Anglican Evangelical Clergy 1797-1837' (Cambridge University Ph. D. thesis, 1979), p. 98.

[9] High Churchmen tended to label as Zwinglian anyone who eschewed placing emphasis on the elements as instrumental in conveying Christ to the communicant. Thus Receptionists and Memorialists were often put in the same category. William Goode, Rector of All Hallows, Thames Street, and a prolific academic theologian, commented on this problem in *The Divine Rule of Faith* (London, 1853). Peter Toon, *Evangelical Theology 1833-1856* (London, 1977), pp 195-196, 200. This is also discussed by Ervine,

1830s, sometimes labelled Evangelicals who held those views as Zwinglian, purely because they denied the real, bodily presence of Christ in the elements.[10] While it is thus sometimes difficult to identify accurately the beliefs of all Evangelicals, Bickersteth's *Treatise on the Lord's Supper*, written in 1824, and probably the most widely read publication on the eucharist by Evangelicals, illustrated what many have since identified as Receptionism.[11] He sought to emphasise both the memorial aspect of the communion service as a representation of the objective work of Christ, and the resulting union with Christ which the rite conferred on the faithful. The eucharist was thus a time of special blessing along the lines of Waterland and a step away from the starker doctrine of Hoadly.[12] At the other end of the Receptionist scale, William Palmer, a High Churchman of Worcester College, Oxford, spoke in 1833 not only of Christ being mystically present at the communion service but also suggested that the elements were instrumental in conveying Christ to the recipient. He thus gave purchase to both Receptionism and to higher doctrines of the real presence.[13] Again, within Virtualism, there was variation. Some like the eighteenth-century Daniel Brevint, Dean of Lincoln, who in turn influenced John Wesley, emphasised the mysterious presence of Christ in the elements less than Johnson. Rather, he referred to the bread and wine as 'glorious instruments Divine', 'raised' by the Holy Spirit so that they could 'convey' God's grace rather than Christ himself.[14] There was thus a range of views as to the presence of Christ in the Anglican Communion service, drawing from different schools, and not always clear-cut.

Unfortunately there are no surviving sermons by early nineteenth-century Scottish Episcopal Evangelicals illustrating their position, apart from some writings by D. T. K. Drummond, the future incumbent of St Thomas's, Edinburgh, who showed an affinity with Bickersteth. In 1829,

---

'Doctrine and Diplomacy', pp. 86-99. See also Härdelin, *Tractarian Understanding of the Eucharist*, p. 127 where it is asserted that J. B. Sumner, Bishop of Chester, was Zwinglian because he rejected any presence of Christ's body and blood in the elements.

[10] Härdelin, *Tractarian Understanding of the Eucharist*, p. 127. Toon, *Evangelical Theology*, p. 200.

[11] Ervine, 'Doctrine and Diplomacy', pp. 86-88. E. M. Culbertson, 'Evangelical Theology 1857-1900 (University of London, Ph. D. thesis, 1991), pp. 276-277, illustrates the Receptionist theology of Nathaniel Dimock, who was accused of Zwinglianism by his opponents at the end of the nineteenth century.

[12] Edward Bickersteth, *Treatise on the Lord's Supper* (London, 1824), pp. 1, 62, quoted in Ervine, 'Doctrine and Diplomacy', pp. 93-97.

[13] William Palmer, 'The Oxford Movement of 1833', p. 642. *The Contemporary Review* 43 (1883), pp. 636-659, quoted in Härdelin, *Eucharist*, p. 128.

[14] C. J. Cocksworth, *Evangelical Eucharistic Thought in the Church of England* (Cambridge, 1993), pp. 65-66. A. J. MacDonald (ed.), *The Evangelical Doctrine of Holy Communion* (London, 1936), pp. 287-290.

The Doctrine of the Scottish Communion Office

while he was a student at Oxford, Drummond possibly expressed a higher view than Hoadly. In a letter to his wife, while he described the bread and wine as 'the precious memorials of the dying love of our Saviour', he also prayed that by receiving them she might in her 'spirit be strengthened and refreshed, and that every spiritual and temporal blessing might be showered down' upon her.[15] Again, in 1840, his understanding of the service as a time of particular spiritual significance was evident when he preached that Christ, when 'he took bread he so thought of you...as to institute an ordinance for your joy and consolation' and that believers would find in it 'rivers of water in a dry place, the shadow of a great rock in a weary land, a refuge from the heat and a shelter from the storm'.[16] Drummond thus taught that the communion service was a special time of closeness to Christ. Although difficult to categorise accurately, he was probably nearer to Receptionism than to Memorialism.

While Evangelicals like Drummond and Bickersteth made little attempt at defining the nature of Christ's presence, they had, nonetheless, a very powerful awareness of Christ at the communion service. This was evident even in the 1850s and 1870s when the maturing Tractarian doctrine of the real, objective presence of Christ in the elements might have caused a reaction towards Hoadlyism. But, in 1852, Drummond was still speaking of the communion service as 'the refreshing from [Christ's] presence',[17] and there is no evidence to suggest his view altered. In 1853 Drummond's wife, Harriet, published *The Upper Room Furnished or a Help to the Christian at the Lord's Supper*, which was reprinted in 1875. In the introduction, Drummond referred to the communion service as 'this deepest melody of the Gospel of Love' where Christ, in the words recorded in the Bible, appealed to the communicant saying, 'Come for all things are ready'.[18] The sentiment that Christ was present in person to welcome his people and commune with them at the service was a recurring message of the book. In a chapter headed 'What think ye, that He will not come to the feast?' Harriet enlarged on the theme. She called upon some of the old eighteenth-century Calvinist writers who had held a strong doctrine of the presence of Christ. Robert Hawker of Plymouth was brought forward with his impassioned teaching: 'thy Jesus will be there. He spreads the feast, and he will be present at it. He waits to be gracious – he waits to be kind to thee...Come then thou gracious Lord, and sit down with me this day at thy table'. Indeed, the meeting with Christ was found to be so personal and vibrant that John Willison, the minister of South Church, Dundee, was

---

[15] *Memoir*, p. xxi.

[16] D. T. K. Drummond, *The Last Scenes in the Life of our Lord and Saviour* (London, 1850), p. 59.

[17] *Memoir*, p. lxxx.

[18] From the parable of the great supper, Luke 14.17.

quoted: 'Let Him there kiss me with the kisses of His lips, and enable me to embrace Him in the arms of my faith, saying, This is my Beloved, and this is my Friend!'[19] Evangelicals like the Drummonds believed that Christ was present in person at the communion service, and that the experience of meeting him there was emotional, personal and nourishing to faith.

C. H. Terrot, Bishop of Edinburgh and a High Churchman, expressed something like Receptionism in 1844, writing, rather plainly, that 'I fix my faith on sacramental grace, and believe that God does convey the benefits of Christ's death to the worthy communicant by mere bread and wine'.[20] In contrast, Bishop Alexander Jolly of Moray in 1831 published *The Christian Sacrifice in the Eucharist*, propounding the clearly Virtualist understanding of Johnson that the bread and wine 'become the body and blood of Christ in spirit and power...by the sanctifying power of the Holy Spirit for the communication or conveyance of pardon, grace and glory'.[21] Within the Scottish Episcopal Church in the nineteenth century there were thus both Receptionists and Virtualists.

The History of the Scottish Communion Office

Johnson's Virtualism was often associated with the Nonjuring beliefs of those who refused to take the oath of allegiance to William and Mary and left the Anglican Church in 1688. In 1716 the Nonjurors split into two parties. While one group was content to carry on using the 1662 Anglican Prayer Book as an adequate expression of its beliefs, the other, led by Thomas Brett and Jeremy Taylor, wanted to restore four practices, or usages, that had been present in the 1549 Edwardian liturgy, but had been discarded by the Reformers thereafter to remove any suggestion of Roman Catholicism.[22] These were the prayer of oblation or offering of the consecrated bread and wine to God; the prayer of invocation with its epiclesis, asking for the descent of the Holy Spirit on the elements; the use of the mixed chalice; and prayers for the faithful departed.

The so-called Usagers were typical High Churchmen with a regard for tradition and antiquity in the interpretation of the faith where the Bible was not absolutely clear. As there was no actual liturgical guidance in scripture for the communion service, they looked to the Eastern Church, whose

---

[19] Harriet Drummond, *The Upper Room Furnished* (Edinburgh, 1875), pp. ix-xi, 61-66.

[20] William Walker, *Three Churchmen* (Edinburgh, 1893), p. 125.

[21] William Walker, *Memoirs of Bishops Jolly and Gleig* (Edinburgh, 1878), p. 139.

[22] Edward Cardwell, *The Two Books of Common Prayer, set forth by authority of Parliament in the Reign of King Edward the Sixth, compared with each other* (Oxford, 1838), p. xxiv, quoted in Drummond, *Office Examined*, p. 8.

The Doctrine of the Scottish Communion Office 221

ancient rites included the usages, for a model to follow.[23] Regarding these services as the historical sources closest to the days of the apostles, the Usagers understood them to possess patristic authority.

The resulting English Nonjuring Communion Service, compiled by Thomas Brett and Jeremy Taylor in 1718, was based on the Eastern Clementine liturgy, which Brett believed had been used in the time of the Apostles, and on the 1549 service of Edward VI, together with references to the 1552 and 1662 English offices and Laud's service for Scotland of 1637.[24] The service differed from that of the 1662 office in that it contained a three-fold consecration of the elements which followed the order in the Eastern liturgies. Starting from the words of institution, it proceeded to an oblation of the bread and wine to God. The Nonjurors believed this ancient liturgical practice was indicative that Christ had offered himself as a sacrifice at the Last Supper rather than on the cross, which was merely the place of his death. While not upholding transubstantiation, the final part of the consecration consisted of a prayer of invocation with an epiclesis asking the Holy Spirit to descend on the bread and wine, making them equivalent in virtue, power and efficacy to Christ's natural body, capable of conveying grace.

The Scottish Nonjurors formed close links with Brett and Taylor, and in 1744, Bishop Thomas Rattray of Dunkeld wrote a similar liturgy for Scotland.[25] In 1755 Bishop William Falconar of Moray produced a modified version of Rattray's service, and revised it again in 1764 with the help of Bishop Robert Forbes of Caithness. This liturgy was to become widely adopted among the Nonjuring clergy of northeastern Scotland, while the 1662 Book of Common Prayer service was used in the qualified Episcopal chapels elsewhere in the country.[26] Thus, by 1764 the Nonjuring clergy of Scotland had their own liturgy which was expressive of their particular beliefs. It contained the four usages which the Usager party so prized, and was to be the cause of vigorous dispute with Evangelicals in the nineteenth century.

However, the Scottish Office diverged from the English Nonjuring service of 1718 in one very important respect which was, again, to have repercussions in the nineteenth century. Table 7.1[27] shows the forms of invocations in the Clementine Liturgy, the 1549 liturgy of Edward VI, the English Nonjuring liturgy of 1718, and the Scottish Communion Office of 1764.

---

[23] J. D. Smith, *The Eucharistic Doctrine of the Later Nonjurors* (Cambridge, 2000), pp. 10-11. Dugmore, *Eucharistic Doctrine*, pp. 146-147.

[24] Smith, *Later Nonjurors*, p.11. For Laud's Liturgy, see Chapter 1, p. 29.

[25] See Chapter 1, p. 30 for an account of the historical details surrounding this.

[26] Dowden, *Scottish Communion Office*, pp. 23-77.

[27] See Chapter 7, p. 222.

Reference to Table 7.1 highlights a problem noticed by Brett when compiling the English service of 1718. He detected that the Clementine invocation, like other Eastern liturgies he had studied, left out the words 'be unto us', while the 1549 English prayer, and the Roman one from which it was derived, included them. Brett warned that this gave a loophole for the 'zealous transubstantiators' to read the Clementine invocation in a literal manner expressive of their own theology. He suggested that the words 'that they who are partakers thereof may be confirmed in godliness, may obtain remission of their sins' in the Clementine invocation were the real equivalent of 'be unto us'. Accordingly, his recommendation that this phrase should be inserted in the English Office of 1718 was agreed to. However, the Scottish Office of 1764 failed to do this and asked only that the elements 'may become the body and blood of thy most dearly beloved Son'.[28] In 1884, Bishop John Dowden of Edinburgh, who was not an Evangelical and was a foremost liturgical scholar of the Scottish Episcopal Church, wrote that the invocation in the 1764 Scottish liturgy was unusually 'abrupt and bald with neither antiquity nor the analogy of other Offices to countenance it'.[29] The Scottish Communion Office was thus innovative in its form of epiclesis and had the potential of being understood as promoting the doctrine of transubstantiation. This was to cause serious problems in the nineteenth century.

Table 7.1 Types of Invocation

Clementine Liturgy send down upon this sacrifice Thy Holy Spirit…that He may declare this bread the Body of Thy Christ, and this cup the Blood of Thy Christ, that they who partake thereof may be confirmed in godliness, may obtain remission of sins, etc.
The First Liturgy of Edward VI, 1549 with thy Holy Spirit and Word, vouchsafe to bless and sanctify these thy gifts and creatures of bread and wine, that they may be unto us the body and blood of thy most dearly beloved Son Jesus Christ etc.
The English Nonjuring Office 1718 send down thine Holy Spirit…upon this sacrifice, that he may make this bread the Body of Thy Christ, and this cup the Blood of thy Christ: that they who are partakers thereof may be confirmed in godliness, may obtain remission of their sins etc.

---

[28] Dowden, *Scottish Communion Office*, p. 164.
[29] Dowden, *Scottish Communion Office*, pp. 164-165.

> *Scottish Office 1764*
> vouchsafe to bless and sanctify with thy Word and Holy Spirit, these thy gifts and creatures of bread and wine, that they may become the body and blood of thy most dearly beloved Son.

Source: John Dowden, *Scottish Office 1764* (Oxford 1922), pp. 127, 188 and 218, and D. T. K. Drummond, *Sketch of Episcopacy* (Edinburgh, 1845), endplate.

In Scotland, after the Usager party had joined with the qualified chapels in 1804, the reunited Church continued to use the 1764 service.[30] In 1811 the canon law of the Church declared it to hold primacy over the Book of Common Prayer, the decision being ratified in 1828 and 1838. With the Scottish Communion Office of 1764 as the official service of the Church from 1811, it would have been expected that some disputation over its doctrine of oblation and invocation would have occurred between Evangelicals, together with orthodox High Churchmen, and the former Nonjuror Usagers in Scotland during the first three decades of the century. But although there were some minor skirmishes,[31] serious trouble did not break out until 1842.

Part of the explanation for the delay in hostilities lies in the fact that there were several different editions of the Scottish Communion Office. There was one from 1723 and another from 1735. A service published in 1801 contained an invocation asking, less abruptly, that the bread and wine 'may become the spiritual body and blood of Christ'.[32] The various canons fixing the Scottish Office as primary always failed to state which service was meant. Drummond claimed that, until 1842 when Edward Craig, the former incumbent of St James's, Edinburgh, told him that the 1764 office was the official one, he had never seen it and had always assumed Laud's liturgy to be the authorised service. He pointed out that he had not attended Terrot's institution as bishop in 1841, which had taken place in Aberdeen and where the service was used, and that it was quite possible never to come in contact with it since all the southern clergy used the Book of

---

[30] See Chapter 1, p. 31. In the eighteenth-century Anglican Church there had been some, like Johnson, who, though supporting the doctrines of invocation and oblation taught by the Usagers, read the 1662 Prayer Book as consonant with their beliefs. By the early nineteenth century they were not a large group and there was very little controversy over the doctrine of the Communion Service in England at that time, with Receptionism being the dominant doctrine. See Ervine, 'Doctrine and Diplomacy', pp. 86-87.

[31] See Chapter 7, p. 224 below.

[32] D. T. K. Drummond, *Historical Sketch of Episcopacy from 1688 to the Present Time* (Edinburgh, 1845), pp. 64-65.

Common Prayer.³³ Dispute over the theology of the Scottish Communion Office, we may conclude, did not break out until 1842 because its content was not widely known to potential objectors before that date. It was Craig, then resident in England, who brought the matter to light.

When the situation became clear in 1842, some of the Evangelical Episcopal clergy and laity reacted vehemently. Many were to leave the Scottish Episcopal Church for conscientious reasons connected with the Scottish Communion Office.³⁴ The dispute was inflamed further because the Tractarians were propounding a similar theology to the Virtualism of the Scottish Office. In 1838 J. H. Newman had written in his *Letter to Faussett* that the consecrated elements 'are instruments of life...conveying grace' although Christ was not shut up in them,³⁵ and Pusey wrote in 1839 that the Articles of the Church of England taught a real presence 'conveyed by means of the elements'.³⁶ Alongside this, the sacrificial theology of the Tractarians was also similar to that of the Nonjurors. In 1837, in *Tract 81*, Pusey taught that the primitive Church performed 'an oblation under the form of ...bread and wine, according to our blessed Lord's holy institution', and that it was capable of bringing 'down blessings upon us'. He even commended the sacrificial theology of Alexander Jolly, Bishop of Moray, Ross and Caithness, as upholding these ideas.³⁷

Evangelical Scottish Episcopalians feared, as will now be discussed, that in 1842 there was a ready-made communion office, authorised as the primary rite of the Scottish Episcopal Church, to which they had to assent when signing the canons of the Church, and through which advancing Tractarian ideas could be transmitted. At a time of increasing links with the Church of England, cemented by the act of 1840,³⁸ these Churchmen sought to reaffirm their Protestantism.

Disputes Over The Scottish Communion Office of 1764

Although the main body of protest was against the Scottish Communion Office of 1764, there had been unrest among Churchmen as early as 1723 over the adoption of the usages. Some Scottish clergy, influenced by the English Nonjurors, began to incorporate these practices into the Book of

---

[33] *Scottish Episcopal Times*, 23 March 1844. Drummond, *Scottish Communion Office Examined*, pp. 42-43. D. T. K. Drummond to W. E Gladstone, 1 April 1873, Scottish *Guardian*, 11 April 1873.

[34] See Chapters 8 and 9.

[35] Härdelin, *Eucharist*, pp. 137-138.

[36] *Ibid.*, p. 136.

[37] *Ibid.*, pp. 204-205. Peter Nockles, 'Scottish Episcopal Church and the Oxford Movement', *Journal of Ecclesiastical History* 47, (1996), p. 664.

[38] See Chapter 1, p. 31.

Common Prayer, despite strong condemnation from others who warned of 'fatal rocks whereon others have been shipwrecked before'.[39] Trouble resurfaced in 1796 in northeastern Scotland where the Scottish Communion Office of 1764 was used. Primus John Skinner informed Patrick Torry, the incumbent of Peterhead, that the invocation was causing complaints from the English qualified clergy 'as if we favoured transubstantiation'. Skinner decided to insert the phrase 'be unto us', after the fashion of Laud's Office, in order to appease such feeling. Around the same time it appears that the incumbent at Brechin, Norman Sievewright, had objected to the theology of the Scottish Office on similar grounds, but the details of the dispute are not clear.[40] Opposition to the usages was not unknown in the eighteenth and early nineteenth centuries.

But, as discussed above, the major dispute arose in 1842. It was marked by the publication in that year of two pamphlets by Evangelical Episcopalians. Craig's *On the Important Discrepancy between the Church of England and the Scottish Episcopal Community* and Drummond's *The Scottish Communion Office Examined* dissected the theology of the Scottish Office of 1764 in detail.[41] The question with which Craig and Drummond were concerned was whether the Nonjuring compilers of the Scottish service, like the Tractarians, had drifted away from Reformation theology towards a more Roman Catholic understanding.[42] Their investigations centred on the structure and language of the prayers of oblation and invocation since, according to Drummond, 'numerous and urgent were the objections raised against this portion of the service by the Reformers during the reign of Edward the Sixth'.[43] The aim was to show that the Scottish Communion Office was not compatible with mature Reformation doctrine.

In order to facilitate the investigation, Drummond drew up the collation of services reproduced in Table 7.2.[44] This contains the disputed portions of the English liturgies of 1549, 1552, and 1662, and of Laud's Scottish liturgy (1637) and of the Scottish Office (1764) – all of which are represented by bold type and superscript note numbers.

---

[39] George Grubb, *Ecclesiastical History of Scotland*, Volume III (Edinburgh, 1861), pp. 388-392. Edward Craig, *On the Important Discrepancy between the Church of England and the Scottish Episcopal Community showing the Schismatical Character of a Subscription by English Clerics to the Scottish Communion Office of 1765* (Edinburgh, 1842), p. 6. Rowan Strong, *Episcopalianism in Nineteenth-Century Scotland* (Oxford, 2002), pp. 14-15.

[40] J. M. Neale, *The Life and Times of Patrick Torry* (London, 1856), pp. 25, 91.

[41] Craig and Drummond put the date of the disputed service as 1765. This was shown later by John Dowden to have been a mistake: it should have been 1764.

[42] Drummond, *Scottish Communion Office Examined*, p. 3. Craig, *Important Discrepancy* pp. 4-5.

[43] Drummond, *Scottish Communion Office Examined*, p. 8.

[44] See Chapter 11, pp. 378-383

The Prayer of Oblation

Craig and Drummond objected to the inclusion of the Oblation[45] in the Prayer of Consecration in the Scottish Office, as being clearly suggestive of a sacrificial offering. Concerning the structure of the service, they argued that a less obvious oblation was present in the 1549 and 1637 rites, and maintained that its omission from the 1552 and 1662 services indicated the opposition of the Reformers.[46] Besides this striking difference, Drummond drew attention to the sacrifice of praise and thanksgiving.[47] The Scottish Office placed it before the administration of the bread and wine. In the 1552 and 1662 services it occurred at the end and thus could not be understood as applying to the elements.[48] Thus the structure of the Scottish rite seemed to be designed to support sacrificial doctrine.

The difficulty for Evangelicals with such teaching was that it ran contrary to their belief in the centrality of the cross, that Christ's death there had been a once-and-for-all-time sacrifice. Drummond pointed parrticularly to the 1662 service as emphasising this doctrine by the use of the words 'there' and 'one' in its Prayer of Consecration – that Christ 'made there, that is on the cross, his one oblation for sin'.[49] The fact that the Scottish Office replaced the word 'one' with 'own', and omitted 'there', was indicative that its theology did not centralise the cross in the same way[50]. Moreover, the Scottish service had a sacerdotal emphasis which was unacceptable to Evangelicals. The idea that the bread and wine were offered up to God by a priest 'as an intercessor between God and the people' was contrary to Evangelical teaching that Christ's death had abolished the need for any such intermediaries. Christ had performed the priestly duties for all time on the cross, and any repetition of sacrifices denied the efficacy of his work.[51] Thus Craig pointed to what he saw as the danger of the Scottish Office, that it could 'only bring the mind down to earth...away from the great offering' of Christ on the cross.[52] The prayer of oblation in the Scottish Communion Office of 1764, absent from the Book of Common Prayer, was thus contrary to Evangelical belief.

---

[45] see note[4] in bold in Table 7.2, p. 381, column 2

[46] Drummond, *Scottish Communion Office Examined*, pp. 9-22. Craig, *Important Discrepancy*, pp. 15-20.

[47] see note[5] in bold in Table 7.2, p. 382, columns 1-3 and p. 383, columns 1-2

[48] Drummond, *Scottish Communion Office Examined*, p. 19.

[49] *Ibid.*, p. 46.

[50] see note[2] in bold and underlined in Table 7.2, p. 378, columns 1-3 and p. 379, columns 1-2

[51] Drummond, *Scottish Communion Office Examined*, p. 12. See also Chapter 4, pp. 129-131.

[52] Craig, *Important Discrepancy*, pp. 18-19.

The language of the 1764 service was also an important factor. Craig and Drummond firstly drew attention to the preceding rubric of the Scottish Office. The words 'offer up'[53], which were absent from both of the Edwardian services and from the 1662 English liturgy, implanted, it was argued, a sacrificial intention in the service. But the main thrust of the polemic focused on the words 'which we now offer unto Thee' in the Oblation of the Scottish Office. Because the corresponding prayers of oblation in the 1549 and 1637 services lacked the word 'offer', the language of the Scottish service by contrast was argued to convey a more distinctly sacrificial tone.[54] Craig pointed out that the words of the Scottish service ran close to those of the Roman Catholic Mass, that it left itself 'open to imply all that the Romish Office fearlessly asserts'.[55] As such he considered it was a dangerous passage, subversive of the ideals of the Reformers who had sought to remove all hints of continuing sacrifices offered by the clergy.[56] Liturgical language was considered by Craig and Drummond to be important in conveying doctrine.

A critique of the Scottish Nonjuring theology which underpinned the Scottish Office was also mounted. Drummond, continuing his analysis of the language of the Prayer of Consecration, argued that the use of the word 'own' and the omission of 'there' was expressive of the particular belief that Christ had offered himself as a sacrifice at the Last Supper rather than on the cross.[57] He maintained that the phrase 'these thy holy gifts' described a material sacrifice while the word 'memorial' made it commemorative.[58] These observations were consolidated by quoting the Catechisms of Aberdeen and Moray which taught that the sacrifice thus rendered engaged 'God to apply the blessings and benefits of Christ's death and sacrifice to our souls and bodies, and to preserve them both unto everlasting life'.[59] Thus, as Craig and Drummond both explained, the Oblation was understood by Scottish Churchmen to be propitiatory: it made 'amends for human sin...putting God in mind as it were of the all-sufficient sacrifice of his Son', detracting from Christ's death.[60] Although Craig had objected to the link of the language of the Scottish Office with Roman

---

[53] see note[1] in bold in Table 7.2, p. 379, column 2
[54] Drummond, *Scottish Communion Office Examined*, pp. 10-11. Craig, *Important Discrepancy*, pp. 20-23.
[55] Craig, *Important Discrepancy*, pp. 23-24.
[56] *Ibid.*, pp. 16-19.
[57] Drummond, *Scottish Communion Office Examined*, p. 48.
[58] *Ibid.*, p. 11.
[59] *Ibid.*, pp. 47-50.
[60] Craig, *Important Discrepancy*, p. 21. See also, Drummond, *Scottish Communion Office Examined*, pp. 14-15.

Catholicism, the main thrust of both his criticism and Drummond's was against Nonjuring, Usager sacrificial doctrine.

The Prayer of Invocation

In a similar manner, Craig and Drummond analysed the prayer of invocation[61] in the Scottish Office. In connection with the structure of the services, both considered the omission of an invocation from the 1551 and 1662 services as an important indication that it was unfavourable to the Reformers.[62] Additionally, Drummond pointed out that in the First Liturgy of Edward and Laud's service, the invocation occurred before the words of institution, whereas in the Scottish Communion Office it was placed 'after they have become the symbols of Christ's body and blood'. He claimed that this indicated that 'the bread and wine are supposed to undergo some ulterior change beyond being made symbols or figures', and labelled it as 'a doctrine of transubstantiation…not the doctrine as professed by the Church of Rome…but a doctrine of transubstantiation nonetheless'.[63] The structure of the Scottish Office appeared to speak of a change in the elements.

Language, again, was an important part of the argument. Both contenders drew attention to the fact that the 1549 and 1637 services had invocations which differed from the Scottish Office by the insertion of the words 'unto us'. Echoing Brett's earlier caution over the 1718 English liturgy,[64] Drummond maintained that the inclusion of these words made the 1549 and 1637 invocations less descriptive of a definite change in the elements, 'that almost any doctrine may be supposed to be expressed in the words "be unto us"…ranging between the extreme view of the bread and wine being mere symbols on the one hand, to being literally changed into "the body and blood and soul and divinity" of Christ on the other'. In comparison he felt that the word 'become' in the Scottish Office, without any qualification, conveyed forcibly the single idea of a transformation in the elements.[65] Craig argued similarly. He turned to the trial of Laud who, when charged with introducing transubstantiation into the 1637 service, had defended himself by appealing to the words 'unto us' as negating that meaning.[66] For Craig and Drummond, the language of the Scottish invocation was suggestive of a change of some sort in the bread and wine.

---

[61] see note[3] in bold and part underlined in Table 7.2, p. 378, columns 1 and 3 and p. 381, column 2

[62] Craig, *Important Discrepancy*, p. 24. Drummond, *Scottish Communion Office Examined*, p. 20.

[63] Drummond, *Scottish Communion Office Examined*, pp. 27-32.

[64] See Chapter 7, pp. 221-222.

[65] Drummond, *Scottish Communion Office Examined*, pp. 22-26.

[66] Craig, *Important Discrepancy*, pp. 27-28.

Evangelicals resisted these ideas because, like Bishop John Jewel of Salisbury in the sixteenth century, they believed that 'it is not the creatures of bread and wine, but the soul of man that receiveth the grace of God'.[67] For Evangelicals with their strong doctrine of conversion, faith was the only way by which God's presence was known. They were aware that Christ was with them at the communion service because his Spirit acted directly on their minds and emotions rather than through the bread and wine as the Virtualist Scottish Office taught. The idea that an intermediary medium, under sacerdotal influence, like the bread and wine of the communion service, could be efficacious in the same way was contrary to their belief. They saw it as a completely unnecessary doctrine, and, worse, misleading about the way of salvation.

Craig and Drummond displayed some of the interpretations that might ensue from the Scottish Communion Office. Craig claimed that the Scottish invocation actually asserted the change in the elements to be one of transubstantiation in a manner 'more broadly than it is by Rome herself', because the Roman Catholic prayer for the elements included the more inclusive words 'unto us'.[68] While not pressing Craig's charge of full transubstantiation, Drummond suggested that the Scottish Office taught some sort of change in the elements which was in the same general class and rationale as transubstantiation. He thus implied that a dangerous range of teaching was opened up.[69] Virtualism fell within this category. Referring to the catechism from Moray, he quoted it as teaching the bread and wine after the invocation to be 'the spiritual body and blood of Christ', while the Aberdeen catechism referred to them as the 'mystical body and blood of our Redeemer...that they really and truly become the body and blood of Christ...to all intents and purposes'.[70] Drummond opposed Virtualism, quoting Waterland's argument that once 'the old notion of a sacrament as imparting a sign...wore off,...many different modifications of one and the same error' were adopted. He acknowledged that, while the Virtualists he had quoted in the catechisms denied 'a change of the elements into the natural body' of Christ, nonetheless the language used seemed to teach 'a change into a spiritual body of some sort'. He suggested their interpretations fitted closely with one of Waterland's categories of 'subtle evasions' used by Churchmen to describe the elements as 'the very body and blood of Christ' – namely that the bread and wine had 'become another personal body'.[71] Thus Craig understood the prayer of invocation as the Roman Catholic doctrine of transubstantiation. Drummond, on the other

---

[67] *Ibid.*, p. 52.
[68] *Ibid.*, p. 24.
[69] Drummond, *Scottish Communion Office Examined*, pp. 27-30.
[70] *Ibid.*, pp. 49-50.
[71] *Ibid.*, pp, 52-53.

hand, demonstrated it to be Virtualism, which he labelled a modification of transubstantiation because it taught that the elements underwent a spiritual transformation. All notions of the elements being changed in any way so as to become instrumental in conferring blessing on the recipients were firmly rejected by Evangelicals.

Having expounded their view of the Scottish Office, Drummond and Craig then argued that it opposed scripture, ancient practice and the formularies of the Church of England. Drummond believed that the Bible discountenanced sacrificial practices. He quoted Hebrews 10.12, with its emphasis on Christ's death as the one offering for sin acceptable to God, and 1 Peter 2.5 and Romans 12.1, with teaching that God did not desire material gifts from his people but, rather, the daily offering of lives for his service.[72] As for the function of the bread and the wine, he argued for a figurative interpretation of the words, 'This is my body…this is my blood', spoken by Christ at the Last Supper, emphasising that these were uttered in the course of a Passover meal which was itself a visual celebration.[73] Other instances of Christ using non-literal phrases, such as the expressions 'I am the door', 'I am the true vine', were brought forward to explain that Christ used the elements solely as visual aids which would speak to human minds, explaining the atonement.[74] Evangelicals wished to demonstrate that the Bible was on their side.

Drummond also drew upon second-century accounts of celebrations of the Lord's Supper to discountenance the sacrificial aspect of the Scottish service. Justyn Martyr, a Christian living in Rome around 155 A. D., the African Church father, Tertullian, and the Alexandrian, Origen, were brought forward as never mentioning oblations in their accounts of eucharistic gatherings. Likewise, following again the writings of Jewel, he quoted the Catholic Fathers of the first six centuries as referring to the elements as signs, not sacrifices. Less evidence was produced concerning the invocation. Drummond relied, instead, on demonstrating that in the liturgy of St Ambrose, the fourth-century Bishop of Milan, the bread and wine did not 'become' the body and blood of Christ, but were referred to as 'figures' only.[75] Thus Drummond attempted to show that the Eastern liturgies used by the Nonjurors were not reflective of the practice of the early Church.

As for the doctrine of the Church of England, besides the obvious conclusion that the absence of the usages from the 1662 English service indicated the distaste of the Reformers, other evidence was considered. Drummond called attention to Stephen Gardiner, Bishop of Winchester, and

---

[72] *Ibid.*, pp. 16, 22.

[73] *Ibid.*, p. 25.

[74] *Ibid.*

[75] *Ibid.*, pp. 17-18, 30-31.

an opponent of the Reformation, who had defended the 1549 English service as 'not distant from the Catholic faith'.[76] Likewise he recorded that the managers at the trial of Laud had objected to the oblation of an 'unbloody' sacrifice contained in the 1637 service as a 'Popish corruption'.[77] Further proof centred on Brett, who had said that the Church of England had 'wilfully omitted to make the prayer of oblation'.[78] The absence of an invocation and oblation from the Book of Common Prayer was argued to be a mark of its Protestantism.

The formularies of the Anglican Church were also claimed to oppose the teaching of the Scottish Office. The fact that the Reformers had clearly rejected carnal transubstantiation in Article XXVIII, was extended to include Virtualism.[79] Article XXXI on the 'one oblation of Christ finished upon the Cross' was quoted as opposing the material sacrifice of the Scottish Office. The Homilies were discussed as rejecting sacrifices with their teaching that 'we must then take heed, lest of the memory it be made a sacrifice'.[80] Drummond and Craig were convinced that the Scottish Office fell outside the boundaries set by the Church of England.

Attention was also drawn to the parallels between the teaching of the Scottish Office and Tractarian theology. Craig, alarmed that Tractarianism was 'an ominous movement', summed up its doctrines as 'the peculiarities of the…Nonjurors'.[81] The danger of the Tractarian movement was, according to Drummond, that it negated the gains made by the Reformers. He pointed to Newman's dictum that the Reformers 'had mutilated the tradition of 1,500 years', to R .H. Froude who had denounced the English service as 'a judgement on the Church' and to John Keble who had said that the Reformers had 'given up altogether the Ecclesiastical tradition regarding certain very material points…in the doctrine of the Holy Eucharist'.[82] Craig thus summed up Nonjuring theology 'as stepping-stones towards Rome'.[83] Evangelicals understood Tractarian eucharistic teaching and that of the Scottish Office to veer towards Roman Catholicism and to be un-Anglican.

The analyses of Drummond and Craig thus focused on showing that the Scottish Communion Office of 1764 taught doctrines which were absent from the Book of Common Prayer. While the Anglican service could be used conscientiously by Evangelicals, Drummond and Craig argued that the

---

[76] *Ibid.*, p. 8.
[77] *Ibid.*, p. 13.
[78] *Ibid.*, pp. 35-36.
[79] *Ibid.*, pp. 32-33. Craig, *Important Discrepancy*, pp. 11-13.
[80] Drummond, *Scottish Communion Office Examined*, p. 20.
[81] Craig, *Important Discrepancy*, p. 34.
[82] Drummond, *Scottish Communion Office Examined*, pp. 36-37.
[83] Craig, *Important Discrepancy*, pp. 34-35.

Scottish Office was altogether more exclusive because its prayers of oblation and invocation excluded Evangelical theology. As such, Drummond and Craig found it impossible to support subscription to the Scottish Episcopal Church while it sanctioned the use of the service, particularly at a time of rising Tractarian controversy over eucharistic doctrine.

Minor Points of Difference

Concerning the idea of praying for the dead, Drummond highlighted the omission of the phrase 'militant here on earth' in the prayer for Christ's Church in the Scottish Office[84]. The removal of this prayer from a position in the Book of Common Prayer after the participation of the elements to a place before it in the Scottish Office substantiated his view that the ancient usage had been deliberately reinstated in the service. Drummond pointed to the Reformers having dispensed with such prayers as 'a superstitious, gross, and a Jewish error', and that the Scottish Office was not in the spirit of the Reformation.[85]

In 1847 the author 'Justitia', J. D. Miller, the assistant minister at St Paul's, Aberdeen, quoted Bishop Alexander Jolly of Moray as having taught in his *Catechism* that the mixed chalice represented the 'blood and water which flowed from the dead body of Christ'. For Evangelicals like Miller this came far too near the belief that the real blood of Christ was present at the eucharist.[86]

Finally, Miller commented that, in the Scottish Episcopal Church, 'the communicant was taught to place his hands in the form of a cross' at reception of the elements. Evangelicals regarded this as encouraging the idea of receiving the actual body of Christ on 'a throne to receive the King'.[87] The Scottish Communion Office was understood by Evangelicals to encompass non-Protestant doctrine in minor details as well as major features, and it was increasingly unacceptable to them.

Bagot's Analysis

Daniel Bagot, the Evangelical incumbent of St James's, Edinburgh, however, sought to find a loophole in interpreting the Scottish Communion Office which would pacify his fellow clergy and enable them to stay in the Church. His aim was to show that, like the English Office, its Scottish

---

[84] see note[6] in bold in Table 7.2, p. 382, columns 1-3 and p. 383, columns 1-2
[85] Drummond, *Scottish Communion Office Examined*, pp. 54-55.
[86] [J. D. Miller], 'Justitia', *Peculiarities of the Scottish Episcopal Church* (Aberdeen, 1847), p. 4.
[87] *Ibid.*

The Doctrine of the Scottish Communion Office 233

counterpart was open to a wide range of interpretation which would satisfy Virtualists and Evangelicals alike.[88] Firstly, Bagot examined the language and structure of the service. He suggested, in contrast to Drummond, that the word 'memorial' in the prayer of oblation made it clearly non-sacrificial, that it was merely a remembrance of the sacrifice of Christ. He proposed that the bread and wine could be understood to be a thankoffering for the fruits of the earth, presented by priest and people alike, simply asking God to bless them for his own use. Substantiating his argument by looking at the structure of the service, he argued that the gifts offered in the oblation were not yet consecrated, and thus could not be regarded as sacrificial. This was because the rubric, operating in the situation where more bread and wine were needed, directed that the prayer should be recited to the end of the invocation. It was thus only at the end of the invocation that the bread and wine were consecrated.[89] Therefore Evangelicals could use the oblatory prayer without scruple.

Drummond was not convinced. Concerning the structure, he thought that the paragraphing of the prayer indicated a natural break before the oblation, showing that the consecration had occurred previously when the priest had been directed to take 'the cup into his hand', and to lay 'his hand upon every vessel' while reciting 'this is my body...this is my blood'. It was at this point that the elements had been made 'authoritative representations' of Christ's body and blood, and they were thereafter offered to God as a sacrifice.[90] Thus whereas Bagot had argued that the consecration was not effective until after the invocation, Drummond thought that the language and structure of the oblatory prayer constituted a clear rendering of the Nonjuring belief that Christ had offered himself as a sacrifice at the Last Supper.[91]

Bagot sought to defend the invocation by reference to the small print in the service book. On the first page he found that the congregation should 'spiritually eat the flesh of Christ and drink His blood', and that the introductory rubric referred to the service as a 'sacrament'. He thus denied that the word 'become' meant transubstantiation of any kind. He offered a further suggestion that the invocation prayer was equivalent to Christ's own words at the Last Supper. These were not meant in 'a Romish sense' but sacramentally, imparting the inward and spiritual grace of Christ's body

---

[88] Bagot's analysis was reported in *A Letter to Some of the Members of the Vestry of St James's Chapel in Reference to the Scottish Communion Office* (Edinburgh, 1842), on 16 November 1842. The substance was repeated in a correspondence between Bagot and Drummond reported in the *Scottish Episcopal Times* from 3 February to 23 March 1844, and it is the latter that will be used in this account since it contains Drummond's reply.

[89] *The Scottish Episcopal Times*, 3 February 1844.

[90] *Ibid.*, 24 February 1844.

[91] *Ibid.*

and blood to the elements. Finally, Bagot suggested that, following Drummond's analysis, the words of the Anglican and Presbyterian services could also be read literally as suggestive of transubstantiation. He encouraged the reader to approach such statements in a spirit of compromise.[92]

Drummond replied that he had never argued that the Scottish Office taught transubstantiation in the way of the Roman Catholic Church, but that he had shown that some change in the elements was indicated by the structure of the service. For him therefore it was not that 'there are statements in [the service] which *look* like error', but that statements existed 'which *are* erroneous and heterodox'.[93] Bagot's arguments had not convinced Drummond that there was doctrinal similarity between the Scottish Communion Office and the Book of Common Prayer.

Bagot took refuge in the Thirty-Nine Articles to which all Scottish Episcopal clergy submitted, stating that, as they spoke against transubstantiation and any form of sacrifice, they provided 'a screen' for the Scottish Church from the accusation that it upheld doctrines contrary to those of Anglicanism. But Drummond pointed out that this was no line of defence since the Nonjuring doctrines of the Scottish Office existed in print and were upheld by clergy in Scotland, regardless of the requirement to sign the Articles. False subscription to the Articles could occur.[94]

Bagot was obviously trying to work for a peaceable settlement within the body of the Church in an attempt to calm things down in his congregation at St James's, Edinburgh, where some members were hoping to remove him and replace him with Drummond.[95] But his analysis, while quietening the dispute at St James's, did not win the support of all Evangelicals and many followed Drummond and Craig.[96] By 1844, when Bagot was the incumbent at Newry, Ireland, he seemed unconvinced by his own analysis. He suggested that the invocation could be worded more satisfactorily as 'that they may become the Sacrament of the body and blood of Christ' and, referring to the service as 'obnoxious', he hoped that it would be removed or altered at the next General Synod.[97] From 1842, Evangelical condemnation of the Scottish Communion Office was widespread.

---

[92] *Ibid.*, 10 February 1844.
[93] *Ibid.*, 16, 23 March.
[94] *Ibid.*, 23 March 1844.
[95] A Member of the Congregation, *A Letter to the Members of the Congregation of St James's Chapel in Reference to Certain Resolutions Which Have Been Entered into by Some Members of the Vestry of that Chapel* (Edinburgh, 31 December 1842).
[96] See Chapter 8 pp. 263-265.
[97] *Scottish Episcopal Times*, 10 February 1844.

High Church Response to Craig, Drummond and Bagot

The analyses by Craig, Drummond and Bagot called for a response. In 1843, among Virtualists, Patrick Cheyne of St John's Chapel, Aberdeen, defended the doctrine of the Scottish Communion Office as a clear demonstration of 'the sacrifice in the Eucharist; the real, spiritual presence and participation of Christ's Body and Blood; and the commemoration of the faithful departed'.[98] For Cheyne, the purpose of the invocation was 'to make the symbols what Christ made them – the instruments of conveying Himself to the spirit of the receiver'.[99] He understood the office to have been 'designed to preserve and witness [to] those great truths, more fully and consistently than the present English Office, or the Scottish Office of 1637'.[100] Pointing to the Edwardian liturgy of 1549, Cheyne went on to say that 'Cranmer and his associates...acted under threat' and the revised liturgy 'was a sad indication of the downward progress of the Church of England towards the error of [Zwingli]'.[101] Later, on 7 August 1844, Cheyne preached on similar lines before the Synod of Aberdeen, which afterwards asked him to publish the sermon. In it he called for the Scottish Episcopal Church to uphold publicly its own eucharistic doctrine against Evangelical 'discordant utterances...of doctrines...plainly and confessedly anti-Catholic', criticising his church for taking 'refuge under the indefinite and halting testimony of the English Liturgy'.[102] Cheyne, as a Virtualist, saw the Scottish Office as superior to the English.

However, Cheyne defended the Scottish Office against charges of Romanism. He pointed out that, since Roman Catholics believed the elements to be transubstantiated when the words, 'This is my Body...This is my Blood' were uttered by the priest, they would regard the subsequent Scottish invocation as blasphemous. But Cheyne was also anxious to show the Catholicity of the Scottish rite by pointing out that it expressly asked the Holy Spirit to change the elements. In this respect he maintained that it was clearer in intent than the Roman Mass which had no such prayer.[103] For Cheyne, the Scottish Office was plainly Catholic and superior to the Roman rite because it was more explicit.

While Michael Russell, Bishop of Glasgow and Galloway, never 'concealed [his] preference for the Scottish Office',[104] other Virtualists

---

[98] Patrick Cheyne, *The Authority and Use of the Scottish Communion Office Vindicated* (Aberdeen, 1843), p. 9.
[99] *Ibid.*, p. 31.
[100] *Ibid.*, p. 9.
[101] *Ibid.*, p. 13. (I thank Margaret Lye for pointing out this reference)
[102] Patrick Cheyne, *Holiness and the True Reforming Power of the Church* (Aberdeen, 1844), p. 23.
[103] Cheyne, *Authority and Use of Scottish Communion Office* pp. 16-17.
[104] William Walker, *Three Churchmen* (Edinburgh, 1893), p. 75.

sought to provide a vindication for it on biblical grounds. James Christie, the incumbent of Trinity Church, Turiff, argued in 1844 that Christ's words 'This is my body...This is my blood' at the Last Supper were not figurative because 'a mere symbol can communicate nothing', and that the oblation was clearly taught in the gospels.[105] Another approach was to repudiate any connection of the office with the doctrine of transubstantiation. Christie contended that all the catechisms pronounced the bread and wine to be only 'Christ's body and blood in virtue, power and efficacy', that there was no change in the elements beyond that.[106] Again, Christie, like Cheyne, pointed to the significant position of the invocation after the oblation as being anti-Roman.[107] Bishop Patrick Torry of St Andrews, Dunkeld and Dunblane also investigated the latter point in some depth from 1843 to 1845. While upholding the Scottish Office as a 'mark of distinction as an independent national Church', he maintained, along with Cheyne, that Roman Catholics would recoil from the service.[108] Virtualists, like Evangelicals, defended their views on biblical and doctrinal grounds.

Fearing links made with the Church of England by the act of 1840 might be damaged by the controversy, some orthodox High Churchmen were anxious to uphold the office. In 1843, C. H. Terrot, Bishop of Edinburgh, while acknowledging that 'no-one pretends that the formularies are perfect', added harshly that 'malevolent criticism can produce apparent discrepancies'.[109] E. B. Ramsay, incumbent of St John's, Edinburgh, and

---

[105] James Christie, *The Oblation and Invocation in the Scottish Communion Office Vindicated in answer to a Pamphlet entitled An Important discrepancy by the Rev E. Craig* (London and Aberdeen, 1844) pp. 26, 51-53.

[106] James Christie, *A Vindication of the Church in Scotland being an Exposure of D. T. K. Drummond's "Historical Sketch of Episcopacy"* (London, 1847), pp. 62-64. See also, John Alexander, *Letter to the Rt. Rev. William Skinner, Bishop of Aberdeen, Primus of the Church in Scotland, on the Eucharistic Doctrine Exhibited in the Scottish Communion Office as it is Affected to the School of Archdeacon Wilberforce and the Teaching of the Great Anglican Divines* (Edinburgh, 1857), p. 53. Here Alexander acknowledges 'a virtue...power...and opertion of the Flesh and Blood of Christ being mystically united to the signs...Thus far we go in acknowledging a change in the elements by consecration'.

[107] Cheyne, *Authority and Use of Scottish Communion Office*, pp. 16-17. Christie, *Oblation and Invocation*, p. 19. See also Francis Garden, *Vindication of the Scottish Episcopate* (Edinburgh, 1847), pp. 19-20, 28. Here, Garden, incumbent of St Paul's, York Place, Edinburgh (1844-1850) and editor of the Tractarian *Christian Remembrancer* from 1841 endeavoured to show that the Scottish Invocation could be understood as saying nothing different 'from our Lord's own words', but also admitted to finding its language 'wrong and dangerous' presumably inferring that it was suggestive of transubstantiation.

[108] Bishop Torry to Dean Torry, 27 April 1843 and 7 November 1845, NAS, CH12/12/2391 and CH12/12/2395.

[109] C. H. Terrot, *A Dissuasive from Schism* (Edinburgh, 1843), pp. 8-9.

Dean of the diocese, assured his congregation in December 1842 that the Scottish rite was 'a highly spiritual service, identical in doctrine with the Communion Service of the Church of England' and pointed to Bagot's 'very able and Christian Letter upon the subject'.[110] Again, John Boyle of St Mark's, Portobello, possibly more of a central Churchman, argued similarly that while the Scottish service 'may seem to lean to Romish error, when read as a whole...it is impossible to regard it otherwise than as echoing the words and breathing the spirit of Protestant truth'.[111] Non-Evangelicals maintained that the doctrine of the Scottish service hardly differed from that of the English Office.

Scottish Evangelical Episcopal Response

In turn, Drummond and J. D. Hull, the incumbent of Huntly Chapel, asked Bishop William Skinner of Aberdeen to disclaim Cheyne's sermons of 1843. When no such declaration occurred, Drummond assumed the views to have been 'tacitly approved'[112] and Hull declared that the Scottish Episcopal Church was 'moving down an inclined plane...shortly [to be] in a position to fit it for union with Rome'.[113] Evangelicals called for an official response on the doctrine of the Communion Office of 1764 by the Scottish Episcopal Church.

Drummond, in particular, countered the doctrinal arguments which had been offered in defence of the Scottish Office. He continued to attack Virtualism, staunchly maintaining in 1845 that the rationale of Roman and

---

[110] E. B. Ramsay, *The True Position of the Scottish Episcopal Church* (Edinburgh, 1842), pp. 35-36. Ramsay is often difficult to pin down. See E. B. Ramsay, *The Scripture Doctrine of the Eucharist* (Edinburgh, 1858), p. 11. Here he goes some way towards Evangelical belief but still puts stress on the elements: 'we do not speak of changes in the elements in substance...but...a channel of intimate union or communication is in these sacred elements formed'. Ramsay's exposition probably puts him at the 'high' end of Receptionism. See also John Marshall, *A Few Remarks Addressed at the Request of Others to the Congregation of St James's Episcopal Church, Edinburgh* (Edinburgh, 1843), p. 9 where Marshall, incumbent of Blairgowrie (1841-1843), pressed that the Scottish Invocation expressed nothing different from Christ's words at the Last Supper. See also W. E. Aytoun, *The Drummond Schism Examined and Exposed* (Edinburgh, 1842), p. 28. Aytoun, Professor of Rhetoric at Edinburgh University, argued that the Scottish Office, based on the Clementine Liturgy, which he claimed to date 'from the foundation of the Church itself', could not be accused of upholding transubstatiation since 'the dogma...was never heard of until the eighth century'.

[111] John Boyle, *A Plea for the Episcopal Church in Scotland in a Brief Defence of the Scottish Communion Office* (Edinburgh, 1843), pp. 8-9.

[112] Drummond, *Sketch*, p. 52.

[113] J. D. Hull, *Popery in the Scotch Episcopal Church* (Aberdeen, 1844), p. 5.

Nonjuring theology was 'unAnglican' in that both connected 'the grace of the sacrament with the elements instead of looking for it in the persons only'.[114] As for the position of the prayer of invocation saving the Scottish Office from teaching transubstantiation, Drummond quoted Waterland that 'the Romish divines have frequently laid hold of what is said...in the prayer of invocation as found in some of the old Greek liturgies...as favourable with their tenet of transubstantiation' because the language used was very strong and 'is said to make the bread the body and the wine the blood of Christ'.[115] By 1849,[116] Drummond's views on this point had crystallised, and he pressed firmly, as Craig had done in 1842, that the Scottish service implied actual transubstantiation. Ironically, Cheyne's analysis aided his argument. He agreed with Cheyne that Roman Catholics thought the words of consecration to effect transubstantiation, and that there was no express prayer in the Roman rite asking for this change, whereas the Scottish invocation was specific in its request. Thus, for Drummond, what was only implied in the Roman mass was plainly expressed in the Scottish Office.[117] Proceeding from this point, Drummond argued that the former service was more acceptable to Evangelicals. He then suggested that because of the position of the oblation in the Scottish service, which was a sacrifice of only the symbolic body and blood of Christ, a subsequent, distinct invocation to make the bread and wine something more than signifiers was required.[118] Thus he concluded that, while a Roman Catholic might recoil from the Scottish service, 'it does not appear that a Scottish Episcopalian may not receive the doctrine of transubstantiation' from it, 'provided the period of change is deferred'.[119] For Drummond, the Scottish Communion Office, based on Greek liturgies, while not Roman, was nonetheless Catholic. It clearly asked for the elements to undergo a change, and its language was suggestive of full transubstantiation even though its Nonjuring authors had not intended this. Thus he argued that the service exhibited 'ultra-Romanism'.[120]

---

[114] *Reprint of Four Articles Taken by Permission from the London Record with an Introduction by the Rev. D. T. K. Drummond Containing Remarks Recently Addressed by the Rev. F. Garden to the Rt. Rev. Lord Bishop of Cashel* (Edinburgh, 1845), pp. 8-12, 26.

[115] *Ibid.*, pp. 7-8.

[116] The occasion prompting this detailed theological analysis was a deputation of English Episcopalians to the House of Lords, 22 May 1849, endeavouring to obtain concessions from the Anglican Church. See Chapter 10, pp. 323-326.

[117] *Episcopacy in Scotland: Revised Report of the Debate in the House of Lords May 22 1849* (London, 1849), p. 199.

[118] *Ibid.*, p. 202.

[119] *Ibid.*, p. 206.

[120] *Ibid.*, p. 199.

While Robert Montgomery, former incumbent of St Jude's, Glasgow, applauded Christie's analysis,[121] many other Evangelicals eventually followed Drummond. Somewhat dramatically, in 1856, Richard Hibbs, incumbent of St Vincent's, Edinburgh, declared of the Scottish Office, 'here is Christ corporally present upon the Altar'.[122] C. B. Gribble, of St Jude's, Glasgow, in 1858, found 'the Scottish Communion Office so near to the Romish doctrine of Transubstantiation as to render it hard for the most ingenious sophistry to show the distinction'.[123] In 1861 F. W. B. Bouverie, of St Paul's, Aberdeen, feared that the Scottish service could only 'impose on the simple minded, by making them believe that the word or touch of a priest can convert bread and wine into flesh and blood'.[124] The defence of the Scottish Office against charges of Romanism pushed the Evangelical polemic towards establishing that the service not only taught Virtualism, of which it disapproved, but could, indeed, be interpreted as containing the extreme doctrine of transubstantiation.

Many Scottish Episcopalians continued to fear that the dispute would damage their growing links with the Church of England. As early as September 1843, the Synod of Moray, Ross and Argyll, under Bishop David Low, called for a General Synod to examine a petition from its clergy for the removal of the Scottish Office for the sake of harmony, while not opposing its doctrines.[125] However, given the general mood of instability, the suggestion was not pursued.[126] The situation, already inflamed, became worse for the Scottish Episcopal Church in October 1843 when the *English Churchman*, a periodical favoured by the Tractarians, announced 'we implore every Scottish Bishop to part with the Catholic Communion Office only with life itself'.[127] The growing discord was marked when seventeen presbyters from the diocese of Aberdeen, including Cheyne and Christie, signed a protest against 'deprecation of the Scottish

---

[121] Robert Montgomery, *The Scottish Episcopal Church and the English Schismatics* (London, 1847), pp. 28-29.

[122] Richard Hibbs, *Scottish Episcopal Romanism* (Edinburgh, 1856), pp. 80-81.

[123] C. B. Gribble, *A Mistake Corrected. A Letter to the Rev Dr Champneys, Head Master of the Collegiate School, Glasgow* (Glasgow, 1858), p. 10.

[124] F. W. Bouverie, *Can They be Made One? A Question in Reference to the Church of England and the Scottish Episcopal Church* (Aberdeen, 1861), p. 17.

[125] David Low himself supported relinquishing the Scottish Office for the sake of peace in the Church. Low's churchmanship is not clear. He was born at Brechin and attended Marischal College, Aberdeen and underwent theological training under George Gleig, future Bishop of Brechin, 1810-1840, an opponent of Edward Craig in 1820 over Evangelical doctrine. William Blatch, *A Memoir of the Right Rev. David Low* (London, 1855), pp. 5-17, 273-274. Chapter 8, p. 247.

[126] Papers of the College of Bishops, NAS, CH 12/60/3 p. 119. Drummond, *Sketch*, p. 50.

[127] *English Churchman*, October 1843. Quoted in Drummond, *Sketch*, p. 51.

Liturgy' in November 1843, while only five other clergy opposed its use.[128] Two years later alternative suggestions emerged. In private letters to W. E. Gladstone in 1845 and 1846, E. B. Ramsay of St John's, Edinburgh, remarked that although he did not think the Scottish Office contained 'Romish sentiments', it would be better 'to state on authority which the Office is – no authorised edition ever having been declared', revealing that 'I strongly incline to the opinion now held of many that Laud's Office...is the genuine edition'.[129] Thus by 1845, although the Scottish Episcopal Church had produced no official statement, there were well-defined factions of support and opposition for the Scottish Communion Office among the Scottish High Churchmen.

By the 1850s the Tractarians had developed their eucharistic theories further. They discarded Virtualism as inadequate and instead looked to giving more weight to the idea of the real presence of Christ in the elements. In 1853, Robert Wilberforce spoke of a 'real, objective presence' of Christ in the bread and wine, meaning a 'substantial presence' not a 'symbolic, virtual presence'.[130] Pusey, in the same year, spoke of a spiritual, but objective, presence which was united to the bread and wine to form a single compound, so that Christ was received by all communicants whatever their faith.[131] Advanced Tractarianism thus taught doctrine that could be defined, in Drummond's terms, as a type of transubstantiation.[132]

The topic now under investigation was whether these ideas could be read into the English and Scottish Communion Offices. Regarding the former, Evangelicals were happy that their own beliefs were clearly expressed in the Book of Common Prayer even though the Tractarians matched it to their own theology. There was little agitation at the time calling for an alteration of the Communion Service. A campaign begun in 1860, led by Robert Grosvenor, Baron Ebury, a Low Churchman, to revise the liturgy concentrated only on the services for burial, baptism, marriage and visitation of the sick.[133] Most Evangelicals followed Hugh McNeile of

---

[128] To the Rt. Rev. Bishop of Aberdeen and Primus, William Skinner. Protest by Eighteen Presbyters of the Diocese of Aberdeen against Deprecation of the Scottish Liturgy, November 1843, NAS, CH12/12/2188. Drummond, *Sketch*, p. 50.

[129] E. B. Ramsay to W. E. Gladstone, 1 May 1845, British Library, Gladstone Papers, Volume CXCVIII Add. MSS 44,283 f. 99. E. B. Ramsay to W. E. Gladstone, 1 January 1846, British Library, Gladstone Papers, Volume CXCVIII Add. MSS 44,283 f. 143.

[130] Härdelin, *Eucharist,* pp. 156-157. Robert Wilberforce, *The Doctrine of the Holy Eucharist* (London, 1853), pp. 228ff., quoted in, Härdelin, *Eucharist*, p. 165. Toon, *Evangelical Theology*, pp. 197-198.

[131] E. B. Pusey, *The Presence of Christ in the Eucharist*, (Oxford 1853), pp. 22, 47, 69, quoted in, Härdelin, *Eucharist*, p. 167. Toon, *Evangelical Theology*, p. 197.

[132] See Chapter 7, p. 229.

[133] Robert Grosvenor, *On the Revision of the Liturgy: The Speech of Lord Ebury in the House of Lords, 8 May 1860* (London, 1860), p. 23.

Liverpool who explained that any seemingly controversial phrases in the Anglican service were ambiguous only because 'they were intended to be fervently devotional', and should be approached as such.[134] Evangelicals in England felt their beliefs were clearly represented in the Anglican service.

But in Scotland the situation was different. The Scottish Office faced a two-pronged attack. Evangelicals believed it, unlike the English Office, to be inimical to their theology, and Tractarians began to claim it was conducive to their advancing ideas.[135] Cheyne, still a supporter of the Scottish Office, appeared to embrace Tractarianism in 1857, preaching that the 'Real Presence' was 'the whole Christ, God and Man truly and substantially present under the form of bread and wine [and] the sacrifice of the Eucharist is absolutely the same as the Sacrifice of the Cross'.[136] Bishop T. G. S. Suther of Aberdeen, alarmed that this would alienate the Church of England, called Cheyne to trial before the diocesan Synod in June 1858.[137] On 2 December 1858, distancing itself from Cheyne, the Scottish Episcopal Church suspended him for preaching doctrines similar to Roman Catholicism.[138]

But the climax of the issue in Scotland revolved around Bishop A. P. Forbes of Brechin. In his Charge of 5 August 1857 Forbes attempted to affirm the advanced Tractarian view that Christ was 'really present in the Holy Sacrament as the supernatural Bread which cometh down from

---

[134] *Record*, 8 November 1871.

[135] Virtualist theologians, like George Forbes, incumbent of Burntisland, striving to protect the Scottish Office, argued that advanced Tractarianism was linked to Luther's consubstantiation, a material change, whereas the Scottish Office asked only for a transformation of the quality of the elements enabling them to act as the body and blood of Christ. G. H. Forbes, *Panoply,* Volume II, pp. 150-153, 210; Volume III, p. 252. G. H. Forbes, *A Short Explanation of the Communion Office of the Church of Scotland adapted to the Revised Edition* (Burntisland, 1863), p. 12. This however did not answer Evangelical objections to a change of any sort in the elements being asked for. Again, Forbes's subsequent recommendation that the bread and wine should be received carefully so 'that not the smallest crumb fall to the ground. And do not wipe your lips with a handkerchief after having partaken of the chalice' would not have assured Evangelicals that he held anything but a high eucharistic doctrine. See Forbes, *Short Explanation*, p. 12.

[136] Patrick Cheyne, *Six Sermons on the Doctrine of the Most Holy Eucharist* (Aberdeen, 1858), p. 22. G. N. Pennie, 'The Trial of the Rev Patrick Cheyne for Erroneous Teaching on the Eucharist in Aberdeen in 1858', *Records of the Scottish Church History Society*, 23 (1987), pp. 77-93.

[137] Rowan Strong, *Alexander Forbes of Brechin* (Oxford, 1995), pp. 124-125. Cheyne's trial followed the precedent set by the Church of England in 1856 when G. A. Dennison, vicar of East Brent in Somerset, had preached views similar to Cheyne's, and was found guilty of teaching doctrine repugnant to the Church of England.

[138] Strong, *Forbes*, pp. 124-125.

Heaven'.[139] He concluded that the Book of Common Prayer, although 'a sad mutilation' of the 1549 liturgy, nevertheless upheld the doctrine of the real, objective presence taught by the Tractarians.[140] Turning to Virtualism, he found it to be an inadequate expression of the real presence.[141] But as for the Scottish Communion Office itself, he described it as expressive of more than Virtualism, that it was the 'interpreter of the English Office'. He explained that, for him, the Scottish Office adequately expressed his current views in bearing 'witness not only to the two great Christian doctrines of the Eucharistic Sacrifice and Real Presence, but to the whole Vincentian theory',[142] and that any calls from 'the Drummondite[s]' to relinquish it would be as casting 'to the swine the precious pearl committed to our keeping'.[143] Forbes's sermon was a clear statement that the Scottish Communion Office, more adequately than the English service, could be interpreted as containing advanced Tractarianism.

Some of the Tractarian leaders in England, along with Forbes, upheld the Scottish Office as conducive to their developed views. In 1862 the Scottish Episcopal Church, now looking to cement its links with the Anglican Church, held negotiations towards revising the service to make it more acceptable to objectors.[144] One of the suggestions was to change the invocation to that of the Eastern liturgy of St James with its less objective language. John Keble wrote to William Forbes of Medwyn, the Bishop of Brechin's elder brother that, if this were accomplished, the congregation should all say 'Amen' after the invocation 'as a distinct and constant acknowledgement of the Real Presence'. But Keble preferred that 'you will see your way to support the real old fashioned followers of Bishop Jolly' and that 'if the unrevised liturgy can be allowed, it ought to be'.[145] Prominent Tractarians, in 1862, understood the Scottish Office to be a suitable expression of their matured doctrine of the real, objective presence. Drummond's argument of 1842, that the Scottish Office opened the way to a range of high eucharistic theology, had been vindicated.[146]

---

[139] A. P. Forbes, *A Primary Charge Delivered to the Clergy in his Diocese at the Annual Synod of 1857* 2nd Edition (London, 1858), pp. 2-3.

[140] Strong, *Forbes*, pp. 102-104.

[141] Forbes, *Charge*, pp. 20-21.

[142] The threefold test of Catholicity, 'oecumenicity, antiquity, and consent'. See F. L. Cross, *The Oxford Dictionary of the Christian Church* (London, 1958), p. 1423.

[143] Forbes, *Charge*, pp. 58-61.

[144] See n. 63, Chapter 10, p. 329.

[145] Two letters on the subject of the Revision of the Scottish Office addressed in 1862-1863 to William Forbes Esq. of Medwyn by the Late John Keble, NAS, CH/12/13/87, added as an appendix to a letter from Rev A. D. Murdoch to the Bishop of Edinburgh, 1 June 1889.

[146] See Chapter 7, pp. 229.

The Doctrine of the Scottish Communion Office 243

When Forbes was brought to trial for alleged heretical views before the Synod of Scottish Bishops in September 1857, Evangelicals took the opportunity of pressing their case for abolition of the Scottish Office. Before proceedings commenced, Bishops C. H. Terrot of Edinburgh, Alexander Ewing of Argyll and the Isles, and W. J. Trower of Glasgow and Galloway issued a declaration stating that

> we hold and teach that the Body and Blood of Christ are not so present in the consecrated Elements of bread and wine as to be therein the proper object of such supreme adoration as is due to God alone.[147]

A layman, John Carmichael, under the pseudonym 'Veritas', probably a master at the High School of Edinburgh, criticised the declaration as imprecise, and asked for a clear exposition of the doctrines held by the bishops stating whether they themselves supported Forbes's views.[148] Drummond likewise informed Ramsay on 23 February 1858 that the declaration was 'worthless', that its use of 'so' and 'such' could have meant that the Scottish Episcopal Church upheld any theology from Trower's view that there was a 'supernatural presence to the elements'[149] to Ramsay's Receptionist view that 'in the Eucharist Christ's presence is spiritually manifested in the heart of the faithful communicant'. In the absence of a clear statement from the Church, Drummond urged Ramsay 'to demand the removal once and forever...of the Scotch Communion Office'.[150] A pastoral letter from the bishops in May 1858, calling their clergy to teach the 'essential mystery of Christ's Eucharistic presence, while there was no requirement to believe the presence was a substantial one',[151] did not improve matters. Scottish Evangelicals in 1858 looked for something much firmer. They queried the beliefs of the Scottish bishops and demanded the abolition of the Scottish Communion Office, believing it to exclude their own theology and to be top-heavy in its accommodation of a range of theology from Virtualism to advanced Tractarian views.

Eventually Forbes, since he had asked only for toleration of his views, rather than for the express authority of the Scottish Episcopal Church, was merely censured and entreated to be more careful. As Rowan Strong points

---

[147] *Declaration of the Doctrine of the Holy Eucharist signed by the Bishops of Edinburgh, Argyll, and Glasgow* (Edinburgh, 1858).

[148] [John Carmichael], 'Veritas', *Romanism and Scottish Episcopacy* (Edinburgh, 1858), p. 10.

[149] See W. J. Trower, *A Remonstrance Addressed to Archibald Campbell Esq. of Blythswood on Certain Resolutions to which his Name is Appended, Published in the Glasgow Herald of Nov. 21 1856* (Glasgow, 1856), p. 14.

[150] D. T. K. Drummond, *Letter to the Rev. Dean Ramsay in Reference to the Primary Charge of Bishop Forbes and the Declaration of Bishops Terrot, Ewing, and Trower* (Edinburgh, 1858), pp. 5, 8.

[151] *Scottish Ecclesiastical Journal*, May 1858, Supplement 1-2.

out, this meant that he was neither effectively condemned nor silenced and that Tractarianism could be freely propagated in the Scottish Episcopal Church.[152] In reality, Scottish High Churchmen were wrestling with the issue of formal acceptance by the Church of England. They had to juggle this against the problem of causing offence to their Virtualist clergy if they condemned the Scottish Office outright. But the verdict left many Evangelicals feeling, increasingly, that their theology was not recognised by the Church, unless they chose to read the Scottish Office as Bagot had recommended. For most Evangelicals the problems were clear-cut – they found the Scottish Communion Office totally unacceptable.

Conclusion

In some ways the problems surrounding the Scottish Communion Office were similar to those connected with the baptismal rite of the Book of Common Prayer. However, Evangelicals believed the latter service to be a product of the ongoing thought of the Reformation in which there had been positive steps away from Roman Catholicism. But the Scottish Communion Office, with its particular structure and language, was regarded as a retrograde step towards beliefs which Cranmer and his associates had discarded. Whereas Evangelicals produced a reading of the baptismal service to match their theology, most found it impossible to be reconciled to the Scottish Office. Firstly, its oblation was understood to demean the Evangelical belief in the infinite merit of Christ's death on the cross. Secondly, while some Evangelicals had a strong sense of Christ's presence and special blessing at their communion services, they repudiated the Scottish invocation because it connected such experience with the elements rather than with the hearts of believers. Drummond classed the prayer as 'a doctrine of transubstantiation', since it asked for a specific change in the bread and wine, and he placed Virtualism within this category. Many Evangelicals found it impossible to read the service according to their own theology.

It is evident that the rise of Tractarianism in the 1840s exacerbated the opposition by causing a strong Protestant reaction against anything approaching Roman Catholicism. But it is clear that the chasm between Evangelicals and the Virtualist authors of the rite was so great that the dispute would in any case have occurred whenever the service became widely known. Indeed, Laud had expressed similar concerns in the seventeenth century, followed by Brett and Low Churchmen in the eighteenth and early nineteenth centuries – problems in the 1840s were by no means a new phenomenon.

---

[152] Strong, *Forbes*, pp. 153, 158.

Evangelicals acknowledged that Roman Catholics might be uneasy about using the Scottish Office because of the order of its prayers. Nonetheless, they pressed that its structure and language, unlike that of the Book of Common Prayer, so plainly suggested transubstantiation that even the ordinary communicant would sense that meaning. Thus the Scottish Office, although based on Greek rather than Roman form, was understood to be Catholic.

In essence Evangelicals were asking for a service, such as they believed the Anglican rite to be, which would encompass their own theology. Replacement of the word 'become' by 'be unto us' in the invocation would probably have lessened the problem of the suggested change in the elements, but the dilemma surrounding the oblation would have remained. The language and structure of the Scottish Communion Office were fundamentally unacceptable to Evangelicals.

Chapter 8

Secession

Introduction

For three or four decades, mainly after 1842, the Scottish Episcopal Church was disturbed by a numerically small group of clergy and laity who left its confines and set themselves up as English, rather than Scottish, Episcopal congregations, loyal to the Church of England. The controversies surrounding their departure concerned matters of theology and church practice. Issues such as the suitable use of the set services of the Church and the doctrine of the Communion Office were at the centre of the disputes. But, in the decades before these problems occurred, there was already disagreement between some Evangelicals and High Churchmen in Scotland, and the later events arose out of an already inflamed atmosphere of mistrust.

A major difficulty was presented by the differences of doctrine between Evangelicals and High Churchmen. The *Scottish Episcopal Review and Magazine*, as early as 1820, referred to Evangelicals as 'precise, pretending, and censorious religionists who have annoyed and afflicted us severely for a few years past, and have really changed a pleasant society...into a group of hostile combatants'.[1] Again, in 1837, there was continued condemnation when Evangelicals were designated as 'thin skinned and...vindictive', and their preaching as containing 'omissions, exaggerations and unscriptural peculiarities'.[2] The problems revolved, in part, around the Evangelical doctrine of conversion.[3] This was illustrated in 1822, when letters from a clergyman were published describing a young man 'being pounced upon by the keen-scented hawks of modern Evangelicalism' in an effort to bring him to faith.[4] The doctrine of baptism was a related problem area. The chasm of belief between Evangelicals and High Churchmen in Scotland over this issue has already been analysed in the discussion of the arguments in Edinburgh between Edward Craig, of St James's, and James Walker, of St Peter's, in the 1820s.[5] Sometimes it was apparent that High Churchmen in Scotland did not fully understand what Evangelical teaching upheld. In

---

[1] *Scottish Episcopal Review and Magazine*, October 1820.
[2] *Stephen's Episcopal Magazine*, June 1837, December 1837.
[3] See Chapter 4, pp. 117-122.
[4] *Scottish Episcopal Review and Magazine*, April 1822.
[5] See Chapter 6, pp. 199-203.

these early decades, since there were so few Evangelicals in the Scottish Episcopal Church,[6] High Churchmen tended to be wary of them as an alien force. This was the case in 1820 when Craig dismissed the allegation of Bishop George Gleig of Brechin that he had altered the words of administration in the service for Holy Communion to 'the body of our Lord Jesus Christ which was given for sinners', in an attempt to conform to the doctrine of limited atonement.[7] However, since neither Craig nor most of the other Scottish Episcopal Evangelicals were predestinarians,[8] Gleig's understanding was obviously ill founded. Such differences between Evangelical and High Church doctrine led to growing tension in the Scottish Episcopal Church during the 1820s.

By the 1830s it was clear that there was a divergence between some Evangelical Scottish Episcopalians and High Churchmen over the understanding of Church order. High Churchmen, who upheld the catholicity of the Church, were strong believers in its corporate unity and discipline, and they promoted its claims of apostolic succession as the guarantee of the truth of its teaching.[9] Typically, Bishop Alexander Jolly, of Moray, in 1828 wrote that 'the Church [is] one Body animated by...the Spirit of Unity...and the Apostolic succession, which is to be traced in the line of Episcopacy, [is] essential to the Constitution of Christ's Church'.[10] Similar concern was not uncommon among many early nineteenth-century Anglican Evangelicals who often upheld apostolicity, although their adherence to the idea of the invisible church made up of true believers tended to mean that, according to the *Record* in 1833, they attached 'an inferior degree of importance to it'.[11] Again, many followed the teaching of Charles Simeon, vicar of Holy Trinity, Cambridge, from 1782 to 1836, who had taught respect for the Church as an institution. The fear that French Revolutionary fervour could grip Methodism, leading to an overthrow of the British Crown as had been achieved by Puritanism in the seventeenth century, was the core of such beliefs. As a result, Anglican Evangelicals were often wary of close interaction with their counterparts in other

---

[6] See Chapter 1, pp. 26-28.

[7] *Correspondence Between Right Reverend Bishop Gleig and Rev Edward Craig Respecting an Accusation Lately Published in a Charge Delivered to the Clergy of the Episcopal Communion of Brechin* (Edinburgh, 1820), pp. 1-15.

[8] See Chapter 4, pp. 139-143. *Cf ENCS*, p. 213, where it is implied that all Evangelicals held the belief.

[9] P. B. Nockles, *The Oxford Movement in Context: Anglican High Churchmanship, 1760-1857* (Cambridge, 1994), pp. 25-26, 155-156.

[10] Alexander Jolly to Charles Fyvie, 23 October 1828, NAS, CH12/14/149. Fyvie was incumbent of Inverness in 1828. From 1842 to 1848 he was Dean of Moray and Ross. D. M. Bertie, *Scottish Episcopal Clergy 1689-2000* (Edinburgh, 2000), p. 264.

[11] *Record*, 12 December 1833. See also, Grayson Carter, *Anglican Evangelicals: Protestant Secessions from the Via Media, c. 1800-1850* (Oxford, 2001), pp. 13-14.

denominations, believing separation from the Anglican Church, with its apostolic line, to be sinful. From around the 1820s, however, these ideas began to give way when Evangelicals like Edward Irving and Robert Haldane criticised what they perceived to be lukewarm faith among their contemporaries. Holding, also, to the advent hope that Christ would soon return in person, some regarded it as less important to maintain the unity and discipline of the Church at the expense of more aggressive evangelism and fervent faith.[12]

Various Evangelical Scottish Episcopalians appear to have been affected by the new views. Fuelled by their alienation from some aspects of Scottish Episcopalian doctrine they were sometimes led into joint ventures with non-Anglicans before similar co-operation was universally evident among their counterparts in England. Craig's position as an examiner of missionaries for David Nasmith's newly formed Edinburgh City Mission in 1832 meant that he worked alongside the Edinburgh clergy David Dickson of St Cuthbert's, Church of Scotland, John Brown of Broughton Place Secession Church and William Innes of Elder Street Baptist Church.[13] Granted the shared established status of Anglicanism and Scottish Presbyterianism might have appealed to some Evangelicals, relations with Thomas Chalmers were, nevertheless, particularly warm. Letters to Chalmers from Craig reveal that they met on a social as well as formal basis. D. T. K. Drummond, of Trinity Chapel, Edinburgh, interacted similarly. In April 1842 B. W. Noel, incumbent of St John's, Bedford Row, London, who had been instrumental in persuading Anglicans to support Nasmith's interdenominational London City Mission, stayed at Drummond's home where he was entertained to dinner together with Chalmers. Again, Drummond obtained free tickets to enable impoverished Episcopalians to attend Chalmers's divinity classes, at which Daniel Bagot, of St James's, Edinburgh, suggested that his own *Catechism on Popery* might be of use.[14] At a time when some Evangelical Scottish Episcopalians

---

[12] Donald M. Lewis, *Lighten their Darkness: The Evangelical Mission to Working-Class London* (New York, 2001), pp. 11-12. Charles Smyth, *Simeon and Chuch Order: A Study of the Origins of the Evangelical Revival in Cambridge in the Eighteenth Century* (Cambridge, 1940), p. 290. Grayson Carter, *Anglican Evangelicals: Protestant Secessions from the Via Media c. 1800-1850* (Oxford, 2001), pp. 13-14. See also Chapter 4, pp. 134-148. Charles Simeon, although holding strict views on Church order, did preach in the Church of Scotland, but only on the principle that it was the Established Church in Scotland. Smyth, *Simeon*, pp. 300-301.

[13] *Edinburgh Almanack* (Edinburgh, 1833-1842). See, Lewis, *Lighten Their Darkness*, pp. 52-53. See Chapter 5, p. 168 for Edinburgh City Mission.

[14] Letters to Thomas Chalmers from Edward Craig, 1823-1833, New College Library, Edinburgh, Thomas Chalmers Papers, CHA 4.71.33; 4.92.15,17; 4.136.50,51,52; 4.156.36,37,38; 4.177.16,17; 4.202.72. CHA 104.35. Letters from D. T. K. Drummond to Thomas Chalmers, 1836-1842, New College Library, Edinburgh,

felt distanced from their High Church colleagues, they grew closer to Churchmen of other denominations.

A particular problem concerning Church discipline arose for Drummond over the use of the Book of Common Prayer. Most High Churchmen were liturgically conservative, wanting to preserve the existing forms of service as a safeguard against doctrinal error. In general Evangelicals, although also adhering to the Prayer Book in public worship, did not feel constrained to use it in more informal settings. Prayer meetings and Bible studies were a regular part of their ministry and, at these, the forms of service in the Prayer Book were generally replaced by extempore prayer offered by the incumbent and laity. These meetings, which were a legacy of the Evangelical Revival of the eighteenth century when the Methodists began weekly class meetings for the discussion of spiritual experiences,[15] were used by both Drummond and Bagot.[16] Drummond had difficulties with Scottish Episcopal High Church understanding in the 1830s because his meetings went beyond the usual form into the area of evangelisation. The editor of the official Scottish Episcopal newspaper filed a complaint against him in 1835 for holding such events in a room in Princes Street in Edinburgh without using the liturgy.[17] Bishop James Walker of Edinburgh did not pursue the matter, probably because Drummond was acting within Canon XIX, laid down in 1828, which, although requiring the use of the liturgy in public worship in church, did not insist on it at other times:

> As in all the ordinary parts of divine service it is necessary to fix, by authority, the precise form, from which no Bishop, or Presbyter, or Deacon, shall be at liberty to depart by his own alterations or insertions, lest such liberty should produce consequences destructive of "decency and order," it is hereby enacted, that in the performance of Morning and Evening Service the words of the English Liturgy shall be strictly adhered to.[18]

Drummond, although obeying the letter of the law, because his meetings could not be classified as morning or evening services, was, however, felt by some High Churchmen to be pushing the boundary too far.

Thomas Chalmers Papers, CHA 4.249.29,30,31;4.262.52,53; 4.290.48; 4.303.15,17. For letter regarding B. W. Noel, see CHA 4.303.15. Daniel Bagot to Thomas Chalmers 1837, New College Library, Edinburgh, Thomas Chalmers Papers, CHA 4. 258. 52, 54,56.

[15] D. W. Bebbington, *Evangelicalism in Modern Britain* (London, 1993), pp. 24-25.

[16] *Correspondence Between Rt Rev C. H. Terrot and Rev D. T. K Drummond* (Edinburgh, 1842), p. 11.

[17] *Ibid.*, p. 24.

[18] George Grubb, *An Ecclesiastical History of Scotland* Vol. IV (Edinburgh, 1861), pp. 132, 184. This law had its roots as far back as 1811 to check irregular practices in daily church services which even some High Churchmen were introducing.

On 18 November 1837 Walker summoned Drummond to answer another accusation concerning failure to use the liturgy. David Moir, Bishop of Brechin, and J. B. Pratt, of St James's, Cruden, Aberdeenshire, objected because he had held informal, non-Prayer Book mission services for fishermen in Usan, near Montrose, and was, moreover, encroaching on the territory of another Episcopalian, Patrick Cushnie. Their complaint was that of orthodox High Churchmen with a reverence for the liturgy and church order.[19] But the case revealed a further problem. Drummond's meetings at Usan were held in co-operation with the local Presbyterian minister, James Brewster.[20] Such practice was clearly at odds with High Churchmen who, loyal to the doctrine of apostolic succession, eschewed any co-operation with non-Anglicans whom they believed to have been in a state of schism from the church catholic since the Reformation. But Drummond defended himself, announcing in 1842, 'I esteem it a privilege to act with...all them that love the Lord Jesus Christ in sincerity'.[21] Thus Drummond's activities at Usan, although possibly objectionable to some Simeonite Evangelicals, would certainly have been unacceptable to High Churchmen like Moir. While Walker once more declined to take matters further, showing considerable latitude for a High Churchman, there was, nevertheless, a growing tension by 1838 among some Scottish Episcopalians concerning conduct of services.

The rise of Tractarianism was an important factor in exacerbating such issues for Evangelicals because there were obvious links between Oxford teaching and that of the Scottish High Churchmen. The shared Tractarian and High Church emphasis on episcopal order and discipline[22] would have caused Evangelicals like Drummond, after his problems with Moir in 1838, to have felt increasingly ill at ease in the Scottish Episcopal Church. Additionally, although most Evangelicals were not aware of the affinity between Tractarian eucharistic belief and the Scottish Communion Office of 1764, they would have been conversant with its links to Laud's liturgy

---

[19] Many earlier Evangelicals had, in fact, held similar views to Moir. Charles Simeon considered that clergy had enough to do in their own parishes. Henry Venn, vicar of Huddersfield, had given up helping Wesleyans with field preaching after 1771. Bebbington, *Evangelicalism*, pp. 31, 65, 76.

[20] D. T. K. Drummond, *Historical Sketch of Episcopacy in Scotland from 1688 to the Present Time* (Edinburgh, 1845), p. 75. D. T. K. Drummond, *Reply to Resolutions of Clergy of the Scottish Episcopal Church of the Diocese of Edinburgh* (Edinburgh, 1842), pp. 11-12. John Pratt to Alexander Jolly, 21 December 1836. NAS, CH12/30/203. *Memoir*, p. xl.

[21] D. T. K. Drummond, *A Sermon for the Times Preached in Trinity Chapel, Dean Bridge* (Edinburgh, 1842), p. 98.

[22] P. B. Nockles, 'Our Brethren in the North: The Scottish Episcopal Church and the Oxford Movement', *Journal of Ecclesiastical History*, 47 (1996) p. 660. Nockles, *Oxford Movement in Context*, pp. 218-219.

which they understood to be the service still used in the northeast of Scotland, and this, conceivably, would have been likely to concern them.[23] Similarly, the belief in baptismal regeneration held by High Churchmen was also espoused in E. B. Pusey's *Scriptural Views of Baptism* in *Tract 67* (1836),[24] doubtless leading Bagot to spearhead his spirited defence of Evangelical doctrine in 1836.[25] These similarities in the 1830s between Oxford and Scottish Episcopal High Church theology were likely to have led some Evangelicals to fear that their church might forge close links with the Tractarians whom they saw as undermining the Reformation base of Anglicanism.

Again, by 1834, the Tractarians began to extend the doctrine of apostolic succession, placing a high sacramental understanding on it, similar to that of the earlier Nonjurors, with an emphasis on special grace being transmitted down the line of bishops.[26] Many Evangelicals, as a result, distanced themselves further from the doctrine, but others continued to uphold it robustly. For instance, W. M. Wade, of Holy Trinity, Paisley, preached in 1840 that 'our Lord imparted the authority which he had on earth, to his Apostles, by whom it was transmitted to our day',[27] and in 1847, Robert Montgomery, the incumbent of St Jude's, Glasgow, from 1837 to 1843, 'maintained the apostolical claims of an Episcopate with unflinching boldness'.[28] It is not surprising therefore that Wade appears to have been in open conflict on the topic with his Presbyterian neighbour, Dr Robert Burns of the High Kirk, Paisley.[29] By the late 1830s it seems that there was a noticeable split in the Evangelical party in Scotland over apostolic succession, with Wade and Montgomery continuing to uphold it, while Drummond, Craig and Bagot, who were willing to work alongside non-Anglicans, veered away from it. Drummond's co-operation with the Presbyterian, James Brewster, in the mission at Usan was typical of an Evangelical with a low view of the doctrine of apostolic succession.

A related problem arose on 18 December 1841, when the Scottish Episcopal Church advertised the foundation of Glenalmond College, an establishment for general education and the training of ordinands. The bishops who signed the document described themselves as belonging to the

---

[23] See Chapter 7, p. 220.

[24] Nockles, *Oxford Movement in Context*, pp. 231-235.

[25] See Chapter 6, p. 203.

[26] Nockles, *Oxford Movement in Context*, pp. 150-152.

[27] W. M. Wade, *The Truth Spoken in Love Relative to Episcopacy and the Anglican Liturgy* (Paisley, 1840), p. 7.

[28] Robert Montgomery, *A Letter on the Recent Schisms in Scotland with a Documentary Appendix and an Introduction Addressed to the Lord Bishop of Llandaff* (London, 1847), p. 10.

[29] Wade, *Truth Spoken in Love*, pp. 3-8.

Secession 253

Reformed Catholic Church in Scotland, rather than the Episcopal Church, as had been their custom. Some Evangelicals protested strongly, questioning whether Scottish High Churchmen were wise in thus apparently lining up with Tractarian teaching on the necessity of apostolic succession for the existence of a valid church. The *Christian Observer* remarked that the bishops had seemed to assert by their new title that there 'is not and cannot be, any church which is not episcopal' and that they 'in effect hold that the established Church of Scotland is no part of Christ's Catholic Church and that it is not Reformed'.[30] Protests were sent to the *North British Advertiser* in January 1842 by Drummond and one of his congregation, R. K. Greville. Drummond commented that the title was not that to which he had sworn obedience when he had joined the Church and that it aimed 'a blow against multitudes in this country, who, though not Episcopalians, belong nevertheless to 'Reformed' Churches, and are (in the best sense of the term) members of the Catholic Church'.[31] The pressure of such public censure caused the title to be removed. By 1842, certain Evangelicals in the Scottish Episcopal Church were obviously alarmed by what they understood to be a public declaration by the Scottish bishops of a distance between themselves and non-Anglicans.

Two events in 1842 would, again, have indicated to Evangelicals that some Scottish bishops were attracted by Tractarian theology. In his Charge of 4 May 1842, the Bishop of Glasgow and Galloway, Michael Russell, had included a statement which seemed to support the Oxford Movement: 'the doctrines which have been revived in the south have always been professed by Episcopalians in Scotland…Scotland escaped the malign influence which affected the Church of England'. When he added that these Tractarian doctrines had not 'been condemned by any who by learning or research have qualified themselves to pronounce judgement', it appeared to the *Christian Observer* that he was an ally of Tractarianism.[32] Likewise, even the more orthodox High Churchman C. H. Terrot, Bishop of Edinburgh, was accused of giving too much latitude to Oxford ideas in his Charge of 13 April 1842, when he expressed doubts that the 'anonymous Editors of newspapers and magazines' had any authority 'to examine and judge the religious opinions of the faithful'. In this, the *Christian Observer* branded him as propounding 'high priest-craft' and 'low popery', and of treading too close to Tractarian ideas.[33] But in 1840 Wade, already seeming to accommodate Tractarianism on the topic of apostolic succession, in like manner showed some latitude when he announced that the Oxford *Tracts* were 'to my certain knowledge, often grossly misquoted and

---

[30] *Christian Observer*, 1842, pp. 59-60.
[31] Drummond, *Sketch*, pp. 68-69.
[32] *Christian Observer*, October 1842, p. 638.
[33] *Ibid.*, pp. 638-639.

misrepresented'.[34] Such analysis from an English-based periodical, and an apparent shift of allegiance by an Evangelical, would have served to heighten tension in Episcopal Scotland.

In fact, Charles Wordsworth, Bishop of St Andrew's from 1853 to 1893, commented of the Oxford Movement that 'the more the leaders were discountenanced in England, the more they looked to our Scottish Church as the field in which they were to carry on their operations'.[35] In the 1830s, these sentiments seem to have been confirmed by various contacts between Tractarians and Scottish Episcopal clergy. W. J. Copeland, Fellow of Trinity College, Oxford,[36] visited Bishop David Low of Ross and Argyll in 1838 and also, in the same year, an Inverness-shire clergyman, Charles Fyvie. *Tracts for the Times* were sent by J. H. Newman to James Walker, Bishop of Edinburgh, in the early 1830s, and R. H. Froude's *Remains*, with its criticisms of the Reformation, was endorsed by John Torry, Dean of Fife, Dunkeld and Dunblane, and incumbent of Coupar Angus, in 1838.[37] All this came at a time when some High Churchmen in England were beginning to distance themselves from the Tractarians, feeling that their views were too extreme. By contrast, some in the Scottish Episcopal Church appeared to be drawing closer to them, leading to a mounting mood of tension and mistrust.

Again, the growing discontent of Evangelicals in the Church of Scotland over the patronage issue and the amount of state control over the affairs of the Church cannot be discountenanced as a contributory cause of Evangelical unrest in the Scottish Episcopal Church in the late 1830s. The increasing friendship of Drummond and Bagot with Thomas Chalmers, together with the willingness of the former to work with Presbyterian Evangelicals such as James Brewster at Usan, would have highlighted shared concerns. When Chalmers set up an embryonic fund-raising Free Church congregation in Morningside, Edinburgh, by December 1842[38] the sense of importance of making a stand on matters that were close to Evangelical concern was very probably clearly focused for many, particularly in Edinburgh. The religious climate of the age was one of increasingly sharply defined theological identity.

---

[34] Wade, *Truth Spoken in Love*, p. 16. See also Chapter 1, p. 18 for Wade's other views.

[35] Charles Wordsworth, *Annals of My Life, 1847-1856* (London, 1893), p. 62.

[36] W. J. Copeland became curate of Farnham, Essex, in 1849. Although always retaining connections with the old High Church party, he became a close ally of J. H. Newman, editing Newman's *Parochial and Plain Sermons* (1868). See P. B. Nockles, *The Oxford Movement in Context: Anglican High Churchmanship, 1760-1856* (Cambridge 1994), n.1, p. 1.

[37] Nockles, 'Scottish Episcopal Church', pp. 667-670.

[38] S. J. Brown, *Thomas Chalmers* (Oxford, 1982), pp. 296-337, especially p. 332.

Secession

The Scottish Episcopal General Synod at Edinburgh in 1838 was a fourth cause of yet more discord. Evangelicals were, because of their small numbers, unlikely to influence decisions made at General Synods which consisted of all the bishops, the deans whom they appointed, and six presbyters – one from each diocese – chosen by the clergy assembled at the Diocesan Synods.[39] In 1838, the presiding bishops were William Skinner (Aberdeen), George Gleig (Brechin), James Walker (Edinburgh), Michael Russell (Glasgow and Galloway), David Low (Moray, Ross and Argyll) and Patrick Torry (Fife, Dunkeld and Dunblane). The Synod made three important changes to the canons of the Church. The new Canon XXVIII contained the following clause which seemed to be a concession to orthodox and Virtualist High Churchmanship alike but gave little purchase to Evangelicals:

> And it is farther decreed that, if any clergyman shall officiate or preach in any place publicly without using the Liturgy at all, he shall, for the first offence, be admonished by his Bishop and, if he perseveres in this uncanonical practice, shall be suspended until, after due contrition, he be restored to the exercise of his clerical function.[40]

This amendment to the old canon of 1828, by the addition of the words 'in any public place' seemed to decrease what was allowable in any form of worship. Now, not only was the liturgy to be used at morning and evening services, but it was also implied that it was to be employed whenever any sort of public engagement was undertaken. Some Evangelicals found no difficulty with the new law. In 1840 Wade expressed his readiness to introduce some lectures by Montgomery to the Paisley Widow and Orphan Society by reading the liturgy for him before the meeting. He regarded this as a safeguard against 'heretical factions, passionate or selfish approaches to the throne of God'.[41] But, by 1841, Drummond was having trouble with the canon. He had been invited to address the Edinburgh Association of Young Men as part of a course they were holding on religious, moral and scientific subjects.[42] This large event, for which an entrance fee was

---

[39] Drummond, *Sketch*, pp. 38-40.

[40] *Code of Canons of the Episcopal Church in Scotland, as Revised, Amended, and Enacted by an Ecclesiastical Synod, Holden for that Purpose, at Edinburgh, on the 29th Day of August, and Continued by Adjourment till the 6th September, Inclusive, in the Year of Our Lord 1838* (Edinburgh, 1838), p. 34.

[41] Wade, *Truth Spoken in Love*, pp. 3-6.

[42] The Association was possibly part of the movement of inter-denominational societies aimed at religious and moral instruction started by the evangelist David Naismith in Glasgow in 1824. The *Scotsman*, 21 December 1844 reported the Edinburgh society as having over one hundred members, divided into seven groups in different districts of the city. In that year three to four hundred 'essays' were delivered which closed with 'prayer and praise and were aimed at the 'religious, moral and intellectual

required, was to be held in the parish church of St George's, Edinburgh. No prayers were to be offered, the emphasis being on lectures delivered by both laymen and clergy. The Edinburgh Episcopal clergy R. Q. Shannon (St George's), E. B. Ramsay (St John's), John Sandilands (St John's), G. M. Yorke (St Paul's, York Place), H. S. Beresford (St Mark's, Portobello) and T. G. S. Suther (St George's), led by Terrot, remonstrated with Drummond on the grounds that he would be 'infringing the Canon Law of our Church' if he took part without using the liturgy, because it was a public event. Drummond, although 'astonished' at the ruling, withdrew from the engagement, feeling that he was severely limited by Canon XXVIII.[43]

The second change made at the 1838 Synod was the removal of the word 'Protestant' from most of the canons. Initially the Tractarians had respected the Reformers, but their growing belief in antiquity as being the reference point for doctrine made them uneasy with the Reformation, evidenced in 1838 by John Keble's refusal to countenance the Martyrs' Memorial in Oxford. Although, generally, orthodox High Churchmen by the late 1830s felt that Tractarian disparagement of the Reformation made them look un-Protestant,[44] Evangelicals in Scotland increasingly suspected that, there, the High Churchmen were more sympathetic to Tractarian teaching. Although in 1838 Evangelicals appeared not to have noticed the removal of the term 'Protestant', by 1844, after the problems leading to Drummond's resignation from the Scottish Episcopal Church – which will form the substance of the rest of this chapter – many felt it had been a concession towards the Oxford Movement. Drummond pointed out that the word 'Protestant' had occurred seventeen times in the canons of 1828, but not once in 1838 and that, 'considering the pressure of Tractarian principles, this was significant and startling enough'.[45] Thus Evangelicals, who had scant representation at Synod, might have felt that their views were not accommodated.

The status of the Scottish Communion Office of 1764 constituted a third change. Although the rite was retained as the primary service of the Church in accordance with the canons laid down in 1811, Canon XXI now decreed that not only was the service to be used at all consecrations of bishops but

---

improvement' of young men. See also N. M. de S. Cameron, *Dictionary of Scottish Church History and Theology* (Edinburgh, 1993), p. 902. The *Edinburgh Courant*, 23 December 1843, describes the Edinburgh Young Men's Society for Religious, Moral, and intellectual Improvement. Its meetings included: 'The best methods for cultivating the mind'; The causes and tendencies of war'; 'The present aspect of the religious world'.

[43] Drummond, *Sketch*, p. 155.
[44] Nockles, *Oxford Movement in Context*, pp. 122-126.
[45] Drummond, *Sketch*, p. 67.

Secession

also at the openings of General Synods.⁴⁶ While the Communion Office did not become an issue until 1842, the bishops who valued the service – Skinner, Gleig, Walker, Torry – and possibly Low and Russell at that time,⁴⁷ together with the northeastern clergy who used it, had been able to promote a change in the canon law that Evangelicals could do little to prevent.

In conclusion, the years from 1820 to 1842 saw serious tensions between some Evangelicals and High Churchmen in the Scottish Episcopal Church. With the advance of Tractarianism and the impetus given by the rising storm in the Church of Scotland over patronage, it seemed that the time was ripe by 1842 for Evangelicals to make a clear statement of belief and standards. While it has not been possible to find any references to the opinions of Evangelicals like G. M. Drummond of St Mark's, Portobello, or W. P. MacFarquahar of Dumfries, who left Scotland in 1839 and 1845 respectively, some like Wade and Montgomery shared a degree of common ground with High Churchmen and seemingly worked within the confines of the Scottish Episcopal Church without dispute. But Drummond, who wished to try new methods of evangelism, did not. In August 1841 Terrot wrote to William Skinner, Bishop of Aberdeen, that he had hopes that Drummond was 'disposed to be more at one with us than he had previously been'.⁴⁸ But the disagreements of the earlier years, which had resulted in some Evangelicals becoming increasingly uncomfortable in the Scottish Episcopal Church, were inflamed into a major dispute at the end of 1842 revolving around yet further evangelistic activities by Drummond.

---

⁴⁶ George Grubb, *An Ecclesiastical History of Scotland*, IV (Edinburgh, 1861), p. 193. Canon 28 enjoined the use of the surplice, formerly only recommended, in public reading of prayers and administration of the sacraments. *Ibid*. Initially this does not appear to have been combated by Evangelicals in Scotland, but became an issue after the impact of Ritualism when E. C. Dawson sought to introduce it for preaching at St Thomas's, Edinburgh, in 1887. See Chapter 7, pp. 223.

⁴⁷ For Skinner, see Chapter 9, pp. 286-288. For Gleig, see William Walker, *Memoirs of Bishops Jolly and Gleig* (Edinburgh, 1878), pp. 264-265. For Walker, see Frederick Goldie, *A Short History of the Scottish Episcopal Church* (Edinburgh, 1976), pp. 112-113. For Russell, see Chapter 7, p. 235, Chapter 8, p. 253, Chapter 9, pp. 289-293. For Low, see Chapter 9, pp. 296-297. For Torry, see Chapter 7, p. 236, Chapter 9, p. 293-295, n. 64.

⁴⁸ Charles Terrot to William Skinner, 18 August 1841, NAS, CH12 /12 2303.

The First Disruptions

Arradoul

Although it has been customary to regard Drummond's church, St Thomas's, Edinburgh, as the first of the English Episcopal chapels in the nineteenth century, there was an earlier incident resulting in the formation of a new, separate congregation at Arradoul, in the diocese of Aberdeen. The issues surrounding it concerned doctrine, not evangelism.

From the correspondence of Bishop Alexander Jolly of Moray it would seem that the chapel at Arradoul, where opposition to the Scottish Communion Office arose as early as 1831, was severed from the Church at that time. Jolly wrote to 'Mr Shand of Arradoul' on 6 November 1834, mentioning that the Duchess of Gordon, resident in nearby Huntly, had written to him about 'Mr Gordon of Cairnfield', an influential layman, who was not happy to communicate at his family church at Arradoul where the Scottish Office was used. Gordon was, according to the Duchess, opposed to the rite for similar reasons to her own which were concerned with greater familiarity and affection for the Book of Common Prayer. In 1834 she had introduced the Anglican communion service into her chapel at Fochabers, not because she believed that the Scottish Office differed 'in any material point from that of the Church of England, but...we have been more accustomed to the latter...[also] our numerous friends and servants from England, who, with the family of Mr Gordon of Cairnfield, are in the same case, and feel the distraction of thought occasioned by the different order in which the prayers are placed'.[49] Thus unfamiliarity with the Scottish Communion Office was a problem for Gordon at Arradoul.

But it seems that Gordon's difficulty eventually went deeper. John Hay Forbes, Lord Medwyn,[50] intervened by sending him a book explaining that the doctrine of the Scottish Office was no different from that of the English, but Gordon was not convinced. Jolly continued that Gordon 'pleads conscience for withdrawing from [the Church] totally, and thereby decides that it is sinful in itself'. He described Gordon as 'having mutilated the congregation at Arradoul'. Gordon pressed for the English service to be

---

[49] The letters are reproduced in: John Archibald, *The History of the Episcopal Church of Keith in the Seventeenth, Eighteenth and Nineteenth Century with other Reminiscences of the Dioceses of Moray and Ross* (Edinburgh, 1890), pp. 109-112. *Cf* ENCS, pp. 275-276. 'Mr Gordon of Cairnfield' was possibly Adam Gordon. See J. Gordon (ed.), *The New Statistical Account of Scotland* (Edinburgh, 1845), Volume 13, p. 253.

[50] John Hay Forbes, a leading Edinburgh advocate of the Court of Session, was father of A. P. Forbes, Bishop of Brechin, 1847-1875, and George Hay Forbes, incumbent of Burntisland, 1848-1875.

adopted at Elgin so that he could take communion there, but while some of the Elgin congregation supported him, he got no support from Jolly.[51] As a result, he set up a breakaway congregation at Arradoul.

Mention is made in the records of All Saints, Buckie, of a meetinghouse at Arradoul in 1834 and again in the 1870s.[52] A search has been made of the local newspapers of the time but nothing has been found reporting either congregation. It is difficult therefore to judge how far the news of the problem at Arradoul in 1834 travelled, and whether Evangelicals further south came to know much about it. But it can be safely assumed that in 1831 the doctrine of the Scottish Office was thought by some lay Episcopalians in the northeast of Scotland to be seriously divergent from that of the Church of England, causing them to leave the Scottish Episcopal Church. It represents an early dispute on eucharistic matters by a Scottish layman who seemed to have been influenced by links with England.

However, from 1850 to 1854, a chapel at Arradoul in the same category as St Thomas's, Edinburgh, allied to the Church of England but separate from the Scottish Episcopal Church, was recorded.[53] It is likely that it was the descendant of Gordon's chapel of the 1830s. In the 1850s it appears to have been under lay supervision since the *Edinburgh Almanack* for those years gives no entry for the incumbent. Its founding in the early 1830s was very much a forerunner of events which were to escalate a decade later when the theological climate was more intense as a result of increasing Tractarian activity and when matters of doctrine became paramount.

Edinburgh

For the sake of clarity, the preliminary part of this section will provide a brief outline of the events which constituted the second disruption. There will be no analytical discussion at this stage. This will be offered in the succeeding section, headed: 'Factors surrounding the conflict'.

EVENTS

The second disruption in the Scottish Episcopal Church in the nineteenth century came at the end of 1842. Unlike at Arradoul, it was a clash over the understanding of the correct conduct of worship and was a continuation of the trouble between Drummond and the Church authorities. In 1838 Drummond, then joint incumbent, with George Coventry, of Trinity Chapel, Edinburgh, resurrected his evangelistic meetings of 1835 as mid-

---

[51] Archibald, *Episcopal Church of Keith*, pp. 109-112.
[52] Aberdeen and Orkney Diocese Congregations (1989), NAS, Survey 2698 for All Saints, Buckie. This records the Minute Book for All Saints, p. 64, as mentioning the Arradoul meeting house in 1834 and again in the 1870s.
[53] *Edinburgh Almanack*, 1850-1854.

week events in a hall in Clyde Street, where the liturgy of the Church was replaced by extempore prayers. They became very popular, and on occasions fifty to sixty people had to be turned away.[54] But it was only on 3 October 1842 that Terrot, who had become Bishop of Edinburgh in June, officially admonished Drummond for the practice. Drummond claimed that he was not transgressing Canon XXVIII because his meetings were not public, since they were privately announced to none but his own congregation, and were held in a non-public room which he himself hired for the purpose. That others attended who had not been invited was, according to Drummond, because no one was turned away if space remained in the hall.[55] Drummond asked why these particular meetings had been singled out for censure, since other gatherings such as his young people's Bible class and missionary prayer meetings, which followed a similar informal pattern, were regarded by Terrot as private, and were thus allowed to continue. He also asked why Daniel Bagot, of St James's, Edinburgh, was allowed to hold an informal communion service where extempore prayer was used.[56]

Drummond made no secret that he preached for conversion at Clyde Street. He described his practice as consistent with the command in the Bible: 'Do the work of an evangelist, make full proof of thy ministry'. As to their effectiveness, he said that they were 'the gate of heaven to souls',[57] and that 'not a few have been roused there to the inquiry what must I do to be saved?'[58] The extempore prayer, where individuals expressed their own concerns over their spiritual condition in response to Drummond's preaching, contributed to an informal atmosphere so that 'a bond of sympathy and love is formed between those who attend', resulting in 'a freedom of expression and a particularity in prayer' among the participants as they made known their innermost concerns. Because those who attended had been helped by the format, Drummond considered extending them to evening meetings for servants and working people, and adding to their ministry by including a monthly informal service of Holy Communion.[59]

Terrot, uninfluenced by Drummond's arguments, maintained that the Clyde Street meetings were public and were therefore forbidden by the law of the Church. Drummond decided that he was left with three options: to give up the meetings; to defy Terrot and be suspended according to the law as laid down in Canon XXVIII; or to resign. Feeling that Terrot was not

---

[54] *Correspondence Between Terrot and Drummond*, p. 24.

[55] *Ibid.*, pp. iii-iv, p. 10 and p. 15.

[56] *Ibid.*, pp. 11-13.

[57] D. T. K. Drummond, *Reasons for Withdrawing from the Scottish Episcopal Church with a Full Reply to the Charge of Schism* (Edinburgh, 1842), p. 4.

[58] *Correspondence Between Terrot and Drummond* pp. 29-30.

[59] *Ibid.*, pp. 29-30.

going to give way, he chose the last option on 20 October 1842, and three days later preached a farewell sermon to the congregation of Trinity Chapel. On 24 October he circulated a private letter to the congregation listing the events which had led up to his resignation. The sentiments contained in the letter clearly showed that he regarded the matter as closed: 'And now beloved in the Lord, I tremble, as I feel that I must write the word, farewell'.[60] The dispute appeared to have come to an end but from now on events escalated, and the Evangelical party in Edinburgh began to split into two factions – one pro-Drummond, and the other against him.

On 24 October 1842, a 'Committee of Friends', composed of supporters of Drummond, was set up.[61] Their position in Scottish society will be analysed later on. At this stage it is sufficient to note that they were middle- and upper-class men. John Wauchope, Lt-Col. H. F. Holcombe, J. Keith, Montague Stanley, Robert Pitcairn, Andrew Wood, James Mylne, and J. Neil Dyce were all members of Drummond's congregation at Trinity Chapel. From Bagot's church, St James's, Captain Francis Grove, a vestryman, and Bagot's brother-in-law, James Cunningham, a trustee, joined them, although without Bagot's express consent. They met to consider what action to take and, in particular, to look into whether an Anglican congregation, separate from the Scottish Episcopal Church, could be set up in Edinburgh.[62] Grove and Cunningham denied that they, at this point, intended to join such a congregation; they were merely present in an advisory capacity. It was decided to put an advertisement in the newspapers in order to ascertain the level of support for such a congregation.[63] By 29 October, Cunningham had withdrawn his name from the list of those intending to take seats, followed by Grove on 9 November, in accord with a request from Bagot.[64]

Soon after, the Committee of Friends asked Bagot to convene a meeting of the Edinburgh clergy to draw up a resolution which would enable Drummond to return to the Scottish Episcopal Church. Bagot agreed but warned that Dean E. B. Ramsay of St John's, Edinburgh, insisted that a remonstrance against Drummond's actions, signed by all of them, should accompany it. The Committee, still anxious to obtain the resolution, complied.[65]

---

[60] *Ibid.*, p. vii.
[61] *Statement by the Committee of Mr Drummond's Friends* (Edinburgh, 1842), p10. *Statement of the Proceedings of the Majority of the Vestry of St James's, 7 January 1842* (Edinburgh, 1842), p. 2.
[62] *Statement by Committee*, p. 10. *Statement of Vestry of St James's*, p. 9.
[63] *Statement by Committee*, p. 11.
[64] F. Grove and J. Cunningham, *Supplementary Statement 19 January 1843*, pp. 1-3.
[65] *Scottish Episcopal Times*, 17 February 1844.

A deputation of Ramsay, Bagot, G. M. Yorke, and John Boyle,[66] visited Drummond at his home, 4, Bruntsfield Place, Edinburgh, on Tuesday 1 November 1842. Drummond's old friend, R. K. Greville, attended as an advisor. Ramsay read the resolution, stating that Drummond had resigned 'totally without cause', because it was considered that his meetings had been public, not private, and hence transgressed the law of the Church. Drummond refused to enter into discussion about the remonstrance which contained a condemnation of all plans to form a new congregation because he 'had neither by deed or word identified himself' with such a move. Instead, he confirmed that he was 'willing to declare what he would consider as a sufficient opening for his return to the Scottish Episcopal Church'. Reiterating that Terrot had not explained 'in what the publicity of [the] meetings' consisted, Drummond stated that he was prepared 'to take steps for the restricting of these meetings to members of [his] own congregation', providing they were held in Clyde Street Hall 'or any other private room for social prayer without the Liturgy', as a way out of the deadlock. Greville moved that 'this seemed to be a fit subject for mediation', and the deputation 'resolved to wait upon the Bishop to inform him of Mr Drummond's sentiments'.[67] However, Terrot's reply on the next day did not satisfy Drummond. Its suggestion, that one of the other clergy could read the liturgy before the meetings, confirmed to Drummond that Terrot regarded that 'every meeting to which the congregation is generally invited is public...even in my own house'.[68] It seemed to Drummond that there was no way of forgoing the liturgy at his meetings.

The Edinburgh clergy published their resolution and remonstrance, both addressed to Drummond, on 3 November 1842 in *The Edinburgh Courant; The Edinburgh Advertiser; The Witness; The North British Advertiser; The Record; The Ecclesiastical Gazette;* and *The Irish Ecclesiastical Gazette.* The remonstrance was particularly severe against any notion of forming a new congregation which it labelled as 'Independent' rather than 'Episcopal', and that it involved 'the commission of a great sin of schism...likely to engender animosity...and [that] Divine blessing could hardly be expected'.[69] The Committee of Friends advertised on 4 November for the taking of seats in the new congregation.[70] On the same day, Drummond replied to the resolutions and remonstrance in *Reply to Resolutions of the Clergy of the Scottish Episcopal Church of the Diocese*

---

[66] John Boyle was incumbent of St Mark's, Portobello, 1842-1854.

[67] 'Memorandum of a conversation between Dean Ramsay etc and Mr Drummond', DRO, D5550/3/5/13. D. T. K. Drummond, *Reply to Resolutions of the Clergy of the Scottish Episcopal Church of the Diocese of Edinburgh* (Edinburgh, 1842), p. 8.

[68] Drummond, *Reply to Resolutions*, pp. 8-9.

[69] *Record*, 10 November 1842.

[70] *Statement of Committee*, p. 11.

Secession 263

of Edinburgh. In this he denied that his resignation was without cause, recounting the events leading up to it. He rejected suppositions that he had any connection with the new congregation. But suddenly and importantly, the whole dispute took on a new dimension when Drummond announced that 'an English clergyman' had drawn his attention 'to a fact...connected with Canon XXI', concerning the Communion Service, which provided 'an insuperable barrier...to the possibility of my ever returning' to the Scottish Episcopal Church.[71] It was later revealed that the person involved was Edward Craig, former incumbent of St James's, Edinburgh.[72] The confines of the problem had gone beyond the issue of Church practice into the realms of doctrine.

By 8 November the Committee of Friends advertised that enough sittings had been obtained to justify the opening of a new chapel on 20 November 1842.[73] On 12 November they wrote to Drummond inviting him to become their pastor, having been assured by 'eminent ecclesiastical authorities in England that all legal and technical difficulties' regarding the status and privileges of the incumbent and congregation as members of the Church of England were removed, and 'persuaded that the tie which has so long existed between [many friends] and you should not be broken.[74] On the same day the *Statement by the Committee of Mr Drummond's Friends* was released, denouncing Terrot's actions as 'a grievous infringement of the Christian liberty, both of ministers and laymen', and saying that Drummond had been invited, and had accepted, to become their 'pastor'.[75]

Unrest broke out among the vestry at St James's after the revelation by Drummond concerning the communion service. On 15 November 1842, Bagot discussed matters with its members, but they were not convinced by his doctrinal analysis.[76] To their surprise, Bagot published the contents of these discussions on 16 November in a pamphlet entitled *A Letter Addressed to some Members of the Vestry of St James's Chapel*. It contained the ideas he had put forward to them showing how he thought the Scottish Communion Office could be read in a favourable light by Evangelicals.[77] This was followed, on 21 November, by Drummond's pamphlet *Reasons for Withdrawing from the Scottish Episcopal Church with a Full Reply to the Charge of Schism*, where he spoke of the Scottish

---

[71] Drummond, *Reply to Resolutions*, pp. 3-13.

[72] See Chapter 7, p. 223.

[73] St Thomas's Church, Edinburgh, Archives, 'Advertisement'.

[74] John Wauchope to D. T. K. Drummond, 12 November 1842, DRO, D5550/3/12. *Statement by Committee*, p. 10.

[75] *Statement by Committee*, pp. 8, 10.

[76] *Statement of Vestry of St James's*, p. 1.

[77] Daniel Bagot, *A Letter to Some Members of the Vestry of St James's Chapel in Reference to the Scottish Communion Office* (Edinburgh, 1842), pp. 1-2.

Office teaching 'the naked doctrine of transubstantiation'.[78] Around this time Craig, resident in England, printed *On an Important Discrepancy between the Church of England and the Scottish Episcopal Community* containing similar sentiments. But sometime towards the beginning of December 1842 Drummond published a second pamphlet, *The Scottish Communion Office Examined*, where he took the less extreme view that the Scottish Episcopal Church taught '*a* doctrine of transubstantiation'.[79] The vestry members at St James's pressed Bagot for further discussion on the communion service, but were refused.[80] Alexander Stuart, James Cunningham, Francis Grove, Thomas Robertson and Smith Fergusson of the vestry issued a statement on 13 December criticising Bagot for taking part in the remonstrance against Drummond, and stating that they believed the Scottish Communion Office to be 'anti Protestant and unscriptural'.[81]

Matters deteriorated at St James's on 17 December when Bagot refused to give Christmas communion to the protestors on the vestry.[82] They replied on 21 December in 'friendly and affectionate terms', saying they were 'contending for what appear to be vital principles' and asking Bagot's help in getting rid of the 'obnoxious Canons of the Scottish Episcopal Church'.[83] In January 1843, Joseph Moule, a member of the congregation at St James's, sent a letter to the congregation denouncing Drummond and Craig and arguing that the Scottish Communion Office was not abhorrent. He accused the majority of the vestry of trying to remove Bagot in an effort to replace him with Drummond.[84] Another communication on similar lines was published anonymously by 'Sigma'.[85]

On 19 January 1843 Cunningham and Grove wrote a letter denying any intention of joining Drummond's congregation.[86] However, from February to May 1843 the Vestry of St James's explored whether the chapel could be removed, legally, from the Scottish Episcopal Church, but it was judged impossible by the Lord Advocate, Andrew Rutherford. Bagot, who was not paid a stipend during this time,[87] resigned on 10 June and took up a position

---

[78] Drummond, *Reasons for Withdrawing*, p. 12.

[79] See Chapter 7, p. 225.

[80] *Statement of Vestry of St James's*, p. 4.

[81] *Ibid.*, p. 2.

[82] *Ibid.*, p. 3.

[83] *Ibid.*

[84] J. Moule, *A Second Letter to the Members of the Congregation of St James's Chapel* (Edinburgh, 1843), pp. 5-8.

[85] 'SIGMA', *A Brief Review of a Statement of the Majority of the Vestry of St James's Chapel, Edinburgh* (Edinburgh, 18430.

[86] Grove and Cunningham, *Supplementary Statement*, pp. 1-3.

[87] *Scottish Episcopal Times*, 10 February 1844, p. 38. St James's Minute Book 1843, p. 176, St James's Church, Edinburgh, Archives.

Secession 265

at Newry in Ireland.[88] Grove and Cunningham remained as trustees of the chapel.[89]

While the building of Drummond's new church, St Thomas's, was in process, the congregation met in the Mainzierian Hall, South St David Street.[90] On 17 March 1843 the foundation stone was laid at Rutland Street, Edinburgh. The building was to hold 800 people and the seats were quickly filled. It claimed legality as an English Episcopal Church, loyal to the Church of England, under the Toleration Act of 1712,[91] opening for public worship on 24 December 1843.[92] By 1844 Grove was a trustee, having left St James's over the matter of the Communion Office.[93] Such is the outline of the events, but further analysis is required to isolate the underlying factors which drove them.

FACTORS SURROUNDING THE CONFLICT

The factors surrounding the formation of St Thomas's in 1842 owed their existence to various influences. Many of them had been apparent in the previous decades while others were the product of the circumstances at the particular time. However, as in the 1820s and 1830s, the Evangelical Scottish Episcopalians were not a homogenous group. They were representative of different opinions and not all of them felt that Drummond had a strong enough reason to go as far as resigning his incumbency over the problem of evangelistic meetings. Among them, Bagot and Robert Montgomery were particularly vocal.

Bagot's position was rather unclear. In some ways he would have been expected to have taken a similar line to Drummond. He had been quite abrasive in the arguments over baptism in the 1830s. The editor of *Stephen's Episcopal Magazine* wrote to Drummond in 1836 that he had received a letter on the matter from Bagot 'in a style and language very unbecoming a clergyman', while Drummond's communication was 'friendly [and] respectful'.[94] It seems strange that Bagot became more of a peacemaker in Drummond's dispute. It might have been that Bagot hoped for elevated office in the Church, possibly seeing it as a way of promulgating Evangelical views. Certainly Wade, in Paisley, who appears

---

[88] St James's Minute Book, 10 June 1843, p. 211. St James's Church, Edinburgh, Archives.

[89] *Ibid.*, p. 214.

[90] *Memoir*, p. xli.

[91] R. L. Stuart, *English Episcopalianism in Scotland Explained and Justified* (Edinburgh, 1877), pp. 7-14. See Chapter 1, p. 29.

[92] The name St Thomas's was probably chosen since the date of opening was just three days after St Thomas's Day, 21 December.

[93] List of Trustees, St Thomas's Church, Edinburgh, Archives.

[94] T. Stephen to D. T. K. Drummond, LPL, MS1537 f. 12.

to have passed no comments on the events of 1842, was appointed Dean of Glasgow and Galloway in 1843, and it seems that his milder Evangelicalism and willingness to work within the legal confines of the Church made him more acceptable than Drummond. However, it is more likely that Bagot's concerns were to preserve his congregation. Although he took a strong line on maintaining the unity of the Church, defending the Scottish Communion Office, and announcing that 'I have promised obedience to the Bishop under whom I serve, and that obedience I shall faithfully render',[95] once he had returned to Newry, Ireland, in 1844, he took a more favourable view of Drummond's objections to the service.[96] The overriding reason for his stand was probably, therefore, that he feared his own congregation would break up over the affair if he did not intervene, especially after the Trustees unsuccessfully tried to remove St James's from the Scottish Episcopal Church.[97] Bagot's position emerges as one of expediency.

Montgomery, however, was a clearer example of an Evangelical who upheld ecclesiastical discipline. On the issue of Drummond's meetings, Montgomery, in a particularly virulent pamphlet written in 1847, emphasised the principle that 'the liberty of an individual member must sometimes be surrendered, in order to procure and maintain the collective unity of the whole body'.[98] While Edward Bickersteth, the incumbent of Watton, Hertfordshire praised Drummond as having 'honoured the authority of Christ...[because he] refused to renounce it for the authority of man',[99] and the Committee of Friends regarded Drummond as having 'acted rightly [in a] grievous infringement of Christian liberty',[100] Montgomery's position, in line with his strong adherence to the apostolicity of the Church,[101] was to maintain unity and to submit to ecclesiastical direction.

Certainly, the Anglican Evangelical press did not, initially, back Drummond fully. The *Christian Observer* and *Christian Guardian* in 1842 notably omitted all mention of the disputed evangelistic meetings. Even the *Record*, the mouthpiece of strict Evangelicalism, warned Drummond that 'in the present age of endless division...nothing but necessity justifies' such

---

[95] Bagot, *Letter to Some of the Members of the Vestry*, p. 13.
[96] See Chapter 7, p. 234.
[97] See Chapter 8, p. 264.
[98] Robert Montgomery, *The Scottish Church and the English Schismatics* (London, 1847), p. 115.
[99] Edward Bickersteth, *The Episcopal Church in Scotland* (Edinburgh, 1843), p. 12. This publication was extracted from *The Churchman's Monthly Review* (London, 1843).
[100] *Statement by Committee*, pp. 8-9.
[101] See Chapter 8, p. 252.

Secession

action.[102] Thus, although a Presbyterian magazine wished him 'God speed...in the name of common evangelism',[103] there was by no means universal support from Anglican Evangelicals for Drummond. Some, valuing Church unity, were willing to compromise over the conduct of evangelistic services.

However, Drummond considered that the failure to reach agreement over his meetings gave sufficient reason to leave the Scottish Episcopal Church. Several factors connected to this decision can be isolated. Firstly, there were his continuing differences of opinion with High Churchmen concerning church practice. Drummond's self-defence centred on an attack against formalism which he condemned as 'eating, like a canker, into the very heart of religious truth...which makes liturgical service the...beginning, middle, and end of all true worship...degrading it to the office of the gaoler'.[104] In this he almost echoed Tractarian criticisms of contemporary High Churchmanship, denouncing dryness in worship and non-dynamic faith.[105] Drummond argued that the liturgy was not always the most appropriate method of ministry, that there were times when the church service was not ideally suited to meeting every need. He did not oppose the regular Sunday-by-Sunday use of the liturgy in formal worship saying, 'I shall ever adhere strictly to the liturgy of the Church of England in the public services of the sanctuary'.[106] But he was willing, in other settings, to use 'the privilege of prayer *without* the liturgy'.[107] He considered that to insist on the liturgy on all occasions 'was imposing a burden which God has not imposed...that God is a free Spirit, and so should ours be in pouring out our voluntary devotions on *all* occasions', and that 'this liberty and a public liturgy should go hand in hand together'.[108] Drummond felt that the words of Canon XXVIII seemed to limit such informal worship and acted as 'a barrier...against the free exercise of my ministry'.[109] He agreed with orthodox High Churchmen in regarding the liturgy as a basic safeguard against malpractice and possible unscriptural innovations. But he pressed for abandoning formalism in favour of more flexibility within what he understood to be scriptural limits, especially at evangelistic services where he found that an informal approach was more conducive to conversions.

---

[102] *Record*, 3 November 1842, 17 November 1842. It was less surprising that the *Christian Guardian*, which was mainly a devotional and theological publication, also omitted any reports on Drummond's evangelistic meetings.

[103] An article, written in the 'name of the Church of Scotland', in an unnamed publication, dated April 1843, p. 79, NLS, included in Dowd. 531 (40).

[104] Drummond, *Reasons for Withdrawing*, pp. 5-6.

[105] Chapter 1, p. 5.

[106] Drummond, *Sketch*, p. 72.

[107] *Ibid.*, p. 72.

[108] *Ibid.*

[109] Drummond, *Reasons for Withdrawing*, p. 7.

Drummond's meetings were an attempt to enliven the ministry of the Church.

Many Evangelicals supported Drummond's views. Bickersteth, referring in January 1843 to the disputed gatherings, commented that Drummond was entitled 'in private rooms...to use or not use forms just as he found most profitable to the people of his charge'.[110] In similar vein the *Record*, on 3 November 1842, while not supporting Drummond's resignation over the affair, referred to such occasions as 'a sacred cause' which did not allow people to 'rest peacefully in their worldliness and sin',[111] and a Presbyterian publication criticised the Scottish Episcopal Church for attempting 'to crush evangelism [and] living religion'.[112] Again, Bagot worked hard to find a way in which the meetings could continue. Some historians have tended to underestimate the store that Evangelicals set by such events. For instance, Reginald Foskett refers to Drummond's refusal to use the liturgy as 'rather narrow-minded',[113] and Rowan Strong describes the Edinburgh furore of 1842 as prompted by 'an absurdly small' incident.[114] Although Drummond seems to have been the only Evangelical Episcopalian in Scotland holding such meetings in 1842, it was the case that many of his counterparts understood them to be an effective way of bringing people to faith. The Scottish High Church party, by contrast, feared that such events could lead to unscriptural practices since the well-tried and tested restraints of the liturgy were being breached. The dispute over Drummond's evangelistic meetings was representative of strongly held beliefs on both sides, which Foskett and Strong do not analyse sufficiently. It was a particularly important issue over which Drummond was unwilling to compromise because he regarded his meetings as a vital dimension of his evangelistic ministry.

A further aspect of this factor was that Drummond's activities would not necessarily have been such a problem in the Church of England, despite similar restrictions imposed by the Act of Uniformity of 1662.[115] As

---

[110] Bickersteth, *Episcopal Church in Scotland*, p. 12.

[111] *Record*, 17 November 1842.

[112] Part of an unnamed publication, dated April 1843, p. 79, NLS, included in Dowd. 531 (40).

[113] Reginald Foskett, 'The Drummond Controversy 1842', *Records of the Scottish Church History Society* 16 (1969), p. 102.

[114] Rowan Strong, *Episcopalianism in Nineteenth-Century Scotland* (Oxford, 2002), p. 215.

[115] In fact non-liturgical services and meetings were outlawed in England until 1872 when an act was passed negating the restrictions in the Act of Uniformity. Shortened services were authorised, and sermons or lectures could be preached or delivered without the prayer and services appointed by the Book of Common Prayer. Thus while the Church of England, prior to 1872, was lenient on such matters, the Scottish

Secession

Drummond pointed out, even the High Churchman W. F. Hook, of Leeds, held similar types of mid-week meetings in a hired room. At these, only a few portions of the liturgy were read, followed by an exposition on selected verses from the Bible.[116] In fact, Drummond, as a newly ordained clergyman, had used his particular brand of evangelistic meetings effectively in Gloucestershire in 1830. The Bishop of Bristol, Dr Robert Gray, who was not an Evangelical, gave sanction and 'entered warmly and cordially into this and other plans I was pursuing for ministerial usefulness'. Drummond maintained, also, that 'there is not a Diocese in England in which such meetings do not exist – I believe there is not one Bishop of that Church who has thought it right to prohibit them'.[117] Bickersteth confirmed this claim in January 1843 when he commented that 'on this principle...many of the most excellent ministers in our Church...in every diocese in England, are continually acting'.[118] Drummond's meetings were thus probably innovative only in Scotland, and it seems that the Scottish Episcopal Church was less lenient than the Church of England in allowing them to proceed unhindered.

The problem in Scotland was, in part, the result of the continuing numerical superiority of the High Church party. As had been evident earlier in the century, High Churchmen in Scotland were unaccustomed to working alongside Evangelicals and were therefore unlikely to countenance their ideas. This was well illustrated when Bagot was unable to influence his High Church colleagues in Edinburgh to any great extent over the problem of Drummond's meetings, with the result that his deputation offered very little ground in the way of a compromise. Instead, Scottish High Churchmen continued strictly to uphold the traditional regard for order and discipline in worship. For instance William Blatch, the incumbent at St John's, Pittenweem, in 1855, argued that 'injury was inflicted on the Church'[119] by Drummond's meetings, and W. E. Aytoun, Professor of Rhetoric at Edinburgh University, commented that 'if everyone be allowed to follow out his own whims and crochets in defiance of constituted authority and written law, there is an end to the Church'.[120] Thus Terrot, characteristically adhering to such ideals, felt that he was 'bound...to obey

---

Episcopal Church was strict. See *A Plea for Union Among Episcopalians in Scotland by a Member of the Church of England* (Edinburgh, 1882), p. 28.

[116] Drummond, *Sketch*, pp. 73-74. See Nockles, *Oxford Movement in Context*, pp. 35, 126, 252-253 for Hook's Churchmanship.

[117] *Correspondence Between Terrot and Drummond*, pp. 24-25.

[118] Bickersteth, *Episcopal Church in Scotland*, p. 12.

[119] William Blatch, *A Memoir of the Rt. Rev David Low* (Edinburgh, 1855), p. 266.

[120] W. E. Aytoun, *The Drummond Schism Examined and Exposed* (Edinburgh, 1842), p. 17.

and enforce' canon law and bring Drummond into obedience with it.[121] Compared to the Church of England, the Scottish Episcopal Church provided particularly infertile ground for the cultivation of Evangelical innovations.

Secondly, as earlier, doctrine was an important factor in the conflict. While Drummond's resignation was the result of his refusal to relinquish his evangelistic meetings, his understanding of the theology of the Scottish Communion Office cemented his conviction that he had been right to secede, because it afforded 'a full and perfect justification' in the matter.[122] His *Scottish Communion Office Examined*, which was a more mature opinion than his earlier *Reasons for Withdrawing from the Scottish Episcopal Church*, was crucial in this respect.[123] Its analysis, showing the similarity of the office to current Tractarian theology, appeared to substantiate the former concerns of some Scottish Evangelicals that the Scottish Episcopal Church was allied to the Oxford Movement. Drummond's antipathy to Catholic doctrine confirmed his decision to separate from the Scottish Episcopal Church.

In fact, Drummond's analysis was to prove instrumental in consolidating his cause. Although Bagot's defence of the office was mirrored by Montgomery in an attempt to prevent St Jude's, Glasgow, from following Drummond,[124] and W. M. Wade in Paisley and the other Scottish Evangelicals appear to have made no comment on the matter at all, others were won over. Among the laity, it has been shown that, together with the 'Committee of Friends', the majority of the vestry at St James's endorsed Drummond's argument. In England, Bickersteth allied with Drummond, describing the *Scottish Communion Office Examined* as 'able' and leaving 'a most painful expression...of the present character of the Scottish Communion Office'. In contrast, he found Bagot's *Letter to Some Members of the Vestry of St James's Chapel* to be unsatisfactory because while 'conscientious minds may quiet their scruples in this way, it is not satisfactory to us; nor will it be so, we think, to his readers generally'. Again, while agreeing with the sentiments of Craig's *Important Discrepancy between the Church of England and the Scottish Episcopal Community* Bickersteth found it 'somewhat sharp', a sentiment which would probably have enhanced Drummond's position as one of moderation in the public mind.[125] By January 1843, the *Record* had also accepted

---

[121] *Correspondence Between Terrot and Drummond*, pp. 9-10.

[122] D. T. K. Drummond, *The Scottish Communion Office Examined and Proved to be Repugnant to Scripture and Opposed to the Articles, Liturgy, and Homilies of the Church of England* (Edinburgh, 1842), p. 44.

[123] See Chapter 7 for a full analysis.

[124] See Chapter 7, p. 239.

[125] Bickersteth, *Episcopal Church in Scotland*, pp. 8-9.

Drummond's argument as sufficient reason, unlike the prayer meeting issue, for his secession. In April, the milder *Christian Observer*, although not reporting directly on the Scottish dispute, argued that the Scottish Episcopal Church 'teaches directly and explicitly what the Tractarians wish to fasten upon ours by implication'.[126] It is likely therefore that Bickersteth, the *Record* and the *Christian Observer* swayed an increasing number of Evangelicals to ally with Drummond. Certainly, among Drummond's private correspondence, which is by no means complete, a letter from E. S. Greville, of Matlock, in February 1843, remarked on his 'very responsible position' in Scotland, and assured him of 'much prayer'.[127] It could well have been representative of a fairly large body of Evangelical opinion in Drummond's favour by this time. Thus Drummond's analysis of the Scottish Communion Office was not only vital in confirming his decision to secede but also in winning the support of others. Whereas some had doubted that he had reason to resign over the prayer meetings, the issue of the Scottish Communion Office probably won many of them over.

But the affair surrounding the foundation of St Thomas's also highlighted another doctrinal point. After the decision to form St Thomas's, the High Church party in the Scottish Episcopal Church rapidly labelled Drummond and his followers as schismatics. Terrot put the case clearly in a letter to Drummond: 'my opinions and the laws of the church are of as different authority in my estimate as they can be in yours'.[128] He viewed 'private interpretation of Scripture [and] private convictions of expediency which scoff at the notion of Catholic obligation' as a violation of the unity of the Church.[129] But events showed that Drummond did, in fact, value such cohesion just as highly as his High Church counterparts and Evangelicals like Montgomery. He did not take the charge of schism lightly, and he presented his defence very thoroughly on various grounds. The first point he made was the legal one that he had been ordained in the Church of England, not the Scottish Episcopal Church. The churches, despite an Act of 1840 which gave some reduction in the restrictions on Scottish Episcopal clergy officiating in England,[130] remained separate bodies with their own codes of canons. Drummond claimed that the advice of ecclesiastical lawyers in England assured him that he was within his rights to resign from the Scottish Episcopal Church without affecting his position as an Anglican clergyman. He maintained that he had not, on legal grounds, committed an

---

[126] *Christian Observer*, April 1843. The *Christian Guardian* did not report on the matter.

[127] R. S. Greville to D. T. K. Drummond, 8 February 1843, DRO, D5550/3/5/26.

[128] *Correspondence Between Terrot and Drummond*, p. 16.

[129] C. H. Terrot, *A Dissuasive from Schism* (Edinburgh, 1843), p. 8.

[130] Drummond, *Sketch*, p. 129.

act of schism – he had not withdrawn from the church in which he had been ordained.[131]

To convince himself and others that he did take the matter very seriously he then proceeded to argue his position on the same ecclesiastical grounds as those held by High Churchmen. These involved the very strict analysis of seventeenth-century divines such as John Tillotson, Archbishop of Canterbury, Gilbert Burnet, Bishop of Salisbury, and Edward Stillingfleet, Bishop of Worcester, all of whom had written that schism was permissible in a church which was found to impose sinful conditions, corruptions and errors. When Terrot likewise allowed that schism was not a sin if a church insisted on 'sinful terms of communion',[132] Drummond replied that his own 'convictions imperatively demand that I pursue the course which Bishop Terrot declares is both lawful and right'.[133] Drummond considered that both the restrictive law expressed in Canon XXVIII and the content of the Scottish Communion Office justified ignoring Terrot's strictures on schism. In this he was supported, again, by Bickersteth who announced that Drummond had 'fully replied to the charge of schism'.[134] Drummond, convinced of the non-schismatic nature of his protest, argued that he was justified in his separation.

A third factor surrounding the defection involved the concern of High Churchmen over the growing popularity of Evangelicals within the Scottish Episcopal Church. Certainly many of the incoming clergy subsequent to Craig had evoked a measure of praise. Bagot continued to attract large numbers at St James's, Edinburgh. Drummond at St Paul's, Carrubber's Close, Edinburgh, in 1836 was commended as 'zealous, faithful and affectionate' in his work among the congregation there, and, subsequently in 1837, at Trinity Chapel, Edinburgh, he was similarly popular. Montgomery at St Jude's, Glasgow, had a considerable following,[135] and there was the continuing unobtrusive work of W. M. Wade at Paisley and the clergy at Fochabers. Concern over this rising tide of Evangelicalism had been expressed in 1836 by J. B. Pratt, a native of the northeast and incumbent of Cruden in the diocese of Aberdeen. Writing to Alexander Jolly at nearby Fraserburgh he complained that the Scottish Episcopal Church was veering towards Evangelicalism which might result in

---

[131] Drummond, *Reasons for Withdrawing*, p. 15.

[132] Terrot, *Disuasive*, p. 6.

[133] D. T. K. Drummond, *An Address in Reference to a Dissuasive from Schism* (Edinburgh, 1843), p. 7.

[134] *Ibid.*, pp. 20-31. Bickersteth, *Episcopal Church*, p. 7.

[135] For Craig and Bagot see Chapter 1, pp 16-17. For Drummond see Copy of Minute of Vestry Meeting at St Paul's Episcopal Chapel, Carrubber's Close, Edinburgh, 29 December 1836, referring to the work of Mr Drummond and his wife, DRO, D550/3/5/10. For Montgomery, see Chapter 9, pp. 289-290.

Secession 273

'primitive truths of the Church [being] given up'.[136] Evangelical opposition to baptismal regeneration and Drummond's low view of apostolic succession and his willingness to work with Presbyterians were probably the cause of Pratt's alarm, although he possibly, too, feared for the future of the Scottish Communion Office. He undoubtedly spoke for others who regarded Evangelical clergy, all in Anglican orders and loyal to the Church of England, to be an Anglicising influence which would eventually result in the Scottish Episcopal Church losing its identity and customs, thus becoming a mere outpost of the Church of England.[137] As in earlier decades, some Scottish Episcopalians did not welcome Evangelicals, leading to an atmosphere of mistrust.

In fact Drummond felt that he was being particularly singled out by the Church authorities for censure and that he would be tolerated only if he obeyed the strict letter of the law. Terrot admitted to Drummond on 3 October 1842 that he was acting 'not on my own spontaneous motion, but in consequence of suggestions from a quarter which I am bound to respect'.[138] His obvious discomfort over the matter was expressed in the same letter: 'I must confess that I have felt an extreme unwillingness to interfere in this matter'.[139] Likewise, at the end of the correspondence on 21 October 1843, he wrote, 'if you knew how much pain it has given me, you would not wonder at my not having performed it sooner'.[140] However, Terrot did not necessarily disagree with the complaint from a legal point of view. He was enough of a High Churchman to desire to uphold the sentiment of consistency in worship: 'At the same time, I should not have been influenced by such suggestions, had I not been conscientiously convinced that they were just'.[141] But the point seemed to be that, while Terrot himself might have been willing to turn a blind eye to Drummond's activities, others in the Scottish Episcopal Church were not. Terrot's own statements appeared to suggest to Drummond that there was an influential individual or movement in the Scottish Episcopal Church seeking to keep Evangelical activities such as his under tight control.

Drummond suspected that Bishop Moir was the likely instigator of the complaint about his evangelistic meetings, pointing to his opposition to events at Usan in 1837.[142] Suspicion of Moir was also expressed in the *Scotsman* on 7 December 1842. It reported that all Moir's 'ingenuity will not explain away the remarkable co-incidence of time, place and

---

[136] J. B. Pratt to Alexander Jolly, 21 December 1836, NAS, CH12/30/203.
[137] Strong, *Episcopalianism*, pp. 290-293).
[138] *Correspondence Between Terrot and Drummond*, p. 9.
[139] *Ibid.*, p. 10.
[140] *Ibid.*, p. 33.
[141] *Ibid.*, p. 9.
[142] Drummond, *Reply to Resolutions*, pp. 11-12. See also Chapter 8, p. 250-251.

circumstance attending the enactment of that strange clause [in the canon of 1838]'.[143] There also seems to have been similar concern about law and order in the Church in the diocese of Aberdeen where Skinner, the Primus since June 1841, was bishop. The diocesan minutes of 10 April 1839 reported very prominently that the aim of the forthcoming General Synod was 'to simplify and enforce order and discipline, not to introduce, but to repress innovations, to clear existing irregularities, and as far as possible to maintain inviolate the recognised principles of our Church'.[144] Moir and Skinner, reacting to complaints such as Pratt's, were thus probably responsible for trying to curtail Evangelical activity, and so for having instigated the formulation of Canon XXVIII at the 1838 Synod.

Some Evangelicals began to question why Drummond, alone, was singled out and suspicion arose that there was a plot to remove him from the Scottish scene. While contemporary High Churchmen applauded Terrot for upholding the law of the Church,[145] Evangelicals questioned Terrot's motives. One anonymous clergyman wrote to the *Record* that 'a resolution to get rid of Mr Drummond, if possible, was previously tacitly adopted'.[146] On 26 November 1842 the *Scotsman* hinted 'we fear that the solution may be found in the fact of Mr Drummond's extraordinary popularity' that he was 'too popular for the taste of his superiors and equals'.[147] Rumours were thus circulating that Drummond's brand of Evangelicalism and the following he was attracting were unacceptable to the Scottish Episcopal Church.

There is evidence to support the view of the *Scotsman*. It is possible that some High Churchmen might have feared that Drummond's popularity would result in a strong Evangelical wing gathering around him. Drummond was Scottish by birth, although in English orders, whereas Bagot and Montgomery, other obvious leaders of the Evangelical party, were Irish and English respectively, and Sir William Dunbar, newly arrived at St Paul's, Aberdeen, although Scottish, had been born and brought up in England[148]. Drummond was thus more likely to remain in Scotland than they. Moreover Drummond was no ordinary Scotsman; he was very well connected, belonging to a branch of the nobility of Perthshire,[149] and according to some genealogies in direct line of descent from Scottish

---

[143] *Scotsman*, 7 December 1842.

[144] Handwritten Minutes of the Diocese of Aberdeen, 4 November 1783-19 August 1840, p. 267, 10 April 1839. St Paul's Church, Aberdeen, Archives, MS 3320/1/2.

[145] For example, see Aytoun, *Schism Examined*, pp. 5-17.

[146] *Record*, 1 December 1842.

[147] *Scotsman*, 26 November 1842.

[148] See Chapter 9, p. 285

[149] *Memoir*, pp. xv-xvi.

Secession 275

royalty.¹⁵⁰ The photographer Vernon Heath recorded a striking example of such influence in the 1850s when Drummond left him 'letters of introduction to some of the best-known people in Perthshire'.¹⁵¹ Additionally, Drummond's family homes were at Aberuchill Castle, near Crieff in Perthshire, and in Edinburgh, so his contacts were widespread,¹⁵² and it was likely that he would remain in the capital city where he had a considerable following. Support for Drummond's views from a powerful section of Scottish society would have been very disruptive for the Scottish Episcopal Church.

Again, Drummond appeared to possess the personal qualities which would inspire. The *Scotsman* in 1877 recorded him as 'held in warm esteem...his ever courteous and engaging manners alike tending to cement many cordial friendships'.¹⁵³ Even some who disagreed with his theological position acknowledged his character and charisma. Montgomery allowed that he was 'pious and amiable in all relations of private life'.¹⁵⁴ An anonymous Episcopalian presbyter from Edinburgh wrote in 1871 of his 'deep feelings of personal respect and regard for him',¹⁵⁵ and a Scottish Episcopal High Churchman writing in the *Perthshire Constitutional* in 1877 described him to be 'as good a man as ever served [the Scottish Episcopal Church] yet'.¹⁵⁶ The joint suspicion in the minds of some Evangelicals, that the Scottish Episcopal Church was seeking to limit Evangelical activity both by its canon law and by possibly getting rid of Drummond as a potential leader, was a factor in increasing the ferment.

Drummond's certainty that he was a marked man was illustrated by his refusal to take his case to the Church courts. While Professor W. E. Aytoun put the opinion that Drummond could have appealed to the Diocesan Synod where he considered that a fair hearing would have been given,¹⁵⁷ Drummond replied that, according to Canon XXXVI, Terrot in Synod would be required to ask the opinion of his presbyters, and since the Edinburgh clergy had shown that they supported Terrot, he saw little purpose in pursuing this course of action. In reply to the additional charge that he could have appealed to the College of Bishops, Drummond answered that this would have been pointless since four out of the six members had made it quite plain that they considered him to be in the

---

¹⁵⁰ *History of the Family of Drummond* (London, 1842).
¹⁵¹ Vernon Heath, *Recollections* (London, 1892), pp. 117-119.
¹⁵² *Memoir*, pp. i-xvi.
¹⁵³ *Scotsman*, 11 June 1877.
¹⁵⁴ Montgomery, *English Schismatics*, p. 70.
¹⁵⁵ *Scottish Guardian*, 1 September 1871.
¹⁵⁶ *Perthshire Constitutional*, 13 June 1877.
¹⁵⁷ Drummond, *Reply to Resolutions*, pp. 14-16. Aytoun, *Schism Examined*, pp. 11-12.

wrong.[158] Thus Drummond argued that various High Churchmen were intent on crushing his particular activities. Overall, then, mistrust and suspicion were potent factors in the secession of 1842.

A fourth factor surrounding events was that lay-people made a particular contribution to the founding of St Thomas's. In October 1842 the Committee of Friends looked into the correspondence between Drummond and Terrot and concluded that they themselves were 'aggrieved in their Christian liberty by the effect which had been given to the canon'.[159] As a result they considered the possibility of forming a Church of England congregation in Edinburgh, where there would be no restriction of the evangelistic prayer meetings they valued. When legal authorities advised that such a congregation would be 'consistent with the rules of the Church of England', and in the light of the problem of the Scottish Communion Office, the decision to form a congregation went ahead.[160] It was not until 12 November that John Wauchope, the chairman of the Committee, wrote to Drummond inviting him 'to become our Pastor'.[161] From the small beginnings of the Edinburgh Episcopal Evangelical movement in 1820, centred around the ministry of Craig, a vibrant and assertive group of lay-people had arisen by 1842. Its members were knowledgeable about doctrinal issues and were willing to push for a church where they could conscientiously worship according to their own beliefs. The laity in Edinburgh, not Drummond, appears to have been the driving force behind the move to set up St Thomas's.

Moreover, the group of Drummond's friends was influential, consisting of professional people and members of the gentry. H. F. Holcombe was a lieutenant-colonel in the Army; Francis Grove a captain in the Royal Navy; J. Keith and Andrew Wood were medical doctors; Robert Pitcairn, James Cunningham and James Mylne were lawyers; Montague Stanley was a well-known former actor; John Wauchope was heir to the Edmonstone estate at Newton, Midlothian; and J. Neil Dyce was also of gentry status.[162] They did not necessarily wield great power in Edinburgh, but the lawyers among them could check legal matters concerning the new congregation. Additionally they were wealthy enough to give generously towards the building of St Thomas's and were sufficiently respected in the community to provide the movement with credibility.[163] Without the impetus of such

---

[158] Drummond, *Reply to Resolutions*, pp. 14-16.

[159] *Statement by the Committee*, p. 10.

[160] *Ibid.*, pp. 10-11.

[161] John Wauchope to D. T. K. Drummond, 12 November 1842, DRO, D5550/3/5/12.

[162] *Statement by Committee*, p. 16. Professions obtained from the *Post Office Directory for Edinburgh*, 1842.

[163] See Chapter 3, p. 91-92.

Secession 277

lay support, Drummond would probably have left Scotland and continued his ministry elsewhere.

It is also evident that many of the original congregation at St Thomas's were Presbyterians. Although it has proved impossible to identify them, the writer in the *Perthshire Constitutional* in 1877 suggested that the storms in the Church of Scotland in the early 1840s drove a number of such people to St Thomas's where 'there appeared to many the quiet unruffled harbour where those might find rest and peace and good, who did not care for entering the fierce Presbyterian warfare'.[164] Again, some were probably attracted by a growing desire for beauty in worship compared to the rather plain services in their own churches. Presbyterian input, at a time of conflict in the Church of Scotland, was thus an important factor in making St Thomas's a viable proposition.

A final factor to be considered was that Drummond's position was marked by an astonishing degree of confidence given the fact that, until Bickersteth gave his backing in January 1843, he seemed to be rather isolated, having the support of only lay people in Edinburgh. Convinced as Drummond was concerning the need to evangelise unhindered and to oppose all hints of Tractarianism, various influences can be pinpointed as probable contributors to his conviction that secession was justified. Although Drummond's premillennial theology was possibly immature in 1842, Bickersteth's was developed and, in 1837, he wrote to Drummond, warning 'how short our time is to work for our Heavenly Master with freedom'.[165] The need to gather converts before Christ's return was paramount, and Bickersteth's influence in this respect was significant. Again, the Romanticism of the times, with its spirit of adventure and the desire to make a stand on issues, might have enhanced Drummond's decision.[166] More importantly, though, there is reason to suppose that prominent Evangelicals in England, some of whom Drummond knew through the Church Missionary Society, had previously given him a sense of his position. Drummond's personal correspondence in the 1830s and early 1840s includes letters from Henry Blunt, vicar of Holy Trinity, Sloane Street, London, regarded as perhaps the most influential congregation in the capital. Hugh McNeile, then curate-in-charge of St Jude's, Liverpool, and Hugh Stowell of Manchester, who had made inroads into imposing a strong Evangelicalism on those cities, were also frequent correspondents. A letter from Francis Close of Cheltenham in 1840, offering Drummond a large church in the area, with one thousand eight hundred seats and a stipend of £200-£300, but at the same time pointing to the 'important part [he] played

---

[164] *Perthshire Constitutional*, 13 June 1877. *Memoir*, p. xli.
[165] See Chapter 4, p. 145 for Drummond's premillennialism. See also, Edward Bickersteth to D. T. K. Drumond, 16 April 1837, DRO, D5550/3/5/26.
[166] *Cf.* David Newsome, *The Victorian World Picture* (London, 1997), pp. 155-158.

in Scotland', is also notable.[167] Theological, cultural and personal influences all appear to have contributed towards Drummond's confidence in seceding from the Scottish Episcopal Church.

Conclusion

The formation of St Thomas's in 1842 arose out of an atmosphere of mistrust between Evangelicals and High Churchmen evident in the previous decades. The continuing conflict with prevailing High Church opinions, especially in northeastern Scotland, where Skinner and Moir were bishops, over how to conduct evangelism without using the liturgy, was the initial and most important factor in the events. Drummond appears to have been particularly innovative in this respect, and while the Scottish Episcopal Church was willing to accommodate evangelism in the context of normal services it would not condone Drummond's activities, seeing them as disruptive of the discipline of the Church. It looked for a more quiescent Evangelicalism, along the lines of Wade in Paisley, supportive of apostolic succession and ecclesiastical discipline.

It also seems likely that some Scottish High Churchmen became increasingly reluctant to allow Drummond to gain too much popularity, fearing he might form a strong, and possibly disruptive, Evangelical following within the Church. There is substantial evidence to show that, in the late 1830s and early 1840s, some were anxious to curtail Evangelical activity, and that they saw Drummond as a potential leader of a vibrant and influential group.

The doctrine of the Scottish Communion Office, brought to light by Craig, was an aspect of Evangelical antipathy to Catholic doctrinal emphases. It became a determining issue for Drummond who, nevertheless, regarded the restriction on his evangelistic activities as sufficient reason, on biblical grounds, to withdraw from the Church. But other Evangelicals felt that the Scottish Communion Office gave far more cogency to his secession. The support of the *Record*, the *Christian Observer* and ultimately many other Evangelicals, including the influential Bickersteth, all of whom were swayed by Drummond's *Scottish Office Examined*, was vitally important to the cause of English Episcopalianism.

Despite his problems with the Scottish Episcopal Church, Drummond remained faithful to the Church of England, and claimed that he was not a schismatic. In a similar way the laity, who seem to have driven the events in Edinburgh, were all loyal Anglicans. By contrast, the distance between Drummond and the Scottish Episcopal Church was evident when he was

---

[167] H. Blunt to D. T. K. Drummond, 5 November 1834. H. Mc Neile to D. T. K. Drummond, 31 March 1839, 24 December 1839. H. Stowell to D. T. K. Drummond, 10 April 1839. F. Close to D. T. K. Drummond, 20 March 1840, DRO, D5550/3/5/26.

cheered on the platform of the Free Church Assembly when it first met in the Canonmills of Edinburgh in 1843.[168] While many Scottish High Churchmen, and even some Evangelicals, could not countenance Drummond, the Free Church honoured him. The affinity between Evangelical Episcopalians like Drummond and their counterparts in other denominations, evident earlier in the century, was thus increasingly cemented. But importantly, while Drummond could have been tolerated in the Church of England, many of the numerically dominant High Churchmen in the Scottish Episcopal Church refused to condone his activities. The factors surrounding the formation of St Thomas's in 1842 were multi-faceted.

---

[168] Montgomery, *English Schismatics*, p. 84.

Chapter 9

Continuing Disruption

After the foundation of St Thomas's, Edinburgh, in 1842, the years up to 1887 witnessed the planting of a further twenty-two English Episcopal churches, including the re-emergence of the Arradoul congregation in 1854, and the establishment of Evangelicalism at St Peter's, Montrose, a qualified church.[1] Table 9.1 lists these churches, their relationship to the Scottish Episcopal Church and the presiding bishop at the time of their commencement.[2] It can be seen that, although the origins of Galloway House chapel are unknown, nine congregations had at one time been part of the Scottish Episcopal Church, while twelve were totally new gatherings.

Secession was not unusual in the nineteenth century. In the period 1830 to 1840 forty-four clergy, who had become more clearly Calvinistic or opposed to the baptismal service, are known to have left the Church of England. Most of these joined the Baptists or Plymouth Brethren. In the following decade, the numbers dropped to around sixteen.[3] In proportion to the sizes of the Anglican and Scottish Episcopal Churches, the Episcopal disruption in Scotland was on a far larger scale. It is thus a particularly noteworthy event, and although it might have been influenced by the example of the secessions in England it was, in many respects, unique to Scotland.

The problems leading to the formation of St Thomas's had revolved around church discipline, evangelism and, ultimately, the doctrine of the Scottish Communion Office. In an age when Tractarianism was evolving into Ritualism some Churchmen found the expression of advancing eucharistic ideas in the Scottish Office disturbing,[4] and it will be seen that eucharistic unrest was the underlying reason for the burgeoning English Episcopal movement. Additionally, reference to Graph 9.1[5] shows that the number of English Episcopal chapels reached peaks around 1854 and 1875. The following analysis will thus examine both the impact of the continuing,

---

[1] See Chapter 1, pp. 29, 31.
[2] See Chapter 9, p. 283
[3] Grayson Carter, *Anglican Evangelicals* (Oxford, 2001), pp. 339-403. *Cf.* Chapter 6, p. 220.
[4] Chapters 7, 10.
[5] See Chapter 9, p. 282.

broad doctrinal issues and the various factors which consolidated specific bursts of separatist activity.

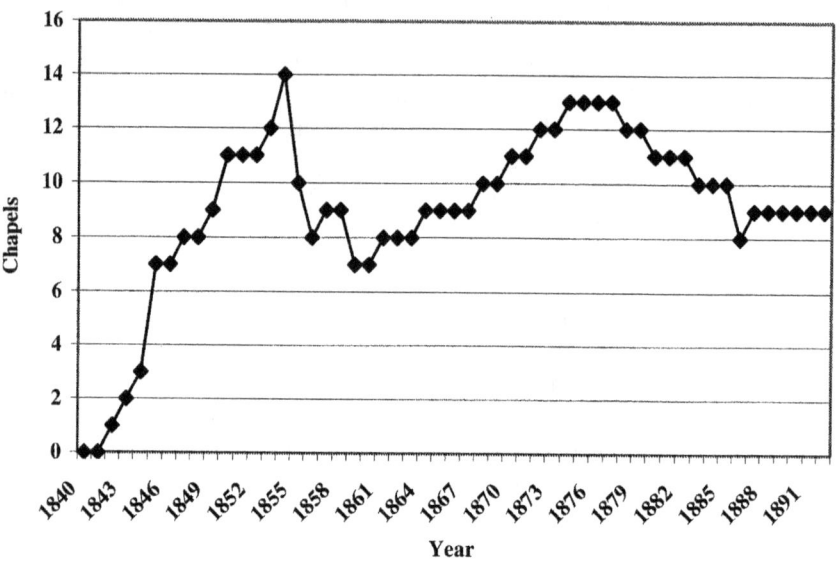

Graph 9.1

English Episcopal Chapels

Table 9.1 English Episcopal Chapels, 1842-1988

	CHURCH	DATE	ORIGIN	BISHOP AT FOUNDATION
1	St Thomas's, Edinburgh, and Canongate Mission	1842-1988	New	C. H. Terrot
2	St Paul's, Aberdeen	1843-1898	S. E. C.	William Skinner *
3	St Jude's, Glasgow	1844-1894	S. E. C.	Michael Russell *
4	Dunoon	1845-1900	New	Alexander Ewing (1847)
5	Huntly	1845-1854	S. E. C.	David Low +
6	Nairn	1845-1879	S. E. C.	David Low +
7	Gask	1845-1855	New	Patrick Torry *
8	Fochabers	1847-1855	S. E. C.	David Low +
9	Galloway House	1848-?	?	Michael Russell*
10	Crieff	1849-1854	New	Patrick Torry *
11	Corrimony	1850-1854	New	David Low +
12	Arradoul	1850-1854	S. E. C.	William Skinner *
13	Old Deer	1853-1858	S. E. C.	William Skinner *
14	St James's, Aberdeen	1854-1897	New	William Skinner *
15	Selkirk	1854-1858	S. E. C.	C. H. Terrot
16	St Vincent's, Edinburgh	1857-1882	New	C. H. Terrot
17	Wemyss Bay	1861-1932	New	Alexander Ewing
18	St Silas's and Partick Mission, Govan, Glasgow	1864-1987	New	W. S. Wilson
19	St John's, Dundee	1868-1885	S. E. C.	A. P. Forbes *
20	Hunters Quay	1870-1905	New	Alexander Ewing
21	Cally	1872-1885	New	W. S. Wilson
22	Johnstone	1874-1877	New	W. S. Wilson
23	Balmacara	1887-1916	New	J. B. K. Kelly
24	Montrose	Qualified		

S. E. C. Scottish Episcopal Church
* Scottish Communion Office supporter
+Diocese with strong Scottish Communion Office support
Source: David Bertie, Scottish Episcopal Clergy 1689-2000 (Edinburgh, 2000), pp. 655-658.

St Paul's, Aberdeen

St Paul's, Aberdeen, established in 1720 as a qualified chapel using only the Book of Common Prayer, was totally outside the jurisdiction of the Scottish Episcopal Church. Its status was jealously guarded, as revealed by the designation of funds donated at its foundation by 'Mr Rickarton of Auchnacant', given on the understanding that St Paul's remained qualified. The intensity of feeling was evident since, if the status of the church were altered, Rickarton's gift was to be transferred to the infirmary and workhouse of Aberdeen.[6] The early members of St Paul's were mainly native Scots, with 'hardly any English' in the congregation,[7] a situation which probably remained at least until 1867 when membership lists show 58% with evidently Scottish names.[8]

St Paul's, unlike most of the qualified congregations, resisted joining the Scottish Episcopal Church at the convocation of Laurencekirk in 1804. Similarly, when James Walker, the future Bishop of Edinburgh from 1830 to 1841, posed the possibility in 1822, lay members and managers voted against it.[9] Reasons for this reluctance were probably diverse. In the eighteenth century the northeast of Scotland was a centre of Nonjuring theology and adherence to the Scottish Communion Office. Qualified chapels such as St Paul's would have been aware of doctrinal differences, leading them to be cautious of union whenever the question arose. But Evangelicalism does not appear to have been a reason for opposition. A letter written by one of the congregation in 1843 refers to the movement becoming established only after 1840 when Sir William Dunbar was appointed as incumbent. Before that, under John Brown, 'the laws of the Church were strictly obeyed...if there was lack of Evangelical preaching as some nowadays would think, the seat rental was greater than it has been

---

[6] Sir William Dunbar, *A Letter to the Managers and Constituent Members and Congregation of St Paul's Chapel, Aberdeen, by the Rev Sir William Dunbar Bart. S. C. L. Presbyter of the Church of England to which is added Bishop Skinner's Declaration that Sir William Dunbar has placed himself in a State of Open Schism and the Warning of His Reverence to "All Faithful People to Avoid all Communion with the said Sir William Dunbar in Prayers and Sacraments"* 3rd edition (Aberdeen, 1843), pp. 6-7.

[7] Harry Allen, 'Aberdeen's Aristocratic Church'(n. pub. 1927), p. 5.

[8] 'Roll of Members, St Paul's Church, Aberdeen', St Paul's Church, Aberdeen, Archives. In 1860 the proportion was 57%.

[9] James Walker, *A Friendly Call to Union Addressed to the Managers of St Paul's Chapel, Aberdeen*, (Edinburgh, 1823). *Scottish Episcopal Review and Magazine*, 1822, pp. 603-605.

Continuing Disruption

ever since'.[10] Thus before 1840, St Paul's was a thriving church composed mainly of Scots who, for historical reasons, valued its qualified status and attachment to the Church of England.

But when the incumbency of St Paul's fell vacant in 1840, the managers agreed to union with the Scottish Episcopal Church on 22 October in the hope of securing 'better candidates to supply the present vacancy'.[11] However, current events caused controversy. The links of the Scottish Episcopal Church with the Oxford Movement[12] led one manager to warn that 'a talented Puseyite' might be appointed if union were established.[13] Another, possibly in reaction to the canons passed by the 1838 Synod,[14] 'could not get over the difficulty of being a member of a Church which...recognises the Scottish Communion Office as of primary authority'. Although only two managers were firmly opposed to the motion, those who assented were by no means wholly enthusiastic. One voted in favour only because he saw 'no end to jarring otherwise'. Retaining the distinctive personality of the church was a consideration for some who were concerned about 'the power of Bishops...to alter the Services in the Chapels under their jurisdiction'. They pressed 'that we retain the entire management of our funds', and the congregational right of appointing clergy 'in which the Bishop is not allowed to interfere'.[15] At St Paul's there was therefore a distinct fear that union with the Scottish Episcopal Church would not accommodate a clearly Anglican churchmanship. Additionally, it is apparent that the use of the Scottish Communion Office was resisted there before it became an issue in Edinburgh. Thus the agreed union guaranteed the sole use of the Anglican liturgy and placed the choice of incumbent and oversight of funds firmly in the hands of the managers.[16] A noticeable distrust of the Scottish Episcopal Church, emanating from both past history and current events, permeated St Paul's in 1840.

Sir William Dunbar, curate of Stoke-on-Trent, accepted the charge of St Paul's on 26 May 1842, putting his signature to the Deed of Union.[17] Dunbar, an Evangelical, born in 1804, was the sixth baronet in the line of Dunbar of Durn, Banffshire. After education at Magdalen Hall, Oxford,

---

[10] *Answer to a Letter to the Managers, Constituent Members and Congregation of St Paul's Chapel, Aberdeen, by the Rev. Sir William Dunbar, Bart, S. C. L., Presbyter of the Church of England* (Aberdeen, 1843), p. 15.

[11] Dunbar, *Letter*, p. 7. There is a discrepancy with David Bertie, *Scottish Episcopal Clergy 1689-2000* (Edinburgh, 2000), p. 650, which places the vacancy in 1840.

[12] See Chapter 8, pp. 251-254.

[13] Dunbar, *Letter*, pp. 7-8.

[14] See Chapter 8, pp. 255-257.

[15] Dunbar, *Letter*, p. 9.

[16] D. T. K. Drummond, *Historical Sketch of Episcopacy in Scotland from 1688 to the Present Time* (Edinburgh, 1845), pp. 157-158.

[17] *Ibid.*, p. 83.

from 1828 to 1830, he was ordained into the Church of England.[18] He overlapped with D. T. K. Drummond, of St Thomas's, Edinburgh, at Oxford by one year. But the fact that Dunbar seemed to know more about the Scottish Communion Office than Drummond in early 1842, refusing the incumbency of St Paul's initially because of the differences between it and the English service,[19] suggests that they did not know each other well. After discussions with the managers Dunbar considered himself, according to the Deed of Union, 'not bound, in consequence of my *conditional* and *qualified* subscription of the Canons of the Scottish Episcopal Church, to adopt them to the same extent as the Scottish Episcopal presbyters'.[20] His attitude evolved out of a strong opposition to the Scottish Communion Office 'on scriptural as well as on the grounds of my ordination vow [to use only the English Office]'.[21] While there is no evidence to suggest that Dunbar influenced events in Edinburgh, his opposition to the Scottish Office, like that of his congregation, predated Drummond's.

The Scottish Communion Office was a major cause of discontent at St Paul's after union. It was probably the overriding reason for the troubles which befell the church, whereas in Edinburgh it had been only secondary. Dunbar objected to its use soon after his arrival in Aberdeen in 1842. He told William Skinner, Bishop of Aberdeen and Primus, that he was uneasy about preaching in St Andrew's, Aberdeen, where the Scottish Office was the adopted rite.[22] Later, in 1842, Skinner caused outrage in the congregation at a confirmation of candidates from St Paul's by departing from the strict order of the Book of Common Prayer.[23] When, in April 1843, he agreed to confirm St Paul's candidates only in St Andrew's, feelings ran high. Dunbar objected to his young people attending because he felt that there was a risk that they would 'consider of slight or secondary importance subjects of which, in my conscience, I considered essential', and the parents of the children expressed a wish 'to keep their mark of distinction'.[24] Thus by 1843 Dunbar's personal opposition to the Scottish Communion Office, probably exacerbated by events in Edinburgh, provided a focus for discontent in Aberdeen.

Additional factors, similar to those operating in Edinburgh, increased unrest. Church discipline, coupled with Dunbar's growing mistrust of his

---

[18] D. M. Lewis (ed.), *The Blackwell Dictionary of Evangelical Biography*, Volume I (Oxford, 1995), p. 330.

[19] C. P. Miles, *An Address to the Members of St Jude's, Glasgow (In Reply to Bishop M. Russell's Affectionate Address)* (Glasgow, 1844), p. 17.

[20] Dunbar, *Letter*, p. 11.

[21] *Ibid.*, p. 12.

[22] *Ibid.*, pp. 11-12.

[23] Drummond, *Sketch*, p. 84.

[24] Dunbar, *Letter*, pp. 22-23.

bishop, was a particular area of dispute. When Dunbar expressed his reservations about preaching at St Andrew's in 1842, Skinner suggested that he should leave the service immediately after his sermon. But afterwards Skinner surprised Dunbar by disapproving of his withdrawal and strongly advising against such action in the future. Dunbar was left with the distinct impression that he had been misled.[25] Matters worsened when Dunbar asked Skinner if he would infringe Canon XI, requiring personal residence of incumbents, by inviting English Evangelical clergy to assist at St Paul's in his absence. Skinner, probably wary of dissension over the Scottish Office, answered in the affirmative unless their 'principles and clerical character...be correct and consistent with the Scottish Episcopal Church'.[26] Prayer meetings were a problem, as they had been in Edinburgh. Dunbar asked Skinner if Canon XXVIII, on uniformity of public worship, would prevent him from 'meeting a few of the poor and infirm members of the congregation on a weekday in the vestry or schoolroom' when he would use extempore as well as Prayer Book collects. Skinner replied that Dunbar 'might go to their houses and do so, but...had no business to use any other than the Prayer Book in the schoolroom'.[27] Skinner's insistence 'that if you wish to be an Episcopalian, act up in all things to your profession by strict adherence to the liturgical rites and ecclesiastical discipline of your Church',[28] illustrated the chasm between Scottish High Churchmen and some Evangelicals over Church discipline.

The impact of Tractarianism, as in Edinburgh, was a further factor troubling Dunbar. In May 1843 he declined to make a collection for the Scottish Episcopal Church Society, fearing that the money might be used to buy *Tracts for the Times*, several of which were already in the Aberdeen diocesan library.[29] His refusal to allow the merger of St Paul's school with Episcopal foundations in Aberdeen, and his reluctance to 'read the Bishop's Pastoral Letters whether I approve them or not', was part of the same concern.[30] Increasing activity by the Oxford Movement, and its links with the Scottish Episcopal Church, caused Evangelicals like Dunbar to express their own churchmanship more vigorously.

Again, some might have regarded Dunbar, like Drummond, as a threat to the stability of the Church because of his success and popularity. As already noted, Dunbar was well connected by birth. He was a respected and gifted clergyman, as was evident in a letter of September 1843 from his former congregation in Stoke-upon-Trent, describing his 'irreproachable life and

---

[25] Dunbar, *Letter*, pp. 11-12.
[26] *Ibid.*, pp. 14-15.
[27] *Ibid.*, p. 15.
[28] *Ibid.*, pp. 37-38.
[29] *Ibid.*, p. 13.
[30] *Ibid.*, pp. 16, 24.

conversation...the graces of humility, meekness and love [and] the eminent success with which it pleased the Head of the Church to crown your labour'.[31] Skinner might well have feared that Dunbar was capable of gathering a following, leading to a breach of unity in the Church.

By 12 May 1843 Dunbar resigned his charge on the legal grounds that Skinner's insistence on the use of the Scottish Communion Office interfered with the Deed of Union.[32] The constituent members of St Paul's approved the decision and voted by a large majority on 27 June 1843 to make the Deed null and void. Hence the church joined the English Episcopal movement.[33] The Diocesan Synod, held at Aberdeen on 9 August 1843, supported Skinner in a declaration of effectual excommunication of Dunbar which warned faithful people to avoid all communion with him 'lest they be partakers with him in his sin [of open schism], and thereby expose themselves to the threatening denounced against those who cause divisions in the Church'.[34] Bishop David Moir and his clergy of the Brechin diocese backed the edict, reporting from their Synod on 7 September 1843 that 'evils of a still greater magnitude' would ensue if such proceedings 'be allowed to pass without...some public notice and censure'.[35] The seriousness with which High Churchmen in Scotland viewed disruption of the unity of the Church was thus evident. Conversely, many Evangelicals were enraged. Drummond argued that Skinner had no right to denounce Dunbar, who was an ordained clergyman of the Church of England, and that Dunbar had every reason to resign from the Scottish Episcopal Church 'in honesty to the constituent members' and to return 'to the position which he had occupied before he was inducted'.[36] Dunbar's excommunication intensified an already unsettled atmosphere in the Scottish Episcopal Church.

As with Drummond's case at Edinburgh, both Evangelical practice and theology were the main agents in Dunbar's disagreement. While it is true that some of the congregation were probably eager to maintain the qualified personality of St Paul's, Gavin White's suggestion that Dunbar was 'an innocent victim' in the events at Aberdeen and was acting as a spokesman for the congregation,[37] is unfounded. It has been shown here that Dunbar's own doctrinal convictions caused him to resist the Scottish Communion Office and Tractarian influences. Dunbar was certainly not a pawn in the

---

[31] *Ibid.*, p. 53.
[32] *Ibid.*, p. 33.
[33] Drummond, *Sketch*, p. 86.
[34] *Ibid.*, pp. 88-89.
[35] Report from Bishop David Moir, NAS, CH12/60/3.
[36] Drummond, *Sketch*, p. 87.
[37] Gavin White, *The Scottish Episcopal Church: A New History* (Edinburgh, 1998), p. 76.

hands of his congregation. Because of his Evangelicalism, he had his own difficulties with the Scottish liturgy and discipline of the Church.

St Jude's, Glasgow

In 1844, St Jude's, Glasgow, severed itself from the Scottish Episcopal Church. It had been founded in September 1838 with Robert Montgomery, a curate of Hugh McNeile in Liverpool, as incumbent. Montgomery had arrived at St Mary's, Glasgow, in the summer of 1838 to act as a locum for George Almond. Although not universally popular, some regarded him as of 'real genius' and with 'remarkable power in the pulpit' and St Mary's was soon filled to excess. Accordingly, one hundred and fifty-eight of the congregation set up St Jude's, Glasgow, with Montgomery as its pastor in that year. W. F. Burnley, a wealthy Glasgow merchant, and George Burns, the founder of the Cunard shipping company, contributed money towards the chapel which was to be part of the Scottish Episcopal Church, having the special function of reaching the poor of Glasgow. Michael Russell, Bishop of Glasgow and Galloway, a High Churchman, gladly gave his support because the existing three Episcopal chapels provided insufficient accommodation for the ten thousand Episcopalians then living in the city.[38]

By September 1843 repercussions emanating from the secessions of Drummond and Dunbar were evident in Glasgow. Montgomery, together with the Glasgow clergy George Almond and Isaac Hitchin, of St Mary's, and L. P. Mercier, of St Andrew's, wrote to Russell asking him to use his influence to procure the removal of the Scottish Communion Office. They feared it was 'a stumbling block, in their congregations, and predicted that it would cause 'serious evils of lay agitation and secession'.[39] In the autumn of 1843, Montgomery left St Jude's for the Percy Chapel, London. C. P. Miles, from Bishop Wearmouth, County Durham, replaced him. Initially, Miles was not particularly antagonistic to the Scottish Communion Office, informing Russell that he was willing to compromise because 'the objectionable phrase is explained by other portions of the service even as certain strong phrases in the English service are in like manner qualified. Still, I shall rejoice...when the stumbling block is removed'. Further assurances from Russell that the Scottish Communion Office would soon be demoted satisfied Miles that he could take up the appointment at St

---

[38] Edwin Hodder, *Sir George Burns Bart* (London, 1892), pp. 128-129. Chapter 2, p. 41. Michael Russell, *An Affectionate Address to the Managers and Congregation of St Jude's* 2nd Edition (Glasgow, 1844), pp. 3-5.

[39] *Record*, 6 November 1843.

Jude's.[40] Thus the Scottish Communion Office was not the primary cause of Miles's arguments with the Scottish Episcopal Church.

Miles's main problems revolved around Skinner's edict on Dunbar which he regarded as typical of 'the bitter spirit of Anti-Christ during the height of Roman supremacy and intolerance'.[41] Miles maintained that, as far as the Church of England was concerned, the document was a 'dead letter without the remotest legal efficacy' because Dunbar had subsequently officiated freely in several English pulpits.[42] Understanding that Skinner had acted 'unjustly and shamefully', Miles decided to test the views of the other Scottish bishops. He regarded the 'liberty of God's children to be at stake', and warned that if the Scottish episcopate sanctioned Skinner's proceedings 'I will instantly withdraw my subscription'[43] to the Church, pleading, 'if Sir William Dunbar can bring sinners to heaven...why, oh! why, should he be decried as schismatic, and branded excommunicate?'[44] In effect Miles was challenging what he considered to be an extreme example of legalism in the Church which superseded other ministerial functions that he, as an Evangelical, understood to be paramount.

On 16 June 1844 Miles preached at St Paul's, Aberdeen. Skinner immediately complained to Russell in Glasgow and Miles sought to cover himself, arguing that there were no Scottish canons preventing him from preaching for Dunbar, a fellow Anglican.[45] The dispute continued, and on 2 October Russell pointed out, with typical High Church regard for law and order, that although 'there is no canon directly forbidding such intercourse it is irregular, and so far illegal'.[46] Just as Terrot had advised Drummond to apply to the Church courts for clarification, Russell directed Miles on 23 September 1844 to make an 'appeal in the Episcopal College' if he considered Skinner's conduct 'uncanonical'. But Miles, without specifying his reasons, ignored the plea.[47] The differences of opinion between High Churchmen and Evangelicals over the necessity of imposing strict law were as apparent in this dispute as they had been in Edinburgh and Aberdeen.

But in addition to his objection to Dunbar's excommunication, Miles's attitude to the Scottish Office had 'materially altered'. After visiting Dunbar in Aberdeen, he considered 'that the doctrines of the glorious

---

[40] Russell, *Affectionate Address*, pp. 6-7. C. P. Miles, *An Address to the members of St Jude's Congregaion, Glasgow. [In reply to Bishop M. Russell's Address]*, (Glasgow, 1844), p. 55.

[41] Miles, *Address in Reply to Bishop Russell's Address*, p. 24.

[42] *Ibid.*, p. 9.

[43] *Ibid.*, pp. 47, 73.

[44] *Ibid.*, p. 35.

[45] C. P. Miles, *A Second Letter Addressed to the Members of St Jude's Congregation, Glasgow* (Glasgow, 1844), pp. 31-34. Drummond, *Sketch*, pp. 100-101.

[46] Miles, *Address in Reply to Bishop Russell's Address*, pp. 54-55.

[47] *Ibid.*, pp. 43-44.

Continuing Disruption 291

Reformation are seriously discountenanced and reprobated by the Episcopal Church in Scotland'.[48] As a result, Miles objected to Russell's support for the use of the office at the consecration of the Marchioness of Lothian's chapel, St John's, Jedburgh, in 1844, especially because of the 'extremely unusual display' that accompanied it. The 'appearance of four bishops, and about forty clergymen all vested in surplices', some of them Oxford Movement supporters, caused Miles to question Russell's own position.[49] He asked Russell whether his promise given at the commencement of his appointment still held, that 'a considerable amendment respecting the communion office would be effected'.[50] But Russell, who had 'never concealed my own preference for the Scottish Office',[51] merely replied on 23 September 1844 that 'perhaps I should propose that the Scotch Communion Office should not be made imperative at the opening of General Synods'.[52] The doctrine of the Scottish Communion Office compounded Miles's difficulties.

Miles, doubtful that the question of the Scottish Office would be resolved, resigned the incumbency of St Jude's on 5 October 1844. His reasons rested on Russell's public approval of Skinner's edict against Dunbar and his unsatisfactory reply about the future of the Scottish Communion Office.[53] Thereupon the managers withdrew St Jude's from the Scottish Episcopal Church and joined the English Episcopalians, with Miles as their chosen incumbent.[54] On 26 December 1844 Russell issued a document in which he 'reject[ed]...Miles and publicly declar[ed] that he is no longer a clergyman of the Scottish Episcopal Church'. In similar vein to Skinner's edict against Dunbar, Russell warned Episcopalians everywhere to avoid professional communion with Miles.[55] Both sides had now publicly declared separation.

Various factors can be isolated as consolidating Miles's resolve to resign. Laymen at St Jude's influenced events. Burns and Burnley, who had probably previously complained about the Scottish Communion Office to Montgomery, were in constant consultation with Miles throughout the events leading up to his resignation. Seemingly condoning his involvement with Dunbar, they eventually pressed for association with the English

---

[48] *Ibid.*, p. 42.
[49] *Ibid.*, p. 53.
[50] *Ibid.*, p. 42.
[51] Michael Russell to William Skinner, 31 May 1844 in William Walker, *Three Churchmen* (Edinburgh, 1893), p. 75. See also Chapter 7, p. 233.
[52] Miles, *Address in Reply to Bishop Russell's Address*, pp. 44-45.
[53] *Ibid.*, p. 59. Drummond, *Sketch*, pp. 101-102.
[54] Hodder, *Burns*, pp. 167-168.
[55] Drummond, *Sketch*, pp. 108-109.

Episcopalians.[56] Thus, as in Edinburgh and Aberdeen, lay involvement helped to drive events at St Jude's.

The apparent legality of the English chapels was also an important factor encouraging Miles in his decision. While the Church of England had not repudiated the protection of English Episcopalianism afforded by the Toleration Act of 1712, Russell warned that all Episcopal clergy needed a licence from a bishop if they were to minister according to Article XXIII and Canon 48 of the Anglican Church. Miles, however, sought to provide contrary evidence. He pointed to 'peculiars' such as a chapel in London 'in the hands of the Dean and Chapter of St Paul's and, consequently, not under the jurisdiction of the Bishop of London'; to proprietary chapels, such as the Percy Chapel, which were in a similar position; and to naval, army and convict ship chaplains who likewise were unlicensed. Miles concluded that 'several hundreds of English clergymen...are in communion with the Church of England, and sanctioned by a law altogether incomprehensible to Bishop Russell'.[57] The legal standing of English Episcopalianism was sufficiently cogent to Miles to justify his separation.

Support from Evangelicals outside Scotland for Drummond and Dunbar was a factor in Miles's decision. Terrot communicated to the Church Missionary Society in January 1844 that some Edinburgh Episcopalians threatened to withdraw support from the society if deputation members preached at St Thomas's, Edinburgh, and St Paul's, Aberdeen. However, Edward Bickersteth, a committee member of the society, was convinced that the Scottish Episcopal Church was guilty of doctrinal error in its communion service.[58] He argued the importance of remaining faithful to Drummond and Dunbar, the former having been the impetus for the Edinburgh auxiliary branch which contributed about half the annual money received from Scotland.[59] Bickersteth agreed to preach for the society in an unofficial capacity at St Paul's on 21 April 1844 and at St Thomas's on 28 April 1844. Terrot complained to John Kaye, Bickersteth's diocesan at Lincoln, that this was 'causing weakness and disunion' in Scotland. But Bickersteth, convinced of the need for the English Episcopal movement, remarked to Drummond that this was 'a false move against the truth'. He wrote to Kaye on 10 April 1844 upholding Drummond as 'guilty of no schism' and 'peculiarly faithful to his Saviour and to his promises as a minister of the Church of England'. He even pleaded for a bishop to oversee the English Episcopalians because the 'one real remedy where English clergymen multiply out of England is the increase of English

---

[56] Hodder, *Burns*, p. 167. Miles, *Address in Reply to Bishop Russell's Address*, p. 6.

[57] Miles, *Second Address*, pp. 19-23.

[58] See Chapter 8, pp. 268-268, 270-271.

[59] *Correspondence between Bishop Terrot and the Church Missionary Society* (n. p., 1844), p. 3.

Bishopricks'.[60] Support from Bickersteth, coupled with the knowledge that Kaye had received affirmation of English Episcopalianism, would have encouraged Miles to follow Drummond and Dunbar.

However, Montgomery was very critical of Miles. Whereas H. M. Villiers, Rector of St George's, Bloomsbury, and future Bishop of Carlisle and Durham, wrote to Burnley on 29 November 1844 opposing Russell, saying, 'you may stick a piece of lawn on any man and make him a bishop, but the knowledge of the truth and the love of Christ cannot thus be given',[61] Montgomery thought differently. In a letter to a manager of St Jude's in 1844 he maintained that 'schism is a treason to Christ' and he severely criticised the position taken up by Miles.[62] However, although Daniel Bagot, too, had opposed Drummond's defection, there is no other evidence of overt Evangelical criticism of the English Episcopalians. The apparent growing support for the separatists by the end of 1844 was a probable factor encouraging Miles's defection, despite the criticism of his predecessor.

Thus the foundation of St Jude's English Episcopal Church sprang primarily from what Miles considered to be undue interference by Skinner in the affairs of St Paul's, Aberdeen. Miles's eventual rejection of the theology of the Scottish Communion Office was an additional, though cementing, cause. The part played by the laity, the influence of Bickersteth, and the apparent legality of the English Episcopalians were important consolidating factors. The case surrounding St Jude's was similar to that of St Thomas's which also centred on freedom of practice for clergy and congregations, the doctrine of the Scottish Communion Office being secondary, though important in its own right.

Other English Episcopal Chapels, 1845-1855

The period 1845 to 1855 was marked by increasing hostility to the Scottish Communion Office which spilled over into congregations not known for their Evangelicalism. Occasionally a group of party men in a congregation organised protests against the Scottish Office. This was evident at St John's, Perth, which had existed as a qualified chapel since 1750, united with the Scottish Episcopal Church in 1804, severed again in 1810 and re-united in 1847, retaining the use of the Anglican liturgy.[63] Particular

---

[60] E. Bickersteth to D. T. K. Drummond, 10 April 1844, E. Bickersteth to the Bishop of Lincoln, 10 April 1844, DRO, D5550/3/5/26.

[61] Hodder, *Burns*, p. 165.

[62] Robert Montgomery, *Letter to one of the Managers of St Jude's: The Glasgow Schism* (London, 1844), p. 574.

[63] St John's was successfully united with the city's regular Episcopal church in 1804. The congregation was never fully settled, due to the disparate churchmanship of its

outrage was expressed when the Scottish rite was introduced at the Tractarian cathedral in Perth, causing their diocesan, Patrick Torry of St Andrews, Dunkeld and Dunblane, a Scottish Office supporter,[64] to react critically on 1 February 1849.[65] Again, at nearby Kirriemuir Torry reported that Drummond's advice had been sought with a view to secession, but had come to nothing.[66] Isolated groups of Evangelicals were sometimes active in agitation against the Scottish Communion Office.

At other times opposition could come from one or two people only. St Catherine's, Blairgowrie, also under Torry's oversight, had been in abeyance since 1773. It was reopened in 1841 under John Marshall, the former incumbent of Kirkcaldy, and, until he left in 1843, the Scottish Office was in regular use. When J. P. Alley, an Englishman, was appointed in 1845, the congregation applied to Torry for permission to use the Anglican communion service but was refused. For nearly three years the sacrament was not celebrated due to congregational opposition. In January 1846 Torry arranged for Thomas Walker, of Blair Atholl, to administer the Scottish Office whereupon the whole congregation, apart from one young woman, walked out in protest.[67] On 27 March 1846 the Episcopal College,

---

members and union was revoked in 1810 when H. A. Skete, of Wooller, Northumberland, was appointed. On the incumbency of George Wood, of Ingram, Durham, in 1847 a vote for union was carried with one hundred and eight in favour, seventeen against, and thirty abstentions. A party under Lord Mansfield, Major Jelf Sharp, Joseph Ranson and William Archer, left St John's in protest, and the remaining congregation broke into two factions, one High Church in favour of Torry and the other desirous to join the English Episcopal Movement, even though the Book of Common Prayer was used at St John's and Wood himself was not a supporter of the Scottish Office. It is not clear whether the Drummondites stayed at St John's. G. T. S. Farquhar, *The Episcopal History of Perth, 1689-1894* (Perth, 1894), pp. 233-250, 274. St John's Minute Book, November 1848, 'Pastoral Address by George Wood', St John's Church, Perth, Archives.

[64] In 1849 Torry sanctioned and contributed to the production of the *Book of Common Prayer According to the use of the Church of Scotland* compiled by Alexander Lendrum, incumbent of Muthill and Crieff. It contained the Scottish Communion Office as its official liturgy and was supported by Tractarians such as John Mason Neale of Sackville College, East Grinstead. All the other Scottish bishops denounced it, wishing to distance the Church from the advancing doctrine of the Oxford Movement. D. M. Bertie, *Scottish Episcopal Clergy, 1689-2000* (Edinburgh, 2000), pp. 331, 464. 'John Mason Neale: A Memoir', *Society of St Margaret's Magazine* (London, 1887-1895), pp. 120-121. Frederick Goldie, *A Short History of the Episcopal Church in Scotland* (London, 1951), pp. 120-121. Strong, *Episcopalianism*, pp. 302-303.

[65] St John's Minute Book, 1 February 1849, St John's Church, Perth, Archives.

[66] Patrick Torry to Dean Torry, 6 May 1847, NAS, CH 12/12/2402. William Perry, *George Hay Forbes* (London, 1927), p. 41.

[67] *Nairnshire Mirror*, 10 January 1846. [J. D. Miller], 'Justitia', *Peculiarities of the Scottish Episcopal Church* (Aberdeen, 1847), pp. 49-50.

Continuing Disruption

after an appeal by the congregation, requested Torry to allow the use of the English service. He agreed but feared the demise of the Scottish Office, complaining that he had been 'concussed into a compliance'.[68] Later it was reported that the opposition had been due to one individual who later became a Presbyterian. When he left, the congregation asked for the Scottish Office to be reinstated.[69] Again, at St Paul's, Carrubber's Close, Edinburgh, John Hay Forbes, Lord Medwyn, and his son, William, were staunch supporters of the Scottish Office, coming from an old Nonjuring family. In 1846 the incumbent, John Alexander, agreed to their wishes and introduced it alongside the English service which had previously been used alone. A member of the congregation, William Edwards, together with his family, left St Paul's claiming that the English Office was under threat.[70] Such incidents illustrate increasing disturbance in the Scottish Episcopal Church over the desirability of the Scottish and English Communion Offices.

The worsening atmosphere in the Church led some Evangelicals to feel increasingly ill at ease. J. H. Crowder, Daniel Bagot's successor at St James's, Edinburgh, resigned in May 1846 because 'I am compelled on certain public occasions to hear, and by my presence certainly to sanction, teaching against which my soul revolts as utterly opposed to the will of God'.[71] St James's remained in the Scottish Episcopal Church after Crowder left, still hampered from withdrawal by the terms of its foundation deed.[72] But it gradually lost its overt churchmanship when Evangelicals failed to offer themselves for its incumbency,[73] and similar situations occurred when W. P. McFarquhar left St John's, Dumfries, in 1845 and J. H. Maynard retired from Crieff in 1848.[74] The defections of Drummond, Dunbar and Miles led some Evangelicals to distance themselves from Scottish Episcopacy.

Apart from disturbances such as these, dispute over the doctrine of the Scottish Communion Office was the cause of continuing defection to the English Episcopal movement during the period 1845 to 1855. Table 9.1 shows that English Episcopal chapels were founded at Dunoon, Huntly, Nairn, Gask, Fochabers, Galloway House, Crieff, Corrimony, Arradoul[75] and Old Deer. Christchurch, Dunoon, Argyll, with seats for one hundred

---

[68] J. M. Neale, *The Life and Times of Patrick Torry* (London, 1856), pp. 219-223.
[69] *Aberdeen Journal and General Advertiser for the North of Scotland*, 20 January 1847.
[70] [J. D. Miller], 'Justitia', *Peculiarities*, p. 51. Strong, *Episcopalianism*, pp. 236-246.
[71] *Record*, 4 May 1846.
[72] See Chapter 8, p. 264.
[73] See Chapter 1, p. 9.
[74] See Chapter 1, pp. 6, 9-10.
[75] See Chapter 8, pp. 258-259.

and eighty, was founded by W. F. Burnley, benefactor of St Jude's, Glasgow. Several visitors to this popular resort on the Clyde asked for an Episcopal church there in 1845. Burnley's idea was that the church, open in the summer and served by visiting clergy, should be a distinctly Anglican place of worship. It would contrast with what he considered would be provided at the proposed Holy Trinity Scottish Episcopal Church under H. G. Pirie.[76] Burnley's intention was thus to ensure that the Anglican communion service should be available at Dunoon.

Trouble broke out at Huntly in the diocese of Moray, Ross and Caithness under Bishop David Low in 1845. J. D. Hull, ordained in the diocese of Down and Connor in the Church of Ireland, moved to Scotland from Poulton-Le-Fylde in Lancashire some time after 1839, when he became chaplain to the Duchess of Gordon at Gordon Castle, near Huntly. In 1842 he was appointed to the incumbency of the Episcopal chapel in Meadow Street, Huntly, while still remaining chaplain.[77] Hull held strong Evangelical convictions,[78] but initially he attempted to prevent the breach between Skinner and Dunbar in Aberdeen, assuming that the Church of England and the Scottish Episcopal Church were substantially the same.[79] But when Hull became acquainted with the Scottish Communion Office he found its doctrine offensive. He wrote to Low 'avowing my dislike of it', but was assured by him that a 'measure that would modify, if not wholly remove, such scruples' was in prospect.[80] Problems resurfaced for Hull in 1843 when Patrick Cheyne, of Aberdeen, published his *Vindication of the Scottish Office*.[81] Joining with the protest of Drummond, Hull objected to Low that Cheyne's doctrines were 'repudiated by all true Protestants',[82] and concluded that he could not swear obedience to the Scottish Episcopal Church. Although Low, born in the northeast of Scotland, had gradually come to recommend the surrender of the Scottish Office for the sake of

---

[76] *Record*, 20 July 1846. David McCubbin, 'Holy Trinity Dunoon, Consecrated 11 September 1850: A Barrier Against Schism', *Argyll and the Isles* (Autumn 1990), pp. 10-11.

[77] P. W. Scott, *The History of Strathbogie* (Aberdeen, 1977), p. 137.

[78] See Chapter 6, p. 203. Besides calling for a revision of the baptismal service, Hull petitioned, in 1839, for alterations to the burial service which he claimed implied that unbelievers were members of 'the household of faith', and to the Athanasian Creed because its damnatory clauses declared that people 'cannot be saved' unless they accepted the doctrine of the Trinity. J. D. Hull and W. W. Hull, *Observations on a Petition for the Revision of the Liturgy* (London, 1840), pp. 36-37.

[79] J. D. Hull to Bishop David Low, Easter Tuesday 1845, *Record*, 24 April 1845.

[80] *Ibid.*

[81] See Chapter 7, p. 235.

[82] Hull to Low, *Record*, 24 April 1845.

Continuing Disruption

expediency,[83] Hull was dissatisfied. He resigned his charge on 25 March 1845, most of his congregation following him,[84] and together they formed an English Episcopal Church which continued to meet at Meadow Street, Huntly.[85] Difference of opinion over the Scottish Communion Office was the main reason for the formation of the church here.

Problems arose in 1845 at the Episcopal chapel at Nairn which, like Huntly, was in Low's diocese. It had been started in that year as the result of popular demand from lay people. Augustus Clarke of Achveid, William Brodie of Brodie and Mrs Campbell, lessee of Kilvaroch Castle, were the trustees. Clarke, an Englishman and an Anglican, assured by Alexander Ewing, the incumbent at nearby Forres, that the Church of England and Scottish Episcopal Church were in full communion, agreed to put the chapel under Low's superintendence. But when Low tried to arrange that all save Scottish Episcopalians were to be excluded from the trusteeship of the chapel, Clarke, presumably influenced by events surrounding the previous defections, examined the doctrines of the Church more closely. The Scottish Communion Office soon became the main focus of concern. Clarke denounced it as teaching that 'the body and blood of Christ are really present on the Lord's table' and objected to its sacrificial aspects and prayers for the dead as un-Anglican.[86] Accordingly, the chapel became an English Episcopal establishment by July 1845 with John Hitchcock as incumbent in 1846.[87]

The chapel at Gask, Perthshire, located in Torry's diocese, opened officially on 24 March 1846. It stood within the grounds of Gask House, the Oliphant family home, and was built at the sole expense of the Baroness of Nairne, Caroline Oliphant, and her nephew, James Blair Oliphant.[88]

---

[83] William Blatch, *A Memoir of the Right Rev David Low* (Edinburgh, 1855), pp. 272-273.

[84] *Record*, 24 April 1845. *Aberdeen Journal and General Advertiser for the North of Scotland*, 23 July 1845.

[85] *Record*, 17 May 1845. John Archibald, *History of the Episcopal Church of Keith in the 17th, 18th and 19th Centuries with Other Reminiscences of the Diocese of Moray and Ross* (Edinburgh, 1890), pp. 118-120.

[86] *Nairnshire Mirror*, 10 January 1846, 23 February 1845. *Aberdeen Journal and General Advertiser for the North of Scotland*, 30 July 1845. George Bain, *History of Nairnshire*, Second Edition (Nairn, 1928), pp. 426-427. William Blatch, *Memoir of Bishop Low* (Edinburgh, 1855), pp. 283-298.

[87] See Chapter 1, p. 18.

[88] On September 21 1843 the Baroness wrote to her niece, Rachel Oliphant, 'what do you think of our Scottish Church now...we have need of a few excellent bishops'. Later, on 13 December 1844, she again expressed her dissatisfaction with the Scottish Episcopal Church: 'if we had [Luther] now our Scottish Church would not wear the Romish aspect that it does'. Her leanings towards Evangelicalism were again exhibited when she sent part of her plate, sometime around 1844, to be 'turned into money to help

James's early churchmanship is unclear but by the opening of the chapel he had joined the English Episcopalians, calling on Dunbar to read the prayers and Drummond to preach the evening sermon.[89] Thus Evangelicalism was his probable churchmanship by then. His wife, Henrietta, also appeared to be an Evangelical since, after his death in 1847, she joined the Free Church at Aberuthven.[90] Their perception of the Scottish Communion Office was unlikely to have matched Torry's, and was thus the probable explanation for connecting Gask chapel to the English Episcopalian movement.

At Fochabers, Aberdeenshire, similar concerns clearly prevailed. The church there had been opened on 1 August 1834 under the patronage of the Duke and Duchess of Gordon.[91] Although initially putting it under the jurisdiction of Low, the duchess appointed only Church of England clergy since she was anxious that they should preach 'the same Evangelical doctrines, scriptural in their essence and according to the literal and natural sense of the articles of the Church of England'. She did not think it 'possible to find a Scottish Episcopalian who would preach those doctrines which I believe essential to salvation'.[92] By 1847 the duchess, who had become a member of the Free Church, decided that the Scottish Communion Office was doctrinally unacceptable. As she explained to a member of the congregation 'I have been led to the convictions which preclude me from giving any countenance or assistance with the Scottish Episcopal Church which I believe to be in error'.[93] Thereupon she placed the chapel in the English Episcopal movement, very probably taking advice from Hull, with G. F. Williamson, formerly at Colney Heath, Hertfordshire, as her appointed incumbent. The congregation petitioned her without success for the reinstatement of their old connection with Scottish Episcopalianism. When the duchess closed the church in 1848, rather than granting their wishes, they were forced to attend the chapel at Buckie in the diocese of Aberdeen. They pointed out to the duchess in December 1848 that they had never wanted to use the Scottish Office, and that all chapels but two in the diocese of Moray used the Book of Common Prayer, as was the case at Buckie. But while they argued that the Scottish rite posed no

---

the sustention Fund of the new Free Church'. James's early religious sentiments are less clear, since between 1834 and 1837 he fathered some illegitimate children. M. E. M. Graham, *The Oliphants of Gask. Records of a Jacobite Family* (London, 1910), pp. 441-449.

[89] *Record*, 6 April 1846.

[90] Graham, *Oliphants*, pp. 446-462.

[91] J. B. Craven, *History of the Episcopal Church in the Diocese of Moray* (London, 1889), p. 307.

[92] Duchess of Gordon to members of the congregation at Fochabers, 27 April 1847, pp. 1-2. Archives of Gordon Chapel, Fochabers, NAS, CD 44/38/86/8.

[93] Duchess of Gordon to Edward Wagstaffe, 23 December 1848, Archives of Gordon Chapel, Fochabers, NAS, CD 44/38/86/6.

threat to them, the revelation that, at Buckie, 'the Scottish Office [was] bound into the English Prayer Book by individuals for their own convenience' probably cemented the resolve of the duchess.[94] Her opposition to the Scottish Communion Office appears to have been the main reason for severing Fochabers chapel from the Church.

While no details of the church at Galloway House have been found,[95] the congregation established at Crieff, Perthshire, in 1849 was a clear outcome of eucharistic agitation. In 1846 a new Episcopal church, St Michael's, opened under Torry's jurisdiction with Alexander Lendrum as incumbent. Strong support for the Scottish Office was reflected in the church's deed of 1847 which stated that the Scottish Communion Office 'on every occasion of administration...shall be used', and that if an incumbent allowed the use of the Communion Office of the Church of England or any other Office...he shall...forfeit all right to the incumbency of the said church'.[96] In Crieff, the English Office was, in effect, forbidden. By September 1848 several local Episcopalians and visitors in the town expressed a wish to worship in an Episcopal chapel in connection with the Church of England, where the English rite would be used. Drummond was invited to speak on the subject in August 1848. As a result, on 27 September 1848, a committee of Lord Elibank, George Drummond Graeme of Inchbrakie, James Gillespie Graham of Ochill, Henrietta Oliphant of Gask, William Macdonald Macdonald of St Martin's and Rossie Castle and a member of St Peter's, Montrose, Robert Speir of Culdees Castle, and Captain Francis Grove from St Thomas's, Edinburgh, announced that a congregation would be formed at Crieff under 'a faithful and efficient minister of the Church of England'.[97] The new English Episcopal Chapel was set up in 1849 with A. C. Rainey, an old friend of Drummond's, as incumbent. He was in Irish orders, formerly from the diocese of Cashel under Bishop Daly.[98] Opposition at St Michael's to the Scottish Communion Office, which by its foundation deed was the only service to be offered there, was the major cause of the formation of the English Episcopal chapel at Crieff.

Three small English Episcopal congregations, formed around 1850, probably arose for similar reasons. Thomas Ogilvy, a landowner in Low's diocese, with a house at Corrimony, in the northeast of Glen Urquhart, Ross

---

[94] Letter from the Congregation of Fochabers to the Duchess of Gordon, December 1848, Archives of Gordon Chapel, Fochabers, NAS, CD GG/38/86/4. *Cf. ENCS*, pp. 275-283.

[95] See Chapter 1, p. 12 for Galloway House.

[96] Deed of St Michael's Church, Crieff, 1847, Perth City Library Archives, MS 103/11/12.

[97] *Scottish Magazine and Churchman's Review* (December 1848), pp. 622-626.

[98] St Peter's Minute Book, 16 December 1850, p. 178, St Peter's Church, Montrose, Archives. *Scottish Magazine and Churchman's Review*, 1853, p. 495.

and Cromarty, was a member of St Thomas's, Edinburgh.[99] He opened an English Episcopal chapel in his Highland home in 1850, presumably because he agreed with Drummond's analysis of the Scottish Office. Similar concerns probably prevailed at Arradoul, Aberdeenshire, given its previous history, and at Selkirk. Certainly there had been constant agitation in Selkirkshire between Episcopalians and Presbyterians over the theology of the baptismal and communion services, together with apostolic succession, ever since the consecration of the Episcopal chapel at Jedburgh, in 1844.[100] In 1854, one of the Murray family of Philiphaugh, a relative of Lord Elibank,[101] withdrew the new chapel in Selkirk, of which he was a chief subscriber, from the Scottish Episcopal Church.[102] Corrimony, and possibly Selkirk and Arradoul, were, therefore, seemingly set up in response to the climate of hostility to the Scottish Communion Office.

Thus eucharistic agitation was the major factor in the defections to English Episcopalianism in the period 1845 to 1855. Sometimes it seems to have been aggravated by the presence of a bishop who was a supporter of the Scottish Office. This was apparent at Gask and Crieff under Torry[103] and at Arradoul and Old Deer under Skinner. Again, Huntly, Nairn, Fochabers and Corrimony, all in Moray, Ross and Caithness, were in a diocese where there was much agitation over the Scottish Office. It had led some of the clergy, in 1843, along with Low, in 1845, to distance themselves from the rite.[104] The situation, hardly a comfortable one, could only have added to the resolve of some Evangelicals to secede. The Scottish Communion Office was a bar to peace in Episcopal Scotland in 1845 to 1855.

Nonetheless it is apparent that, once more, other considerations cemented the resolve of the Evangelicals involved. For instance Hull, like Miles, regarded the case against Dunbar as 'uncanonical',[105] and, on 16 February 1845, officiated for him at St Paul's, Aberdeen, inviting him back to preach at Huntly.[106] Again, Hull, having already withdrawn from the Church in March 1845, refused to attend the Diocesan Synod called to

---

[99] Thomas Ogilvy, *Dying Scenes in my own Family* (Privately printed, 1854), p. 46.

[100] Kenneth M. Phin, *Letter to the Right Honourable Lord John Scott on the Recent Movement of the Scottish Episcopacy in the Counties of Roxburgh and Selkirk* (Edinburgh, 1856), p. 24. *Inverness Advertiser*, 24 October 1854.

[101] See Chapter 10, p. 323.

[102] *Inverness Advertiser*, 24 October 1854.

[103] See Chapter 7, p. 236 for Torry's analysis of the Scottish Communion Office. With Alexander Lendrum, incumbent of Muthill, he produced a Scottish Prayer Book in 1851, which included the Scottish Communion Office as its only eucharistic rite. See Strong, *Episcopalianism*, pp. 302-303.

[104] See Chapter 7, p. 239 and Chapter 9, p. 297.

[105] J. D. Hull to David Low, Easter Tuesday 1845, *Record*, 24 April 1845.

[106] *Record*, 17 May 1845.

discuss his case in April. As a result, the Synod excommunicated him on 23 April 1845, on the grounds of 'acts of irregularity, and...forgetting his ordination vows and solemn promise of canonical obedience'.[107] The difference in attitude between some Evangelicals and High Churchmen concerning the necessity of obedience to Church laws was as evident in Huntly as it had been in Edinburgh, Aberdeen and Glasgow.

Meanwhile, Clarke in Nairn cited the 'angry spirit...exhibited by some of the Bishops and clergy' towards himself and English Episcopalians as compounding his decision.[108] Tractarian innovations, regarded as un-Protestant, also added to the ferment. In 1845 Hull included 'the systematic expunging of the term Protestant' from the canons of 1838, and the ceremonial at the opening of the church at Jedburgh, in this category.[109] Novelties at Lendrum's chapel in Crieff – the adoption of 'altars, crucifixes and ladies of charity' – did not appeal to Evangelicals in the area.[110] Trouble broke out at Old Deer in the diocese of Aberdeen, under Dunbar's antagonist, William Skinner. A group led by Admiral Ferguson, of Pitfour, split off from the Scottish Episcopal congregation in 1850 and set up an English Episcopal chapel in the town under James Newsam from Bristol. The reason for their defection was because the incumbent, Arthur Ranken, did not 'perform divine service according to the form and manner of the Church of England'.[111] Although Ranken used only the Book of Common Prayer, he appears to have introduced a range of rubrical directions, commenting: 'had your pastor submitted to square his theology to the popular puritan pattern; to cut and to carve and abbreviate the Church service after the approved model of a London Proprietary Chapel where religion is made easy...perhaps we might have enjoyed peace'.[112] In 1843 Drummond had said 'I have not separated from the Scottish Episcopal Church because it has too many or too few vestments, too many or too few lights, because its sermons are too short or its prayers too long, but because its restrictions are too severe'.[113] But by 1845, with the increasing success

---

[107] *Ibid.*

[108] Augustus Clarke to David Low, 23 December 1845, *Nairnshire Mirror*, 10 January 1846.

[109] *Record*, 24 April 1845.

[110] *Christian News*, 22 March 1849.

[111] *Scottish Ecclesiastical Journal*, May 1851, October 1853.

[112] Arthur Ranken, *The Church of England in Scotland. A Pastoral Address to the Congregation of St Drostane's Church, Deer, Diocese of Aberdeen* (Edinburgh, 1853), pp. 1-7, 12.

[113] Drummond, *Sketch*, pp. 80-81.'Ultra-Rubicans' by 1845 commonly informed on Sunday the Holy Days and Fasts for the next week. They held Daily Offices, private baptism, weekly offertory and ridiculed changing to the black gown for preaching. Some English Tractarians by 1845 were noted for bowing and kneeling and the use of pictures,

of Tractarianism, such innovations were causing Evangelicals to feel uncomfortable in the Scottish Episcopal Church. Thus the years 1845 to 1855 saw the establishment of nine English Episcopal churches. Hostility to the Scottish Communion Office, exacerbated by what Evangelicals saw as unnecessary restrictive episcopal discipline and rising Tractarian influence in the Church, was the main reason for the defections.

Internal Disruptions, 1854-1865

Between 1854 and 1864, three new English Episcopal chapels were opened as a result of internal conflicts in the major congregations of St Paul's, Aberdeen, St Thomas's, Edinburgh and St Jude's, Glasgow. Trouble erupted at St Paul's in 1854. As will be explained later, Dunbar was disillusioned with the Church of England because he felt it offered little support to English Episcopalianism. He had quarrelled with others in the group over the matter in 1848, leading to a split in his congregation.[114] The matter seemed to sour relations between Dunbar and his curate, S. A. Walker, since the two had hardly been on speaking terms after Walker's appointment in the same year.[115] In January 1854 Walker resigned and a disruption ensued with nearly a third of the congregation leaving on 12 January 1854 because they 'were not satisfied with the sole ministrations of Dunbar and they could not with advantage to their spiritual condition continue to attend St Paul's'.[116] They set up another English Episcopal chapel in the city which first met in Sinclair's Hall, under Abel Woodroofe, from southern Ireland, who had occasionally officiated at St Paul's.[117] In May 1854, they bought Free Greyfriars Church in Crown Street, naming it St James's.[118]

Matters got worse at St Paul's when the managers invited a previous temporary assistant, A. B. Campbell, to return after Walker's resignation. Initially Dunbar was favourable, presumably feeling he and Campbell could co-operate. But it appears that Dunbar still had opponents at St Paul's, including a vestryman who was on good terms with Campbell. When the vestryman delivered a letter late to Dunbar from Campbell, Dunbar suspected that a plot was brewing to depose him. Campbell remarked that

---

crucifixes and candles. See J. S. Reed, *Glorious Battle: the Cultural Politics of Victorian Anglo-Catholicism* (London, 1998), pp. 29-32.

[114] See Chapter 9, p. 313.

[115] *Scottish Magazine and Churchman's Review*, August 1848.

[116] 'History of St James's from the Minute Books', pp. 1-2, St James's Church, Aberdeen, Archives.

[117] *Aberdeen Journal and General Advertiser for the North of Scotland*, 18 January 1854.

[118] 'History of St James's from Minute Book', pp. 3-4.

Continuing Disruption

Dunbar should examine the reasons 'lest there be some great ministerial defect in yourself',[119] commenting that 'Lady Dunbar...would join me in counselling a conciliatory course'. Thereupon, Dunbar grew increasingly impatient accusing Campbell of 'an act of gratuitous impertinence unbecoming in a gentleman'.[120] As a result, another group left St Paul's and joined St James's in May 1854.[121] It seems that the split with the English Episcopalians in 1848, which cast doubt on Dunbar's loyalty to the Church of England, was probably the cause of the protracted problems at St Paul's.

The affair at St Thomas's concerned a dispute in 1854 between Drummond's assistant, Richard Hibbs, and some members of the congregation, and ultimately with Drummond himself. The arguments were intense and dragged on until 1858. Hibbs had left St Paul's, Covent Garden, London, in 1853, when Drummond appointed him because of congregational growth at St Thomas's.[122] Hibbs's problem appeared to be his 'violence of manner' when preaching.[123] On the Day of National Humiliation, 29 November 1853, he 'gave offence' when he pressed 'upon the wealthy congregation...the urgent claims of the Lazarus in the Old Town of Edinburgh'.[124] In the sermon he repeated critical views he had published in 1851 on the Poor Law Amendment Act of 1834 and the role of the guardians.[125] The content of Hibb's pamphlet, illustrated by remarks such as 'millionaires...set on their pinnacles of gold by the hands of the million',[126] caused Daniel Ainslee, a vestryman, 'to declare with considerable emphasis and warmth of manner, his objection'.[127] More antagonism arose when Hibbs criticised some members of the congregation who had attended the Italian Opera in Edinburgh, an event which he regarded as 'immoral'.[128] But Drummond had also appealed on the Day of National Humiliation: 'enlarge and increase the means at the disposal of the Mission [in the Canongate]...not indeed as a work of merit, but as a

---

[119] A. B. Campbell, *An Authenticated Statement of Circumstances Connected to the Late Abortive Attempt to Elect a Second Minister in St Paul's Chapel, with Correspondence Relating thererto* (Aberdeen 1854), pp. 12-20.

[120] *Ibid.*, pp. 12-15.

[121] *Aberdeen Herald*, 20 May 1854. *Scottish Ecclesiastical Journal*, October 1854.

[122] *Correspondence Between the Rev. D. T. K. Drummond and the Rev. Richard Hibbs* (Edinburgh, 1854), p. 3.

[123] *Truth Vindicated. Pamphlets Concerning the Dispute Between the Rev. Richard Hibbs and the Rev. D. T. K. Drummond* (London, 1858), p. 57.

[124] Hibbs, *Truth Vindicated*, p. 56.

[125] Richard Hibbs, *God's Plea for the Poor: Observations Concerning the Poor and the New Poor Law* (London, 1851), pp. 22-24.

[126] Hibbs, *Plea for the Poor*, pp. 9, 12.

[127] Hibbs, *Truth Vindicated*, p. 57.

[128] Hibbs, *Truth Vindicated*, p. 56.

thanksgiving for God's sparing mercy to you';[129] and since he appointed Hibbs after the publication of the disputed pamphlet, the two probably held similar sentiments on the Poor Law. Again, Drummond was also a strong critic of the theatre,[130] and thus it appears that the main complaint against Hibbs was the tone of his preaching. The congregation was used to being challenged, but it was not accustomed to the robust approach of Hibbs.

Discontent also existed among some Presbyterian members of St Thomas's because Hibbs used appointed readings from the Prayer Book rather than adopting a freer approach. This prompted Hibbs to remark, 'I am not Free Church enough to please some'.[131] Hibbs's problems at St Thomas's thus escalated, and Drummond wrote to him on 6 February 1854, asking him 'to weigh the question in your own mind, whether your present position is the right one' and suggesting he take some time to reflect on the matter.[132] Hibbs replied in a strongly worded letter on 8 February 1854, the tone of which was unacceptable to Drummond who, on 9 February, asked him to leave immediately.[133] A deputation from the vestry, consisting of J. H. Balfour, Daniel Ainslie and James Walker met with Hibbs on 28 February 1854 in an attempt to persuade him to withdraw his letter of 8 February, in which they had identified thirteen charges against Drummond such as 'duplicity', 'unchristian conduct', leading Hibbs into 'ruinous expense', and 'fostering antipathy' against Hibbs in reply to his preaching against 'the opera, worldliness and hypocrisy'. However, Hibbs refused to comply.[134] On 7 March 1854 Hibbs published all his private correspondence on the matters, together with a letter to the congregation containing strong criticism of Drummond. At the close of the same week he announced that he would open a new chapel in Edinburgh. Initially it met in a hired room until 1857 when St Vincent's, was built in St Stephen's Street, in the New Town of Edinburgh under the patronage of William Forbes Skene, Historiographer Royal for Scotland.[135]

More trouble broke out when it was discovered that Hibbs had slightly altered his letter of 8 February before publication, making it less severe. At Hibbs's request the printer compared the letters on 21 June 1854, but he confirmed that there were twenty six discrepancies and that sixteen of them altered 'the meaning invariably in one direction'. Hibbs threatened to take

---

[129] D. T. K. Drummond, *The Three Voices. A Sermon Preached on Tuesday November 29 1853 being the Day of Humiliation for the Pestilence* (Edinburgh, 1853), pp. 8-9.

[130] See Chapter 5, pp. 177-178.

[131] *Correspondence between Drummond and Hibbs*, pp. 17-18.

[132] *Ibid.*, pp. 11-12.

[133] *Ibid.*, p. 19.

[134] Copy of Vestry Minute, 28 February 1854, DRO, D5550/3/5/26.

[135] Hibbs, *Truth Vindicated*, pp. 28, 31.

the matter to court, but from 7 July 1854 Drummond refused to make the disputed letter public, finally giving in on 4 November 1854. After this, the matter seems to have been dropped by Hibbs until 1858 when, apparently unprovoked, he published the complete correspondence with further accusations against Drummond and the vestry, but no further unrest ensued.[136]

The dispute was so severe that Drummond opted for silence throughout. Together with a letter to the *Record* in September 1855 when, following numerous enquiries from clergy in England, he declared that Hibbs's chapel was nothing to do with St Thomas's,[137] the only statement he made was on 18 October 1855. Anxious to restore stability, Drummond addressed his congregation explaining, 'I thought it better to run the risk of being both misrepresented and misunderstood than to encourage a controversy...by an unseemly discussion'.[138] The affair with Hibbs could have escalated into a public brawl, damaging to the English Episcopal movement.

The disruption at St Jude's was less acrimonious. It concerned its status as a Church of England congregation. Shortly before Miles left in 1863, the vestry decided to repay the debt owing to George Burns and W. F. Burnley, its patrons, and to draw up a new constitution plainly stating its English Episcopal position. G. K. Flindt,[139] Miles's replacement, objected to some of its clauses, although it is unclear what his concerns were. Flindt, rather than forcing matters, offered to resign, but Burns and Burnley decided to leave St Jude's after a financial settlement and found a new Glasgow church which, never having been part of the Scottish Episcopal Church, could be defended from charges of schism. Sir Archibald Campbell of Blythswood acted as chairman of the proceedings and until St Silas's was built, the congregation met in the Queen's Rooms, Glasgow, with W. T. Turpin, former chaplain of Albert Hospital, Dublin, as its first incumbent.[140]

Factors similar to those concerning the foundation of the earlier chapels contributed to these mid-century disruptions. Doctrine was very prominent. All the chapels were set up as part of the Church of England. One of the main aims at St Vincent's was to provide protection 'against

---

[136] *Correspondence between Drummond and Hibbs*, pp. 6-9.

[137] *Record*, 29 September 1855.

[138] Hibbs, *Truth Vindicated*, pp. 23-24.

[139] Gustavus Flindt was formerly curate of Keynsham, Somerset, 1853-1857. D. M. Bertie, *Scottish Episcopal Clergy, 1689-2000* (Edinburgh, 2000), p. 258.

[140] *Record*, 18 November 1863. Also, a paper attached to the inside fly leaf of St Silas's Register Book, Mitchell Library, Glasgow, TD 1250/6. Turpin graduated from Trinity College, Dublin, in 1857 *Graduates of University of Dublin* (Dublin, 1869), p. 573. *Clergy List 1865* (London, 1865).

Tractarianism',[141] and notably the ethos of the founders of St Silas's in November 1863 was 'to uphold the integrity of their position as members of the Church of England, enjoying her liturgy, and benefiting by her orthodox doctrines, as secured to the Church by her canons'.[142] The problem of the Scottish Communion Office remained paramount.

The involvement of the laity in steering the events, particularly in Aberdeen and Glasgow, was important. Moreover, Presbyterians were once more part of the new congregations – both 'Established and Free' were present in force, for instance, at St Vincent's.[143] But the laity, who formed the governing body of trustees and vestry of the churches, and were the wealthiest and best educated members, could also cause problems for the incumbent who was in effect their servant. While the early days of the English Episcopal movement had been marked by the way the vestries tended to support their clergy as they worked together to consolidate the cause, later, when the congregations became more established, the consensus tended to fragment. This was apparent at St Paul's and St Thomas's in particular. For instance, at the latter, Hibbs remarked to Drummond, 'I have stood by you on every occasion, always defending you whenever disparaged. It had been easy for me to make a party against you'.[144] In such a setting it was not difficult for the wishes of the vestry to become the rule of the church, even if the bulk of the congregation and incumbent wanted something different – as Hibbs remarked, 'it is a notorious fact that for some time past...a small minority have endeavoured to rule the majority'.[145] The English Episcopal movement remained as much one of the laity as of the clergy, but this tended to foster internal divisions.

However, new factors were evident. While mission and preaching the gospel message were important – one of the aims of St Vincent's was reaching the increasing numbers of English and Irish families moving into Edinburgh[146] – an underlying problem was evident. The English Episcopalians would have benefited from superintendence by a bishop. A warning voice from outside might have defused difficult situations. A letter

---

[141] Hibbs, *Truth Vindicated*, p. 13.

[142] *Cf.* Gavin White, *The Scottish Episcopal Church A New History* (Edinburgh, 1998), pp. 77-78. It is quite wrong to assume with White that St Silas's entered into no more 'mere fulminations about the Scottish Liturgy and parliamentary authority'. The Vestry there were among the most outspoken against the Scottish Communion Office and continually strove for official recognition by the Church of England for the rest of the century. They represented some of the most vociferous resistance to moves towards union with the Scottish Episcopal Church. See Chapter 10, pp. 336, 350-354.

[143] Hibbs, *Truth Vindicated*, p. 31.

[144] *Correspondence between Drummond and Hibbs*, p. 18.

[145] *Ibid.*, p. 16.

[146] Hibbs, *Truth Vindicated*, p. 13.

written to Drummond by a fellow clergyman from England makes this clear: 'with us there would have been an immediate appeal to the Bishop of the Diocese',[147] and an episcopal appointment was to remain a goal for the separatists for many years.[148] Internal squabbles might have been solved by hierarchical oversight.

Additionally, lack of such supervision placed too much responsibility on individual incumbents. Incoming clergy, such as Hibbs and Campbell, did not always adapt to the environment and established leaders, with no superior to turn to, became mentally and physically exhausted and unable to deal with internal problems. Dunbar's odd behaviour towards Campbell probably indicates some sort of mental breakdown. A medical report on Drummond in August 1849 revealed no organic disease but recommended 'good food, kind friends, cheerful society'.[149] But he was so ill by 1852 that his congregation enabled him, with his family, to spend five months in Switzerland and Italy. Then in 1855, during the problems with Hibbs, he was again unable to cope and spent further time on the continent.[150] Differences of opinion were almost inevitable in any congregation, but the English Episcopal clergy had to deal with these alongside all their normal clerical duties and defence of their position in Scotland. They were under an unusual amount of strain, which probably made it more difficult for them to deal with disagreements when they arose.

These events could have had a detrimental effect on the image of English Episcopalianism. The *Scottish Episcopal Journal*, referring to St Paul's and St Thomas's in 1854, remarked, 'it is ever the fate of those who once perversely do wrong to fall into deeper sin', and highlighted the unpleasant tone of the published correspondence as 'calculated to startle those who follow what is popularly called 'Evangelicalism' as exhibiting Christianity in its mildest and purest form'.[151] However, St Thomas's continued to flourish, and its eight hundred seats were filled even after some of the congregation left to form St Vincent's,[152] which was also a viable cause. There was an initial drop in the numbers at St Paul's,[153] but eventually the two Aberdeen congregations survived until the 1890s, as did St Jude's. English Episcopalianism remained attractive, despite internal mid-century problems.

---

[147] *Ibid.*, p. 21.

[148] See Chapter 10, p. 352.

[149] Medical report from A. Hood to D. T. K. Drummond, 16 August 1849, DRO, D5550/3/5/26.

[150] *Memoir*, pp. lxxiii, xc.

[151] *Scottish Ecclesiastical Journal*, October 1854.

[152] *Memoir, passim.*

[153] *Aberdeen Herald*, 20 May 1854.

Later Disruptions, 1861-1887

The causes of the earlier disruptions recurred later in the century. The doctrine of the Scottish Communion Office remained paramount, especially since some advanced Tractarians and Ritualists found it conducive to their theology of the real presence.[154] The English Episcopalians were active in pressing for a revision of the Scottish canons to remove the service from the Church,[155] and their new congregations founded during this period – Wemyss Bay; St John's, Dundee; Hunter's Quay; Cally; Johnstone; and Balmacara – grew up against this background.

Nevertheless, outbursts against Ritualism and the Scottish rite did not always result in the formation of English Episcopal chapels. When a visiting archdeacon from England, John Alexander Matthias, visited St Saviour's Scottish Episcopal Church, Bridge of Allan, near Stirling, on Good Friday, 1873, he wrote to Charles Wordsworth, Bishop of St Andrews, Dunkeld and Dunblane, that the service 'disgusted me'. He refused contact with its incumbent, Thomas Boyle, and by Easter Sunday he hired a hall 'where unritualistic service could be celebrated'.[156] Trouble continued at St Saviour's, with a congregation setting itself up at Wells House in 1876 under C. H. Johnstone, formerly of St Saviour's, Coalpit Heath, Gloucestershire, who eventually re-united the two congregations in 1879.[157] In 1885 there was dissension at Trinity Episcopal Church, Paisley, near Glasgow, where 'a portion of the congregation...who object to alleged Puseyite innovations' in the services considered forming an English Episcopal chapel 'in connection with St Silas's as we are bound in duty to Protestantism'.[158] Although nothing further appears to have happened there, the episode in Paisley, together with that in Bridge of Allan, illustrates continuing doctrinal dissension in the Scottish Episcopal Church.

However, when similar problems broke out at St Mary Magdalene's, Blinshall Street, Dundee, in 1867, secession followed. The bulk of the congregation was composed of Ulstermen who were employed in the developing textile industries.[159] Coming from the Church of Ireland they possessed a distinctly Protestant, if not clearly Evangelical, churchmanship.[160] A. P. Forbes, Bishop of Brechin, appointed fellow Tractarians and encouraged the frequent use of the Scottish Communion

---

[154] See Chapter 7, pp. 241-244. Chapter 10, pp. 335-336, 343-347, 359.

[155] See Chapter 10, *passim*.

[156] *Record*, 25 April 1873.

[157] Bertie, *Scottish Episcopal Clergy*, pp. 316, 631, 647. Malcolm Allan, a member of St Saviour's, Bridge of Allan, directed me to these references.

[158] *Scottish Guardian*, 30 January 1885.

[159] Chapter 2, p. 39.

[160] William Humphrey, *Recollections of Scottish Episcopalianism* (London, 1896), p. 35.

Continuing Disruption 309

Office in an attempt to consolidate his diocese.[161] Thus William Humphrey, a Tractarian, who later became a Roman Catholic, took up the incumbency of St Mary's in 1867.[162] Humphrey replaced another Tractarian, David Greig, who had already split the congregation by appealing to the young people, while their parents remained 'sternly Protestant'.[163] However, although it is not clear whether Humphrey introduced the Scottish Communion Office to St Mary's by 1867, he had certainly introduced Ritualistic practices of which a reporter in the *Dundee Advertiser* wrote: 'it was downright Roman Catholic Popery...Mr Humphrey should leave at once...he had better take his bonnets with him...They are just as much use as his candlesticks'.[164] It was all too much for the Orangemen of the congregation. A group left St Mary's in 1868, and formed a new congregation, St John's, within the Scottish Episcopal Church, with D. J. Mulkerns, an Irish convert from Roman Catholicism, as incumbent. It met in halls, first in Barak Street, then in Lindsay Street, and ultimately in a new iron church in Logie Den.[165] Eventually, in 1870, the congregation broke away to form an English Episcopal church, because its members 'could not remain and worship God in the way their fathers taught them, and their life would have been rendered bitter if they did'.[166] Ritualism at St Mary's, compounded with the use of the Scottish Communion Office in the diocese of Brechin, appears to have been the cause of the separation of St John's.

Likewise, the services at Emmanuel Church, Hunter's Quay, Argyll, established in 1870 by C. J. Anderson, a local benefactor,[167] were recalled by the Bishop of the Arctic, Archibald Lang, a child attender, as 'plain' compared to those of 'the Episcopal Church in Scotland [which] was considered very ritualistic'.[168] Similarly, the chapel at Wemyss Bay presented 'the Church of England to the Scottish people as a thoroughly Protestant, Evangelical and Scriptural Church'.[169] When Horatio Murray Stewart opened his chapel at Cally House, Dumfries, as an English

---

[161] John Quinn, 'The Mission of the Churches to the Irish in Dundee 1846-1886', (M. Litt. thesis, University of Stirling, 1993), pp. 134-135. Forbes was ambivalent about ritual, forbidding the use of vestments in his diocese, because the Scottish canons appeared to disallow them, but wearing them in England where he considered the law to be more lax. Rowan Strong, *Alexander Forbes of Brechin* Oxford, 1995), p. 84.

[162] Humphrey, *Recollections*, pp. 34-35, 43-44.

[163] Quinn, 'Mission to Irish', p. 142.

[164] *Dundee Advertiser*, 31 December 1867.

[165] Unnamed newspaper cuttings, October to December 1869, Lamb Collection, 183 (2).

[166] Unnamed newspaper cuttings, undated but possibly 21 November 1874, Lamb Collection, 183 (2).

[167] *Dunoon Herald and Corval Advertiser*, March 1905.

[168] Archibald Fleming, *Archibald of the Arctic* (London, 1957), pp. 18-19.

[169] Hodder, *Burns*, p. 260.

Episcopal church for the neighbourhood in 1872 it might have been a reaction to the ritualistic services at St John's, Dumfries, where 'choral displays, banners, ceremony and pomp' were the norm at that time.[170] Parallel concerns prevailed in the English Episcopal chapel at Johnstone, near Glasgow, opened in 1874 for Irish immigrants working in the textile mills. The chief subscriber of £500, C. H. Bousefield, of Messrs. Finlayson, Bousfield and Company and a trustee of St Jude's,[171] together with the incumbent Alfred Daniel repudiated 'any connection with those professing ritualistic doctrine'.[172] Again, at Balmacara, Ross and Cromarty, begun in 1887 as a specific project of St Silas's, Glasgow, the services were advertised as conducted in the Presbyterian form, emphasising their doctrine and practice as Protestant.[173] English Episcopalianism, stimulated by a reaction both against the Scottish Communion Office and Ritualism in the Scottish Episcopal Church, opened seven churches, including St Silas's, Glasgow,[174] in the period 1861 to 1887.

Consolidating Factors, 1845-1887

After 1842 the English Episcopalians did not command the good will of all the Anglican bishops, some of whom distinctly censured them. For instance, when the chapel at Nairn left the Scottish Episcopal Church in 1845, the Bishop of London, C. J. Blomfield, withdrew his subscription of £5 towards its building because it was not 'approved by the Bishop' in Scotland. Likewise, Henry Phillpotts, Bishop of Exeter, declared the chapel to be in a state of 'manifest schism' and the 'notion of [it] being in connection with the Church of England, unless through the Bishop of Moray, is monstrous'.[175] On 19 August 1845 William Howley, Archbishop of Canterbury, replied to a letter from Alexander Ewing, incumbent of Forres in Low's diocese, concerning the legal status of the English Episcopalians. In it he gave support to the Scottish Episcopal Church as being 'in communion with the united Church of England and Ireland' under the Act of 1840. Of the English Episcopalians he said 'we know nothing. In order to prove their right...they should be able to show what Bishop in England has authority by law or custom, to regulate their worship, and to

---

[170] *Dumfries and Galloway Courier*, 23 January 1872. *Cf.* Jean S. Maxwell, *The Centenary Book of St John's, Dumfries* (Dumfries, 1968), pp. 33, 45-58. *Glasgow Herald*, 8 September 1877.

[171] *Glasgow Herald*, 15 January 1874. *Scottish Guardian*, 10 July 1885.

[172] *Glasgow Herald*, 15 January 1874.

[173] *St Silas's Magazine*, August 1889. St Silas's Church, Glasgow, Archives.

[174] See pp. 305-306 above.

[175] *Aberdeen Journal and General Advertiser for the North of Scotland*, 10 September 1845.

direct or control their ministers in respect of discipline or doctrine'.[176] The secessionists lacked substantial Episcopal approval.

However, the English Episcopalians replied to such criticism strongly. Hull wrote to Phillpotts on 13 September 1845, disclaiming all accusation of schism and placing it at the door of Scottish Episcopalianism on the grounds of 'so foul and fatal a tide of heresy'. He challenged the Church of England, asking 'why was not the strong arm of authority...exerted to close the floodgate that was letting in error upon the country?'[177] Drummond answered Howley on 17 September 1845, asserting that the Act of 1840 did not negate the protection afforded to the seceders by that of 1712.[178] Thus the English Episcopalians, increasingly entering into confident debate with the highest authorities to substantiate the legality and spiritual cogency of their separation, would probably have rallied others to their cause.

Again, three deputations of English Episcopalians to England in 1846, 1849 and 1872, and two legal opinions obtained in 1871 and 1873, all of which will be discussed in Chapter 10, were important in contributing to the viability of the movement.[179] The 1846 visit brought the affairs in Scotland into focus for English Evangelicals. Limited concessions granted by the Archbishop of Canterbury, J. B. Sumner, at the 1849 event, and support elicited in 1872, together with ratification of the movement obtained by the legal opinions, helped to solidify the separatist cause by bringing it clearly into the public domain.

Likewise, the allegiance of clergy outside Scotland in the face of the censure from Howley and some of the English bishops was crucial. Edward Bickersteth's earlier commendation of Drummond and Dunbar[180] was mirrored in his support for Hull in 1845, when he wrote, 'I cannot but rejoice that you and your people have left the Scottish Episcopal Church which has manifested such departures from the faith in fostering papal corruptions...I doubt not that the Lord will bless the separation'.[181] When Robert Daly, the Bishop of Cashel in the south of Ireland, condoned the English Episcopalians in 1845, he, too, provided an important boost to the

---

[176] *Ibid.*

[177] J. D. Hull, *A Letter Respectfully Addressed to the Rt. Rev. the Lord Bishop of Exeter* (London, 1845), pp. 9-10.

[178] *Record*, 2 October 1845.

[179] Chapter 10 discusses these points in detail. The English Episcopalians petitioned for episcopal oversight in 1849 but Sumner did not concede to their wishes. However, his sympathy for their position and his promise to accept them into incumbencies in his diocese did much to give confidence to their cause. See Chapter 10 pp. 320-326. Again, in 1872, English and Irish Evangelicals assured the deputation of clerical assistance. See pp. 341-343. The important legal documents of 1871, see p. 338, and 1873, see p. 342, clarified the legal and doctrinal issues surrounding English Episcopalianism.

[180] See Chapter 8, pp. 268-271. See also Chapter 9, pp. 292-293.

[181] *Record*, 29 April 1845.

movement. His correspondence with Low and C. H. Terrot, Bishop of Edinburgh, published in the *Record* from June to December 1845, set out his opposition to the Scottish Communion Office, regretting that 'the Scottish Episcopal Church has departed so widely from the doctrines of the Church of England', and pointing to the danger 'when the Tractarian movement in England is doing so much toward an approximation to the Church of Rome'.[182] By 25 November he asserted to Low that the Scottish Office 'justifies the separation from the Scottish Episcopal Church'.[183] His intervention could only have stimulated the English Episcopal cause.

Clerical visits to the separatist pulpits also provided impetus to the movement. For instance, Dunoon was regularly manned, even in the face of opposition from some Anglican bishops. In 1846 the Bishop of Down and Connor, Richard Mant,[184] disciplined one of his presbyters, William MacIlwaine, a friend of Hull's, for preaching there. H. G. Pirie, the Scottish Episcopal incumbent at Dunoon, informed Mant of the situation because he saw it as 'unsettling...my own infant flock'. But MacIlwaine defended his action since he believed the Scottish Communion Office to be 'unscriptural and alien'.[185] In the same year the Bishop of Limerick, Dr Edward Knox, censured his presbyter G. G. Gubbins, and Bishop G. H. Law of Bath and Wells criticised John East from St Michael's, Bath, for involvement at Dunoon, while at Crieff, in 1853, Arthur Isham, rector of Turville, Buckinghamshire, was reprimanded by Samuel Wilberforce, Bishop of Oxford, after a complaint from Lendrum that he had preached at Rainey's English Episcopal church.[186] Again, Wemyss Bay had no problems from 1861 in filling its pulpit. Some of the clergy were high ranking Evangelicals: the future bishop of Rochester, Canon A. W. Thorold; the Bishop of Jerusalem, Samuel Gobat; the future Dean of Lichfield, W. W. Champneys; J. W. Bardsley, who was to become Bishop of Sodor and Man;

---

[182] Robert Daly to David Low, August 1845, Blatch, *Low*, pp. 299-300. Low countered Daly by directing attention to the 1840 Act which had drawn the Scottish Episcopal Church closer to the Church of England, and by arguing that the Scottish Communion Office was 'almost identical with Cranmer's first Office of Edward VI' and was preferred by many Anglicans to the 1662 version. Similarly, C. H. Terrot proposed to Daly that the first Edwardian liturgy had 'satisfied Cranmer and Ridley...which they gave up in deference to the curiosity of others'. David Low to Robert Daly, 25 August, 30 August 1845, Blatch, *Low*, pp. 302-306. C. H. Terrot to Robert Daly, 10 November 1845, *Record*, 24 November 1845. See Chapter 7 for theology of the Communion Service.

[183] Robert Daly to David Low, 25 November 1845, *Record*, 15 December 1845.

[184] See Chapter 6, p. 194.

[185] *Record*, 20 July 1846.

[186] *Ibid.* McGubbin, 'Holy Trinity Dunoon', pp. 10-11. *Scottish Magazine and Churchman's Review*, 1853, p. 495. Speech delivered by D. T. K. Drummond at Exeter Hall, *Record*, 16 December 1872.

and Dr T. P. Boultbee, Principal of the London College of Divinity, all preached at Wemyss. Lord Shaftesbury was also a frequent visitor there.[187] The continued support for English Episcopalianism by Evangelicals outside Scotland was probably a notable factor in encouraging new recruits to the movement.

Importantly, by 1848, Drummond had emerged as a respected leader of the separatists, holding more moderate views than Dunbar, who would have been the other natural choice. The different approach of the two was clearly shown at the meeting of the English Episcopalians at Montrose on 12 April 1848, when Dunbar complained that Archbishop Sumner had not been supportive of their cause. Additionally, he did not agree that the deputation of 1849 should press for provision of a bishop,[188] arguing that it would be equivalent to an acknowledgement of irregularity. He disapproved of Drummond, who had complied with the wishes of C. J. Blomfield by not officiating in London. Dunbar told Drummond that he had lost all confidence in him as a leader, and that in this he had the support of a leading member of St Paul's congregation, Admiral Duff. Rumours appeared in the newspapers that Drummond had been very critical of Dunbar's remarks about Sumner, and had tried unsuccessfully to soften the atmosphere by writing a conciliatory letter to Duff, which succeeded only in provoking a sharp correspondence from Dunbar. By August 1848 Dunbar and Duff, with some supporters at St Paul's, cut themselves off from the main body of English Episcopalians who were united behind Drummond.[189] The desire to work in association with the Church of England had always been paramount with Drummond.[190] Dunbar, by contrast, seemed poised to push for independence, possibly influenced by events surrounding the formation of the Free Church of England in 1845.[191] The English Episcopal movement under Drummond until 1877, remaining firmly loyal to the Church of England and representative of a non-extreme position, was likely to attract would-be supporters.

Drummond's loyalty to Anglicanism was important since Presbyterians were often operative in setting up English Episcopal congregations. At Nairn, of the twenty-one who voted, nine were Episcopalians, of whom only four supported merger with the breakaway churches. Of the others who opted for separation, one was a minister of the Established Church, and eleven were Presbyterian laypeople.[192] Again, at Crieff there were

---

[187] Hodder, *Burns*, pp. 387 ff., 510-511.

[188] See Chapter 10, pp. 322-326.

[189] *Scottish Magazine and Churchman's Review*, August 1848.

[190] See Chapter 8, pp. 271-272.

[191] Carter, *Anglican Evangelicals*, pp. 356-390.

[192] *Aberdeen Journal and General Advertiser for the North of Scotland*, 13 August 1845.

many Presbyterian supporters, evidenced when Lendrum wrote to Torry, on 3 March 1846, saying, 'the Presbyterians at Crieff...are circulating Cashel's letter'.[193] Two of those who signed the petition in the town calling for the English Episcopal Chapel were Presbyterians. One of these was Henrietta Oliphant of Gask, but it is not clear who the other was.[194] With such support, English Episcopalianism might have been tempted to sever its connection with the Church of England, along the lines suggested by Dunbar. Drummond's leadership, however, stamped the movement as clearly Anglican.

Again, established English Episcopalians assisted new recruits. At St Peter's, Montrose, Dunbar and S. C. Baker, curate of St Thomas's, Edinburgh, filled the pulpit when it became vacant in 1844. Drummond, Dunbar, Miles and his assistant, Charles Gribble, were thanked by the church for 'countenance, support and able assistance', in the search for a new incumbent. The post was refused by Baker, but Robert Wade of Tralee, Southern Ireland, a friend of Drummond's, was appointed.[195] A collection for St John's, Dundee, was taken at St Thomas's in 1870. Although Drummond was prevented by illness from preaching there in 1872, on 19 November 1876 he addressed the 'very large Sabbath School' and preached at 'a communion with nearly 100 communicants'.[196] Those contemplating joining the English Episcopal movement were assured of help from the group.

Evangelicalism and English Episcopalianism

The English Episcopal movement, as shown by the discussion here, was clearly Evangelical. In the early stages, from 1842 to 1860, the churchmanship of Drummond, Dunbar, Miles, J. D. Hull at Huntly, J. H. Hitchcock at Nairn and Thomas Ogilvy of Corrimony has been demonstrated previously.[197] In this chapter it has been shown, additionally, that the founders of St James's, Aberdeen, W. F. Burnley, the patron of Dunoon, the Oliphants of Gask, the Duchess of Gordon, A. C. Rainey at Crieff and George Burns at Wemyss Bay were also Evangelicals.[198] Again,

---

[193] Alexander Lendrum to Patrick Torry, 3 March 1846, NAS, 12/12 2398.

[194] *Scottish Magazine and Churchman's Review*, December 1848.

[195] St Peter's Minute Book, 10 May 1845-December 1850, *passim.*, St Peter's Church, Montrose, Archives.

[196] D. T. K. Drummond to Lord Shaftesbury, 30 November 1876, DRO, D5550/3/5/26.

[197] See Chapter 1, pp. 17-19. Chapter 4, *passim*.

[198] It has been assumed, in the absence of published writings, that the clergy surrounding Dunbar at St Paul's and St James's, Aberdeen, were Evangelicals since he was unlikely to have appointed non-Evangelicals. W. F. Burnley's association with St Jude's and St Silas's, Glasgow, and St Thomas's, Edinburgh mark his Evangelicalism.

Continuing Disruption

the Earl of Galloway exhibited his Evangelicalism at the Debate in the House of Lords in 1849 when referring to the 'invisible...real Church of Christ...born again of the Spirit'.[199] Likewise, the credentials of Joseph Mulkerns at St John's, Dundee, were made clear by the incumbent of St Luke's, Holliscroft, Sheffield, S. G. Potter, an Evangelical who had 'preached...in the pulpits of the Established, Free, and United Presbyterian Churches'.[200] He applauded Mulkerns in 1874 as 'a pious, godly, Protestant missionary of truth'.[201] After Mulkerns left St John's, Bishop T. H. Gregg, of the Reformed Church of England, preached there on 11 December 1879 and, in May 1880, because of financial difficulties, St John's officially joined Gregg's church.[202] Thus Mulkerns introduced a distinctly Evangelical churchmanship to the Orangemen of St John's. Again, Archibald Lang recalled the 'evangelical' teaching at Hunters Quay as being the first step to his subsequent conversion,[203] and Adam Gray, a nearby Free Church minister approved so greatly of its ministry, conducted on 'Evangelical lines', that he declined to open a chapel of his own there until Emmanuel closed in 1905.[204] The Evangelicalism of Murray Stewart at Cally was evident in his support of the Church Missionary Society and Gatehouse Auxiliary Bible Society,[205] and in the appointment in 1872 of Drummond's son-in-law, C. T. Moor, as incumbent.[206] Alfred Daniel, at Johnstone, was also clearly Evangelical since Drummond and other English Episcopalians influenced his subsequent appointment to St Peter's, Montrose, in 1876.[207] At Balmacara the concern, clearly expressed, was 'that some who go only thinking of Nature, may be led to Nature's God'.[208] While it has not been possible to fix the precise churchmanship at

---

Ibid., pp. 155, 156, 165. St Thomas's Minute Book, *passim*, St Thomas's Church, Edinburgh, Archives.

[199] *Episcopacy in Scotland: Revised Report of the Debate in the House of Lords on May 22, 1849* (London, 1849), p. 86. See also Chapter 1, p. 12, Chapter 9, p. 295, Chapter 10, pp. 323-326 for the details of the deputation to the House of Lords.

[200] *Ibid.*

[201] Unnamed Newspaper, S. G. Potter to Alexander Forbes, 12 November 1874, Lamb Collection, 183 (2).

[202] R. D. Fenwick, 'The Free Church of England, Otherwise called the Reformed Episcopal Church 1845-1927', (Ph. D. thesis, University of Lampeter, 1995), pp. 140-141.

[203] Fleming, *Arctic*, pp. 18-24.

[204] *Dunoon Herald and Corval Advertiser*, 3 March 1905.

[205] *Dumfries and Galloway Courier*, 22 October 1872, 26 November 1872.

[206] D. T. K. Drummond to C. T. Moor and H. Drummond to C. T. Moor, August 1875, DRO, D5550/3/4/9.

[207] St Peter's Minute Book, 1871-1876, *passim*, St Peter's Montrose, Archives.

[208] *St Silas's Magazine*, August 1889, St Silas's Church, Glasgow, Archives.

Arradoul,[209] Old Deer or Selkirk, Evangelicalism was, or became, the theological complexion of all the other later chapels, as it had been earlier in the movement.

Conclusion

The Scottish Communion Office, compounded with Ritualism after 1860, was the over-riding cause of defections to the English Episcopal movement from 1842 to 1887. Its doctrinal content, known to Dunbar and the congregation of St Paul's, Aberdeen, before Drummond's problems in Edinburgh in 1842, was totally unacceptable to the congregations shown in Table 9.1.

Various factors consolidated the decision to defect. After the censure from Howley and some of the English bishops, the deputations of the English Episcopalians in 1846 and 1849 were probably important in winning support, as indicated by their proximity to the numerical peak in 1854 shown on Graph 9.1. The similar event of 1872, together with the legal clarification of the movement obtained in 1871 and 1873, added to the further increase of activity by 1875. Again, clerical support from England and Ireland, Drummond's leadership and the help offered by some of the richer congregations to poorer ones, all contributed to the growing movement.

However, the peak of the English Episcopalians around 1854 was due to the incorporation of only the small congregations situated at Huntly, Nairn, Dunoon, Gask, Fochabers, Crieff, Corrimony, Arradoul and Old Deer. When they closed down after 1854 because of their limited numbers or removal of patrons,[210] the movement suffered the diminution shown on the graph. Ironically, the mid-century internal divisions repaired this loss by providing large, flourishing churches. St James's, Aberdeen, contributed to the 1854 peak and thereafter, together with St Vincent's, Edinburgh, and St Silas's, Glasgow, it provided substantial numerical input leading up to the second apex around 1875. Thereafter, the drop shown on Graph 9.1 is explained by various factors such as the change in the Scottish canon law in 1890 which enabled Evangelicals to subscribe to the Church without condoning its doctrines, as explained in Chapter 10.[211]

Dioceses where bishops were Scottish Office supporters were particularly prone to disturbance. This was the case in Aberdeen, St Andrews, Dunkeld and Dunblane, and Brechin under William Skinner, Patrick Torry and A. P. Forbes respectively. David Low's diocese, unsettled because he and some of his clergy had distanced themselves from

---

[209] See Chapter 8, pp. 258-259.
[210] See Chapter 2, pp. 41-45.
[211] See Chapter 10, p. 359.

Continuing Disruption 317

the Scottish rite for the sake of peace, was another trouble spot. However, the disputes spilled over to include diocesans who were not openly defenders of the Scottish Office. Alexander Ewing of Argyll and the Isles, in whose jurisdiction Dunoon, Wemyss Bay, and Hunters Quay stood, was notable in this respect, but C. H. Terrot, who presided over St Thomas's and St Vincent's Edinburgh, and Selkirk is difficult to categorise.[212] The disparate views and locations are evidence of the depth of antagonism to the Scottish Communion Office which emerges as the prominent factor in the growth of English Episcopalianism.

---

[212] See Chapter 7, p. 236.

Chapter 10

From Secession to Partial Union, 1846-1900

Two issues dominated English and Scottish Episcopalianism from the 1840s onwards. The fate of the Scottish Communion Office, after its doctrinal differences from the English Office became apparent in 1842, was paramount to Scottish Churchmen and was increasingly debated on both sides of the Border. All hopes of reconciliation between English and Scottish Episcopalians hung on the resolution of this problem. But until materialisation, both groups of Churchmen were equally anxious to show that they were the true representatives of Anglicanism in Scotland. For the former group this would encourage Anglican clergy to its pulpits and enable participation in English religious societies. Increasingly, also, there was the problem of obtaining confirmation for candidates. While St Jude's, Glasgow, received 'young people to...communion...although they may not have received external confirmation',[1] families, in particular newcomers from England used to more official arrangements, found the system unattractive. The consequent threat of leakage to the Scottish Episcopal Church prompted English Episcopalians to campaign for episcopal superintendence. Therefore their immediate aim in the 1840s was to gain the support of the Church of England by a full explanation of their position. Showing that they were loyal to the doctrines, formularies and discipline of their mother Church was vital. While there was continued emphasis on the problem of holding evangelistic meetings, English Episcopalians increasingly drew attention to what they considered to be un-Anglican and non-biblical in the Scottish Communion Office as the cause of their separation. Spiritual and practical concerns thus motivated the English Episcopalians in their quest for recognition by the Church of England.

For their part, many Scottish Episcopalians, looking at the greater wealth and social advantages of the English Church and to the possibility of attracting high-calibre English-trained clergy to Scotland, pressed for the abolition of the remaining clerical disabilities imposed by the act of 1840.[2] But the Scottish Communion Office had caused serious misgivings on the

---

[1] C. B. Gribble, *A Mistake Corrected: A Letter to the Rev. Dr Champneys, Headmaster of the Collegiate School, Glasgow* (Glasgow, 1858), p. 19.

[2] Rowan Strong, *Alexander Forbes of Brechin: The First Tractarian Bishop* (Oxford, 1995), pp. 186, 190-191.

part of some clergy in England.³ Thus Scottish Episcopalians, if they were to gain further concessions, had to convince the Anglican hierarchy of their doctrinal conformity. Recognition by the Church of England would bring rich rewards for Scottish Episcopalians.

Matters were played out against the changing religious climate of Britain. Ritualism took root in the Scottish Episcopal Church in the 1860s, evoking condemnation from Evangelicals, orthodox High Churchmen and Virtualists alike.⁴ At a similar time the image of Evangelicalism became blurred when some of its adherents became more willing to work alongside High Churchmen and gradually adopted practices which had previously been disclaimed.⁵ The resulting tensions added to the particular problems in Scotland in the years 1846 to 1900.

Concessions from the Church of England, 1845-1863

The support for the Scottish Episcopal Church by the Archbishop of Canterbury, William Howley, in 1845, and the various complaints surrounding visits of Anglican clergy to the separated churches,⁶ determined the English Episcopalians to acquaint the Church of England with the facts about their secessions. Accordingly, in May 1846, they formed a clerical and lay association.⁷ D. T. K. Drummond of St Thomas's, Edinburgh, Sir William Dunbar of St Paul's, Aberdeen, and C. P. Miles of St Jude's, Glasgow, accompanied by R. K. Greville, a layman from St Thomas's, were appointed to visit England and bring the case for English Episcopalianism to the attention of the Anglican Church.⁸

Setting out on 8 June 1846, the deputation gained considerable support from notable English Evangelicals. Hugh McNeile and W. W. Ewbank at Liverpool and Hugh Stowell at Manchester convened public meetings. Sixteen clergy together with laymen at the Evangelical stronghold of Clifton, and Francis Close at Cheltenham, arranged similar events. Further

---

³ See Chapters 8 and 9

⁴ Rowan Strong, *Episcopalianism in Nineteenth-Century Scotland* (Oxford, 2002), pp. 242-246, 258-259.

⁵ D. W. Bebbington, *Evangelicalism in Modern Britain* (London, 1993), pp. 146-149.

⁶ See Chapter 9, pp. 308-308.

⁷ This was probably based on the early societies for Anglican Evangelical clergy and laymen in the eighteenth century, providing a focus and cell of activity. The best known was the Eclectic Society, founded in 1783 in London. See K. Hylson-Smith, *Evangelicals in the Church of England, 1734-1984* (Edinburgh, 1989), p. 34.

⁸ *Report of a Deputation Appointed at a Meeting in Aberdeen, May 1846, of Ministers and Lay Members of the Church of England Representing the Congregations Adhering to her Forms and Doctrines in Scotland, in order to visit England and Communicate with the Bishops and Other Parties in the Established Church, on the Subject of their Ecclesiastical Position in Scotland* (Edinburgh, 1847), pp. 1-4.

gatherings at Bath, Exeter, Plymouth, Hereford and Northampton followed. In all these cities the deputation reported 'assurances of support [and] an earnest desire for information'.[9] Finally, in London, the delegates met Howley and the Archbishop of York, Edward Harcourt, plus nine Anglican bishops of whom C. R. Sumner of Winchester, J. B. Sumner of Chester and George Davys of Peterborough were Evangelicals.[10]

Legal and doctrinal differences between the Scottish Episcopal Church and the Church of England were presented to substantiate the case for separation. Among the former, the power of the General Synods 'to change, fundamentally, the laws and regulations' of the Church was criticised as contributing to an unstable constitution. Emphasis was given to the excommunication of Dunbar by William Skinner, Bishop of Aberdeen, in 1844, highlighting that Dunbar 'was never summoned before the Diocesan Synod to explain his case'. But doctrine provided the central focus of concern. A synopsis was given showing that the Scottish Communion Office contained a prayer for some sort of change in the elements, a sacrificial aspect and prayers for the dead, all foreign to the Book of Common Prayer. Additionally, the Scottish Confirmation Service was now contested because the catechism of Alexander Jolly, Bishop of Moray from 1798 to 1838, taught that it validated the efficacy of baptism, and a sermon preached in August 1844 by Patrick Cheyne, of St John's, Aberdeen, uncensured by Skinner, was argued to uphold the revival of auricular confession. The apostolic succession claimed by the Scottish Episcopal Church for its episcopate was analysed by Drummond and shown to be invalid since it could be traced no further back than 1661.[11] Divergences between the Scottish Episcopal Church and the Church of England were central to the argument.

The deputation claimed that the English prelates had become more conversant with matters at the meeting.[12] For instance when Howley, now showing some sympathy for English Episcopal concerns, suggested its clergy should return to England, he was assured that the problems were wider because the laity desired to worship as Anglicans in Scotland.[13] On doctrinal issues one bishop,[14] who had previously opposed English

---

[9] *Ibid.*, pp. 5-8.

[10] The bishops attending the 1847 deputation were: C. J. Blomfield (London); C. R. Sumner (Winchester); J. B. Sumner (Chester); George Davys (Peterborough); Richard Bagot (Bath and Wells); John Lonsdale (Lichfield); Edward Stanley (Norwich); Samuel Wilberforce (Oxford); Edward Denison (Salisbury). *Report of a Deputation*, p. 5.

[11] *Ibid.*, pp. 19-25, 27-31, 33, 39-51. The sermon referred to by Patrick Cheyne was probably *Holiness and the True Reforming Power of the Church* (Aberdeen, 1844).

[12] Unsympathetic views were not recorded.

[13] *Ibid.*, p. 6.

[14] No names are given in the report of the deputation.

Episcopalianism, was said to have acknowledged that he had never realised the 'real character' of the Scottish Communion Office but now believed 'it was the strongest fact he had heard in the whole case'. Another was won over by the argument on apostolic succession which he considered would place the Scottish Episcopal Church outside the Anglican communion; and one lamented that the Scottish Episcopal Church showed 'nothing short of ecclesiastical despotism' over Dunbar's excommunication. Two others declared that they would have no objections to an interchange of pulpits between their clergy and the separatists.[15] The deputation of 1846 considered that its aim of attracting 'the sympathy of clergymen and laymen in the Church'[16] had been successful.

While no official reaction from the Scottish Episcopal Church has been found, James Christie, incumbent of Trinity Chapel, Turriff, Aberdeenshire, probably spoke for many in rebutting any gains claimed by the English Episcopalians. He passionately defended the doctrine of the Scottish Communion Office, labelling the analysis of the deputation as one of 'malice and all uncharitableness'. Drummond's argument on the invalidity of Scottish Orders was sternly repudiated as the work of 'the hooded snake [who] rears his envenomed crest'.[17] While Dunbar's excommunication was upheld as 'scriptural' and 'consonant with the English Church and her greatest Divines', Dunbar himself was accused of ministering 'unto the Devil' and therefore unlikely to 'inherit the Kingdom of God'.[18] Thus Christie forcefully upheld Scottish Episcopalianism as being the true representative of Anglicanism in Scotland, both in terms of its doctrine and legal practices. But, in effect, with no concessions granted, the debate had not progressed far since Drummond's secession in 1842.

However, in 1849 the English Episcopalians won ground as a result of the case surrounding Dunbar's excommunication.[19] Dunbar raised an action for damages of £5000 against Skinner in February 1849 at the Court of Session in Edinburgh.[20] Lord Fullerton judged that in Presbyterian Scotland 'the jurisdiction of a bishop of the Protestant Episcopal Church...has no existence' and consequently he found Skinner's language of

---

[15] *Report of a Deputation*, pp 7-8, 13. To illustrate further support, the deputation reported that 'a metropolitan Rector (a dignitary in the Church, one whose extensive erudition is known throughout the literary world) expressed "I have examined into the Scottish Episcopal question. I have satisfied myself of the truthfulness of the charges alleged against the Scottish Episcopal Church, and I consider the succession of the Scottish bishops as of no more value than three ciphers"'. *Ibid.* p. 50.

[16] *Ibid.*, p. 35.

[17] James Christie, *A Critical Analysis of a Report of a Deputation into England in 1846* (London, 1847), p. 23.

[18] *Ibid.*, pp. 14-17.

[19] See Chapter 9, p. 284.

[20] *Record*, 15 February 1849.

excommunication to be 'unpardonable'.[21] Importantly, therefore, Scotland's highest court had declared that the Scottish Episcopal Church had only limited powers. The English Episcopalians could now claim that the Scottish bishops had no legal authority over them and that they should be allowed to invite Anglican clergy to their pulpits unhindered. The case for English Episcopalianism had seemingly been advanced.

Encouraged by the appointment of the Evangelical, J. B. Sumner, as Archbishop of Canterbury, the English Episcopalians organised an ambitious deputation to the House of Lords on 22 May 1849. Led by Lord Elibank of Innerleithen, it consisted of twelve laymen, Drummond, Miles and his future curate, C. B. Gribble.[22] A petition signed by 'six hundred male representatives of Episcopal families, including some of the most influential of landed proprietors, merchants, and professional men in Scotland'[23] was presented in the hope of securing recognition by the Church of England. English Episcopalianism, by 1849, was increasingly confident.

Firstly, the deputation suggested that its clergy might be 'inducted to the charge of their congregations' either by Sumner or by the bishops from whom they had received ordination. This would protect them from repetitions of the recent excommunications of Dunbar, Miles and J. D. Hull in Huntly.[24] Secondly, it asked for visits by Anglican bishops 'not as legally exercising any territorial jurisdiction, but as ecclesiastically performing episcopal functions in their congregations'.[25] Such a measure would provide a unifying influence and the rite of confirmation. However, although the petitioners hoped that at least one of these requests would be granted, they concluded with a plea for adoption of 'any other course of proceedings which to your Lordships may appear most expedient'.[26] Any concession would be a gain.

---

[21] *Episcopacy in Scotland. Revised Report of the Debate in the House of Lords on May 22 1849* (London, 1849), pp. 21, 39.

[22] *Revised Report*, pp. xii-xiii. Dunbar was absent. See Chapter 9, pp. 313-314 for his reservations about the deputation. The laymen were: James Baird, baronet; Brodie of Brodie; Evan Baillie, of Dochfour; George D. Graeme of Inchbrachie; William Macdonald Macdonald of Rossie Castle; John Hamilton of Sundrum; Arthur Kinnaird, M. P. for Perth and a member of the Free Church; J. K. Greville who had been on the 1847 deputation; James Cunningham, W. S., of Edinburgh: George Burns, merchant of Edinburgh; W. F. Burnley, merchant of Glasgow; and J. H. Balfour, M. D., Professor of the University of Edinburgh.

[23] *Revised Report*, p. viii.

[24] *Revised* Report, pp. viii, 243. See Chapter 9, pp. 284, 288. Hull was excommunicated at the Synod of Moray, Ross and Argyll, under Bishop David Low, on 23 April 1845. *Record,*, 17 May 1845.

[25] *Revised Report*, p. 243.

[26] *Ibid.*, p. 244.

The debate was well attended. Sumner was joined by the Archbishops of York and Dublin, Thomas Musgrave and Richard Whately respectively, together with twelve bishops.[27] Of these, along with Sumner, Robert Daly of Cashel and T. V. Short of St Asaph were Evangelicals.[28] The Duke of Argyll, and the Earls of Minto, Harrowby, Powis and Galloway were also present. The eminent attenders were indicative of the importance assigned to the debate.

The Whig, Henry Peter, Lord Brougham, put the case for the petitioners.[29] His opening speech set out both legal and doctrinal concerns. Using the evidence from Dunbar's case, Brougham was able to argue that the introduction of an English bishop to Scotland would not break the Act of Union. He emphasised that a superintending bishop for the separatists would not imply political or territorial episcopacy, any more than Scottish Episcopalians could claim such rights for their bishops in Presbyterian Scotland.[30] Secondly, he maintained that the doctrine of the Scottish Communion Office, 'if it did not come to transubstantiation, was a very near approach to it'.[31] The petitioners' claims were presented as constitutionally and doctrinally legitimate.

The Bishops of Salisbury, London and Exeter, Edward Denison, C. J. Blomfield and Henry Philpotts respectively, were unconvinced by Brougham's arguments concerning the Act of Union.[32] Wilberforce spoke out for the doctrine of the Scottish Office as being clearly non-Roman, because it asked for a change in only the quality of the elements, not the substance. Philpotts put the orthodox High Church view that all members of the Church of England were in communion with every other branch of the Church, and so he believed the English Episcopalians to be schismatics. But others supported the petitioners. Daly, who had thrown in his lot with the

---

[27] The Bishops of Salisbury (Edward Denison), who was also deputed to speak for the Bishop of London (C. J. Blomfield); Worcester (Henry Pepys); Exeter (Henry Philpotts); Cashel (Robert Daly); Oxford (Samuel Wilberforce); Norwich (Edward Stanley); Hereford (R. D. Hampden); Manchester (J. P. Lee); St Asaph (T. V. Short); Gloucester and Bristol (J. H. Monk) and Meath (Edward Stopford), were present. *Revised Report*, p. iv.

[28] D. M. Lewis, *The Blackwell Dictionary of Evangelical Biography*, Volume II (Oxford, 1995), pp. 1011, 1061.

[29] Rosemary Goring, *Chambers Scottish Biographical Dictionary* (Edinburgh, 1992), p. 251. Brougham was a suitable choice because, being a very broad-minded Scottish Presbyterian, he would have had sympathy with the theological stance of the English Episcopalians. Additionally, he had debating and organisational experience, having entered Parliament in 1818 and having assisted in carrying the Reform Bill of 1832.

[30] *Revised Report*, pp. 10-12.

[31] *Ibid.*, pp. 1-18, 29-31.

[32] *Ibid*, pp. 29, 30, 49.

English Episcopalians in 1845,[33] was critical of the doctrine of the Scottish Communion Office and upheld the petitioners as true members of the Church of England in Scotland.[34] The Earl of Galloway, an English Episcopalian,[35] assured the debate that there was no threat to the Act of Union if the separatists were granted a bishop with spiritual, rather than territorial, oversight.[36] The Earl of Harrowby thought it possible for English Episcopalians to have a bishop similar to those operating in the colonies, and declared the Scottish episcopate to be arrogant in its territorial assumptions. The Presbyterian Duke of Argyll likewise hoped the situation would be remedied, but opposed the idea of English bishops coming to Scotland, fearing this would be 'inexpedient'. Instead he urged the Anglican Church to 'protect' the English Episcopalians from the use of the Scottish Office.[37] Thus confusion over legal matters and the usual divide over doctrine were evident, but there were also constructive suggestions for helping the petitioners.

Sumner expressed sympathy with Anglican clergymen in Scotland who had to subscribe to a different set of canons from those of their mother Church. He added that he believed the Scottish liturgy to be different from that of the Church of England 'in at least one...important particular'.[38] However, he acknowledged that the Church of England and the Scottish Episcopal Church were in communion, and he refused to place the petitioners under his jurisdiction. His decision was to accept English Episcopal clergymen into his diocese, providing they brought sufficient testimonial of conduct and orthodoxy.[39] Sumner's position was thus one of compromise, possibly since legal and constitutional matters were unclear and because his role as Archbishop demanded the preservation of peace in the Church. But, on a positive note for the petitioners, he had made a plain criticism of the Scottish Communion Office, and had announced that English Episcopalians would be welcome in his diocese.

Again, encouragingly for the deputation, it won support from non-Evangelical anti-High Churchmen. Musgrave, Henry Pepys, Bishop of Worcester, and Edward Stanley, Bishop of Norwich, offered help along the lines of Sumner. Pepys even challenged the Scottish Episcopal Church, 'why retain an obnoxious clause, when you profess that our own [service] is identical with [yours]?'[40] After the debate, the Bishop of Llandaff, Edward

---

[33] See Chapter 9, p. 308.
[34] *Revised Report*, pp. 58-67.
[35] *Ibid.*, p. 232.
[36] *Ibid.*, pp. 86-88.
[37] *Ibid.*, pp. 38-41.
[38] *Ibid.*, p. 35.
[39] *Ibid.*, p. 35. *Cf.*, *ENCS*, pp. 222-224.
[40] *Ibid.*, pp. 36, 97, 103-104.

Copleston, the Bishop of Hereford, R. D. Hampden, and the Bishop of Chester, John Graham, pledged similar allegiance.[41] The deputation considered that their position was now 'publicly acknowledged and authoritatively established'. They admitted that 'direct legislation on...their claims was surrounded with considerable difficulty' and professed to be reasonably encouraged by the outcome of the debate.[42] There was thus support for English Episcopalianism from Evangelicals and non-Evangelicals, but seemingly little hope of attaining the episcopal superintendence it desired. Even Sumner, a fellow Evangelical, was pragmatic.

Scottish Episcopal reaction was fiercely critical of the limited concessions granted to the deputation. Picking up on doctrinal and constitutional matters, *The Scottish Magazine and Churchman's Review* referred to Sumner's position as 'this lamentable falling off from the principles of genuine catholicity', and dismissed Daly's doctrinal contribution as a mere reiteration of 'stupid falsehoods'. It ridiculed the desire of the English Episcopalians for a bishop of their own, ironically doubting that they 'would give heed to him'. Philpotts was praised for his 'fair and intelligible' contribution concerning the legal arguments of the petitioners who were reported as working for a 'repeal of that part of the Act of Union which prohibits English Bishops from exercising any authority in Scotland'. In conclusion it declared that the English Episcopalians had been 'led by a malignity' against the Scottish Episcopal Church.[43] Individual clergy entered the debate. A. J. D. D'Orsey, of the Anderston Mission in Glasgow, complained to Brougham that 'you and your ally the Bishop of Cashel do our poor Church the greatest injustice when you recklessly charge her with errors she indignantly repudiates'.[44] William Taylor, the incumbent of Forfar, added that the deputation had no cause for complaint since the English Office was allowed, under Canon

---

[41] *Ibid.*, pp. 98-104. Pepys was an outspoken non-Evangelical. Owen Chadwick, *The Victorian Church*, Part 1(London, 1992), p. 600. Stanley was a theological liberal, at one time calling for latitude in interpreting the Thirty-Nine Articles. *Ibid.*, pp. 181-183. Strong, *Episcopalianism*, p. 224. Hampden was a liberal. Owen Chadwick, *The Victorian Church*, Part II (London, 1992), p.76. Musgrave had some Evangelical sympathies. He supported the Gorham judgement, and tried to prevent the Convocation of York meeting until his death in 1860. *Ibid.*, pp. 315-316, 324. The Earl of Harrowby was a moderate Evangelical, liberal towards Roman Catholics. *DEB*, Volume I, p. 525.

[42] *Revised Debate*, pp. ix-x.

[43] *Scottish Episcopal Magazine and Churchman's Review*, July 1849.

[44] A. J. D. D'Orsey, *A Letter to the Rt. Hon. The Lord Brougham in reply to his Attack on the Scottish Church in the House of Lords, May 22 1849* (London, 1850), pp. 6-11.

XXI of the Scottish Church, in any congregation desiring it.[45] The debates of 1846 and 1849, which brought some encouragement to the English Episcopalians, continued to uncover not only doctrinal but also constitutional problems.

The latter difficulties crystallised in 1856 during a visit of the Bishop of Jerusalem, Samuel Gobat, an Evangelical, to the dissenting chapels. Gobat's task was to collect contributions to the Jerusalem Diocesan Missionary fund, but he also agreed to confirm candidates from St James's and St Paul's, Aberdeen, and St Jude's, Glasgow, and possibly others.[46] William Skinner, Bishop of Aberdeen, and Primus, wrote to Sumner on 28 June 1856, entering an 'official protest' against Gobat, and asking Sumner to declare a 'breach of unity'.[47] On 4 July 1856, Joshua Kirkman of St Paul's, Aberdeen, defended Gobat, pointing out to Sumner, 'if only our wide separation from...the Episcopal Church of Scotland...were generally known in England, we should not be so isolated'.[48] In reply, Sumner assured Kirkman that he had no jurisdiction to prevent Gobat's intervention in Scotland.[49] The Episcopal Synod of 28 August 1856 accordingly pressed Sumner to make 'some expression of censure' towards Gobat, reminding him that the Scottish Episcopal and Anglican churches were 'in full fellowship and communion', and shared the same doctrinal basis.[50] But Sumner again emphasised that, as Gobat was not a bishop of the province of Canterbury, it was impossible 'to entertain the complaint', and expressed no criticism of his activities.[51] The dilemma of episcopal supervision was resolved for the English Episcopalians later in the year by the Evangelical Bishop of Carlisle, H. M. Villiers. While uncertain of the legal connotations of visiting Scotland, he agreed to confirm separatist candidates if they

---

[45] William Taylor, *A Letter to Henry, Lord Brougham of Vaux in Reference to his Lordship's Speech in the House of Lords on 22 May Respecting Episcopacy in Scotland with a Postscript on Sir William Dunbar's Protest* (Edinburgh, 1849), pp. 6-7.

[46] St James's Minute Book, June 1856, St James's Church, Aberdeen, Archives. *Morning Herald*, 22 September 1856. Edwin Hodder, *Sir George Burns Bart.* (London 1892), p. 260.

[47] Bishop Skinner to the Archbishop of Canterbury, 28 June 1856, St James's Church, Aberdeen, Archives.

[48] Joshua Kirkman to J. B. Sumner, 4 July 1856, St James's Church, Aberdeen, Archives.

[49] The Archbishop of Canterbury to the Rev. Joshua Kirkman, 23 July 1856, St James's Church, Aberdeen, Archives.

[50] Bishops of the Scottish Episcopal Church to the Archbishop of Canterbury, (n. d., but included with the deliberations of the Synod of 1856). St James's Church, Aberdeen, Archives.

[51] J. B. Sumner to W. Skinner, 13 October 1856. St James's Church, Aberdeen, Archives.

travelled to England.[52] Villiers received no censure from Sumner, presumably because his activities posed no legal dilemma. Seven years on from the deputation of 1849, and in the absence of an official investigation, the constitutional problems remained. But support from Villiers strengthened the position of the English Episcopalians.

For its part the Scottish Episcopal Church continued to examine the case for removal of the remaining clerical disabilities. In 1857, after four years of work, A. P. Forbes, Bishop of Brechin, William Skinner, Bishop of Aberdeen, and Charles Wordsworth, Bishop of St Andrews, Dunkeld and Dunblane, presented a document to Parliament.[53] But despite the support of W. E. Gladstone, Samuel Wilberforce, Bishop of Oxford, and W. K. Hamilton, Bishop of Salisbury,[54] opinion was so much against them that they were unable to secure a seconder in the House of Commons. C. H. Terrot, Primus and Bishop of Edinburgh, blamed opposition from English Evangelicals, highlighting the production of papers by the Protestant Defence Society against the Scottish Office. Ironically, too, he pointed to English High Church concern over threat to the Act of Union if Scottish Episcopalians won concessions.[55] The Scottish Episcopal Church, like the English Episcopal movement, met formidable doctrinal and constitutional barriers in its quest for a close relationship with the Church of England.

In the uncertainty surrounding legal matters, doctrine became increasingly central. The continued Tractarian interest in the Scottish Office, epitomised in 1857 by the charge of A. P. Forbes, Bishop of Brechin,[56] convinced some in the Church of England and the Scottish Episcopal Church that the service was an impediment to closer union of the two churches. The Archbishop of Dublin, Richard Whately, not an Evangelical, wrote to Sumner in 1857 saying, 'the Scottish Episcopal Church might be recognised as a branch of ours if they would consent completely to remove all points of difference, great or small'.[57] Dean E. B. Ramsay, of St John's, Edinburgh, expressed similar sentiments in 1859, admitting that the language of the Scottish epiclesis was 'unfortunate... and created an insuperable difficulty with many excellent and conscientious persons', and that the office did not follow the order of events at the Last

---

[52] This function was continued from 1860 to 1869 by Samuel Waldegrave, Bishop of Carlisle. *Glasgow Herald*, 6 April 1861. *Memoir*, p.cxxvi

[53] Rowan Strong, *Alexander Forbes of Brechin: The First Tractarian* Bishop (Oxford, 1995), p. 112. The reference given runs as follows: Unlisted papers. Bishop Terrot's report on the deputation to London in regard to the legal disabilities, dated 24 July 1857, to be added to NAS, CH 12.

[54] *Record*, 27 April 1857.

[55] Strong, *Forbes*, p. 112.

[56] Chapter 7, p. 241.

[57] E. B. Ramsay, *The Present State of our Canon Law Considered* (Edinburgh, 1859), pp. 17-18.

Supper.⁵⁸ This was a significant shift from his views in the 1840s when he had firmly opposed the English Episcopalians.⁵⁹ Many High Churchmen increasingly spurned the Scottish Communion Office.

In 1859, possibly fearing that the Scottish Office was to be abandoned, an un-named Scottish bishop⁶⁰ and his brother approached Drummond investigating whether the English Episcopalians might drop their campaign given sufficient guarantees. Assurance was promised that the difficulties surrounding evangelistic meetings would be overcome. Concerning the Scottish rite, the bishop suggested 'a concordat, by which English clergymen joining the Scottish Episcopal Church might be protected against [its] use'. Drummond replied that this would not meet the difficulty of signing the canons 'which declare that the Office be sound' and pressed for its 'entire removal'. The bishop remarked, 'Ah! This reconciliation is hopeless for I would rather part with life itself than with the Scotch Office', to which Drummond answered, 'I would rather part with life itself than have anything to do with it'.⁶¹ Only removal of the Scottish Office from the canons of the Church would satisfy Drummond.

In anticipation of the Scottish Episcopal General Synod planned for July 1862, Sumner wrote to Terrot asking, 'whether in your opinion the Consecration Service, which differs from that of the English Church, would be authoritatively set aside [since] if that were done, a great obstacle would be removed' concerning the disabilities on Scottish clergy.⁶² The Scottish bishops considered various courses of action. Among these, Alexander Ewing of Argyll and the Isles wanted abolition of the rite. A. P. Forbes of Brechin recommended keeping the *status quo* and Charles Wordsworth of St Andrews, Dunkeld and Dunblane suggested a rewording of the epiclesis to that of the 1549 Book of Common Prayer or the liturgy of St James.⁶³

---

⁵⁸ *Ibid.*, p. 19.

⁵⁹ See Chapter 7, p. 236.

⁶⁰ Probably the Bishop of Brechin, A. P. Forbes.

⁶¹ D. T. K. Drummond to the Archbishop of Canterbury, 13 July 1869, LPL, Tait 162, pp. 240-243. Also LPL, H 5340.

⁶² J. B. Sumner to C. H. Terrot, 5 February 1862. Brechin Diocesan Archives, Dundee University, 1.3.561. Quoted in Strong, *Forbes*, p. 165.

⁶³ A. P. Forbes, Bishop of Brechin, staunch supporter of the Scottish Office, opposed all moves to depose it. At the other end of the spectrum, Alexander Ewing, Bishop of Argyll and the Isles, although not an Evangelical, agreed with the English Episcopalians. He argued that 'it is impossible to have two offices meaning different things', and pressed for complete abolition. Charles Wordsworth, Bishop of St Andrew's, Dunkeld and Dunblane, with his idea of rewording the epiclesis suggested either following the path laid out by Forbes's brother George Hay, incumbent of Burntisland, to adopt the less stark invocation of the Eastern liturgy of St James ('Send down, O Lord, Thy Spirit, the same all – holy one, upon us and upon these thy holy gifts set forth – that coming He may by His holy and good and glorious presence, hallow and

However, at the meeting of the Synod in February 1863, after sustained argument from Forbes and Gladstone, of whom the former objected to Wordsworth's idea as a 'distinct surrendering to the Drummondites',[64] Canons XXIX and XXX were drawn up whereby the Scottish Office was retained, but in a secondary position behind the English service. A concession to its use was granted in new congregations, and to those already using it, providing there was a majority in favour.[65] The Scottish Communion Office had been reprieved in spite of the strong recommendation from Sumner.

The canons of 1863 were thus a compromise aimed at pleasing all. The *Scottish Episcopal Journal* declared that 'Mr Drummond has been deprived of every possible excuse for remaining separate' and that an influential member of one of the English Episcopal congregations 'saw nothing to prevent a reunion' now that the Scottish Office had been deposed.[66] Ramsay was less optimistic. He had predicted before the Synod that reconciliation would take time, regretting that reform had not occurred 'ten or fifteen years ago'.[67] He was proved right. The English Episcopalians all refused union. For some, like Drummond, evangelistic meetings remained a problem since they were still outlawed by Canon XXXI.[68] But the Scottish

---

make this bread the Body of Christ ... and this cup the precious Blood of Christ ... that they may be to all who partake of them the remission of sins unto everlasting life.' See John Dowden, *The Scottish Communion Office, 1764* (Oxford, 1922), p. 186). Alternatively he suggested using the prayer from the first liturgy of Edward VI which contained the phrase that the elements 'may be unto us the body and blood of Christ'. Drummond and Craig had put this latter alternative forward in 1842 as being acceptable to Evangelicals. Forbes objected to Wordsworth's ideas, seeing them as making Christ's objective presence less obvious, and a distinct surrendering to the English Episcopalians. But there was clearly a body of opinion in the Scottish Episcopal Church ready to relinquish the Scottish Office for the sake of expediency. In the final vote on 10 February 1863, C. H. Terrot, anxious to secure better ministerial applicants to his diocese, voted for demotion of the Office to a secondary position. W. S. Wilson, Bishop of Glasgow and Galloway, followed similarly in the Upper House, as did E. B. Ramsay, Dean of Edinburgh, in the Lower House. See Chapter 7; *Scottish Ecclesiastical Journal,* 29 January 1863; Strong, *Forbes*, pp 169, 174-177; A. J. Ross, *Memoir of Alexander Ewing* (London, 1877), p. 349.

[64] Strong, *Forbes*, pp. 174-177.

[65] *The Code of Canons of the Episcopal Church in Scotland as Adopted, Enacted, and Sanctioned by a General Synod Holden at Edinburgh on the 8th Day of July 1862, and Continued by Successive Adjournments and Propogations Until the 13th Day of February 1863* (Edinburgh, 1863), pp. 29-30.

[66] *Scottish Ecclesiastical Journal*, 26 March, 30 April 1863.

[67] Ramsay, *Present Position*, pp. 22-23.

[68] *A Paper Printed by Order of the Vestry for Circulation in the Congregation of St Thomas's English Episcopal Chapel, Edinburgh* (Edinburgh, 1875), p. 4. St Thomas's Church, Edinburgh, Archives.

Office took centre stage. While it was sanctioned, albeit in a secondary position, the separatists understood there was no certainty that it 'may not be brought forward into the more prominent position which it [previously] occupied...in a future revision of the Canons'.[69] English Episcopalian agitation against the Scottish Communion Office, combined with Tractarian allegiance to it, had resulted in its deposition. But while it remained canonically endorsed, it was problematical for Evangelicals.

The Duke of Buccleuch's Bill, 1864

The Scottish Episcopal authorities were sufficiently confident that enough had been achieved by the canons of 1863 to appoint the Duke of Buccleuch and Queensberry to introduce, on 10 May 1864, a bill to remove the disabilities inhibiting the ministry of Scottish clergymen in England.[70] Although there were six Church of England Evangelical bishops,[71] C. T. Longley, a non-Evangelical, had succeeded Sumner as Archbishop of Canterbury in 1862. Unlike Sumner, Longley appeared unperturbed by doctrinal concerns and supported the bill because of historical links between Anglicanism and Scottish Episcopalianism.[72] Although his understanding of the issues did not seem to be extensive, his favourable response was an important influence.

Among the various opinions expressed at the debate, some were to affect English Episcopalianism in the future. A. C. Tait, Bishop of London, and a Scot,[73] regretted that the Scottish Office had been retained. He supported the bill only in the hope that greater inter-communion with the Church of England would lead the Scottish Episcopal Church 'to give up its eccentricities of doctrine'.[74] Charles Baring, the Evangelical Bishop of Durham, also 'felt bound, however reluctantly, to move that the bill be read a second time',[75] although he regarded the Scottish Office as 'entirely antagonistic to the Communion Service of the Church of England'. While accepting that it was based on Greek liturgies, he claimed that 'anyone

---

[69] R. L. Stuart, *English Episcopalianism in Scotland Explained and Justified* (Edinburgh, 1877), pp. 20-21.

[70] Buccleuch was an ideal person to present the Bill. He was an Episcopalian, but also a benefactor of the Church of Scotland. Strong, *Forbes*, p. 185.

[71] The Evangelical bishops in 1864 were: C. T. Baring (Durham), Robert Bickersteth (Ripon), J. T. Pelham (Norwich) Samuel Waldegrave (Carlisle), J. C. Wigram (Rochester), Francis Jeune (Peterborough).

[72] *Hansard's Parliamentary Debates, Volume CLXXV, 4 May-20 June 1864*, p. 623.

[73] Although a Broad Churchman, Tait, the son of a Presbyterian Scottish landowner, was sympathetic to Evangelicals. Nigel M. de S. Cameron (ed.), *Dictionary of Scottish Church History and Theology* (Edinburgh, 1993), p. 813.

[74] *Ibid.*, pp. 617-623, 627-630.

[75] *Ibid.*, p. 627.

observing the language of the Scotch Episcopalian Service...would come to the conclusion that it was founded on the doctrine of the Church of Rome'.[76] Baring's position was revealed later in a letter to the *Record* in 1892, which stated that he believed that English Episcopalians were protected against using the Scottish Office after 1863 since it was no longer the official service of the Church.[77] Maybe, also, he agreed with Tait that inter-communion would finally serve to remove the office. But possibly he was typical of some Evangelicals who were beginning to show willingness to compromise on certain issues and work alongside those of different churchmanship,[78] a suspicion endorsed by Lord Shaftesbury in 1876. Referring to Baring's recommendation of the canons of 1863 to the English Episcopalians, Shaftesbury commented, 'he of Durham has imbibed the poisonous air of Sacerdotalism and has succumbed'.[79] But Baring's opinion in 1864 undoubtedly swayed some waverers, and the bill was given royal assent on 29 July 1864.[80] Scottish-ordained clergy could now hold benefices in the Church of England.

Aftermath, 1864-1869

The bill of 1864 brought the Scottish Episcopal Church and the Church of England closer. In 1866 Tait, while visiting Glasgow, pronounced that 'the Scottish Episcopal Church is the only real, authorised representative in this country of the Church of England'.[81] Again, in 1869, when Archbishop of Canterbury, he admitted that he had discouraged an Irish prelate from holding confirmations for English Episcopalians, and had advised a clergyman who was about to preach in a separatist chapel 'to have nothing further to do with it'.[82] Tait, in accord with his position at Buccleuch's debate of 1864, probably hoped that such censures might encourage English Episcopalians to join the Scottish Episcopal Church and help to remove the Scottish Office.

---

[76] *Ibid.*, pp. 623-627.

[77] W. S. Moncrieff to the editor, 5 January 1892, *Record*, 15 January 1892.

[78] Bebbington, *Evangelicalism*, pp. 146-150.

[79] Lord Shaftesbury to John Burns, 13 November 1876, DRO, D5550/3/5/26.

[80] The Archbishop of York, William Thompson, an Evangelical, warned that if the bill were successful it would be regarded as a 'theological triumph' for the Scottish Office. He believed that 'the Scotch Church would have done well...if they had excluded the use of the Scotch Communion service' in 1863, and he registered any support he might give only on the understanding that he was not 'sanctioning the Scotch Office'. *Hansard*, p. 622.

[81] The Archbishop of Canterbury to D. T. K. Drummond, 13 November 1866, *Record*, 4 January 1867.

[82] *Chronicle of Convocation*, 18 June 1869, pp. 382-384.

Similarly, Longley, when attending the laying of the foundation stone of Inverness Cathedral in 1866, declared the Scottish Episcopal Church to be 'the only true representative of the Church of England in Scotland'. Answering a request from Drummond for clarification, Longley remarked of English Episcopalianism, 'I do not believe that a Church not governed by bishops can truly represent the Church of England'.[83] Drummond argued against Longley. He drew a parallel between the separatists and the recent South African Colenso judgement made by Lord Romilly, Master of the Rolls, in November 1866. Romilly had concluded that where the Church of England existed as a voluntary association, as in South Africa, it did not mean that its members 'may adopt any doctrines and ordinances they please, and still belong to the Church of England'. Drummond argued that Romilly had thus inferred that to join a church in communion with the Church of England, but holding different doctrine and rules, was 'a declaration of virtual secession'.[84] Longley accordingly qualified his original remarks by describing the Scottish Episcopal Church as 'a more true representative of the Church of England than certain congregations which were under no bishop'.[85] But it was clear that, since the canon law of 1863, despite legal anomalies, the Scottish Episcopal Church had found greater favour with its Anglican neighbour while the English Episcopalians were increasingly distanced.

The time seemed ripe to encourage English Episcopalians to return to the Scottish Episcopal Church. But the separatists were not receptive since they feared that the Scottish Office was taking root more strongly despite the

---

[83] D. T. K. Drummond to the Archbishop of Canterbury, 29 October 1866. The Archbishop of Canterbury to D. T. K. Drummond, 31 October 1866. *Record*, 4 January 1867.

[84] D. T. K. Drummond to the Archbishop of Canterbury, 19 November 1866. *Record* 4 January 1867. The cause of Romilly's judgement (November 1866) in the Judicial Committee of the Privy Council concerned the deposition for heresy in November 1863 of J. W. Colenso, the first Bishop of Natal, South Africa, by Robert Gray, Bishop of the Cape of Good Hope. Colenso's book, *Commentary on the Epistle to the Romans* (1855) had denied traditional atonement theology and had claimed that conversion and baptism were meaningless. In 1862 he had published the first part of *The Pentaeuch and the Book of Joshua Critically Examined*, challenging the historical accuracy of parts of the Bible. Gray, in a *Declaration* in 1849, had designated himself as merely in communion with the Church of England. As such, Romilly judged that Gray had no jurisdiction in South Africa to dismiss Colenso, a bishop of the Church of England. See Peter Hinchliff, *The Anglican Church in South Africa* (London, 1963), pp. 83-89. Anthony Ive, *A Candle Burns in Africa: The Story of the Church of England in South Africa* (Natal, 1992), pp. 19, 38-45. F. L. Cross (ed.), *The Oxford Dictionary of the Christian Church* (London, 1958), pp. 308-309.

[85] The Archbishop of Canterbury to D. T. K. Drummond, 5 December 1866. *Record*, 4 January 1867.

restrictions of 1863. In 1845 it had been estimated that around thirty out of the ninety existing congregations used the rite. By 1867, although the actual proportion of churches using it had decreased, forty-four out of one hundred and sixty-four churches had adopted it, albeit with fourteen of these alternating it with the English Office.[86] Some English Episcopalians argued that such support gave no 'security that it may not again be brought forward'.[87] Further, the Scottish Office was used in some of the most ritually advanced churches in Scotland. Table 10.1[88] shows areas of Ritualistic activity in the Scottish Episcopal Church from the 1860s to the 1880s, indicating the innovations adopted and the known use of the Scottish Communion Office.[89] It can be seen that there were already, by the 1860s, centres of Ritualism combined with the use of the Scottish Communion Office, notably in Aberdeen and Edinburgh.[90] In Edinburgh, with ten Scottish Episcopal churches, the two Ritualistic centres of St Columba's and All Saints accounted for 20% of the congregations in the city. This was considerably greater than the estimated 2.4% of churches using vestments in London in 1869.[91] While figures for Scotland indicate that, overall, Ritualism took hold later there than in England,[92] its presence in Aberdeen and Edinburgh from the 1840s to the 1860s would have been acutely felt in the Presbyterian ethos, and news of it would have travelled quickly in an age of improving communication. The increasing use of the Scottish Office, together with the rise in Ritualism in Scotland, would have exacerbated feeling against the Scottish Episcopal Church in the 1860s.

---

[86] Stuart, *English Episcoplianism*, p. 22. D'Orsey, *A Letter*, p. 8.

[87] Stuart, *English Episcopalianism*, p. 21.

[88] See Chapter 10, p. 335-336.

[89] *Scottish Episcopal Church Directory* (Edinburgh, 1879) was used to suggest the use of the Scottish Communion Office at Cove and St Andrew's, Glasgow, because earlier editions were not available.

[90] Suther had endeavoured to restrict the activities of F. G. Lee and John Comper at St John's and St Mary's, but eventually allowed Comper to minister at St Margaret's totally unrestrained. Strong, *Episcopalianism*, pp. 261-262.

[91] Owen Chadwick, *The Victorian Church*, Part II (London, 1992), p. 318.

[92] Strong, *Episcopalianism*, p. 261.

Table 10.1 Ritualism in Scotland, 1860-1880

CHURCH	INCUMBENT	RITUAL
Aberdeen, St John *Scottish Office*	F. G. Lee (1859-61) John Comper (1862-7)	Coloured vestments Coloured stoles Lighted altar candles
Aberdeen, St Margaret *Scottish Office*	John Comper (1867-1898)	Linen vestments Lighted altar candles
Aberdeen, St Mary *Scottish Office*	F. G. Lee (1861-64)	Coloured vestments Lighted altar candles
Cove, Aberdeen *Scottish Office*	William Humphrey (1864-67) T. I. Ball (1867-74)	Coloured vestments Lighted altar candles
Bridge of Allan *Scottish Office*	J. T. Boyle (1855-79)	Linen vestments Lighted altar candles
Cumbrae *Scottish Office*	G. C. White (1851-53) Alexander Ewing (1853-67) J. G. Cazenove (1867-75)	Coloured altar frontals Lighted altar candles Altar cross Stone credence table
Dalmahoy	W. G. Bullock (1869-1908)	Unlighted candles, Gregorian chant
Dumbarton	William Stephens (1858-1901)	Weekly Communion
Dumfries	Archibald McEwen (1846-83)	Reredos, carved angels Eastern Position genuflections
Dundee, Mary Magdalene	William Humphrey (1867-68) G. W. Anstiss (1868-70) J. W. Hunter (1871-80)	Lighted candles Biretta
Edinburgh, St Columba *Scottish Office*	John Alexander (1846-69) H. J. Palmer (1869-72) C. E. Bowden (1872-88)	Coloured vestments Lighted candles
Edinburgh, All Saints *Scottish Office*	A. D. Murdoch (1867-1906)	Coloured vestments Lighted Candles
Glasgow, St Andrew *Scottish Office*	J. F. S. Gordon (1844-91)	Coloured vestments Lighted altar candles
Muchalls *Scottish Office*	W. H. B. Proby (1861-65)	Chancel added, 1865 Unspecified ritual changes

Perth, St Ninian's Scottish Office	Canons: Joseph Haskoll (1848-50) J. C. Chambers (1850-53) Henry Humble (1853-76)	Stone altar Jewelled cross Linen vestments Lighted altar candles East end hung with silk

Sources: D. T. K. Drummond, *Letter to the Very Rev the Dean of Carlisle* (Edinburgh, 1876), pp. 15, 33-36. Rowan Strong, *Episcopalianism in Nineteenth-Century Scotland* (Oxford, 2002), pp. 170-171, 235-263, especially 258-259 and 260-261, 309. Nigel Yates, *Anglican Ritualism in Victorian Britain, 1830-1910* (Oxford, 1999), pp. 124-137, 414. *Scottish Ecclesiastical Journal*, 26 June 1862. *Scottish Episcopal* Journal, 24 September 1863. *Scottish Guardian*, May 15 1865. *Dundee Advertiser*, 31 December 1867. *Scottish Episcopal Church Directory* (Edinburgh, 1879).

Thus, not surprisingly, when, in 1864, T. G. S.. Suther, Bishop of Aberdeen and Orkney, issued an invitation to St Paul's and St James's, Aberdeen, 'to join the Scottish Episcopal Church', it was 'very courteously declined' by St James's because 'it would lead to dissention in the congregation'.[93] One correspondent in the *Scottish Episcopal Journal* put the problem in Aberdeen down to 'the ritual practised and tolerated at St Mary's which outdid even 'the excessive ritual at St Ninian's Cathedral, Perth'.[94] Similar moves were made in 1870 to 1873, but the offer was again refused when Thomas Bannerman, a founder and benefactor of the church, objected because of the doctrine of the Scottish Communion Office.[95] In 1866, E. C. Wrenford at Nairn also rejected similar approaches from Suther because 'subscription to the canons involved an expression of assent to...the objectionable office'.[96] In the 1860s English Episcopalians maintained that the doctrine of the Scottish Communion Office, compounded with its growing usage and connection to Ritualism, was an obstacle to union.

Attempt at Reconciliation, 1870-1872

At the Convocation of Canterbury in June 1869, the High Churchman, Samuel Wilberforce, Bishop of Oxford, presented a petition from Scottish Episcopalians objecting to Anglican clergy 'invading' their dioceses and officiating for English Episcopalians.[97] But while Wilberforce warned that he would reprimand any offending clergyman in his diocese, Tait, the

---

[93] St James's Minute Book, August 1864, St James's Church, Aberdeen, Archives. See also 'Bishop of Aberdeen and Orkney in Synod', *Scottish Guardian*, October 1865.

[94] *Scottish Episcopal Journal*, 24 September 1863.

[95] Margaret and Mary Massie, who were also members of St James's, were vocal in their objections to the proposed union. St James's Minute Book, 1870-1873, *passim*. St James's Church, Aberdeen, Archives.

[96] *Record*, 15 November 1872.

[97] *Chronicle of Convocation*, 18 June 1869, p. 382.

Archbishop of Canterbury, preferred to take a conciliatory stance. Seconded by John Jackson, the Bishop of London, who feared any 'irritation in the breasts of the members of the congregations in question', he informed Robert Eden, Primus of the Scottish Episcopal Church, that visits to English Episcopalians should be made 'by private negotiation'.[98] While Wilberforce actively opposed English Episcopalians, Tait and Jackson preferred pacification.

In July 1869 Drummond, probably prompted by Tait's discussions with Eden, informed the former of English Episcopal concerns. The advance of Anglo-Catholicism in Britain, plainly evident in the Ritualist movement, led him to re-emphasise that the Scottish Episcopal Church insisted on 'a term of communion, which if it existed in England, would make it impossible to resist the efforts of that party who seek to establish in our Church the dogma of the real presence objectively'.[99] Regarding Drummond's letter as 'important', Tait forwarded it to Alexander Ewing, Bishop of Argyll and the Isles,[100] who circulated it among the other Scottish bishops.[101] By April 1870 Drummond, convinced that his letter to Tait had initiated discussions in the Scottish Episcopal Church concerning union,[102] sent a private statement to the English Episcopalians setting out the 'obstacles which make separation necessary at the present moment'.[103] He pressed for elimination of the Scottish Office from the canons and for a resolution of the problem of evangelistic meetings.[104] While Tait hoped for reconciliation, Drummond's ground remained unchanged.

However, some English Episcopalians disagreed with Drummond. At St Jude's, Glasgow, there had been a depletion of the congregation and funds after the formation of St Silas's in 1863. Consequently, James McCann, its new incumbent, attempted to reunite with the Scottish Episcopal Church in 1870. Many at St Jude's who, like Drummond, found no security in the

---

[98] *Ibid.*, pp. 383-384.

[99] D. T. K. Drummond to A. C. Tait, 13 July 1869, LPL, Tait 162, pp. 240-243. Also, LPL H 5340. Rowan Strong's argument that contemporary Evangelicals in Scotland believed that many traditional congregations were 'hotbeds of Anglo Catholicism' is misleading. Drummond's letter to Tait clearly indicated that the concern was not that Anglo Catholicism was rife in Scotland, but that the Scottish Communion Office was a natural expression of that particular theology which was at present making inroads into the Church of England. See Strong, *Episcopalianism*, p. 261.

[100] A. C. Tait to D. T. K. Drummond, 26 July 1869, LPL, Tait 162, pp. 240-243. Also, LPL, H 5340.

[101] D. T. K. Drummond, 'Statement', 26 April 1870, LPL, Tait 176, pp. 126-131. Also, LPL, H5320 D7.

[102] *Statement*, 26 April 1870, LPL, H5320 D7, p. 1. Also, LPL, Tait 176, pp. 126-131.

[103] *Ibid.* p. 1.

[104] *Ibid.*, pp. 9-10.

1863 canons, objected. But others joined McCann in forming a new Scottish Episcopal church, St Paul's, Glasgow. While McCann declared his opposition to the doctrine of the Scottish Office – there was no divergence of opinion on this matter – he, like Charles Baring, Bishop of Durham, regarded the 1863 canons as giving sufficient protection against its use.[105] Again, Thomas Worthington left St James's, Aberdeen, in 1873, to become diocesan chaplain for Edinburgh, after disagreement with the managers over congregational matters.[106] Clearly, by 1870 some separatists considered the canons of 1863 to provide a safety net against the Scottish Office and that, possibly, the issue of evangelistic meetings could be dealt with more satisfactorily within a united Church.[107] Baring's accommodating analysis of 1864 had taken root, leading to a weakness in the English Episcopal movement.

Nevertheless, the majority of English Episcopalians showed little inclination to abandon their cause at this stage. When Drummond's letters of 1869 initiated no response from the Scottish Episcopal authorities, the separatists searched for permanent episcopal superintendence. 'Bishop Smith', possibly B. B. Smith, an American bishop of moderate Evangelical views, was approached.[108] Smith informed Tait that he had declined only because of 'the ecclesiastical anomalies'.[109] In February 1870, seemingly in response to Smith's hesitation, the separatists requested A. J. Stephens, Q. C., to provide an analysis of their legal position concerning episcopal oversight and the Act of Union.[110] He was asked whether an Anglican bishop would, on appointment by the English Episcopalians, commit an act of secession and if, in such an event, the congregations would cease to be

---

[105] *Record*, 6, 15, 22, November 1872, 2 December 1872.

[106] Worthington had removed the Sunday School and library to the Gallowgate, presumably to attract local residents to St James's, and had also insisted that the collection had to be taken during the service rather than at the church door, in order to accord with practice in the Church of England. St James's Minute Book, 1872-1873, *passim*, St James's Church, Aberdeen, Archives.

[107] There is some indication that Frederick Courtenay at St Jude's, Glasgow, agreed to the Bishop of Glasgow and Galloway, W. S. Wilson, confirming his candidates in 1875. Gavin White, *The Scottish Episcopal Church: A New History* (Edinburgh, 1998), p. 78. However, Courtenay left in 1876, to be replaced by John Bennett who must have discontinued such links because St Jude's was active in the Association of English Episcopalians after its formation in 1877.

[108] D. M. Lewis (ed.), *The Blackwell Dictionary of Evanglical Biography*, Vol. II (Oxford, 1995), p. 1022.

[109] Bishop Smith to A. C. Tait, 5 August 1870, LPL, Tait 176, pp. 107-108.

[110] Dr A. J. Stephens was regarded by Edward Garbett, editor of the *Record* 1853-1867, as the greatest ecclesiastical lawyer of his day. *The Churchman*, December 1880, p. 466. See also Frederic Boase, *Modern English Biography*, Vol. III (Truro, 1901), p. 728.

members of the Church of England and be open to legal censure. On 22 February 1871, Stephens answered all these questions in the negative.[111] The English Episcopalians had received an endorsement of their legal position and an assurance on constitutional matters. It was now obvious that they might press for their own bishop, invite clergy to their pulpits, and remain in their present position indefinitely unless the situation was resolved.

After more letters from Drummond referring to the opinion of Stephens and complaining of Scottish Episcopal censure on visiting clergy,[112] Tait was exasperated. On 15 December 1871 he sent all Drummond's correspondence to Bishop Robert Eden of Moray, Ross and Caithness, Primus of the Scottish Episcopal Church, asking him 'to take some steps to reconciliation'.[113] Drummond's continued doctrinal objections, the opinion of Stephens, the prohibitions adopted by some Scottish clergy against the separatists, and Tait's desire for settlement were thus crucial factors in the forthcoming negotiations for reconciliation in 1872.

The new Coadjutor of Edinburgh, Henry Cotterill,[114] informed Tait in January 1872, that his intervention had initiated plans for a discussion at a 'conference of the Bishops at Perth on 16 January 1872', where he himself would present a plan for union.[115] Cotterill's idea was to omit all discussions about the Scottish Office, and to invite the English Episcopalians to join the Scottish Episcopal Church 'on their own ground, providing their clergy will promise due canonical obedience to the laws of the Church of England as here applicable', with Tait being 'the referee' in difficult cases. He believed that Drummond's assistant, W. S. Moncrieff, was in favour of the suggestion, although he did not think Drummond would be enthusiastic. As for the other separatists, he was hopeful that,

---

[111] *Record*, 12 April 1871.

[112] D. T. K. Drummond to A. C. Tait, 14 April 1871, LPL, Tait 176, pp. 109-110. D. T. K. Drummond to A. C. Tait, 27 November 1871, LPL, Tait 176, p. 119.

[113] A. C. Tait to Robert Eden, 15 December 1871, LPL, Tait 176, pp. 124-125.

[114] Cotterill had the reputation of being an Evangelical when he was appointed by J. B. Sumner as Bishop of Grahamstown, South Africa, in 1856. At that time it was hoped that he would mediate successfully in the dispute between J. W. Colenso, the Bishop of Natal, and Robert Gray, the Bishop of Cape Town. Cotterill joined forces with Gray against Colenso in the trial held in 1863 over Colenso's theology, which deprived Colenso of his Bishopric. (See n. 84 above). Cotterill eventually prepared a constitution for the 'Church of the Province of South Africa', founded in 1871. This included the Third Proviso whereby the C. P. S. A. was not bound by the decisions of any legal tribunal other than its own. This made the C. P. S. A. legally different from the Church of England. Peter Hinchliff, *The Anglican Church in South Africa* (London, 1963), pp. 93-114. Anthony Ive, *A Candle Burns in Africa: The Story of the Church of England in South Africa* (Natal, South Africa, 1992), pp. 5-57.

[115] Henry Cotterill to A. C. Tait, 5 January 1872, LPL, Tait 183, pp. 158-161.

once within the Church, they would realise the advantages of synodical involvement and would tone down their complaints. Within the Scottish Episcopal Church, he predicted that A. P. Forbes, Bishop of Brechin, would concur because it would leave the Scottish Office untouched.[116] Cotterill, by omitting reference to the Scottish Communion Office, hoped to please all parties.

Drummond wrote to Tait on 31 January 1872 with an alternative. By contrast he regarded the immediate resolution of the Scottish Office issue as vital. He suggested that 'the Scotch Bishops pass a resolution declaring the Communion Office of their canons to be the Office of Laud's Service Book for Scotland'. Drummond insisted that 'though we infinitely prefer our own Office to that of Laud, and shall never use the latter, yet we could not make it the cause of separation'.[117] His plan was a reiteration of his stance in 1842, when he had argued that the words 'become unto us' in Laud's service, together with its less obvious oblation, opened up an interpretation acceptable to Evangelicals.[118]

Drummond's idea found favour among some orthodox High Churchmen in Scotland, especially as he did not ask for removal of the Scottish Office in congregations already using it. E. B. Ramsay and his curate, D. F. Sandford, at St John's, Edinburgh, were enthusiastic, and pressed C. H. Terrot, Bishop of Edinburgh, not to dismiss it 'without very serious consideration [because] the present form has not been moulded by Synodical or Episcopal authority'.[119] Charles Wordsworth, Bishop of St Andrews, Dunkeld and Dunblane, was also supportive, informing Drummond that as the proposal 'would be a gain in every way...I shall do all I can to urge it, especially at our next General Synod'.[120] However, some unnamed leading English Episcopalians[121] felt that 'Mr. D. had gone too far in this'. But E. C Wrenford of Nairn backed Drummond, suggesting that, if this plan were rejected, the separatist clergy might hold a licence from Tait and at the same time accept 'episcopal services from the Scotch Bishops'.[122] Wrenford's proposal appeared to attract little attention, and while it is not apparent how many other English Episcopalians supported Drummond, it is clear that his stance represented an intermediate position

---

[116] *Ibid.* Also, Henry Cotterill to D. F. Sandford, 19 January 1872, DRO, D5550/3/5/26.

[117] D. T. K. Drummond to A. C. Tait, 31 January 1872, LPL, Tait 183, pp. 164-167.

[118] See Chapter 7, p. 225.

[119] D. F. Sandford to Charles Terrot, February 1872, LPL, Tait 183, pp. 168-171.

[120] D. T. K. Drummond to A. C. Tait, 16 November 1872, LPL, Tait 183, p. 210.

[121] 'Private document printed by order of the vestry for circulation in the congregation of St Thomas's English Episcopal Chapel, Edinburgh, 11 June 1875', p. 4, St Thomas's Church, Edinburgh, Archives.

[122] E. C. Wrenford, *The Two Branches of the Episcopal Communion in Scotland:Subjection, No, Not for an Hour* (London, 1872), p. 8.

in the group between the extremes of Moncrieff, who was willing to enter the Scottish Episcopal Church with the Scottish Office intact, and others who wanted only the English service.[123]

Cotterill's idea was not without opposition from Scottish Episcopalians. A rumour went round that he wanted 'to sacrifice the Scottish Office' in order to conciliate the English Episcopalians. Some bishops were also worried that they would take on the position of deputies to Tait and could not accept any notion of 'the see of Canterbury as having a quasi patriarchal position with regard to us'.[124] Scottish Office supporters pressed for autonomy in Scotland, probably fearing that outside involvement could lead to abandonment of the Scottish liturgy.

But it was Cotterill's suggestion which won most support. Already, on 20 January 1872, Sandford had informed Moncrieff that Tait, along with John Jackson, Bishop of London, and Charles Baring, Bishop of Durham, favoured it.[125] On 15 March 1872, Tait wrote to Drummond encouraging him to accept Cotterill's plan, stressing that 'all hopes of union would probably be sacrificed if the question of the Scottish Office were brought forward at the present'.[126] However, although Cotterill had the support of an influential sector of the Church of England, a meeting of the English Episcopalians held in Montrose in May 1872, consisting of clergy and laymen from six congregations, rejected his ideas, informing Tait that it did 'not consider it necessary to make proposals' for intercommunion.[127] The process of working towards union had reached a stalemate.

Afterwards, Baring wrote to Cotterill saying he would continue to confirm English Episcopal candidates only 'out of respect to Mr Drummond', but that he would cease to do so should Drummond resign.[128] More problems arose for the separated congregations over the issue of visiting clergy. Despite the opinion of Stephens in 1871, trouble broke out when E. P. Hathaway of St Ebbe's, Oxford, officiated at the separatist chapel at Nairn in July 1872. The Bishop of Oxford, J. F. Mackarness, assured the Scottish Episcopalians that Hathaway had ignored his 'expressed wish'.[129] The English Episcopalians, threatened with the

---

[123] Cf. Strong, *Episcopalianism*, p. 230 where it is suggested that Drummond 'rather gloried' in his separation'. His conciliatory stance in 1872 seems to contradict this view.

[124] Henry Cotterill to A. C. Tait, 6 March 1872, LPL, Tait 183, pp. 178-181.

[125] D. F. Sandford to W. S. Moncrieff, 20 January 1872, DRO, D5550/3/5/26.

[126] A. C. Tait to D. T. K. Drummond, 15 March 1872, LPL, Tait 183, p. 193.

[127] W. S. Moncrieff to A. C. Tait, 20 May 1872, LPL, Tait 183, p. 202.

[128] W. S. Moncrieff to the Editor, 5 January 1892, *Record*, 15 January 1892.

[129] J. F. Mackarness to William West, 16 July 1872. *Record*, 31 July 1872. Opposition to English clergy visiting the English Episcopalians was a continuing problem. In 1872 Gordon Calthrop, from London, was discouraged by G. R. Mackarness, Bishop of Argyll and the Isles, and John Jackson, Bishop of London, from officiating at Dunoon, *Record*, 13 December 1872. Cotterill tried to prevent J. C. Miller

withdrawal of episcopal oversight, and harassed in their clerical arrangements, were in an increasingly difficult position.

Accordingly, Drummond, Moncrieff, E. D. Hutton of St Silas's, Glasgow, Joseph Mulkerns, of St John's, Dundee, and H. J. Knapp, of Montrose, along with lay representatives, convened a meeting of the Church Association and Clerical Lay Union at Exeter Hall on 12 December 1872, in order to protest against cases like Hathaway's, and to gain increased support from English Evangelicals. At the meeting the chairman, the Hon. W. Ashley, was joined by forty-seven Evangelical clergy.[130] Ashley highlighted the Scottish Communion Office as the bar to union. Edward Garbett[131] and Canon Edward Hoare[132] expressed sympathy for the petition, and R. P. Blakeney[133] summed up proceedings by supporting the deputation and calling for a memorial to be submitted to the Anglican episcopate, entreating that 'no impediment may be thrown in the way of clergymen who propose to minister to the congregations of their brethren in Scotland'.[134] The main purposes of the meeting had thus been realised, despite the opposition of prominent Evangelicals such as Baring. The episode was evidence of the high level of support that English Episcopalians could still muster.[135]

In 1873 the English Episcopalians, looking for consolidation, asked Stephens, aided by Alexander Haldane, a lawyer and editor of the *Record*, to examine the theology of the Scottish Communion Office and confirm

---

from visiting St Thomas's, Edinburgh, for the Church Missionary Society in 1876. Miller maintained that 'Drummond and other valued friends are the champions of truth', and proceeded with his tour. J. C. Miller to Henry Cotterill, 15 March 1876, DRO, D/5550/3/5/26. H. W. Jermyn, Bishop of Brechin, warned the incumbent elect for Montrose, W. Bates, of Ripley, Derbyshire, that 'you cannot canonically minister without a license from me'. Bates withdrew, and the incumbency was not settled for a sustained length of time until T. S. Connolly, the Church Missionary Society secretary for North Lancashire, was appointed from 1881 to 1913. H. W. Jermyn to W. Bates, 22 November 1876, *Record,* 4 December 1876.

[130] Apologies for absence included Bishops Ryan, Alford and Anderson; Deans Hugh McNeile, Francis Close, Robert Payne Smith, and W. W. Champneys; Archdeacon Prest; Canons Battersby, J. C. Ryle and Sale.

[131] Edward Garbett was Vicar of Christ Church, Surbiton, 1863 to 1877, and Editor of the *Record* from 1853 to 1867. Lewis, *Dictionary of Evangelical Biography*, Vol. I, pp. 423-424.

[132] Edward Hoare was Canon of Canterbury Cathedral, 1868, CMS stalwart, and incumbent of Holy Trinity, Tunbridge Wells, 1853 to 1879. *Ibid.*, pp. 559-560.

[133] Author of *The Book of Common Prayer in its History and Interpretation with Special Reference to Points of Dispute in the Present Day* (London, 1865). On p. 157 he had described the Scottish Communion Service as 'a decided retrogression towards Rome'.

[134] *Record*, 16 December 1872.

[135] Baring did not attend the meeting. Reasons are not given.

From Secession to Partial Union, 1846-1900 343

whether their stance was justified. Stephens and Haldane published their findings in May 1873, announcing that, in the consecration of the elements and the doctrine of sacrifice, 'important doctrinal differences do exist' between the Scottish and Anglican rites.[136] Thus some stability was restored to English Episcopalianism by 1873, with legal opinions confirming both its validity to exist in Scotland and its stance on the Scottish Communion Office.

Divisions within English Episcopalianism

As we have seen, the seeming equilibrium of English Episcopalianism in 1873 disguised an increasing fragility which was to continue for the rest of the century. McCann and Worthington[137] had joined the Scottish Episcopal Church in 1870 and 1873 respectively, and in 1872 Moncrieff had sided with Cotterill's attempt to encourage the separatists into the church.[138] Moncrieff's position is not entirely clear although in 1900 he admitted his agreement with Baring that the 1863 canons provided a sufficient safety net for Evangelicals.[139] However, by the 1870s, McCann and Worthington appear more certainly to have accepted Baring's position. Thus, while continuing to be suspicious of the theology of the Scottish Communion Office, some clergy were beginning to consider compromise, adopting Baring's accommodating stance.

Nevertheless, there were other factors which contributed to the softening mood. One that seems to offer a plausible explanation, and appears to have influenced Moncrieff as he revealed in 1900[140], is that, in the 1860s, some Tractarians preferred the Book of Common Prayer, based on Roman liturgy, to the Scottish Office as a vehicle for their beliefs.[141] Despite the counter-arguments of English Episcopalians that the order of the prayers in the Scottish rite did not detract from the belief of an objective presence in the elements,[142] some advanced Churchmen regarded the Scottish consecration as flawed. However, the Anglo-Catholic Provost T. I. Ball of Cumbrae Cathedral, spoke for others in 1900, arguing that 'all Roman

---

[136] *Extract of the Opinion of Dr Stephen and Mr Alexander Haldane on the 'Case of English Episcopalians in Scotland' May 1873*. Quoted in Stuart, *English Episcopalianism*, pp. 31-37.

[137] See Chapter 10, p. 338.

[138] See Chapter 10, pp. 337-340.

[139] *Record*, 8 June 1900.

[140] *Record*, 22 June 1900.

[141] John Keble to E. B. Pusey, 4 May 1862. Pusey to Keble correspondence, Pusey House Archives. Quoted in Rowan Strong, *Alexander Forbes of Brechin* (Oxford, 1995), p. 172.

[142] See Chapter 7, pp. 235-236. See also, C. P. Miles, *The Scottish Episcopal Church Antagonistic to the Church of England* (Glasgow, 1857), pp. 20-21.

liturgists of name' maintained that the Greek rites on which the Scottish Office was based, effected transubstantiation.[143] Certainly, therefore, the Scottish Office appealed to some Anglo-Catholics.

It is possible to gauge the depth of such support. While the presence of non-Ritualistic Anglo-Catholics in the Scottish Episcopal Church is difficult to trace, the more vivid ceremony of Ritualists themselves is easily identified and gives an indication of overall Anglo-Catholic presence. Table 10.1[144] shows that in the 1870s and 1880s the use of the Scottish Office combined with ritualistic activity was evident in at least nine churches: Aberdeen (St Margaret's; Cove), Bridge of Allan, Cumbrae, Edinburgh (St Columba's; All Saints), Glasgow (St Andrew's), Muchalls and Perth (St Ninian's). Table 10.2[145] records the centres of Ritualism in the Scottish Episcopal Church in 1900[146] when it appears that around twenty-one Ritualists used the Scottish Office compared to only nine who officiated from the English liturgy alone.[147] Thus, although the issue of the Scottish consecration unsettled some like Moncrieff, it is not likely that the majority of the separatists were lulled into apathy concerning the Scottish Office because some claimed it to be non-Catholic – a substantial number of Anglo-Catholics were prepared to use it.

---

[143] T. I. Ball to the editor. *Scottish Guardian*, 3 August 1900. Reproduced in *Record*, 10 August 1900.

[144] See Chapter 10, p. 335-336.

[145] See Chapter 10, pp. 345-347.

[146] Not all who held Anglo-Catholic beliefs were Ritualists. There were therefore likely to have been several more Anglo-Catholics than Table 10.2 indicates. J. S. Reed, *Glorious Battle* (London, 1998), p. 70. Nigel Yates, *Anglican Ritualism in Victorian Britain 1830-1910* (Oxford, 1999), pp. 157-158.

[147] This information, collected from the *Year Book for the Scottish Episcopal Church in Scotland, 1900*, appears to have omissions. For instance, Old St Paul's, Edinburgh, is not recorded. Also, caution should be applied when attributing the use of the Scottish or English Offices alone since the entries are rather erratic.

Table 10.2 Ritualism in Scotland, 1900

DIOCESE	SCOTTISH OFFICE/ ENGLISH OFFICE	ENGLISH OFFICE	INCUMBENT	RITUAL
Aberdeen	Banorchy-Terman		J. C. D. Fraser	Coloured stoles, lit candles
	Deer		J. H. Burn	Lights, linen vestments, seasonal colours, mixed chalice
	Fraserburgh		Henry Fyfe	Most ritual points
Argyll and the Isles	Ardchattan *Scottish Office only*		Duncan Munro	Linen vestments, lights
	Ballachulish		Donald Cameron	Linen vestments, Gregorian chant
	Connel Ferry		Charles Pressley-Smith	Linen vestments, lights
	Inverary		E. G. H. Little	Linen vestments
	Nether Lochaber *Scottish Office only*		J. R. Vincent	Vestments, candles
Brechin	St John the Baptist *Scottish Office only*		J. J. Dunbar	Vestments, lights
	St Mary Magdalene		Francis Burdon	Colours
	St Salvador		G. M. Duncan	Lit candles with SO
		Laurencekirk	W.W. Malachi	Coloured stoles, mixed chalice
		Montrose	Charles Grub	Altar lights, colours

Edinburgh	Cathedral		J. S. Wilson	All ritual points
	St Columba		H. H. Flower	All ritual points
		Christ Church, Trinity	P. M. Herford	Altar lights, mixed chalice, coloured stoles, Joules chants
Glasgow and Galloway	St Bride		T. M. R. Younghughes	Five ritual points
	St Gabriel		John Leal	All ritual points
	Newton *Scottish Office only*		Dugald Macdonald	Five ritual points
		Castle Douglas	A. C. Manston	Altar lights
		Clyde Bank	W. H. Jenkins	Vestments
		St Michael	G. F. Garwood	Mixed chalice, coloured stoles
		Kilmarnock	A. F. Blood	Mixed chalice
		Newton Stewart	G. E. Roberts	Coloured lights, stoles
Moray, Ross and Caithness	Tain		G. A. Breguet	Vestments, lights, colours
	Thurso		W. L. Walker	Sarum colours
St Andrew's, Dunkeld and Dunblane	St Ninian's Cathedral, Perth		A. E. Campbell	Vestments, lights
	St Andrews		E. G. A. Winter	Coloured stoles
	Taymouth		William Arbuthnot	Mixed chalice, lights, colours
		Kinross	H. J. Williams	Vestments, lights
TOTAL	21	9 using ENGLISH OFFICE alone		

Source: Year Book of the Episcopal Church in Scotland, 1900

Six Ritual Points: Eastward Position by celebrant at Eucharist, full eucharistic vestments, lighted candles on altar, use of unleavened wafer bread, use of incense, mixing of water and wine in the chalice. Other Ritual practices included; coloured altar frontals, altar crosses, crucifixes, holy water, elevation of elements, statues and credence tables.

However, larger processes affecting the Church of England were more damaging to English Episcopalianism. In 1867, the Church Association brought W. J. E. Bennett, the incumbent of Frome, to court for speaking of a real presence of Christ in the elements which, consequently, deserved outward expressions of adoration. After he modified his language, the Privy Council ruled that he had not spoken with sufficient clarity to indicate prosecution for propagating non-Anglican doctrine. But Evangelicals were dismayed, fearing that licence had been given for Anglo-Catholic teaching in the Church of England.[148] While acknowledging the seriousness of events in the Church of England, Drummond continued to maintain that Evangelicals could safely read their own theology in the English rite. Remarking on the outcome of events to Tait in 1872, Drummond wrote that, 'in England...I am not required personally to give even an indirect sanction to [Bennett's] views. But in the Scottish Episcopal Church...the Scottish Communion Office gives exact expression to [them]'.[149] However, in 1876, Cotterill pointed to different opinions circulating since the Bennett judgement, that 'the English Episcopalians had not a leg to stand on', and that if they protested against the Scottish Office because it was attractive to Anglo-Catholicism, they were bound to find the English rite similarly objectionable.[150] Cotterill's argument was taken up by William Forbes Skene, Historiographer Royal for Scotland and benefactor of St Vincent's, Edinburgh, who wrote anonymously in 1882 that in the Church of England there were 'forms and ceremonies adopted by extreme High Churchmen...which symbolise a doctrine not diverse from that expressed by the Scotch Communion Office and yet the Evangelical party have not thought of leaving the Church on that account'.[151] T. K. Talon, the incumbent of St Vincent's, agreed, maintaining that if toleration of the Scottish Office 'forms a fair bar to union, such a view should drive those who make this objection from the Church of England on account of its toleration of High Church Ritualism'.[152] Under such circumstances Skene

---

[148] Kenneth Hylson-Smith, *Evangelicals in the Church of England 1734-1984* (Edinburgh, 1989), pp. 127-132. Drummond and Gustavus Flindt, of St Silas's, Glasgow, attended a meeting of the Church Association at the National Club, Whitehall, in 1872 to protest against the judgement.

[149] D. T. K. Drummond to the Archbishop of Canterbury, 7 August 1872, LPL, Tait 183, p. 208.

[150] Henry Cotterill to Canon Miller, 16 March 1876, DRO, D5550 3/5/26.

[151] *A Plea for Union among Episcopalians in Scotland by a Member of the Church of England,* (Edinburgh, 1882), p. 24.

[152] T. K. Talon, *Reasons for Joining the Episcopal Church of Scotland*, (Edinburgh, 1882), p. 6.

proposed that it was better to join the Scottish Episcopal Church 'bearing witness to Evangelic truth'.[153] Thus by the late 1870s the argument that the Scottish Communion Office, unlike the English service, was inimical to Evangelical belief had become less of an issue for some who considered that Ritualism in England made the Scottish Episcopal Church seem distinctly less sinister.

Again, High Church concern for the visible unity of the Church might have begun to cause doubts about separation among some Evangelicals. Certainly Cotterill's sermons after 1860 continually warned that 'divisions in our Church...must be fatal to its growth', and in 1877 his charge to the diocese of Edinburgh focused on 1 Corinthians 12 and Ephesians 4 as speaking of the Church as a 'corporate...unity', and warned against clergy who 'presumptuously imagine that [their] knowledge is perfect and complete, and judge those who perchance see other parts of God's truth'.[154] In this respect Cotterill's influence could have been considerable, leading for instance, in part, to Moncrieff's changing position.

Similarly, some Evangelicals were, possibly, increasingly influenced by High Church views of the Scottish liturgy. In 1900 Moncrieff admitted to agreeing with Charles Wordsworth, former bishop of St Andrews, Dunkeld and Dunblane, that the Scottish Communion Office, although 'chosen so as to cause unnecessary offence', and preferring its rewriting, was 'perfectly defensible upon the plainest Scriptural and theological grounds'.[155] Working alongside High Churchmen sometimes led to dilution of a clear Evangelical doctrinal identity.

Drummond warned English Episcopalians of the outcome of such accommodation, 'that the differences so fundamental and essential, as we believe them to be, between us and the Scottish Episcopal Church, may gradually be lost sight of, and our congregations finally absorbed in a Church...which is to this day unreformed'.[156] G. T. Fox, a leading Evangelical from Durham, wrote to Drummond in 1876 on the topic: 'St Thomas's was never more needed than now', and drew attention to 'silly Evangelicals, captivated by sacerdotalism [which] poisons their minds'.[157]

---

[153] *Plea*, p. 25.

[154] Henry Cotterill, *Charge of the Lord Bishop of Grahamstown at his Third Visitation*, (Grahamstown, 1863), pp. 14-15. Henry Cotterill, *True Position of the Episcopal Church in Scotland being a Charge Delivered to the Synod of the Diocese of Edinburgh, May 2 1877* (Edinburgh, 1877), p. 22. See also Henry Cotterill, *The Unity of Christians Essential to the Conversion of the* World (Edinburgh, 1879), pp. 4-8. Henry Cotterill to W. E. Gladstone, 12 July 1876, British Library, Gladstone Papers, Add. MS 44 450 f. 245.

[155] *Record*, 22 June 1900, 6 July 1900, 3 August 1900.

[156] *Record*, 23 October 1876.

[157] G. T. Fox to D. T. K. Drummond, 1 June 1876, DRO, D5550/3/5/26.

The image of Evangelicalism was considered by some to become blurred when its proponents sought to co-operate with High Churchmen.

A serious problem occurred over such matters in 1875 at St Thomas's, Edinburgh, when Cotterill organised a mission for the diocese. This was typical of a movement in the 1870s when Anglo-Catholics began to organise their own parish-based outreach, often causing disagreement among Evangelicals concerning their co-operation.[158] Cotterill's Edinburgh mission commenced on 10 January 1875 with the involvement of High Churchmen, Ritualists and the Cowley Fathers, an Anglo-Catholic preaching order. When it was announced, at the close of 1874, as an exclusively Scottish Episcopal event, Drummond and Moncrieff agreed 'to defer to another time any evangelistic services...for St Thomas's'. Drummond was not 'prepared to incur the responsibility of arrangements over which I have no control',[159] and while he did not rule out future involvement he considered the matter closed.

But Moncrieff continued to show the same willingness to co-operate with Cotterill as had been evident in 1872 in the discussions towards union. Moncrieff's actions revealed the deepening rifts in the Evangelical party over the matter of accommodation. Without informing Drummond, he attended the services at St John's, Edinburgh, under the teaching of W. D. Maclagan, who had played a prominent part in a similar mission in London in 1874. Maclagan's preaching involved distinctly sacramental emphases. Typically he taught that 'in baptism there was the beginning of restoration [and] through Holy Communion...Christ became formed in us'. He recommended a booklet, *The Narrow Way*, which explained that confirmation 'makes you a perfect Christian' and that the communion

---

[158] In contrast to Evangelical events, where the emphasis was on the doctrine of conversion from a sinful nature, Anglo-Catholic missions focused on the renewal of baptismal vows and confession of individual sins to a priest, culminating with a corporate celebration of the Eucharist. A. W. Thorold opened up his church at St Pancras in London for a such mission in 1871. But a large event held in London in 1874 caused heated controversy among Evangelicals concerning the extent of their involvement. The *Record* urged participation but the *Rock,* was sceptical, fearing Evangelicals might compromise their beliefs. When six hundred Evangelicals protested against the use of the confessional at the mission some Evangelicals withdrew their support, but Sholto Douglas-Campbell, of All Souls, Marylebone, and a future incumbent of St Silas's, Glasgow, participated. John Kent, *Holding the Fort: Studies in Victorian Revivalism* (London, 1978), pp. 236-237. Anne Bentley, 'The Transformation of the Evangelical Party in the later Nineteenth Century', (University if Durham Ph. D. thesis, 1971), pp. 301-311. *Record*, 23 June 1873, Quoted in Bentley, 'Transformation of the Evangelical Party', p. 303. *Rock*, 14 November, 19 December 1873, Quoted in Bentley, 'Transformation of Evangelical Party', p. 304.

[159] D. T. K. Drummond, *Letter to the Very Rev. the Dean of Carlisle* (Edinburgh, 1876), pp. 4, 31-32.

elements were changed by consecration. While Moncrieff wrote to Drummond that Maclagan's address was 'most impressive', and that the whole mission was a 'great work', Drummond considered it to exhibit an 'evangelical-High Church-sacerdotal compound, or mingle-mangle of dangerous teaching'.[160] John Burns of Wemyss Bay criticised Moncrieff's involvement with 'a party with whom no true-hearted Protestant would desire to have any connection'.[161] However, Moncrieff was supported by Canon Tristram of the Church Missionary Society who, on a visit to St Thomas's, told him 'I intensely sympathise with you',[162] while J. C. Miller, another official of the society, wrote to Drummond, 'what is Moncrieff about...he forgot that he was compromising himself as well as others'.[163] Accommodation with High Churchmen seriously divided Evangelicals.

The difficulties led to turmoil in the congregation at St Thomas's, many of whom were newcomers. On 4 March 1875, the vestry decided that it would be advisable to prepare a document giving the details of the basis of St Thomas's position relative to the Scottish Episcopal Church.[164] But on 30 March Moncrieff announced that he found the statement misleading because not enough prominence was given to the canons of 1863,[165] and on 17 April six vestrymen resigned in support of him, stressing that it was important to do 'all that is possible to encourage inter communion among Christians'.[166] By 11 June 1875 the statement was circulated to the congregation, with the canons of 1863 reported in some detail,[167] but a protest against it was organised by Moncrieff's supporters.[168]

The vestry had always been reluctant to allow Drummond's resignation 'even when his health broke down' in 1872.[169] But now they, and Drummond, realised that peace would be restored only in the event of his retirement. In such circumstances, Moncrieff's position would be terminated according to his deed of contract. By 9 July Drummond's decision had been accepted and Moncrieff departed to a living in Baring's diocese of Durham. There was still considerable support for Drummond, as

---

[160] *Ibid.*, pp. 7-13, 17, 31.

[161] John Burns to the Editor, 28 January 1875. *Record*, 1 February 1875.

[162] W. S. Moncrieff to Mr Davidson, 15 March 1875, LPL, Tait 290 p. 242.

[163] J. C. Miller to D. T. K. Drummond, 30 January 1875, DRO, D5550/3.5/26.

[164] Minute of Vestry Meeting, St Thomas's Church, Edinburgh, 4, 18 March 1875, LPL, Tait 290, p. 244.

[165] Drummond, *Dean of Carlisle*, p. 19.

[166] H. Davidson to the Vestry, 17 April 1875, LPL, Tait 290, p. 248. W. S. Moncrieff to Mr. Davidson, 17 April 1875, LPL, Tait 290, p. 250.

[167] 'Private Paper for the Information of the Congregation of St Thomas's English Episcopal Chapel, printed by order of the Vestry', 11 June 1875. St Thomas's Church, Edinburgh, Archives.

[168] Lillian Craig to Mr Drummond, 19July 1875, DRO, D5550/3/5/26.

[169] Harriet Drummond to Harriet Moor, 28 June 1875, DRO, D5550/3/4/8.

evidenced by an invitation to oversee the Bible and Sabbath classes for the young people, the presentation of a gift of one thousand sovereigns, a pension of £200 a year, plus other costly gifts.[170] But the problem of how far to go in accommodating different doctrines had led to the breaking up of the incumbency and congregation of St Thomas's.

Very seriously, the dispute spilt over into an unpleasant personal dispute. Drummond, appearing to maintain a conciliatory stance, wrote to Henry Davidson, one of the resigning vestrymen, that 'nothing that has passed can change my feelings of esteem and friendship towards yourself and of real and loving interest in all belonging to you'.[171] But Moncrieff complained to Davidson that 'when poor Mr Wood was buried, Drummond...refused to go to the grave because he could not stand the exposure, but he led... Mr Hope Grant's funeral in the open air in a shower of sleet and was not a bit the worse!'[172] Again, a member of St Thomas's informed Drummond in December 1875 that rumours, probably emanating from Moncrieff, were circulating that he was negligent in pastoral visiting. Drummond was appalled at the accusation 'of unfaithfulness in the high and holy responsibilities of the Christian ministry'. He pointed out that the vestry had notified Moncrieff on his engagement in 1870, and again after his own near fatality in 1872, that he would bear the responsibility for congregational work.[173] Confiding in T. K. Talon, of St Vincent's, Edinburgh, in June 1877, Drummond revealed that some of Moncrieff's supporters 'had come to pass [me] by in the street' and 'have broken my heart'. Talon, remarking that Drummond had died just six days later, said, 'if I had not heard it from his own lips of his treatment at the close, I would not have believed it'.[174] The correspondence is indicative of the deeply damaging disarray among some Evangelicals by 1875 over co-operation with High Churchmen. Together with Baring's confidence in the protection offered by the canons of 1863, the problem of rising Anglo-Catholicism in the Church of England and Cotterill's influence in Edinburgh, increasing Evangelical accommodation with High Churchmen led to English Episcopal splits in the 1870s.

---

[170] Excerpt from a minute of the vestry meeting 9 July 1875, DRO, D 5550/3/5/23/1. D. T. K. Drummond to the congregation, (n. d), DRO, D5550/3/4/8. *Memoir*, pp. cxxxiv-cxl.

[171] D. T. K. Drummond to H. Davidson, 30 April 1875, LPL, Tait 290, p. 254.

[172] W. S. Moncrieff to Mr Davidson, 15 March 1875, LPL, Tait 290, p. 242.

[173] D. T. K. Drummond to Dearest Friend, 13 December 1875, DRO, D5550/3/5/26.

[174] T. K. Talon to E. C. Dawson, (n. d.), DC.

An English Episcopal Bishop

After Drummond's resignation Baring refused confirmation to English Episcopal candidates. E. H. Beckles, the retired Bishop of Sierra Leone, accepted the position of bishop to the separatists on 19 February 1877 following an approach from Lord Shaftesbury, a personal friend of John Burns of Wemyss Bay Chapel.[175] The English Episcopalians, in response, formed the Association of English Episcopalians on 6 March 1877 in order to collect money to pay a salary to Beckles and to 'promote the interests' of the various congregations. From St Thomas's, Edinburgh, Sir J. D. Wauchope was elected president, R. L. Stuart, secretary, and, together with Drummond, they made up the Executive Council. Congregational representatives from each church also served on the committee.[176] A. F. Kinnaird, tenth Baron Kinnaird, a prominent Free Churchman,[177] and Shaftesbury both linked themselves with the Association as speakers at its

---

[175] *Glasgow Herald*, 24 February 1877.

[176] Congregational representatives of the Association of English Episcopalians were: Professor Balfour (St Thomas's, Edinburgh), G. J. Doddrell and R. C. Todd (St Jude's, Glasgow), W. F. Skene and Major Wyld (St Vincent's, Edinburgh), J. Burns (Wemyss Bay Chapel), Thomas Clavering and George Black (St Silas's, Glasgow), R. Walker and A. Melville Watt (St Peter's, Montrose), W. F. Burnley (Dunoon), G. Compton and J. P. Kay (St James's, Aberdeen), Alfred Guthrie and Omar Boyd (St John's, Dundee), Edmund Bell (Mission Chapel, Partick, Glasgow). Nairn and Cally were to be invited to name two representatives. D. T. K. Drummond was also a representative. 'Meeting of the Representatives of English Episcopal Congregations in Scotland, held in the Religious Institution Rooms, Glasgow, on Tuesday, 6 March 1877' (For Private Circulation), DC. Also held in, NAS, CH12.16.126.

In the first year of the Association of English Episcopalians, the capital fund contributed by congregations amounted to £1367.14.0, and receipts of annual subscriptions from individuals totalled £338.18.1, out of which a annual salary was paid to Beckles of £316.0.0. Contributions were: St Thomas's (£699), Montrose (£500), Dunoon (£250), St Silas's (£96.8.6), St Jude's (£62.6.0), Wemyss Bay (£50), Cally (£10), St John's (£10). *First Annual Report of the Association of English Episcopalians in Scotland* (Edinburgh, 1878), p. 10, DC.

Frederic Peake, St Silas's, Glasgow, (1880-1886) and John Burns of Wemyss Bay English Episcopal Chapel took out a successful injunction against the dissolution of the Association raised by St Thomas's in 1884. St Thomas's Minute Book, 7 April 1884, 28 January 1886, St Thomas's Church, Edinburgh, Archives. In 1899 the Association was revamped after a petition from H. C. Knox, incumbent of St Silas's, Glasgow, (1899-1901) and T. S. Connolly, Incumbent of St Peter's, Montrose, (1881-1913). By 7 June 1900 Davidson, Edwards and Gaff, of St Thomas's, Edinburgh, were elected as lay representatives of the newly constituted Association. *Ibid.*, 6 December 1899, 7 June 1890.

[177] D. M. Lewis (ed.), *The Blackwell Dictionary of Evangelical Biography 1730-1860*, Vol. II (Oxford, 1995), p. 650.

From Secession to Partial Union, 1846-1900 353

annual meetings and by offering verbal support for its cause.[178] The Association thus commanded considerable respect from British Evangelicals.

However, matters erupted when the Convocation of York censured Beckles on 19 April 1877, declaring his appointment as 'an intrusion within the Dioceses of the Bishops of Northern Britain who are in full communion with this Church'.[179] The Convocation of Canterbury followed similarly on 26 April 1877, but Tait, conciliatory as ever, recommended caution, seeing the matter as a 'very awkward one',[180] and left Beckles to continue his episcopal work unhindered.

For his part, Beckles declared that Convocation had not shaken his resolve and John Burns announced that 'the star chamber of Convocation is no terror in Scotland'.[181] But Robert Allen, the incumbent of St James's, Aberdeen, and his vestry were alarmed at proceedings and declined to allow Beckles to confirm their candidates 'on the very eve' of the event.[182] Allen applied for, and received, a licence allowing him to preach in Scottish Episcopal pulpits and enabling Suther to perform episcopal duty for St James's, but the issue split the congregation.[183] Although Beckles himself carried on his ministrations until 1887, after which J. C. Ryle performed episcopal oversight from Liverpool,[184] the events at St James's revealed

---

[178] *First Annual Report of Association of English Episcopalians*, p. 9.

[179] Copy of Resolution of the Convocation of York, 19 April 1877, NAS, CH 12.59.22. *Cf. ENCS*, p. 230.

[180] *Chronicle of Convocation* (London, 1887), pp. 94-99, 102-104, 129-130. The Bishop of St Asaph, Joshua Hughes, pointed out that the English Episcopalians had 'been fully recognised by Parliament' and, disagreed with Tait over the extent of protection afforded by the 1863 canons against the Scottish Office in which 'there is a certain amount of difference...from our own'.

[181] John Burns to the Editor of the *Times*. *Glasgow Herald*, 3 May 1877.

[182] Beckles confirmed a total of 299 candidates in April 1877: 22 (St Thomas's), 47 (St Vincent's), 36 (St Silas's), 33 (St Jude's), 60 (St John's), 31 (Montrose), and in September 1877 8 (Cally). He officiated at Wemyss and Dunoon in the summer, at Drummond's funeral in Edinburgh in June 1877, and in other congregations in December 1877. *First Annual Report*, pp. 6-7, *Scottish Guardian*, 28 February 1896.

[183] St James' Church Minute Book, 1872 *passim*. St James's Church, Aberdeen, Archives. Edward Bannerman, a benefactor of St James's, appealed unsuccessfully to the Court of Session for an annulment of the licence, so disrupting the congregation.

[184] It has been impossible to find the exact circumstances surrounding Beckles by 1887. The mantle of episcopal oversight of the English Episcopalians in 1887 passed over to J. C. Ryle, Bishop of Liverpool, but he did not travel to Scotland to perform confirmations. Instead, his first recorded confirmation service for the separatists appears to have been held in Liverpool, December 1887, for St Silas's candidates. A. T. Pullin of St Luke's, Glasgow, complained to E. W. Benson, Archbishop of Canterbury, that Ryle had arranged the time of the service purely to suit the needs of the group from St Silas's.

fragility in the English Episcopal movement when individual clergy, overwhelmed by opposition from the Anglican hierarchy, moderated their objections to the Scottish Office.

Moves to Unite, 1882

The process of accommodation by English Episcopalians came to a head in 1882. Several factors contributed to the mood. Drummond died in 1877. The absence of his strong resistance to any compromise towards union while the Scottish Office existed probably contributed to some English Episcopalians considering other options. Baring's influence towards a more conciliatory stance, based on the 1863 canons, began to flower, culminating in his attendance at the diocesan Synod in Glasgow in 1878 where he 'acted the part of a peacemaker and mediator, urging upon both sides mutual forbearance and concession'.[185] Again, there were often problems in manning English Episcopal churches after the censure on Beckles, since some English clergy were reluctant to visit.[186] Additionally, in Edinburgh some congregations reported leakage to the Scottish Episcopal Church which had become more attractive to Evangelicals after the mission of 1875, with extempore prayer meetings, often attended by Cotterill himself, no longer unusual.[187] Under such circumstances, W. F. Skene of St Vincent's, Edinburgh, warned that English Episcopalianism was 'likely to divide away both financially and numerically'.[188] Union with the Scottish Episcopal Church became more appealing by 1880.

The new mood took root under Skene's guidance. Following Baring's counsel of peace, Skene published his ideas in 1882.[189] While strongly opposing the doctrine of the Scottish Office as implying 'a material change of some kind',[190] he agreed with Baring that the canons of 1863 gave protection.[191] However, again probably following Baring's conciliatory stance at the Synod of 1878, he asked for concessions to prevent any recurrence of the strictures placed on Drummond's evangelistic meetings in

---

A. T. Pullin to E. W. Benson, 12 December 1887, LPL, Benson Papers, Volume 59, ff. 324, 326.

[185] Talon, *Reasons*, pp. 9-10. W. F. Skene to E. C. Dawson, 23 October 1882, DC.

[186] Talon, *Reasons*, p. 9.

[187] Daniel Sandford to W. F. Skene, 10 April 1882. DC. J. F. Montgomery to W. F. Skene, 23 January 1882, DC.

[188] W. F. Skene to E. C. Dawson, 10 July 1882, DC.

[189] *A Plea for Union Among Episcopalians Within Scotland* (Edinburgh, 1882). Cf. *ENCS*, pp. 232-234, which deals with correspondence in July 1881 between Skene and Bishop George Mackarness of Argyll and the Isles.

[190] *Plea*, p. 13.

[191] *Ibid.*, pp. 22-24.

1842.[192] By 29 April 1882 Skene informed E. C. Dawson, the new incumbent of St Thomas's, Edinburgh, that the 'bishops now sincerely regret the mistaken steps which led to separation, and would gladly meet with such concessions as can reasonably be acquired'.[193] Skene eventually formulated a plan to bring before the bishops. He suggested all reference to the Scottish Office being removed from Canon XXX so that it merely allowed all congregations joining the Scottish Episcopal Church 'to continue to use such services and religious meetings as they have hitherto been in the habit of using'.[194] It was an effort towards creating a broad Church, encompassing different beliefs.

But some English Episcopalians rejected Skene's plans. John Burns of Wemyss Bay Chapel declared he could have no part 'in a system which...tolerates the abomination of desolation of the idolatrous Scottish Communion Office'.[195] W. F. Burnley at Dunoon was concerned that such developments would involve him in taking out a licence from G. R. Mackarness, Bishop of Argyll and the Isles, and risking interference with services and the choice of visiting preachers.[196] There was still considerable feeling against union among some English Episcopalians who feared it would lead to a compromise of their distinctive beliefs.

Given such opposition, Skene and Dawson came up with a further suggestion for Canon XXX, asking that Evangelicals subscribing to the Scottish Episcopal Church might 'except their signatures from Canon XXX' but nevertheless be licensed by the Church. Among the bishops, Cotterill was doubtful that it would be workable, but H. W. Jermyn of Brechin, supported by G. R. Mackarness of Argyll and the Isles,[197] assured Skene that 'there is a strong desire...to go as far as possible', and felt that Scottish Office supporters would favour the suggestion because it did not demote the Office further.[198] But after a meeting in August, the bishops reported that the idea was impossible unless similar provision was allowed to Scottish Office devotees when signing allegiance to Canon XXIX declaring the English Office to be the authorised service.[199] The problem of appeasing all sides was considerable.

The eventual declaration from the bishops, released on 28 November 1882, was found by Skene to be 'specious and short of what was required'. Nevertheless, concerning Canon XXXI, Evangelical clergy were

---

[192] *Ibid.*, pp 28-29.
[193] W. F. Skene to E. C. Dawson, 29 April 1882, DC.
[194] W. F. Skene to E. C. Dawson, 2 June 1882, DC.
[195] John Burns to E. C. Dawson, 12 June 1882, DC.
[196] Wm. Burnley to E. C. Dawson, 10 July 1882, DC.
[197] Strong, *Episcopalianism*, pp. 232-234.
[198] W. F. Skene to E. C. Dawson, 10 July 1882, DC.
[199] W. F. Skene to E. C. Dawson, 25 August 1882, DC.

guaranteed freedom to conduct evangelistic services on weekdays as well as Sundays. But the problem of the communion office as enshrined in Canon XXX was only partially resolved. English Episcopalians were assured that 'those who by their subscription promise obedience to the Canons, do not thereby commit themselves either to an approval of the distinctive features of the said Communion Office or to any acceptance of doctrine which can be supposed inconsistent with the Book of Common Prayer'. Scottish Office supporters were allowed to continue to use the service.[200] In effect, the Scottish Office remained authorised but the English Episcopalians were offered an escape clause.

Reactions to the declaration were mixed. Eventually, Skene decided that after its friendly spirit 'separation was no longer justifiable'.[201] Talon regarded it 'as a satisfactory solution' and placed St Vincent's in the Scottish Episcopal Church.[202] But, for others, the Scottish Communion Office remained a stumbling block. Richard Hibbs, the former incumbent of St Vincent's, fulminated that he would never have allowed 'the chapel to pass from under my control...had I thought it possible that the congregation...would one day betray the Protestant cause',[203] and most other English Episcopalians followed him. Notable among the opposition at St Thomas's were the old members like J. H. Balfour who feared that a compromise of the principles 'for which St Thomas's has so long contended' was involved.[204] A partial alliance called 'the Concordat' was entered upon at St Thomas's, whereby congregational independence was retained while allowing Cotterill to perform confirmations and Dawson to interchange pulpits with Scottish Episcopalians.[205] However, there was so much opposition even to this concession that Cotterill made it a purely verbal, rather than written, contract.[206] In Glasgow, Frederic Peake and William Williams at St Silas's and St Jude's respectively declined all association whatsoever with the declaration. Peake contested Scottish Episcopal teaching on 'baptism...the divine institution of the episcopacy and the continued sanction of the Scottish Communion Office'.[207] Likewise George and John Burns at Wemyss Bay Chapel held aloof because the declaration continued 'to recognise and sanction' the Scottish Office.[208]

---

[200] 'Declaration of Scottish Bishops' 28 November 1882, DC. Cf. *ENCS*, p. 235.

[201] W. F. Skene to the editor, 17 March 1883, *Record*, 22 March 1883.

[202] Talon, *Reasons*, pp. 10-11.

[203] Richard Hibbs to the Editor, 5 March 1883, *Record*, 9 March 1883.

[204] St Thomas's Minute Book, 30 December 1882, St Thomas's Church, Edinburgh, Archives. *Record*, 16 February 1883.

[205] St Thomas's Minute Book, February to March 1883. St Thomas's Church, Edinburgh, Archives. *Record*, 16 February 1883

[206] E. C. Dawson to John Dowden, 9 February 1892, DC.

[207] Frederic Peake to John Burns, 19 December 1882, DC.

[208] John Burns to R. L. Stuart, 21 December 1882, DC.

From Secession to Partial Union, 1846-1900 357

Montrose, under T. S. Connolly, stayed independent because 'a powerful party in the congregation...would rather do without confirmation than receive it from a Scotch Bishop'.[209] O. F. Walton, the chaplain at Cally, rejected union,[210] and it was not until 1885 that the new chaplain, H. E. Eardley, under Dawson's influence, joined the Scottish Episcopal Church. Again, feeling ran so high at St John's, Dundee, that, when facing huge financial problems in 1885, it shunned the Scottish Episcopal Church and opted to unite with the Church of Scotland, adopting the name of St Thomas's Chapel of Ease.[211] W. F. Burnley, at Dunoon, took out a licence only in 1889, again with advice from Dawson.[212] Thus St Vincent's, Edinburgh, alone accepted the declaration.

Contrary to Rowan Strong's suggestion that the declaration 'broke the decades-long theological...logjam between the Church and the congregations of the English Episcopalians',[213] it had only very limited effect. Most English Episcopalians agreed with the *Record* that there had been 'an attempt to varnish over fundamental differences', and with Fox,[214] who again warned that the separatists would 'become...wheedled into the reception of corrupt doctrines'.[215] With the continued oversight of Beckles until 1887, the majority of English Episcopalians were settled in their decision to refuse any compromise of their beliefs concerning the Scottish Office.

Revision of Liturgy and Canons, 1890

In 1875 Drummond wrote to Moncrieff's supporter, Henry Davidson, 'the question just comes to this, shall the protest of St Thomas's be maintained, or shall it have a decent burial in the tomb of the Capulets?'[216] His fears materialised vividly in 1885 when J. M. Danson, of St Andrew's, Aberdeen, petitioned the Episcopal Synod at Edinburgh for the elevation of the Scottish Office.[217] In the same year, a similar request was received from

---

[209] E. C. Dawson to John Dowden, 23 April 1883, DC.

[210] *Record*, 2 March 1883.

[211] *Dundee Advertiser*, 25 May 1885. *Scottish Guardian*, 14 April, 22 May, 29 May 1885. D. M. Bertie, *Scottish Episcopal Clergy, 1689-2000* (Edinburgh, 2000), p. 656.

[212] E. C. Dawson to John Dowden, 18 May 1889, DC.

[213] Strong, *Episcopalianism*, p. 235.

[214] See Chapter 10, p. 348 for G. T. Fox.

[215] *Record*, 2 March 1883. G. T. Fox to the Editor, 26 March 1883, *Record 30 March 1883*.

[216] Quoted in Henry Davidson to D. T. K. Drummond, 3 May 1875, LPL, Tait 290, p. 256.

[217] *Scottish Guardian* 1885, p. 435. Danson had been the incumbent of St Mary's, Aberdeen, from 1874 to 1880, following H. J. Palmer who had been appointed to St

the dioceses of Moray, Ross and Caithness, and Aberdeen and Orkney, for 'perfect equality' with the English rite.[218] Similarly, James Christie, the incumbent of Turriff, asked John Dowden, Bishop of Edinburgh, in 1886 that the office be returned to primacy 'without any revision, any alteration' of its text.[219] Some Scottish clergy, particularly in the northeast, were anxious for the resurrection of the Scottish Communion Office to a primary position.

But Dowden revealed that many Scottish bishops, fearing trouble with the Church of England, felt primacy could not be granted 'without serious danger unless the Scottish Office was revised'.[220] Problems surrounding revision were immense. As Dowden put it, 'the form of Invocation was, of course, the crucial point'.[221] Dowden's own view was that the invocation as it stood favoured High Church doctrine and excluded Evangelical understanding. Countering suggestions that the prayer was non-Roman, he maintained that 'the consecration once complete is as patient as the English Office...of Transubstantiation, or Consubstantiation, or the real spiritual Presence of the Anglican divines, or the Presence in power and efficacy of the Nonjurors...but it is less patient of a Zwinglian gloss than the English Office'.[222] Thus the central difficulty was how to make the prayer acceptable to a range of beliefs.

Work began in 1887 in preparation for the General Synod planned for 1890. The issues raised by Drummond and Craig in the 1840s were to be re-examined and the opinion of Evangelicals was sought. Dowden wrote to Dawson in December 1887 that he hoped the words 'be unto us' might be restored in place of 'become' in the invocation.[223] The liturgical expertise of H. A. Wilson of Magdalene College, Oxford, who had been chaplain to his father, W. S. Wilson, Bishop of Glasgow and Galloway, from 1879 to 1888, and William Bright, of Christ Church, Oxford, the former warden of Trinity College, Glenalmond, was called upon. After prolonged discussions it was decided to reword the invocation, replacing 'become' with 'be' and adding a supplementary phrase to make it closer to ancient Greek liturgies. The agreed form was:

Vouchsafe to bless and sanctify, with Thy Holy Spirit, this Bread and this Cup, that they may *be* the Body and Blood of Thy most dearly beloved

---

Columba's, Edinburgh, from 1869 to 1872, a Ritualist church. See Strong, *Episcopalianism*, pp. 236-247.

[218] *Scottish Guardian*, 27 November 1885.

[219] James Christie to John Dowden, 20 December 1886, NLS, Dep. 171.13.

[220] John Dowden, *The Scottish Communion Office 1764* (Oxford 1922), p. 88.

[221] Dowden, *Scottish Office*, p. 94.

[222] Dowden, *Scottish Office*, p. 229. See Chapter 7, p. 217, n. 9 for an explanation of labelling both Receptionists and Memorialists as Zwinglian.

[223] John Dowden to E. C. Dawson, 11 December 1887, DC.

Son, that so whosoever shall receive the same may be sanctified both in soul and body, and preserved unto everlasting life.[224]

But there was opposition to the amendment. Wilson explained that it might be taken to exclude Virtualist theology and that of 'those who hold...something more'.[225] Speaking for Anglo-Catholics, A. D. Murdoch, of All Saints, Edinburgh, confirmed Wilson's concern, informing Dowden 'this revision...practically eliminates the objective idea'.[226] A. G. Douglas, Bishop of Aberdeen and Orkney, highlighted national pride as an issue: 'God forbid that we should part with the inheritance of our fathers'.[227] The new invocation was fraught with problems.

Dawson at St Thomas's was not satisfied either. Warning that the 'old fires are by no means damped out', he acknowledged that the new invocation was an improvement, but he considered that it did 'not at all materially affect the doctrinal teaching upon which the objectors to the Office have protested', and pressed for the words 'be unto us' to be inserted instead. He warned Dowden that if the proposed office were raised to primacy then 'three or four of the English bishops would support a separation'. As a solution he suggested a change in the canons whereby when the Scottish Office was used on official occasions, 'the English Office shall also be used at about the same hour as an alternative service'.[228] Evangelical opinion on the doctrine of the Scottish Communion Office remained a problem.

Disagreement from all sides over the new liturgy was so intense that any hope of revision was abandoned.[229] Attention was turned instead to rewriting the canons along the lines suggested in 1882. Accordingly an important amendment was made to the new Canon XII concerning subscription to the Thirty-Nine Articles and obedience to the tribunals of the Church:

> The form of subscription promising obedience to the Canons of this Church implies only obedience to their requirements, and not necessarily

---

[224] Dowden, *Scottish Office*, pp. 94-98, 242.

[225] H. A. Wilson to My Lord Bishop, 29 May 1889, NAS, CH12/16/127/8. See Chapter 7, pp. 220-222 for an analysis of various invocations.

[226] A. D. Murdoch to John Dowden, 1 June 1889, NAS, CH 12/13/87/1. All Saints in 1875, under Murdoch, had coloured vestments, lighted candles, Gregorian chant and daily communion.

[227] *Scottish Guardian*, 31 January 1890.

[228] E. C. Dawson to John Dowden, 18 May, 22 May 1889, DC.

[229] Dowden, *Communion Office*, p. 96.

approval of everything therein contained, or that may be supposed to be inferred there-from.[230]

A clause was added to the new Canon XXXV to allow for evangelistic meetings:

> When a sermon is to be preached, or a lecture given on a weekday, or on a Holy day or Sunday...it shall be lawful for the Minister to use only the Litany or other portion of the Prayer Book which he may think desirable and proper for the occasion.[231]

The terms of the declaration of 1882 were now official, albeit expressed in less explicit language. A seeming compromise, which enabled the Scottish Communion Office to remain intact for those who valued it but also offered protection to Evangelicals, had been reached. Moreover, evangelistic meetings could now proceed unhindered. As such, the Canon Law of 1890 was the result of fifty years of conflict between English Episcopalians and marked a considerable concession towards Evangelical belief.

After 1890

The altered canons of 1890 did not immediately entice the remaining English Episcopal chapels into the Scottish Episcopal Church. Doubtless they made it easier for St Paul's and St James's, Aberdeen, to take the step in 1898 when financial difficulties made such a move essential.[232] At St Silas's, Glasgow, the incumbent, Sholto Douglas-Campbell Douglas, looked into the possibility of obtaining a licence in 1890 but was impeded by congregational opposition.[233] St Silas's, along with St Jude's, Wemyss, Dunoon and Montrose, thus opted for continued independence.

At St Thomas's, Edinburgh, the issue of Dawson's verbal licence of 1882 complicated the situation.[234] In 1886 Dowden, then Bishop of Edinburgh, insisted on a written agreement. But Daniel Ainslie, a long-serving member of the vestry, and others were already 'making such determined efforts to break the informal license' that Dawson and two of the three trustees agreed to Dowden's demand only in secret.[235] When Dawson was elected as diocesan representative at the General Synod of

---

[230] *Code of Canons of the Scottish Episcopal Church in Scotland as amended, Adopted and Enacted By a General Synod Holden at Edinburgh in the Year of Our Lord 1890* (Edinburgh, 1890), p. 16.

[231] *Ibid.*, p. 41.

[232] St James's Minute Book, 1898, *passim*, St James's Church, Aberdeen, Archives.

[233] W. T. Harrison to E. C. Dawson, 6 November 1890, DC.

[234] See Chapter 10, p. 356.

[235] E. C. Dawson to John Dowden, 9 February 1892, DC.

1890 the new arrangement became known, leading to uproar on the vestry.[236]

On hearing of Dawson's problems, Dowden offered him the incumbency of St Peter's, Edinburgh, in the Scottish Episcopal Church. By November 1890 Dawson and a large group of the congregation accepted the suggestion while the trustees of St Thomas's, on the casting vote of Sir J. D. Wauchope, a founder of the church, seemingly concerned that issues of doctrine remained unresolved,[237] severed connection with the Scottish Episcopal Church because the new canons '[are] always subject to review'.[238] Thus, at the end of the nineteenth century, St Thomas's, St

---

[236] 'Copy of a Letter Published in the July 1890 Number of the Church Magazine by the Rev E. C. Dawson', St Thomas's Church, Edinburgh, Archives.

[237] St Thomas's Minute Book, 10 October 1890, St Thomas's Church, Edinburgh, Archives.

[238] *Ibid.*, 2 January 1891. The situation at St Thomas's was particularly discordant. By June 1890 Dowden agreed to issue the church with a concordat but only with an accompanying official licence to Dawson. The vestry rejected this proposal and Dawson resigned on 27 June 1890, arguing that the licence was a natural outcome of the concordat. Dawson informed the vestry on 16 July 1890 that he would not return to St Thomas's unless it were constituted as an incumbency of the Scottish Episcopal church. A congregational vote was taken on 6 August 1890 to ascertain the support for total union of St Thomas's with the Scottish Episcopal Church, with Dawson as incumbent. Out of 272 voting papers taken up 175 opted for union, 30 for a concordat, 5 for total separation, 7 declined to vote, 51 papers were not returned, and there were 4 dead papers. At a meeting of the vestry on the same day a vote in favour of union was obtained, but the trustees were not unanimous with Sir John Don Wauchope considering that the proposed union was *ultra vires* of the trustees. On 3 September 1890 Wauchope suggested that a friendly suit should ascertain whether the buildings of St Thomas's could be handed over to the Scottish Episcopal Church. A motion was moved by the vestry on 10 October for joining the Scottish Episcopal Church without awaiting the result of Wauchope's friendly suit. Three members of the vestry were absent, and the resulting vote was a split of four in favour and four against. Wauchope's casting vote decided against the motion. Dawson's appointment as incumbent of St Thomas's was thereupon dissolved and he and his supporters joined St Peter's, Edinburgh, in the Scottish Episcopal Church. When Wauchope applied to Dowden for a concordat whereby St Thomas's would remain independent but with its incumbent holding an official licence, Dowden refused, regarding the canons of 1890 as sufficient protection for St Thomas's in pursuing an Evangelical ministry. The events show, again, the splits in the Evangelical party over the extent of co-operation with Churchmen holding different views. *Ibid.* June 1890-January 1891.

St Thomas's was severely depleted after Dawson and his supporters left. In 1876, after Drummond's dispute with Moncrieff, the total income had been £1120.13.3. In 1877, under the unpopular G. W. Butler, the seat rents were still £556.1.6 and the total income was £847.4.4. In 1889, under Dawson, seat rents had risen to £745.17.9 and the total income was £1256.14.3. After Dawson left, in 1892, the seat rents dropped to £245.14.0 and although the total income was £1199.12.7, £610 of it came from private

Silas's, St Jude's,[239] Montrose, Wemyss, and Dunoon, represented a continuing conservative Evangelicalism which resisted compromise with Churchmen of differing beliefs.

It has not been possible to discover how long St Vincent's, Edinburgh, St Paul's and St James', Aberdeen, maintained a clear Evangelical identity within the Scottish Episcopal Church. At St Peter's, Edinburgh, Dawson catered for a range of churchmanship. Among the invited speakers were Evangelicals such as Henry Wace, Dean of Canterbury, and Robert Bickersteth, Bishop of Ripon. But, in 1890, the church was reported as having full choral services and communion services with the Eastern position, practices not seen in more conservative Evangelical churches.[240] It seems likely, therefore, that Dawson's churchmanship diluted after he joined the Scottish Episcopal Church.

By contrast, W. L. Holland, a staunch Evangelical, was appointed to St Thomas's, Edinburgh, in 1891. His firm beliefs led him to resign from the Church of England in March 1895, because he could not reconcile its traditions and ceremonies with the 'simple teaching of the New Testament'.[241] H. J. Colclough, who replaced him, entered into an acrimonious correspondence with Moncrieff in 1900 concerning the Scottish Communion Office. Colclough concluded the controversy by refusing compromise because he could not 'approve or defend the teaching of the Scottish Office, and therefore we choose to remain...separate.'[242] The English Episcopalians remained as a clear Evangelical group, unwilling to co-operate in a Church which sanctioned the Scottish Office.

---

gifts from members of the congregation. By 1899, under the more settled ministry of H. J. Colclough, seat rents were still only £244.16.11 and income was £843.15.8. *Ibid*, 26 June 1891, 8 January 1892, 20 December 1900.

[239] St Jude's was in considerable financial difficulty by 1884 and was to be sold. It sold bonds to English Evangelicals, but was unable to pay the interest. The bond-holders tried to sell the building unsuccessfully in 1884. However the church continued under William Robinson as incumbent in 1885. Eventually the bond-holders rented the church to the Free Presbyterians in 1893 and sold it to them in 1909. *Scottish Guardian*, July 1885, 1893. *Glasgow Herald*, 1909. Quoted in Gavin White, *The Scottish Episcopal Church. A New History*. (Edinburgh, 1998), p. 78.

[240] *Scottish Guardian*, 7 April 1893. *Year Book for the Episcopal Church in Scotland* (Edinburgh, 1900). *Scottish Standard Bearer*, February 1897. *Scottish Chronicle*, 15 October, 1920.

[241] St Thomas's Minute Book, 27 March 1895, St Thomas's Church, Edinburgh. Archives. Holland appears to have devoted himself to writing after leaving St Thomas's.

[242] H. J. Colclough to Editor, 6 August 1900. *Record*, 10 August 1900.

Conclusion

Within the Church of England, although some raised constitutional problems concerning the Act of Union as barriers to episcopal oversight for English Episcopalians, no official legal analysis contradicting that of Stephens was ever provided. It is likely, therefore, that these matters were not genuinely insurmountable and that the case offered by Stephens was valid. However, the desire for peace and unity, always a pressing concern for Church leaders, was probably the most likely cause of hesitation among members of the Church of England in granting concessions to the separatists.

The English Episcopal movement, at its strongest in 1849 to 1856 after its deputations to London and the granting of episcopal oversight by Villiers, undoubtedly played an important part in the deposition of the Scottish Office in 1863. But by the 1870s the rise of Anglo-Catholicism in the Church of England possibly made some separatists less hostile to the Scottish Episcopal Church. This, combined with willingness to work with High Churchmen, led some to take refuge in the canons of 1863, the declaration of 1882, and the canonical provision of 1890, and so to join the Scottish Episcopal Church. But no English Episcopalians, apart from Moncrieff, appear to have faltered in their belief that the Scottish Communion Office taught doctrines foreign to the Book of Common Prayer.

The theology of the Scottish Office was therefore the crux of the situation in Scotland and it was vital that the Scottish Episcopal Church found a solution. While the synod of 1890 conceded to English Episcopal concern over evangelistic meetings, the resistance of Anglo-Catholic and Virtualist clergy to any widening of the wording of the Scottish rite to include Evangelical belief was a serious bar to union. For the sake of the three words 'be unto us' instead of 'become' the hope of encouraging all the remaining separatists into the Church was lost. Of those who did join, some failed to maintain the clear Evangelical image of earlier days, exemplified by E. C. Dawson's adoption of the Eastern position and full choral services at St Peter's, Edinburgh. St Thomas's, Edinburgh, and St Silas's, Glasgow, separate from the Scottish Episcopal Church, had no difficulty in attracting clear-cut Evangelicals to their incumbencies at the end of the century. With the episcopal oversight of J. C. Ryle in Liverpool, who in 1883 had refused to attend the Scottish Episcopal Church imploring its adherents to 'overthrow every office in which they differ from the Church of England',[243] the main thrust of such Evangelicalism in Scotland remained in the English Episcopal movement.

---

[243] J. C. Ryle to the editor, *Scottish Guardian*, 10 September 1883. See also LPL, Benson Papers, Volume 5, f. 240.

Chapter 11

Conclusion

The part played by Evangelical Episcopalianism in nineteenth-century Scotland was far-reaching. Both in terms of the numbers of its adherents and the impact of its theology on individual lives, it was a significant movement. But, despite such influence, it is evident that Evangelicalism did not rest easily in the Scottish Episcopal Church and was subject to a turbulent history. In particular, between 1842 and 1870, doctrinal differences led those who held strict, but not extreme, Evangelical views to take refuge outside the confines of the Scottish Church, preferring to ally with the Church of England.

While there is some evidence of a mild Evangelical presence in the Scottish Episcopal Church, such as that of W. M. Wade at Paisley from 1817 to 1845, Chapter 1 showed that strict, more robust Episcopal Evangelicalism was a late implant in Scotland, with the arrival of Edward Craig and G. T. Noel in 1818. At that time the dominant party was composed of High Churchmen, mainly orthodox in the south and Virtualist in the north, the descendants of those who had been unreceptive to the doctrines of the eighteenth-century Evangelical revival. From a small beginning, however, Evangelical clergy peaked at 13.3% of Episcopalians by mid-century, declining to 3.7% by the end of the century, most of whom can be designated as holding firm views. English clergy were, noticeably, the numerically dominant group.

Although Evangelicalism grew in the Scottish Episcopal Church, it was always in the minority. After 1842 the breakaway English Episcopalians, among whom English clergy were again the most numerous, represented by far the largest sector. With ninety-one incumbents at their churches during the century, they far outstripped the known Scottish Episcopal Evangelicals, who numbered only twenty-eight, some of whom later became, or had been, English Episcopalians. Nonetheless, the separatist group was not a major presence in Presbyterian Scotland. Limited as it was by its size, the substantial financial support it required was not easily obtained.

Chapter 2 showed that Evangelical churches were generally found in cities, important towns and holiday centres because these places provided congregations large enough to ensure viability. Where Evangelical congregations existed in smaller locations, they were under the patronage of wealthy local aristocrats and landowners. The limited penetration of

Episcopal Evangelicalism in Scotland was, in part, due to its small number of adherents in a country where Presbyterianism was the established denomination.

In Chapter 3 it was shown that the desire to pass on the Evangelical message meant that churches were active in reaching a large cross-section of society. The skilled working class, some of whom were probably recruited as a result of the 1859 to 1860 and 1874 revivals, was never absent from their congregations, and St Thomas's, Edinburgh, and St Silas's, Glasgow, made outstanding contributions in reaching the unskilled working class in their mission churches in the Canongate and Partick.

Many Scottish Evangelical Episcopalians emerged, in Chapter 4, as strong exponents of the core theology of their party, putting particular stress on the doctrine of conversion, the centrality of the cross in the redemption of mankind, the place of the Bible in formulating doctrine, and the desire to pass on the Christian gospel. Various influences moulded additional positions in theology. The group was shown to be typical of the mild Calvinism of Evangelical Anglicanism, but to be more like Scottish Presbyterianism in its early identification with verbal inspiration of the Bible and revival movements. Apart from T. H. Wilkinson at St John's, Greenock, from 1829 to 1831, the group did not adhere to the innovations of Edward Irving, Henry Drummond and Thomas Erskine. Additionally, the ministry of D. T. K. Drummond was shown to have included sustained teaching on incarnation and sanctification themes. Overall, although most Scottish Evangelical Episcopalians emerge as strict representatives of their faith, they were the sort of Churchmen who would have been able to exist in the Church of England without too many qualms. They were not extremists.

Chapter 5 investigated the lifestyle of some middle-class Evangelical Episcopalians in Scotland, for whom biblical standards emerged as the guiding principle. Family relationships were noticeably loving and attractive. Individuals were often knowledgeable in the realm of the arts and science, but time spent on such activities was not allowed to encroach on religious pursuits. While working assiduously for religious conversions, the group also undertook purely philanthropic causes and was prominent in the temperance and sabbatarian crusades, providing what it considered to be wholesome alternatives to harmful influences in society.

During the decades after 1820, Chapter 6 showed that issues arose in Scotland which conflicted with strict Evangelical belief. These were often exacerbated by an increasing antagonism to Roman Catholicism and an identification of the Pope as the antichrist, at a time of increasing concessions to Catholics and rising premillennial beliefs. As a result, any doctrine leaning towards Rome was severely resisted. Many Scottish Evangelical Episcopalians took on a firmly Protestant stance, joining the Reformation Society to argue for the reformed basis of the Church of

Conclusion

England. Accordingly, the group was active in rejecting any notion of baptismal regeneration, with the Edinburgh clergy Edward Craig, Daniel Bagot and D. T. K. Drummond in open dispute with High Church Scottish Episcopalians in the 1820s to 1830s. Even after the Gorham case in 1847 to 1851, when some Evangelicals expounded a slightly softer doctrine, the Evangelical Episcopalians in Scotland remained hardliners, apart, possibly, from T. K. Talon of St Vincent's, Edinburgh, who showed some adherence to less rigid views. Most of them were thus nearer to Scottish Presbyterians over the issue of infant baptism than to those Anglican Evangelicals who were willing to give some accommodation to High Church doctrine, and they were noticeably at odds with their more numerous High Church colleagues.

Evangelical aversion to anything approximating to Roman Catholic theology was felt strongly in the issue of the Scottish Communion Office of 1764, as discussed in Chapter 7. Drummond and Craig analysed the Scottish Office in detail from 1842 to 1843. They objected that the sacrificial aspect of its prayer of oblation demeaned the once-for-all nature of Christ's death on the cross, and that the invocation suggested a change in the elements to incorporate some sort of presence of Christ, countering Evangelical belief that the human heart was the site of such interaction. Drummond, while acknowledging that the Scottish invocation did not teach the actual doctrine of transubstantiation as held by Roman Catholics, placed it in the same general class because it prayed for a distinct change to the elements beyond being symbols of Christ's body and blood. Craig was more critical, arguing that the language of the invocation, which asked that the bread and wine 'might become the body and blood' of Christ, expressed the Roman doctrine plainly. Both he and Drummond preferred the wording of Laud's service of 1637 that the bread and wine 'might be unto us the Body and Blood of thy most dearly beloved Son'. They claimed that this phraseology would encompass their own theology as well as doctrinally higher beliefs. With the growing interest and support of the Tractarians in the 1840s for the Virtualist theology of the Scottish Office, Drummond and Craig feared that it was a safe haven for such doctrine. The problems did not ease even when many Tractarians, such as A. P. Forbes, Bishop of Brechin, relinquished Virtualism in favour of a more objective understanding of Christ's presence in the elements, because they continued to support the Scottish Office as a vehicle for their advanced views. Evangelicals regarded the episcopal Declaration of 1857 opposing Forbes as inconclusive, and pressed for the removal of the rite. They believed that, in an age of increasing Catholic doctrine, the Scottish Communion Office eclipsed their beliefs, while the Anglican Book of Common Prayer was more comprehensive.

In the light of these problems, Chapters 8 and 9 discussed the disruptions surrounding those Evangelicals who left the Scottish Episcopal Church from 1842 to 1887. In all, twenty-five English Episcopal congregations were set up in addition to the qualified chapel of Montrose which came under Evangelical leadership in the 1840s. Although the main cause of Drummond's secession in Edinburgh was the outlawing of non-liturgical evangelistic meetings by the 1838 Synod, the allegiance of the Tractarian party in 1842 to the Scottish Communion Office was clearly an important impetus to secession. Even after demotion of the service to a secondary position behind the Book of Common Prayer in 1863 Evangelicals, and then only some of them, were not prepared for another eight years to return to the Scottish Episcopal Church. The disruptions were thus a vivid expression of the desire among Scottish Evangelicals to preserve what they understood to be Protestant beliefs.

Chapter 10 discussed the continuing conflicts surrounding English and Scottish Episcopalians and the various attempts made by both to gain recognition from the Church of England as its legitimate representative in Scotland. While showing that its opponents could not substantiate legal objections to the English Episcopal movement, the doctrine of the Scottish Communion Office was isolated as the pivot on which all events and discussions hinged. The continued English Episcopalian agitation against the Scottish rite, the acknowledgement by the Archbishop of Canterbury, J. B. Sumner in 1849, that the Scottish Office differed in at least one important respect from the English service, together with rising and more extreme Catholic views of the service, were all shown to have led to its demotion in 1863 to a secondary position.

Various influences were argued to have drawn some English Episcopalians into the Scottish Episcopal Church. The impact of the changes of 1863 was not immediate since fear that the service could be resurrected as the official rite of the Church, together with the lack of provision for the free exercise of evangelistic services, kept many strict Evangelicals at bay. But by the 1870s, encouraged by Charles Baring, Bishop of Durham, a few considered that the new canon law did offer enough protection against the Scottish Communion Office and that matters concerning non-liturgical meetings could best be dealt with within a united Church. Secondly, the revelation that some, although not all, Anglo-Catholics preferred the English Office because its form of consecration was nearer to the Roman Catholic model, together with the decision in England that the Ritualist, W. J. E. Bennett, had not clearly contradicted the Anglican Articles, certainly made the Scottish Communion Office seem less sinister to some Evangelicals. Thirdly, by the 1870s, a different mood was apparent in British Evangelicalism, shaking the previously firm base of the movement, when some of its members became more willing to work with High Churchmen, co-operating with them in events like church missions. Two English Episcopal clergy were particularly influenced by such doubts and accommodation. W. S. Moncrieff's apparent drift towards

Conclusion

High Church eucharistic theology and the eventual acceptance by T. K. Talon at St Vincent's, Edinburgh, of the terms of an unofficial agreement drawn up by the Scottish bishops in 1882, whereby any clergyman signing the Scottish canons did not commit himself to allegiance to the doctrine of the Scottish Communion Office and was guaranteed freedom to conduct evangelistic services, were examples of the change in mood.

However, Chapter 10 culminated by showing that the Scottish Communion Office continued to remain a major bar to wholesale Evangelical involvement in the Scottish Episcopal Church. While, in 1890, the new canon law allowed freer practice of evangelistic meetings, efforts to revise the language of the prayer of invocation in a direction acceptable to High Churchmen and Evangelicals alike were shown to have been unsuccessful. The only way for hostile Evangelicals to join the Church was to sign the canons of 1890 in which the reservation suggested in 1882 was made official. Nevertheless, most English Episcopalians declined. With the support of J. C. Ryle, Bishop of Liverpool, from the late 1880s and the continuing provision of clergy to English Episcopal incumbencies the movement was given stability, with St Thomas's, Edinburgh, and St Silas's, Glasgow, remaining separate from the Scottish Episcopal Church until the late twentieth century.

The problem of maintaining an Evangelical stance in the Scottish Episcopal Church in the nineteenth century, elucidated in the material summarised here, is thus clearly apparent. The fact that English clergy dominated the Evangelical movement illustrates that native Scots, more intimately aware than others of the religious climate in their land, probably considered the cause of Evangelical Episcopalianism in Scotland to have been surrounded by insurmountable difficulties. Even so, English clergy did not remain long in Scotland and, having given a few years in pursuit of the cause, they then proceeded to livings elsewhere. Various reasons can be put forward to explain the difficulty, and have already been alluded to in the foregoing discussion. Partly it was the result of Evangelicalism being a recent implant into a dominant High Church environment. The mistaken marking out, in 1820, by George Gleig, Bishop of Brechin, of Craig as a hyper-Calvinist,[1] was indicative of ignorance concerning the nature of Evangelicalism, leading to a blanket categorisation. Again, Drummond's original reason for secession in 1842 was the insistence by his bishop, C. H. Terrot, on obedience to the strict letter of the law concerning the conduct of church services, a requirement to which most authorities of the Church of England at that time, more used to working alongside Evangelicals, turned a blind eye.[2] Additionally, interaction with Scottish Presbyterianism

---

[1] See Chapter 8, p. 248.
[2] *Ibid,.* pp. 268-270.

influenced some Evangelicals and made their beliefs stand out as obviously different from those of High Churchmen. Evangelical views on baptism early in the century,[3] and the developing stance of Drummond and J. D. Hull on the inerrancy of the Bible in the 1830s and 1840s,[4] together with involvement in inter-denominational city missions,[5] were examples of this. The dominant High Church party was thus likely to have been suspicious of the Evangelical newcomers in the early part of the century, making it difficult for relationships to flourish.

However, although it is possible that such intricacies might have diminished over time, as the various groups became better acquainted, it is evident that the Scottish Communion Office of 1764 was the major and continuing obstacle to the involvement of firm Evangelicals in the Scottish Episcopal Church. It is true that, initially, Daniel Bagot was able to read the service in a way that embraced his Evangelical beliefs, and others, like Robert Montgomery, were loathe to break the unity of the Church. But ninety-one English Episcopal clergy over the span of sixty years found it impossible to reconcile their theology with that of the Scottish rite and left the Church. While these Churchmen were comfortable enough with the wide sweep of doctrine in the Anglican Communion Service, with its multiple shades of theological emphasis, they saw the Scottish Office as the exclusive territory of those High Churchmen who leant towards Virtualism and sacramentalism.

It seems almost certain that the Scottish Communion Office would have produced problems for many Evangelicals whenever the implications of its language and structure had become evident. It is true that hostility to the service was exacerbated by its support from the Tractarians, but even in calmer times Evangelicals would have been likely to object to it. In fact, as has been discussed, Evangelical discomfort with the language of the prayer of invocation had been, and would be, matched even by High Churchmen. William Laud, Archbishop of Canterbury in 1637, the Nonjuror, Thomas Brett, in 1718 and John Dowden, Bishop of Edinburgh in 1890, all recognised that the prayer of invocation needed careful wording if a wide range of churchmanship were to be satisfied.[6] If High Churchmen recognised such snares, it is hardly surprising that Evangelicals found the Scottish Communion Office unacceptable.

While many Evangelicals thus found it difficult to remain members of the Scottish Episcopal Church, the English Episcopal movement provided them with more fertile ground. Within its fold, Evangelicals achieved a degree of success. For instance, English Episcopalianism can be regarded

---

[3] Chapter 6, pp. 195, 202-203.
[4] See Chapter 4, p. 149.
[5] See Chapter 8, pp. 249-250.
[6] See Chapter 7, pp. 221-222 and Chapter 10, pp. 357-359.

Conclusion 371

as having played an important part in the development of the Scottish Episcopal Church. Its agitation over the years against the Scottish Communion Office and the difficulty of holding non-liturgical evangelistic meetings was almost certainly a prominent factor in the eventual rewording of canon law in 1890 and in the development of the Scottish Episcopal Church into a wider body. Again, the separatists probably acted as a reference point for strict Evangelicalism. Their endorsement by Lord Shaftesbury and clergy such as G. T. Fox and J. C. Ryle in the 1880s, together with the continued supply of clergy to St Thomas's, Edinburgh, and St Silas's, Glasgow, in the twentieth century, when the churchmanship of some Evangelicals became blurred as a consequence of accommodation of High Church views, illustrates this point.[7] English Episcopalianism exerted an important influence.

Such success of English Episcopalianism can be attributed to various factors. Firstly, the continued opposition to the Scottish Communion Office suggests that the analysis made by Drummond and Craig in 1842 was accepted as basically sound for the rest of the century. Within Evangelicalism it appealed both to the moderate, but strict, Edward Bickersteth and to the more extreme Hugh McNeile, to the dogmatic Calvinistic *Record* as well as to the more liberal *Christian Observer*.[8] When Dowden argued in 1890 that the service favoured all shades of Catholic churchmanship but excluded lower views, he appeared to vindicate the Evangelical dilemma.[9] The points raised in 1842 by Drummond and Craig were still valid after fifty years of scrutiny.

Secondly, apart possibly from Sir William Dunbar, all the English Episcopalians were united in their desire to remain in the Church of England.[10] Their stance, from the beginning of the movement in 1842, was in line with that of Ryle, in 1891, that secession from the Church of England was unnecessary 'so long as the Articles and the Prayer Book are not altered'.[11] English Episcopalians were thus unlike those Anglican groups in the eighteenth and nineteenth centuries, such as Lady Huntingdon's Connexion in 1771, the Western Schism of 1815, the Free Church of England in 1843 and individuals such as B. W. Noel of Bedford

---

[7] See Chapter 1, p. 22 and Chapter 10, pp. 348, 354, 357, 360-363.

[8] See Chapter 8, pp. 270, 272, 292 and Chapter 10, p. 320. From 1843 the *Record* continually supported English Episcopalianism. See also, *Christian Observer* May 1857. After 1863 the *Christian Observer* appears to have withdrawn some of its support, possibly aligning itself with Charles Baring, Bishop of Durham, who felt that the demotion of the Scottish Communion Office in 1863 provided the English Episcopalians with protection against its use.

[9] Chapter 10, p. 358.

[10] See Chapter 9, pp. 313-314.

[11] J. C. Ryle, *Is All Scripture Inspired?* (London, 1891), pp. 62-63.

Row, London, in 1848, who seceded over issues ranging from the doctrine of baptism to the right to preach the gospel unfettered by the establishment connection.[12] Nor was there an exact parallel with the Free Church of Scotland which separated from the Church of Scotland over the problem of patronage. Although this difficulty could have hampered Evangelical advancement in the Scottish Kirk, it did not prevent the free exercise of evangelism in the manner imposed by the Scottish Episcopal authorities on Drummond. Again, granted the seriousness of the patronage dispute,[13] the fundamental doctrinal problem of the Scottish Communion Office, faced by the separatist Episcopalians, was possibly an even deeper issue affecting subscription to the Church. By contrast, the English Episcopalians bore some resemblance to the nineteenth-century Church of England congregations in South Africa. This body, which was, however, not uniformly Evangelical, refused to join the autonomous Church of the Province of South Africa, formed in 1870, on the grounds that the latter was not subject on spiritual matters to the Privy Council but only to its own courts. Partly fearing an upsurge of Tractarian theology in the South African Church, the separatist group there regarded itself as the true doctrinal representative of Anglicanism in South Africa, never severing itself from its mother Church.[14] English Episcopalianism, likewise, always stayed loyal to the Church of England.

Thirdly, the leadership of Drummond was important. While he and the English Episcopalians were not representative of outlandish theological doctrines they may, possibly, be placed in the general category of 'Recordites', that group of pro-Establishment Tory Churchmen, allied to the *Record* newspaper, which propounded moderate Calvinist and anti-Catholic views and was prone to secession.[15] Certainly, the English Episcopalian cause was regularly and vigorously defended in the *Record*, and it owed much of its success to that newspaper above all other Evangelical publications.[16] Recordites were often described as representative of a 'cold, tough Protestantism' with a negative approach to new ideas.[17] But, importantly, Drummond belied such blanket classification, exemplified by his willingness to compromise over the

---

[12] Grayson Carter, *Anglican Evangelicals: Protestant Secessions from the Via Media, c. 1800-1850* (Oxford, 2001), pp. 35, 135-150, 312-390.

[13] S. J. Brown, *Thomas Chalmers* (Oxford, 1982), pp. 303-337.

[14] Peter Hinchliff, *The Anglican Church in South Africa* (London, 1963), pp. 93-129.

[15] Grayson Carter, *Anglican Evangelicals: Protestant Secessions from the Via Media, c. 1800-1850* (Oxford, 2001), pp. 24-25, 56-57, 176, 192.

[16] The *Christian Observer, Christian Guardian* and the *Churchman* did not cover the events surrounding English Episcopalianism in as great detail or volume as the *Record*. The *Churchman*, from 1880-1900, did not report on English Episcopalianism.

[17] Peter Toon, *Evangelical Theology 1833-1856: A Response to Tractarianism* (London, 1977), p. 77.

Conclusion

eucharistic issue in 1872 when offering Laud's liturgy. Again, he was known by many Evangelicals for 'a piety which placed him among the foremost of those who walked closely with God in his day',[18] and even among High Churchmen who were unable 'to accord entire sympathy to the peculiar position which he occupied' he was praised for his 'modesty, prudence, temperance and charity'.[19] While, admittedly, English Episcopalianism fragmented after the 1870s, Drummond was particularly noteworthy in presenting the movement as an attractive, though strict, form of Evangelicalism, to Churchmen with varying beliefs.

Fourthly, although many Evangelical Episcopalians had serious scruples with the Scottish Episcopal Church, there was, nevertheless, some affinity between the camps. Importantly, these Evangelicals did not necessarily approach the communion service as a bare rite. For example Drummond taught that the ordinance was a time of drawing near to Christ, which resulted in spiritual nourishment and rejoicing for the blessings received. Despite the emphasis within Evangelical teaching that Christ dwelt in the hearts of believers, and was not found connected with the outward symbols of bread and wine, clergy like Drummond clearly expected that Christ would be present at the service, ministering to his people. Similarly, there was the shared conscientiousness in building up faithful congregations, albeit from the different perspectives of the need for conversion as opposed to the sufficiency of sacramental grace. In 1894 W. E. Gladstone, who deplored the disruptions that led to the English Episcopal movement, admitted that 'within that obscure and abstractedly unblessed fold there grew up, as I had occasion to know, some young people of a singular holiness'.[20] Similarly, in the rural northeast of Scotland, the Scottish Episcopalian, J. B. Pratt of Cruden, gathered a devout following over the forty-three years of his incumbency.[21] Again, the success achieved by St Thomas's, Edinburgh, and St Silas's, Glasgow, in reaching the underprivileged with the gospel would have been applauded by David Aitchison, A. J. D. D'Orsey, A. P. Forbes and John Comper who engaged with similar problems in Glasgow, Dundee and Aberdeen respectively.[22] Importantly, also, English Episcopalianism, like its Scottish counterpart, was notably socially influential. Some of the clergy such as Dunbar, Sholto

---

[18] Review of *Sparkling Rills by the Wayside or Thoughts on the Book of Psalms* (London, 1879), edited by Harriet Drummond, in the *Churchman*, May, 1881.

[19] *Perthshire Constitutional*, 13 June 1877.

[20] W. E. Gladstone, *Later Gleanings a New Series of Gleanings of Past Years*, Second edition, (London, 1898), p. 293. The quote is taken from an article written in 1894 entitled 'The Place of Heresy and Schism in the Modern Church'.

[21] Rowan Strong, *Episcopalianism in Nineteenth-Century Scotland* (Oxford, 2002), pp.52-58.

[22] See Chapter 3, pp. 87-91.

Douglas at St Silas's in the 1890s, and Drummond were from the upper echelons of Scottish society. Patrons such as the Duchess of Gordon, the Oliphants of Gask, Lord Elibank of Innerleithen, and laity like Sir George Burns and Sir J. D. Wauchope all added to the social acceptability of the movement. Similarly, a number of Evangelicals were eminent in different fields. While Scottish Episcopalianism could claim the allegiance of W. E. Aytoun, Professor of Logic at Edinburgh University, the English Episcopalians could number J. H. Balfour, the Edinburgh Professor of Medicine and Botany, W. F. Skene, Historiographer Royal for Scotland, and George Burns, the founder of the Cunard shipping line.[23] There were both spiritual and secular similarities between English and Scottish Episcopalians, contributing to an image of respectability for the former.

The foregoing analysis thus adds considerably to the existing secondary literature on the subject which has not delved deeply into the theological concerns of all the parties involved. By recognising the theological gulf between Evangelicals and the Scottish Episcopal Church, the secession of the English Episcopalians is placed in a more comprehensive light. Reginald Foskett's contention, for example, that Drummond was misguided in his assumption that the law of the Church could be disregarded for the sake of preaching the gospel, becomes a wider issue. The conversion of souls was always the primary concern for Evangelicals, and for many, like Drummond, it over-rode Church discipline. Again, Gavin White proposed that, because English Episcopalians desired to remain part of the Church of England, they were more 'establishment than anything else', not really Evangelical and unlike the contemporaneous Free Churchmen.[24] The detailed analysis given in Chapters 4 and 9 has, by contrast, placed the main protagonists of the separatist Episcopalians firmly within the Evangelical camp. Its members were certainly committed Churchmen, but their first loyalty was to Christ as the head of the church on earth. Their fervent preaching on conversion, the cross and the Bible, together with their active missionary involvement, reveals them as distinct Evangelicals in nineteenth-century Scotland.

While Gavin White's remark that the prayer of invocation in the Scottish Communion Office raises 'all sorts of problems'[25] is very apt, Peter Nockles's suggestion that such concerns 'provided a stick' with which

---

[23] Chapter 9 gives numerous other examples of high-ranking English Episcopalians.

[24] Gavin White, *Records of the Scottish Church History Society* 28, (1998) 'The Nine Lives of the Episcopal Cat. Changing Self-Images of the Scottish Episcopal Church', p. 88. Gavin White, *The Scottish Episcopal Church. A New History* (Edinburgh, 1998), p. 78.

[25] Gavin White, *The Scottish Episcopal Church. A New History* (Edinburgh, 1998), p. 27.

Conclusion

Drummond 'could beat his theological opponents'[26] needs to be interpreted with care. The knowledge that eighteenth and nineteenth-century theologians, with different doctrinal beliefs, saw the office as fundamentally different from the English service and top heavy in a Virtualist to Anglo-Catholic direction, suggests that the Evangelical polemic was not without basis. Similar reservations should be borne in mind when reading Rowan Strong's analysis that the Evangelicals concentrated their objections on the 'supposed transubstantiation' of the Scottish Office.[27] The different structure and content of the Scottish from the English rite has been shown to have opened it up to such charges from a whole range of Churchmen. The problem of framing a comprehensive liturgy was at the heart of the dispute.

Once the Evangelical position is fully dissected, Strong's serious allegations that Drummond was 'opinionated' in arguing for his evangelistic meetings and that 'he rather gloried' in his separation from the Scottish Episcopal Church, can be challenged.[28] The former assertion falls into the same misconception of Evangelical belief as Foskett's. But the latter is potentially more damning, since Drummond's fellow Evangelicals, with their strong sense of human sinfulness, would have been highly critical of such ostentation. The event needs to be placed in context if it is to be understood. The incident referred to the elderly Drummond's speech at Exeter Hall in 1872. Here, he brought the case for English Episcopalianism into the public arena once again after some English bishops had criticised their clergy for preaching at the separatist churches. He alluded to the enthusiastic ovation he had received in 1843 from the platform of the first assembly of the Free Church. His point, clearly made, was that the Free Churchmen 'were deeply interested in the stand' he was making 'for the Protestant faith'. The substance of the remark was far from self-aggrandisement. Instead it aimed at showing that many Scottish Evangelicals, of varying denominations, saw the English Episcopalian position as one of maintaining the Reformation roots of British Christianity. Certainly Drummond received supportive cheering from the floor of Exeter Hall, but no hint of criticism of his speech from any quarter, along the lines of Strong, has been found in the available public and private literature.[29] Evangelicalism in the 1840s and beyond, in response to rising Catholic belief, was deeply imbued with a desire to be identified with the Reformation, and English Episcopalianism was part of that trend.

---

[26] Peter Nockles, *Journal of Ecclesiastical History* 47, (1996), 'Scottish Episcopal Church and the Oxford Movement', pp. 676-677.

[27] Strong, *Episcopalianism*, p. 221.

[28] *Ibid.*, pp. 220, 230.

[29] *Record*, 16 December 1872. See Chapter 10, p. 342-342.

Importantly, also, it has been demonstrated that Scottish Evangelical Episcopalianism, although demanding a rigorous and serious application of faith, was by no means devoid of attractiveness in the private sphere. While it seems that little research has been undertaken concerning the daily lives of High Church Scottish Episcopalians, it has been possible to add an important contribution in the case of Evangelicalism in nineteenth-century Scotland. Doreen Rosman's contention in *Evangelicals and Culture*, that Evangelical family life and interests were not always restrictive, has been further supported by the analysis in Chapter 5, which provides alternative examples to those of Ian Bradley in *The Call to Seriousness* and Ford K. Brown in *Fathers of the Victorians*, which categorised a darker side of Evangelicalism.[30] Evangelical faith was certainly intensely felt, but it is evident that private and public persona did not always contradict within Evangelical Episcopalianism in Scotland.

The history of Scottish Evangelical Episcopalianism in the nineteenth century reflects that of the British movement generally. It demonstrates that Evangelicalism was never uniform. Again, the eventual drift of some English Episcopalians into the Scottish Episcopal Church mirrors the rifts in the British party when its conservative branch began to break up by the end of the century because some were willing to compromise and accommodate higher churchmanship. The following extract, which formed part of a letter headed 'Last Words', was found among Drummond's papers after his death in 1877, together with a request that it be read to his friends. It sums up the concerns of conscience that had formed the substance of the English Episcopalian dispute and continued to do so for an enduring sector of firm Evangelicals in nineteenth-century Scotland:

> St Thomas's Chapel was built and the congregation formed as a distinct testimony in favour of the simplicity of the ordinance of the Lord's Supper, and of direct antagonism to everything which could in any way or from any quarter affect that simplicity by the mysticism of unscriptural teaching, and the presence more or less developed of superstitious practice. Our position rested on the rock of the inspired Scriptures of God, accepting thankfully those views of divine truth for which our Protestant forefathers rejoiced to die.[31]

---

[30] Ian Bradley, *The Call to Seriousness* (London, 1976), pp. 186-189. Ford K. Brown, *Fathers of the Victorians* (Cambridge, 1961), pp. 462-467. Doreen M. Rosman, *Evangelicals and Culture* (London, 1984), pp. 97-115.

[31] *Memoir*, pp. clxxxii-clxxxiii.

Conclusion

The preservation of the Protestant tradition had always been at the heart of the problem in Scotland. While the issue of evangelistic services was resolved in 1890, the failure to deal with the difficulties surrounding the Scottish Communion Office meant that the Scottish Episcopal Church, as it entered the twentieth century, was unable to match, easily, the doctrinal breadth of the Church of England. Those Evangelicals who left the English Episcopal movement for the Scottish Church found it difficult to maintain their distinctive beliefs and it became increasingly problematical to appoint Evangelical clergy to their incumbencies. But conservative Evangelicalism flourished if it remained independent. As in earlier decades, the Scottish Episcopal Church was not a natural home for a large group of Evangelicals for whom doctrinal compromise ran counter to conscience.

Table 7.2

1549	1552	1637
FIRST LITURGY OF EDWARD VI	**REVISED LITURGY OF EDWARD VI**	**SCOTTISH SERVICE BOOK LAUD**
RUBRIC Then shall the Minister take so much bread and wine as shall suffice for the persons appointed to receive the Holy Communion, laying the bread upon the corporas, or else in the paten, or in some comely thing prepared for that purpose; And putting the wine into the chalice, or else in some fair or convenient cup prepared for that use, (if the chalice will not serve,) putting thereto a little pure and clean water, and settting both the bread and the wine upon the altar.	[No corresponding Rubric]	RUBRIC And the Presbyter shall then **offer up**[1] and place the bread and wine prepared for the Sacrament upon the Lord's Table, that it may be ready for that Service.
PRAYER OF CONSECRATION[2] O God, heavenly Father, which, of they tender mercy, didst give thine only Son, Jesu Christ to suffer death upon the cross for our redemption; **who made there (by his one oblation once offered)**[2] a full, perfect, and sufficient sacrifice, oblation, and satisfaction for the sins of the whole world; and did institute, and in his holy Gospel command us to celebrate, a perpetual memory of that his precious death, until his coming again; Hear us, (O merciful Father,) we beseech thee; and with thy Holy Spirit and Word, **vouchsafe to bless and sanctify these thy gifts and creatures of bread and wine, that they may be unto us the body and blood of thy most dearly beloved Son Jesus Christ**[3] who, in the same night that he was betrayed, took bread: and when he had blessed, and given thanks, he brake it, and gave it to his disciples, saying, Take, eat;	**PRAYER OF CONSECRATION**[2] Almighty God, our heavenly Father, which of thy tender mercy, didst give thine only Son Jesus Christ to suffer death upon the cross for our redemption; who made **there (by his one oblation of himself once offered)**[2] a full, perfect, and sufficient sacrifice, oblation, and satisfaction for the sins of the whole world, and did institute, and in his holy Gospel, command us to continue, a perpetual memory of that his precious death, until his coming again: Hear us, O merciful Father, we beseech thee; and grant that we, receiving these thy creatures of bread and wine, according to thy Son our Saviour Jesus Christ's holy institution, in remembrance of his death and passion, may be partakers of his most blessed body and blood; who, in the same night that he was betrayed, took bread; and when he had given thanks, he brake it, and gave it	**PRAYER OF CONSECRATION**[2] Almighty God, our heavenly Father, which, of thy tender mercy, didst give thy only Son Jesus Christ to suffer death upon the cross for our redemption, **who made there (by his one oblation of himself once offered)**[2] a full, perfect, and sufficient sacrifice, oblation, and satisfaction for the sins of the whole world; and did institute, and in his holy Gospel command us to continue, a perpetual memory of that his precious death and sacrifice, until his coming again: Hear us, O merciful Father, we most humbly beseech thee, and of thy Almighty goodness **vouchsafe so to bless and sanctify, with thy word and Holy Spirit, these thy gifts and creatures of bread and wine, that they may be unto us the body and blood of thy most dearly beloved Son;**[3] so that we receiving them according to thy Son our Saviour Jesus Christ's

Endplate

Collation of Communion Offices

1662	1764
ENGLISH LITURGY	SCOTTISH COMMUNION OFFICE
RUBRIC	RUBRIC
And when there is a communion, the Priest shall then place upon the table so much bread and wine as he shall think sufficient.	And the Presbyter shall then **offer up**[1] and place the bread and wine, prepared for the Sacrament, upon the Lord's Table.
PRAYER OF CONSECRATION[2]	**PRAYER OF CONSECRATION**[2]
Almighty God, our heavenly Father, who, of thy tender mercy, didst give thine only Son Jesus Christ to suffer death upon the cross for our redemption, **who made there (by his one oblation of himself once offered)**[2] a full, perfect, and sufficient sacrifice, oblation, and satisfaction, for the sins of the whole world; and did institute, and in his holy Gospel command us to continue, a perpetual memory of that his precious death, until his coming again: Hear us, O merciful Father, we most humbly beseech thee; and grant that we, receiving these thy creatures of bread and wine, according to thy Son our Saviour Jesus Christ's holy institution, in remembrance of his death and passion, may be partakers of his most blessed body and blood: who, in the same night that he was betrayed, took bread; and when he had given thanks, he brake	All glory be to thee, Almighty God, our heavenly Father, for that thou, of thy tender mercy, didst give thy only Son Jesus Christ to suffer death upon the cross for our redemption; **who (by his own oblation of himself once offered)**[2] made a full, perfect, and sufficient sacrific, oblation, and satisfaction, for the sins of the whole world, and did institute, and in his holy Gospel command us to continue, a perpetual memorial of that his precious death and sacrifice until his coming again. For, on the night that he was betrayed he took bread; and when he had given thanks, he brake it, and gave it to his disciples, saying, Take, eat, THIS IS MY BODY, which is given for you: DO this in remembrance of me. Likewise, after supper, he took the cup; and when he had given thanks, he gave it to them, saying, Drink ye all of this, for THIS

is my body which is given for you: Do this in remembrance of me. Likewise, after supper, he took the cup, and when he had given thanks, he gave it to them, saying, Drink ye all of this; for this is my blood of the New Testament, which is shed for you, and for many for the remission of sins: Do this, as oft as ye shall drink it, in remembrance of me. Wherefore, O Lord and heavenly Father, according to the institution of thy dearly beloved Son our Saviour Jesu Christ, we, thy humble servants, do celebrate and make here before thy Divine Majesty, with these thy holy gifts, the memorial which thy Son hath willed us to make; having in remembrance his blessed passion, mighty rersurrection, and glorious ascension; rendering unto thee most hearty thanks for the innumerable benefits procured unto us by the same; entirely desiring thy Fatherly goodness mercifully to accept this our sacrifice of praise and thanksgiving, &c.	to his disciples, saying, Take, eat; this is my body which is given for you; do this in remembrance of me. Likewise, after supper, he took the cup: and when he had given thanks, he gave it to them, saying, Drink ye all of this; for this is my blood of the New Testament, which is shed for you and for many for remission of sins: Do this, as oft as ye shall drink it, in remembrance of me.	holy institution, in remembrance of his death and passion, may be partakers of the same his most precious body and blood; who, in the night that he was betrayed, *took bread*; and when he had given thanks he brake it, and gave it to his disciples, saying, Take, eat, this is my body, which is given for you: do this is remembrance of me. Likewise, after supper, *he took the cup*, and when he had given thanks, he gave it to them, saying, Drink ye all of this; for this is my blood of the New Testament, which is shed for you and for many for the remission of sins: Do this, as oft as ye shall drink it, in rememebrance of me. Wherefore, O Lord and heavenly Father, according to the institution of thy dearly beloved Son our Saviour Jesus Christ, we, thy humble servants, do celebrate and make here before thy Divine Majesty, with these thy holy gifts, the memorial which thy Son hath willed us to make, having in remembrance his blessed passion, mighty resurrection, and glorious ascension, rendering unto thee most hearty thanks for the innumerable benefits procured unto us by the same. And we entirely desire thy Fatherly goodness mercifully to accept this our sacrifice of praise and thanksgiving, &c.

Endplate

it, and gave it to his disciples, saying Take, eat, this is my body which is given for you; do this in remembrance of me. Likewise, after supper, he took the cup; and, when he had given thanks, he gave it to them, saying, Drink ye all of this; for this is my blood of the New Testament, which is shed for you and for many for the remission of sins: Do this, as oft as ye shall drink it, in remembrance of me.	IS MY BLOOD of the New Testament, which is shed for you and for many for the remission of sins: DO this, as oft as ye shall drink it, in remembrance of me. Wherefore, O Lord, and [**The Oblation**][4] heavenly Father, according to the institution of thy dearly beloved Son, our Saviour Jesus Christ, we, thy humble servants, do celebrate and make here before thy Divine Majesty, **with these thy holy gifts, which WE NOW OFFER UNTO THEE, the memorial thy Son hath commanded us to make;**[4] having in remembrance his blessed passion, and precious death, his mighty resurrection, and glorious ascension; rendering unto thee most hearty thanks for the innumerable benefits procured unto us by the same. And we most humbly beseech thee, O [**The Invocation**][3] merciful Father, to hear us, and of thy Almighty goodness **vouchsafe to bless and sanctify with thy Word and Holy Spirit, these thy gifts and creatures of bread and wine <u>that they may become the body and blood of thy most dearly beloved Son.</u>**[3] And we earnestly desire thy Fatherly goodness mercifully to accept this our sacrifice of praise and thanksgiving, &c.

FORM OF ADMINISTRATION	FORM OF ADMINISTRATION	FORM OF ADMINISTRATION
The body of our Lord Jesus Christ, which was given for thee, preserve thy body and soul unto everlasting life.	Take and eat this in remembrance that Christ died for thee, and feed on him in thy heart, by faith, with thanksgiving.	The body of our Lord Jesus Christ, which was given for thee, preserve thy body and soul unto everlasting life.
[Not in this sevice.]	[Not in this sevice.]	[Not in this sevice.]
OFFERING UP OF PRAISE[5] [Used **before**[5] communicating.]	**OFFERING UP OF PRAISE**[5] [Used **after**[5] communicating.] O Lord and heavenly Father, we, thy humble servants, entirely desire thy Fatherly goodness mercifully to accept this our sacrifice of praise and thanksgiving. &c.	**OFFERING UP OF PRAISE**[5] [Used **before**[5] communicating.]
Let us pray for the whole state of Christ's Church.[6] [This prayer is *before*[6] the consecration of the elements.]	**Let us pray for the whole state of Christ's Church militant here on earth.**[6] [This prayer is *before*[6] the consecration of the elements.]	**Let us pray for the whole state of Christ's Church militant here on earth.**[6] [This prayer is *before*[6] the consecration of the elements.]

Endplate

FORM OF ADMINISTRATION	FORM OF ADMINISTRATION
The body of our Lord Jesus Christ, which was given for thee, preserve thy body and soul unto everlasting life. Take and eat this in remembrance that Christ died for thee, and feed on him in thy heart, by faith, with thanksgiving.	The body of our Lord Jesus Christ, which was given for thee, preserve thy body and soul unto everlasting life. The body of our Lord Jesus Christ, which was given for thee, preserve thy body and soul unto everlasting life.
[Not in this service.]	PRAYER AFTER COMMUNICATING Having now received the precious body and blood of Christ, let us, &c.
OFFERING UP OF PRAISE[5] [Used **after**[5] communicating.] O Lord and heavenly Father, we, thy humble servants, entirely desire thy Fatherly goodness mercifully to accept this our sacrifice of praise and thanksgiving, &c.	**OFFERING UP OF PRAISE**[5] [Used **before**[5] communicating.]
Let us pray for the whole state of Christ's Church militant here on earth.[6] [This prayer is **before**[6] the consecration of the elements.	Let us pray for the whole state of Christ's Church.[6] [This prayer is used ***after***[6] the elements are consecrated, and *before* they are consumed.]

N. B. All sections in this table which are in bold and with superscript note numbers are editorial and refer to the discussion on pages 226-232.

Bibliography

PRIMARY SOURCES

(a) MANUSCRIPTS

CHURCH RECORDS

Aberdeen	St James's	Aberdeen City Archives, MS DD15/3
	St Paul's	Aberdeen University Library, MS 3320/8
Crieff	St Columba's	Held in church
	St Michael's	Perth City Library, MS 103/11
Edinburgh	St James's	Held in church
	St Paul's, Carrubber's Close,	
		Edinburgh City Archives, MS ED 10
	St James's, Back of Castle	
		National Archives of Scotland, CH12/48
	St Thomas's	Held in church
	St Vincent's	Held in church
Fochabers	Gordon Chapel	Held in church
Glasgow	St Jude's	Mitchell Library, Glasgow, MS TD 66
	St Silas's	Mitchell Library, Glasgow, MS TD 1250
Greenock	St John's	Held in church
Montrose	St Peter's	Montrose Public Library, MS 549
Paisley	Holy Trinity	Held in church
Perth	St John's	Held in church

OTHERS

Benson Papers, Lambeth Palace Library, London
Brechin Diocesan Archives, Dundee University Library
Thomas Chalmers letters, New College Library, University of Edinburgh
Church Missionary Society Papers, Birmingham University Library
E. C. Dawson Papers, Dawson Collection, St Mary's Cathedral, Edinburgh
John Dowden Papers, National Library of Scotland, Edinburgh
D. T. K. Drummond Papers,   Derbyshire Record Office
                             Edinburgh University Library
                             National Library of Scotland
                             Tait Papers, Lambeth Palace Library

Gladstone Papers, Add. MSS, British Library, London
John Hope Papers, National Archives of Scotland, Edinburgh
Scottish Reformation Society Archives, Magdalen Chapel, 41 Cowgate, Edinburgh
Tait Papers, Lambeth Palace Library, London
Scottish Episcopal Church, Episcopal Chest, Jolly Kist, College of Bishops and General Synods, National Archives of Scotland, Edinburgh

(b) PUBLISHED WORKS

JOURNALS AND NEWSPAPERS

Aberdeen Free Press
Aberdeen Herald
Aberdeen Journal and General Advertiser for the North of Scotland
Bannfshire Journal and General Advertiser
Border Advertiser
British and Foreign Evangelical Review
Bulwark
Christian Guardian
Christian Lady's Magazine
Christian News
Christian Observer
Christian Remembrancer
Churchman
Churchman's Monthly Review
Clergy List
Contemporary Review
Crieff Journal
Dumfries and Galloway Courier
Dundee Advertiser
Dunoon Herald and Corval Advertiser
Edinburgh Advertiser
Edinburgh Almanack
Edinburgh Evening Courant
Edinburgh Evening Express
Elgin Courant
Elgin Courier
Elgin and Morayshire Courier
English Churchman
Glasgow Christian News
Glasgow Mail
Glasgow Herald
Greenock Advertiser

Bibliography

Inverness Advertiser
Inverness Courier
Johnstone Gleaner and Advertiser
Morning Herald
Nairnshire Mirror
National British Mail
Ninth Report of the Edinburgh Association in Aid of the United Brethren's Mission for the Year 1831 (Edinburgh, 1832).
North British Daily Mail
Oban Times
Paisley and Renfrewshire Gazette
Perthshire Advertiser
Perthshire Courier
Perthshire Constitutional
Post Office Directory (Aberdeen, Edinburgh, Glasgow, Montrose)
Proceedings of the Church Missionary Society
Protestant
Protestant Magazine
Record
Rock
St Silas's Magazine, August 1889.
Scottish Episcopal Church Directory (Edinburgh, 1879).
Scottish Reformation Society, The Truth of God against the Papacy (Edinburgh, 1860).
Scotsman
Scottish Ecclesiastical Journal
Scottish Episcopal Journal
Scottish Episcopal Review and Magazine
Scottish Episcopal Times
Scottish Guardian
Scottish Magazine and Churchman's Review
Scottish Standard Bearer
Society of St Margaret's Magazine
Southern Reporter
Stephen's Episcopal Magazine
Scottish Episcopal Magazine and Churchman's Review
Stephen's Episcopal Magazine and Ecclesiastical Journal
Strathearn Herald
United Presbyterian Magazine
Western Standard

NEWSPAPER COLLECTIONS

Lamb Collection, Local Studies Department, Central Library, Wellgate, Dundee

WORKS PUBLISHED BEFORE 1900

Addison, Berkeley, *An Earnest and Solemn Remonstrance Addressed to the Rev D. T. K. Drummond* (Edinburgh, 1843).
  Remarks on Bishop Wordsworth's Recent Letter Reprobating the Author's Conduct for Taking Part in the Public Meetings of the Scottish Reformation Society (Edinburgh, 1853).
  Address to the Rev. Sir William Dunbar...with reference to Bishop Skinner's having declared him to be apart from Christ's mystical body [From the Parish Church of Stoke-on-Trent and from St Paul's Chapel, Aberdeen] (Aberdeen, 1843).
  Address from the Protestant Association of the Members of the United Church of England and Ireland in Scotland (Glasgow, 1851).
  Announcement by the Committee of the Friends of the Rev. D. T. K. Drummond: A Temporary Place of Worship will be Opened on the 20th Instant in the Local School, no. 10 Young Street, Charlotte Square (17th November 1842).
Alexander, John, *Letter to the Rt. Rev. William Skinner, Bishop of Aberdeen, Primus of the Church in Scotland, on the Eucharistic Doctrine Exhibited in the Scottish Communion Office as it Stands Affected to the School of Archdeacon Wilberforce and the Teaching of the Anglican Divines* (Edinburgh, 1857).
Archibald, John, *The History of the Episcopal Church of Keith in the Seventeenth, Eighteenth and Nineteenth Century with other Reminiscences of the Dioceses of Moray and Ross* (Edinburgh, 1890).
Aytoun, W. E., *The Drummond Schism Examined and Exposed* (Edinburgh, 1842).
B. P. P. *1851 Census Great Britain, Population* Volume II (London, 1853).
Bagot, Daniel, *A Protestant Catechism* (Edinburgh, 1836).
  A Catechism Explanatory of the Leading Truths of the Gospel (Edinburgh, 1839).
  A Letter to Some Members of the Vestry of St James's Chapel in Reference to the Scottish Communion Office (Edinburgh, 1842).
  The Inspiration of Holy Scripture (London, 1878).
Baker, S. C., *Early Grace Illustrated in the Memoir of David Tod* (Edinburgh, 1846).
  Hope Founded on the Word (London, 1860).
  A Pastor's Word against Ritualistic Innovations (London, 1868).
Balfour, J. H., *The Plants of the Bible* (London, 1866).
Bennett, John *The Second Advent* (London, 1878).
Bickersteth, Edward, *Treatise on the Lord's Supper* (London, 1824).
  The Episcopal Church in Scotland (Edinburgh, 1843).

Bibliography 389

Birks, T. R., *Memoir of the Rev. Edward Bickersteth, Late Rector of Watton., Herts.,* Volume II (London, 1852).
Blatch, William, *A Memoir of the Right Rev. David Low* (London, 1855).
Bligh, E. V., *Lord Ebury as a Church Reformer* (London, 1891).
Boase, Frederic, *Modern English Biography, Containing Memoirs of Persons Who Have Died Since 1850, with an Index of the Most Interesting Matters* (Truro, 1892-1921).
Bouverie, F. W., *I Will Not Hear* (London, 1859).
Can They be Made One? A Question in Reference to the Church of England and the Scottish Episcopal Church (Aberdeen, 1861).
Boyle, John, *A Plea for the Episcopal Church in Scotland in a Brief Defence of the Scottish Communion Office* (Edinburgh, 1843).
The Sacrament of the Body and Blood of Christ Doctrinally Explained According to the Homily of the Church of England (London, 1860).
Brown, David, *Christ's Second Coming: Will it be Premillennial?* (Edinburgh, 1846).
Budd, Henry, *A Sermon Preached Before C. M. S. 30 April 1827* (London, 1827).
Calvin, John, *Tracts Relating to the Reformation* Volume II, Translated by H. Beveridge (Edinburgh, 1844).
Campbell, A. B., *An Authenticated Statement of Circumstances Connected to the Late Abortive Attempt to Elect a Second Minister in St Paul's Chapel, with Correspondence Relating Thereto* (Aberdeen 1854).
Candlish, R. S., *The Aims and Principles of the Work of the Scottish Reformation Society* (Edinburgh, 1891).
Cardwell, Edward, *The Two Books of Common Prayer, Set Forth by Authority of Parliament in the Reign of King Edward the Sixth, Compared with Each Other* (Oxford, 1838).
[Carmichael, John] 'Veritas', *Romanism and Scottish Episcopacy* (Edinburgh, 1858).
Catalogue of the General and Theological Library of the late D. T. K. Drummond, 5 February 1878 (Edinburgh, 1878).
Cazenove, J. G., *Bishop Cotterill. Reprinted from the Proceedings of the Royal Society of Edinburgh* (Edinburgh, 1888).
Cheyne, Patrick, *The Authority and Use of the Scottish Communion Office Vindicated* (Aberdeen, 1843).
Holiness and the True Reforming Power of the Church (Aberdeen, 1844).
Six Sermons on the Doctrine of the Most Holy Eucharist (Aberdeen, 1858).
Christie, James, *The Oblation and Invocation in the Scottish Communion Office Vindicated in answer to a Pamphlet entitled An Important discrepancy by the Rev E. Craig* (London and Aberdeen, 1844).

A Critical Analysis of a Report of a Deputation into England in 1846 (London, 1847).
A Vindication of the Church in Scotland being an exposure of D. T. K. Drummond's "Historical Sketch of Episcopacy" (London, 1847).
Chronicle of Convocation (London, 1869, 1887).
Church Missionary Society Record (London, 1835, 1841).
Code of Canons of the Episcopal Church in Scotland (Edinburgh, 1811, 1828, 1838, 1863, 1877, 1890, 1911, 1929).
Correspondence Between Right Reverend Bishop Gleig and Rev Edward Craig Respecting an Accusation Lately Published in a Charge Delivered to the Clergy of the Episcopal Communion of Brechin (Edinburgh, 1820).
Correspondence Between Rt. Rev C. H. Terrot and Rev D. T. K Drummond (Edinburgh, 1842).
Correspondence Between the Rev D. T. K. Drummond and the Rev Richard Hibbs (Edinburgh, 1854).
Cotterill, Henry, *Charge of the Lord Bishop of Grahamstown at his Third Visitation* (Grahamstown, 1863).
A Charge Delivered in the Cathedral Church, Grahamstown, June 29, 1871 (Grahamstown, 1871).
The Genesis of the Church (Edinburgh, 1872).
True Position of the Episcopal Church in Scotland being a Charge Delivered to the Synod of the Diocese of Edinburgh, May 2 1877 (Edinburgh, 1877).
The Unity of Christians Essential to the Conversion of the World (Edinburgh, 1879).
Craig, Edward, *The Religious Instruction of the Poor, The Duty of the Rich* (Edinburgh, 1819).
Plain Pastoral Addresses on Regeneration (Edinburgh, 1823).
A Reply to the Rev. James Walker M.A. Rendered Necessary by his Serious Expostulation on the Subject of Baptismal Regeneration (London, 1826).
The Gospel Message Plainly Stated (Edinburgh, 1830).
A Letter to Thomas Erskine Esq. In Reply to his Recent Pamphlet in Vindication of the West Country Miracles (Edinburgh, 1830).
A Friendly Address to Roman Catholics occasioned by an Introductory Address from the Rev Mr M'Kay to the Congregation of St James's Episcopal Chapel (Edinburgh, 1831).
The Religious Instruction of the Poor, Gospel Message Plainly Stated, Christian Circumspection (Edinburgh, 1832).
On the Important Discrepancy between the Church of England and the Scottish Episcopal Community showing the Schismatical Character of a Subscription by English Clerics to the Scottish Communion Office of 1765 (Edinburgh, 1842).

Cuninghame, William, *A Dissertation on the Seals and Trumpets of the Apocalypse* (London, 1813).
Davidson, A. J., (ed.), *The Autobiography of Samuel Davidson, D.D. LL.D.* (Edinburgh, 1899).
E. C. Dawson, *The Bands That Bind Us to our Belief* (Edinburgh, 1891).
Declaration of the Clergy Against Alteration of the Prayer Book Second edition, (London, 1860).
D'Orsey, A. J. D., *A Letter to the Rt. Hon. The Lord Brougham in reply to his Attack on the Scottish Church in the House of Lords, May 22 1849* (London, 1850).
Drummond, D. T. K., *Last Scenes in the Life of our Lord and Saviour*, (London, 1841, 1850, 1878).
Reasons for Withdrawing from the Scottish Episcopal Church with a Full Reply to the Charge of Schism (Edinburgh, 1842).
Reply to Resolutions of Clergy of the Scottish Episcopal Church of the Diocese of Edinburgh, in which the Rev. D. T. K. Drummond is Declared to have Separated himself from that Church Totally Without Cause (Edinburgh, 1842).
Sermon for the Times, preached in Trinity Chapel, Dean Bridge, with Introduction and Copious Appendix (Edinburgh, 1842).
The Scottish Communion Office Examined and Proved to be Repugnant to Scripture and Opposed to the Articles, Liturgy and Homilies of the Church of England (Edinburgh, 1842).
Address to the Congregation of St Thomas's English Episcopal Chapel in Reference to a Dissuasive from Schism, &c by the Right Rev. C. H. Terrot, D. D. Bishop (Edinburgh, 1843).
Historical Sketch of Episcopacy from 1688 to the Present Time (Edinburgh, 1845).
Destitution in the Highlands of Scotland. A Sermon preached in aid of the Fund for the Destitute Highlanders (Edinburgh, 1847).
Memoir of Montague Stanley A. R. S. A. (Edinburgh, 1848).
Preacher in the House; or Family Sabbath Readings (Edinburgh, 1851).
Scenes and Impressions in Switzerland and the North of Italy (Edinburgh, 1853).
The Three Voices. A Sermon Preached on Tuesday November 29 1853 being the Day of Humiliation for the Pestilence (Edinburgh, 1853).
Statement Relative to the Correspondence Between the Rev. D. T. K. Drummond and the Rev. Richard Hibbs (Edinburgh, 1854).
The Engravings of the New Testament or the Parabolic Teaching of Christ (Edinburgh, 1855).
Letter to the Rev Dean Ramsay in Reference to the Primary Charge of Bishop Forbes and the Declaration of Bishops Terrot, Ewing, and Trower (Edinburgh, 1858).

The Jewish Sabbath. What it was not, and what it was (Edinburgh, 1862).

'Some Remarks on the Malt Process'. *The Photographic News*, 22 January, 1864.

Letter to the Very Rev the Dean of Carlisle (Edinburgh, 1876).

A Serious Inquiry into the Nature of the Stage (Edinburgh, 1876).

Sparkling Rills by the Wayside, ed. Harriet Drummond (Edinburgh, 1879).

Drummond, D. T .K. and Robert Kaye Greville, *The Church of England Hymn Book* (Edinburgh, 1838).

Drummond, Harriet, *Peace for the Christian Mourner: or Extracts from Various Christian Authors on the subject of Affliction. With a Preface by the Rev D. T. K. Drummond and an Original Paper on Christian Consolation by the Rev Hugh White, Curate of St Mary's, Dublin* (London, 1840).

Peace for the Dying Christian: or Extracts from Various Authors on the Subject of Death, with Preface by B. W. Noel and an Introductory Notice by D. T. K. Drummond (Edinburgh, 1845).

The Christian's Anchor: or I Will Hope Continually (Edinburgh, 1851).

Christian Experience Being the Second Series of Peace For the Dying Christian (Edinburgh, 1855).

Emily Vernon, or, Filial Piety Exemplified (Edinburgh, 1855. New York, 1855).

Lucy Seymour: or, It is more Blessed to Give than to Receive (Edinburgh, 1847, 1849), (London, 1870).

Wilmot Family: or, 'They that Deal Truly are His Delight' (Edinburgh, 1848. London, 1870).

Glen Isla, or The Good and Joyful Thing (London, 1870).

Louisa Morton, or, Children Obey your Parents in all Things (London, 1871).

The Upper Room Furnished, or, a Help to the Christian at the Lord's Table (Edinburgh, 1875).

Dunbar, Sir William, *Pulpit Recollections or Miscellaneous Sermons* (London, 1841).

A Letter to the Managers and Constituent Members and Congregation of St Paul's Chapel, Aberdeen, by the Rev Sir William Dunbar Bart. S. C. L. Presbyter of the Church of England to which is added Bishop Skinner's Declaration that Sir William Dunbar has placed himself in a State of Open Schism and the Warning of His Reverence to "All Faithful People to Avoid all Communion with the said Sir William Dunbar in Prayers and Sacraments" 3rd edition (Aberdeen, 1843).

Answer to a Letter to the Managers, Constituent Members and Congregation of St Paul's Chapel, Aberdeen, by the Rev Sir William

Bibliography 393

Dunbar, Bart, S. C. L., *Presbyter of the Church of England* (Aberdeen, 1843).
An Address to the Congregation of St Paul's Chapel, Aberdeen, by their minister. Delivered on the occasion of Bishop Skinner having pronounced him to be in a state of open schism.
A Sermon Preached in Kew Church, 21 June 1863 (Private, 1863).
Episcopacy in Scotland: Revised Report of the Debate in the House of Lords May 22 1849 (London, 1849).
Euchologion: A Book of Common Order Being Forms of Worship Issued by the Church Service Society (Edinburgh, 1867).
Extract of the Opinion of Dr Stephen and Mr Alexander Haldane on the 'Case of English Episcopalians in Scotland' May 1873.
Farquhar, G. T. S., *The Episcopal History of Perth, 1689-1894* (Perth, 1894).
First Annual Report of the Association of English Episcopalians in Scotland (Edinburgh, 1878).
Forbes, A. P., *A Primary Charge Delivered to the Clergy in his Diocese at the Annual Synod of 1857* 2nd Edition (London, 1858).
Forbes, G. H., *Panoply,* Volumes II and III.
A Short Explanation of the Communion Office of the Church of Scotland adapted to the Revised Edition (Burntisland, 1863).
Frere, James Hatley, *A Combined View of the Prophecies of Daniel, Esdras, and St John,* (London, 1815).
Garden, Francis, *Vindication of the Scottish Episcopate* (Edinburgh, 1847).
Gladstone, W. E., *Later Gleanings: A New Series of Gleanings of Past Years,* Second edition, (London, 1898).
Goode, William, *The Nature of Christ's Presence in the Eucharist,* Volume II (London, 1856).
Grant, James, *Cassell's Old and New Edinburgh,* Volume II (London, n.d.).
Greville, R. K., *An Appeal to Christians on the Subject of Dramatic Entertainments* (Edinburgh, 1830).
Facts Illustrative of Drunkenness in Scotland (Edinburgh, 1834).
The Sabbath Alliance: Statement and Proceedings of the Sabbath Alliance from its formation November 1 1847 to March 31 1848 (Edinburgh, 1848).
A Letter to the Marquis of Clanricarde, Post Master-General, on the Desecration of the Lord's Day in the Post Office (Edinburgh, 1850).
Letter on the Opening of the Crystal Palace on Sundays (Edinburgh, 1853).
Waifs of Fair Edina or the Mystery of St Leonards (Edinburgh, 1898).
Greville, R. K. and Huie, Richard, *The Amethyst* (Edinburgh, 1832).
Gribble, C. B., *Christ Glorified* (London, 1841).

A Letter to His Grace the Archbishop of Canterbury (with His Lordship's reply) relative to the Spiritual Necessities of Seamen (London, 1856).

A Mistake Corrected. A Letter to the Rev Dr Champneys, Head Master of the Collegiate School, Glasgow (Glasgow, 1858).

Groome, F. H., *Ordnance Gazetteer of Scotland* Volume I-V (London, 1894).

Grosvenor, Robert, *On the Revision of the Liturgy: The Speech of Lord Ebury in the House of Lords, 8 May 1860* (London, 1860).

Grove F. and J. Cunningham, *Supplementary Statement 19 January 1843* (Edinburgh, 1843).

Grubb, George, *Ecclesiastical History of Scotland,* Volume I-IV (Edinburgh, 1861).

Handley, J. E., *The Irish in Modern Scotland* (Cork, 1847).

Hansard's Parliamentary Debates, Volume CLXXV, 4 May-20 June 1864.

Heath, Vernon, *Recollections* (London, 1892).

Hebden, A. H. R., *The Lord's Supper According to the Bible and the Prayer Book* (London, 1871).

Baptism the Prayer Book Explaining Itself (London, 1871).

Baptism: Are We Right? (London, 1874).

Hibbs, Richard, *The Substance of a Series of Discourses on Baptism, Preached Prior to a General Confirmation, in which it is shown that the teaching of the Church of England on the subject is consentient with Holy Scripture* (London, 1848).

God's Plea for the Poor Concerning the Poor and the New Poor Law (London, 1851).

Scottish Episcopal Romanism (Edinburgh, 1856).

Hill, Rowland, *Journal Through the North of England and Parts of Scotland with Remarks on the Present State of the Established Church* (London, 1799).

Extracts of a Journal of a Second Tour from England through the Highlands of Scotland and the North Western Parts of England (London, 1800).

History of the Family of Drummond (London, 1842).

Hoadly, Benjamin, *The Works of Benjamin Hoadly published by his Son, John Hoadly,* Volume I-III (London, 1773).

Hodder, Edwin, *Sir George Burns Bart. His Times, His Friends* (London, 1892).

Holland, W. L., *Walled Up Nuns and Nuns Walled Up* (Edinburgh, 1895).

The Beauty of Holiness (Stirling, 1895).

Hull, J. D., *The Church of God:A Book for the Age* (London, 1840).

Popery in the Scotch Episcopal Church (Aberdeen, 1844).

A Brief Reply to the Rev P. Cheyne's Preface to the Second edition of his Sermon (Aberdeen, 1845).

Bibliography

A Letter Respectively Addressed to the Rt Rev The Lord Bishop of Exeter (London, 1845)
The Cluster Crushed (London, 1867).
Hull J. D. and William Winstanley Hull, *Observations on a Petition for the Revision of the Liturgy of the United Church of England and Ireland in a report of the discussion in the House of Lords,* Second Edition (London, 1840).
Humphrey, William, *Recollections of Scottish Episcopalianism* (London, 1896).
Hutton, E. D., *Burning Questions of the Day* (London, 1882).
Irving, Edward, *Babylon and Infidelity Foredoomed* (Glasgow, 1828).
The Orthodox and Catholic Doctrine of Our Lord's Human Nature (London, 1830).
Jenkins, Charles, *Cathedral Monthly Paper* (Edinburgh, 1895).
'John Mason Neale: A Memoir', *Society of St Margaret's Magazine* (London, 1887-1895).
Johnson, John, *The Unbloody Sacrifice,* Volume I (London, 1714-1718).
Kirk, J. F., *Supplement to Allibone's Critical Dictionary of English Literature and British and American Authors* (Philadelphia, 1891).
Kirkman, Joshua, *The Scriptures the only Rule of Faith* (Aberdeen, 1857).
Address to the London Clerical Conference (London, 1872).
Quit You Like Men (London, 1873).
Lawson, J. P., *History of the Scottish Episcopal Church from the Revolution to the Present Time* (Edinburgh, 1843).
Lathbury, Thomas, *A History of the Nonjurors: Their Controversies and Writings* (London, 1845).
Layman, *The Drummond Schism Examined and Exposed* (Edinburgh, 1842).
Lias, J. J., *The Atonement Viewed in the Light of Certain Modern Difficulties: the Hulsean Lectures for 1883, 1884* (Cambridge, 1884).
Lewis, Thomas, *The Christian Triumphant in Death: A Sermon Occasioned by the Decease of Mr David Naismith, founder of City Missions* (London, 1840).
MacFarquhar, W. P., *Sermons* (Edinburgh, 1844).
Manning, H. E., *Sermons III* (London, 1850).
Marshall, J., *A Few Remarks Addressed at the Request of Others to the Congregation of St James's Episcopal Church, Edinburgh* (Edinburgh, 1843).
McCann, James, *Anti-Darwinism,* (Glasgow, 1869).
Salvation (Glasgow, 1873).
McNeile, Hugh, *Sermon Preached Before the London Society for the Propagation of Christianity among the Jews* (London, 1826).
Miles, C. P., *An Address to the Members of St Jude's, Glasgow [In Reply to Bishop M. Russell's Affectionate Address]* (Glasgow, 1844).

Reply to Bishop Russell A Second Address to the Members of St Jude's Congregation (Glasgow, 1844).
Third Address by C. P. Miles in Reply to a Statement by Bishop Russell in his Appendix to his Original Pamphlet where he Offers an Apology for Certain Discrepancies Contained in His Letters (Glasgow, 1844).
The Voice of the Glorious Reformation, Second Edition, (London, 1844).
The Scottish Episcopal Church Antagonistic to the Church of England (Glasgow, 1857).
[Miller, J. D.] 'Justitia', *Peculiarities of the Scottish Episcopal Church* (Aberdeen, 1847).
Member of the Congregation, *A Letter to the Members of the Congregation of St James's Chapel in Reference to Certain Resolutions Which Have Been Entered into by Some Members of the Vestry of that Chapel* (Edinburgh, 31 December 1842).
Montgomery, Robert, *Letter to one of the Managers of St Jude's: The Glasgow Schism* (London, 1844).
The Gospel Before the Age or Christ With Nicodemus (London, 1844).
The Scottish Episcopal Church and the English Schismatics (London, 1847).
A Letter on the Recent Schisms in Scotland with a Documentary Appendix and an Introduction Addressed to the Lord Bishop of Llandaff (London, 1847).
Moule, J., *A Second Letter to the Members of the Congregation of St James's Chapel* (Edinburgh, 1843).
Murray, E. C. G. *Strange Tales: From Vanity Fair by Silly Billy* (London, 1875).
Neale, J. M., *The Life and Times of Patrick Torry* (London, 1856).
New Directory for the Public Worship of God (Edinburgh, 1898).
New Statistical Account of Scotland (Edinburgh, 1845).
Noel, G. T., *The Gospel. A Revelation of Mercy to the Guilty. A Sermon Delivered at Charlotte Episcopal Chapel, January 22 1818* (Edinburgh, 1818).
A Brief Inquiry into the Prospects of the Church of Christ in Connexion with the Second Advent of our Lord Jesus Christ (London, 1828).
Ogilvy, Thomas, *Dying Scenes in My Own Family* (privately printed, 1854).
Payne Smith, R., *Sermon Preached at Trinity Episcopal Chapel, Edinburgh, 27th June* (Edinburgh, 1852).
Peddie, Mrs Robert (ed.), *A Consecutive Narrative of the Remarkable Awakening in Edinburgh* (London, 1874).
Pennie, G. N., 'The Trial of the Rev Patrick Cheyne for Erroneous Teaching on the Eucharist in Aberdeen in 1858', *Records of the Scottish Church History Society*, 23 (1987).

Bibliography

Phin, Kenneth M., *Letter to the Right Honourable Lord John Scott on the Recent Movement of the Scottish Episcopacy in the Counties of Roxburgh and Selkirk* (Edinburgh, 1856).

Plea for Union among Episcopalians in Scotland by a Member of the Church of England, (Edinburgh, 1882).

Presbyterian Forms of Service Issued by the Devotional Service Association in Connection with the United Presbyterian Church (Edinburgh, 1894).

Proby, W. H., *Annals of the Low Church Party* (London, 1888).

Proceedings of the Church Missionary Society for Africa and the East (London, 1816-1900).

Pusey, E. B., *Tract 67*.
The Presence of Christ in the Eucharist, (Oxford 1853).
Parochial and Cathedral Sermons (Oxford, 1882).

Ramsay, E. B., *The Present State of our Canon Law Considered* (Edinburgh, 1859).
The Scripture Doctrine of the Eucharist (Edinburgh, 1858).

Ranken, Arthur, *The Church of England in Scotland. A Pastoral Address to the Congregation of St Drostane's Church, Deer, Diocese of Aberdeen* (Edinburgh, 1853).

Reports on Speeches delivered at a meeting on Wednesday December 23 1835 for the Purpose of forming a Protestant Society for that City and its Vicinity (Edinburgh, 1835).

Reports of the Proceedings of the Edinburgh Protestant Association read at a Public Meeting of the Association and those friendly to its objects, held in the West Church on Friday 6 December 1839, with an appendix containing the speeches of the Rev H. McNeile of Liverpool (Edinburgh, 1839).

Reports of the Commissioners of Religious Instruction, Scotland, *PP*, (1836-1839).

Report of the Speeches of Counsel, and the Opinion of the judges in the First Division of the Court of Session. March 3, 1849 (Edinburgh, 1849).

Report of a Deputation Appointed at a Meeting in Aberdeen, May 1846, of Ministers and Lay Members of the Church of England Representing the Congregations Adhering to her Forms and Doctrines in Scotland, in order to visit England and Communicate with the Bishops and Other Parties in the Established Church, on the Subject of their Ecclesiastical Position in Scotland (Edinburgh, 1847).

Report of a Discussion Regarding Ragged Schools, July 2 1847 (Edinburgh, 1847).

Reprint of Four Articles Taken by Permission from the London Record with an Introduction by the Rev D. T. K. Drummond Containing Remarks Recently Addressed by the Rev F. Garden to the Rt Rev Lord Bishop of Cashel (Edinburgh, 1845).

Robertson, J. S. S., *Lectures on the Philippians* (London, 1849).
Rogers, Charles, *Memorial and Recollections of the Rev Edward Bannerman Ramsay* (London, 1873).
Ross, A. J., *Memoir of Alexander Ewing* (London, 1877).
Russell, Michael, *An Affectionate Address to the Managers and Congregation of St Jude's* 2nd Edition (Glasgow, 1844).
Ryle, J. C., *Is All Scripture Inspired?* (London, 1891).
'Sigma', *A Brief Review of a Statement of the Majority of the Vestry of St James's Chapel, Edinburgh* (Edinburgh, 1843).
Statement by the Committee of Mr Drummond's Friends (Edinburgh, 1842).
Statement of the Proceedings of the Majority of the Vestry of St James's, 7 January 1842 (Edinburgh, 1842).
Stuart, A. Moody, *Life and Letters of Elisabeth, Last Duchess of Gordon* (London, 1865).
Stuart, R. L., *English Episcopalianism in Scotland Explained and Justified* (Edinburgh, 1877).
Sumner, G. H., (ed.), *Principles at Stake* (London, 1868).
Sumner, J. B., *Apostolical Preaching Considered, in an Examination of St Paul's Epistles* (London, 1815).
Talon, T. K., *Papists' Conspiracy and England's Protest, England's Shield* (London, 1848).
Sermons (London, 1866).
The Established Church in Ireland, being the Substance of a Lecture delivered in Edinburgh on May 1868 (Edinburgh, 1868).
Reasons for Joining the Episcopal Church of Scotland, (Edinburgh, 1882).
Taylor, William, *A Letter to Henry, Lord Brougham of Vaux in Reference to his Lordship's Speech in the House of Lords on 22 May Respecting Episcopacy in Scotland with a Postscript on Sir William Dunbar's Protest* (Edinburgh, 1849).
Teape, C. R., *Confession and Absolution in the Anglican Church* (Edinburgh, 1868).
Effect of Ritualism in Clergy and Laity (Edinburgh, 1882).
Terrot, C. H., *A Dissuasive from Schism* (Edinburgh, 1843).
The Position of Popery in Great Britain and the Means in Scotland for Resisting it, being the Report of the Operations of the Scottish Reformation Society for the Year 1863 (Edinburgh, 1864).
The Second Prayer Book of Edward VI issued 1552 (Editor's preface is signed James Parker) (Oxford, 1883).
Thompson, Henry, *The Life of Hannah More,* (London, 1838).
Trower, W. J., *A Remonstrance Addressed to Archibald Cambell Esq. of Blythswood on Certain Resolutions to which his Name is Appended, Published in the Glasgow Herald of Nov 21 1856* (Glasgow, 1856).

Bibliography

Truth Vindicated. Pamphlets Concerning the Dispute Between the Rev Richard Hibbs and the Rev D. T. K. Drummond (London, 1858).
Turpin, W. T., *Gospel Papers* (London, 1883).
Wade, W. M., *Ten Sermons Preached in Trinity Episcopal Chapel, Paisley,* (Paisley, 1839).
The Truth Spoken in Love Relative to Episcopacy and the Anglican Liturgy (Paisley, 1840).
Walker, James, *A Friendly Call to Union Addressed to the Managers of St Paul's Chapel, Aberdeen,* (Edinburgh, 1823).
A Serious Expostulation with the Rev. Edward Craig, M.A., in Reference to the Doctrine Falsely Attributed (in a remonstrance addressed) to the Rev James Walker, Humbly submitted to the Judgement of the Bishops and Clergy and Earnestly tendered to the consideration of the Laity of the Episcopal Communion in Scotland (Edinburgh, 1826).
Walker, William, *Memoirs of Bishops Jolly and Gleig* (Edinburgh, 1878)
The Life of the Right Reverend Alexander Jolly D.D. (Edinburgh, 1878).
The Life and Times of the Rev John Skinner at Linshart, Longside (London, 1883).
Three Churchmen (Edinburgh, 1893).
Waterland, Daniel, *A Review of the Doctrine of the Eucharist* (Oxford, 1896).
Westcott, B. F., Bishop of Durham, *The Incarnation: A Revelation of Human Duties* (London, 1892).
The Incarnation and Common Life (London, 1893).
Wilberforce, Robert, *The Doctrine of the Holy Eucharist* (London, 1853).
Witherspoon, John, *A Serious Inquiry into the Nature of the Stage with a Preface by D. T. K. Drummond* (Edinburgh, 1876).
Wordsworth, Charles, *Annals of My Life 1847-1856* (London, 1893).
Wrenford, Edwin, *The Two Branches of the Episcopal Communion in Scotland: Subjection, No Not for an Hour, A Letter to the Archbishop of Canterbury* (London, 1872).
First Fruits of Sacred Song (London, 1876).
Carminia Regia (London, 1878).

WORKS PUBLISHED AFTER 1900

A History of the Free Church of England otherwise called the Reformed Episcopal Church (no author, Suffolk, 1960).
Allen, Harry, *'Aberdeen's Aristocratic Church'* (Aberdeen, 1927).
Anson, P. F., *Fashions in Church Furnishings 1840-1940* (London, 1960).
Bain, George, *History of Nairnshire, Second Edition* (Nairn, 1928).
Balleine, G. R., *A History of the Evangelical Party in the Church of England* (London, 1951).
Banks, J. A., *Victorian Values. Secularism and the Size of Families* (Aldershot, 1994).

Banon, Alan, *Old Nairn* (Nairn, 1999).
Beales, Derek and Geoffrey Best (eds.), *History and Society and the Churches* (Cambridge, 1985).
Bebbington, D. W., *Evangelicalism in Modern Britain* (London, 1993).
Holiness in Nineteenth-Century England (Cumbria, 2000).
Bentley, James, *Ritualism and Politics in Victorian Britain: The Attempt to legislate for Belief* (Oxford, 1978).
Berkhof, Louis, *Systematic Theology* (London, 1959).
Bertie, D. M., *Scottish Episcopal Clergy, 1689-2000* (Edinburgh, 2000).
Best, G. F. A., *Shaftesbury* (London, 1964).
Mid-Victorian Britain 1851-1875 ((London, 1987).
Bossy, John, *The English Catholic Community 1750-1850* (London, 1975).
Bradley, Ian, *The Call to Seriousness* (London, 1976).
Brown, C. G., *Religion and Society in Scotland since 1707* (Edinburgh, 1997).
'The Cost of Pew Renting: Church-going and Social Class in Nineteenth-Century Glasgow', *Journal of Ecclesiastical History* 38 (1987), pp. 347-361.
Brown, F. K., *Fathers of the Victorians* (Cambridge, 1961).
Brown, S. J., 'Thomas Chalmers and the Communal Ideal in Victorian Scotland' in T. C. Smout (ed.), *Victorian Values* (Oxford, for the British Academy, 1992), pp. 61-80.
Thomas Chalmers and the Godly Commonwealth in Scotland (Oxford, 1982).
Broxap, Henry, *The Later Nonjurors* (Cambridge, 1924).
Cameron, N. M. de S., *Dictionary of Scottish Church History and Theology* (Edinburgh, 1993).
Carter, Grayson, *Anglican Evangelicals: Protestant Secessions from the Via Media c. 1800-1850* (Oxford, 2001).
Chadwick, Owen, *The Victorian Church:Part I 1829-1859* (London, 1992).
The Victorian Church, Part II (London, 1992).
The Mind of the Oxford Movement (London, 1960).
Checkland, S. G., *The Gladstones: A Family Biography* (Cambridge, 1971).
Cheyne, A. C., *The Transforming of the Kirk* (Edinburgh, 1983).
(ed.), *The Practical and the Pious* (Edinburgh, 1985).
Cocksworth, C. J., *Evangelical Eucharistic Thought in the Church of England* (Cambridge, 1993).
Cole, Gilbert, *A Church for Golden Acre* (Edinburgh, 1988).
Cross, F. L. (ed), *The Oxford Dictionary of the Christian Church* (London, 1958).
Davidoff, Leonore and Catherine Hall, 'Ye are all one in Christ Jesus', *Family Fortunes:Men and Women of the English Middle Class 1780-1850* (London, 1987).

Bibliography 401

Dicey, A. V., *Lectures on the Relation between Law and Public Opinion in England* (1905).
Dictionary of National Biography Volume XV (London, 1909).
Doubleday, H. A. (ed.), *The Complete Peerage* Volume IX (London, 1936).
Dowden, John, *The Scottish Communion Office 1764* (Oxford, 1922).
Drummond, A. L. and James Bulloch, *The Scottish Church 1688-1843* (Edinburgh, 1973).
The Victorian Church in Scotland 1843-1874 (Edinburgh, 1975).
Dugmore, C. W., *Eucharistic Doctrine from Hooker to Waterland* (London, 1942).
Eeles, F. C., *Alcuin Club Collection XVII: Traditional Ceremonial and Customs Connected with the Scottish Liturgy* (London, 1910).
Elwell W. A., (ed.), *Evangelical Dictionary of Theology* (Grand Rapids, 1984).
Fleming, Archibald, *Archibald of the Arctic* (London, 1957).
Foot, M. R. D. (ed.), *The Gladstone Diaries* (Oxford, 1968-1994).
Foskett, Reginald, 'The Drummond Controversy 1842', *Records of the Scottish Church History Society*, 16 (1969), 99-109.
Fraser, W. Hamish and R. J. Morris (ed.), *People and Society in Scotland, 2. 1830-1914* (Edinburgh, 1987).
Froom, L. E., *The Prophetic Faith of our Fathers*, III (Washington, DC, 1946).
Gammie, Alexander, *Churches of Aberdeen: Historical and Descriptive* (Aberdeen, 1909).
Gifford, John, Colin MacWilliam and David Walker, *The Buildings of Scotland* (London, 1984).
Goldie, Frederick, *A Short History of the Scottish Episcopal Church* (Edinburgh, 1976).
Goring, Rosemary, *Chambers Scottish Biographical Dictionary* (Edinburgh, 1992).
Graham, M. E. M., *The Oliphants of Gask: Records of a Jacobite Family* (London, 1910).
Grisbrooke Jardine, G. W., *Anglican Liturgies of the Seventeenth and Eighteenth Centuries* (London, 1958).
Handley, J. E., *The Irish in Modern Scotland* (Cork, 1947).
Hanson, P. F., *Fashions in Church Furnishings 1840-1900* (London, 1960).
Härdelin, Alf, *Tractarian Understanding of the Eucharist* (Uppsala, 1965).
Harris, H. W. *A Short History of St Mark's Church, Portobello* (Portobello. 1928).
Harrison, Brian, *Drink and the Victorians* (London, 1971).
Hay, George, *The Architecture of Scottish Post-Reformation Churches* (Oxford, 1957).

Hillis, Peter, 'Presbyterianism and Social Class in Mid-Nineteenth Century Glasgow: A Study of Nine Churches', *Journal of Ecclesiastical History*, 32 (1981), pp. 46-64.
Hilton, Boyd, *The Age of Atonement: The Influence of Evangelicalism on Social and Economic Thought 1785-1865* (Oxford, 1988).
Hinchliff, Peter, *Anglican Church in South Africa: An Account of the History and Development of the Church of the Province of South Africa* (London, 1963).
Holland, W. L., *Bunyan's Sabbatic Blunders* (London, 1900).
Kenneth Hylson-Smith, *Evangelicals in the Church of England 1734-1984* (Edinburgh, 1988).
Hylson-Smith, Kenneth, *High Churchmanship in the Church of England* (Edinburgh, 1993).
Ive, Anthony, *A Candle Burns in Africa* (South Africa, 1992).
Jalland, Pat and John Hooper (eds.) *Women from Birth to Death: the Female Life Cycle in Britain, 1830-1914* (Brighton, 1986).
Jeffrey, K. S., *When the Lord Walked the Land* (Carlisle, 2004).
Kent, John, *Holding the Fort: Studies in Victorian Revivalism* (London, 1978).
Kiernan, Victor, 'Evangelicalism and the French Revolution', *Past and Present*, no. 1, (1952).
Lees, L. H., *Exiles of Erin: Irish Immigrants in Victorian London* (Manchester, 1979).
Lewis, D. M. (ed.), *The Blackwell Dictionary of Evangelical Biography*, Volumes I and II (Oxford, 1995).
Lighten Their Darkness: The Evangelical Mission to Working-Class London, 1828-1860 (Cumbria, 2001).
Lochhead, Marion, *Episcopal Scotland in the Nineteenth Century* (London, 1996).
MacDonald, A. J. (ed.), *The Evangelical Doctrine of Holy Communion* (London, 1936).
Luscombe, Edward, *The Scottish Episcopal Church in the Twentieth Century* (Edinburgh, 1996).
MacLaren, A. A., *Religion and Social Class. The Disruption Years in Aberdeen* (London, 1974).
Martin, R. H., *The Pan-Evangelical Impulse in Britain 1798-1830 with Specific Reference to Four London Societies* (Oxford, 1974).
Maxwell, Jean S., *The Centenary Book of St John's, Dumfries* (Dumfries, 1968).
McGrath, A. E., *Reformation Thought* Third Edition (Oxford, 1999).
McGubbin, David, 'Holy Trinity Dunoon, Consecrated 11 September 1850: A Barrier Against Schism', *Argyll and the Isles* (Autumn, 1990).
Morris, R. J., *Class, Sect and Party. The Making of the Middle Class, Leeds* (Manchester, 1990).

Newsome, David, *The Parting of Friends* (London, 1966).
The Victorian World Picture (London, 1997).
Nockles, P. B., *The Oxford Movement in Context: Anglican High Churchmanship 1760-1857* (Cambridge, 1994).
'Our Brethren in the North: The Scottish Episcopal Church and the Oxford Movement', *Journal of Ecclesiastical History*, 47 (1996), pp. 655-682.
Orr, J. E., *The Second Evangelical Awakening in Britain* (London, 1953).
Ousby, Ian, *The Cambridge Guide to Literature in English* (Cambridge, 1993).
Parsons, Gerald, *Religion in Victorian Britain Study Guides 1-4*, (Manchester, 1988).
Perry, William, *The Scottish Liturgy: Its Value and History* (Edinburgh, 1922).
George Hay Forbes (London 1927).
Powicke, Sir M. P. and Fryde, E. B. *Handbook of British Chronology* (London, 1961).
Prochaska, F. K., *Women and Philanthropy in Nineteenth-century England* (Oxford, 1980).
Quinlan, M. J., *Victorian Prelude* (1941).
Reed, J. S., *Glorious Battle* (London, 1998).
Rosman, D. M., *Evangelicals and Culture*, (London, 1984).
Rowell, Geoffrey, *Hell and the Victorians* (Oxford, 1974).
The Vision Glorious (Oxford, 1983).
Russell, G. W. E., *A Short History of the Evangelical Movement* (London, 1915).
Ryle, J. C., *Knots Untied* (London, 1959).
Scott, P. W., *The History of Strathbogie* (Aberdeen, 1977).
Smith, J. C. and W. Wallace (eds.), *Robert Wallace: Life and Last Leaves* (London, 1903).
Smith, J. D., *The Eucharistic Doctrine of the Later Nonjurors: A Revisionist View of the Eighteenth-Century Usagers Controversy* (Cambridge, 2000).
Smout, T. C., *A History of the Scottish People 1560-1830* (London, 1985).
A Century of the Scottish People 1830-1950 (London, 1987).
(ed.), *Victorian Values; A Joint Symposium of the Royal Society of Edinburgh and the British Academy, December 1900* (Oxford, 1992).
Smyth, Charles, *Simeon and Church Order: A Study of the Origins of the Evangelical Revival in Cambridge in the Eighteenth Century* (Cambridge, 1940).
Stevenson, Sara, *Scottish Photography*, Bulletein 2 (Edinburgh, 1992).
Strawley, J. H., *The Early History of the Liturgy* (Cambridge, 1947).
Strong, Rowan, *Alexander Forbes of Brechin* (Oxford, 1995).
Episcopalianism in Nineteenth-Century Scotland (Oxford, 2002).

Toon, Peter, *Evangelical Theology 1833-1856* (London, 1977).
Voll, Dieter, *Catholic Evangelicalism* (London, 1963).
White, Gavin, 'New Names for Old Things: Scottish Reaction to Early Tractarianism', in Derek Baker (ed.), *Studies in Church History: Rennaissance and Renewal in Christian History* (Oxford, for the Ecclesiastical History Society, 1977), pp. 329-337.
    The Scottish Episcopal Church: A New History (Edinburgh, 1998).
    'The Nine Lives of the Episcopal Cat: Changing Self-Images of the Scottish Episcopal Church', *Records of the Scottish Church History Society*, 28, (1998).
White, J. F., *The Cambridge Movement: The Ecclesiologists and the Gothic Revival* (Cambridge, 1962).
Williamson, Elizabeth Anne Riches and Malcolm Higg, *The Buildings of Scotland, Glasgow* (Harmondsworth, 1990).
Wolffe, John, *The Protestant Crusade in Great Britain 1829-1860* (Oxford, 1991).
    Evangelicals, Women and Community, Open University Study Guide, (Milton Keynes, 1994).
    (ed.), *Evangelical Faith and Public Zeal* (London, 1995).
    Religion in Victorian Britain, Volume V (Manchester, 1997).
Wrigley, E. A., *Nineteenth Century Society: Essays in the Use of Quantitative Methods for the Study of Social Data* (London, 1972).
Yates, Nigel, *Anglican Ritualism in Victorian Britain 1830-1910* (Oxford, 1999).
Year Book for the Scottish Episcopal Church in Scotland, 1900.

UNPUBLISHED DISSERTATIONS

Bentley, Anne, 'The Transformation of the Evangelical Party in the Church of England in the Later Nineteenth Century' (Durham University Ph. D. thesis, 1971).
Culbertson, E. M., 'Evangelical Theology 1857-1900', (London University Ph. D. thesis, 1991).
Ervine, W. J. C., 'Doctrine and Diplomacy: Some Aspects of the Life and Thought of Anglican Evangelical Clergy 1797-1837', (Cambridge University Ph. D. thesis, 1979).
Fenwick, R. D., 'The Free Church of England, otherwise called the Reformed Episcopal Church circa 1845 to 1927' (Lampeter Ph. D. thesis, 1995).
Hardman, B. E., 'The Evangelical party in the Church of England, 1855-1865', (Cambridge University Ph. D. thesis, 1964).
Jeffrey, Linda, 'Women in the Churches of Nineteenth-Century Stirling' (University of Stirling M. Litt. thesis, 1996).
Nockles, P. B., 'Continuity and Change in Anglican High Churchmanship in Britain 1792-1850' (Oxford University D. Phil. thesis, 1982).

Bibliography

Quinn, John, 'The Mission of the Churches to the Irish in Dundee 1846-1886,' (M. Litt. thesis, University of Stirling, 1993).

Index

Aberdour, 18, 19
Act of Union, 324, 325, 326, 338
activism, 122–29
Addison, Berkeley, 189, 194
Agnew, Sir Andrew, 170
Ainslie, Daniel, 168, 173, 211, 304, 360
Aitchison, David, 122
Alexander, John, 188
Alexander, W. L., 188
All Saints, Edinburgh, 334
Allen, Robert, 13, 353
Alley, J. P., 294
Almond, George, 47, 48, 49, 50, 51, 289
Anderson, C. J., 44, 309
Andrewes, Bishop Lancelot, 133
Anglo-Catholicism, 337, 343–44, 347, 359. *See* Ritualism; conversion, 7
anti-Catholicism, 183–93
anti-slavery, 166
apostolic succession, 248, 252, 266, 273, 321
architecture, 205–10; English Episcopal, 207
Arminianism. *See* election
Arradoul, 17, 45, 259, 281
art, 180
assurance, 121
Astley, C. T., 162
atonement. *See* cross, doctrine of
Atonement Controversy, 1841-45, 142
Aytoun, Professor W. E., 269, 275
Bagot, Daniel, 16, 18, 49, 51, 132, 137, 142, 150, 168, 185, 203, 232, 233, 244, 249, 252, 254, 260, 263, 264, 265, 268, 270, 272, 274, 293
Baker, S. C., 11, 125, 131, 138, 210
Balfour, Professor J. H., 124, 125, 128, 136, 149, 173, 356
Ball, T. I., 343

Balmacara English Episcopal chapel, 42, 45, 310
Balmer, Robert, 142
baptism, 119, 193–205, 247, 273, 367
Baptists, 281
Bardsley, J. W., 312
Baring, Bishop Charles, 14, 331, 332, 341, 354, 368
Beckles, Bishop E. H., 14, 211, 352–54, 357
Begg, James, 189
Bennett, John, 146
Bennett, W. J. E., 347, 368
Beresford, H. S., 256
Bible: inerrancy, 148; inspiration, 131, 147–51; verbal inspiration, 147, 148
Bible Women, 132
biblicism, 131–33
Bickersteth, Bishop Robert, 362
Bickersteth, Edward, 132, 137, 138, 144, 196, 217, 266, 268, 269, 270, 277, 292, 311, 371
Biddulph, T. T., 195, 197, 198
Birks, T. R., 150
Black, Alexander, 148
Black, C. M., 19
Blakeney, R. P., 342
Blatch, William, 269
Blomfield, Bishop C. J., 310, 313
Blunt, Henry, 277
Bonar, Andrew and Horatius, 144
Book of Common Prayer, 1549. *See* Church of England
Book of Common Prayer, 1662. *See* Church of England
Botanic Garden, Edinburgh, 172
Boultbee, Dr T. P., 313
Bousefield, C. H., 44, 310
Bouverie, F. W. B., 11, 52, 239
Boyle, John, 237
Boyle, Thomas, 308

Brett, Thomas, 220, 222, 370
Brevint, Daniel, 218
Brewster, James, 251, 252, 254
Bridge of Allan, 308
Bright, John, 134
Bright, William, 358
Brougham, Lord Henry Peter, 324
Brown, John, 142, 249
Bruce, A. B., 142
Buckmaster, Thomas, 173
Budd, Henry, 134, 195, 197
Bugg, George, 196, 197
Bulteel, Henry, 140
Burnet, Bishop Gilbert, 272
Burnley, W. F., 44, 170, 173, 289, 296, 305, 355, 357
Burns, Dr Robert, 252
Burns, George, 127, 128, 146, 159, 167, 173, 181, 289, 305, 356
Burns, John, 125, 127, 163, 173, 350, 352, 355, 356
Burns, Mrs. George, 167, 168
Cally English Episcopal chapel, 45, 309
Calvin, John, 215
Calvinism. *See* election
Campbell, A. B., 302
Campbell, John Macleod, 141
Campbell, Sir Archibald of Blythswood, 187, 305
Candlish, R. S., 173, 187, 189
Canongate Mission, Edinburgh, 91, 123, 132, 192
Carmichael, John, 243
Catholic Emancipation Act, 1829, 183, 186
Chalmers, Thomas, 165, 174, 186, 249, 254
Champneys, W. W., 312
Cheyne, Patrick, 235, 236, 239, 296
children, 159–64
Christian Guardian,, 266
Christian Institute for Young Men, 169
Christian Observer,, 253, 266, 271, 278, 371
Christian Remembrancer, 5
Christie, James, 236, 239, 322, 358

Church Missionary Society, 7, 127, 277, 292; Scotland, 45–56
Church of England, 268, 273; Book of Common Prayer, 1549, 222, 329; Book of Common Prayer, 1662, 30, 215, 250, 258, 370; Convocation of Canterbury, 1869, 336; Convocation of Canterbury, 1877, 22, 353; Convocation of York, 1877, 22, 353; South Africa, 372; Thirty-Nine Articles, 31, 216, 231
Cleland, Jeannie, 159
Clementine liturgy, 221, 222
Close, Francis, 277, 320
Colclough, H. J., 362
Colenso judgement, 333
Collins, William, 174
Colonial and Continental Society, 127
conversion, 117–22
Copeland, W. J., 254
Corrimony English Episcopal chapel, 45, 299
Cottage for Incurables, Maryhill, 169
Cotterill, Bishop Henry, 21, 339, 341, 347, 356
Coventry, George, 50, 51, 168, 187, 189, 259
Cowley Fathers, 349
Craig, Edward, 9, 15, 16, 37, 47, 48, 54, 130, 131, 134, 135, 142, 145, 149, 153, 166, 168, 184, 185, 186, 197, 198, 199, 200, 202, 203, 223, 225, 227, 228, 229, 247, 252, 263, 270, 365, 369, 371
Cranmer, Archbishop Thomas, 215, 235
Crieff English Episcopal chapel, 42, 299, 312, 313
cross, doctrine of, 129–31
Crowder, J. H., 18, 295
Cuninghame, William, 143
Cunningham, James, 261
Cunningham, William, 148, 187, 189
Cushnie, Patrick, 251
D'Orsey, A. J. D., 90, 122, 326
Daly, Bishop Robert, 311, 324
Danson, J. M., 357
Darby, J. N., 145

Index

Darwin, Charles, 150
Davidson, A. B., 148
Davys, Bishop George, 321
Dawson, E. C., 10, 11, 19, 55, 211, 355, 358, 359, 360
Day of Humiliation, 1853, 303
Dicey, A. V., 154
Dick, John, 148
Dickens, Charles, 153, 171
Dickson, David, 249
Dods, Marcus, 148
Douglas, Bishop A. G., 359
Douglas, Sholto Douglas-Campbell, Lord Blythswood, 13, 53, 128, 360
Dowden, Bishop John, 222, 358, 360, 370
Drummond, D. T. K., 8, 9, 11, 20, 118, 119, 120, 123, 124, 126, 127, 130, 135, 138, 142, 145, 146, 149, 150, 154, 155, 157, 158, 160, 165, 166, 167, 169, 170, 173, 175, 177, 178, 179, 184, 185, 187, 189, 198, 203, 211, 223, 225, 227, 228, 229, 233, 234, 237, 243, 249, 252, 254, 255, 256, 265, 259-79, 286, 303, 307, 311, 313, 330, 337, 339, 341, 347, 354, 357, 366, 369, 371, 372; and Craig, Edward, 263; Anglo-Catholicism, 238, 349-51; apostolic succession, 252; background and character, 274, 372; Church Missionary Society, 48, 50, 51, 52, 54, 127-29, 292; Church of England, 17, 244, 265, 268, 271, 301, 313, 333, 371; evangelism, 123-26, 250-51, 259-65, 266-69; family life, 154-64; Laud's Office, 1637, 340; schism, defence against, 271-72; Scottish Communion Office, 1764, 218, 224-45, 263, 270-71, 329, 337-38, 347-49
Drummond, G. M., 9, 16, 54, 169, 257
Drummond, Harriet (Moor, Owen), 120, 123, 133, 139, 157, 162, 167, 171, 179, 182
Drummond, Henry, 140, 141
Drummond, Henry, son of D. T. K. Drummond, 161
Drummond, Mrs. Harriet, 132, 157, 158, 159, 161, 162, 163, 168, 179, 182, 199
Duke of Buccleuch's Bill, 1864, 331
Dunbar, Sir William, 9, 11, 17, 51, 52, 119, 123, 274, 285-89, 290, 313, 321, 322, 371; background and character, 287-88; Church of England, 285, 302, 313; Scottish Communion Office, 1764, 286-87
Dunblane, 19, 42
Duncan, John, 148
Dunfermline Abbey, 207
Dunlop, John, 174
Dunoon, Christchurch, English Episcopal chapel, 42, 295, 312
Eardley, H. E., 357
East, John, 312
Ecclesiological Society, 206
Eden, Bishop Robert, 339
Edinburgh Association of Young Men, 255
Edinburgh City Mission, 168, 249
Edinburgh Protestant Association, 1836, 187
Edinburgh Protestant demonstration, 1850, 189
Edinburgh Protestant Society, 1845, 188
Edinburgh Society for Clothing the Industrious Poor, 167
Edwards, Jonathan, 2, 137
election or predestination, 139-43; Church of Scotland, 140; Scottish Episcopal Church, 140
Elibank, Lord, 299, 323
Elliott, E. B., 145
English Episcopal: accomodation with High Churchmen, 348; Association of English Episcopalians, 1877, 352; Church of England, 310, 313, 371; churches, 1842-1900, 11-14; clergy, 1842-1900, 11-14; clerical and lay association, 1846, 320; definition, 8, 22; Deputation, 1846, 311, 320-23; Deputation, 1849,

311, 323–27; divisions, 1873, 343; Evangelicalism of, 314; Exeter Hall, 1872, 342; lay involvement, 276, 306; legal opinion, 1871, 311, 316, 339; legal opinion, 1873, 311, 316, 342; Toleration Act, 1712, 29, 205, 265, 292, 311
Episcopal Free School, 169
Erskine, Thomas, 141, 148
Essays and Reviews, 149
Evangelical Alliance, 20, 150
Evangelical Episcopalianism: strength in Scotland, 23–24, 26–28
Evangelical Revival, 3
Evangelicalism: characteristics, 1; history, 2
Evangelicals: Anglican, 3, 266; class, lower middle, 93; class, skilled working, 85; class, unskilled working, 87; class, upper middle, 91; English Episcopal clergy, 1842-1900, 11–14; English Episcopal congregations, 1842-1900, 11–14; evangelism, 122–29, 247, 259–61, 371; identification, 6; location in Scotland, 37–45, 365; Scottish Episcopal clergy, 1800-1900, 9–10, 15; Scottish Episcopal congregations, 1800-1900, 9–10; Scottish lay, 22, 25, 37
Ewbank, W. W., 320
Ewing, Bishop Alexander, 130, 243, 329
excommunication, 288, 291, 300
extempore prayer, 260
Faber, G. S., 140
Faithfull, V. G., 20
Fasque, 20, 44
Ferguson, J. W., 187
Flindt, G. K., 12, 52, 124
Fochabers, 45, 258, 298
Forbes, Bishop A. P., 122, 137, 150, 153, 204, 241, 308, 328, 329
Forbes, Bishop Robert, 221
Forbes, John Hay, Lord Medwyn, 258, 295
Forbes, William, 242
Foster, Henry, 147, 195

Fox, G. T., 348, 371
Free Church of Scotland, 45, 123–25, 279
Froude, R. H., 231, 254
Fyvie, Charles, 202
Gaelic School Society, 132
Galloway House, 299
Garbett, Edward, 342
gardening, 181
Gask English Episcopal chapel, 45, 297
Gaussen, Louis, 148
gender roles, 154–59
Gillespie, Thomas, 3
Gladstone family, 163
Gladstone, John, 20
Gladstone, W. E., 20, 160, 240, 328, 330
Glasgow City Mission, 168
Gleig, Bishop George, 4, 16, 118, 121, 248, 255
Glenalmond College, 252
Gobat, Bishop Samuel, 14, 312, 327
Gordon of Cairnfield, 258
Gordon, Elisabeth Brodie, Duchess of, 17, 42, 125, 155, 258, 296, 298
Gordon, James Edward, 186
Gorham judgement, 156, 196, 198; Scottish Episcopal Church, 204–5
Graham, J. G., 299
Gray, Bishop Dr Robert, 269
Gregg, Bishop T. H., 315
Greville, E. S., 271
Greville, R. E., 163
Greville, R. K., 119, 161, 166, 168, 170, 172, 173, 174, 177, 187, 189, 253
Gribble, C. B., 12, 128, 239
Grimshaw, William, 3
Grosvenor, Baron Robert, 240
Grove, Captain Francis, 169, 173, 187, 261, 276, 299
Gubbins, G. G., 312
Guthrie, Thomas, 168, 192
Hackney Phalanx, 133
Haldane, Alexander, 342
Haldane, Robert, 140, 141, 147, 249
Hamilton, Bishop W. K., 328

Index

Harris, Howell, 2
Hathaway, E. P., 341
Hawker, Robert, 137, 140, 219
Heath, Vernon, 275
Hebden, A. H. R., 11, 199
Hibbs, Richard, 11, 165, 166, 197, 198, 239, 303–5, 356
Hill, Rowland, 4, 5
Hitchcock, John, 9, 12, 18, 297
Hoadly, Bishop Benjamin, 216
Hoare, Edward, 342
Holland, W. L., 150, 185, 211, 362
Hook, W. F., 269
House of Shelter, Glasgow, 169
Howley, Archbishop William, 310, 320
Hull, J. D., 12, 17, 42, 50, 51, 52, 120, 137, 145, 146, 149, 153, 158, 185, 203, 237, 296, 311, 370
Humphrey, William, 193, 309
Hunter's Quay, 42, 309
Huntly English Episcopal chapel, 208, 297
Hutton, E. F. D., 18, 122, 123
Huxley, T. H., 151
incarnation, 133–36
Innes, William, 249
Institute for Young Men, Edinburgh,, 177
invisible church, 248
invocation, types of, 223
Irish: immigration, 39
Irish Church Bill, 1833, 186
Irving, Edward, 17, 134, 140, 143, 249
Jackson, Bishop John, 337, 341
Jedburgh, 300
Jermyn, Bishop H. W., 355
Jews' Society, 127, 143
Johnson, John, 216
Johnstone, C. H., 308
Johnstone, James, 56
Jolly, Bishop Alexander, 130, 136, 194, 203, 220, 224, 232, 248, 258, 272
justification by faith, 120
Kaffraria, 128
Kaye, John, 292
Keble, John, 132, 231, 242, 256

Kirkman, Joshua, 149
Kirriemuir, 294
Knox, Bishop Dr Edward, 312
Lang, Bishop Archibald, 309, 315
Laud, Archbishop William, 370
Laud's liturgy, 1637, 29, 30, 223, 251, 340, 373
Law, Bishop G. H., 312
Law, William, 133, 135
Lendrum, Alexander, 299, 312
Lias, J. J., 136
lifestyle, 366
London Reformation Society, 186
Longley, Archbishop C. T., 331, 333
Low, Bishop David, 189, 239, 254, 255, 297, 312
Luther, Martin, 215
Lux Mundi, 134
Macdonald, W. M., 299
MacFarquahar, W. P., 257
MacIlwaine, William, 312
Mackarness, Bishop G. R., 355
Mackarness, Bishop J. F., 341
MacKay, A. M., 19
Maclagan, W. D., 349
Maclaurin, John, 3
MacLeod, Norman, 172
Magdalene Asylum, Edinburgh, 164
Manning, H. E., 133
Mant, Bishop Richard, 194, 312
Marshall, E. E., 19
Marshall, H. J., 14, 52, 146
Matthias, J. A., 308
Maynard, J. H., 9, 295
Maynooth question, 186, 188
McCann, James, 19, 129, 151, 337
McColl, Donald, 202
McFarquhar, W. P., 9, 18, 49, 51, 295
McGavin, William, 184
McNeile, Hugh, 140, 145, 187, 240, 277, 289, 320, 371
Melvill, Henry, 196
Memorialism, 216
Methodism, 2–3, 248; English Calvinistic Methodist Connexion, 3; Scotland, 3
Midwifery Dispensary and Lying-in Hospital, Edinburgh,, 169

Miles, C. P., 9, 12, 18, 52, 117, 133, 142, 187, 197, 199, 289–93; Scottish Communion Office, 1764, 289–91
millenarianism, 143–47; postmillennialism, 143; premillennialism, 126, 143–47, 184, 192, 277
Miller, J. C., 350
Miller, J. D., 133, 232
Moir, Bishop David, 251, 273, 288
Moncrieff, W. S., 11, 119, 125, 339, 343, 348, 350, 362, 368
Montgomery, Robert, 9, 17, 49, 50, 51, 118, 149, 179, 252, 257, 265, 270, 272, 274, 289, 293
Moor, C. T., 14, 176, 181
More, Hannah, 177
Morrison, James, 142
Mulkerns, D. J., 13, 309
Murdoch, A. D., 359
Musgrave, Archbishop Thomas, 324
Mylne, James, 168
Nairn English Episcopal chapel, 18, 42, 208, 297, 310, 313
Nasmith, David, 249
National Bible Society of Scotland, 131
naval and army chaplains, 292
Naval and Military Bible Society, 131
Neale, J. M., 15, 206
New Town Dispensary, Edinburgh, 169
Newman, J. H., 7, 132, 216, 224, 231, 254
Nicholson, George, 196, 197
Noel, B. W., 249, 371
Noel, G. T., 15, 134, 141, 145, 164, 365
Nonjurors, 252. *See* Scottish Communion Office, 1764; Virtualism; English, 30, 221; English liturgy, 1718, 220–21; Scottish, 29, 221, 223; Scottish liturgy 1744, 1755, 1764, 221
novels, 178
Ogilvy, Thomas, 126, 299
Old Deer, Aberdeenshire, 37, 45

Oliphant family, 297
opera, 303
original sin, doctrine of, 118
Outdoor Blind Society, Glasgow, 169
Oxford Movement, 5, 133, 136, 151, 242, 251, 254, 256, 267, 270, 285, 287, 291, 301, 328
Paisley, 308
Palmer, William, 218
pantomimes, 178
Partick Mission, Govan, Glasgow, 91, 123, 208; social class, 83
Payne Smith, Robert, 9, 20
Peake, Frederic, 13, 356
Pepys, Bishop Henry, 325
Percy Chapel, London, 292
philanthropy, 164–70
Philiphaugh, Selkirkshire, Murray of, 42, 190, 300
Phillpotts, Bishop Henry, 194, 196, 310
Photographic Society of Scotland, 181
Pirie, H. G., 312
Pitlochry, 42, 43
Plymouth Brethren, 281
poetry, 179
Poole, G. A., 187
Poor Law Amendment Act, 1834, 303
Poor Law Amendment Act, Scotland, 1845, 167
population, Scottish, 38
Portobello, 42, 43
Pratt, J. B., 251, 272, 274
prayer meetings, 250, 259–60
Presbyterianism, 151, 267, 273, 304, 313, 369
Protestant Association, 1835, 186
Protestant Defence Society, 328
Puritans, 137, 248
Pusey, E. B., 137, 194, 224, 240, 252
Qualified chapels, 29, 31, 284
Queensberry Lodge, Edinburgh, 169
Ragged Schools, 168, 192
Rainey, A. C., 12, 299
Rainy, Robert, 173
Ramsay, E. B., 6, 119, 243, 256, 261, 328, 340; Scottish Communion Office, 1764, 236, 240, 328–30

Index 413

Rattray, Bishop Thomas, 221
Receptionism, 218
Record, 5, 266, 270, 278, 371, 372
recreation, 177–82
Reformation, the, 231
Relief Church, 4
revivals: 1859-60, 85, 89, 124; Moody and Sankey, 1873-75, 85, 125
Ritualism: Evangelicals, 210–12; Scottish Episcopal Church, 210–12, 334–36, 345–47
Robertson, J. S. S., 19, 119, 122, 128, 149
Rollo, Lord, 19
Romaine, William, 3
Roman Catholicism, 144, 215, 366. *See* anti-catholic
Rose, George, 187
Royal Edinburgh Asylum for the Insane, 169
Royal Edinburgh Hospital for Sick Children, 169
Royal Maternity Hospital, Edinburgh, 169
Rulerson, William, 202
Russell, Bishop Michael, 235, 253, 255, 289–93
Ryle, Bishop J. C., 2, 14, 148, 353, 363, 369, 371
sabbatarianism, 170–74
Sabbath Alliance, 173
sanctification, 136–39
Sandford, Bishop Daniel, 194, 202
Sandford, D. F., 20, 340
Sandilands, John, 256
Scott, John, 195
Scott, Thomas, 195
Scottish Communion Office, 1764, 8, 19, 31, 155, 215, 223, 247, 256, 263, 266, 270, 286, 289, 294, 296, 297, 306, 309, 319, 321, 324, 328, 329, 331, 333, 338, 340, 342, 348, 354, 358–60, 367, 368, 370, 371; Anglo-Catholicism, 337, 343–44, 347, 359; antiquity, 230; disputes, 224; invocation, 228–32; oblation, 226–28; prayers for the dead, 232; Ritualism, 308; scripture, 230;

Tractarianism, 240–42; transubstantiation, 235, 238–39; Virtualism, 220–32, 359, 370
Scottish Episcopal Church. *See* Scottish Communion Office, 1764. *See* Virtualism; Church of England, 31, 319, 327, 333; Declaration, 1882, 19, 355; Evangelical Revival, 4; General Synod, 1811, 31; General Synod, 1838, 255; General Synod, 1863, 329, 368; General Synod, 1890, 19, 358; High Churchmanship, 4, 369; history, 29; mission, Edinburgh, 1875, 349; Thirty-Nine Articles, 31
Scottish Reformation Society, 189–92; members, 1851-1880, 190
Scripture Readers' Society of Ireland, 132
Secession Church, 4
Secker, Archbishop Thomas, 136
Shaftesbury, Lord, 166, 313, 332, 352, 371
Shannon, R. Q., 256
Sherwood, Ellen, 128, 139, 161, 162, 179
Short, Bishop T. V., 324
Simeon, Charles, 16, 137, 140, 143, 195, 248
Sinclair, John, 187
Skene, W. F., 20, 347, 354, 356
Skinner, Bishop John, 225
Skinner, Bishop William, 204, 255, 274, 286, 290–93, 327, 328
Skinner, John, of Linshart, Longside, 15, 122
Smith, Bishop B. B., 338
Smith, Robert and Hannah Pearsall, 124, 139
Smith, W. C., 172
Smith, William Robertson, 148
Society for Giving Higher Education to the Blind of Scotland, 170
Speir, Robert, 299
St Andrew's, Edinburgh, 19
St Catherine's, Blairgowrie, 294
St Columba's, Edinburgh, 334

St James's, Aberdeen, 19, 40, 208, 302; social class, 81
St James's, Edinburgh, 16, 205; social class, 79
St John's scheme, Glasgow, 167
St John's, Dumfries, 310
St John's, Dundee, 40, 309, 314
St John's, Jedburgh, 207, 291
St John's, Perth, 293
St Jude's, Glasgow, 19, 39, 40, 69, 206, 289–93; lay involvement, 291; social class, 82
St Mary Magdalene's, Dundee, 308
St Ninian's, Perth, 336
St Paul's, Aberdeen, 40, 71, 72, 284–89, 302; lay involvement, 287; social class, 78
St Paul's, Carrubber's Close, Edinburgh, 38; social class, 83
St Paul's, Glasgow, 19
St Peter's, Edinburgh, 19
St Peter's, Montrose, 86, 281, 314; social class, 79
St Silas's, Glasgow, 18, 40, 208–9, 305; social class, 82
St Thomas's, Edinburgh, 40, 73, 129, 155, 207–10, 265; factors surrounding foundation, 265; lay involvement, 276; Presbyterians, 277; schism, 271–73; social class, 80
St Vincent's, Edinburgh, 19, 208–10, 304; social class, 81
Stanley, Montague, 160, 164, 177, 261
Stephens, A. J., 338, 342
Stillingfleet, Bishop Edward, 272
Stowell, Hugh, 320
Stuart, G. P., Earl of Moray, 18
Sumner, Archbishop J. B., 165, 195, 204, 311, 313, 323, 325, 329
Sumner, Bishop C. R., 321
Suther, Bishop T. G. S., 241, 256, 336
Tait, Archbishop A. C., 331, 332, 336, 340, 347
Talon, T. K., 19, 138, 142, 149, 185, 199, 347, 351, 356, 369
Taylor, Bishop Jeremy, 136
Taylor, Jeremy, 220

Teape, C. R., 20, 189, 211
temperance, 174–76; Edinburgh Society for Suppressing Intemperance, 175; Edinburgh Temperance Society, 174; Forbes-Mackenzie Act, 1853, 176; Free Church Temperance Society, 175; Gatehouse Total Abstinence Society, 176
Terrot, Bishop C. H., 188, 220, 253, 260, 262, 269, 273, 290, 312, 329, 340; and Drummond, D. T. K., 259–65, 275; Scottish Communion Office, 1764, 236, 243
theatre, 177, 304
Thorold, A. W., 312
Tillotson, Archbishop John, 272
Torry, Bishop Patrick, 202, 204, 225, 255, 294, 299
Torry, John, 254
Tractarianism. *See* Oxford Movement
transubstantiation, 215, 234
Trower, Bishop W. J., 150, 204, 243
Turpin, W. T., 130
United Secession Church, 142
Usagers, 220
Usan, Montrose, 123, 251
Venn, John, 147
Villiers, Bishop H. M., 14, 144, 293, 327
Virtualism, 4, 216, 220, 229. *See* Scottish Communion Office, 1764; Virtualism
Wace, Henry, 148, 362
Wade, Robert, 314
Wade, W. M., 9, 18, 47, 49, 69, 252, 253, 255, 257, 265, 270, 272, 365
Waldegrave, Bishop Samuel, 14
Walker, Bishop James, 199–201, 202, 250, 254, 255
Walker, S. A., 11, 302
Walker, Samuel, 3
Walker, William, 15
Wallace, Robert, 171
Walton, O. F., 357
Ward, William, 15
Wardlaw, Robert, 56
Water of Leith, Edinburgh, school, 165

Index

Waterland, Daniel, 217, 238
Wauchope, Sir John Don, 169, 189, 211, 261, 276, 361
Way, Lewis, 143
Wemyss Bay English Episcopal chapel, 42, 208–9, 309, 312
Wesley, John and Charles, 2
Western schism, 1815, 196
Whately, Archbishop Richard, 324, 328
Whitefield, George, 2
Wilberforce, Bishop Samuel, 20, 312, 328, 336
Wilberforce, Robert, 240
Wilberforce, William, 177
Wilkinson, Bishop G. H., 153

Wilkinson, T. H., 9, 17, 56
Williams, Rowland, 150
Williamson, G. F., 298
Willison, John, 219
Wilson, H. A., 358
Wilson, H. B., 150
Woodd, Basil, 195
Woodroofe, Abel, 13, 302
Wordsworth, Bishop Charles, 184, 189, 254, 308, 328, 329, 340, 348
Worthington, Thomas, 13, 19, 338
Wrenford, E. C., 12, 120, 179, 336, 340
Yorke, G. M., 256
Zwingli, Huldrych, 215
Zwingliansm, 216

Studies in Evangelical History and Thought
(All titles uniform with this volume)
Dates in bold are of projected publication

Andrew Atherstone
Oxford's Protestant Spy
The Controversial Career of Charles Golightly
Charles Golightly (1807–85) was a notorious Protestant polemicist. His life was dedicated to resisting the spread of ritualism and liberalism within the Church of England and the University of Oxford. For half a century he led many memorable campaigns, such as building a martyr's memorial and attempting to close a theological college. John Henry Newman, Samuel Wilberforce and Benjamin Jowett were among his adversaries. This is the first study of Golightly's controversial career.
***2006** / 1-84227-364-7 / approx. 324pp*

Clyde Binfield
Victorian Nonconformity in Eastern England
Studies of Victorian religion and society often concentrate on cities, suburbs, and industrialisation. This study provides a contrast. Victorian Eastern England—Essex, Suffolk, Norfolk, Cambridgeshire, and Huntingdonshire—was rural, traditional, relatively unchanging. That is nonetheless a caricature which discounts the industry in Norwich and Ipswich (as well as in Haverhill, Stowmarket and Leiston) and ignores the impact of London on Essex, of railways throughout the region, and of an ancient but changing university (Cambridge) on the county town which housed it. It also entirely ignores the political implications of such changes in a region noted for the variety of its religious Dissent since the seventeenth century. This book explores Victorian Eastern England and its Nonconformity. It brings to a wider readership a pioneering thesis which has made a major contribution to a fresh evolution of English religion and society.
***2006** / 1-84227-216-0 / approx. 274pp*

John Brencher
Martyn Lloyd-Jones (1899–1981) and Twentieth-Century Evangelicalism
This study critically demonstrates the significance of the life and ministry of Martyn Lloyd-Jones for post-war British evangelicalism and demonstrates that his preaching was his greatest influence on twentieth-century Christianity. The factors which shaped his view of the church are examined, as is the way his reformed evangelicalism led to a separatist ecclesiology which divided evangelicals.
2002 / 1-84227-051-6 / xvi + 268pp

July 2005

Jonathan D. Burnham
A Story of Conflict
The Controversial Relationship between Benjamin Wills Newton and John Nelson Darby

Burnham explores the controversial relationship between the two principal leaders of the early Brethren movement. In many ways Newton and Darby were products of their times, and this study of their relationship provides insight not only into the dynamics of early Brethrenism, but also into the progress of nineteenth-century English and Irish evangelicalism.

2004 / 1-84227-191-1 / xxiv + 268pp

Grayson Carter
Anglican Evangelicals
Protestant Secessions from the Via Media, c.1800–1850

This study examines, within a chronological framework, the major themes and personalities which influenced the outbreak of a number of Evangelical clerical and lay secessions from the Church of England and Ireland during the first half of the nineteenth century. Though the number of secessions was relatively small—between a hundred and two hundred of the 'Gospel' clergy abandoned the Church during this period—their influence was considerable, especially in highlighting in embarrassing fashion the tensions between the evangelical conversionist imperative and the principles of a national religious establishment. Moreover, through much of this period there remained, just beneath the surface, the potential threat of a large Evangelical disruption similar to that which occurred in Scotland in 1843. Consequently, these secessions provoked great consternation within the Church and within Evangelicalism itself, they contributed to the outbreak of millennial speculation following the 'constitutional revolution' of 1828–32, they led to the formation of several new denominations, and they sparked off a major Church–State crisis over the legal right of a clergyman to secede and begin a new ministry within Protestant Dissent.

2007 / 1-84227-401-5 / xvi + 470pp

J.N. Ian Dickson
Beyond Religious Discourse
Sermons, Preaching and Evangelical Protestants in Nineteenth-Century Irish Society
Drawing extensively on primary sources, this pioneer work in modern religious history explores the training of preachers, the construction of sermons and how Irish evangelicalism and the wider movement in Great Britain and the United States shaped the preaching event. Evangelical preaching and politics, sectarianism, denominations, education, class, social reform, gender, and revival are examined to advance the argument that evangelical sermons and preaching went significantly beyond religious discourse. The result is a book for those with interests in Irish history, culture and belief, popular religion and society, evangelicalism, preaching and communication.
2005 / 1-84227-217-9 / approx. 324pp

Neil T.R. Dickson
Brethren in Scotland 1838–2000
A Social Study of an Evangelical Movement
The Brethren were remarkably pervasive throughout Scottish society. This study of the Open Brethren in Scotland places them in their social context and examines their growth, development and relationship to society.
2003 / 1-84227-113-X / xxviii + 510pp

Crawford Gribben and Timothy C.F. Stunt (eds)
Prisoners of Hope?
Aspects of Evangelical Millennialism in Britain and Ireland, 1800–1880
This volume of essays offers a comprehensive account of the impact of evangelical millennialism in nineteenth-century Britain and Ireland.
2004 / 1-84227-224-1 / xiv + 208pp

Khim Harris
Evangelicals and Education
Evangelical Anglicans and Middle-Class Education in Nineteenth-Century England
This ground breaking study investigates the history of English public schools founded by nineteenth-century Evangelicals. It documents the rise of middle-class education and Evangelical societies such as the influential Church Association, and includes a useful biographical survey of prominent Evangelicals of the period.
2004 / 1-84227-250-0 / xviii + 422pp

Mark Hopkins
Nonconformity's Romantic Generation
Evangelical and Liberal Theologies in Victorian England
A study of the theological development of key leaders of the Baptist and Congregational denominations at their period of greatest influence, including C.H. Spurgeon and R.W. Dale, and of the controversies in which those among them who embraced and rejected the liberal transformation of their evangelical heritage opposed each other.
2004 / 1-84227-150-4 / xvi + 284pp

Don Horrocks
Laws of the Spiritual Order
Innovation and Reconstruction in the Soteriology of Thomas Erskine of Linlathen
Don Horrocks argues that Thomas Erskine's unique historical and theological significance as a soteriological innovator has been neglected. This timely reassessment reveals Erskine as a creative, radical theologian of central and enduring importance in Scottish nineteenth-century theology, perhaps equivalent in significance to that of S.T. Coleridge in England.
2004 / 1-84227-192-X / xx + 362pp

Kenneth S. Jeffrey
When the Lord Walked the Land
The 1858–62 Revival in the North East of Scotland
Previous studies of revivals have tended to approach religious movements from either a broad, national or a strictly local level. This study of the multifaceted nature of the 1859 revival as it appeared in three distinct social contexts within a single region reveals the heterogeneous nature of simultaneous religious movements in the same vicinity.
2002 / 1-84227-057-5 / xxiv + 304pp

John Kenneth Lander
Itinerant Temples
Tent Methodism, 1814–1832
Tent preaching began in 1814 and the Tent Methodist sect resulted from disputes with Bristol Wesleyan Methodists in 1820. The movement spread to parts of Gloucestershire, Wiltshire, London and Liverpool, among other places. Its demise started in 1826 after which one leader returned to the Wesleyans and others became ministers in the Congregational and Baptist denominations.
2003 / 1-84227-151-2 / xx + 268pp

Donald M. Lewis
Lighten Their Darkness
The Evangelical Mission to Working-Class London, 1828–1860
This is a comprehensive and compelling study of the Church and the complexities of nineteenth-century London. Challenging our understanding of the culture in working London at this time, Lewis presents a well-structured and illustrated work that contributes substantially to the study of evangelicalism and mission in nineteenth-century Britain.
2001 / 1-84227-074-5 / xviii + 372pp

Herbert McGonigle
'Sufficient Saving Grace'
John Wesley's Evangelical Arminianism
A thorough investigation of the theological roots of John Wesley's evangelical Arminianism and how these convictions were hammered out in controversies on predestination, limited atonement and the perseverance of the saints.
2001 / 1-84227-045-1 / xvi + 350pp

Lisa S. Nolland
A Victorian Feminist Christian
Josephine Butler, the Prostitutes and God
Josephine Butler was an unlikely candidate for taking up the cause of prostitutes, as she did, with a fierce and self-disregarding passion. This book explores the particular mix of perspectives and experiences that came together to envision and empower her remarkable achievements. It highlights the vital role of her spirituality and the tragic loss of her daughter.
2004 / 1-84227-225-X / xxiv + 328pp

Don J. Payne
The Theology of the Christian Life in J.I. Packer's Thought
Theological Anthropology, Theological Method, and the Doctrine of Sanctification
J.I. Packer has wielded widespread influence on evangelicalism for more than three decades. This study pursues a nuanced understanding of Packer's theology of sanctification by tracing the development of his thought, showing how he reflects a particular version of Reformed theology, and examining the unique influence of theological anthropology and theological method on this area of his theology.
2005 / 1-84227-397-3 / approx. 374pp

Ian M. Randall
Evangelical Experiences
A Study in the Spirituality of English Evangelicalism 1918–1939
This book makes a detailed historical examination of evangelical spirituality between the First and Second World Wars. It shows how patterns of devotion led to tensions and divisions. In a wide-ranging study, Anglican, Wesleyan, Reformed and Pentecostal-charismatic spiritualities are analysed.
1999 / 0-85364-919-7 / xii + 310pp

Ian M. Randall
Spirituality and Social Change
The Contribution of F.B. Meyer (1847–1929)
This is a fresh appraisal of F.B. Meyer (1847–1929), a leading Free Church minister. Having been deeply affected by holiness spirituality, Meyer became the Keswick Convention's foremost international speaker. He combined spirituality with effective evangelism and socio-political activity. This study shows Meyer's significant contribution to spiritual renewal and social change.
2003 / 1-84227-195-4 / xx + 184pp

James Robinson
Pentecostal Origins
Early Pentecostalism in Ireland in the Context of the British Isles
Harvey Cox describes Pentecostalism as 'the fascinating spiritual child of our time' that has the potential, at the global scale, to contribute to the 'reshaping of religion in the twenty-first century'. This study grounds such sentiments by examining at the local scale the origin, development and nature of Pentecostalism in Ireland in its first twenty years. Illustrative, in a paradigmatic way, of how Pentecostalism became established within one region of the British Isles, it sets the story within the wider context of formative influences emanating from America, Europe and, in particular, other parts of the British Isles. As a synoptic regional study in Pentecostal history it is the first survey of its kind.
2005 / 1-84227-329-1 / xxviii + 378pp

Geoffrey Robson
Dark Satanic Mills?
Religion and Irreligion in Birmingham and the Black Country
This book analyses and interprets the nature and extent of popular Christian belief and practice in Birmingham and the Black Country during the first half of the nineteenth century, with particular reference to the impact of cholera epidemics and evangelism on church extension programmes.
2002 / 1-84227-102-4 / xiv + 294pp

Roger Shuff
Searching for the True Church
Brethren and Evangelicals in Mid-Twentieth-Century England

Roger Shuff holds that the influence of the Brethren movement on wider evangelical life in England in the twentieth century is often underrated. This book records and accounts for the fact that Brethren reached the peak of their strength at the time when evangelicalism was at it lowest ebb, immediately before World War II. However, the movement then moved into persistent decline as evangelicalism regained ground in the post war period. Accompanying this downward trend has been a sharp accentuation of the contrast between Brethren congregations who engage constructively with the non-Brethren scene and, at the other end of the spectrum, the isolationist group commonly referred to as 'Exclusive Brethren'.

2005 / 1-84227-254-3 / xviii+ 296pp

James H.S. Steven
Worship in the Spirit
Charismatic Worship in the Church of England

This book explores the nature and function of worship in six Church of England churches influenced by the Charismatic Movement, focusing on congregational singing and public prayer ministry. The theological adequacy of such ritual is discussed in relation to pneumatological and christological understandings in Christian worship.

2002 / 1-84227-103-2 / xvi + 238pp

Peter K. Stevenson
God in Our Nature
The Incarnational Theology of John McLeod Campbell

This radical reassessment of Campbell's thought arises from a comprehensive study of his preaching and theology. Previous accounts have overlooked both his sermons and his Christology. This study examines the distinctive Christology evident in his sermons and shows that it sheds new light on Campbell's much debated views about atonement.

2004 / 1-84227-218-7 / xxiv + 458pp

Kenneth J. Stewart
Restoring the Reformation
British Evangelicalism and the Réveil at Geneva 1816–1849
Restoring the Reformation traces British missionary initiative in post-Revolutionary Francophone Europe from the genesis of the London Missionary Society, the visits of Robert Haldane and Henry Drummond, and the founding of the Continental Society. While British Evangelicals aimed at the reviving of a foreign Protestant cause of momentous legend, they received unforeseen reciprocating emphases from the Continent which forced self-reflection on Evangelicalism's own relationship to the Reformation.
2006 / 1-84227-392-2 / approx. 190pp

Martin Wellings
Evangelicals Embattled
Responses of Evangelicals in the Church of England to Ritualism, Darwinism and Theological Liberalism 1890–1930
In the closing years of the nineteenth century and the first decades of the twentieth century Anglican Evangelicals faced a series of challenges. In responding to Anglo-Catholicism, liberal theology, Darwinism and biblical criticism, the unity and identity of the Evangelical school were severely tested.
2003 / 1-84227-049-4 / xviii + 352pp

James Whisenant
A Fragile Unity
Anti-Ritualism and the Division of Anglican Evangelicalism in the Nineteenth Century
This book deals with the ritualist controversy (approximately 1850–1900) from the perspective of its evangelical participants and considers the divisive effects it had on the party.
2003 / 1-84227-105-9 / xvi + 530pp

Haddon Willmer
Evangelicalism 1785–1835: An Essay (1962) and Reflections (2004)
Awarded the Hulsean Prize in the University of Cambridge in 1962, this interpretation of a classic period of English Evangelicalism, by a young church historian, is now supplemented by reflections on Evangelicalism from the vantage point of a retired Professor of Theology.
2006 / 1-84227-219-5 / approx. 350pp

Linda Wilson
Constrained by Zeal
Female Spirituality amongst Nonconformists 1825–1875

Constrained by Zeal investigates the neglected area of Nonconformist female spirituality. Against the background of separate spheres, it analyses the experience of women from four denominations, and argues that the churches provided a 'third sphere' in which they could find opportunities for participation.

2000 / 0-85364-972-3 / xvi + 294pp

Paternoster
9 Holdom Avenue,
Bletchley,
Milton Keynes MK1 1QR,
United Kingdom
Web: www.authenticmedia.co.uk/paternoster

July 2005

www.ingramcontent.com/pod-product-compliance
Lightning Source LLC
Chambersburg PA
CBHW052049290426
44111CB00011B/1677